what's language got to do with it?

what's language got to do with it?

Keith Walters

The University of Texas
at Austin

Michal Brody

CIESAS Programa Peninsular,
Yucatán, México

W. W. NORTON & COMPANY

New York   London

W. W. Norton & Company has been independent since its founding in 1923, when William Warder Norton and Mary D. Herter Norton first published lectures delivered at the People's Institute, the adult education division of New York City's Cooper Union. The Nortons soon expanded their program beyond the Institute, publishing books by celebrated academics from America and abroad. By mid-century, the two major pillars of Norton's publishing program—trade books and college texts—were firmly established. In the 1950s, the Norton family transferred control of the company to its employees, and today—with a staff of four hundred and a comparable number of trade, college, and professional titles published each year—W. W. Norton & Company stands as the largest and oldest publishing house owned wholly by its employees.

Editor: Marilyn Moller
Assistant Editor: Nicole Netherton
Production Manager: Diane O'Connor
Project Editor: Dexter Gasque
Copy Editor: Katharine Ings
Photo Researcher: Meredith Coeyman
Covers, Design, Layout: Anna Palchik

Composition by PennSet, Inc.
Digital art file services by Jay's Publishers Services and Bukva Imaging Group
Manufacturing by Maple-Vail Book Group

Library of Congress Cataloging-in-Publication Data
What's language got to do with it? / [edited by] Keith Walters, Michal Brody.
      p. cm.
    Includes bibliographical references and index.

    ISBN 0-393-97884-2 (pbk.)
    ISBN 0-393-92663-X (Instructor's Edition)

    1. Language and languages. I. Walters, Keith, 1952– II. Brody, Michal.
P107.W5 2005
400—dc22

                                                          2004061725

W. W. Norton & Company, Inc., 500 Fifth Avenue, New York, N.Y. 10110
www.wwnorton.com

W. W. Norton & Company Ltd., Castle House, 75/76 Wells Street, London W1T 3QT

Preface

What's Language Got to Do with It? represents our best effort to create a reader about language that will engage students on multiple levels, helping them think critically and analytically about the language that is all around them and through which they construct their identities as individuals and as members of groups of all kinds. Few things give us greater pleasure than seeing students become excited about language, helping them investigate the many roles it plays in their lives and the lives of those they love, and learning from them as they teach us about their understanding of language and how it functions from their perspective.

The topics and texts we've included here come from our own teaching. We are both sociolinguists and teachers of writing, with training in rhetoric and a strong anthropological bent, seeking to understand how humans use language as tool and symbol. We are convinced that every course can and should be a writing course, a fact reflected in how we've designed this book, especially in thinking about possible writing assignments.

In designing the book, we have sought topics and readings that will engage students and teachers. Because arguments about language issues are easily politicized, one of our goals could be cast in almost Ciceronian terms: to give students the tools they need to think in an informed fashion and make decisions about language issues that shape and are shaped by political contexts. Most of the students we teach are already taxpayers, and nearly all will become parents. Certainly, all will work in a more globalized economy than those of us who teach them have ever experienced. They will help make decisions about funding for schools and for public services that involve language issues in some way. Their lives, including the languages they speak, will be influenced by as-yet-undeveloped technologies. We hope that the information and skills they take from this book—the questions they learn to ask and the ways of questioning they come to practice—will prove useful beyond the course in which the book is used. Hence, we repeatedly turn students' attention to how they and others around them use language.

KEY FEATURES OF THIS BOOK

• **It covers fresh, important language issues**—language and globalization, the languages used in Deaf communities, languages and national identities, the multiple languages now spoken in the United States, and more. These are issues that engage the attention of scholars working on questions of language in society today and that will, we trust, be of interest to students.

• **It looks at language in the context of writing**, with Chapter 1 on Language as Argument and Chapter 2 on How Writing Changes Language.

• **It includes discussions of many languages in addition to English** (ASL, Azeri, Chinese, French, German, Luiseño, Oneida, Sahnish, Spanish, Vietnamese, Yiddish, and more) as well as language varieties (such as Ebonics) and language practices (such as Spanglish).

• **It takes a global focus on language issues**, considering those in the United States and in many other countries. It likewise examines the global spread of English and its effect both on English itself and on other languages.

• **It includes real-world readings as well as academic ones**—more than half the readings are essays, of the kind that students will be assigned to write, but the book also includes many other genres, including cartoons, news articles, ads, census data, Web sites, radio scripts, poetry, stories, handbook guidelines, and more. In addition, there are two essays by students.

• **It prompts students to think about their own use of language,** helping them to recognize language as one of the most significant resources human beings draw on in the construction of their own identities—and to consider their own language practices.

Because of our training, we seek to present and encourage perspectives on language supported by current theory and research in the disciplines that take language seriously. We have often found that students, especially undergraduates, assume that opinions about language are just that—individual opinions, each of which is equally valid because "in America, everyone is entitled to their own opinion." Such a perspective, we believe, confuses a sort of intellectual agnosticism—it's not clear what to believe about language or why—with a deeper understanding of the notion of "a balanced perspective." For us, within the realm of intellectual debate, balance is about representing the various sides of an issue critically. Anyone who has ever had a linguistics course accepts the validity of certain facts that fly in the face of assumptions that most people, even highly educated ones, often make about language. We encourage readers to constantly question their assumptions about language, and at the same time recognize that knowledge based on research and theory carries weight of a sort that mere opinion, even when based on received wisdom, does not and should not.

A NOTE ABOUT DOCUMENTATION

We've tried to sample a wide array of genres and the uses of language they represent, and also to include many examples of the kind of writing students using this book will be expected to do themselves. Many of the texts include documentation, partly because we wanted some research-based readings in our collection. We have consciously retained the systems of documentation used by the authors of these pieces rather than seeking to convert them to a single format. If the truth be told, differences in documentation practices represent more than just different ways of doing bibliographic entries. The larger issue is an epistemological one: the styles of documentation used in different disciplines encourage readers to construct knowledge in different ways. Those with training in literature and *belles-lettres* are used to writing about texts using the present tense—after all, literary texts speak their truth eternally in some sense—and the current MLA documentation system of document-internal reference focuses on the author and title of the work. Those trained in the social sciences are used to writing and reading about earlier research in the past tense—the data were collected in the past, and the knowledge claims made about them were made in the past—and the system of documentation focuses on the researcher who made the claim and when she or he made it. These observations remind us that systems of documentation across disciplines are conventions, a fact students need to come to appreciate as part of their education—in the same way that they have to learn to use whatever conventions you, as a teacher, may require in your course.

ACKNOWLEDGMENTS

We are grateful to many people for making this book a reality. We thank first those whose teaching got us interested in language. For Michal, these teachers include Judy Kaplan-Weinger, Teddy Bofman, Audrey Reynolds, and Shahrzad Mahootian at Northeastern Illinois University in Chicago; Keith's first teacher of linguistics was Ann Sharp, now retired from Furman University in Greenville, South Carolina. We likewise thank the many students we have taught at UT and elsewhere—and who have taught us so very much about the importance of language.

Throughout the process of creating this work, we have been richly blessed in many, many ways, particularly by our collaboration with Marilyn Moller, our editor at Norton, and Nicole Netherton, the assistant editor there. Indeed, it is no overstatement to claim that the book in your hand is there only because of Marilyn's faith that such a book needed to be done, and that we could do it, and because of her assistance at every step. We'd learned much from working with Marilyn on an earlier project, and we were especially excited to undertake this one, which reflects so closely many of our most cherished personal and professional interests. Nicole, a former student of Keith's and a former classmate of Michal's, has been a delight, giving us crucial assistance and frank commentary when we needed it most. We will miss the emails coming and going several times daily about every aspect of the book. All textbook authors should be as lucky as we have been in this regard.

We are especially grateful to Shirley Brice Heath for writing a foreword to our book. Over the years, her research has taught us much about the complex relationships between language, culture, and identity, and the many meanings of literacy across cultures and communities.

We are grateful for the thoughtful comments we received from reviewers: Valerie Balester (Texas A&M University), Irene Clark (University of Southern California), LuMing Mao (Miami University of Ohio), Jaime Mejía (Texas State University), Peter Murphy (Murray State University), Kathy Overhulse Smith (Indiana University), and Peter Vandenberg (DePaul University).

Anytime a book, especially a textbook, is published, it represents a true team effort because people working for the publishers, both full-time and freelance employees, take care of a million or more details, everything from seeking permissions to design and layout to copyediting (yes, textbook writers need copyeditors too!) to overseeing every stage of the book's production. Here we wish to thank Meredith Coeyman, Eileen Connell, Courtney Fitch, Dexter Gasque, Katharine Ings, Marian Johnson, Diane O'Connor, Anna Palchik, Rich Rivellese, Nancy Rodwan, and Katrina Washington.

We thank our life partners, Jonathan Tamez and Mucuy Kak Moó Marín, for helping us see this textbook through and for sharing with us their own love of the languages they speak.

Surely one of the greatest blessings of this project has been the opportu-

Contents

1 Language as Argument   *1*

PUNCTUATION. PERIOD. *97*

The period tells you that . . . you got all the writer intended to parcel out and now you have to move along. But with a semicolon there you get a pleasant little feeling of expectancy; there is more to come; read on; it will get clearer.

POLICING USAGE IN THE COMICS *109*

According to Mom, " 'no problem' is basically an inappropriate response to 'thank you.' "

Dear Grammar Lady, Is it OK to use "can" in the expression "Can I help you?" or is "May I help you?" the only correct thing to say?

A scrupulous writer, in every sentence that he writes, will ask himself . . . What am I trying to say? What words will express it? What image or idiom will make it clearer? Is this image fresh enough to have an effect?

Informalization has steadily denatured many words once considered dirty. . . . Even fastidious grandmothers now say, when confessing error, that they "screwed up."

③ Technology and (versus?) Language *133*

Once you start down the email path, there's no going back.

The language of instant messaging is creeping into student papers, and some teachers are not amused.

⑥ His and Hers
Language and Gender 333

7 Language in Deaf Communities *393*

8 Languages and National Identities *447*

9 Globalizing English 501

Foreword

by Shirley Brice Heath

Neither as teachers nor as students of writing do we turn naturally to thinking about the structures and uses of language. This book asks us to do just that, however, and to understand language as a crucial means of argument, technology, and identity.

But before we roll up our sleeves and think about these important aspects of language, I want to ask that we first consider some of our very first feelings about what language does within us. Remember your grandmother's voice as she announced she had made a favorite dessert? Can you sense again emotions that came with the last cheer at a winning high-school homecoming game? And what about times when you were moved by the force of someone else's words—a fervent religious or political leader, an inspirational teacher, or an astute friend? All our memories, emotions, and motivations depend on language—the words that swirl in our own heads as well as those we hear from others. Language lies deeply within our hearts as well as our heads.

This is why, as we begin to study composition, we do not think first about taking language and its functions apart; we know it best for how it makes us feel. Yet its instrumental powers—what we can do with it—matter, perhaps more than any other human capacity.

Language is like other parts of our very being that we just accept and expect to work well for us. Consider physical fitness. We usually do not think much about either language or our bodies until there is some kind of breakdown or problem.

We just expect our bodies to be healthy and to function according to our intentions. We certainly do not want to have to study how our bodies work in order to make them perform better.

Similarly, we may well resist any focused awareness of the workings of language. We just expect that the ways we put words together will keep on giving us what we expect.

To entertain the idea that we might have reason to think deeply about how language works might even strike some of us as unpleasant. We do not want to reflect on what might happen when what we say is not what we mean—or what others hear us say. Breakdowns in the form of quarrels, misunderstandings, or instances of miscommunication, however, draw our attention to the fact that we have to work with words to make what may be in our hearts and minds match up with what our listeners hear.

When we want to argue a point and to persuade others, we have to plan, think, and perhaps even rehearse how we will use language. It's not unlike running a marathon, when we certainly have to think about the state of our physical fitness and to plan, think, and train. Language and physical fitness work much the same way in this regard.

As we come to formulate in our minds what we actually want our words to *do*, as opposed to what they just *say*, we need to think ahead. We have to assess our ways with words. As with physical fitness, we are likely to realize that we have to "train" to meet goals. We have to become consciously aware of our own uses and possible misuses of language and learn a great deal more about how we and others use language as a means of argument, technology, and identity.

We rarely think of the need to practice or "train" in our native language, assuming perhaps that it "comes naturally." In fact, training is essential if our language is going to help us achieve particular goals. Composition classes, as well as courses in the history of language or in ways that language, culture, and class work together, provide time for just such training and practice. Writing, as well as particular kinds of speaking, calls for particular sorts of training in the structures most effective for certain uses and forms of text production.

One lesson we have to learn as we grow older is that spoken words can never be taken back. Though the words themselves have no physical permanence, their memories, emotions, and motivations linger. Written words, though mostly permanent, open themselves to alteration, endless amplification, and ongoing interpretation. Therefore, their composition requires special training to guide us in putting our spoken words together effectively. Topics and exercises in this book, from considering how certain combinations of words structure arguments to pondering the global spread of English, set out the bases for that training.

But it is here that the parallels of physical fitness and language move apart. Training to run a marathon helps prepare for a single event. Training in language, on the other hand, has lasting effects. To be sure, what is learned in language training has to be "kept up." Language needs regular infusions of new and different forms, content, and occasions of use—and it benefits, to a great extent, from a balance of the familiar and routine with the unfamiliar, new, and unpredictable. It can even benefit, strangely enough, from long periods when there is no outward appearance of its use. Meditation, retreats, long walks for silent reflection, and silent prayer are some occasions that make our language stronger and more powerful—both for managing ourselves and for relating to others. All are occasions when we rehearse ways of using language—whether as argument, entertainment, or some other purpose—in a kind of communication tool box we call upon when we write or speak for particular effects or outcomes.

Competence with this language tool box comes through study and training with experts. In a sense, we apprentice ourselves to those we read and hear whose words have received accolades for their effectiveness, thereby creating the capacity to keep on learning language while "keeping up" what we have learned before. From such study come habits of language that undergird fluency, competence, and accomplished discourse across situations, needs, and audiences. Gradually, we absorb into our heads and hearts a deepening understanding of how language works and what its special powers might be. We learn to invoke those powers.

Most important, with this understanding, we accumulate instances of language use that remain with us as models. We may have grandparents who studied epigrams and famous quotations or memorized long passages of the Bible. We ourselves may have studied exemplary writings and been asked to model a piece of our own writing on that of other authors. All such occasions bring more demonstrations of effective language use into our familiarity. Many of the pieces in this volume may be ones we might not ordinarily take note of, and their inclusion here expands that world of words and models.

As we learn to play with language, manipulate its parts, and compare its effects in different situations, we internalize—with sufficient practice and motivation—habits of communication that remain with us. Pick up any magazine about business, search any Web site of business consultants, or read articles in newspapers that report on economic affairs. Communication dominates all other topics. Managers, workers, union representatives, auditors, stockholders, members of regulatory boards—all have to convey information, recommendations, and summative reports clearly and effectively. To do so requires knowing not only "what to say" but also how to say it. We have to use words to argue, persuade, and appeal to specific audiences.

Students in composition classes may not now think of themselves as entering business or pursuing a career in communication. Yet the hard fact remains that whatever they do—in friendship, family life, civic roles, or employment—habits of communication and the ability to take in and respond to what others say will significantly define their lives. Some think of oral and written communication skills as bedrock material for life-long learning—and language as a means to keep on learning, to gain and use information across wide reaches, and to enrich our lives for the moment as well as in the future.

What's Language Got to Do with It? covers many important topics in language—globalization, nationalism, multilingualism, and more. Taking on these topics and gaining facility with language depends in large part on our ability to listen. When and if we truly listen, we increase the likelihood of taking in that which is in the hearts and heads of others. And listening well bears other benefits as well.

Speaking well, reflecting what we know in either oral or written language, and being judged an effective communicator do not come as natural parts of human development. To gain proficiency in these areas requires not only practice and motivation, but also dedication and conscious awareness of what is to be gained by listening rather than just hearing.

Students often bemoan the numerous "extra" events, such as public lectures, panels of experts, or debates, that their professors expect them to attend. Perhaps they assume that they need an interest in the subject of these occasions to make it worth their while to go and listen. Not so. Whether or not they are engaged with the topic or the personality or even the outcome of such events, they can as listeners learn how others communicate in genres or situations that they themselves are likely to face in the years ahead. Later in life, well beyond their current classroom experiences, they will, no doubt, give talks—to fellow workers, fellow worshippers in a religious organization, city council members, and school boards. They will serve on panels and be brought into debates within committees or with a child and a group of his or her friends. On these occasions, they will be glad to remember back to strategies they heard—and learned—from these expert speakers, debaters, and panelists.

In all the various roles and genres of speaking we assume in life, we meet issues of gender differences in both communication styles and expectations. We attend events for which interpreters using American Sign Language are positioned at the front of the auditorium. We encounter varieties of language different from our own, ones that differ by ethnicity, region, occasion, age (of speakers and listeners), and genre (whether rap lyrics, sermons, or political debates). As students, workers, homeowners, citizens, we regularly have to confront new uses of technology and widely varying influences and demands from these on the languages we ourselves use.

New technology not only adds vocabulary to our language; it also alters meanings of old words, integrates new symbols, and expands media forms. In other words, it is impossible to avoid hearing about and also living with and practicing the topics and issues covered within *What's Language Got to Do with It?* But we have to *listen* to amplify our understanding of these issues and to be able to answer the more personal question of "what exactly do these language matters have to do with me?"

Of all the language issues confronted in this book, perhaps the most troublesome are the ways in which written language diverges from spoken language. Here is where practice in producing as well as listening to language must be supplemented by extensive experience in *reading* a wide variety of written texts. What we see with the eye when we read remains with us not only in the verbal content we remember, but also in the visual images and forms of presentation. These images shape everything we read and everything we write. Try to form an image of a page or chapter you are reading. As you do so, you think of chapter title; layout; photographs, charts, and other illustrations; the list of references at the end. Whenever we write, we need to have a visual image of what the end product will *look like.*

When we say look *like,* we naturally invoke comparison to what we've seen before. The shaping of paragraphs (some short, some long) as well as the frames of their openings (some brittle and catchy, some filled with definitions, and others offering transition) invite the eye into the text and engage the reader in the physical action of scanning lines of the page with the eye. When we read, our eyes move; however, when we *look* at a page, brochure, or theater program, we focus first on the image of the whole and embed that in our memory. It is through this accumulation of images that we come to know automatically what various forms of written text are as we meet them in our daily lives. If we go to a movie theater and the ticket taker hands us a single sheet of paper, we know this is not a program, but an announcement, notice, or advertisement of some type. Should the ticket taker give us a piece of paper roughly 4 inches by 7 inches in folded form, we know that we have in our hand a brochure or flyer. When we go to live performances, we know what to expect in a playbill that gives the biographies of performers as well as the history of past performances and schedule of forthcoming events. Reading is then not merely a matter of accumulating or remembering words, but of impressing in the brain visual images of the text as a whole: of knowing *what it looks like.*

What's Language Got to Do with It? The most important subtext of this book is this: language is acquired, shaped, interpreted, and changed through interaction and engagement. For those among us who have learned English as a supplement to some other mother tongue, watching English-language television could do no good without engaging with the words heard on the screen. Learning as a spectator and not as a participant will not work for language. Talking back to the speakers on English-language films or television or radio, along with seeking every possible opportunity to converse with native speakers, amounts to engaged interaction.

Language has to be at least two-way, and often it is multi-directional, reaching more than one audience or respondent. Language has to be learned in meaningful, motivated interactions. We can acquire language only by stepping into roles that mean something to us. When we do so, we speak eloquently and with clarity and force, and we feel the effects of our efforts. Here is where our hearts know the words in our heads have reached others.

One peculiar but everyday example will illustrate what we mean by stepping into meaningful roles to learn language more effectively. For centuries, historians have studied the marginal notes that readers scribble on the pages of books. These seemingly simple notes portray interacting, arguing, agreeing, or disagreeing readers who took on the role of discussant, conversationalist, or listener with a writer. Underlining or using a yellow marker does not count as interaction, for when we underline we are not forming words, offering ideas, or asking questions.

Writing in response to reading is an assignment often given by professors. Such assignments should not be viewed as busy-work, but as occasions for conversations. The hope is that students might think of themselves as being in a coffee shop or on a hike with the writer, engaged in dialogue. Stuffed in their pockets are illustrations, text excerpts, or references within the writing that they do not understand, agree with, or consider relevant to their own experiences. Students should consider seriously the meaning of *dialogue* and imagine how the author might reply to their questions, explain points needing clarification, or receive proposals to expand the text. Whether in the margins of a book or on the page of an assignment, this kind of writing, if taken as true dialogue, helps internalize what it means to debate ideas and meaning with others.

Conversation that focuses on a single topic, draws in information from sources other than a speaker's own opinion, and reflects the intake of ideas from others is becoming an endangered art. As the percentage of households with two parents who work outside the home increases, the likelihood that children will grow up with extensive experience in extended adult-child conversations with a single topic as focus decreases. Single-parent households face special constraints in finding the time to anchor such conversations. Multiple televisions and computers in homes contribute to the decline of direct face-to-face talk. The loss of family mealtimes as a regular feature of each day has been a major force in cutting off meaningful conversations. Much talk between the young and the adults in a household amounts to instructions, requests, schedule maintenance, or other brief interactions. The decline in proximity of extended family members—the uncle whose passion is the history of baseball, or the grandparent who built the first bowling alley in the county—has also cut off opportunities for the young to talk with adults whose interests and experiences amount to expertise. Being expert involves both content and process, in mind and body; the combination almost always results in good stories of both successes and failures.

As conversational experiences decline among young people, and as more students arrive at college without having had extensive opportunities to hold their own in long conversations focused on content and process, college classes swell with insecure writers and speakers. Composition classes are a place for taking some steps to make up for the missing years of long talks with caring, knowledgeable adults. Here students can put themselves in roles, settings, and tasks that will build oral language experiences—both listening and talking. Without oral language competence and experience, students cannot hope to write fluently or to do work that brings writer, reader, and ideas together effectively. Talking more, listening better, and thinking more about texts add up to the essential practice needed to support confident, fluent writing. Text-messaging, cell phones, email, and other abbreviating forces on extended language have in certain ways curtailed practice in extended conversations of substance. The hours, weeks, and years of practice missed in childhood and adolescence can be overcome by purposefully assuming the role of a learning, listening, active conversationalist during the college years. Just as a foreign-language learner gains conversational ease and fluency from spending time and talking with native speakers, so do we all learn language by interacting with other competent speakers and by seeing what they see, reading what they read, and attending to the ways they use language to navigate their worlds.

These words of *foreword* you are now reading amount to words of *foretelling* and *forewarning*—for both instructors and students. Students should not expect reading the chapters in this book to make them better writers unless they take on roles and opportunities to listen and talk outside the classroom. Inspiration and imaginative challenges from instructors can stimulate this essential, *real* practice. Students need talking and listening occasions that are as wide-ranging as possible—from news reports on several different radio stations to televised political programs to on-campus debates. Instructors need to follow-up these occasions of listening with conversations in class and by having students report on debates they have had with friends about issues and societal problems. *What's Language Got to Do with It?* will come most alive when students also attend campus talks, panels, and debates, and bring a couple of friends to office hours to continue those debates and conversations.

What's language got to do with it? The answer to this question relates to the roles we hope students will want to play as they move through life. As family member, employee, citizen, and friend, their language represents and reflects them more than any other aspect of their being. They can have no stronger distractor or deterrent to achieving the goals they set and their instructors encourage than their facility with language. Students need to remember that language can be their greatest ally, protector, and advocate. But it can also hold them back, trip them up, and inadvertently set limits on where they can go and what they can become.

Language counts. Making it count depends on learning more about how it works or does not work, what it means and why, and what its most powerful features are. All of us benefit by deepening these understandings. Students, I especially hope that you will take the *it* of this book's title to be *you* and all that you hope to be, know, and achieve.

Introduction
What's Language Got to Do with It?

What's language got to do with it? Just about everything, we contend. In fact, we'd bet that people talk—and argue—about language a lot more than they realize. In a *People* survey of pet peeves in summer 2004, a third of the twenty-four celebrities queried gave answers relating to language. Billy Bob Thornton said his pet peeve was people who say "in sync." Kevin Pollak's was people in the service industry "who don't speak English." For Will Smith, it was "poor grammar." He explained, however, "It's okay if you're making a choice [to use it], ebonically speaking. But not knowing proper grammar is a tough one for me." (Notice that he doesn't condemn Ebonics, a variety of American English, or those who choose to use it, but criticizes speakers of Ebonics who *can't* make a choice because they haven't mastered Standard English.) Director John Waters complained that people who say "*pitcher* instead of *picture*" drive him crazy. Others didn't mention language specifically, but complained about how language gets used—or doesn't. Language—it's everywhere.

The readings in this book seek to give you the tools you need to think analytically about language, to have informed opinions about many issues relating to language and language use—rather than *just* opinions—and to think critically about the powerful influence language exerts on who you and others are. To achieve these goals, we have assembled texts of all sorts—articles, Web pages, cartoons, poems, advertisements, advice columns, letters to the editor, fiction, postcards, and even the very first crossword puzzle—as starting points for examining how language gets used in daily life and why.

Although we present these selections in nine chapters, three themes run through many of the chapters and readings. These themes include, first, the ways that language and especially word choices function as arguments; second, the fact that language is itself a technology, one that changes over time and that is changed in important ways by other technologies, whether by simply writing it down with a pencil, using it for instant messaging, or using it in the outsourcing of jobs to other countries; and, third, the roles that language plays in shaping who you are as a member of groups of various sorts. Keep all three themes in mind as you examine the selections.

WHAT'S LANGUAGE GOT TO DO WITH ARGUMENT?

Even before Massachusetts first married same-sex couples in 2004, a growing number of Americans had begun supporting the creation of civil unions as a means of guaranteeing that lesbian and gay couples would have legal status and receive certain legal rights. Proponents of such unions represented a range of ideological and political beliefs, but they were clear about one thing: a civil union was not to be confused or equated with a marriage. For various reasons, these proponents argued that the term "marriage" can or should be used only in reference to adult heterosexual couples. Whatever else this debate represents, it is an argument about language and the power of words: what words can or cannot mean, and why. As those on both sides of this argument well understand, words, labels, and metaphors are not innocent things that simply reflect social realities; rather, they create those realities in many important ways.

Language and linguistic choices are at the heart of many arguments. Arguments can take various forms, from words to images to a combination of both, in order to present a certain view of reality, real or imagined. From this perspective, argument is not just a fight to the end, with one side leaving the other bloody on the sidewalk. Rather, it includes ways of engaging others by offering them a particular perspective on an issue and asking them to see that issue and the world (temporarily, at least) from that perspective.

"These are trees" reads a small, neat sign taped to a napkin holder at a coffee shop near our campus. We bet this sign does more good than the large placard a few doors down imploring patrons not to waste napkins. Why? Perhaps the language of the first sign makes a more complex, interesting, and artful argument. It invites, indeed requires, the reader to engage in a chain of reasoning to answer several questions: How are napkins trees? Why are the owners reminding me of this fact? What am I supposed to do? Because the sign is small, readers also have to do some work, getting close enough to read its simple message. In contrast, the second sign, while polite with its "Please don't waste napkins," invites no such reasoning. There's nothing thought-provoking about yet another message not to be wasteful—even if it is justified. The two arguments have the same goals—to save money for the shops' owners (and perhaps for their patrons) and maybe even to help the environment—but the real difference between these arguments is the language—the words—through which they are conveyed. The words of the first argument and the implied links they establish between product and desired action work together to make the reader pause, take note, think, and consider a response. This argument *talks* in a way that makes it more likely, in our experience, that customers will think twice about its message than they will about the message of the second sign. The texts in chapter 1, "Language as Argument," present you with opportunities to scrutinize how this process works and to come to appreciate why it is important—not only in debates in the political realm but in every part of life.

WHAT'S LANGUAGE GOT TO DO WITH TECHNOLOGY?

Language itself is a technology. It permits its users to communicate all sorts of things quickly, efficiently, and sometimes unambiguously. At the same time, new technologies change language. As many of the readings in this book demonstrate, writing is also a technology, and it changes language that comes to be written down. How has the existence of punctuation, itself a technology, changed how we use and understand language? As you'll learn, the earliest alphabetic texts weren't just written without punctuation; they were written in the way that oxen plow: left to right on one line, right to left on the next, and back to left to right—and with no spaces between words, to boot.

Additionally, writing down a language encourages and reinforces the belief that there is a single correct way it should be used. It also opens the way for a corollary to that belief: that those who don't use language the "correct" way are somehow less intelligent, not as hardworking, less moral, maybe even less clean. And of course, what is considered correct changes over time. Just a few decades ago, usage manuals proscribed the split infinitive—Captain Kirk would not have dared "to boldly go"; rather, he'd have needed "to go boldly." Split infinitives are no longer taboo, however, and they show up in academic prose as well as in the *New York Times*. Even though most of us realize that language, even written language, changes constantly, it is almost second nature for us to judge others on the correctness of their language use. (If we were a bit more honest, we'd come to admit that "what is correct" in fact almost always means what we believe we do.)

And the birth of new technologies changes language in novel ways. How are email and instant messaging influencing written language? Once upon a time, not so long ago, *wrt* was a meaningless string of letters, but for many of us who compose email in English, it now means "with respect to" or "with regard to." How does the use of *wrt* spread to new contexts, whether student essays or the notes a teacher writes on the board? Will *wrt* follow in the footsteps of the Latin abbreviations *e.g.* "for example" and *i.e.* "that is," to become part of "standard" English, the variety of English expected for formal writing and speaking? (Notice that most people who use such abbreviations know they come from Latin, but they don't know what the abbreviations mean in Latin—and don't need to.) Will our attitudes change so much that the next edition of this book will use *wrt* in place of "with respect to"? Stay tuned.

Similarly, we can ask how instant messaging is changing our notion of what written language is or should be. As you'll see in some of our readings, the language of IMs is already showing up in cartoons. Will someone one day write a novel constructed of nothing but IMs? As we come up with new ways to communicate, how does language follow? The evolution of language and technologies proceeds in complicated—and often controversial—ways, a claim that the texts in chapter 2, "How Writing Changes Language," and chapter 3, "Technology and (versus?) Language," invite you to evaluate.

WHAT'S LANGUAGE GOT TO DO WITH WHO YOU ARE?

That language is a big part of everyone's identity is not news. If you name ten groups you belong to, odds are that language plays an important role in the sense of membership you have with each one. People in every country likely feel a special bond with those who speak the same regional, social, or ethnic dialect they do. Most people are convinced that females and males use language differently. Friends develop in-group slang. Bilinguals don't just speak two languages; rather, they know when to use each and even how to mix them, depending on where they are and whom they are with. Those who are religious often use language differently from those who aren't, and it's as much a matter of what they don't say (for example, avoiding swear words) as what they do (using expressions like "Thank you, Jesus" or "In-sha'-Allah"). If you're Deaf or know someone who is, you realize that Deaf identity is predicated on using American Sign Language. As African Americans know all too well—and Will Smith's comments remind us—someone will always have an opinion about the variety or varieties of language they use. These cases show us that, whatever else it does, the language we use says something about who we are, giving others some idea of the groups we identify with as well as those we don't. Four chapters in this book deal most directly with language and identity. Chapter 4, "Multilingual USA," considers what it means to be bilingual in the United States today and what it means that more than 1 out of 5 Americans report speaking a language other than English at home. Chapter 5, "Talking While Black," examines the choices African Americans make anytime they speak. Chapter 6, "His and Hers: Language and Gender," explores patterns of language use between males and females—and also language used *about* females and males. And chapter 7, "Language in Deaf Communities," shows why debates about deafness are ultimately always debates about language.

Language even comes to stand in for entire groups or nations. One can't be *québécois* without speaking the French of Canada—in contrast to the French spoken in France or Tunisia. And many Americans believe you can't claim to be a true American if you can't speak English. (Some Americans go so far as to argue that "good" Americans speak *only* English—and that means American English, thank you.) From a very different perspective, one of the longest-running battles about language in this country concerns the use of Native American names and images in sports. If a college calls its team the Braves and students chant war cries at games, are these practices evidence of respect for the first Americans or a lack of it? The texts in chapter 8, "Language and National Identities" challenge you to examine language to see how closely linked it is to belonging to a nation.

As English becomes more widely used around the world, does it serve any less as a marker of identity for those who speak it as a native language? And who, by the way, gets to make the rules? Will native speakers of English ever gain the skills they need to work with or for people who do *not* speak English as their first language? How will English change as "the whole world" comes to speak and use it? And what consequences does the spread of English have for other languages? Its spread in what is today the United States nearly destroyed the languages of the country's original peoples, the Native Americans—not because of anything about English itself but because of the attitudes and policies of English speakers. How have those changes influenced these groups' understanding of who they are? The book's closing chapter, "Globalizing English," examines these issues and others: what will happen to English—and to native and nonnative speakers of English—if the whole world does eventually speak English?

WHAT'S LANGUAGE GOT TO DO WITH WRITING?

At the most basic level, all writing—whether essays or grocery lists—depends on language (and almost always written *words*). At a deeper level, it's worth remembering that, images aside, written texts are *only* language—scribbles on a page for those who don't know how to read the language in which the text is written. Yet, for readers who know the code, texts have the power to move us to act, to cry, to laugh. Successful communication, including successful writing, depends on mastery of myriad skills, nearly all of which are related to language in one way or another—whether it is the mastery of particular varieties of language, particular genres of text, or particular strategies of argumentation. The assignments in this book will help you hone your analytic skills and develop your abilities as a communicator and writer, especially when it comes to your use of language.

If, after using this book, you find yourself noticing and reflecting on language around you—your language, the lyrics of the music you listen to, the signs in places you shop, the language of a novelist or poet you read, or the language of politicians or advertisements or even those who teach you, we'll have succeeded, and you'll have learned that language has got pretty much everything to do with it.

chapter 1

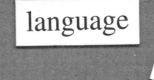 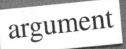

i f most folks think about language at all, they assume it works like a window—a clear pane of glass—beyond which we see reality as it truly is. In this chapter (and throughout this book), we'll take a very different perspective, assuming that something as mundane as word choice makes an argument, often a powerful one.

Kenneth Burke (1887–1995), a scholar of literature, rhetoric, and religion, suggests that words and phrases act as terministic screens encouraging or even forcing us to see reality in particular ways, ruling out alternatives. As Burke points out, words don't just reflect particular views of reality; they actually complete arguments. If, for example, someone refers to a fetus as an "unborn child," it's logical for that person to believe that abortion should be banned because in his or her eyes, it is the murder of a child. If someone else thinks of abortion as a "right" that women should have in order to have control over their own bodies, that person probably doesn't even use the term "unborn child." Similarly, some may refer to homosexuality as a "disease." But lesbians and gay men who perceive that to be just who they are would not likely use such a term like "disease" to talk about homosexuality. In all these cases, the arguments complete themselves: by choosing language like "unborn child," "right," "disease," or "who I am," you set up chains of propositions leading inevitably (or nearly so) to particular conclusions.

This chapter begins with selections that focus on just such word choices. Clyde Haberman demonstrates how and why Israelis and Palestinians and their respective supporters can't agree even on terms for talking about the political situation that divides them on one level and unites them on another. Examining a less explosive situation, Kendra Hamilton considers why some people identify themselves as "Hispanic" while others prefer the term "Latino."

Moving beyond words alone, several selections consider the power of metaphors in argument. In a selection from The Argument Culture, the well-known sociolinguist Deborah Tannen examines and critiques the ubiquitous metaphor of argument as battle, for example, the ideas that there are (only) two sides to every question and that one side must win while the other loses. Otto Santa Ana, also a sociolinguist, analyzes the roles metaphors about immigration played in newspaper writing in a heated California vote about the rights of immigrants. Cliff Rothman reflects on the subtle and not-so-subtle ways that advertisers, through their choice of words and images, court lesbian and gay customers. The Web site <wordscanheal.org> documents an effort to put an end to gossip and similar linguistic behaviors because, its creators contend, doing so will prevent another Columbine. From the vantage point of history, Anna Quindlen carefully scrutinizes the ways that word choices in New York Times articles over the past century and a half have both supported and undermined the struggles of various groups for civil rights. In a short text from 1915, the suffragist Alice Duer Miller uses sexist metaphors and rhetoric to explain why some women at the time opposed votes for men—all as a way of humorously arguing for women's right to vote. The chapter ends with an article by Michiko Kakutani that looks at genres of language use, especially argument, as she considers whether and how today's college students actually debate social and political issues.

If these readings succeed, you'll never take words or windows for granted again.

••

In this feature story from August 2001, Clyde Haberman, a former bureau chief for the
New York Times in Jerusalem and current columnist, explains the delicacy and signifi-
cance of labeling places or events in the Middle East. As noted in the introduction to this
chapter, Kenneth Burke claims that words, especially names or labels, often work as
"terministic screens," predisposing us to see things in certain ways. In chapter 2, George
Orwell will rail against what he considers dishonest use of language by those committed
to political causes. Were Orwell alive today, we can safely imagine he would not see any
of the lexical choices discussed in this selection as neutral or innocent.

••

CLYDE HABERMAN

In the Mideast This Year, Even Words Shoot to Kill

WARS MAY BE FOUGHT WITH GUNS, mortars, bombs and the rest of the standard arsenal, but near-wars are more subtle. Besides all the usual tools of battle, they have one more: language. And in the near-war that has enmeshed Israelis and Palestinians, this is the weapon that may help decide who wins.

The importance of words was amply evident last week after the Israeli Army fired missiles at Hamas offices in the West Bank, killing eight Palestinians, among them two small boys who happened to be at the scene. It was regrettable about the boys, Israeli officials said, but the target was a leader of the militant Islamic group, who they say was the brains behind terrorist operations. While the United States and other countries condemned this calculated killing, the latest in a series of such attacks, Israel insisted on its right and obligation to protect its own people, by disposing of suspected terror masterminds before it's too late.

The merits of that argument aside, how might one describe that anti-Hamas strike in Nablus?

Easy, Palestinian officials said. It was a cold-blooded assassination. But just as one person's terrorist has long been another's freedom fighter, one side's "assassination" is the other's "active self-defense," a term favored by some Israeli officials.

Foreign Minister Shimon Peres became practically apoplectic when an ⁵ Israeli television interviewer used the A-word. Israel does not assassinate people, Mr. Peres said angrily. It goes after leaders who dispatch young men to blow themselves up in the midst of Israelis. "Suicide bombers cannot be threatened by death," he said. "The only way to stop them is to intercept those who send them."

"Interception" is much preferred by some in the Israeli government, the implication being that the army intervenes merely to stop a terrorist act already in progress. Another word of choice is "liquidation." But this has an unpleasant ring for some, almost a Mafia taint. Indeed, a prominent spokeswoman for the Palestinians, Hanan Ashrawi, said that "they're behaving like mobsters, turning their army into hit men."

When Prime Minister Ariel Sharon's security cabinet met last week, time was given to coming up with a better name for these targeted killings, which Mr. Sharon promised to continue if he deemed them necessary. Among the candidates was "actions to prevent the killing of Jews." Presumably, the hunt for an acceptable label is not over.

All this goes beyond mere political spin, though each side in this near-war is out to persuade the world that it is the true victim. The use of language touches the psychology of the conflict, not only how Palestinians and Israelis view each other but also how they judge themselves. No way, for example, is Israel about to pronounce itself an assassin state, no matter how much the wisdom and morality of its strategy is questioned abroad.

It takes but a single word to show how far Israelis and Palestinians have tumbled from more hopeful—some would say more naïve—days. Think back to 1993, to the Oslo peace agreement and the memorable White House handshake between Yitzhak Rabin and Yasir Arafat to seal the deal. They were peace "partners," they said, and they clung to that word almost as if it were a talisman, through repeated suicide bombings by Palestinian terrorists and the massacre of Palestinian worshipers by an Israeli settler. "Partner" now lies in the graveyard of "peace process." Mr. Sharon is not about to use it, and his predecessor, Ehud Barak, wrote the other day that he doubted Mr. Arafat would ever qualify again as a "partner for peace."

Nuanced phraseology is hardly unique to Israelis or Palestinians. Had ¹⁰ the Nablus strike been the work of American forces, one could easily imagine a Pentagon statement describing the unintended deaths of the two boys as "collateral damage." Still, the arsenal of words is an essential element of this conflict.

The very land being fought over has long been up for linguistic grabs. Is it the West Bank, the choice of Palestinians and a convention followed by most foreigners? Or is it Judea and Samaria, ancient names preferred in Israel (except perhaps by those who refer to the area as "the territories")?

Whatever the land is called, it has been essentially sealed off for months, along with the Gaza Strip. Most days, Israeli roadblocks make it difficult, to the point of impossibility, for Palestinians to move between towns. This, the Israelis call a "closure." Or else they say that the Palestinians are being "shut in" their villages. Palestinians are more graphic about their confinement. Plain and simple, they say, they are "under siege."

The boundary between Israel and the West Bank has been called the "green line" since 1949, when it was traced on a map in green ink as part of a cease-fire ending what Israel calls its War of Independence. But in the peace talks of the 1990s, many Israelis—not to mention Palestinians—saw the "green line" as a likely border of an emerging Palestinian state. Since actual borders remain subject to negotiation, at least from Israel's perspective, Israeli officials have begun to shy from "green line." The term in vogue now is "seam line." The boundary remains the same, but to Israeli ears, "seam line" doesn't sound so much like a fixed border between two states.

When a suicide bombing occurs, Israelis fall victim to a "terrorist." Palestinians have a new "martyr." If a Palestinian dies in a mysterious explosion at his house or office, his neighbors are often quick to attribute it to an "Israeli attack" by missiles or artillery shells. The Israeli version just as often is that the man died in a "work accident," meaning that he blew himself up inadvertently while making a bomb.

Palestinians interrogated by Israeli security agents say they have been subjected to "torture." Israel says it applies "moderate physical pressure," and only when it has to. After the Nablus raid, Palestinian security courts sentenced several men to death for being "collaborators" with Israel. On the Israeli side, such men tend to be described as "cooperators" or "aiders." 15

Israelis worry about Palestinian "extremists." Palestinians talk about their "activists." Palestinians hold "demonstrations." Israelis send the police to contain these "disturbances."

Palestinians want "observers," the implication being an international force to watch over them. The Israeli government will accept "monitors," a word that suggests they will be Americans only, filing reports from a distant office and not actually going to the scene to actually see what they are supposed to be monitoring.

Then there is the difficulty that the Sharon government seems to have with what to call its strategy. Hardliners on the Israeli right are demanding an all-out assault on the Palestinian Authority, but the prime minister refuses to go that far. His has come to be known as a policy of "restraint." But "restraint" makes an old warrior like Mr. Sharon wince, and so he leans toward other expressions, including "active self-defense."

"'Restraint' has bad connotations going back to the 1930s," explained Amiel Ungar, a political science professor at Judea and Samaria College, in the West Bank settlement of Ariel. In those pre-state days, Professor Ungar said, it referred to Jews' staying inside their communities, not attacking Arabs and waiting instead to be hit first before responding.

Clearly, however, the more crucial fault lines are between Israelis and Palestinians. "We see in the language the huge discrepancy in psychology and emotions that each side brings to the conflict," said Yaron Ezrahi, a political theorist with the Israel Democracy Institute in Jerusalem. "Every act, gesture, or word used by one side is destined to be mistranslated in the other system. So we have endless systemic misunderstandings."

There is one word at least that both sides share. In Hebrew, it is "shalom," in Arabic "salaam." Either way, it means peace. It is the most overused and underachieved word in the region.

about the text

1. According to Haberman, how are words weapons in the Middle East? Give examples of terms that both sides use as weapons.

2. What does the expression "one person's terrorist has long been another person's freedom fighter" mean (paragraph 4)? In what ways does Haberman go beyond the generalization to show the power of words in the conflict?

3. Yaron Ezrahi contends that there is a "huge discrepancy" between the "psychology and emotions that each side brings to the conflict," and that "every act, gesture or word used by one side is destined to be mistranslated in the other system," resulting in "endless systematic misunderstandings" (paragraph 20). What are the origins of the discrepancy of which he speaks? What are the consequences of the "misunderstandings"?

on language use

4. Haberman's article uses several terms that refer to the parts of the Middle East in which conflict occurs: the West Bank, Judea and Samaria, and the territories (paragraph 11). There are others: the Gaza Strip, the occupied territories, Palestine. Research who prefers each label and why. Why are these labels important to both sides? What argument(s) does the labeling of the land itself make?

5. Investigate some of the terms currently used to discuss the conflict, and analyze the consequences of the use of the differing terms. A good place to start would be the label for the border with the West Bank. Think, for example, about the differences between "fence" and "wall."

for writing

6. Among the most complex set of labels are those used for Arabs who blow themselves up in public areas. The Western press refers to these individuals as "suicide bombers" while the Arab press uses the term "martyrs." Write an essay about how each side uses labels, explaining how they came about and what the denotations and connotations of each term are.

7. In paragraph 10, Haberman notes that nuanced phraseology can be found anywhere there are differences of opinion and commitment. Take another conflict—for example, immigration or privatizing social security—and look for terms used by one or both sides. Write an essay analyzing how the terms predispose listeners or readers to see the situation and solutions in partisan ways.

KENDRA HAMILTON

You Say "Hispanic," I Say "Latino"

In this article from the maga-zine Black Issues in Higher Education (September 2001), Kendra Hamilton, *the assistant editor, examines the terms of self-reference preferred by various Spanish-speaking Americans. She pays special attention to the labels "Hispanic" and "Latino." As their comments make clear, those who fall into these groups often have strong preferences for one term or the other, and their reasons are not necessarily shared, even by those who choose the same label.*

AT A GROCERY STORE in San Antonio the "Mexican" food section has a new name. "They're calling it the 'Hispanic' food section. But I don't see any 'Hispanic' food—no Bolivian food, no Cuban food," says Marcia Miller, a public affairs officer at the University of Texas-Austin—"just the same old chilies and refried beans."

Major grocery chains aren't the only ones jumping on the "Hispanic" bandwagon. It has long been the term of choice for government and the media—but its vagueness can offend.

"It's (Hispanic) not an identity, it's not a race, it's not an ethnicity," explains Dr. Maria DeGuzmán, a Spanish-born conceptual artist and assistant professor of Latina/o Literature(s) and Culture(s) at the University of North Carolina-Chapel Hill. "It's an umbrella term that's trying to unite people who share a history, with many fractures and divergences within that history."

And there are plenty for whom it's pretty close to being a fighting word. Writers such as Gloria Anzaldúa, Sandra Cisneros and Denise Chavez are on record as being strongly and proudly "Latina"—not "Hispanic."

And so is Elizabeth Jones, a fourth-year student at the ⁵ University of Virginia who runs the school's Hispanic-Latino Peer Mentoring program—though neither her name nor her appearance label her as such.

Jones has an Anglo name, and she also happens to look Black. Although she currently lives in Arlington, Va., she was born in San Jose, Costa Rica—"in Limon, where most of the Blacks live." She's fully bilingual in English and Spanish and learning Portuguese as well.

"Dislike" might be too strong a word to describe Jones' reaction to the word "Hispanic"; however, she does take issue with the term. "Hispanic says you're a division of Spain, but I'm from Latin America, specifically Central America." Jones is from a section of Costa Rica whose ethnic mix includes Jamaicans who immigrated to work in the coffee industry and intermarried with Indians.

"'Hispanic' doesn't encompass anything about the Jamaican and Indian parts of my background," Jones says. "For me, Latina tells you more about my heritage and culture."

REGIONAL AND CULTURAL DIFFERENCES

There are areas of the United States in which "Hispanic" is considered a highly descriptive term.

"I take a census informally among my students every year. They seem to 10
like Hispanic," says Dr. Rolando Hinojosa-Smith, the Ellen Garwood professor of English at UT-Austin and something of an institution among Southwestern writers. "But then we Texans are ornery. 'Chicano' never caught hold here when that term was popular back in the '70s. And as far as I know, neither has 'Latino.'"

This is somewhat confusing for cultural outsiders—so much so that it may be tempting to see the debate as a sort of "you say to-may-to, I say to-mah-to." But the social, historical and political dimensions of the debate are quite complex, and with the Hispanic, Latino, and Latin American populations less than a percentage point away from being the largest U.S. minority—12 percent of the U.S. population, compared with 12.9 percent for African Americans—calling the whole thing off is not an option.

So what precisely is the difference between Hispanic and Latino?

Dr. Alicia Borinsky, an Argentina-born writer and literary scholar who writes in Spanish and English and is a professor of Latin American and Comparative Literature at Boston University, says there is a generation gap in usage. "Latin Americans of an older generation dislike both terms and prefer to be recognized by their countries of origin—Venezuela, Mexico, etc.," she says.

Region has a part to play as well, says Dr. Pablo Davis, an Argentian American born in New York who is an assistant dean of students at the University of Virginia. "Hispanic is preferred in the West"—Texas and the desert Southwest—"and Latino is preferred in the East, particularly in the Caribbean and among Puerto Ricans and Dominicans."

But the crucial difference is less one of age or of regional taste than one 15
of race and politics.

"Sometimes, and this is particularly true of the West, 'Hispanic' is used by people who want to emphasize the European part of their heritage. This is absolutely true in New Mexico—people say Hispanic there with a fairly clear intention to indicate, 'We're not Indian, and we're not mestizo.[1] We're from the old Spanish families,'" Davis explains.

DeGuzmán agrees. "In one sense, 'Hispanic' has its uses because it reminds people that 'we' have been here a long time. People tend to forget that the first printing press was in Mexico City, that the first U.S. city was St. Augustine. "But," she adds, "there's also that class/caste prejudice of associating 'Latino' with immigration, of seeing 'Latino' as downwardly mobile, of wanting to claim *emblanquecimiento*"—(pronounced em-BLAHN-kay-see-me-ento)—or literally 'en-Whitening.'"

"It's absolutely a matter of positionality in the political space," argues Dr. Silvio Torres-Saillant, associate professor of English and director of the Latino-Latin American Studies program at Syracuse University. "People who call themselves 'Latino' are firmer about staking their claim as a community fighting for inclusion and empowerment."

Some say "Hispanic" and some say "Latino." Which should the general public use? Or is choosing necessary, or even desirable?

DeGuzmán, who personally prefers "Latina," offers a conditional yes. "To 20 the extent that it allows you to form (academic) disciplines, bring people together, protect their rights, fight for their visibility, I would say, yes, it's absolutely justified," she says.

But Torres-Saillant is a bit more cautious. Offering the rise of "Hispanic" as an example, he points out that the pan-hemispheric connotations of that term—while not actively destructive—have actually served the interests of corporate America over and above those of the Latino community.

"If you can have people in Buenos Aires being moved by the same images as people in San Antonio, (as a corporation) you've got it made," he says.

And given Latin America's troubled history of Negrophobia, anti-Indian prejudice, and White supremacy, even celebrations of racial mixing with the current vogue for all things "mestizo" "become suspect when in saying the word, one then chooses the image of a European to represent it," Torres-Saillant adds.

"This is a strategy that quells the yearning for justice and inclusion. It tells us that we are all one, that we are all mixed, that racial boundaries are not discernible," says Torres-Saillant. "But let's imagine a scenario in which there's no way to tell the difference, shall we say, between the ruling class in Nigeria and underserved and disempowered communities in places like

---

1. **mestizo** having ancestors of both European (usually Iberian) heritage and indigenous or Indian heritage, from an Old Spanish word meaning "mixed."

Harlem and the Bronx. You would be worried, wouldn't you? Because how can one fight for the empowerment of the disinherited if you do not have to have the capacity to tell who they are?"

But there's still a practical question lingering in the background for cul- 25 tural outsiders. Davis, who oversees UVA's Hispanic-Latino Peer Mentoring Program as part of his duties, says, "I tend to sacrifice elegance for completeness and inclusion. When people ask, I say that I work with Hispanic, Latino, and Latin American students."

But if that sounds like too much of a mouthful, one could always plunge ahead with one of the three—keeping in mind the generational, regional, and sociopolitical contexts, as well as Borinsky's rule of thumb.

"I do not mind whatever term is used, as long as it is mentioned in a spirit of generosity," she says.

| **about the text** |

1. What do the terms "Hispanic" and "Latino" denote and connote for those interviewed here? What are the sources of those meanings? Why is the distinction important?

2. What is the history of the term "Hispanic"? Why is Latin America called "Latin America"? (Remember that Portuguese, not Spanish, is the main language of Brazil.) In what ways do the labels "Hispanic" and "Latino" reflect and create a linguistic division from a colonial past?

| **on language use** |

3. Consider two other minority groups in the United States—African Americans and Asian Americans. What are some terms of self-reference that have been used by members of these groups? What might account for variations in these naming practices?

4. We recall a sign posted several years ago by an Asian American students' association entitled "The Ten Things Asian Americans

Hate Most." Number 1 on the list was "the hyphen." Why all the fuss about a hyphen?

5. Outsiders who do not wish to offend (and even more so those who wish to demonstrate support or solidarity), often find it difficult to choose terms. Why? How might outsiders decide which term or terms to use or not use?

| **for writing** |

6. Some cultural theorists argue that one of the most important freedoms a group can have is the freedom to name itself. What does this claim mean? Why might it be true? Take a social group in the United States (not necessarily one based on race or heritage) and explore this claim in an essay.

7. In paragraph 23, Professor Silvio Torres-Saillant comments on "Latin America's troubled history of Negrophobia, anti-Indian prejudice and White supremacy." Research and write an essay comparing the consequences of one of these topics in Latin America and the United States.

DEBORAH TANNEN

Fighting for Our Lives

A sociolinguist at Georgetown University, Deborah Tannen is the author of the best-selling You Just Don't Understand: Women and Men in Conversation (1990). In this selection from the opening chapter of her 1998 book, The Argument Culture: Moving from Debate to Dialogue, Tannen focuses on metaphor and its power to influence perceptions. She examines American culture's propensity to treat nearly every interaction as a metaphorical or potential debate that one side must lose, asking whether such a practice limits our society's possibilities in important ways. As you read, think about the metaphors you use to describe your own interactions.

METAPHORS: WE ARE WHAT WE SPEAK

CULTURE, IN A SENSE, is an environment of narratives that we hear repeatedly until they seem to make self-evident sense in explaining human behavior. Thinking of human interactions as battles is a metaphorical frame through which we learn to regard the world and the people in it.

All language uses metaphors to express ideas; some metaphoric words and expressions are novel, made up for the occasion, but more are calcified in the language. They are simply the way we think it is natural to express ideas. We don't think of them as metaphors. Someone who says, "Be careful: You aren't a cat; you don't have nine lives," is explicitly comparing you to a cat, because the cat is named in words. But what if someone says, "Don't pussyfoot around; get to the point"? There is no explicit comparison to a cat, but the comparison is there nonetheless, implied in the word "pussyfoot." This expression probably developed as a reference to the movements of a cat cautiously circling a suspicious object. I doubt that individuals using the word "pussyfoot" think consciously of cats. More often than not, we use expressions without thinking about their metaphoric implications. But that doesn't mean those implications are not influencing us.

At a meeting, a general discussion became so animated that a participant who wanted to comment prefaced his remark by saying, "I'd like to leap into the fray." Another participant called out, "Or share your thoughts." Everyone laughed. By suggesting a different phrasing, she called attention to what would probably have otherwise gone unnoticed: "Leap into the fray" characterized the lively discussion as a metaphorical battle.

Americans talk about almost everything as if it were a war. A book about the history of linguistics is called *The Linguistics Wars*. A magazine article about claims that science is not completely objective is titled "The Science Wars." One about breast cancer detection is "The Mammogram War"; about competition among caterers, "Party Wars"—and on and on in a potentially endless list. Politics, of course, is a prime candidate. One of innumerable possible examples, the headline of a story reporting that the Democratic National Convention nominated Bill Clinton to run for a second term declares, "DEMOCRATS SEND CLINTON INTO BATTLE FOR A 2D TERM." But medicine is as frequent a candidate, as we talk about battling and conquering disease.

Headlines are intentionally devised to attract attention, but we all use military or attack imagery in everyday expressions without thinking about it: "Take a shot at it," "I don't want to be shot down," "He went off half cocked," "That's half the battle." Why does it matter that our public discourse is filled with military metaphors? Aren't they just words? Why not talk about something that matters—like actions?

Because words matter. When we think we are using language, language is using us. As linguist Dwight Bolinger put it (employing a military metaphor), language is like a loaded gun: It can be fired intentionally, but it can wound or kill just as surely when fired accidentally. The terms in which we talk about something shape the way we think about it—and even what we see.

The power of words to shape perception has been proven by researchers in controlled experiments. Psychologists Elizabeth Loftus and John Palmer, for example, found that the terms in which people are asked to recall something affect what they recall. The researchers showed subjects a film of two cars colliding, then asked how fast the cars were going; one week later, they asked whether there had been any broken glass. Some subjects were asked, "About how fast were the cars going when they bumped into each other?" Others were asked, "About how fast were the cars going when they smashed into each other?" Those who read the question with the verb "smashed" estimated that the cars were going faster. They were also more likely to "remember" having seen broken glass. (There wasn't any.)

This is how language works. It invisibly molds our way of thinking about people, actions, and the world around us. Military metaphors train us to think about—and see—everything in terms of fighting, conflict, and war.

This perspective then limits our imaginations when we consider what we can do about situations we would like to understand or change.

Even in science, common metaphors that are taken for granted influence how researchers think about natural phenomena. Evelyn Fox Keller describes a case in which acceptance of a metaphor led scientists to see something that was not there. A mathematical biologist, Keller outlines the fascinating behavior of cellular slime mold. This unique mold can take two completely different forms: It can exist as single-cell organisms, or the separate cells can come together to form multicellular aggregates. The puzzle facing scientists was: What triggers aggregation? In other words, what makes the single cells join together? Scientists focused their investigations by asking what entity issued the order to start aggregating. They first called this bosslike entity a "founder cell," and later a "pacemaker cell," even though no one had seen any evidence for the existence of such a cell. Proceeding nonetheless from the assumption that such a cell must exist, they ignored evidence to the contrary: For example, when the center of the aggregate is removed, other centers form.

Scientists studying slime mold did not examine the interrelationship between the cells and their environment, nor the interrelationship between the functional systems within each cell, because they were busy looking for the pacemaker cell, which, as eventually became evident, did not exist. Instead, under conditions of nutritional deprivation, each individual cell begins to feel the urge to merge with others to form the conglomerate. It is a reaction of the cells to their environment, not to the orders of a boss. Keller recounts this tale to illustrate her insight that we tend to view nature through our understanding of human relations as hierarchical. In her words, "We risk imposing on nature the very stories we like to hear." In other words, the conceptual metaphor of hierarchical governance made scientists "see" something—a pacemaker cell—that wasn't there.

Among the stories many Americans most like to hear are war stories. According to historian Michael Sherry, the American war movie developed during World War II and has been with us ever since. He shows that movies not explicitly about war were also war movies at heart, such as westerns with their good guy–bad guy battles settled with guns. *High Noon*, for example, which became a model for later westerns, was an allegory of the Second World War: The happy ending hinges on the pacifist taking up arms. We can also see this story line in contemporary adventure films: Think of *Star Wars*, with its stirring finale in which Han Solo, having professed no interest in or taste for battle, returns at the last moment to destroy the enemy and save the day. And precisely the same theme is found in a contemporary low-budget independent film, *Sling Blade*, in which a peace-loving retarded man becomes a hero at the end by murdering the man who has been tormenting the family he has come to love.

PUT UP YOUR DUKES

If war provides the metaphors through which we view the world and each other, we come to view others—and ourselves—as warriors in battle. Almost any human encounter can be framed as a fight between two opponents. Looking at it this way brings particular aspects of the event into focus and obscures others.

Framing interactions as fights affects not only the participants but also the viewers. At a performance, the audience, as well as the performers, can be transformed. This effect was noted by a reviewer in the *New York Times*, commenting on a musical event:

> **Showdown at Lincoln Center.** Jazz's ideological war of the last several years led to a pitched battle in August between John Lincoln Collier, the writer, and Wynton Marsalis, the trumpeter, in a debate at Lincoln Center. Mr. Marsalis demolished Mr. Collier, point after point after point, but what made the debate unpleasant was the crowd's blood lust; humiliation, not elucidation, was the desired end.

Military imagery pervades this account: the difference of opinions between Collier and Marsalis was an "ideological war," and the "debate" was a "pitched battle" in which Marsalis "demolished" Collier (not his arguments, but him). What the commentator regrets, however, is that the audience got swept up in the mood instigated by the way the debate was carried out: "the crowd's blood lust" for Collier's defeat.

This is one of the most dangerous aspects of regarding intellectual interchange as a fight. It contributes to an atmosphere of animosity that spreads like a fever. In a society that includes people who express their anger by shooting, the result of demonizing those with whom we disagree can be truly tragic.

But do audiences necessarily harbor within themselves a "blood lust," or [15] is it stirred in them by the performances they are offered? Another arts event was set up as a debate between a playwright and a theater director. In this case, the metaphor through which the debate was viewed was not war but boxing—a sport that is in itself, like a debate, a metaphorical battle that pitches one side against the other in an all-out effort to win. A headline describing the event set the frame: "AND IN THIS CORNER . . ." followed by the subhead "A Black Playwright and White Critic Duke It Out." The story then reports:

> the face-off between August Wilson, the most successful black playwright in the American theater, and Robert Brustein, longtime drama critic for *The New Republic* and artistic director of the American Repertory Theatre in Cambridge, Mass. These two heavyweights had been battling in print since last June. . . .
> Entering from opposite sides of the stage, the two men shook hands and came out fighting—or at least sparring.

Wilson, the article explains, had given a speech in which he opposed Black performers taking "white" roles in color-blind casting; Brustein had written a column disagreeing; and both followed up with further responses to each other.

According to the article, "The drama of the Wilson-Brustein confrontation lies in their mutual intransigence."[1] No one would question that audiences crave drama. But is intransigence the most appealing source of drama? I happened to hear this debate broadcast on the radio. The line that triggered the loudest cheers from the audience was the final question put to the two men by the moderator, Anna Deavere Smith: "What did you each learn from the other in this debate?" The loud applause was evidence that the audience did not crave intransigence. They wanted to see another kind of drama: the drama of change—change that comes from genuinely listening to someone with a different point of view, not the transitory drama of two intransigent positions in stalemate.

To encourage the staging of more dramas of change and fewer of intransigence, we need new metaphors to supplement and complement the pervasive war and boxing match metaphors through which we take it for granted issues and events are best talked about and viewed.

MUD SPLATTERS

Our fondness for the fight scenario leads us to frame many complex human interactions as a battle between two sides. This then shapes the way we understand what happened and how we regard the participants. One unfortu-

---

1. **intransigence** refusal to compromise.

nate result is that fights make a mess in which everyone is muddied. The person attacked is often deemed just as guilty as the attacker.

The injustice of this is clear if you think back to childhood. Many of us still harbor anger as we recall a time (or many times) a sibling or playmate started a fight—but both of us got blamed. Actions occur in a stream, each a response to what came before. Where you punctuate them can change their meaning just as you can change the meaning of a sentence by punctuating it in one place or another.

Like a parent despairing of trying to sort out which child started a fight, people often respond to those involved in a public dispute as if both were equally guilty. When champion figure skater Nancy Kerrigan was struck on the knee shortly before the 1994 Olympics in Norway and the then-husband of another champion skater, Tonya Harding, implicated his wife in planning the attack, the event was characterized as a fight between two skaters that obscured their differing roles. As both skaters headed for the Olympic competition, their potential meeting was described as a "long-anticipated figure-skating shootout." Two years later, the event was referred to not as "the attack on Nancy Kerrigan" but as "the rivalry surrounding Tonya Harding and Nancy Kerrigan." 20

By a similar process, the Senate Judiciary Committee hearings to consider the nomination of Clarence Thomas for Supreme Court justice at which Anita Hill was called to testify are regularly referred to as the "Hill-Thomas hearings," obscuring the very different roles played by Hill and Thomas. Although testimony by Anita Hill was the occasion for reopening the hearings, they were still the Clarence Thomas confirmation hearings: Their purpose was to evaluate Thomas's candidacy. Framing these hearings as a two-sides dispute between Hill and Thomas allowed the senators to focus their investigation on cross-examining Hill rather than seeking other sorts of evidence, for example by consulting experts on sexual harassment to ascertain whether Hill's account seemed plausible.

SLASH-AND-BURN THINKING

Approaching situations like warriors in battle leads to the assumption that intellectual inquiry, too, is a game of attack, counterattack, and self-defense. In this spirit, critical thinking is synonymous with criticizing. In many classrooms, students are encouraged to read someone's life work, then rip it to shreds. Though criticism is one form of critical thinking—and an essential one—so are integrating ideas from disparate fields and examining the context out of which ideas grew. Opposition does not lead to the whole truth when we ask only "What's wrong with this?" and never "What can we use from this in building a new theory, a new understanding?"

There are many ways that unrelenting criticism is destructive in itself. All of society loses when creative people are discouraged from their pursuits by unfair criticism. (This is particularly likely to happen since, as Kay Redfield Jamison shows in her book *Touched with Fire*, many of those who are unusually creative are also unusually sensitive; their sensitivity often drives their creativity.)

If the criticism is unwarranted, many will say, you are free to argue against it, to defend yourself. But there are problems with this, too. Not only does self-defense take time and draw off energy that would better be spent on new creative work, but any move to defend yourself makes you appear, well, defensive. For example, when an author wrote a letter to the editor protesting a review he considered unfair, the reviewer (who is typically given the last word) turned the very fact that the author defended himself into a weapon with which to attack again. The reviewer's response began, "I haven't much time to waste on the kind of writer who squanders his talent drafting angry letters to reviewers."

The argument culture limits the information we get rather than broaden- 25 ing it in another way. When a certain kind of interaction is the norm, those who feel comfortable with that type of interaction are drawn to participate, and those who do not feel comfortable with it recoil and go elsewhere. If public discourse included a broad range of types, we would be making room for individuals with different temperaments to take part and contribute their perspectives and insights. But when debate, opposition, and fights overwhelmingly predominate, those who enjoy verbal sparring are likely to take part—by calling in to talk shows, writing letters to the editor or articles, becoming journalists—and those who cannot comfortably take part in oppositional discourse, or do not wish to, are likely to opt out.

This winnowing² process is easy to see in apprenticeship programs such as acting school, law school, and graduate school. A woman who was identified in her university drama program as showing exceptional promise was encouraged to go to New York to study acting. Full of enthusiasm, she was accepted by a famous acting school where the teaching method entailed the teacher screaming at students, goading and insulting them as a way to bring

---

2. **winnowing** separating the good from the bad, the valuable from the worthless. The original process involved throwing grain into the air so that the wind would blow away the lighter chaff, or covering, while the heavier and valuable grain fell back to the ground.

out the best in them. This worked well with many of the students but not with her. Rather than rising to the occasion when attacked, she cringed, becoming less able to draw on her talent, not more. After a year, she dropped out. It could be that she simply didn't have what it took—but this will never be known, because the adversarial style of teaching did not allow her to show what talent she had.

POLARIZING COMPLEXITY: NATURE OR NURTURE?

Few issues come with two neat, and neatly opposed, sides. Again, I have seen this in the domain of gender. One common polarization is an opposition between two sources of differences between women and men: "culture," or "nurture," on one hand and "biology," or "nature," on the other.

Shortly after the publication of *You Just Don't Understand*, I was asked by a journalist what question I most often encountered about women's and men's conversational styles. I told her, "Whether the differences I describe are biological or cultural." The journalist laughed. Puzzled, I asked why this made her laugh. She explained that she had always been so certain that any significant differences are cultural rather than biological in origin that the question struck her as absurd. So I should not have been surprised when I read, in the article she wrote, that the two questions I am most frequently asked are "Why do women nag?" and "Why won't men ask for directions?" Her ideological certainty that the question I am most frequently asked was absurd led her to ignore my answer and get a fact wrong in her report of my experience.

Some people are convinced that any significant differences between men and women are entirely or overwhelmingly due to cultural influences— the way we treat girls and boys, and men's dominance of women in society. Others are convinced that any significant differences are entirely or over-whelmingly due to biology: the physical facts of female and male bodies, hormones, and reproductive functions. Many problems are caused by fram-ing the question as a dichotomy: Are behaviors that pattern by sex biological or cultural? This polarization encourages those on one side to demonize those who take the other view, which leads in turn to misrepresenting the work of those who are assigned to the opposing camp. Finally, and most dev-astatingly, it prevents us from exploring the interaction of biological and cul-tural factors—factors that must, and can only, be understood together. By posing the question as either/or, we reinforce a false assumption that biolog-ical and cultural factors are separable and preclude the investigations that would help us understand their interrelationship. When a problem is posed in a way that polarizes, the solution is often obscured before the search is under way.

★ ★ ★

AN ETHIC OF AGGRESSION

In an argument culture aggressive tactics are valued for their own sake. For example, a woman called in to a talk show on which I was a guest to say, "When I'm in a place where a man is smoking, and there's a no-smoking sign, instead of saying to him 'You aren't allowed to smoke in here. Put that out,' I say, 'I'm awfully sorry, but I have asthma, so your smoking makes it hard for me to breathe. Would you mind terribly not smoking?' Whenever I say this, the man is extremely polite and solicitous, and he puts his cigarette out, and I say, 'Oh, thank you, thank you!' as if he's done a wonderful thing for me. Why do I do that?"

I think this woman expected me to say that she needs assertiveness training to learn to confront smokers in a more aggressive manner. Instead, I told her that there was nothing wrong with her style of getting the man to stop smoking. She gave him a face-saving way of doing what she asked, one that allowed him to feel chivalrous rather than chastised. This is kind to him, but it is also kind to herself, since it is more likely to lead to the result she desires. If she tried to alter his behavior by reminding him of the rules, he might well rebel: "Who made you the enforcer? Mind your own business!" Indeed, who gives any of us the authority to set others straight when we think they're breaking rules?

Another caller disagreed with me, saying the first caller's style was "self-abasing" and there was no reason for her to use it. But I persisted: There is nothing necessarily destructive about conventional self-effacement. Human relations depend on the agreement to use such verbal conventions. I believe the mistake this caller was making—a mistake many of us make—was to confuse *ritual* self-effacement with the literal kind. All human relations require us to find ways to get what we want from others without seeming to dominate them. Allowing others to feel they are doing what you want for a reason less humiliating to them fulfills this need.

Thinking of yourself as the wronged party who is victimized by a law-breaking boor makes it harder to see the value of this method. But suppose you are the person addicted to smoking who lights up (knowingly or not) in a no-smoking zone. Would you like strangers to yell at you to stop smoking, or would you rather be allowed to save face by being asked politely to stop in order to help them out? Or imagine yourself having broken a rule inadvertently (which is not to imply rules are broken only by mistake; it is only to say that sometimes they are). Would you like some stranger to swoop down on you and begin berating you, or would you rather be asked politely to comply?

As this example shows, conflicts can sometimes be resolved without confrontational tactics, but current conventional wisdom often devalues less confrontational tactics even if they work well, favoring more aggressive strategies even if they get less favorable results. It's as if we value a fight for its own sake, not for its effectiveness in resolving disputes.

This ethic shows up in many contexts. In a review of a contentious book, 35 for example, a reviewer wrote, "Always provocative, sometimes infuriating, this collection reminds us that the purpose of art is not to confirm and coddle but to provoke and confront." This false dichotomy encapsulates that belief that if you are not provoking and confronting, then you are confirming and coddling—as if there weren't myriad other ways to question and learn. What about exploring, exposing, delving, analyzing, understanding, moving, connecting, integrating, illuminating . . . or any of innumerable verbs that capture other aspects of what art can do?

★ ★ ★

WHAT OTHER WAY IS THERE?

Philosopher John Dewey said, on his ninetieth birthday, "Democracy begins in conversation." I fear that it gets derailed in polarized debate.

In conversation we form the interpersonal ties that bind individuals together in personal relationships; in public discourse, we form similar ties on a larger scale, binding individuals into a community. In conversation, we exchange the many types of information we need to live our lives as members of a community. In public discourse, we exchange the information that citizens in a democracy need in order to decide how to vote. If public discourse provides entertainment first and foremost—and if entertainment is first and foremost watching fights—then citizens do not get the information they need to make meaningful use of their right to vote.

Of course it is the responsibility of intellectuals to explore potential weaknesses in others' arguments, and of journalists to represent serious opposition when it exists. But when opposition becomes the overwhelming avenue of inquiry—a formula that *requires* another side to be found or a criticism to be voiced; when the lust for opposition privileges extreme views and obscures complexity; when our eagerness to find weaknesses blinds us to strengths; when the atmosphere of animosity precludes respect and poisons our relations with one another; then the argument culture is doing more damage than good.

★　★　★

I do not believe we should put aside the argument model of public discourse entirely, but we need to rethink whether this is the *only* way, or *always* the best way, to carry out our affairs. A step toward broadening our repertoires would be to pioneer reform by experimenting with metaphors other than sports and war, and with formats other than debate for framing the exchange of ideas. The change might be as simple as introducing a plural form. Instead of asking "What's the other side?" we might ask instead, "What are the other sides?" Instead of insisting on hearing "both sides," we might insist on hearing "all sides."

Another option is to expand our notion of "debate" to include more dia- 40 logue. This does not mean there can be no negativity, criticism, or disagreement. It simply means we can be more creative in our ways of managing all of these, which are inevitable and useful. In dialogue, each statement that one person makes is qualified by a statement made by someone else, until the series of statements and qualifications moves everyone closer to a fuller truth. Dialogue does not preclude negativity. Even saying "I agree" makes sense only against the background assumption that you might disagree. In dialogue, there is opposition, yes, but no head-on collision. Smashing heads does not open minds.

There are times when we need to disagree, criticize, oppose, and attack —to hold debates and view issues as polarized battles. Even cooperation, after all, is not the absence of conflict but a means of managing conflict. My goal is not a make-nice false veneer of agreement or a dangerous ignoring of true opposition. I'm questioning the *automatic* use of adversarial formats— the assumption that it's *always* best to address problems and issues by fighting over them. I'm hoping for a broader repertoire of ways to talk to each other and address issues vital to us.

about the text

1. What does Tannen see as the disadvantages of the tendency to view interactions, especially between people who are different or in competition, as battles?

2. What does Tannen mean by her opening claim that "culture . . . is an environment of narratives that we hear repeatedly until they seem to make self-evident sense in explaining . . . behavior" (paragraph 1)? How does her example from Evelyn Fox Keller's work support this claim (paragraphs 9–10)?

3. Tannen claims that "language . . . invisibly molds our ways of thinking about people, actions, and the world around us" (paragraph 9). How—and how effectively—does she support this claim?

4. What is the difference between "hearing 'both sides'" and "hearing 'all sides'" (paragraph 39)? What assumptions does each perspective make about interaction? The nature of argument? Reality? Why are these assumptions made?

on language use

5. Make a list of the metaphors Tannen uses to describe how we typically think of argument in American culture. What do these metaphors contribute to Tannen's own argument?

6. To what extent does Tannen practice what she preaches? In other words, does she structure her critique as a debate one side must win? If not, how does she structure it?

for writing

7. Reread the section entitled "An Ethic of Aggression" (paragraphs 30–35), in which Tannen supports the way a woman asked a man to stop smoking in a no-smoking area. How would you have responded to the man smoking? What are the consequences of responding as the woman did? Of doing so persistently? Write an essay analyzing this situation. You may wish to suggest alternative ways to respond, explaining their appropriateness.

8. Analyze the metaphor(s) used in some event or situation. Does the use of metaphor create an agonistic argument when it need not? Write an essay in which you analyze the situation and the metaphor(s) used to discuss it, being sure to support and/or critique Tannen's claims about metaphor and argument.

••

Otto Santa Ana is a founder of and associate professor in the César Chávez Center for Chicana and Chicano Studies at the University of California at Los Angeles. In the following selection, from his book Brown Tide Rising: Metaphors of Latinos in Contemporary Public Discourse *(2002), Santa Ana analyzes the metaphor of immigration as dangerous waters, a metaphor that frequently appeared in the* Los Angeles Times *during debates about Proposition 187. A 1992 California voter-inititative, Proposition 187 would have severely limited benefits and services available to what Santa Ana calls "undocumented immigrants" (or what those who oppose rights for this group would call "illegal aliens"). The proposition was passed by 59 percent of the voters but was immediately the subject of legal challenges, which found much of it unconstitutional. In the end, changing federal laws and court decisions regarding immigration, and the California governor's refusal to pursue further action, effectively killed Proposition 187.*

In his discussion of the dangerous waters metaphor, Santa Ana provides a range of examples, discusses the essence of the metaphor's ontology, and argues for some of its implications. (Notice that he refers to metaphors in upper-case letters). As you read, think about the language you have used when discussing immigrants to the United States.

••

OTTO SANTA ANA

Immigration as Dangerous Waters
The Power of Metaphor

THE TEXTBOOKS SAY the United States is a nation of immigrants. However, while schoolchildren are steeped in the pageantry of American history, they seldom learn to appreciate the depth of its reprehensible acts and persistent inequities. A case in point is the history of Mexican Americans. For most, it is news that in 1846, when President James Polk initiated the U.S.-Mexican War, between 75,000 and 100,000 Mexicans were already living in the Southwest,[1] including my father's family.

The virulent racism with which nineteenth-century white Americans elevated themselves above all other people also infected relations with Mexicans, leading to the view that the Southwest was rightfully granted to white

---

1. Gutiérrez 1995, p. 13 [Santa Ana's note].

America, and that its Mexican residents were a contemptible mongrel breed.[2] Today's Americans generally are not cognizant that the U.S.–Mexican War ended with the Treaty of Guadalupe Hidalgo, which guaranteed language, property, and citizenship rights to the Spanish-speaking residents of this territory.[3] Moreover, from its establishment in 1848 and on through the twentieth century, the new border between Mexico and the United States was an arbitrary and largely vain restraint on the historic and prehistoric free movement of people north and south.[4] Thus it is particularly painful to have witnessed the continuing mistreatment of Mexicans and Mexican Americans in the twentieth century.

In spite of its overwhelmingly immigrant origin and its self-satisfied adulation of the immigrants' contribution to its strength and wealth, the United States maintains a Janus-faced[5] attitude of self-interest toward immigrants. When the country is in the growth part of the economic cycle, cheap labor is at a premium. During these times, U.S. commerce promotes the virtues of America and its "American Dream" of unbounded opportunity for the hardest worker, no matter who and from what circumstances. When native-born Americans scorn essential labor, workers from other countries are recruited for the lowest-paid and least desirable work. The immigrants come in great numbers, do the work, dream the Dream, and honor their end of the bargain. For example, from 1880 to 1920, with a population much less than 100 million, the United States accepted 24 million immigrants.[6]

However, as the economic cycle wanes, Janus's second face is manifest toward immigrants and their children. Then the immigrant is regaled as a menace. Evidence for this attitude abounds in American history. For example, between 1921 and 1924 Congress set up a restrictive immigration quota system which disfavored immigrants from Eastern and Southern Europe as

---

2. Gutiérrez quotes such nineteenth-century viewpoints as that of South Carolina's well-known Senator John C. Calhoun, who objected to embracing in the United States a large number of Mexicans. For Calhoun, Mexicans consist of "impure races, not as good as the Cherokees or Choctaws" (1995, p. 16) [Santa Ana's note].

3. Griswold del Castillo 1990 [Santa Ana's note].

4. Vélez-Ibáñez 1997, in Chapter I, "Without Borders, the Original Vision" [Santa Ana's note].

5. **Janus** Roman deity presiding over doors, gates, and the beginning of things, Janus was often depicted in profile as having two faces, one looking forward and the other looking backward. Sometimes used metaphorically to describe the mutually contradictory aspects of something.

6. Brownstein and Simon 1993 [Santa Ana's note].

well as Asia and Latin America.[7] These attitudes have also turned punitive. Between 1929 and 1935 authorities mobilized the U.S. military to force the repatriation of 500,000 Mexican immigrants and their U.S.-born children,[8] including my mother.

A post–World War II economic upswing in California did not waver for forty-five years. During that time immigrants were recruited by business and industry to power an unparalleled period of economic growth. Middle-class families also employed immigrants to do the gardening, to clean their homes, and to tend their children. With immigrant labor, the middle class achieved a higher standard of living than they otherwise could afford. Today it is rare for middle-class women in Los Angeles to do their own nails, or for suburban homeowners to cut their own lawns on Saturday morning.

However, with the end of the Cold War in 1989, the expansion period of California's military-based economy also came to a close. Over 830,000 jobs were lost between 1990 and 1993, primarily in the defense sector. A ripple effect from the defense industry layoffs and cut-downs was felt throughout the economy. The economic recession led as well to reductions in state and local governmental incomes and created budgetary shortfalls.[9]

The demographic profile of California has also changed in the last decades, becoming decidedly less "Teutonic"[10] and more multiethnic. While there was a general increase of the proportion of foreign-born residents in the United States from 5 percent in 1970 to 8 percent in 1990, these figures (the highest since 1930) belie a skewed distribution of immigrant residence. Sikhs, Mexicans, and Armenians are not settling in Idaho. Seventy-five percent of foreign-born residents settle in seven states, with California at the top of the list. Nearly 25 percent of all documented immigrants settled in California during the decade of the 1980s. And overall, California's foreign-born population was about 22 percent of the population in the 1990s; in Los Angeles County it was 33 percent. Los Angeles Unified School District officially listed more than seventy-five mother tongues spoken in its kindergartens. While a plethora of cultures is represented, 85 percent of documented immi-

---

7. Higham 1955 [Santa Ana's note].

8. Hoffman 1974, p. 126 [Santa Ana's note].

9. Davis 1995 [Santa Ana's note].

10. The nineteenth-century term for the preferred "race" of European immigrant, with "Alpine" and "Mediterranean" successively lower on the scale of purity (Higham 1955, p. 155) [Santa Ana's note].

gration during the 1980s was from Asia and Latin America. Adding to an already large population of Mexican-origin citizens, the continued browning of California is inevitable. Latinos now make up over 30 percent of the population of the state. They are projected to become a majority by 2040.[11] In Los Angeles the tendency is more pronounced, since Latinos are projected to be the majority by 2007. For Californians brought up with the unspoken belief that American society means a preeminently Anglo-American culture, these demographic changes have been unnerving.

The first nativist reaction to this sense of a changing social order in the 1990s was Proposition 187. This initiative was overwhelmingly passed by the California electorate even though its provisions had been denounced throughout the campaign as unconstitutional. Indeed, it was enjoined by the courts within hours of its enactment. While the laws of the land already dictated sanctions against employers utilizing the labor of undocumented immigrant workers, and the federal government provided for a policing body, the Border Patrol, to apprehend and deport such immigrants, Proposition 187 was designed to supersede and radicalize federal law. It would have denied to undocumented immigrants a range of public benefits, including education and nonemergency health care. It would also have made school administrators, health care workers, social service personnel, police, and other state employees responsible for determining the residence status of any "apparently illegal alien" (to use the controversial phrasing of the referendum) among their clients and for notifying the Immigration and Naturalization Service of suspected undocumented immigrants for deportation.

This chapter presents the findings of an empirical analysis of the public discourse metaphors in California during the Proposition 187 period. Over one hundred *Los Angeles Times* articles were published on Proposition 187, as indexed by the commercial distributor of a CD-ROM version of the newspaper. All of these were included in this study. Two issues stood out for the voters and general public: immigration, namely, the demographic process; and immigrants themselves. Consequently, the public discourse on these semantic domains was examined in terms of metaphor use.

In [this] section, the metaphors for IMMIGRATION are described. One dominant metaphor will be discussed more fully than, and separately from, other less prevalent metaphors. Its ontology[12] will be specified, namely, the se- 10

---

11. Brownstein and Simon 1993 [Santa Ana's note].

12. **ontology** nature or essence.

mantic notions that are imposed on the concept IMMIGRATION by means of the dominant semantic source domain.

* * *

IMMIGRATION AS DANGEROUS WATERS

One of the two key notions debated during the campaigns for and against Proposition 187 was the demographic process of the movement of people, IMMIGRATION. As a concept at the heart of the political contest, this notion was constantly being referred to in the public discourse of the period, and was frequently metaphorized. This metaphorization reveals the worldview that is promulgated in public discourse. In this section the metaphors that construct and reinforce commonly held views of immigration will be displayed.

As will be noted in Table 1, there are dominant, secondary, and occasional metaphors. These are three informal groupings of semantic source domains found in the data, combining all instances of closely related semantic domains under a single heading. The dominant metaphor class is composed of scores of textual instances of metaphor with a similar semantic source domain that occur relatively frequently and appear in a great variety of forms. In the *Los Angeles Times* data sampled, the dominant metaphor comprises

TABLE 1 Immigration Metaphors Published during the Proposition 187 Campaign

Source Domain	Type	Totals	Percentages
DANGEROUS WATERS, e.g., *floods, tide*	dominant	113	58.2
WAR, e.g., *invasion, takeover*	secondary	45	23.2
ANIMAL, e.g., *curbing illegal immigration*		17	8.8
BODY, e.g., *disease, burden*		6	3.1
various metaphors, e.g., AIR, WEED, CRIMINAL, MACHINE, FIRE, etc.	occasional	13	6.7
	TOTAL	194	100

Source: 116 *Los Angeles Times* articles published June 1992–December 1994. The list accounts for immigration metaphors, i.e., the demographic process. It excludes metaphors that target immigrants as people.

the greatest proportion of all instances of metaphors characterizing immigration. The demographic process of immigration to the United States is conceptualized in terms of dangerous moving water.

*   *   *

The major metaphor for the process of the movement of substantial numbers of human beings to the United States is characterized as IMMIGRATION AS DANGEROUS WATERS. Perhaps it should be restated that to characterize the movement of people as moving water might seem quite natural, but such a formulation of movement of people is not the only possible image that can be employed. Moreover, strongly negative connotations associated with immigration in particular had decidedly negative implications for the target population. A few instances are listed below:

1. **awash under a brown tide** (October 2, 1994, A3)
2. Like **waves on a beach**, these **human flows** are literally remaking the face of America. (October 14, 1993, A1)
3. **a sea of brown faces** marching through Downtown would only antagonize many voters (October 17, 1994, A1)
4. In April, Gov. Pete Wilson sued the federal government to recover costs associated with illegal immigrants, claiming that they are sapping the state budget, taking jobs from legal residents and **swamping** hospital emergency rooms. (June 12, 1994, A3)
5. **the human surge** (July 5, 1992, A3)
6. **the inexorable**[13] **flow** (September 22, 1993, A1)

The dangerous waters of immigration come in many forms, *rough seas, treacherous tides, surges.*[14] The DANGEROUS WATERS metaphors do not refer to any aspect of the humanity of the immigrants, except to allude to ethnicity and race. In contrast to such nonhuman metaphors for immigrants, U.S. society is often referred to in human terms. This provides an ironic contrast when

---

13. **inexorable** relentless.

14. Each italicized metaphor appearing in the body of this selection, like the sequentially numbered excerpts, is drawn from the *Los Angeles Times* database. Any exceptions are expressly described as fabrications [Santa Ana's note].

these metaphors appear in tandem, as in excerpt 18, which likens the United States to a person who is defaced by an ocean of immigrants.

Within IMMIGRATION AS DANGEROUS WATERS there are clear subcategories. The first is volume, which emphasizes the relative numbers of immigrants. Individuals are lost in the mass sense of these volume terms. The negative connotation is highlighted in the excerpts that contain strong adjectives such as *relentless* and *overwhelming*.

7. the foreigners who have **flooded** into the country (November 10, 1992, World Report p. 1, col. 2)

8. "I thought that it was a waste of time, frankly," [California Governor] Wilson said of [U.S. Senator Robert] Byrd's line of questioning. "What we ought to be doing is focusing on the fact that federal failure continues to provide this **massive flow of illegal immigrants** into my state and the other states." (July 23, 1994; A3)

9. **the relentless flow of immigrants** (May 30, 1993, A5)

10. **an overwhelming flood** of asylum-seekers have put the country in an angry funk (October 1, 1992, A1)

Note that immigration waters are seen to be dangerous, as when coupling an exacerbating adjective to a neutral noun, as with *inexorable flow*. The second subcategory of DANGEROUS WATERS is movement, which emphasizes the direction of waters, primarily northward as from Mexico to the United States. With regard to the destination of the migration, the nation is conceived as a basin or some kind of container and the migration taken to be an inward-flowing stream, in terms such as *influx*.

11. Residents of the San Fernando Valley are increasingly outraged about illegal immigration—if not immigration generally—in the face of economic hard times, growing congestion, widespread crime and a **dramatic influx of Latinos.** (August 1, 1993, A1)

12. **the tide and flow of illegal immigration** (October 26, 1994, A27)

13. Glenn Spencer . . . says his interest in the subject was sparked about two years ago when he began noticing that an **influx of minorities had flooded the city.** He compiled research and launched a newsletter that he circulated among his neighbors. Ultimately, he formed Valley Citizens Together, but the group changed its name after residents from other parts of Los Angeles wanted to get involved. . . . When asked what motivates him, Spencer points to the photos of his two blond, blue-eyed

grandchildren on the mantel in his orderly living room. "What I'd like to achieve is a little better world for my grandchildren," he said. "I don't want my grandchildren to live in chaos. Isn't that enough?" (November 15, 1994, A1)[15]

14. **the flood of legal and illegal immigrants streaming** into the country (September 7, 1993, A3)

The terms used to characterize the immigration do not describe benefi-   15
cial and enriching flows, but *dramatic influxes* and *floods* that endanger the country. The third subcategory is the control of dangerous waters. Here the intent to reduce the immigration of undocumented workers pursues a correspondence with the dangerous waters metaphor by describing means by which the waters can be held back, or *stemmed*, which means "to make headway against an adverse tide."

15. an attempt to **stem illegal immigration** (December 22, 1994, B1)

16. the opportunistic criminal element that exploits our **porous borders** (November 27, 1992, A3)

17. On the other hand, [Clinton] warned, if the government is unable to "show some more discipline" in its control of illegal immigration, "I'm afraid the genie out of the bottle will be passion to **shut off legal immigration.**" (August 13, 1993, A1)

18. [The] executive director of the Federation for American Immigration Reform . . . said Clinton's approach is akin to "**trying to dam the Mississippi with toothpicks.**" (September 7, 1993, A1)

ONTOLOGY OF *IMMIGRATION AS DANGEROUS WATERS*

The metaphor labeled IMMIGRATION AS DANGEROUS WATERS is a tightly structured semantic relationship. It is a coupling and mapping of the semantic ontology of DANGEROUS WATERS onto the domain of IMMIGRATION. It establishes semantic associations between the two meaning domains, taking the well-developed framework of everyday knowledge of floods and tides and imposing it on an

---

15. In the excerpts throughout the selection, additional metaphors can be noted which will not be discussed in the body of the selection, such as in excerpts 4, *sap*, and 13, *chaos*. Mixing metaphors in nonliterary genres and everyday talk is rarely noticed. There is little sense of confusion of thought, or of anomalous passages. In the excerpts from the *Times*, there is ready mixing of metaphors that are associated with the distinctive NATION AS HOUSE and NATION AS BODY metaphors [Santa Ana's note].

entirely human activity. In schematic form, the mapping, to wit the ontology of immigration to the United States as dangerous waters, is a four-point relationship as follows:

- Immigration corresponds to moving waters.

- America is a landmass or other entity such as a house that is subject to flooding.

- Greater immigration corresponds to an increased threat to America.

- America's vulnerability to flooding corresponds to its susceptibility to change.

Some of the pertinent everyday understandings of this source metaphor, moving water, will be explicitly elaborated in order to present the elements of the source domain that are reinforced with each repetition of the metaphor. These semantic associations obscure or pass over some aspects of the target domain as they highlight others. In the absence of alternative metaphoric imagery, such highlighted features of the source domain, DANGEROUS WATERS, are taken as natural features of the target domain, IMMIGRATION.

Moving water is a fluid. Above all other characteristics, fluids are normally understood and measured in terms of volume and mass, not units. They are most often named with mass nouns, such as *water, milk,* or *beer*.[16] Greater amounts of a fluid are registered in terms of volume, not larger numbers of individuals. The everyday use of such noncount words reflects a motile energy. Water moves, and when placed under pressure cannot be compressed, but forces its way or is channeled in some direction. This dynamism implies kinetic and hydraulic power, and control of the movement of water also requires power. There are naturally occurring masses of water, geophysical bodies such as streams, rivers, ponds, lakes, and oceans, as well as formations created by humans such as channels and reservoirs. With most naturally occurring and all human-made formations, human power and control are involved. The control of water varies from total mastery, such as when people shut off a kitchen faucet, to partial control, as in a hydroelectric dam. Greater volume and movement of water imply greater need for safeguards and controls, and more powerful human agency to control the water (which of

---

16. The exception to noncount measures occurs with the use of quantifiers followed by *of*, such as *two teaspoons of vinegar*, in which case the intrinsic liquid nature of fluids becomes secondary to the extrinsic calibration [Santa Ana's note].

course is not a human force). Insufficient human control of the kinetic energy pent up in volumes of water can lead to flooding and other ravages.

The main effect of invoking the DANGEROUS WATERS semantic domain[17] to characterize the IMMIGRATION domain is to transform aggregates of individuals into an undifferentiated mass quantity. Immigrants are not merely described in terms of a mass noun; they are transfigured. The demographic process, immigration, is also vested with potential kinetic energy that is released in its movement, just as when water is commonly discussed. This misleading association is established by the metaphor. Further, salient features of the human immigration process are omitted with this metaphor. At its most simplistic yet still acceptable association, the potency of workers is in their labor, which is just one of a number of aspects of immigration entirely passed over by the IMMIGRATION AS DANGEROUS WATERS metaphor.

For investigators working within cognitive metaphor theory, metaphors 20 have an "inherent logic."[18] In the case of IMMIGRATION AS DANGEROUS WATERS, three weighty presuppositions[19] will be pointed out. These associations are inherited from WATER, the semantic source domain, but are entirely inappropriate characterizations of the demographic process of immigration. Since people conventionally talk about immigration using this metaphor, the presuppositions are often taken as given and overlooked. Since the power of metaphor increases with repetition of such implicit, but unnatural, associations, it is important to point them out. First, by way of the IMMIGRATION AS DANGEROUS WATERS metaphor, aggregates of human beings are reduced to or remade into an undifferentiated quantity that is not human. Second, as this mass moves from one contained space to another, some sort of kinetic energy is released. The contained space referred to is California, the United States, Los Angeles, or other polities. Recall that political entities are not inherently

---

17. **semantic domain** the range of meanings to which a word applies. For example, the English verb "to turn" can refer to a change of direction ("Turn left at the light") or a change of state ("The leaves turn red each autumn" or "I turned twenty-one last year"). The Spanish verb *voltear*, which means "to turn," refers only to "change of direction"; different verbs— *ponerse* and *cumplir*, respectively, would be used for changes of state. Thus, the semantic domain of the English verb "to turn" differs from that of Spanish *voltear*.

18. Lakoff 1987, pp. 141–144; Johnson 1987, pp. 113–119 [Santa Ana's note].

19. **presuppositions** for example, the sentence *Morgan's wife is Martha* logically presupposes that Morgan is married. We know this "fact" because we know that Martha is a female's name and that someone who has a wife is married. (When we first drafted this example another presupposition was that Morgan was male because, at that time, only heterosexual couples could legally marry in the United States. Marriages of lesbian and gay couples in some jurisdictions in 2004 have removed that presupposition.)

a contained finite space. Third, such movements are inherently powerful, and if not controlled, they are dangerous.

In excerpts 1–18, provided above, the vocabulary of dynamic bodies of water and their movement includes: *tide, sea, flood, influx, flow, waves, drowning, dams, porous, stem,* and *shut off,* to which we can add multiple instances of *swell/ing, absorb, funnel, surge/ing, pour/ing, stream/ing, swamp, pool,* and *safety valve,* among other water terms from the *Los Angeles Times* database.

IMPLICATIONS OF THE METAPHOR

The implications of this metaphor are extensive. Treating immigration as dangerous waters conceals the individuality of the immigrants' lives and their humanity. In their place a frightening scenario of uncontrolled movements of water can be played out with *devastating floods* and *inundating surges* of brown faces.

The impending flood is taken to be washing away something basic to America. What the anti-immigration advocates initially claimed is that immigrants were an economic threat to the United States and California. However, no presuppositions or entailments built into the DANGEROUS WATERS metaphor imply economics. Consequently the impact of the metaphor does not center on commonsense understandings of the U.S. economy. The threat constructed by DANGEROUS WATERS is cultural.

To make this point it may be useful to compare the implied associations of the frequently invoked *flood* metaphor to other metaphors that have unmistakable economic implications. Compare a metaphor that was often found in the database, *immigration as a burden.* Such metaphors clearly refer to the economic state as human body. If the threat felt by the public was principally a matter of economics, as is often taken to be the case by pundits, one would expect that the dominant metaphor in the public discourse on immigration would reinforce a fiscal message. Yet nearly 60 percent of the metaphors in the public discourse on immigration were DANGEROUS WATERS, while less than 5 percent were BURDEN metaphors. By this measure, although the 1990–1993 recession was the catalyst that initiated the xenophobic animus of the decade, the public discourse metaphors of the time did not have a fiscal focus.

Again, immigrants supply the cheap labor to maintain personal living standards that were higher than otherwise attainable for the average Californian, while at the same time sustaining labor-intensive industries, 25 such as garment manufacturing and certain agribusiness concerns, in an increasingly postindustrial state economy. Moreover, there were counterindications to Governor Wilson's[20] warnings. He repeatedly stated during his reelection campaign that California faced economic disaster, based primarily on $3 billion in purported costs incurred yearly by the state due to immigration. Wilson's claims proved grossly overstated. Five years later, Wilson supervised the largest budgetary surplus in California history, over $4.4 billion.[21] Neither the deficit nor the surplus was due in large part to immigrant labor.

Instead of budgetary issues, the principal signal that DANGEROUS WATERS expresses is cultural alarm. The fear is that the *rising brown tide* will wash away Anglo-American cultural dominance. The panic expressed in DANGEROUS WATERS metaphors reflecting the perceived threat to Anglo-American hegemony is also articulated by the overtly anti-immigrant IMMIGRATION AS INVASION metaphor. Together, DANGEROUS WATERS and INVASION account for over 80 percent of all metaphors expressed in public discourse on immigration. Hence the relative absence of anomaly in the ready references to the American "complexion," as in excerpt 2, *these human flows are remaking the face of America*, and to the Californian economic body in excerpt 19, below:

19. Councilwoman Joyce C. Nicholson said illegal immigration is a serious problem and "the state of California is **drowning** in it." (September 17, 1994, B2)

In this excerpt, while the explicit complaint is economic, the metaphor invokes the state as a person drowning in a body of water representing immigration. During the anti-immigrant period, it was considered above-board to critique immigration on economic terms. However, the most frequent metaphors appearing in public discourse did not refer to fiscal arguments. As seen in this excerpt, there is more implied than a metaphorical reference to state finances. Thus in this excerpt the Los Angeles councilwoman openly called for economic relief, while metaphorically warning her constituency about the cultural threat that immigration seemingly posed. It was common to talk explicitly about the economy, all the while invoking the ostensible

---

20. **Pete Wilson** was the governor of California from 1991 to 1999, during the time Proposition 187 was debated.

21. *Los Angeles Times*, July 6, 1998, B4 [Santa Ana's note].

danger to Anglo-American cultural hegemony by the use of the DANGEROUS WATERS metaphor.[22]

Since only a trickle of water can be enough to signal an impending flood, warnings about *rising brown tides* are apt metaphors to inspire fear. All other considerations aside, the hardworking, family-oriented immigrant who believes in the American Dream was concealed with the DANGEROUS WATERS metaphor. This allowed California voters to remain comfortable in their daily interactions with the individual immigrant worker, part of an important workforce in the economy, while feeling justified in supporting the referendum and voting to end the only apparent menace to the social order.

NARRATIVE OF *IMMIGRATION AS DANGEROUS WATERS*

A narrative of the dominant metaphor can also be constructed in which its principal presuppositions and social context are made explicit.[23] This metaphor narrative of immigration to the United States is based on the preceding ontological mapping, which, in cognitive semantic terms, established associations between the semantic domains of DANGEROUS WATERS and IMMIGRATION, as well as with the NATION AS HOUSE metaphor we will discuss presently.

> A flood of immigrants is flowing into the land or house of America. In controlled quantities, America can either channel and absorb the influx unchanged. Because of the enormous volume of these floodwaters, America will be inundated with a sea of people unlike Anglo-Americans. Anglo-America will be engulfed and dispossessed.

The narrative of immigration to the United States is invoked, and its ideological content reinforced, with each repetition of the metaphor. This constitutes the pattern of social inference on—that is to say, the prevalent way to think about—immigration.

---

22. On another note, the use of the term *literal*, in excerpt 2, demonstrates tacit recognition on the part of the writer of the force of metaphor. Since *face of the nation* in excerpt 2 is a metaphor, there is nothing literal to be understood by the term *literally*. In such cases the adverb can only function as an intensifier, meaning "very," or "intensely." Its use is intended to heighten the expressed severity of the effect of cultural change caused by non-European immigration [Santa Ana's note].

23. Lakoff 1993 [Santa Ana's note].

NATION AS HOUSE

Metaphors do not make sense in isolation. This is the case for poetic 30
metaphor.[24] This is also the case with conventional metaphors that give
structure to and reinforce the generally held worldview of U.S. society. These
immigration metaphors are comprehensible, as are all metaphors, because
they are woven layer upon layer in webs of semantic associations, starting
with foundational metaphors that give structure to higher-level ones. This
web of associations and presuppositions constitutes the basis for a semanti-
cally congruent understanding of the world.

Truly original metaphors, such as IMMIGRATION AS TURTLE FOOD or AS RAIN-
FOREST, fail to make sense because few if any conventional semantic associations can be pressed into service to edify the target domain, IMMIGRATION.
Moreover, since these novel metaphors are not woven into the total web of
customary metaphoric associations, the link between the source and target
semantic domains seems abnormal. The technical semantic term is *anomalous*. Its etymological meaning, "abnormal," highlights the contingent (non-
natural) and conventionalized (learned and reinforced to the point of being
naturalized) character of everyday semantic mappings.

Thus the IMMIGRATION AS DANGEROUS WATERS and AS INVASION metaphors,
in order to be comprehensible in public discourse on immigration, must be
associated with some compatible metaphor for the nation. We turn now to
one of these metaphors, NATION AS HOUSE, one of the two most productive
metaphors for the United States, in order to demonstrate its arbitrary and
contingent, non-natural associations. NATION AS HOUSE is also used to refer to
other political entities, such as the state of California. It is invoked in many of
the preceding excerpts that have been provided. A few more of these include:

20. With recent immigration reforms proposed by President Clinton, the gov-
    ernor and other political leaders, the issue has moved to the **nation's
    front burner** and it looms as an explosive topic for debate in the 1994
    elections. (August 22, 1993, A1)

21. The fantasy of Proposition 187 supporters seems to be that once Califor-
    nia is **cleansed** of its illegal menace, welfare recipients can be coerced
    into the fields. (October 2, 1994, A3)

22. "I understand the principles that our country was **built on,** but **our house
    is pretty raggedy** and we need to take care of our own first." (August 20,
    1993, A1)

---

24. Lakoff and Turner 1989 [Santa Ana's note].

In brief, the NATION AS HOUSE metaphor was used or invoked with regularity in the Proposition 187 campaign with respect to the threats posed by IMMIGRATION AS DANGEROUS WATERS. Many linguistic expressions characterize immigrants in terms of chaos, destruction, and other perils to the NATION AS HOUSE.

23. "That's like saying, 'I've got this **great house, but it's on fire, it's built on a fault and the bank is moving in to repossess it.**'" (June 16, 1993, A1)

24. a growing body of evidence that Canada, long a **haven** for the world's oppressed, is banking its lamp unto the nations. (June 18, 1992, A1)

25. When U.S. Atty. Gen. Janet Reno toured Nogales this month to announce a 30 percent increase of Border Patrol forces in Arizona—she described the state as the **"side door"** to California. (January 30, 1995, A1)

26. "[Wilson] **cut a hole in the fence** to allow millions of illegal immigrants in, and now he wants **to patch that hole** because that's what the polls tell him to do." (September 16, 1994, A1)

27. "What are you going to do to **close our borders tight** to illegal aliens and drug-runners?" (June 10, 1993, J1)

28. **"Put up a Berlin Wall!"** cried Vines, an African-American who denies that racism has anything to do with his get-tough stand. He says that any fool can see it: Immigration is bringing this country down. (August 30, 1993, A1)

29. "Lots of folks say we have to **shut the door** now. Others disagree pretty strongly. . . . And so maybe we shouldn't be so quick to **shut the door.**" (October 3, 1993, E1)

The frequency and diversity of (metaphoric) threats to the NATION AS HOUSE, as indicated in Table 1, demonstrate that this immigration metaphor was customarily used to impugn the motivation and character of immigrants to the United States.

The metaphor NATION AS HOUSE came into prominent use in the late fifteenth century and was apt to characterize the emerging European nationhood at a time when the majority of the population did not travel and long-distance communication was dependent on animal transportation. The use of a fixed dwelling place as a metaphoric source for the American political entity is increasingly challenged by the early-twenty-first-century system of rapid global transportation, instant worldwide televisual communication, broadening cross-national regional integration, and an increasingly globalized economy.

However, the inadequacy of NATION AS HOUSE as a metaphor for the United 35
States did not distract from or diminish the impact of the rampant use of the
IMMIGRATION AS DANGEROUS WATERS metaphor during the Proposition 187 period.
DANGEROUS WATERS divests immigrant workers and their families of their humanity, to become at best a natural resource to be controlled and exploited,
and at worst to be feared for the potential damage that *floods* and *rising seas*
of brown faces can visit on the nation. Geological metaphors invoke certain
unwarranted associations about movements of human beings. In the context
of a political campaign, the dehumanizing presupposition of the metaphor
was fully exploited, transfiguring people into fear-inspiring floods and dangerous tides.

REFERENCES

Brownstein, Ronald, and Richard Simon. 1993. "Hospitality turns to hostility.
California has a long history of welcoming newcomers for their cheap labor—until times turn rough." *Los Angeles Times*, November 14, p. A1.

Davis, Mike. 1995. "The social origins of the referendum." *NACLA Report on the
Americas 29* (3): 24–28.

Gibbs, Raymond W., Jr. 1994. *Poetics of the Mind: Figurative Thought, Language
and Understanding.* Cambridge: Cambridge University Press.

Griswold del Castillo, Richard. 1990. *The Treaty of Guadalupe Hidalgo: A
Legacy of Conflict.* Norman: University of Oklahoma Press.

Gutiérrez, David G. 1995. *Walls and Mirrors: Mexican Americans, Mexican Immigrants, and the Politics of Ethnicity.* Berkeley: University of California
Press.

Higham, John. 1955. *Strangers in the Land: Patterns of American Nativism,
1860–1925.* New Brunswick, NJ: Rutgers University Press.

Hoffman, Abraham. 1974. *Unwanted Mexican Americans in the Great Depression: Repatriation Pressures, 1929–1939.* Tucson: University of Arizona
Press.

Johnson, Mark. 1987. *The Body in the Mind: The Bodily Basis of Meaning, Imagination, and Reason.* Chicago: University of Chicago Press.

Lakoff, George. 1987. *Women, Fire and Dangerous Things: What Categories Reveal about the Mind.* Chicago: University of Chicago Press.

Lakoff, George. 1993. "The contemporary theory of metaphor." *Metaphor and Thought*. 2nd ed. Ed. Andrew Ortony, pp. 202–251. Cambridge: Cambridge University Press.

Lakoff, George, and Mark Turner. 1989. *More than Cool Reason: A Field Guide to Poetic Metaphor*. Chicago: University of Chicago Press.

Vélez-Ibáñez, Carlos G. 1997. *Border Visions: Mexican Cultures of the Southwest United States*. Tucson: U of Arizona Press.

about the text

1. Throughout the text, Santa Ana sees the treatment of Latinos, especially those of Mexican origin, by "white Americans" in terms of brown and white. In what ways is such a dichotomy accurate? What drawbacks might it have?

2. Santa Ana begins with a discussion of what Americans learn and don't learn in school about the United States "as a nation of immigrants" (paragraphs 1–9). What metaphors does he use in these paragraphs when discussing America's attitude toward immigrants, especially those of Mexican origin? Why might he have used this discussion to introduce his analysis of the metaphor IMMIGRATION AS DANGEROUS WATERS?

3. According to Santa Ana, the associations of the metaphor IMMIGRATION AS DANGEROUS WATERS fall into three subcategories. What are they? What three "weighty presuppositions" does Santa Ana see for this metaphor? What are the implications of the metaphor and its presuppositions?

on language use

4. Study the examples Santa Ana cites from the *Los Angeles Times*. Explain how the metaphor works in each one. For example, it's easy to explain why the verb *flooded* serves as an example of "dangerous waters" (example 27); "porous borders" (example 16) is less transparent. How do this example and the others cited illustrate the metaphor?

5. How does the NATION AS HOUSE metaphor work? How does it complement the metaphor IMMIGRATION AS DANGEROUS WATERS?

for writing

6. Since September 11, 2001, new metaphors have been added to everyday talk in the United States. For example, never before had the United States been referred to as "our homeland" in public discourse, nor had there ever been an Office of Homeland Security. Write an essay analyzing the meaning and significance of these two metaphors or other metaphors that have come into the language after September 11.

7. Using the Internet, collect ten to twenty editorials about one controversial issue, and read through them to find a recurring metaphor. Write an essay analyzing the use of the metaphor, giving examples and describing the metaphor's essence and how the metaphor functions in everyday discourse.

This selection begins with a New York Times article from August 2001 in which Cliff Rothman, who writes for a variety of newspapers and magazines as well as salon.com, discusses the shifting advertising practices of automakers as they target lesbians and gay men. We are also including the Subaru ad that ran with the article, as well as two ads that ran in magazines and newspapers for the lesbian and gay community. Study these ads, and ask yourself what, if anything, appears to be specifically lesbian or gay about them.

CLIFF ROTHMAN

A Welcome Mat for Lesbian and Gay Customers

After decades of treating gay consumers as the invisible minority they often were, automakers are courting them directly, often with messages that wave the rainbow banner of gay acceptance.

This year, Jaguar, Volkswagen and Volvo began advertising in national gay publications, joining three companies—Saab, Saturn and Subaru—that had signed on earlier. And the commitment often runs deeper than a few strategic ads. Carmakers are sponsoring gay events, awards and causes.

Last year, DaimlerChrysler, Ford and General Motors were sponsors of the annual show of the Lambda Car Club, a group of nearly 2,000 gay collectors. For two years, Jaguar has sponsored media awards given by the Gay and Lesbian Alliance Against Defamation. In June, Volvo provided cars for the Los Angeles gay pride parade.

Subaru, whose cars have long sold well among gay men and lesbians, has taken an increasingly prominent role. It sponsors the Los Angeles gay pride festival and events organized by an advocacy group, the Human Rights Campaign. It was a founding sponsor of the Rainbow Card, an affinity credit card program— co-founded by Martina Navratilova—that has raised more than $1 million for gay causes. Subaru gives discounts of up to $3,000 to cardholders.

"We're clear that we sup- 5 port the health and civic-mindedness of the gay and lesbian community," said Tim Bennett, director of national marketing for Subaru. "We were the first to offer domestic partnership benefits. We're not just here to sell you a car as an exploited segment."

Saab was the first to advertise in the national gay press, in 1994. Saturn dipped its toes in the water a year later, then retreated, but returned in 1999. Although it only recently joined the party. Volvo seems intent on having fun. Last month, it ran an ad in *Genre*, a gay lifestyle magazine, that showed a man's bare upper torso and an S60 sedan. The tagline read: "Lust and logic. Don't they make a lovely couple?"

Subaru, which began gay-specific advertising in 1997, is probably the most visible, and daring. Typical of its sassy tone was a recent ad with the tagline, "Get out. And stay out," a sly wordplay on leaving the closet—and exploring the great outdoors.

"It says, 'We acknowledge you as a consumer; this is the language that you speak,'" said John Nash, president of Moon City Productions, the New York company that created the campaign.

In 1994, Subaru identified gays as one of its five core groups of buyers. "There were educators, health-care professionals, technical professionals, rugged individualists—man vs. nature types—and then gay men and lesbians," Mr. Bennett said.

Research also determined that the gay community was a good market for Saturn, a G.M. division. "It's been under- 10 served," said Tom Eise, senior vice president of Publicis & Hal Riney, which does Saturn advertising.

National gay publications offer prized demographics to advertisers. According to the most recent survey commissioned by Liberation Publications Inc., which owns *Out*, a lifestyle magazine, and *The Advocate*, a newsmagazine, the publications' average reader is a 39-year-old white-collar professional man with a college degree and a household income of $95,000. Readers also have a strong propensity to buy European cars, the survey found.

Yet, however visible many gay people have become, automakers face a marketing conundrum. "How do you reach a group that in many ways wants to remain hidden?" asked Bret Scott, a G.M. engineer who is co-chairman of G.M. Plus, an advocacy group for the company's gay and lesbian employees. "And how do you advertise to a group that is really a sub-set of a lot of other groups of people?"

Relations between the industry and many gay people warmed considerably last year when the Detroit automakers began offering employee benefits to same-sex partners, under a joint agreement with the United Automobile Workers. The change came after Big Three employees jointly petitioned the companies, and the union, on the issue.

"The recognition of gays and lesbians as car consumers is something that has been put on the radar screen of the Big Three companies by their employee resource groups," said Cindy Clardy of Ford Globe, a gay employee group. "We also told Ford not to try and consider direct marketing to gay and lesbian consumers until they had their internal policies in place. You run the risk of being seen as, 'You just want to take our money but you don't care about your gay employees.'"

Throughout the car industry, diversity consultants are popping up. "All the leading companies are taking initiatives to do diversity marketing," said Javelyn Ibarra Baldwin, cultural marketing manager for Jaguar. "They are realizing that they can no longer ignore, or do

marketing or advertising, without having a consideration of all the groups that exist."

Still, most companies do not advertise in the gay press. "We don't do any specific targeting to the gay community," said Karen Vonder Meulen, marketing and events communications manager for BMW. "The community already purchases our cars without having to target them individually."

Though Mazda has a new diversity program, the company is channeling its marketing energies toward three groups—African-Americans, Hispanics and Asians—that showed more marketing potential, said Jyoti Bates, a media and diversity marketing specialist for Mazda.

But industry executives are also sensitive to the possibility of a backlash from the majority of their customers. "They worry that reaching out to gays with a particular model can then affect the rest of the lineup," a senior advertising executive said, adding that the companies aimed their promotions where only gays were likely to see them. "They may view it as a political nightmare to be strongly associated in the market."

But Mr. Bennett of Subaru is pragmatic about his company's explicit stance: "Look, we know that our owner base and our consumers are extremely well educated, and they celebrate diversity. A person who would be offended by our advertising probably would not have bought our car anyway."

Variety makes us strong...

These are the secrets behind nature's genius. From rain forests in the Amazon to modest backyard gardens, each creature and every species helps maintain the health and stability of these wondrous surroundings. And the more diverse the environment, the more beautiful it is to behold.

...Harmony makes us successful

At Delta, we take great pride in the diversity of the people who make us what we are – a company of many cultures, languages, backgrounds and experiences. These differences serve to bring us together, make us stronger and give us a unique understanding and sensitivity to the needs of our customers and the communities we serve.

However, like the most dedicated gardener, we're never satisfied with how our garden grows. We constantly strive to build on our achievements to make Delta fertile ground for our employees, partners and suppliers around the globe.

Delta – sowing the seeds for success worldwide, naturally.

▲ **Delta**

We want to make our position perfectly clear.

This election year, there's a lot of national debate on issues that are important to the GLBT community, including the Federal Marriage Amendment. And, as a political candidate, Pete Coors has expressed his personal position on this issue. Coors Brewing Company's position on this issue differs from Pete Coors'. Coors CEO Leo Kiely outlines the company's official position as follows:

"We do not support discrimination against the GLBT community—via legislation or otherwise."

Let's be clear. We don't support amending the Constitution.

That attitude is in keeping with our actions since 1978, when we adopted an inclusive nondiscrimination policy that recognized the rights of GLBT applicants and employees. We took another important step forward in 1988 and provided corporate support to important GLBT community groups. Today, we're proud to back the efforts of the HRC, GLAAD, GPAC and numerous AIDS organizations.

And we've continued our efforts to be not only a better corporate citizen, but a better place to work as well. More than 10 years ago, we created our Lesbian and Gay Employee Resource Council (LAGER) to provide an employee support network and regularly advise our senior management. We even made history in 1995, when Coors became the first major brewery in America to offer same-sex partner health benefits.

Many people have responded positively to these efforts. In 2001, we received the Colorado Human Rights Campaign Award. And we just received the highest score possible from the Human Rights Campaign's Corporate Equality Index—100. So, while we're not perfect, we're clearly working hard to be a better company.

It's simple. At Coors, we believe supporting the rights of the GLBT community is good for our customers and our employees. And, above all, it's the right thing to do.

Thanks for listening.

Give us your feedback: str8talk@mergemediagroup.com

Coors
Now's the time.

about the texts

1. What are the potential advantages and disadvantages for automakers of ads that target lesbian and gay consumers? Why might these consumers be seen as an attractive target audience?

2. Are there aspects of these ads that you do not understand? Do you find them interesting and appealing as ads? Why (or why not)? How might you respond if these ads appeared in a publication targeted at the general public? Why?

on language use

3. Study carefully the language used in these ads. Which specific uses of language, images, metaphors, or wordplay might appeal to the lesbian or gay reader? Why?

4. As Rothman's article notes, major industries have only recently begun using ad campaigns that target lesbian or gay communities. Find such an ad in a public space, a magazine or newspaper, or on a television program. How does the ad appeal to its target audience? How effective is it?

for writing

5. Choose two magazines targeted at very different audiences (*Maxim* and *Good Housekeeping*, for example), and examine the advertisements for a specific consumer product—cars, clothing, cologne, etc. Write an essay comparing and contrasting the ways in which the ads appeal to their respective readers.

6. Choose a group in American society—an ethnic group or some other identifiable group (e.g., skateboarders, geeks)—and look at how it is represented (or not represented) in the ads of several issues of a specific magazine. Consider both ads that might appeal to members of the group and those that might represent them poorly or inaccurately. Write an essay analyzing what you find, being sure to attach copies of the ads you discuss. If you find no representations of the group, write about why certain groups do not appear in the magazines you examine.

\<wordscanheal.org\>

Words Can Heal is a nonprofit national organization founded in 2001 and endorsed by many actors, politicians, and clergy, including Tom Cruise, Goldie Hawn, Senator Tom Daschle, Senator John Kerry, and the Reverend Robert Schuller, among others. Its goal is "to reduce verbal violence and gossip" and "to promote the value and practice of ethical speech in order to improve our democracy, build mutual respect, honor and dignity in our country." Go to \<wwnorton.com/write/langugage\> to learn more about the organization, its goals, and its methods. Below is the pledge that the Web site challenges its visitors to take.

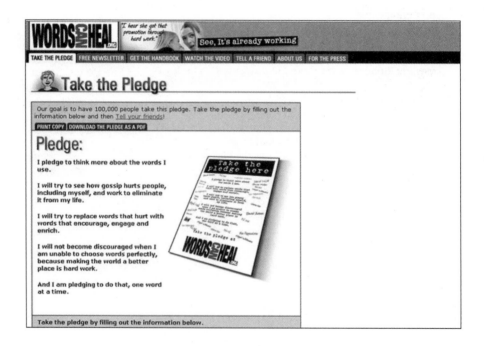

about the text

1. Explore the Web site for Words Can Heal. What assumptions do members of the organization make about the relationship between the way we use language in our daily lives and the nature of the society we live in?

2. Read carefully the press release on this book's Web site. What specific events motivated the creation of this organization? Do you believe organizations like this one do any good? For whom? Why or why not?

3. The press release mentioned in question 2 implies that there are problems in American schools. What are these problems? What are their consequences? How do the creators of the organization hope to respond to the problems?

on language use

4. Watch the video for the Words Can Heal campaign and study the ads for print media on this book's Web site. Which of these appeals to you most? Least? Why?

5. How can we see the assumptions of the organization's creators and members reflected in the ads for the initial campaign? Do you think the ads target specific groups? What kinds of people do you think might find the ads most appealing? Least appealing? Why?

for writing

6. Write an essay in which you evaluate the possible benefits of Words Can Heal. Study the Web site in detail and examine the handbook and kits, which you can find at links on the main site. Consider what this program is likely to accomplish, what it assumes, how valid those assumptions might be, whom this program will likely help, and who will most likely participate.

7. A theme of this chapter, and indeed this book, is that words function as arguments because they articulate certain assumptions that not everyone automatically accepts. In what ways does Words Can Heal illustrate this theme? Write an essay in which you explore how everyday language practices (including efforts to avoid certain language) support the claim that words function as arguments.

ANNA QUINDLEN

Anna Quindlen *is currently a columnist for* Newsweek, *where she writes "The Last Word," the one-page column that closes the magazine each week. She received the Pulitzer Prize for her Op Ed pieces for the* New York Times, *where she worked for many years before leaving to write novels, essays, and children's books. Among her novels is* One True Thing, *which was made into a film starring Meryl Streep and Renée Zellweger. The essay included here is one of several that appeared in the* Times *in a 2001 series marking the paper's 150th year of publication. In it, Quindlen considers "the power of an adjective" and the ways in which the* Times' *changing choice of terms for referring to various social groups teaches us much about American history.*

Some Struggles Never Seem to End

HISTORY is most often described in terms of its signal events: a bloody battle in a small town in Pennsylvania, the murder of an archduke, a day that will live in infamy. Social history is different. It is best understood as the changing by inches of the ways in which Americans live and work and, above all, think of themselves and others. Nowhere in the nation's history is this clearer than in the struggles for civil rights over the last 150 years. Here there is no war between nations, to be settled with signatures on a treaty, but a conflict of hearts and minds that flares up and eases, then flares again.

Certainly there are defining moments that mark progress for women, blacks, gay men, lesbians and others who have suffered discrimination. There was the passage of the 19th Amendment in 1920, when women were granted the right to vote, and the March for Equality in New York half a century later that helped mark the beginning of the second wave of feminism. There was the Warren Court decision of 1954 banning school segregation, the murders of the civil rights giants Martin Luther King Jr. and Malcolm X. There was the Stonewall uprising in Greenwich Village in 1969, when gay men went on a rampage after a bar was raided by the police, and the day the *New York Times* ran an article with the headline "Rare Cancer Seen in 41 Homosexuals," the first inkling that there existed a mortal illness that would come to be known as AIDS.

But the story of these movements is more complex and richer than simply a series of big moments, and the size of the banner headlines is sometimes belied by the subsequent backsliding. After the Supreme Court outlawed segregation, black students needed to be accompanied to classes by police officers to get past jeering classmates, and cities were torn apart by violence fired by the issue of forced busing.

Women gained the right to vote, but it was decades before they were seen as fully sentient human beings, capable not only of choosing office-holders but also of running for office themselves. And the battle that began at the Stonewall Inn continued for gay men and lesbians at home and at the office as they fought to be allowed to work as teachers and ministers, to adopt children and make lifelong commitments to one another, and simply to be left alone.

THE POWER OF AN ADJECTIVE

Some of the victories, as well as the humiliations, can be gleaned from 5 the language used to describe these groups, and the gradual assumption of self-determined names as substitutes for those created by others. The news columns of the *Times* reflected both societal biases and societal changes; as an arbiter of national mores, some argued, the paper subtly contributed to both. At the midpoint of the 20th century its stories about homosexuality referred matter-of-factly to perverts, deviants and undesirables. It took many years for the term homosexual to be used free of pejorative, and it was not until 1987 that the paper acceded to the wishes of homosexuals to be called gay.

The descriptions Negro and colored disappeared in the 1970's, to be replaced with black and African-American, and subconscious assumptions began to be explored by those overseeing news coverage. In 1970 the publisher, Arthur Ochs Sulzberger, asked in a memo to editors: "I am curious: why is it that when the National Guard kills four white students we put it on page 1, and when the National Guard kills six black people we put it on page 32?"

Other subtler biases were addressed, as details about hair color and clothing began to fade from stories about women. It seems quaintly anachronistic—and shocking—to have a 1970 account of the Women's March for Equality interrupted by a small item reporting that Betty Friedan was wearing a three-year-old "raspberry colored shift" and was late in arriving because she had been at the hairdresser.

In 1986 the executive editor, A. M. Rosenthal, posted a long-awaited memo that read in part, "The *Times* believes that 'Ms.' has become a part of the language, and is changing its policy," allowing the new honorific to replace Mrs. and Miss when suitable.

(Left) Landmark civil rights events were often followed by backsliding and violent conflicts, protests, and riots. For decades, the *Times* wrestled both with the events and with the language in which to describe them, as seen in this front page from October 2, 1962. (Below) The *Times* long viewed homosexuality simply as a problem, as this headline from December 17, 1963, shows. By the 1993 protest pictured here, however, the concerns of gays were part of mainstream coverage.

time. A throng of miners applauded as they departed.

The 17 were escorted to waiting cars by Vice President Juan Lechín Oquendo, Archbishop Abel Antezana y Rojas of La Paz, and the United States consul in La Paz, Charles Thomas.

The three had taken part in the tense and difficult, but finally successful, effort to persuade the miners to free their prisoners. In return, the Government agreed to withdraw 4,000 troops surrounding the Catavi mine.

The Government did not yield, however, to the miners' princi-

Continued on Page 2, Column 3 | Continued on Page 6, Column 4

Growth of Overt Homosexuality In City Provokes Wide Concern

By ROBERT C. DOTY

The problem of homosexuality in New York became the focus yesterday of increased attention by the State Liquor Authority and the Police Department.

The liquor authority an-

and restaurants that cater to the homosexual trade. Commenting yesterday on the situation, Police Commissioner Michael J. Murphy said:

"Homosexuality is another one of the many problems con-

Bank, 76 William Street, since he was 14 years old.

Mr. Scorca was picked up by Detectives John Nolan and Joseph Iacovelli of the First Squad early yesterday in Atlantic City, four days after he allegedly attempted to commit suicide.

According to the police, the bank believes that Mr. Scorca had been embezzling its funds for the last five years but that his crime did not come to light until recently.

Mr. Scorca, who stands 5 feet

Even these atmospherics and events are no more than dots to be connected to gain a true picture of the period. What is now known in gay history as Stonewall was seen as a minor melee at the time, although it has come to be considered a landmark in the fight for civil rights for gay Americans.

On the other hand, the Emancipation Proclamation was styled as the be- 10 ginning of the end of discrimination against black men and women, when in truth the nearly 140 years since have been a dizzying succession of advances and setbacks. After the great public parade in New York City for women's suffrage in 1912, the *Times*, editorializing against it, stated unequivocally. "It is not possible to think of women as soldiers and sailors, police patrolmen or firemen."

Of course, after dozens of lawsuits, decades of consciousness-raising, thousands of articles and pamphlets and speeches, the American people do think of women in those jobs. So it is, too, with civil rights for black men and women, who work and live in a polyglot world that scarcely seemed possible only a few decades ago, when armed guards were escorting black students into state universities. There are still the banner headlines, about affirmative action and racial profiling, and there are still glaring inequalities writ large in the world, inequalities between black and white, male and female, gay and straight.

And there are still the small moments that so often tell the true story of the continuing search for equality. A commitment ceremony in Vermont between two women whose families embrace their love for each another. A little girl with steady hands whose father wonders whether she will follow him into the practice of surgery, or the rigors of construction work. A black man who runs a major American city, perhaps one of those riven by riots in the 60's. What creeps up on us is a changing view of our nation and of ourselves, a view that comes to accept freedom based on right and position based on ability, a sometimes uneasy peace between prejudice and justice best understood through the long lens of history.

about the text

1. Quindlen begins her essay by contrasting the way we generally think of history with the best way to understand the history of social movements relating to struggles for civil rights. What, specifically, is her argument? Why is the contrast she describes important?

2. Paragraph 5 offers Quindlen's thesis: "The *Times* reflected both societal biases and societal changes; as an arbiter of national mores . . . [it] subtly contributed to both." What evidence does Quindlen offer for her thesis? How effectively does she distinguish between the ways that the *Times* simultaneously reflected and subtly contributed to both societal biases and changes?

3. What does Quindlen mean when she contends, "Here there is no war between nations, to be settled with signatures on a treaty, but a conflict of hearts and minds that flares up and eases, then flares again" (paragraph 1)? What metaphors does she use here? How do they support her claim?

on language use

4. Likely you have had the experience of realizing that some word or expression you'd used all your life reflected bias against some group. What led you to your realization? Has the realization influenced your behavior in any way? Why or why not?

5. Research press coverage of one of the events Quindlen mentions, and collect three stories from the time. Study them carefully for language. Are the labels used to describe various groups "self-determined names" or names "created by others"? Do other word choices reflect bias?

for writing

6. Think about the language used in discussions of a current controversial social issue —same-sex marriage, abortion, undocumented workers. Write an essay describing how language used to talk about that issue might be seen as biased.

7. Consider again the research you did for question 5; write an essay reflecting on the implications of what you found.

1. Because man's place is in the armory.

2. Because no really manly man wants to settle any question otherwise than by fighting about it.

3. Because if men should adopt peaceable methods women will no longer look up to them.

4. Because men will lose their charm if they step out of their natural sphere and interest themselves in other matters than feats of arms, uniforms, and drums.

ALICE DUER MILLER

Why We Oppose Votes for Men

Alice Duer Miller studied math and astronomy at Barnard College, paying for her education by publishing stories, poems, and essays in national magazines. She began teaching but later devoted her full attention to writing. Miller championed women's suffrage and often wrote about this issue in the New York Tribune; collections of these columns were published as Are Women People? *(1915) and* Women Are People! *(1917). As you read this selection from 1915, note how Miller parodies what was then (and is perhaps still) "common sense" knowledge about women in her argument for why women should be allowed to vote. (American women received the right to vote in 1920 through the Nineteenth Amendment to the U.S. Constitution.)*

5. Because men are too emotional to vote. Their conduct at baseball games and political conventions shows this, while their innate tendency to appeal to force renders them particularly unfit for the task of government.

about the text

1. How is Miller parodying "common sense" knowledge about women? What arguments against women's suffrage were opponents making?

2. How does Miller, in each case, turn stereotypes and everyday wisdom on their heads? How does she answer stereotype with stereotype?

3. How does studying Miller's text help us appreciate the claims made by Anna Quindlen in the previous selection, "Some Struggles Never Seem to End"?

on language use

4. Why is parody such a powerful tool in criticizing positions with which one disagrees? What are the limits of parody? Do you think there are situations in which parody is risky or inappropriate? Why? Give specific examples of subjects you would likely not parody.

5. Many comedians, television programs (such as *South Park*), and movies (such as *Scream* and its sequels) rely on parody. Find an example of effective parody in popular culture and analyze why it works.

for writing

6. Try your hand at parody of Miller's sort on a contemporary issue. Nearly any political or politicized issue will do; rich topics might be gay marriage, the war on terror, Mad Cow Disease, or stem cell research. As you consider possible topics, remember that some may be too risky for parody, and that creating a really clever parody based on common arguments will take some hard and creative thinking.

7. Investigate the rhetoric of the women's suffrage movement. (You can find some examples on the Internet using the keyword "suffrage.") What arguments did American suffragists use in support of their cause? What arguments were used by others against giving women the vote? Can you think of parallels to contemporary situations? Write an essay reporting what you discover.

MICHIKO KAKUTANI

Debate? Dissent? Discussion? Oh, Don't Go There!

Michiko Kakutani *is a book critic for the* New York Times, *where she has worked since 1979. She received the Pulitzer Prize in 1998 for criticism. In this 2002 essay from the* Times, *Kakutani contends that college students are no longer interested in the sort of debate that characterized the college experience of past generations. In contrast to Deborah Tannen, who claims that Americans relish winner-take-all arguments, Kakutani argues that contemporary college students work hard to avoid direct confrontation, at least in the classroom. Thus, she claims that today's students use language and argument in ways quite different from those of earlier generations.*

T HAT FAMILIAR INTERJECTION "whatever" says a lot about the state of mind of college students today. So do the catch phrases "no problem," "not even" and "don't go there."

Noisy dorm and dining room debates are no longer *de rigueur* as they were during earlier decades; quiet acceptance of differing views—be they political or aesthetic—is increasingly the rule.

Neil Howe and William Strauss's book "Millennials Rising"—a survey of the post-Gen X generation—suggests that the young people born in the early 1980's and afterward are, as a group, less rebellious than their predecessors, more practical-minded, less individualistic and more inclined to value "team over self, duties over rights, honor over feeling, action over words."

"Much the opposite of boomers at the same age," the authors write, "millennials feel more of an urge to homogenize, to celebrate ties that bind rather than differences that splinter."

These are gross generalizations, of course, but a student's article titled "The Silent Classroom," which appeared in the Fall 2001 issue of *Amherst* magazine, suggested that upperclassmen at that college tend to be guarded and private about their intellectual beliefs. And in this writer's own completely unscientific survey, professors and administrators observed that students today tend to be more respectful of authority—parental and professorial—than they used to be, and more reticent about public disputation.

"My sense from talking to students and other faculty is that out of class, students are interested in hearing another person's point of view, but not interested in engaging it, in challenging it or being challenged," Joseph W. Gordon, dean of undergraduate education at Yale, said. "So they'll be very accepting of other points of view very different from their own. They live in a world that's very diverse, but it's a diversity that's more parallel than cross-stitched."

The students' reticence about debate stems, in part, from the fact that the great issues of the day—the September 11 terrorist attacks and the war in Afghanistan—do not engender the sort of dissent that the Vietnam War did in an earlier era. It also has roots in a disillusionment with the vitriolic partisanship (that held sway in Washington in the 1990's: the often petty haggling between right and left, Republicans and Democrats, during President Bill Clinton's impeachment hearings and the disputed presidential election of 2000, and the spectacle of liberals and conservatives screaming at each other on television programs like "Crossfire."

"Debate has gotten a very bad name in our culture." Jeff Nunokawa, a professor of English at Princeton University, said: "It's become synonymous with some of the most nonintellectual forms of bullying, rather than as an opportunity for deliberative democracy." He added that while the events of September 11 may well serve as a kind of wake-up call, many of his students say that "it's not politic or polite to seem to care too much about abstract issues."

"Many of them are intensely socially conscientious, caring and committed," he said. "It's just not clear precisely what they wish to commit themselves to."

In a much talked-about article in the *Atlantic Monthly* a year ago, the   10
writer David Brooks argued that elite college students today "don't shout out their differences or declare them in political or social movements" because they do not belong to a generation that is "fighting to emancipate itself from the past," because most of them are "not trying to buck the system: they're trying to climb it." And yet to suggest that the archetypal student today is "the Organization Kid," as Mr. Brooks did, seems too simplistic, ignoring the powerful effect that certain academic modes of thinking—from multiculturalism to deconstruction[1]—have had in shaping contemporary college discourse.

---

1. **Multiculturalism** acknowledging and valuing the fact that a society like America's is composed of groups that maintain—and seek to maintain—distinct identities; critics of this perspective argue that it reduces complex social issues to questions of gender, color, and class. **deconstruction** a method of critical analysis, often applied to literary works, associated with French philosopher Jacques Derrida (1930–2004), which encourages readers to analyze the unstated and often contradictory assumptions made in a text.

Indeed, the reluctance of today's students to engage in impassioned debate can be seen as a byproduct of a philosophical relativism.[2] fostered by theories that gained ascendance in academia in the last two decades and that have seeped into the broader culture. While deconstruction promoted the indeterminacy[3] of texts, the broader principle of subjectivity has been embraced by everyone from biographers (like Edmund Morris, whose biography of President Ronald Reagan mixed fact and fiction) to scholars (who have inserted personal testimony in their work to underscore their own biases). Because subjectivity[4] enshrines ideas that are partial and fragmentary by definition, it tends to preclude searches for larger, overarching truths, thereby undermining a strong culture of contestation.

"How did you say 'Whatever' in the sixties?"

At the same time, multiculturalism and identity politics[5] were questioning the very existence of objective truths and a single historical reality. As the historians Joyce Appleby, Lynn Hunt and Margaret Jacob observed in their book, "Telling the Truth About History," radical multiculturalists celebrated "the virtues of fragmentation," arguing that "since all history has a political—often a propaganda—function, it is time for each group to rewrite history from its own perspective and thereby reaffirm its own past."

During the height of the culture wars of the early 90's, such views led to vociferous showdowns between academic radicals and traditionalists. It also led to the politicization of subjects like history and literature, and ideo-

---

2. **philosophical relativism** the belief that truths of any sort are relative to the situation or context, rather than absolute or eternal.

3. **indeterminacy** the idea that meaning cannot be fully and unambiguously stated.

4. **subjectivity** the idea that one views the world through the lens of one's own experience (rather than from a so-called "objective" perspective).

5. **identity politics** basing claims on what are assumed to be shared experiences by members of a specific social group (e.g., being a woman or an Asian American or a lesbian—or an Asian American lesbian).

logical posturing that could be reductive and doctrinaire in the extreme. Thankfully, these excesses have begun to die down, as bipolar dogmatism has started to give way to a scholarly eclecticism[6]—less concerned with large paradigms, and more focused on narrower issues—but the legacy of multiculturalism and identity politics remains potent on college campuses.

On one hand, it has made students more accepting of individuals different from themselves, more tolerant of other races, religions and sexual orientations. But this tolerance of other people also seems to have resulted in a reluctance to engage in the sort of impassioned argumentation that many baby boomers remember from their college days.

"It's as though there's no distinction between the person and the argument, as though to criticize an argument would be injurious to the person," said Amanda Anderson, an English professor at Johns Hopkins University and the author of a forthcoming book. "The Way We Argue Now." "Because so many forms of scholarly inquiry today foreground people's lived experience, there's this kind of odd overtactfulness. In many ways, it's emanating from a good thing, but it's turned into a disabling thing." 15

"A lot of professors complain about the way students make appeals to relativism today." Professor Anderson added. "It's difficult because it's coming out of genuinely pluralistic orientation and a desire to get along, but it makes argument and rigorous analysis very difficult, because people will stop and say, 'I guess I just disagree.'"

Outside the classroom, it's a mindset ratified by the PLUR ("Peace, Love, Unity and Respect") T-shirts worn by ravers (whose drug of choice is Ecstasy, which induces warm, fuzzy feelings of communion). It is also a mindset reinforced by television shows like *Oprah* that preach self-esteem and the accommodation of others, and by the internet, which instead of leading to a global village, has created a multitude of self-contained tribes—niche cultures in which like-minded people can talk to like-minded people and filter out information that might undermine their views.

At the same time, the diminished debate syndrome mirrors the irony-suffused sensibility of many millennial-era students. Irony, after all, represents a form of detachment; like the knee-jerk acceptance of the positions of others, it's a defensive mode that enables one to avoid commitment and stand above the fray.

What are the consequences of students' growing reluctance to debate? Though it represents a welcome departure from the polarized mudslinging of the 90's culture wars, it also represents a failure to fully engage with the

---

6. **eclecticism** borrowing from several approaches, rather than adhering to a single perspective.

world, a failure to test one's convictions against the logic and passions of others. It suggests a closing off of the possibilities of growth and transformation and a repudiation of the process of consensus building. "It doesn't bode well for democratic practice in this country," Professor Anderson said. "To keep democracy vital, it's important that students learn to integrate debate into their lives and see it modeled for them, in a productive way, when they're in school."

about the text

1. Though Kakutani qualifies her claims ("These are gross generalizations" [paragraph 5], "in this writer's own completely unscientific survey" [paragraph 5]), she makes strong statements about today's students. What are her claims? To what does Kakutani attribute the ways students think about and act toward "impassioned debate"?

2. In paragraphs 11–16, what does Kakutani see as the advantages and disadvantages of multiculturalism? Do you agree that respecting others' points of view and explicitly defending one's own are mutually exclusive? Why or why not?

3. Kakutani argues that students' reluctance to debate could have consequences for the United States as a democracy (paragraphs 18–19). What are her concerns? Do you agree? Why or why not?

4. If Kakutani is right about today's students, what sort of discussion should you expect about this article? Why?

on language use

5. Observe debates or discussions any place where students gather. What sort of language do the students use to acknowledge opinions with which they might disagree? What sort of language do they use to disagree?

6. Kakutani uses metaphors to advance several of her claims. For example:

"They [today's college students] live in a world that's very diverse, but it's a diversity that's more parallel than cross-stitched" (paragraph 6).

"Irony, after all, represents a form of detachment; like the knee-jerk acceptance of the positions of others, it's a defensive mode that enables one to avoid commitment and stand above the fray" (paragraph 18).

Identify these metaphors, or find others. How do they contribute to Kakutani's argument? Edit out the metaphors. What can you conclude about metaphor as a language strategy?

for writing

7. Based on your observations of student debates and discussions, write an essay in which you agree or disagree with Kakutani's position.

8. Kakutani's essay raises a complicated challenge: how to have and hold on to strong convictions in a society where others hold very different sets of convictions based on their experiences. We can find evidence of this challenge both within American society and within the larger world community. Write an essay in which you analyze this challenge, explain how you have sought to deal with it, and consider how successful you have been.

chapter 2

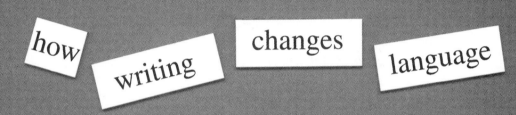

some consequences of literacy

you've likely never considered the fact, but most of the world's languages remain unwritten. Most are spoken or signed languages that have no agreed-upon or widespread writing system—no correct spelling, no dictionaries, no written texts at all. Writing is a technology that has particular benefits—and consequences. As the readings in this chapter demonstrate, writing a language down changes the way its users think about the language, themselves, and others who use the language. In particular, many people have very strong ideas about how their language should be written—and then how it should be used when it is spoken. Such ideas generally include strong value judgments about people who violate the conventions for writing or speaking, whatever they are. (Poor spellers, for example, may be assumed to be dumb or lazy. In fact, some people have dyslexia or other conditions that make spelling especially difficult for them.) This chapter asks you to reflect on some of the ways writing a language down changes both the language and people's attitudes toward it.

The chapter starts with two selections about spelling: one, a Web site, argues that English spellers should rise up, unite, and simply change English spelling by engaging in "freespeling" (with one l), spelling words how they sound; the other, a newspaper article, looks at the ruckus that arose in German-speaking countries when their governments passed laws mandating the simplification of spelling rules. (Imagine the U.S. government decreeing that the rules of spelling will change!) Then comes an article by Simon Winchester about Roget's thesaurus—how it came to be, and why, in Winchester's opinion, it is bad for the English language. We also include a copy of the very first crossword puzzle (Winchester shows the connection between thesauruses, crossword puzzles, and written language) and a series of advertisements for Mercedes-Benz that appeared in the article on Roget. As you'll see, they too are all about written language.

Next are two essays devoted to typographic conventions and punctuation. Ellen Lupton and J. Abbott Miller explain—and demonstrate—

how word spacing, paragraphing, italics, and other typographical conventions have developed over time, and Lewis Thomas shows how and why punctuation functions as it does.

The final group of readings focuses on how writing comes to change the way we speak—and then how we judge the way others speak. We start with some examples from the comics and the Internet and then examine two pieces that look at what they contend is the decline of how we in the Anglophone world use language: George Orwell's "Politics and the English Language" and Jack Rosenthal's "So Here's What's Happening to Language."

Each of these selections challenges you to think analytically about things you daily take for granted, like standardized spelling or the thesaurus or judgments about how people speak. They remind us that standardized varieties of language don't come from nowhere. In fact, they are shaped by many factors, including written language and attitudes that have arisen in response to the existence of writing and written language. When William Caxton set up the first printing press in England in 1476, he decided that his job and that of readers might be easier if words were spelled in a consistent way, thus beginning the standardizing of English spelling (something that happened only centuries later). As this chapter demonstrates, most of us assume standardized English spelling has always existed—until, that is, we read a text written before the eighteenth century or a novel written by an Australian or a sign posted in Singapore. Around the world and even within the United States there's more than one way to spell theater, and catalog, and many other words. The same is true for the way we use language—there's no one right way. But once a language comes to be written down, written standards affect the way we think about the language—and about others who use it. As you read this chapter, think about these and other consequences of being able to read and write.

The Kwestion of Speling

Joining a caravan of reformers, perhaps the best known being the playwright Bernard Shaw, Richard Lawrence Wade is a man with a cause and a plan: the reform of English spelling. Wade is British, and his Web site (**<freespeling.com>**, with one l) tells us that he has worked in television, radio, and advertising. As you browse his site, imagine what English would be like if writers followed Wade's advice. Pay special attention to Wade's arguments for seeking to alter English spelling as well as his advice on how English-language spellers of the world might unite to change the language.

Jody K. Biehl is a journalist living in Berlin. This article, **Crisis of Letters in Germany**, which appeared in the San Francisco Chronicle in November 2000, details some of the consequences of governmental efforts to simplify spelling and punctuation rules in Germany. As you read, imagine what might happen were there to be a "top-down" effort to reform the spelling of English, in the United States.

RICHARD LAWRENCE WADE

<freespeling.com>

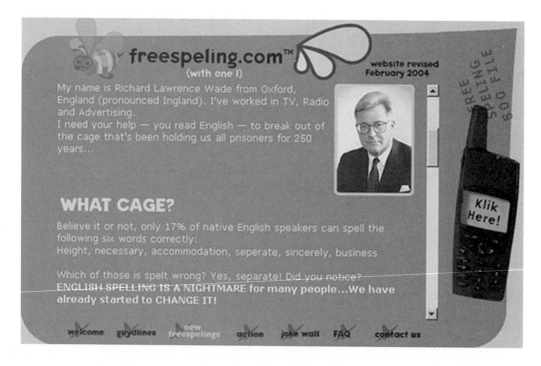

freespeling.com™
(with one l)

website revised
February 2004

My name is Richard Lawrence Wade from Oxford, England (pronounced Ingland). I've worked in TV, Radio and Advertising.
I need your help — you read English — to break out of the cage that's been holding us all prisoners for 250 years...

WHAT CAGE?

Believe it or not, only 17% of native English speakers can spell the following six words correctly:
Height, necessary, accommodation, seperate, sincerely, business

Which of those is spelt wrong? Yes, separate! Did you notice?
ENGLISH SPELLING IS A NIGHTMARE for many people...We have already started to CHANGE IT!

Klik Here!

FREE SPELING 500 FILE

welcome   guydlines   new freespelings   action   joke wall   FAQ   contact us

JODY K. BIEHL

Crisis of Letters in Germany

*Spelling Reforms Have Touched Off an Angry Debate
and Have Left the Public, Students, and Teachers Confused*

German trains may run with uncanny precision, but ask any person standing on the tracks how to spell the word for "train travel" and you might be greeted with a gaze of pure Teutonic panic.

Indeed, this meticulous nation of 83 million inhabitants has not suddenly forgotten how to spell. But the entire country —and the German-speaking nations of Austria and Switzerland—are gripped in a seething debate about the future of their language.

The debate focuses on an international attempt to make German easier by eliminating 100 spelling rules, including those that permit famously long compound words like *Feierabendverkehr* (rush-hour traffic) and *Rettungschwimmeruebungsplatz* (lifeguard training area). The reforms also reduce the number of rules for commas, from an astonishing 52 to nine and replace Americanized spellings for words like "ketchup" and "disco" with the Germanized *Ketschup* and *Disko*. "It is absolute lunacy," said Thomas Steinfeld, chief literary critic for the *Frankfurter Allgemeine Zeitung*, a staunchly conservative newspaper. "Can you imagine telling generations

of people—let alone writers, historians, and other academics —that the way they learned to spell is wrong? It is a linguistic nightmare."

Examples of the new grammar are as complicated as the old rules are long. In general, they break up compound words into various parts, so *Zugfahren* (to ride a train) becomes *Zug fahren*.

Steinfeld insists such shifts 5 alter the meaning of many words. A good comparison, he said, would be to take the English word undercover and break it into under cover.

"You end up not knowing if the person is a spy or if they are going to bed," he said. "You want to ask under cover of what, a blanket?"

In some cases, critics say the new rules push otherwise separated words together, resulting in an awkward situation of having three consonants in a row, as in *Shifffahrt*, the word for navigation.

Language reform is based on a 1960s notion that the way people write German is an automatic clue to their social status. In theory, class barriers disappear by simplifying the language.

The new spelling, which

took effect in 1998 in schools, government offices, and courts of law, has resulted in orthographic chaos in the usually placid world of German publishing. According to Steinfeld, every dictionary published since 1998 is different because publishers are also struggling to understand the new rules and explain away the old ones.

Moreover, teachers com- 10 plain that publishers of classic books often don't adhere to the new rules, leaving students confused and unsure of spelling and grammar.

"Instead of being more modern, we are reverting back to the nineteenth century where there were no standard rules of spelling and every publishing house was free to make up its own style," Steinfeld said.

The changes are happening at a time when many Germans are suffering from what the media describes as "reform fatigue." In recent months, they have seen sweeping changes hit their tax system and have watched in horror as legislators threaten to do away with cushy pensions that have been a popular perk of the West German system since the 1950s. Health insurance and commercial laws are also under scrutiny as Germany struggles to find its way in the global economy.

But fine-tuning the language, it seems, is one step many Germans are not willing to make in the name of modernity.

"We have tried the language reform for the past two years and I think we have to come to the conclusion that people don't want it," said Ulrike Flach, chairman of the education committee in the German parliament. "I think we should stop it now."

But that is not likely to happen any time soon. 15

Since the reforms were agreed upon in 1996 by the cultural ministers of Germany, Austria, Switzerland, and Liechtenstein, the German government has spent more than $200 million to rewrite school textbooks and official brochures. More significantly, several cultural ministers would have to admit that they were wrong.

In recent months, *Frankfurter Allgemeine Zeitung* has enraged government officials by branding the reforms "ridiculous" and "a total failure." In a much-read editorial, the newspaper, which still uses nineteenth-century typeface and refuses to publish photos on its front page, announced that it had abandoned the new rules in favor of classic, rule-bound German.

Leading literary figures, including Nobel laureate Guenter Grass and the conservative Academy of Language and Literature, have rallied around the newspaper, creating a bizarre alliance between political foes. Grass, a leftist who has long refused to be interviewed by *Frankfurter Allgemeine Zeitung* reporters, has quipped that he would happily allow the newspaper to "continue publishing nonsense about me as long as it is written according to the old rules."

In response, Education Minister Klaus Boeger says the anti-reform campaign will have no effect. "We are not in the habit of revoking decisions of the Cultural Ministers' Conference merely because an important newspaper returns to the old spelling rules," he said.

But Karin Wolff, the minister of culture for the state of Hesse, said changes should be made to soften the reforms. Wolff reminded critics that a linguistic transition period is scheduled to last until 2005.

Meanwhile, the latest German standard dictionary, known 20 as the *Duden*, has 5,000 new

The German-speaking Countries

words, incorporates the new spelling rules and has triumphed over what used to be Germany's biggest linguistic battle: the different usage of words in the former communist East and the capitalist West. Before the Berlin Wall fell in 1991, separate dictionaries were published with different entries.

Now, publishing houses in the East and the West are working together. The *Duden 2000* is its third joint edition; the other two were published in 1991 and 1996.

Steinfeld, however, is not thrilled with the new dictionary.

"It is not that I am against learning new words," he said. "I just want the old ones to be spelled correctly."

about the texts

1. List Wade's arguments for spelling reform from his FAQ page. How effective do you find them? Why?

2. How applicable and realistic are Wade's proposals? For example, could freespeling or any other English spelling–reform program accommodate dialects of both British and American English? Why or why not? (By the way, why does Wade keep both of the e's in the first half of "freespeling"? Wouldn't it be simpler if he deleted one of them?)

3. How does Wade link English spelling reform to technology? Do you agree or disagree with his claim? Why?

4. Thomas Steinfeld, a noted German literary critic, claims that the new spellings are "wrong" although Biehl's article acknowledges that German spelling was not standardized until the nineteenth century (much later than English spelling). Why do you think that speakers have such strong feelings about conventions like spelling and attach such strong value judgments to them?

5. According to Biehl, what are the goals of the international spelling reform for the German language? What are the motivations for such a reform? How persuasive do you find these goals and motivations? What are the consequences of the changes in spelling?

on language use

6. What sort of response do you have to Wade's "freespelings"? Aside from the title of the Web site, what was the first freespeling you noticed? Did you find any of the freespelings confusing to read or to pronounce? Why or why not?

7. Do you think arguments like those the German reformers present for spelling reform would be successful in the United States?

8. How often do you read the words "gonna" or "dunno" (as in "We're gonna bake her a cake, but I dunno what kind she likes")? Where do you see them? Newspapers? Novels? Cartoons? E-mails? History books? How often and where do you write them? Do you think these spellings will become standard in ten years? twenty? fifty? never? Why or why not?

for writing

9. Write an essay in which you argue for or against the reform of English spelling. If you argue for reform, should reform be top-down (as in Germany, where the government imposed reform) or bottom-up (as Wade advocates, where writers simply begin to change the language by freespeling)? Why? If you argue against spelling reform, you will need to explain why it is not necessary or why it will not achieve proponents' goals. In either case, consider variation in spelling that already exists— "theatre" and "theater," for example—as well as the advantages and disadvantages of standardized spelling.

10. Take something you've already written and re-render it using freespeling; then ask a friend or classmate to read it to you. Was it easy to understand? Did it become easier toward the end? Discuss the experience with your partner; then write an essay that discusses whether this experience has left you more in favor of freespeling or more opposed. Present reasons for your conclusions.

In this two-part selection, Simon Winchester explains the history of a product of literacy that all of us take for granted, the thesaurus—specifically, the King of Thesauruses, Roget's. Winchester is best known as a journalist and author of books, including The Professor and the Madman: A Tale of Murder, Insanity, and the Making of the Oxford English Dictionary *(1998),* Krakatoa: The Day the World Exploded: August 27, 1883 *(2003), and* The Meaning of Everything: The Story of the Oxford English Dictionary *(2003). These excerpts on Roget and his thesaurus are from the May 2001 issue of the* Atlantic Monthly. *As you read, you'll see that Winchester believes Roget did the English language a disservice in creating the thesaurus. Discover why he believes this and decide if you agree.*

SIMON WINCHESTER

Roget and His Brilliant,[1] Unrivaled,[2] Maligned,[3] and Detestable[4] Thesaurus

| part 1 |

* * *

MORE THAN **30** MILLION COPIES of *Roget's Thesaurus of English Words and Phrases* have been sold since the book was first published, in London, by the firm of Longman, Brown, Green and Longmans, in May of 1852. It is, by any standard, one of the most popular reference books ever written—a "treasure-house" indeed, as *thesaurus* translates from the Greek. Rare is the household without a dog-eared copy somewhere—

---

1. keen, perspicacious, sapient.

2. paramount, predominant, peerless.

3. ill-contrived, mordacious, harmful.

4. deplorable, nefarious, ghastly, accursed [Winchester's notes].

perhaps a holdover from school days; perhaps bought years ago with good intent, along with *Merriam-Webster* and *Bartlett's Familiar Quotations*; perhaps twinned with a book of crossword puzzles or acrostics. The motives for owning *Roget*—improving that essay, finding that eight-letter word beginning with *t*, getting the *mot juste*[5] for that Rotary Club or senate-campaign speech—are manifold.

There have been countless editions. Roget himself presided over twenty-five of the twenty-eight—each one subtly different—that were published during the two decades in which he continued to work on his magnum opus. The book has been published in America continuously since 1854. A considerable industry has arisen alongside *Roget*, devoted to books with a similar function and with similar titles. Many of these works once used the word *Roget* in their titles, as the name of the original author or, quite often, as a purely descriptive term. C. O. Sylvester Mawson's *A Dictionary of Synonyms and Antonyms; Being a Presentation of Roget's Thesaurus . . . in Alphabetical Form* (1931), is one example. Amazon lists 935 works for sale that include *thesaurus* in the title. (An impressive number, one might think—though it is perhaps worth noting that the same catalogue lists 21,782 products that incorporate the word *dictionary* in their titles, and 10,748 that call themselves encyclopedias. *Roget* may sell phenomenally well, but it has much less competition than do many other great works of reference.)

However defining and useful *Roget's Thesaurus* may have proved to be over the past 150 years, it was not the first book of its kind: Actually it would be more accurate to say that earlier books performed the function that *Roget's Thesaurus* is *believed* to perform—a distinction that makes it necessary to focus at the outset on two questions: What exactly was Roget trying to do when he first sat down to assemble his famous work? And what did he in fact achieve?

★ ★ ★

Although [earlier] volumes [had] listed hundreds upon hundreds of almost interchangeable words and phrases, and gave helpful hints as to how each might be suitably employed, none of them—with the possible exception of [one]—took care to examine the subtle notion of the synonym itself. None of the editors wondered—at least not in print—why a language as complex and finely turned as English would include any two words that meant *exactly* the same thing. Was there such a thing as a real synonym? Or

---

5. **mot juste** a French expression borrowed into English, meaning "the exact (or perfect) word."

had every word been created for a unique purpose? Roget, who began as early as 1805 to consider the need for some formal classification of the chaotic entity that was then the English language, was fascinated by these questions. The answers he constructed led him, fifty years later, to the creation of this organizational masterpiece that bears his name.

Consider some of the words that are listed in the *OED*[6] (under *synonym*) as examples of as-near-as-it-comes synonymy. The first are *serpent* and *snake*. Are these words true synonyms? In terms of pure definition, yes—sort of. *Serpent* is defined in the *OED* as "any of the scaly limbless reptiles regarded as having the properties of hissing and 'stinging'; *Zool.* a reptile of the group *Ophidia*; a snake." *Snake* is defined as "one or other of the limbless vertebrates constituting the reptilian order *Ophidia* (characterized by a greatly elongated body, tapering tail, and smooth scaly integument), some species of which are noted for their venomous properties; an ophidian; a serpent." The difference at this level is minuscule: one definition is more comprehensive, mentioning the vertebrated skeleton and the scaly integument: the other is somewhat more colorful, accentuating the hissing noise that the beast is able to emit.

Were this all, one might agree that the two words are perfect synonyms. But the *OED*, complete as always, continues its definition of *serpent*, observing that nowadays, in ordinary use, the word is "applied chiefly to the larger and more venomous species; otherwise only *rhetorical . . .* or with reference to serpent-worship."

Therein is the suggestion of reptilian synonymy blown suddenly asunder. For *serpent* is indeed the word we choose when we want to denote a snake that is bigger and nastier than most, and *snake* is the word we choose to describe any smooth and elongated creature that skitters from beneath the lawnmower blades. We say, on the one hand, "There is a *snake* in the basement" and, on the other, that missionaries were once thrown into "pits filled with *serpents*." But we don't proclaim there to be a *serpent* in the garden shed, and if we told a listener that a missionary was in a pit full of *snakes*, we would realize from the resulting questions—Were they big? Were they venomous?—that we had used the word wrongly, poorly, or incautiously. (This leads to another supposed synonymy: *venom* and *poison*. The words, however, are not exactly synonymous, because one can speak with *venom* yet perhaps not quite with *poison*. *Venom* is both a substance and a tone; *poison* is more a matter of chemistry.)

---

6. **OED** *Oxford English Dictionary*, the most comprehensive dictionary of the English language. Based on historical principles, it seeks to document how usage of each English word developed across time. No other language has a dictionary of comparable coverage.

Examination of any words thought to be synonymous reveals a congruency of range but not an identical meaning. Take some other illustrative related examples from the *OED: ship, vessel; compassion, fellow-feeling, sympathy; enormous, excessive, immense; glad, happy, joyful, joyous; kill, slay, slaughter; grieve, mourn, lament, sorrow.* Some are very close indeed; there is little to distinguish a ship from a vessel, except that one doesn't say *fishing ship* or *war vessel*—suggesting that a *vessel* is likely to be engaged in peaceful activities, whereas a *ship* can have a more menacing role. One cannot quite imagine Nelson's having spoken of *vessels* on the horizon off Cape Trafalgar,[7] or any dockside idler's speaking of the handsome lines of the *ship* that has just brought lobsters back from the Outer Banks. (In truth, he would probably say *boat*.) Others on the list are more obviously distinguishable. Sometimes the distinction is a matter of degree: one *kills* a man; one *slays* his child; one *slaughters* the villagers who sheltered the family. On other occasions the context suggests one choice rather than another: one feels *compassion* for the villagers in such circumstances; but *fellow-feeling* for the brother of the first who had to die.

*   *   *

An awareness of the nuances of synonymy, then, is fundamental to the speaking and writing of good English. Merely cataloguing synonyms, uncritically offering up lists of alternative words from which a speaker or writer may choose, makes for something less happy. Roget realized this back at the beginning of the nineteenth century, when the literate world was awash in dictionaries, thesauri, lexicons, and other guides for the betterment of verbal display. His goal was to make sure that what was written and spoken and read was impeccable. To this end he began a study of the language with the primary aim of classifying it and then distilling from that classification a guide to how it might best be made to work.

Peter Mark Roget, born in London on January 18, 1779, was in myriad [10] ways a most extraordinary man. [He] seems to have been interested in and learned about almost everything. The title page of the first edition of his *Thesaurus* offers tantalizing clues to his brilliance: his geological inclinations are shown only in the string of initials after his name ("M.D., F.R.S., F.R.A.S., F.G.S."), but he is also identified as "Fellow of the Royal College of Physicians; Member of the Senate of the University of London; of the Literary

---

7. **Nelson/Trafalgar** Admiral Horatio Nelson led a decisive British naval victory against Napoleon's navy at Cape Trafalgar, Spain in 1805. Although Nelson was killed in the battle, the victory established the British as a naval superpower.

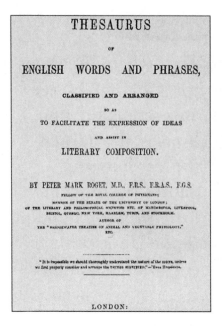

The first edition of *Roget's Thesaurus*, published in 1852

and Philosophical Societies etc. of Manchester, Liverpool, Bristol, Quebec, New York, Haarlem, Turin, and Stockholm. Author of the 'Bridgewater Treatise on Animal and Vegetable Physiology,' etc."

The "etc." shrouds an array of other achievements. Even the sparse *Britannica* entry mentions that Roget invented the so-called log-log slide rule, that he was the secretary of London's fabled Royal Society, and that he was a philologist. A cursory look at his scores of published papers attests to his many other interests (and the fact that he wrote some of these papers in French, German, and Latin as well as English shows his formidable linguistic abilities, stemming from his Swiss Huguenot roots).

★ ★ ★

It remains one of the more curious aspects of Roget's life that in this fury of intellectual and socially reforming energy his deep interest in the English language did not become fully apparent until he was in late middle age. He was nearly seventy when, still living in his London townhouse, he began work on his *Thesaurus*, having just been forced from his post at the Royal Society to make way for younger, cleverer, more energetic scientists.

Roget was by no means bitter—he knew well his own scientific strengths and weaknesses, and he would have been the first to acknowledge that his great achievements to date, largely in the fields of description and classification, had not been marked by brio[8] and inspiration. He settled down to his retirement, and yet equipped himself with a grand plan: if the God in whom he believed so implicitly allowed him sufficient time and energy (he was in fact granted a further twenty-one years, all of them healthy), he, by writing and thinking and organizing, would bestow on the kingdom of language the same order that Linnaeus had given to the kingdoms of animals and plants.

Such an ordering, Roget came to believe, would not just answer an intellectual need—it might well have benefits for society as a whole. He mentioned in the *Thesaurus*'s introduction that it might even help to fulfill his

---

8. **brio** liveliness or vivacity.

long-cherished dream of fostering the birth of a universal language — "that splendid aspiration of philanthropists."

Ever since the turn of the century, when he first began delivering medical lectures in Manchester and London, Roget had carried a succession of notebooks. Few, if any, of the originals survived the fires of World War II. The notebooks contained list after list of words that appeared to Roget to be near synonyms or — as the lists lengthened and the notebooks multiplied — to belong to the same philosophical groupings. Roget's realization as a young man that words could be placed in classes would later underpin his making of the *Thesaurus*. This is the essential difference between Roget's accomplishment and that of the other thesaurus makers before and since: his was a *conceptual* thesaurus, whereas the others were merely arranged alphabetically or otherwise organized to be useful.

Peter Mark Roget in 1835

There is no doubt that Roget aimed to produce a volume that was likely to be helpful to some users. In his preface he used the word *desideratum* — he was creating something he felt was *required* or *desired*. The book was designed "to supply, with respect to the English language, a desideratum hitherto unsupplied in any language; namely, a collection of the words it contains and of the idiomatic combinations peculiar to it, arranged, not in alphabetical order as they are in a Dictionary, but according to the *ideas* which they express."

Tom McArthur, the editor of the monthly magazine *English Today*, wrote in the *Oxford Companion to the English Language* that Roget's clear intent was "not . . . to define or discriminate [words], but to arrange them in synonymous and antonymous groups; it serves as both a word-finder and a prompter of the memory regarding words one knew but could not recall to mind."

Yet — and this is why I feel his book proved an ultimate and unwitting disservice to the language — Roget aimed, in selecting his supposed readership, very high indeed. His sixpenny tracts for diffusing knowledge may well have been intended for the artless and the educationally impoverished. His *Thesaurus*, on the other hand, was meant for users equipped with more finely honed intellects and with a very real lexical intuition. He surely never imagined that businessmen, students, and politicians would one day help to make his book such a commercial success. Had he done so, he might have organized his work in a signally different way.

His nobly Platonic[9] vision was that the language could come to be seen as an ordered part of the cosmos, amply reflective of divine will and inspiration. He took an Aristotelian[10] approach to his task as well, marshaling his subject according to the strictest logic. His organization was clearly of the moment: he believed in all sincerity that from out of the miasma of Victorian intellectual confusion could rise a gleaming pillar of lexical glory, a totem to the God who had made it all.

Once he had established his conceptual framework, he concluded that all words could be placed in one of six classes. "The purpose of this work," he wrote in the introduction to the first edition, "is not to explain the signification of words, but simply to classify and arrange them according to the sense in which they are now used, and which I presume to be already known to the reader." Those six classes indicate his staggering polymathy: Abstract Relations, Space, Matter, Intellect, Volition, Sentient and Moral Powers.

The first three cover the external world: Abstract Relations encompasses concepts such as order, number, and time; Space encompasses words relating to size and movement; Matter encompasses the physical world and the way in which people experience it with the five senses. The second three classes relate to the interior world of human beings: Intellect encompasses matters of the mind; Volition acts of will; and Sentient and Moral Powers (or, as modern *Roget* editors now call it, Emotion, Religion and Morality) the more profound matters of the heart and soul. As we can perhaps already see, it would take an extraordinary mind to discern such order and to impose it on the language we use.

Some might suggest that Roget was rather out of touch in assuming that such things were already known to or understood by his potential readers. Further, such an assumption, they say, casts doubt on Roget's utilitarian ideals. For how on earth could an average user understand something that few trained lexicographers—and, indeed, few philosophers of language— can properly comprehend (let alone agree on) today?

But that seems not to matter: a glance at a modern Longman edition of

---

9. **Platonic** referring to Plato's goals, including the analysis of the nature of the world and things in it.

10. **Aristotelian** referring to Aristotle's method, which always involved creating taxonomies, that is, breaking things down into smaller and smaller categories.

Roget's Thesaurus, published now by Penguin Press (1998) and edited by Betty Kirkpatrick, shows that the classification structure survives. However incomprehensible it may be, it is still the basis for the real *Thesaurus*, a century and a half later. Only in matters of the heart and soul has it been slightly changed, and only, in truth, for cosmetic reasons. The words within have changed, of course, with the times and the fashions—which is true of any thesaurus, dictionary, encyclopedia, or other work of reference that passes through new editions over the years.

---

about the text

1. As becomes clear in this selection, Winchester has little respect for Roget's creation—or at least for its consequences. What criticisms does Winchester offer of the thesaurus?
2. Cite examples from Winchester's article to support each of the following claims:
   (a) There are no such things as synonyms.
   (b) Synonyms exist.
   What examples of your own can you come up with?

on language use

3. Winchester quotes Tom McArthur, a well-known writer about the English language, as claiming that Roget did not intend to define words but to prompt users' memories in order to help them recall a word (paragraph 17). Is this how you use a thesaurus? Some researchers have claimed that one function of literacy is to serve as a "memory prompt"—for example, shopping lists or phone numbers scribbled on matchbook covers help readers (and writers) remember various kinds of things. Give a few other examples of cases in which you use literacy as a memory prompt.

for writing

4. Select a few paragraphs from a paper you have written and revise it using the thesaurus as a guide to making alternate word choices. Submit the original and revised versions along with a short essay describing your experience revising the paragraphs and evaluating the results. Is the revised material better? Why or why not?
5. Using a thesaurus is a good way to find a word that's on the tip of your tongue or to remember a word you already know, but it can also produce disastrous results. In the sentences below, the bold words have been changed by using the synonym feature of Microsoft Word. Try to re-create the original version by using the synonym feature and your own judgment. (The answer is on p. 89). Were there any words that you were unable to recover? If so, which ones? Why? What problems did you encounter? Write a brief essay detailing the drawbacks of using a thesaurus such as the synonym feature of Word. Include recommendations for when the feature should, and should not, be used.

   Frances wondered what **brilliant** her roommate, Pat, to **disperse costume approximately** the living **opportunity**. Meanwhile, Davonne was in the kitchen **thumping** up a **juicy frozen lump**. They were very provoked about the **celebrate** and wanted **the lot** to **exit healthy.**

$$\boxed{\text{part 2}}$$

To ILLUSTRATE THE CLEVERNESS of Roget's extraordinary classification system, let us track in the Penguin edition all the way through a single class of thought to its logical conclusion—to what, if we compared this with the Linnaean system of classifying life, we would call the thought's linguistic species or subspecies. Let us take the conceptual class Volition.

"Volition: the exercise of the will" is first divided into Individual Volition 25 (the will of one) and Social Volition (the will of many). Under Individual Volition are five subclasses: Volition in General, Prospective Volition, Voluntary Action, Antagonism, and Results of Action.

Let us look at Voluntary Action, which may be Simple or Complex, and let us select Simple. The Heads—the paragraphs full of words, organized by part of speech and according to whether they represent the idea or its precise opposite—that fall within this classification are self-explanatory: Action, Activity, Haste, Exertion, Fatigue, Agent, Workshop, and their opposites, which are Inaction, Inactivity, Leisure, Repose, and Refreshment. Agent and Workshop, being neutral aspects, do not have obvious opposites, of course.

Under one of those Heads—let us choose Haste—are about 200 words and phrases that can properly be used to express portions of the range of this single idea. Some of them are nouns: *dispatch, urgency, impetuosity.* Rather more of them are adjectives: *hot-headed, breakneck, slapdash, immediate.* About seventy-five verbs connote individual voluntary simple haste, including *scurry, bustle, fret, cut and run, make oneself scarce, whip, lash, bundle off.* There are a few adverbs, such as *feverishly, on the spur of the moment, with not a moment to lose,* and a very few interjections—*Buck up! Quick march! At the double!*

Within any one paragraph the words are grouped according to the manner and context in which they are used—whether, for example, they are usually employed in colloquial or in formal circumstances. Roget persuaded Longman to allow him to organize the book's Heads into two columns, with words of opposite meaning across from each other. So set against Haste is (no, not Less Speed; there is precious little wit in *Roget*) Leisure. Among those arrayed against *over-hasty* is *deliberate* (though with no phonetic explanation to guard against the verb). Against *expedite* is, among others, *while away.*

In formulating this dual-column plan, however, Roget very promptly came up against a problem that has long plagued semanticists interested in synonymy and antonymy: in countless groups there are in fact not two but three shades of sense—the meaning, its opposite, and a middle ground.

Beginning, middle, and *end* are one obvious example; *past, present,* and *future* are another. And the more the nature of the middle-ground word is subject to scrutiny, the more it changes. In some trinities noted by Roget in his introduction, the central word is the opposite of both the others—*concavity, flatness, convexity,* for example, or *desire, indifference, aversion.* In some groups the middle word is the standard against which the others are measured: *sufficiency* exists between *insufficiency* and *redundance.*

To rub in the difficulty of trying to make semantic order out of English linguistic mayhem, what about groups in which the middle word represents an imperfect state of the other two? *Dimsightedness* is less perfect than both *vision* and *blindness. Semitransparency* is a less perfect state than either *transparency* or its opposite, *opacity.* To take this a little further: *damp* is neither *wet* nor *dry, tepid* is neither *hot* nor *cold*—and neither of these last two middle words has a precise opposite.

So should there have been three columns in Roget's book? Roget originally thought so, but he eventually recognized the practical difficulties and the cost of such an arrangement, to which his publisher was hostile. The plan was dropped. But in and of themselves, such difficulties with the internal classifications of synonymy need not have made *Roget* the force for literary ill that I believe it to be. If anything, those difficulties served to remind people interested in the vocabulary what a superbly complex entity the English language is. They served further to enhance public respect for the language, and to emphasize still more widely the great care that needed to be employed to ensure its best use.

No, the central shortcoming in *Roget's Thesaurus,* as I see it, stems not from the book's troublesome structure but from something quite different— from Peter Mark Roget's Panglossian[11] regard for the intellectual merit of his likely readership. Roget never imagined, for instance, that an Ohio sophomore majoring in political science might one day use his book to find a word with which to pad out a paragraph in a midterm paper. Roget never envisioned that paperback editions of his work would be stuffed into millions of school backpacks and satchels from Huddersfield to Hobart, or that a barely literate board chairman bound for Liverpool would have his secretary's volume by his side as he was writing his report to shareholders on the morning express from Euston.

---

11. **Panglossian** blindly optimistic. (An eponymous term that derives from Dr. Pangloss, a character in Voltaire's play *Candide,* who foolishly believed that we live in "the best of all possible worlds.")

Roget assumed that anyone who might chance upon his *Thesaurus* would be just as clever as he, just as accustomed to precise syntax, to scrupulous grammar, and to confident and impeccable word selection.

Roget assumed, as he organized his work, that anyone who might chance upon it would be just as clever as he, just as accustomed to precise syntax, to scrupulous grammar, and to confident and impeccable word selection. Armed with this naive set of assumptions, he produced a book that was predicated on the misguided belief that, as he wrote in his introduction, users would guide themselves through the thicket of words by relying on what he grandly termed their "instinctive tact." Thus there was no need to explain what any word meant—because his users, with all their "tact," would know that full well already.

And so an icily precise classification was all that was necessary. Definitions would be so cumbersome to include, so time-consuming to assemble, so costly to publish, so unnecessary, so—so *insulting* to his highly accomplished readers. Thus, crucially, Roget, who already possessed a deep knowledge of the English vocabulary, decided not to include them. And yet, of course, neither the Ohio sophomore nor the Liverpudlian businessman had such knowledge. Neither had the ability to make proper use of the volume Roget created. For such as these, the *Roget* that they were persuaded to buy and to use—wrongheadedly and irresponsibly, in my view—provided no more than an unexplained and inexplicable list of *quick fixes*. Each user had a sudden want. Each needed a word. Each reached for the *Roget*—and presto! The way the book is arranged makes it all appear easy, a quick solution in an efficient microsecond. And yet, precisely because the users are ill-versed, and because the book makes utterly invalid assumptions about their knowledge, and offers no help at all in discovering what anything means, the word chosen with each *presto!* is often wrong. Sometimes very wrong. Often slightly wrong. And at the very least, frequently, curiously, and discordantly *off*. For example, a freshman student of mine, who admitted to using *Roget*, attempted to improve the phrase "his earthly fingers" by changing it to "his chthonic digits."

Each time such a wrong is perpetrated by way of Peter Mark Roget, the 35 language, as spoken, written, or read, becomes a little worse, a little more mediocre, and a measure more decayed, disarranged, and unlovely. And that, I suggest, is why all *Rogets* should be shunned.

* * *

Back in the 1850s only a few recognized the potential short-comings of *Roget's Thesaurus*. One of them was Edwin P. Whipple, who wrote a perceptive essay in the 1854 issue of the *North American Review*.

A reference book of this nature and with this express purpose, Whipple [wrote], was certain to spread the contagion of literary mediocrity. What was needed was not *more information* (oh! how today's users of the Internet might consider that anew) but *more inspiration*. Not more words to make easy the *expression* of ideas but more energy to make more probable the *conception* of ideas. Not so much message, not so much medium—but more, many more marvels of true creation.

And Roget, Whipple implied, never had an original thought in his life. He was a mere classifier of the existing order, a pedant, a noble dullard who should no more have been let loose on the language than a civil engineer should be let loose on the west door of Chartres, or an industrial chemist on the manufacture of Haut-Brion.[12]

Under the heading for Haste and Leisure, we find *brusquerie* and its Latin converse, *otium cum dignitate*.

Whatever the carping and the cavils, Roget and his publishers swiftly realized that their creation was a gold mine. The first edition of the *Thesaurus* sold out its initial printing of a thousand copies by the end of the year. A second edition came out the following March, and a third—"cheaper . . . enlarged . . . improved"—went on the streets in February of 1855. This edition—for which Roget rewrote part of the text and added "many thousand" new expressions and subsidiary headings that in his view filled gaps in the original structure—was used as the basis for so many subsequent printings that the steel-and-antimony plates were eventually worn smooth and useless.

The first American edition (1854) was edited by a man named Barnas 40 Sears and published by Gould and Lincoln, of Boston. Roget conceived an immediate dislike for it, writing that "an imperfect edition of this work was published at Boston . . . in which the editor, among other mutilations, has altogether omitted the Phrases . . . and has removed from the body of the work all the words and expressions borrowed from a foreign language, throwing them into an Appendix, where . . . they are completely lost to the inquirer." He would perhaps have been more pleased when the distinctly different International Edition was published in New York, in 1922, by Thomas Crowell (which had bought the rights to the book in 1886 and had published for the

---

12. **Haut-Brion** a variety of very fine French wine.

next three and a half decades what was essentially a facsimile of the original, despite its being manifestly designed for the English-speakers of England). The rationale behind the International Edition was abundantly clear. As C. O. Sylvester Mawson wrote in his preface to Crowell's *Roget's International Thesaurus,* "The English language marches with no frontiers: it is a world possession." So we find words and expressions that were much better known on the Continent than in either America or Britain. Under the heading for Haste and Leisure, for instance, we find *brusquerie* and its Latin converse, *otium cum dignitate.*[13] (In the fifth edition of the *International,* published by HarperCollins in 1992, both these obscure forms have vanished, though the Latin term that was under the Leisure column has been replaced by the Italian *dolce far niente,*[14] which is amply supplemented by the phrases *ride the gravy train* and *lead the life of Riley.*)

Roget's son, John, took over the *Thesaurus* when Roget died, at ninety, in 1869. John was more than modest about his own achievements (his only other publication was "A History of the Society of Water-Colourists," in 1891) and insisted that any changes he made to the great book during what was to be thirty-nine years of work (up until his death, in 1908) were "almost entirely of a practical nature, demanding industry and attention, rather than philosophic culture or the learning of a philologist."

John Roget did, however, engineer one important organizational compromise during his tenure: he extended his father's embryonic system of cross-referencing and fine-tuned it over the years, greatly simplifying a work that was in danger of collapsing under its own weight because of the rapid proliferation of words.

As the editions thundered out, the new words included in them—*electrolier, lorry, motor-car, veldt,* and *outspan* were all added under John Roget's suzerainty[15]—reflected new technologies and the war in Natal and Cape Province.[16] When *television* was added, it was put into the class of concepts that is termed Intellect—the exercise of the mind. (Sour minds might wonder at the propriety of classifying one of the senses of *television* under Intellect,

---

13. **otium cum dignitate** "leisure with dignity," or dignified leisure (Latin).

14. **dolce far niente** "sweet doing nothing," or delightful idleness (Italian).

15. **electrolier** a cluster of electric lights. **lorry** the word used for "truck" in British English. **veldt** in South Africa, an open pasture or piece of land. **outspan** to unyoke a horse or ox; by extension, to encamp. **suzerainty** control or leadership.

16. **war in Natal and Cape Province** war fought by the British in South Africa in the late nineteenth and early twentieth centuries against native Africans and Boers (descendants of Dutch settlers).

particularly if they see on the screen such puzzling phenomena as Jerry Springer, Dan Rather, and Ron Popeil's Pocket Fisherman.)

Peter Mark Roget's primary intent in creating his book was a noble one—avowedly Platonic, Aristotelian, a monument to the Almighty and His purpose. Or at least it was until the very last minute, when Roget decided to include a feature he had earlier intended to forget—a feature that changed for all time the role that this remarkable book would play: an index.

When the index was finished, it was a miserly thing—hastily done, fully 45 advertising the reluctance of its compiler. But because it made the book much easier to use—though in a way very different from what Roget had intended—it was to swell mightily over the coming years. John Roget worked hard to increase the size and scope of the index. Today the index to the British edition is twenty pages longer than the thesaurus itself. The index to *Roget's International Thesaurus*, in America, though set in a typeface two points smaller than that of the main body of the book, still occupies half the number of pages the thesaurus does; it would be far longer were it printed in the same size.

The index is and always has been what everybody uses. The classification system is something of which almost no user of *Roget* is even vaguely aware. I defy all but the specialists among readers of this article to claim that they knew, for example, that *deodorant, henpecked, box-office,* and *consuetude* can be found in a class Roget called Volition, or that *dog collar, privet, fulcrum,* and *clotheshorse* are in the class he called Space. However noble Roget's design, no one uses it and few care about it; if there was once a Platonic ideal for his book, it is subordinate to the relentless usefulness that was brought about at a stroke, by the inclusion of an index. As Roget might well have grumbled, that index represents the chicane[17] that separates the original intent of the book from its present vulgar function.

Roget, however, was not intended to address the want of drawing-room conversation; it met a very different set of needs. The book's real popularity was achieved—and sales figures more than amply confirm this—in the immediate aftermath of one fateful Sunday in December of 1913. That was the day that the popular newspaper the *New York World* published in its supplement *Fun* a small matrix of black and white squares into which readers were directed to write words that, in some clever way, correctly responded to a list of clues printed alongside the matrix. The crossword puzzle had been born.

By the 1920s the craze had spread across America and across the Atlantic by 1930 the venerable *Times* of London had a puzzle, the speed of completing

---

17. **chicane** petty trick.

FUN'S Word-Cross Puzzle.

2–3. What bargain hunters enjoy.
4–5. A written acknowledgment.
6–7. Such and nothing more.
10–11. A bird.
14–15. Opposed to less.
18–19. What this puzzle is.
20–23. An animal of prey,
26–27. The close of a day.
28–29. To elude.
30–31. The plural of is.
8–9. To cultivate.
12–13. A bar of wood or iron.
16–17. What artists learn to do.
20–21. Fastened.
24–25. Found on the seashore.
10–18. The fiber of the gomuti palm

6–22. What we all should be.
4–26. A day dream.
2–11. A talon.
19–28. A pigeon.
F–7. Part of your head.
23–30. A river in Russia.
1–32. To govern.
33–34. An aromatic plant.
N–8. A fist.
24–31. To agree with.
3–12. Part of a ship.
20–29. One.
5–27. Exchanging.
9–25. To sink in mud.
13–21. A boy.

(Answers on p. 89.)

The world's first crossword puzzle was devised by Arthur Wynne, and published in the *New York World* on December 21, 1913.

which was used as a test of ability and intelligence. The provost of Eton,[18] it was said, finished this exercise each morning in the time it took to boil his egg (from cold).

But there were, especially in Britain, strict and unspoken rules. Self-respecting people figuring out the answers to clever crossword puzzles never, ever used dictionaries—or any other reference books. To do so was an admission of defeat. It was simply not done.

Because many of these early crossword puzzles offered monetary re- 50 wards, a goodly number of stupid, callow, competitive, and greedy people did not observe these proprieties. They had a pressing need—to gain standing to win dollars or pounds, to best the fellow next door. They yearned for a tool for looking up unknown words: a book that listed words that were similar to other words, so that if the clue was "habit," they might find the answer in a list that stretched from *cacoëthes* and *consuetude* to *disposition, leaning,* and *mannerism*. Thesauri answered the call. Scores of them were on sale— the 1920s equivalent of the 935 thesauri listed for sale by Amazon eight decades later. And the king of the hill even then was *Roget*.

Roget's Thesaurus, which had come into being as a linguistic example of the Platonic ideal, became instead a vade mecum[19] for the crossword cheat.

It already had other, more insidious shortcomings. By eschewing definitions altogether, and thus suggesting no choices, it fostered poor writing. It offered facile answers to complex liguistic questions. It appealed to a growing desire for snap solutions to tricky verbal situations. It enabled students to appear learned without ever helping to make them so. It encouraged a malaprop society. It made for literary window dressing. It was meretricious.

But a tool for cutting corners? How Peter Mark Roget might have turned in his grave: the book by which he set so much store, his most lasting memorial, was being used for petty and degrading purposes—assisting no one with the language, but boosting the circulation of tabloid dross. And its usage has not widened significantly since (not, that is, in the sense of becoming more than a quick and easy remedy for the lexically distressed— for the literary poseur, if you will). A student in want of a word? No need to expend mental energy, no need to wait until blood prickles from the forehead: *Roget* will supply the answer, will find the syllables to plug the hole, will offer the solution with no delay or fuss. No need to bend, spindle, or mutilate.

---

18. **Eton** elite school in England.

19. **vade mecum** a handbook or bible (Latin: literally, "go with me").

Consider, in conclusion, two simple passages, both drawn from the first chapter of Sir Ernest Gowers's *The Complete Plain Words*[20] (1954), a British-government-issued book that is still the Bible of the best English writing. The first is from a Shakespearean sonnet that begins. "Full many a glorious morning have I seen / Flatter the mountain-tops with sovereign eye," and continues, as Gowers cites, "Kissing with golden face the meadows green / Gilding pale streams with heavenly alchymy."

There was no *Roget* when Shakespeare wrote those lines—or, for that matter, any dictionary. The lines were written perhaps a decade before Robert Cawdrey and his *Table Alphabeticall*,[21] 250 years before Peter Mark Roget and his high lexical ideals. And yet the writing is perfect, in choice and arrangement of words, in thought, timbre, address, and note.

As, on altogether another level, is this—a notice that was once placed inside all British post offices: "Postmasters are neither bound to give change nor authorised to demand it."

No *Roget* was employed here, either. The civil servant who penned those words knew just what he wanted to say, and had a mind lithe and educated enough to come up with a sentence in which every word counts, not one is superfluous, and the whole has a harmony that in its modest way achieves the greatness of poetry.

So, indeed, Peter Mark Roget, physician, chess genius, expert on bees, phrenology,[22] and the kaleidoscope: for all your noble ideals and Aristotelian logic, your book offers comfort only to the few—some clues for crossword cheats, some natterings for speechwriters, and some quick and easy solutions for the making of the middlebrow, the mindless, and the mundane. *Roget* has become no more than a calculator for the lexically lazy; used too often, relied on at all, it will cause the most valuable part of the brain to atrophy, the core of human expression to wither.

---

20. **Complete Plain Words** a usage manual published by Sir Ernest Gowers in Britain, a favorite of conservative users of the language even today.

21. **Table Alphabeticall of Hard Usual English Words.** a 1604 dictionary considered the first monolingual dictionary of English. (Generally, the earliest dictionaries of a language are bilingual dictionaries. Early monolingual dictionaries of English and other European languages included only the difficult words, assuming users would know the easy words.)

22. **phrenology** a nineteenth- and early-twentieth-century pseudoscience that argued that the shape of a person's skull could give clues as to her or his intelligence and personality.

about the text

1. Winchester notes that when one examines synonyms and antonyms in detail, one finds that the lexicon of English isn't categorized by simple opposites, but often by a concept, its opposite, and something in between. Winchester gives several examples of this situation. Give several of your own, consulting *Roget's Thesaurus* if you like.

2. What crucial innovation did Roget's son bring to his father's creation? What does his innovation have to do with literacy? How did it transform the thesaurus?

3. How did the invention of the crossword puzzle create a new use for the thesaurus?

4. What, ultimately, is Winchester's complaint about Roget and his thesaurus? What does he claim the consequences of the thesaurus to be? Examine Winchester's reasoning (paragraphs 32–35). Do you agree? Why or why not? Is Winchester an elitist? Why or why not?

on language use

5. Try doing the first crossword puzzle (the boxes with numbers are spaces for letters, too). What sorts of cognitive skills and knowledge of language does the puzzle require? How do they compare with the skills needed to do a contemporary crossword puzzle? What strategies do you use for figuring out a word when you have one or two letters?

for writing

6. Do you like to do crossword puzzles? Why or why not? Work alone or with a partner, and select a challenging crossword puzzle from a newspaper, magazine, or puzzle book. Solve as much as you can on your own, and then use a thesaurus to help you with the rest. Were you able to complete the puzzle? Why or why not? Write an essay describing how you used the thesaurus—what worked, what didn't, and why. Also, describe the experience of doing the puzzle. Was it fun? frustrating? difficult? easy? Would you solve another puzzle using the thesaurus? Why or why not?

Answer to writing question 5 on p. 79

Frances wondered what motivated her roommate, Pat, to scatter clothes around the living room. Meanwhile, Davonne was in the kitchen whipping up a luscious frosted cake. They were very excited about the party and wanted everything to go well.

Crossword answers

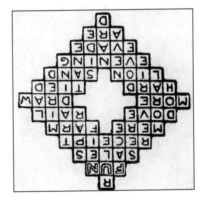

Playing with Words to Sell Cars

These five ads for Mercedes-Benz originally appeared in Winchester's article on Roget in the Atlantic Monthly in May 2001. All were full-page ads, sprinkled at intervals throughout the essay, and each one had a bright, solid-color background, providing a sharp contrast with the dense type blocks on their facing pages. Unlike most magazine ads, which may appear in several different publications and have nothing to do with the content of neighboring pages, these ads were designed specifically for placement within the Winchester essay. Each ad invites you to focus on a single word and involves some kind of word play, with written words. What does a thesaurus have to do with a car? How is it significant that the car being advertised is a Mercedes-Benz and not a Ford or a Chevy? As you look at the ads, think about the relationship between the visual image of the word presented and its meaning — in other words, think about words in their dual role here as symbols representing meaning and as visual images that convey something larger.

cute, prosecute. *Informal:* pull off. See [...] also act, fulfill, function, play, stage.
performance *noun* The act of beginning and carrying through to completion : discharge, effectuation, execution, prosecution. See DO in Index. — See also behavior, interpretation.
performer *noun* See player.
perfume *noun* See fragrance.
perfume *verb* See scent.
perfunctory *adjective* Performed or performing automatically and impersonally : automatic, mechanical. See CONCERN in Index.
perhaps *adverb* See maybe.
periapt *noun* See charm.
peril *noun* See danger.
peril *verb* See endanger.
perilous *adjective* See dangerous.
perimeter *noun* See border, circumference.
period *noun* 1. A specific length of time characterized by the occurrence of certain conditions or events : season, span, stretch, term. See TIME in Index. 2. An interval regarded as a distinct evolutionary or developmental unit : phase, stage. See TIME in Index. — See also age, end, time.
periodic *adjective* See intermittent, recurrent.
periodical *adjective* See intermittent, recurrent.
periodically *adverb* See intermittently.
peripatetic *adjective* See nomadic.
periphery *noun* See border, circumference.
periphrastic *adjective* See wordy.
perish *verb* See die.
perjure *verb* See lie².
perjured *adjective* See perjurious.
perjurer *noun* See liar.

perjurious *adjective* Marked by lying under oath : forsworn, perjured. See TRUE in Index.
perjury *noun* See mendacity.
perk up *verb* See encourage, recover.
permanent *adjective* See continuing.
permeate *verb* See charge.
permissible *adjective* Capable of being allowed : admissible, allowable. *Slang:* kosher. See ALLOW in Index.
permission *noun* The approving of an action, especially when done by one in authority : allowance, approbation, approval, authorization, consent, endorsement, leave², license, permit, sanction. *Informal:* OK. See ALLOW in Index.
permit *verb* 1. To neither forbid nor prevent : allow, have, let, suffer, tolerate. See ALLOW in Index. 2. To give one's consent to : allow, approbate, approve, authorize, consent, endorse, let, sanction. *Informal:* OK. See ALLOW in Index. 3. To afford an opportunity for : admit, allow, let. See ALLOW in Index. — See also enable.
permit *noun* See license, permission.
permutation *noun* See change.
pernicious *adjective* See destructive, virulent.
perorate *verb* See rant.
perpendicular *adjective* See vertical.
perpetrate *verb* See commit.
perpetual *adjective* See continual, endless.
perpetuate *verb* See immortalize.
perpetuity *noun* See endlessness, eternity.
perplex *verb* See complicate, confuse.
perplexed *adjective* See confused.

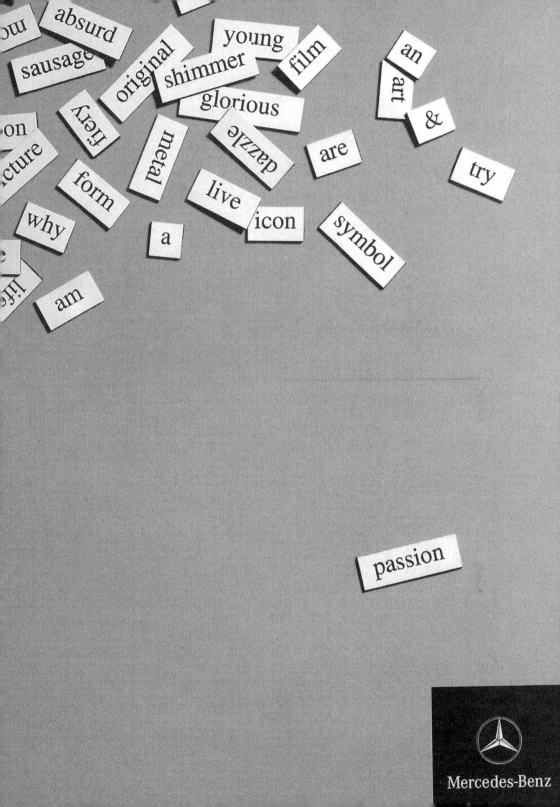

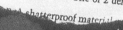

keeping safe or state of being kept safe.
safe·ty (sāf'tē) *n.*, *pl.* **-ties. 1.** The state of being safe. **2.** A device designed to prevent accidents. **3.** *Football.* **a.** A play in which a member of the offensive team downs the ball behind his own goal line. **b.** One of 2 defensive backs.
safe·ty ... shatterproof material.

Mercedes-Benz

about the texts

1. What arguments does this series of ads make for Mercedes-Benz? Why are these arguments especially appropriate for the readership of an article on the thesaurus?

2. How do the ads' creators take what may at first seem like random, everyday instances of written language and use them to create their arguments? What is the source of or inspiration for each of the ads? Why are the ads sequenced as they are?

on language use

3. Which ad do you think is the most creative? Most effective? Why? Do you generally find ads whose message depends on words effective? Why or why not?

4. These ads are for Mercedes-Benz, but could they just as easily be for Ford or Chevy? Why or why not? Almost all car ads in magazines show photos of the cars, but these ads don't. Why might the designers have chosen not to use images of the product itself? What message is conveyed by the absence of photos? Are the ads effective without photos? Why or why not?

for writing

5. Revise these ads to sell a different product —sneakers, perfume, organic food, underwear. What words would you use? You'll need to consider what audience you want to reach.

6. Select a product or service and find examples of both print and radio ads for it (cars, soft drinks, banks, and department stores are likely categories; since radio ads tend to be local, try your local newspaper to find the print ad). Write an essay comparing the language in the two ads. How are they similar? Different? What kinds of information are easier to convey in writing? In spoken language? Include the print ad and a transcript from the radio ad, with your essay.

7. In everyday conversation and writing, we don't use language as Mercedes-Benz does here —single words without context, dictionary definitions, words jumbled together with no sense or order. Yet none of the ads appears unusual to us. Why not? Is it surprising that the ads are for a car and not for, say, perfume or underwear or soft drinks? Why or why not? Write an essay that addresses these questions; then, with one or two classmates, select a product and design an ad using elements similar to those in the Mercedes-Benz ads. (Your ads don't have to be polished and artistic—it's the concepts that count)

Punctuation. Period.

· ·

Lewis Thomas *was a twentieth-century American biologist, physician, and writer. Known especially for his ability to write about biology for nonscientists, he was author of* The Lives of a Cell: Notes of a Biology Watcher *(1974), a collection of essays that had originally appeared in the* New England Journal of Medicine. *So great was his reputation that in 1993 Rockefeller University established the Lewis Thomas Prize to honor scientists "whose voice and vision can tell us of science's aesthetic and philosophical dimensions."* **Notes on Punctuation** *comes from Thomas's 1979 collection of essays,* The Medusa and the Snail: More Notes of a Biology Watcher.

Ellen Lupton *and J. Abbott Miller work collaboratively as artists, designers, and writers, sharing a studio named Design Writing Research. For them, design is a kind of authorship. They serve as co-chairs of the Graphic Design Department in Baltimore's Maryland Institute College of Art.* **Period Styles: A Punctuated History** *comes from their award-winning 1996 book* Design/Writing/Research: Writing on Design. *Part of the effectiveness of this essay results from Lupton and Miller's use of typography to illustrate their subject.*

· ·

LEWIS THOMAS

Notes on Punctuation

THERE ARE NO PRECISE RULES about punctuation (Fowler[1] lays out some general advice (as best he can under the complex circumstances of English prose (he points out, for example, that we possess only four stops (the comma, the semicolon, the colon, and the period (the question mark and exclamation point are not, strictly speaking, stops; they are indicators of tone (oddly enough, the Greeks employed the semicolon for their question mark (it produces a strange sensation to read a Greek sentence which is a straightforward question: Why weepest thou; (instead of Why weepest thou? (and, of course, there are parentheses (which are surely a kind of punctuation making this whole much more complicated by having to count up the left-handed parentheses in order to be sure of closing with the right number (but if the parentheses were left out, with nothing to work with but the stops, we would have considerably more flexibility in the deploying of layers of meaning than if we tried to separate all the clauses by physical barriers (and in the latter case, while we might have more precision and exactitude for our meaning, we would lose the essential flavor of language, which is its wonderful ambiguity)))))))))))).

The commas are the most useful and usable of all the stops. It is highly important to put them in place as you go along. If you try to come back after doing a paragraph and stick them in the various spots that tempt you you will discover that they tend to swarm like minnows into all sorts of crevices whose existence you hadn't realized and before you know it the whole long sentence becomes immobilized and lashed up squirming in commas. Better to use them sparingly, and with affection, precisely when the need for each one arises, nicely, by itself.

I have grown fond of semicolons in recent years. The semicolon tells you that there is still some question about the preceding full sentence; something needs to be added; it reminds you sometimes of the Greek usage. It is almost always a greater pleasure to come across a semicolon than a period. The period tells you that that is that; if you didn't get all the meaning you wanted or expected, anyway you got all the writer intended to parcel out and now you have to move along. But with a semicolon there you get a pleasant little feel-

---

1. **Fowler** (1858–1933) was a lexicographer and the author of *Modern English Usage* (1926).

ing of expectancy; there is more to come; read on; it will get clearer.

Colons are a lot less attractive, for several reasons: firstly, they give you the feeling of being rather ordered around, or at least having your nose pointed in a direction you might not be inclined to take if left to yourself, and, secondly, you suspect you're in for one of those sentences that will be labeling the points to be made: firstly, secondly, and so forth, with the implication that you haven't sense enough to keep track of a sequence of notions without having them numbered. Also, many writers use this system loosely and incompletely, starting out with number one and number two as though counting off on their fingers but then going on and on without the succession of labels you've been led to expect, leaving you floundering about searching for the ninethly or seventeenthly that ought to be there but isn't.

Exclamation points are the most irritating of all. Look! they say, look at 5 what I just said! How amazing is my thought! It is like being forced to watch someone else's small child jumping up and down crazily in the center of the living room shouting to attract attention. If a sentence really has something of importance to say, something quite remarkable, it doesn't need a mark to point it out. And if it is really, after all, a banal sentence needing more zing, the exclamation point simply emphasizes its banality!

Quotation marks should be used honestly and sparingly, when there is a genuine quotation at hand, and it is necessary to be very rigorous about the words enclosed by the marks. If something is to be quoted, the *exact* words must be used. If part of it must be left out because of space limitations, it is good manners to insert three dots to indicate the omission, but it is unethical to do this if it means connecting two thoughts which the original author did not intend to have tied together. Above all, quotation marks should not be used for ideas that you'd like to disown, things in the air so to speak. Nor should they be put in place around clichés; if you want to use a cliché you must take full responsibility for it yourself and not try to job it off on anon., or on society. The most objectionable misuse of quotation marks, but one which illustrates the dangers of misuse in ordinary prose, is seen in advertising, especially in advertisements for small restaurants, for example "just around the corner," or "a good place to eat." No single, identifiable, citable person ever really said, for the record, "just around the corner," much less "a good place to eat," least likely of all for restaurants of the type that use this type of prose.

The dash is a handy device, informal and essentially playful, telling you that you're about to take off on a different tack but still in some way connected with the present course—only you have to remember that the dash is there, and either put a second dash at the end of the notion to let the reader know that he's back on course, or else end the sentence, as here, with a period.

The greatest danger in punctuation is for poetry. Here it is necessary to be as economical and parsimonious with commas and periods as with the words themselves, and any marks that seem to carry their own subtle meanings, like dashes and little rows of periods, even semicolons and question marks, should be left out altogether rather than inserted to clog up the thing with ambiguity. A single exclamation point in a poem, no matter what else the poem has to say, is enough to destroy the work.

The things I like best in T. S. Eliot's poetry, especially in the *Four Quartets*, are the semicolons. You cannot hear them, but they are there, laying out the connections between the images and the ideas. Sometimes you get a glimpse of a semicolon coming, a few lines farther on, and it is like climbing a steep path through woods and seeing a wooden bench just at a bend in the road ahead, a place where you can expect to sit for a moment, catching your breath.

Commas can't do this sort of thing; they can only tell you how the differ-   10
ent parts of a complicated thought are to be fitted together, but you can't sit, not even take a breath, just because of a comma,

ELLEN LUPTON AND J. ABBOTT MILLER

Period Styles

A Punctuated History

GREEK AND LATIN MANUSCRIPTS WERE USUALLY WRITTEN WITH NO SPACE BETWEEN WORDS UNTIL AROUND THE NINTH CENTURY AD ALTHOUGH· ROMAN·INSCRIPTIONS·LIKE·THE·FAMOUS·TRAJAN·COLUMN·SOMETIMES· SEPARATED·WORDS·WITH·A·CENTERED·DOT·   EVEN AFTER SPACING BECAME COMMON IT REMAINED HAPHAZARD   FOREXAMPLE OFTEN A PREPOSITION WAS LINKEDTO ANOTHER WORD   EARLY GREEK WRITING RAN IN LINES ALTERNATING FROM LEFT TO RIGHT AND RIGHT TO LEFT   THIS CONVENTION WAS CALLED BOUSTREPHEDON MEANING AS THE OX PLOWS   IT WAS CONVENIENT FOR LARGE CARVED MONUMENTS   BUT BOUSTREPHEDON HINDERED THE READING AND WRITING OF SMALLER TEXTS AND SO THE LEFT TO RIGHT DIRECTION BECAME DOMINANT   A CENTERED DOT DIVID· ED WORDS WHICH SPLIT AT THE END OF A LINE IN EARLY GREEK AND LATIN MANUSCRIPTS   IN THE ELEVENTH CENTURY A MARK SIMILAR TO THE MOD· ERN HYPHEN WAS INTRODUCED   MEDIEVAL SCRIBES OFTEN FILLED⁑/⁑°(;](;] SHORT LINES WITH MARKS AND ORNAMENTS   THE PERFECTLY JUSTIFIED LINE BECAME THE STANDARD AFTER THE INVENTION OF PRINTING THE EARLIEST GREEK LITERARY TEXTS WERE DIVIDED INTO UNITS WITH A HORIZONTAL LINE CALLED A PARAGRAPHOS   PARAGRAPHING REMAINS OUR CENTRAL METHOD OF ORGANIZING PROSE AND YET ALTHOUGH PARAGRAPHS ARE ANCIENT THEY ARE NOT GRAMMATICALLY ESSENTIAL THE CORRECTNESS OF A PARAGRAPH IS A MATTER OF STYLE HAVING NO STRICT RULES

LATER GREEK DOCUMENTS SOMETIMES MARKED PARAGRAPHS BY PLACING THE FIRST LETTER OF THE NEW LINE IN THE MARGIN   THIS LETTER COULD BE ENLARGED COLORED OR ORNATE

TODAY THE OUTDENT IS OFTEN USED FOR LISTS WHOSE ITEMS ARE IDENTIFIED ALPHABETICALLY AS IN DICTIONARIES OR BIBLIOGRAPHIES ¶ A MARK CALLED CAPITULUM WAS INTRODUCED IN EARLY LATIN MANUSCRIPTS ❦ IT FUNCTIONED VARIOUSLY AS A POINTER OR SEPARATOR ❦ IT USUALLY OCCURRED INSIDE A RUNNING BLOCK OF TEXT WHICH DID NOT BREAK ONTO A NEW LINE ❦ THIS TECHNIQUE SAVED SPACE ❦ IT ALSO PRESERVED THE VISUAL DENSITY OF THE PAGE WHICH EMULATED THE CONTINUOUS UNBROKEN FLOW OF SPEECH

BY THE SEVENTEENTH CENTURY THE INDENT WAS THE STANDARD PARAGRAPH BREAK IN WESTERN PROSE   THE RISE OF PRINTING ENCOURAGED THE USE OF SPACE TO ORGANIZE TEXTS   A GAP IN A PRINTED PAGE FEELS MORE DELIBERATE THAN A GAP IN A MANUSCRIPT BECAUSE IT IS MADE BY A SLUG OF LEAD RATHER THAN A FLUX IN HANDWRITING

EVEN AFTER THE ASCENDENCE OF THE INDENT THE CAPITULUM REMAINED IN USE FOR IDENTIFYING SECTIONS AND CHAPTERS ALONG WITH OTHER MARKS LIKE THE SECTION § THE DAGGER † THE DOUBLE DAGGER ‡ THE ASTERISK ✳ AND NUMEROUS LESS CONVENTIONAL ORNAMENTS § SUCH MARKS HAVE BEEN USED SINCE THE MIDDLE AGES FOR CITING PASSAGES AND KEYING MARGINAL REFERENCES † THE INVENTION OF PRINTING MADE MORE ELABORATE AND PRECISE REFERENCING POSSIBLE BECAUSE THE PAGES OF A TEXT WERE CONSISTENT FROM ONE COPY TO THE NEXT ‡

ALL PUNCTUATION WAS USED IDIOSYNCRATICALLY UNTIL AFTER THE INVENTION OF PRINTING WHICH REVOLUTIONIZED WRITING BY DISSEMI-

5

NATING GRAMMATICAL AND TYPOGRAPHICAL STANDARDS BEFORE PRINTING
PUNCTUATION VARIED WILDLY FROM REGION TO REGION AND SCRIBE TO
SCRIBE THE LIBRARIAN AT ALEXANDRIA WHO WAS NAMED ARISTOPHANES
DESIGNED A GREEK PUNCTUATION SYSTEM CIRCA 260 BC   HIS SYSTEM
MARKED THE SHORTEST SEGMENTS OF DISCOURSE WITH A CENTERED DOT ·
CALLED A COMMA · AND MARKED THE LONGER SECTIONS WITH A LOW DOT
CALLED A COLON . A HIGH DOT SET OFF THE LONGEST UNIT · HE CALLED IT
PERIODOS · THE THREE DOTS WERE EASILY DISTINGUISHED FROM ONE
ANOTHER BECAUSE ALL THE LETTERS WERE THE SAME HEIGHT · PROVIDING A
CONSISTENT FRAME OF REFERENCE · LIKE A MUSICAL STAFF ·

ALTHOUGH THE TERMS COMMA · COLON · AND PERIOD PERSIST · THE
SHAPE OF THE MARKS AND THEIR FUNCTION TODAY ARE DIFFERENT ·
DURING THE SEVENTH AND EIGHTH CENTURIES NEW MARKS APPEARED IN
SOME MANUSCRIPTS INCLUDING THE SEMICOLON ; THE INVERTED SEMI-
COLON ; AND A QUESTION MARK THAT RAN HORIZONTALLY ◡ A THIN
DIAGONAL SLASH / CALLED A VIRGULE / WAS SOMETIMES USED LIKE A COMMA
IN MEDIEVAL MANUSCRIPTS AND EARLY PRINTED BOOKS . SUCH MARKS ARE
THOUGHT TO HAVE BEEN CUES FOR READING ALOUD ; THEY INDICATED A
RISING , FALLING , OR LEVEL TONE OF VOICE . THE USE OF PUNCTUATION BY
SCRIBES AND THEIR INTERPRETATION BY READERS WAS BY NO MEANS
CONSISTENT , HOWEVER , AND MARKS MIGHT BE ADDED TO A MANUSCRIPT
BY ANOTHER SCRIBE WELL AFTER IT WAS WRITTEN .

EARLY PUNCTUATION WAS LINKED TO ORAL DELIVERY. FOR EXAMPLE
THE TERMS COMMA, COLON, AND PERIODOS, AS THEY WERE USED BY ARISTO-
PHANES, COME FROM THE THEORY OF RHETORIC, WHERE THEY REFER TO
RHYTHMICAL UNITS OF SPEECH. AS A SOURCE OF RHETORICAL RATHER THAN

GRAMMATICAL CUES, PUNCTUATION SERVED TO REGULATE PACE AND GIVE EMPHASIS TO PARTICULAR PHRASES, RATHER THAN TO MARK THE LOGICAL STRUCTURE OF SENTENCES. MANY OF THE PAUSES IN RHETORICAL DELIVERY, HOWEVER, NATURALLY CORRESPOND WITH GRAMMATICAL STRUCTURE: FOR EXAMPLE, WHEN A PAUSE FALLS BETWEEN TWO CLAUSES OR SENTENCES.

THE SYSTEM OF ARISTOPHANES WAS RARELY USED BY THE GREEKS, BUT IT WAS REVIVED BY THE LATIN GRAMMARIAN DONATUS IN THE FOURTH CENTURY A.D. ACCORDING TO DONATUS PUNCTUATION SHOULD FALL WHEREVER THE SPEAKER WOULD NEED A MOMENT'S REST; IT PROVIDED BREATHING CUES FOR READING ALOUD. SOME LATER WRITERS MODIFIED THE THEORIES OF DONATUS, RETURNING TO A RHETORICAL APPROACH TO PUNCTUATION, IN WHICH THE MARKS SERVED TO CONTROL RHYTHM AND EMPHASIS. AFTER THE INVENTION OF PRINTING, GRAMMARIANS BEGAN TO BASE PUNCTUATION ON STRUCTURE RATHER THAN ON SPOKEN SOUND: MARKS SUCH AS THE COMMA, COLON, AND PERIOD SIGNALLED SOME OF THE GRAMMATICAL PARTS OF A SENTENCE. THUS PUNCTUATION CAME TO BE DEFINED ARCHITECTURALLY RATHER THAN ORALLY. THE COMMA BECAME A MARK OF SEPARATION, AND THE SEMICOLON WORKED AS A JOINT BETWEEN INDEPENDENT CLAUSES; THE COLON INDICATED GRAMMATICAL DISCONTINUITY: WRITING WAS SLOWLY DISTANCED FROM SPEECH.

RHETORIC, STRUCTURE, AND PACE ARE ALL AT WORK IN MODERN ENGLISH PUNCTUATION, WHOSE RULES WERE ESTABLISHED BY THE END OF THE EIGHTEENTH CENTURY. ALTHOUGH STRUCTURE IS THE STRONGEST RATIONALE TODAY, PUNCTUATION REMAINS A LARGELY INTUITIVE ART. A WRITER CAN OFTEN CHOOSE AMONG SEVERAL CORRECT WAYS TO PUNCTUATE A PASSAGE, EACH WITH A SLIGHTLY DIFFERENT RHYTHM AND MEANING.

10

THERE WAS NO CONSISTENT MARK FOR QUOTATIONS BEFORE THE SEV-
ENTEENTH CENTURY. DIRECT SPEECH WAS USUALLY ANNOUNCED ONLY BY
PHRASES LIKE HE SAID. ,,SOMETIMES A DOUBLE COMMA WAS USED IN MAN-
USCRIPTS TO POINT OUT IMPORTANT SENTENCES AND WAS LATER USED TO
ENCLOSE "QUOTATIONS." ENGLISH PRINTERS BEFORE THE NINETEENTH
" CENTURY OFTEN EDGED ONE MARGIN OF A QUOTE WITH DOUBLE COMMAS.
" THIS CONVENTION PRESENTED TEXT AS A SPATIAL PLANE RATHER THAN A
" TEMPORAL LINE, FRAMING THE QUOTED PASSAGE LIKE A PICTURE.
" PRINTING, BY PRODUCING IDENTICAL COPIES OF A TEXT, ENCOURAGED
" THE STANDARDIZATION OF QUOTATION MARKS. PRINTED BOOKS COM-
" MONLY INCORPORATED MATERIAL FROM OTHER SOURCES.

BOTH THE GREEK AND ROMAN ALPHABETS WERE ORIGINALLY MAJUS-
CULE: ALL LETTERS WERE THE SAME HEIGHT. greek and roman minuscule
letters developed out of rapidly written scripts called cursive, which were
used for business correspondence. minuscule characters have limbs
extending above and below a uniform body. alcuin, advisor to charle-
magne, introduced the "carolingian" minuscule, which spread rapidly
through europe between the eighth and twelfth centuries. during the dissemination of the carolingian script, condensed, black minuscule styles of
handwriting, now called "gothic," were also developing; they eventually
replaced the classical carolingian.

A carolingian manuscript sometimes marked the beginning of a
sentence with an enlarged letter. This character was often a majuscule,
presaging the modern use of minuscule and majuscule as double features
of the same alphabet. Both scripts were still considered separate manners
of writing, however.

"As he Sets on, he [the printer] considers
how to Point his Work,
viz. when to Set, where; where. where to make ( ) where [ ]
and when to make a Break....
When he meets with proper Names of Persons or Places
he Sets them in Italick...
and Sets the first Letter with a Capital,
or as the Person or Place he finds
the purpose of the Author to dignifie, all Capitals;
but then, if he conveniently can,
he will Set a Space between every Letter...
to make it shew more Graceful and Stately."

JOSEPH MOXON 1683

In the fifteenth century, the Carolingian script was revived by the Italian humanists. The new script, called "lettera antica," was paired with classical roman capitals. It became the basis of the roman typefaces, which were established as a European norm by the mid-sixteenth century. The terms "uppercase" and "lowercase" refer to the drawers in a printing shop that hold the two fonts. Until recently, Punctuation was an Intuitive Art, ruled by convenience and Intuition. A Printer could Liberally Capitalize the Initial of Any word She deemed worthy of Distinction, as well as Proper Names. The printer was Free to set some Words entirely in C A P I T A L S and to add further emphasis with extra S P A C E S.

The roman typefaces were based on a formal script used for books. *The cursive, rapidly written version of the Carolingian minuscule was employed for business and also for books sold in the less expensive writing shops. Called "antica corsiva" or "cancelleresca," this style of handwriting was the model for the italic typefaces cut for Aldus Manutius in Venice in 1500. Aldus Manutius was a scholar, printer, and businessman. Italic script conserved space, and Aldus developed it for his internationally distributed series of small, inexpensive books. The Aldine italic was paired with Roman capitals. The Italian typo-*

15

grapher Tagliente advocated Italic Capitals in the early sixteenth century.
Aldus set entire books in italic; it was an autonomous type style, unrelated to
roman. In France, however, the roman style was becoming the neutral,
generic norm, with *italic* played against it for *contrast.* The pairs UPPER-
CASE/lowercase and roman/*italic* each add an inaudible, non-phonetic
dimension to the alphabet. Before *italic* became the official auxiliary of
roman, scribes and printers had other techniques for marking emphasis,
including enlarged, **heavy,** colored, or **gothic** letters. Underlining
appeared in some medieval manuscripts, and today it is the conventional
substitute for italics in handwritten and typewritten texts. S p a c e is
sometimes inserted between letters to declare e m p h a s i s in German
and Eastern European book t y p o g r a p h y . **Boldface** fonts were not
common until the nineteenth century, when display advertising created a
demand for **big, black** types. Most book faces designed since the early
twentieth century belong to families of four: roman, *italic,* **bold roman,**
and ***bold italic.*** These are used for systematically marking different kinds of
copy, such as headings, captions, body text, notes, and references.

Since the rise of digital production, printed texts have become
more visually elaborate—typographic variations are now routinely available to writers and designers. Some recent fonts contain only ornaments
and symbols; Carlos Segura's typeface Dingura (⚲⚲ ⚲⚲⚲⚲ ⚲⚲ ⚲⚲⚲⚲⚲⚲ ⚲⚲ ⚲)
consists of mysterious runes that recall the era of manuscript production.
During the e-mail incunabula, writers and designers have been using
punctuation marks for expressive ends. Punctuated portraits found in
electronic correspondence range from the simple "smiley" :-) to such
subtle constructions as $-) [yuppie] or :-I [indifferent].

about the texts

1. Compare and contrast Lupton and Miller's and Thomas's purposes in writing their essays. How does each essay make its point, paragraph by paragraph?

2. In what ways do these selections demonstrate that punctuation and other typographical conventions are associated with writing and literacy? What are the advantages of each of the following — a single, fixed direction for writing; spaces between words; punctuation; upper- and lower-case letters?

3. What makes each of these essays humorous in some way? Which do you think is more effective? Why?

4. What would be lost if the essay by Lupton and Miller were presented as an encyclopedia entry that followed current typographical conventions?

5. To what extent does Thomas follow or violate his own prescriptions in paragraph 5? (You'll have to analyze each sentence carefully to answer this question.)

on language use

6. Writing conventions are not limited to written language. Speakers, for example, often make quotation marks in the air with their fingers to put a word or comment "in quotes." Why do they do this? Can you think of other cases in which literate conventions influence spoken language?

7. Especially in the past decade, there has been a great deal of play with typography and spelling. Hip-hop culture has been the force behind much of this. For example, the word "phat" has a completely new meaning, one signalled by its spelling. (Is the word used more in speech or in print? Why might that be the case?) Find a half-dozen examples that challenge spelling and/or typographical conventions, and try to explain why writers might engage in these practices.

for writing

8. Some writers, such as the American poet E. E. Cummings, become well known for violating language conventions. Choose two of Cummings's poems and analyze how he violates our expectations about punctuation and capitalization. How does his calculated but playful use of punctuation and capitalization contribute to the power of his poetry? You may analyze the work of some other poet or writer if you prefer. Write an essay about what you discover. Be sure to include copies of the poems you analyze with your completed essay.

9. In both of these selections, the form of the message is an important component of the message itself. Look for at least two other texts that employ this technique, and write an essay in which you describe how the message's form contributes to fulfilling its function. (Advertisements are often fertile ground for using this rhetorical trick.)

Some Americans are obsessed with "correct usage," which they usually label "grammar." These Grammar Police feel a responsibility to correct others' speech—the use of "me" instead of "I," "lie" instead of "lay," "infer" instead of "imply." In this and the next several selections, we'll be examining the beliefs and assumptions these Americans (and other speakers of English) make about matters of correctness in both writing and speaking.

We begin our examination of this topic by going straight to the comics. A number of social scientists argue that if you really want to know what the hot-button issues are in a particular society, look at the things its members laugh about. In this case, we offer a 2001 comic strip from **Jump Start**, by Robb Armstrong, about a young couple—Marcy, a nurse, and Joe, a police officer—their parents, and their kids. In this cartoon, you'll see that Joe's mom is at least a captain in the Grammar Police. Then come three comic strips from Pat Brady's **Rose Is Rose**, also from 2001, which feature Rose, her husband Jimbo, and their son Pasquale. In all three strips, Rose is putting her grammar whistle to use.

about the texts

1. What specific questions of usage are Joe's mom and Rose concerned about? How do their concerns differ?

2. How serious are the "problems" that annoy Joe's mom and Rose? Do they impede communication? Do they matter equally in speaking and in writing? Why or why not?

on language use

3. It is likely no accident that both Joe's mom and Rose are female and that the alleged criminals are all male. Why do you think Americans associate a concern with correctness in language with girls and women?

for writing

4. Are you an officer in the Grammar Police, a criminal, or both? Write an essay in which you describe and analyze occasions on which you have corrected the speech of others or have had your own speech corrected. What purpose did the correction serve? How did it make you feel to correct or be corrected? Did it have any consequences on your subsequent behavior? Why do you think some people routinely correct others' language mistakes? Why might they believe they should?

MARY NEWTON BRUDER

<grammarlady.com>

Mary Newton Bruder, a linguist, teacher of English as a second language, and consultant, was also the Grammar Lady. In 1988 she established the Grammar Hotline, and in 1989 she began writing the "Grammar Hotline Column" for the Pittsburgh Post-Gazette. As her Web site <grammarlady.com> noted, "The Grammar Hotline/Web site is a one-woman, free service, and one of its purposes is to 'remind everyone of the ways to have fun with language.'" As you read this column from April 1990, think about questions you might ask the Grammar Lady and why they matter—to you, to her, or to others.

Dear Grammar Lady: How can we know when to use "some time/sometime/sometimes"?

A: The one-word versions are adverbs which have different meanings as follows: "sometime" means at an indefinite or unspecified time. Ex: Come and see me sometime. The plane arrived sometime in the morning. "Sometimes" means occasionally or now and then. Ex: Sometimes we hear the train in the distance. Do you sometimes wish you had chosen a different line of work? The phrase "some time" is a measure of time: It will take some time for the repairs to be made. The word "some" can be replaced by other expressions of quantity: a little/a lot of/more, etc.

Dear Grammar Lady: Is it OK to use "can" in the expression "Can I help you?" or is "May I help you?" the only correct thing to say?

A: Both are correct; it depends on what you mean. In formal styles, "may" asks permission; so the question is "Will you permit me to help you?" "Can" asks about ability and the question becomes "Am I able to help you?" The clerk in the department store may ask permission to be of service; the passerby, seeing a car with the hood lifted, may inquire about the ability to be of assistance.

Dear Grammar Lady: What is the difference between the adjectives "analytic" and "analytical"?

A: Some of these adjective pairs have taken on different meanings: "a historic moment" (a moment in history) and "historical research" (pertaining to history). Also, "an economic turn-around" (in the economy) and "an economical car" (low cost). However, "analytic" and "analytical" have coexisted for about 400 years with pretty much the same meaning. Except in fixed expressions, such as "analytic geometry," they seem interchangeable according to the sources I have consulted.

Dear Grammar Lady: Is it correct to put the pronoun "me" first in the following sentence in a letter: "Please contact me or John Doe in reference to this matter."

A: Yes. It is only with the conjunction "and" that "me/I" must be placed last. By putting "me" first you are telling the recipient of the letter the order in which to contact you and your colleague.

---

about the text

1. The Grammar Lady's column answers specific usage questions. If someone asked you these questions, would you have been able to answer them? What answers would you have given? What does the Grammar Lady mean in her response to the question about "can" versus "may" when she writes, "The clerk in the department store may ask permission to be of service; the passerby, seeing a car with the hood lifted, may inquire about the ability to be of assistance"? What, exactly, is the difference between "can" and "may" for the Grammar Lady, and why does it matter?

on language use

2. Where do you think the Grammar Lady found the information required to respond to these questions? Why do you think some people value such information? What, if anything, is lost when writers do not distinguish among "sometime," "sometimes," and "some time"? Where do you go for answers to your own usage questions?

for writing

3. Consult several usage manuals about the difference between "between" and "among," "further" and "farther," "shall" and "will," or some other usage question. You can start with the Web site for the *American Heritage Book of English Usage* <bartleby.com/64> or Strunk's *Elements of Style* <bartleby.com/141>. Write an essay in which you compare and contrast the advice given about a single usage issue in three or four usage sites or manuals. Conclude your essay by offering advice based on what you have learned; in perhaps all cases, you'll have to choose among several options, explaining why you believe your choice is the best one.

Likely the most famous modern discussion of the English language, its use, and its misuse, this essay dates from 1946. It was written by George Orwell, the pen name of Eric Blair, who was also a writer of fiction, including Animal Farm *(1945) and* 1984 *(1949), both of which deal with the problems of totalitarian states. Even though the situation that prompted Orwell to write — political discourse at the end of World War II — may seem distant, his concern with clear thinking and clear writing, especially in political rhetoric, remains germane as does his hatred of authoritarianism in any form. As you study his criticisms of the political discourse of the times, think about how politicians, political parties, and spin doctors use language today. See whether you agree with what Orwell says about poor writing, the questions he believes all good writers ask themselves, and the rules he gives for improving one's writing style.*

GEORGE ORWELL

Politics and the English Language

MOST PEOPLE who bother with the matter at all would admit that the English language is in a bad way, but it is generally assumed that we cannot by conscious action do anything about it. Our civilization is decadent and our language — so the argument runs — must inevitably share in the general collapse. It follows that any struggle against the abuse of language is a sentimental archaism, like preferring candles to electric light or hansom cabs[1] to aeroplanes. Underneath this lies the half conscious belief that language is a natural growth and not an instrument which we shape for our own purposes.

Now, it is clear that the decline of a language must ultimately have political and economic causes: it is not due simply to the bad influence of this or that individual writer. But an effect can become a cause, reinforcing the original cause and producing the same effect in an intensified form, and so on indefinitely. A man may take to drink because he feels himself to be a failure, and then fail all the more completely because he drinks. It is rather the same thing that is happening to the English language. It becomes ugly and inaccurate because our thoughts are foolish, but the slovenliness of our language makes it easier for us to have foolish thoughts. The point is that the process is reversible. Modern English, especially written English, is full of bad habits which spread by imitation and which can be avoided if one is willing to take the necessary trouble. If one gets rid of these habits one can think more clearly, and to think clearly is a necessary first step towards political regeneration so that the fight against bad English is not

---

1. **hansom cabs** horse-drawn carriages made for two passengers ("hansom" is from the surname of a nineteenth-century architect who designed and patented the vehicle; "cab" is a shortened form of "cabriolet," an earlier term for a horse-drawn carriage).

frivolous and is not the exclusive concern of professional writers. I will come back to this presently, and I hope that by that time the meaning of what I have said here will have become clearer. Meanwhile, here are five specimens of the English language as it is now habitually written.

These five passages have not been picked out because they are especially bad — I could have quoted far worse if I had chosen — but because they illustrate various of the mental vices from which we now suffer. They are a little below the average, but are fairly representative samples. I number them so that I can refer back to them when necessary.

1. I am not, indeed, sure whether it is not true to say that the Milton who once seemed not unlike a seventeenth-century Shelley had not become out of an experience ever more bitter in each year, more alien [*sic*] to the founder of that Jesuit sect which nothing could induce him to tolerate.

Professor Harold Laski (Essay in *Freedom of Expression*)

2. Above all, we cannot play ducks and drakes with a native battery of idioms which prescribes such egregious collocations of vocables as the Basic *put up with* for *tolerate* or *put at a loss* for *bewilder*.

Professor Lancelot Hogben (*Interglossa*)

3. On the one side we have the free personality; by definition it is not neurotic, for it has neither conflict nor dream. Its desires, such as they are, are transparent, for they are just what institutional approval keeps in the forefront of consciousness; another institutional pattern would alter their number and intensity; there is little in them that is natural, irreducible, or culturally dangerous. But on *the other side*, the social bond itself is nothing but the mutual reflection of these self-secure integrities. Recall the definition of love. Is not this the very picture of a small academic? Where is there a place in this hall of mirrors for either personality or fraternity?

Essay on psychology in *Politics* (New York)

4. All the "best people" from the gentlemen's clubs, and all the frantic fascist captains, united in common hatred of Socialism and bestial horror of the rising tide of the mass revolutionary movement, have turned to acts of provocation, to foul incendiarism, to medieval legends of poisoned wells, to legalize their own destruction of proletarian organizations, and rouse the agitated petty-bourgeoisie to chauvinistic fervour on behalf of the fight against the revolutionary way out of the crisis.   Communist pamphlet

5. If a new spirit is to be infused into this old country, there is one thorny and contentious reform which must be tackled, and that is the humanization and galvinization of the B.B.C. Timidity here will be-

speak cancer and atrophy of the soul. The heart of Britain may be sound and of strong beat, for instance, but the British lion's roar at present is like that of Bottom in Shakespeare's *Midsummer Night's Dream*—as gentle as any sucking dove. A virile new Britain cannot continue indefinitely to be traduced in the eyes or rather ears, of the world by the effete languors of Langham Place,[2] brazenly masquerading as "standard English." When the Voice of Britain is heard at nine o'clock, better far and infinitely less ludicrous to hear aitches honestly dropped[3] than the present priggish, inflated, inhibited, schoolma'amish arch braying of blameless bashful mewing maidens!   Letter in *Tribune*

Each of these passages has faults of its own, but, quite apart from avoidable ugliness, two qualities are common to all of them. The first is staleness of imagery: the other is lack of precision. The writer either has a meaning and cannot express it, or he inadvertently says something else, or he is almost indifferent as to whether his words mean anything or not. This mixture of vagueness and sheer incompetence is the most marked characteristic of modern English prose, and especially of any kind of political writing. As soon as certain topics are raised, the concrete melts into the abstract and no one seems able to think of turns of speech that are not hackneyed: prose consists less and less of *words* chosen for the sake of their meaning, and more and more of *phrases* tacked together like the sections of a prefabricated henhouse. I list below, with notes and examples, various of the tricks by means of which the work of prose-construction is habitually dodged:

DYING METAPHORS

A newly invented metaphor assists thought by evoking a visual image, while   5 on the other hand a metaphor which is technically "dead" (e.g. *iron resolution*) has in effect reverted to being an ordinary word and can generally be

---

2. **B.B.C./Langham Place** the British Broadcasting Company, the national radio station of Britain, whose offices are located in Langham Place. Respected around the world for the quality and objectivity of its news reporting, at the time Orwell was writing, all its announcers used Received Pronunciation, the most prestigious accent of British English.

3. **aitches honestly dropped** a failure to pronounce the initial *h* in a word (e.g., saying "'otel" instead of "hotel" or "'istory" instead of "history"), a highly stigmatized feature of lower-class and some regional dialects of British English.

used without loss of vividness. But in between these two classes there is a huge dump of worn-out metaphors which have lost all evocative power and are merely used because they save people the trouble of inventing phrases for themselves. Examples are *Ring the changes on, take up the cudgels for, toe the line, ride roughshod over, stand shoulder to shoulder with, play into the hands of, no axe to grind, grist to the mill, fishing in troubled waters, on the order of the day, Achilles' heel, swan song, hotbed.* Many of these are used without knowledge of their meaning (what is a "rift," for instance?), and incompatible metaphors are frequently mixed, a sure sign that the writer is not interested in what he is saying. Some metaphors now current have been twisted out of their original meaning without those who use them even being aware of the fact. For example, *toe the line* is sometimes written *tow the line.* Another example is *the hammer and the anvil*, now always used with the implication that the anvil gets the worst of it. In real life it is always the anvil that breaks the hammer, never the other way about: a writer who stopped to think what he was saying would be aware of this, and would avoid perverting the original phrase.

OPERATORS OR VERBAL FALSE LIMBS

These save the trouble of picking out appropriate verbs and nouns, and at the same time pad each sentence with extra syllables which give it an appearance of symmetry. Characteristic phrases are: *render inoperative, militate against, make contact with, be subjected to, give rise to, give grounds for, have the effect of, play a leading part (role) in, make itself felt, take effect, exhibit a tendency to, serve the purpose of,* etc., etc. The keynote is the elimination of simple verbs. Instead of being a single word, such as *break, stop, spoil, mend, kill*, a verb becomes a *phrase*, made up of a noun or adjective tacked on to some general-purposes verb such as *prove, serve, form, play, render.* In addition, the passive voice is wherever possible used in preference to the active, and noun constructions are used instead of gerunds (*by examination of* instead of *by examining*). The range of verbs is further cut down by means of the *-ize* and *de-* formation, and the banal statements are given an appearance of profundity by means of the *not un-* formation. Simple conjunctions and prepositions are replaced by such phrases as *with respect to, having regard to, the fact that, by dint of, in view of, in the interests of, on the hypothesis that;* and the ends of sentences are saved from anticlimax by such resounding commonplaces as *greatly to be desired, cannot be left out* of account, a development to be expected in the near future, deserving of serious consideration, brought to a satisfactory conclusion, and so on and so forth.

PRETENTIOUS DICTION

Words like *phenomenon, element, individual* (as noun), *objective, categorical, effective, virtual, basic, primary, promote, constitute, exhibit, exploit, utilize, eliminate, liquidate* are used to dress up simple statements and given an air of scientific impartiality to biased judgments. Adjectives like *epoch-making, epic, historic, unforgettable, triumphant, age-old, inevitable, inexorable, veritable* are used to dignify the sordid processes of international politics, while writing that aims at glorifying war usually takes on an archaic colour, its characteristic words being: *realm, throne, chariot, mailed fist, trident, sword shield, buckler, banner, jackboot, clarion.* Foreign words and expressions such as *cul de sac, ancien régime, deus ex machina, mutatis mutandis, status quo, gleichschaltung, weltanschauung* are used to give an air of culture and elegance. Except for the useful abbreviations *i.e., e.g.,* and *etc.,* there is no real need for any of the hundreds of foreign phrases now current in English. Bad writers, and especially scientific, political and sociological writers, are nearly always haunted by the notion that Latin or Greek words are grander than Saxon ones, and unnecessary words like *expedite, ameliorate, predict, extraneous, deracinated, clandestine, subaqueous* and hundreds of others constantly gain ground from their Anglo-Saxon opposite numbers.[4] The jargon peculiar to Marxist writing (*hyena, hangman, cannibal, petty bourgeois, these gentry, lacquey, flunkey, mad dog, White Guard,* etc.) consists largely of words and phrases translated from Russian, German or French; but the normal way of coining a new word is to use a Latin or Greek root with the appropriate affix and, where necessary, the -ize formation. It is often easier to make up words of this kind (*deregionalize, impermissible, extramarital, nonfragmentatory* and so forth) than to think up the English words that will cover one's meaning. The result, in general, is an increase in slovenliness and vagueness.

---

4. An interesting illustration of this is the way in which the English flower names which were in use till very recently are being ousted by Greek ones, *snapdragon* becoming *antirrhinum, forget-me-not* becoming *myosotis,* etc. It is hard to see any practical reason for this change of fashion: it is probably due to an instinctive turning-away from the more homely word and a vague feeling that the Greek word is scientific [Orwell's note].

MEANINGLESS WORDS

In certain kinds of writing, particularly in art criticism and literary criticism, it is normal to come across long passages which are almost completely lacking in meaning.[5] Words like *romantic, plastic, values, human, dead, sentimental, natural, vitality,* as used in art criticism, are strictly meaningless in the sense that they not only do not point to any discoverable object, but are hardly ever expected to do so by the reader. When one critic writes, "The outstanding feature of Mr. X's work is its living quality," while another writes, "The immediately striking thing about Mr. X's work is its peculiar deadness,"the reader accepts this as a simple difference of opinion. If words like *black* and *white* were involved, instead of the jargon words *dead* and *living,* he would see at once that language was being used in an improper way. Many political words are similarly abused. The word *Fascism* has now no meaning except in so far as it signifies "something not desirable." The words *democracy, socialism, freedom, patriotic, realistic, justice* have each of them several different meanings which cannot be reconciled with one another. In the case of a word like *democracy,* not only is there no agreed definition, but the attempt to make one is resisted from all sides. It is almost universally felt that when we call a country democratic we are praising it: consequently the defenders of every kind of régime claim that it is a democracy, and fear that they might have to stop using the word if it were tied down to any one meaning. Words of this kind are often used in a consciously dishonest way. That is, the person who uses them has his own private definition, but allows his hearer to think he means something quite different. Statements like *Marshal Pétain*[6] *was a true patriot, The Soviet Press is the freest in the world, The Catholic Church is opposed to persecution* are almost always made with intent to deceive. Other words used in variable meanings, in most cases more or less dishonestly, are: *class, totalitarian, science, progressive, reactionary, bourgeois, equality.*

---

5. Example: "Comfort's catholicity of perception and image, strangely Whitmanesque in range, almost the exact opposite in aesthetic compulsion, continues to evoke that trembling atmospheric accumulative hinting at a cruel, an inexorably serene timelessness . . . Wrey Gardiner scores by aiming at simple bull's-eyes with precision. Only they are not so simple, and through this contented sadness runs more than the surface bittersweet of resignation" (*Poetry Quarterly*) [Orwell's note].

6. **Marshal Pétain** Henri Philippe Pétain (1856–1951) was the leader of France during the Nazi occupation in World War II. After the war, he was found guilty of treason for aiding the Germans; his death sentence was commuted to life imprisonment.

Now that I have made this catalogue of swindles and perversions, let me give another example of the kind of writing that they lead to. This time it must of its nature be an imaginary one. I am going to translate a passage of good English into modern English of the worst sort. Here is a well-known verse from *Ecclesiastes*:

I returned and saw under the sun, that the race is not to the swift, nor the battle to the strong, neither yet bread to the wise, nor yet riches to men of understanding, nor yet favour to men of skill; but time and chance happeneth to them all.

Here it is in modern English:

10

Objective consideration of contemporary phenomena compels the conclusion that success or failure in competitive activities exhibits no tendency to be commensurate with innate capacity, but that a considerable element of the unpredictable must invariably be taken into account.

This is a parody, but not a very gross one. Exhibit (3), above, for instance, contains several patches of the same kind of English. It will be seen that I have not made a full translation. The beginning and ending of the sentence follow the original meaning fairly closely, but in the middle the concrete illustrations—race, battle, bread—dissolve into the vague phrase "success or failure in competitive activities." This had to be so, because no modern writer of the kind I am discussing—no one capable of using phrases like "objective consideration of contemporary phenomena"—would ever tabulate his thoughts in that precise and detailed way. The whole tendency of modern prose is away from concreteness. Now analyse these two sentences a little more closely. The first contains forty-nine words but only sixty syllables, and all its words are those of everyday life. The second contains thirty-eight words of ninety syllables: eighteen of its words are from Latin roots, and one from Greek. The first sentence contains six vivid images, and only one phrase ("time and chance") that could be called vague. The second contains not a single fresh, arresting phrase, and in spite of its ninety syllables it gives only a shortened version of the meaning contained in the first. Yet without a doubt it is the second kind of sentence that is gaining ground in modern English. I do not want to exaggerate. This kind of writing is not yet universal, and outcrops of simplicity will occur here and there in the worst-written page. Still, if you or I were told to write a few lines on the uncertainty of human fortunes, we should probably come much nearer to my imaginary sentence than to the one from *Ecclesiastes*.

As I have tried to show, modern writing at its worst does not consist in picking out words for the sake of their meaning and inventing images in order to make the meaning clearer. It consists in gumming together long strips of words which have already been set in order by someone else, and making the results presentable by sheer humbug. The attraction of this way of writing is that it is easy. It is easier—even quicker, once you have the habit—to say *In my opinion it is a not unjustifiable assumption that* than to say *I think.* If you use ready-made phrases, you not only don't have to hunt about for words; you also don't have to bother with the rhythms of your sentences, since these phrases are generally so arranged as to be more or less euphonious. When you are composing in a hurry—when you are dictating to a stenographer, for instance, or making a public speech—it is natural to fall into a pretentious, Latinized style. Tags like *a consideration which we should do well to bear in mind* or *a conclusion to which all of us would readily assent* will save many a sentence from coming down with a bump. By using stale metaphors, similes, and idioms, you save much mental effort, at the cost of leaving your meaning vague, not only for your reader but for yourself. This is the significance of mixed metaphors. The sole aim of a metaphor is to call up a visual image. When these images clash—as in *The Fascist octopus has sung its swan song, the jack-boot is thrown into the melting pot*—it can be taken as certain that the writer is not seeing a mental image of the objects he is naming; in other words he is not really thinking. Look again at the examples I gave at the beginning of this essay. Professor Laski (1) uses five negatives in fifty-three words. One of these is superfluous, making nonsense of the whole passage, and in addition there is the slip *alien* for *akin*, making further nonsense, and several avoidable pieces of clumsiness which increase the general vagueness. Professor Hogben (2) plays ducks and drakes[7] with a battery which is able to write prescriptions, and, while disapproving of the everyday phrase *put up with*, is unwilling to look *egregious* up in the dictionary and see what it means. (3), if one takes an uncharitable attitude towards it, is simply meaningless: probably one could work out its intended meaning by reading the whole of the article in which it occurs. In (4), the writer knows more or less what he wants to say, but an accumulation of stale phrases chokes him like tea leaves blocking a sink. In (5), words and meaning have almost parted company. People who write in this manner usually have a general emotional meaning—they dislike one thing and want to express solidarity with another—but they are not interested in the detail of

---

7. **plays ducks and drakes** an idiom meaning "to handle or use recklessly" or "to squander"; the expression dates back to the seventeenth century.

what they are saying. A scrupulous writer, in every sentence that he writes, will ask himself at least four questions, thus: What am I trying to say? What words will express it? What image or idiom will make it clearer? Is this image fresh enough to have an effect? And he will probably ask himself two more: Could I put it more shortly? Have I said anything that is avoidably ugly? But you are not obliged to go to all this trouble. You can shirk it by simply throwing your mind open and letting the ready-made phrases come crowding in. They will construct your sentences for you—even think your thoughts for you, to a certain extent—and at need they will perform the important service of partially concealing your meaning even from yourself. It is at this point that the special connection between politics and the debasement of language becomes clear.

In our time it is broadly true that political writing is bad writing. Where it is not true, it will generally be found that the writer is some kind of rebel, expressing his private opinions and not a "party line." Orthodoxy, of whatever colour, seems to demand a lifeless, imitative style. The political dialects to be found in pamphlets, leading articles, manifestos, White Papers,[8] and the speeches of under-secretaries do, of course, vary from party to party, but they are all alike in that one almost never finds in them a fresh, vivid, home-made turn of speech. When one watches some tired hack on the platform mechanically repeating the familiar phrases—*bestial atrocities, iron heel, blood-stained tyranny, free peoples of the world, stand shoulder to shoulder*—one often has a curious feeling that one is not watching a live human being but some kind of dummy: a feeling which suddenly becomes stronger at moments when the light catches the speaker's spectacles and turns them into blank discs which seem to have no eyes behind them. And this is not altogether fanciful. A speaker who uses that kind of phraseology has gone some distance towards turning himself into a machine. The appropriate noises are coming out of his larynx, but his brain is not involved as it would be if he were choosing his words for himself. If the speech he is making is one that he is accustomed to make over and over again, he may be almost unconscious of what he is saying, as one is when one utters the responses in church. And this reduced state of consciousness, if not indispensable, is at any rate favourable to political conformity.

In our time, political speech and writing are largely the defence of the indefensible. Things like the continuance of British rule in India, the Russian

---

8. **White Papers** originally, an official government publication presented to (English) Parliament, so called to distinguish it from revised versions, which were blue. The term now refers to any kind of policy statement issued by government or business.

purges and deportations, the dropping of the atom bombs on Japan, can indeed be defended, but only by arguments which are too brutal for most people to face, and which do not square with the professed aims of political parties. Thus political language has to consist largely of euphemism, question-begging, and sheer cloudy vagueness. Defenceless villages are bombarded from the air, the inhabitants driven out into the countryside, the cattle machine-gunned, the huts set on fire with incendiary bullets: this is called *pacification*. Millions of peasants are robbed of their farms and sent trudging along the roads with no more than they can carry: this is called *transfer of population* or *rectification of frontiers*. People are imprisoned for years without trial, or shot in the back of the neck or sent to die of scurvy in Arctic lumber camps: this is called *elimination of unreliable elements*. Such phraseology is needed if one wants to name things without calling up mental pictures of them. Consider for instance some comfortable English professor defending Russian totalitarianism. He cannot say outright, "I believe in killing off your opponents when you can get good results by doing so," Probably, therefore, he will say something like this:

"While freely conceding that the Soviet régime exhibits certain features 15 which the humanitarian may be inclined to deplore, we must, I think, agree that a certain curtailment of the right to political opposition is an unavoidable concomitant of transitional periods, and that the rigours which the Russian people have been called upon to undergo have been amply justified in the sphere of concrete achievement."

The inflated style is itself a kind of euphemism. A mass of Latin words falls upon the facts like soft snow, blurring the outlines and covering up all the details. The great enemy of clear language is insincerity. When there is a gap between one's real and one's declared aims, one turns as it were instinctively to long words and exhausted idioms, like a cuttlefish squirting out ink. In our age there is no such thing as "keeping out of politics." All issues are political issues, and politics itself is a mass of lies, evasions, folly, hatred and schizophrenia. When the general atmosphere is bad, language must suffer. I should expect to find—this is a guess which I have not sufficient knowledge to verify—that the German, Russian, and Italian languages have all deteriorated in the last ten or fifteen years, as a result of dictatorship.

But if thought corrupts language, language can also corrupt thought. A bad usage can spread by tradition and imitation, even among people who should and do know better. The debased language that I have been discussing is in some ways very convenient. Phrases like *a not unjustifiable assumption, leaves much to be desired, would serve no good purpose, a consideration which we should do well to bear in mind* are a continuous temptation, a packet of aspirins always at one's elbow. Look back through this essay, and for certain you will find that I have again and again committed the very faults I am protesting against. By this morning's post I have received a pamphlet dealing with conditions in Germany. The author tells me that he "felt impelled" to write it. I open it at random, and here is almost the first sentence that I see: "(The Allies) have an opportunity not only of achieving a radical transformation of Germany's social and political structure in such a way as to avoid a nationalistic reaction in Germany itself, but at the same time of laying the foundations of a cooperative and unified Europe." You see, he "feels impelled" to write—feels, presumably, that he has something new to say—and yet his words, like cavalry horses answering the bugle, group themselves automatically into the familiar dreary pattern. This invasion of one's mind by ready-made phrases (*lay the foundations, achieve a radical transformation*) can only be prevented if one is constantly on guard against them, and every such phrase anaesthetizes a portion of one's brain.

I said earlier that the decadence of our language is probably curable. Those who deny this would argue, if they produced an argument at all, that language merely reflects existing social conditions, and that we cannot influence its development by any direct tinkering with words and constructions. So far as the general tone or spirit of a language goes, this may be true, but it is not true in detail. Silly words and expressions have often disappeared, not through any evolutionary process but owing to the conscious action of a minority. Two recent examples were *explore every avenue* and *leave no stone unturned*, which were killed by the jeers of a few journalists. There is a long list of flyblown metaphors which could similarly be got rid of if enough people would interest themselves in the job; and it should also be possible to laugh the *not un-* formation out of existence,[9] to reduce the amount of Latin and Greek in the average sentence, to drive out foreign phrases and strayed scientific words, and, in general, to make pretentiousness unfashionable. But all these are minor points. The defence of the English language implies more than this, and perhaps it is best to start by saying what it does not imply.

To begin with it has nothing to do with archaism, with the salvaging of obsolete words and turns of speech, or with the setting up of a "standard English" which must never be departed from. On the contrary, it is especially

---

9. One can cure oneself of the *not un-* formation by memorizing this sentence: *A not unblack dog was chasing a not unsmall rabbit across a not ungreen field* [Orwell's note].

concerned with the scrapping of every word or idiom which has outworn its usefulness. It has nothing to do with correct grammar and syntax, which are of no importance so long as one makes one's meaning clear, or with the avoidance of Americanisms, or with having what is called a "good prose style." On the other hand it is not concerned with fake simplicity and the attempt to make written English colloquial. Nor does it even imply in every case preferring the Saxon word to the Latin one, though it does imply using the fewest and shortest words that will cover one's meaning. What is above all needed is to let the meaning choose the word, and not the other way about. In prose, the worst thing one can do with words is to surrender to them. When you think of a concrete object, you think wordlessly, and then, if you want to describe the thing you have been visualizing you probably hunt about till you find the exact words that seem to fit. When you think of something abstract you are more inclined to use words from the start, and unless you make a conscious effort to prevent it, the existing dialect will come rushing in and do the job for you, at the expense of blurring or even changing your meaning. Probably it is better to put off using words as long as possible and get one's meaning as clear as one can through pictures or sensations. Afterwards one can choose—not simply accept—the phrases that will best cover the meaning, and then switch round and decide what impression one's words are likely to make on another person. This last effort of the mind cuts out all stale or mixed images, all prefabricated phrases, needless repetitions, and humbug and vagueness generally. But one can often be in doubt about the effect of a word or a phrase, and one needs rules that one can rely on when instinct fails. I think the following rules will cover most cases:

(i) Never use a metaphor, simile, or other figure of speech which you are used to seeing in print.

(ii) Never use a long word where a short one will do.

(iii) If it is possible to cut a word out, always cut it out.

(iv) Never use the passive where you can use the active.

(v) Never use a foreign phrase, a scientific word, or a jargon word if you can think of an everyday English equivalent.

(vi) Break any of these rules sooner than say anything outright barbarous.

These rules sound elementary, and so they are, but they demand a deep change of attitude in anyone who has grown used to writing in the style now fashionable. One could keep all of them and still write bad English, but one could not write the kind of stuff that I quoted in those five specimens at the beginning of this article.

I have not here been considering the literary use of language, but merely 20 language as an instrument for expressing and not for concealing or preventing thought. Stuart Chase[10] and others have come near to claiming that all abstract words are meaningless, and have used this as a pretext for advocating a kind of political quietism. Since you don't know what Fascism is, how can you struggle against Fascism? One need not swallow such absurdities as this, but one ought to recognize that the present political chaos is connected with the decay of language, and that one can probably bring about some improvement by starting at the verbal end. If you simplify your English, you are freed from the worst follies of orthodoxy. You cannot speak any of the necessary dialects, and when you make a stupid remark its stupidity will be obvious, even to yourself. Political language—and with variations this is true of all political parties, from Conservatives to Anarchists—is designed to make lies sound truthful and murder respectable, and to give an appearance of solidity to pure wind. One cannot change this all in a moment, but one can at least change one's own habits, and from time to time one can even, if one jeers loudly enough, send some worn-out and useless phrase—some *jack-boot, Achilles' heel, hotbed, melting pot, acid test, veritable inferno* or other lump of verbal refuse—into the dustbin where it belongs.

---

10. **Stuart Chase** (1888–1985) was a contemporary of Orwell and author of many books on economics, business, and communication. His 1938 *The Tyranny of Words* is still in print.

about the text

1. What assumptions does Orwell make about the relationship between clarity of thought and clarity of written expression? What is his argument?
2. What does Orwell see as the characteristic of sloppy writing?
3. Choose two of Orwell's "dying metaphors" and investigate their origins, using a dictionary. Do their current meanings remain close to the original ones? List some contemporary metaphors Orwell might wish banished.
4. Orwell offers us six rules to improve our writing. Do you think these rules are useful? Why or why not? To what extent will they help "cure" the English language of the decline that Orwell sees it experiencing?

on language use

5. Throughout this selection, Orwell uses many metaphors as he refers to the English language (e.g., that it is living; that it is diseased but can be cured). Make a list of these metaphors and evaluate the appropriateness and limitations of each.
6. Give two examples each of pretentious diction and meaningless words or phrases from textbooks you currently use (perhaps this one). Why would Orwell object to these usages? Following his rules, can you improve each of your examples?

7. Although Orwell's comments apply to all writing, his particular concern is political rhetoric, especially labels he considers dishonest like "transfer of population" or "rectification of frontiers." Give examples of current political terminology that you think fits Orwell's categorization.

for writing

8. Visit a Web site for a social or political cause that you support. Analyze the language of this Web site from Orwell's perspective. Then, write an essay in which you present the specific uses of language Orwell would likely find objectionable and give your own evaluation of them. Be sure to include the URL for the Web site so that your instructor and classmates can visit it.
9. Find a political speech from the Republican and Democratic candidates in the most recent presidential election, preferably on the same topic. Analyze them as Orwell might, beginning with the assumption that both politicians would have used language characterized by "vagueness and sheer incompetence" (paragraph 4). Write an essay in which you analyze the specific usages Orwell would criticize. Which candidate committed the more egregious "crimes"? Why?

Jack Rosenthal currently
serves as president of the New
York Times Company Foundation after twenty-seven years
as a senior editor at that
newspaper. In 1982, he won
a Pulitzer Prize for editorial
writing. In this article, written
in 2001 as part of a series
marking the paper's 150th
birthday, Rosenthal discusses
how the language of the
Times, and news reporting
more broadly, has changed
during the last century.

JACK ROSENTHAL

So Here's What's Happening to Language

WRITTEN ENGLISH, which reigned as America's national language for most of the *New York Times's*
150 years, has been dethroned. The spoken word
now rules, in all its informality and occasional vulgarity.
The effects are felt in politics, public taste, and even in our
writing.

The written language predominated because for generations, there was no other way to communicate over distance than by letters, newspapers, periodicals, or books;
even telegrams were written. With the invention of the telephone in 1876, spoken English started its long, slow march
toward dominance, a march that has accelerated in the last
few years. Now, though widespread literacy has made written English ever more influential, speech sets the standards.

Spoken language is by nature casual, so its ascendancy
has brought informality. Even presidents shrink from oro-
tund oratory—and from formal names. It's hard to imagine
the grandparents of Jimmy Carter and Bill Clinton referring
to Woody Wilson or Herb Hoover. Ask not what your country
can do for you? No. Today's usage would be, Don't ask.

The rapid ascendancy of the spoken language shows
even in public blunders. In 1992, Dan Quayle's problem
was a written one; he couldn't spell potato. Last year, during the New York Senate campaign, Rick Lazio's was oral.
He described Kim Jong I, the North Korean leader, as Kim
Jong the Second.

Full circle: the daily dominance of spoken English is 5
evident even when it's written, in the conversational informality of e-mail.

All of this can be seen as an admirable extension of
democracy. Informalization of language brings closer the
goal of universal discussion of public issues and policy decisions.

So who needs rules? Written language does. When he bought the *New York Times* in 1896, Adolph S. Ochs said he intended to present the news in language that "is parliamentary in good society." The details of his standards have evolved, but the reasons for maintaining them endure.

SESQUIPEDALIAN STUFFINESS

In 1851, the relatively few lettered Americans used writing to do more than communicate. With their class-conscious attention to spelling and sesquipedalian[1] words, they pronounced their membership in the intelligentsia.

So did newspapers. In its first issue, the *New-York Daily Times* gave this stuffy introduction to a letter about "a lamentable riot" in Lancaster, Pa.: "The commonsense view of the subject which characterizes this production will commend it to the candid reader."

A half century later, here's how the *Times* described the San Francisco 10 earthquake in 1906: "A disaster that staggers comprehension and in point of terror and damage is unprecedented on the coast has not yet reached its culmination."

New technologies soon sent the spoken word flying across great distances, yet written language still ruled. Vietnam, television's war, put bloody bodies in front of our eyes, but the voice-overs were usually scripted. The Persian Gulf war probably marked a turning point. As the allied missiles exploded in showers of green light television reporters on rooftops extemporized at length. Since then, producers have come to prize a correspondent's ability to deliver an unscripted "live pop."

As the formality of longhand gave way to the breeziness of speech, deciding what's Fit to Print became complicated. What do you do when a President's X-rated?

Casual language need not be careless or crude, and the *Times*, like other institutions of the written word, remains devoted to maintaining two principal standards. The more colorful one is taste. The more important one is credibility.

Talk of standards often means talk about what is Fit to Print in a family newspaper. The *Times*'s efforts to avoid gratuitous vulgarity have sometimes produced difficult distinctions. During Watergate, the editors confronted the

---

1. **sesquipedalian** long words or words of many syllables (the word's source is a phrase from the Roman poet Horace, *sesquipedalian verba*, "words a foot and a half long").

question of how to describe vulgarities uttered by President Nixon on the White House tapes, in the context of possible impeachment.

Their answer was to publish the expressions in the transcript but not in news articles.

The thinking behind that decision was codified in the 1976 revision of *The New York Times Manual of Style and Usage*, a publication used as an authority by others as well. It said that extreme vulgarity would be published only when essential to "insight into matters of great moment—an insight that cannot be otherwise conveyed." 15

That policy has since weathered two notable tests. In the 1991 hearings on the confirmation of Clarence Thomas to the United States Supreme Court, charges of sexual harassment and coarse expressions were broadcast on national television. The *Times* printed the terms in the transcripts and in the articles.

In 1998, the *Times* printed the full text, including explicit sexual descriptions and slang, of the Starr report, the independent counsel's recommendations to Congress on the impeachment of President Clinton.

Meanwhile, informalization has steadily denatured[2] many words once considered dirty. Several variants of the verb "screw," for example, have become certifiably inoffensive. Even fastidious grandmothers now say, when confessing error, that they "screwed up"; "screwed" has also become a routine term for being victimized.

Television, theater, movies, and especially popular music have sped the colloquialization of language. Once, writers thought twice before using even the formal terms for sexual organs. Now these words blaze on Broadway marquees, and the young women on "Sex and the City" joke about male appendages in the coarsest of terms.

HOLDING THE LINE, AT A PRICE

Still, the *Times* holds the line. "The *Times* virtually never prints obscene words, and it maintains a steep threshold for vulgar ones," write Allan M. Siegal and William G. Connolly in the 1999 edition of the *Manual of Style and Usage*. The greatest concern, they write, is for the newspaper's character: "The *Times* differentiates itself by taking a stand for civility in public dis- 20

---

2. **denatured** altered from their original nature. Associated with biochemistry, the word is used figuratively here.

course, sometimes at an acknowledged cost in the vividness of an article or two, and sometimes at the price of submitting to gibes."

Gibes are also a risk when it comes to correct usage. The phrase "It is I" may be correct grammatically but sounds quaintly ridiculous. The *Times* tries to avoid stilted constructions and welcomes informal feature writing, recognizing what advertising copywriters have long understood: that stiff and stuffy doesn't connect with readers.

In 1991, my wife, who worked in advertising at the time, wrote the slogan "Nobody knows like Domino's how you like pizza at home." I objected, recalling the storm of protest from teachers back in 1954 over a commercial proclaiming that "Winston tastes good—like a cigarette should." Well, my wife insisted, people don't care about things like "like" anymore. She was right. This time, there was not one complaint.

FOR CLARITY AND CREDIBILITY

That may illustrate how completely speech has overcome teachers' standards. Why sweat spelling in the Age of Spell Check? Why teach the subjunctive mode to students who write a spoken language? Why not surrender to the informality of speech?

One reason is clarity. In his "On Language" column, William Safire once illustrated the power of a hyphen: "A small-business man could be a huge fellow who runs a mom-and-pop enterprise, but a small businessman is always a runt." In truth, though, actual ambivalence or confusion is rare.

The better reason is credibility. Guarding it means guarding against even the appearance of carelessness and inconsistency. An announcer in New York once referred to Malcolm X as Malcolm the Tenth. A listener hearing that is less likely to trust other information broadcast by the station.

The same goes for inconsistent usage. Years ago, an astute foreign desk editor at the *Times* wrote that if a newspaper cannot make up its mind between advisor and adviser, or Street, St., and st., readers may well conclude that it cares little more about important distinctions of fact or interpretation.

In the end, writing—no matter how conversational the style—is writing. That means it is permanent. In speech, to be casual is to be friendly. In writing, to follow the rules is to be clear. To "talk it over," means to weigh and test; to put something into "black and white" means to decide, to freeze the thought. Spoken English may soften the strictures of written English, but the need for rules endures. There's a time to say "well, kind of," and a time for writing to right wrongs.

about the text

1. Rosenthal begins his article by discussing the changing relationship between written and spoken language, linking the shift to democratization. Do you agree with his argument? Are there disadvantages to the "informalization" of written language?

2. Rosenthal's article is in many ways a justification of the *Times*'s editorial practice with a focus on several particularly problematic events, including the Watergate tapes, the Thomas confirmation hearings, and the Starr Report (paragraphs 13–17). What new challenges did each of these events present for the *Times*? How did the paper choose to deal with those challenges?

3. What values does Rosenthal contend justify the *Times*'s practices? Do you agree? Why or why not?

4. In paragraph 27, Rosenthal contrasts the notions of being friendly and of being clear. Can one be both? In speaking? In writing? Why do you think Rosenthal uses this contrast?

5. What does Rosenthal mean when he ends his article by claiming that there is a "time for writing to right wrongs" (paragraph 27)?

on language use

6. Rosenthal argues that various technologies have encouraged writers to write much the way they speak. Which specific technologies does he mention? Can you name others? Can you cite other events or developments that support Rosenthal's claim?

7. What assumptions does Rosenthal make with respect to grammar rules and spoken language? Written language? Is he justified in making such assumptions?

8. In paragraph 26, Rosenthal gives the example of a foreign desk editor who claims that if the paper cannot be consistent in its spelling or use of abbreviations, "readers may well conclude that it cares little more about important distinctions of fact or interpretation." Is such a claim logical? Why should consistency in spelling or use of abbreviations stand as evidence of quality of thought or carefulness of fact checking? How do you evaluate the trustworthiness of documents that contain inconsistent spellings or especially informal language?

for writing

9. Many consider the *New York Times* to be the most authoritative print news source in the United States. Examine the issues of the *Times* from your birthdate in 1950 and from the day you were assigned Rosenthal's text. (You can do the latter online; the former will likely require a trip to the library.) Study the lead story, the editorial page, and the front page of your favorite section in each day's paper. Look for evidence of the increasing informality of written journalistic prose and then write an essay in which you compare the language used in the papers from these two dates.

10. Find an article in a local newspaper from fifty years ago. Rewrite it so that it sounds contemporary, rather than half a century old. Then write an essay in which you describe the changes you made in updating the article. Be sure to include both a copy of the original article and your update when you turn in your essay.

chapter 3

technology and (versus?) language

technologies are ways of handling specific problems. Writing itself is a technology, one that permits humans to record and transmit information easily across time and space. Alphabetic writing arose to meet specific needs, in fact, commercial ones. (Other writing systems, like Maya hieroglyphs, arose as part of the development of the Maya science of astronomy.) Scholars estimate that alphabetic writing began in the area that is today Iraq in the fourth century B.C.E., when merchants used clay tokens to indicate things to be counted. When a merchant, for example, sent someone ten vats of oil, he put ten tokens inside a sealed clay "envelope" so that the recipient could verify that he had received the right number of vats. Later, the number of tokens inside was also marked on the outside of the envelope. Conventions developed for using different signs—ovoids, spheres, small cones and so on—to indicate specific contents (ovoids for oil, for example). Over time, people realized they could do away with the tokens inside and rely only on what was written on the outside. This form of counting was the beginning of writing.

The readings in this chapter invite you to consider technologies of many sorts and their impact on spoken and written language. We open with a selection that was written to be read aloud, a common use of writing. In it, Dennis Baron considers how "new technologies of the word" are changing our relationship to language. The next several selections—an essay, three cartoons, and a newspaper feature—examine the ways that instant messaging is changing how we use written language, with IM conventions even beginning to show up in student essays (often to the dismay of teachers).

Next comes an NPR interview with Amy Borkowsky, about her book based on the answering machine messages her mother has left her over the past two decades. Think of the spoken-language genres we owe to answering machines, the messages left by owners and the ones left by callers.

Two essays, one by Geoffrey Nunberg and one by Clive Thompson, challenge us to think about how PowerPoint™ is changing the way we present and understand information visually, perhaps not always for the better! Finally come two newspaper articles that consider technology in religious contexts, documenting how the Internet and personal digital assistants, like Palm Pilots or Blackberries are being used by religious believers as part of the practice of their faith.

The technologies that are the focus of this chapter are all relatively recent inventions. Just a few short decades ago, there was no email; there were no IM's, no smiley faces, and no answering machine messages. Each of these new communicative practices has given rise to new genres of language use but most of them are actually extensions of older genres (the hand-written note and rebuses, for example). Whether we see these technological advances as evidence of decline in language standards or as evidence that such technology will continue to drive changes in language, thinking critically about these technologies and their influence can only help us use them well.

DENNIS BARON

The New Technologies of the Word

Dennis Baron *teaches English and linguistics at the University of Illinois at Urbana-Champaign and has written extensively on technology and literacy. He is the author of* The English-Only Question: An Official Language for Americans? *(1992),* Grammar and Gender *(1987), and* Grammar and Good Taste: Reforming the American Language *(1983).*

This selection is a speech that Baron delivered in 2002 at the annual conference of the International Association of World Englishes, an organization of scholars who study varieties of English and their uses in all parts of the world.

In it, Baron encourages us to think about how we use technologies such as email, cell phones, and instant messaging, and how they influence language. If we take technology to be any tool that enables us to do something more efficiently or effectively, we can see that writing and the instruments of writing—styluses and clay tablets, scrolls, paper, books, pens, typewriters, computers, and Palm Pilots, to name but a few—are technologies that intervene in the process of communication, transforming it as they do.

I AM GOING TO TALK SPECIFICALLY about how electronic technologies are introducing major changes in the practice of American English: the computer has altered the ways we write and read significantly in the past 20 years, and the cell phone is changing spoken interaction in ways that continue to evolve. Both technologies are reconfiguring our notions of public and private language, and both are calling our attention increasingly to what is being called the "digital divide" between haves and have nots—and that is what brings us back to language policy both on the national and the global scale.

I think that the new technologies of the word, as I call them, are reinforcing two trends that we may all be observing in what is going on with English around the world. One is the continued spread of English as a world language (with the caveat so nicely articulated by [scholars] many years ago that world languages, like world empires, come and go). But this accent on global English is balanced by what I see as a new emphasis on the local: both local varieties of English set against the umbrella of World Englishes. And also a renewed emphasis on local languages and varieties in tandem with and in resistance to dominant world and national languages. The new technologies of the word are the tools of the globalizers, working for standardization. But what they produce after their initial spread is often a surprising reinforcement of the local.

Not so long ago the claim was going unquestioned that English was the language of the World Wide Web, and that the web itself embodied a kind of digital imperialism increasing the domination by English of the communication pathways. After all, it was argued, computers were limited in their ability to represent non-Roman alphabets, and anyway it was felt that everyone who had anything important to say was saying it in English. How could we be so naïve—and so colonialist—in what we envision as an increasingly postcolonial world? In any case it has become clear that many languages are now claiming their own space in a cyberspace that is perfectly able to stretch to fit them, and that the effects of technology on language practice apply not just to speakers and writers of English, but to users of any language. What is true across languages is true as well within them: the standard language imposed top down by governments, schools, and cultural norms is everywhere met by the infinite variety of local forms and practices. The computer can transmit norms downward from the top, but it can also empower individuals "at the bottom" as it were to take control of authorship: nowadays you don't have to seize the radio stations and the mimeograph machines to support the revolution. Instead, in this age of digital reproduction, you can simply fire up your PC and send your manifesto into cyberspace.

So, on to technology—

TECHNOLOGY

Language, both written and spoken, depends heavily on technology for its transmission. I would argue that speech itself is a technology, as is writing. And the means we use to transmit speech and writing are technological as well.

Today we tend to think of technology as referring primarily to comput- 5 ers, and when I speak of the new technologies of the word I too will consider the impact of digital technology on our communication practices. But we shouldn't lose sight of the fact that there are other technologies—old technologies of the word, if you will—that remain even today more prevalent than computers—that mediate our communication.

For example, there's the humble wood pencil [hold up pencil], which as Henry Petroski[1] has shown, is a complex technology. True it has no electronics, nor any moving parts, and it costs only a few cents to manufacture and purchase in this age of mechanical reproduction. But a pencil is complex enough that you could not easily replicate one in a home workshop, and even if you could master the technologies of woodworking, chemistry, mineralogy,

---

1. **Henry Petroski** professor of civil engineering and history at Duke University and author of many books on the design and technology of ordinary objects, including *The Pencil: A History of Design and Circumstance* (1992).

painting and engineering necessary to make a do-it-yourself pencil, the materials would cost you something on the order of $50, not a few cents per unit.

So when Bill Henderson, the founder of the Lead Pencil Club,[2] a group dedicated to living "contraption-free in a computer-crazed world," when Henderson urges us to abandon our computers, and the technology that grips our writing, and pick up the simple, old-fashioned, no. 2 wood-cased pencil, as an act of civil disobedience worthy of Henry David Thoreau, he may be anticomputer but he cannot claim to be antitechnology.

Henderson argues, "Henry David Thoreau was the son of a pencil maker and helped his father manufacture pencils. Indeed, it is quite probable that *Walden* was written with a pencil that Thoreau made himself." Here Henderson sketches a romanticized picture of America's favorite individualist: Thoreau helped out around the workshop the way Stradivarius *fils*[3] might have helped his dad make fiddles.

Does little Davey Thoreau want to write an essay today? I don't think he goes out in the yard and whittles himself a length of cedar, mixes up a batch of graphite, thinks important thoughts, then writes them down. Probably the procedure went more like this: Thoreau took a box of pencils home from the factory. If he felt like writing, he took one out and went to work. Not quite so romantic, and very much like what we might do today if we were using a pencil to write with.

Thoreau wasn't a pencil-craftsman so much as he was an engineer and   10 entrepreneur who took a marginal business which churned out a cheap, low-quality product and turned it profitable. Thoreau may have written idealistically, but he spent six months in the Harvard College library researching European pencil technology in an effort to make the Thoreau pencil better and more expensive than any import. And the man who invented civil disobedience, refusing to pay taxes being used to finance an unjust war, used his marketing skills to sell his pencils. Thoreau solicited celebrity endorsements for his pencils, which the patriotic Thoreau wanted to prove better than the imported European models against which he was competing. Ralph Waldo Emerson, Thoreau's friend and the man to whose house Thoreau repaired

---

2. **the Lead Pencil Club** an organization that opposes e mail, voice mail, fax machines, and other "electronic gadgetry." By its very nature, the group has no Web site, but it is described by others; learn more about the group at <www.rit.edu/~cyberwww/8.htm>.

3. **Stradivarius** a violin made by the Stradivarius father and son violin makers in eighteenth-century Italy. The sound created by these violins, widely considered the best in the world, has never been duplicated; **fils** son (French). What does Baron gain by using a French term here?

to relieve the loneliness of those Walden nights, signed up as an endorser of the Thoreau pencil: according to Waldo, one couldn't be self-reliant without one.

Thoreau pencils provided the young nation with a truly transcendental experience, and Henry Thoreau rode the pencil technology bubble till it burst: when his pencils lost market share, Thoreau started selling the graphite that came out of the family graphite mine wholesale to the newly emerging electrotyping industry.

We know that time, for Thoreau, was just a stream he went a-fishing in, and I'd like to think that if Thoreau were alive today, he would reject Bill Henderson's critique of technology as totally missing the point. Not one to give up social criticism, Thoreau would surely abandon pencils and keyboard his complaints about today's overscheduled lives and unjust wars on a laptop that he put together from spare parts in his garage.

NOSTALGIA FOR THE OLD WAYS

Bill Henderson's complaint is a common one: new technologies generate nostalgia for the old ones. Socrates warned that the new technology of writing would work to the detriment of the old technology of memory. We remember this, of course, because Plato wrote it down. One of the common complaints we hear today is that computers signal the death of handwriting. Penmanship, as it was once called in American schools, is no longer practiced with any rigor, except by those few diehards who want to bring back the fountain pen.

Perhaps copying all the letters in a big round hand, as the Ruler of the Queen's Navee[4] did to gain advancement, is a lost art for most of us, but standardized handwriting was a literacy technology just as computer writing is today. From a purely practical standpoint, uniform script was once enforced for scribes and clerks to ensure legibility in documents destined to have multiple readers. Indeed, a copperplate[5]-perfect handwriting in the nineteenth

---

4. **Ruler of the Queen's Navee** a reference to the song "I am the Monarch of the Sea" from the nineteenth-century comic operetta *HMS Pinafore* by Gilbert and Sullivan. Sir Joseph sings of working diligently at menial tasks and eventually climbing the career ladder to become "the ruler of the Queen's Navee."

5. **copperplate** dominant style of penmanship used by the eighteenth- and nineteenth-century clerks and scribes; so named because their models were printed from copperplates. THIS SENTENCE USES A FONT MUCH INFLUENCED BY COPPERPLATE STYLE.

century was a class marker. The rich didn't need a nice round hand, for they didn't work in offices and could afford to allow their handwriting to express their individuality. Once the press freed us from a dependence on hand-copied manuscripts, and the typewriter liberated the office from the tyranny of the inkwell, it was inevitable that handwriting would become a lost art, revived from time to time by people who feel trapped in the present.

THE BIRTH OF GENRES

OK, enough about the old technologies of the word. Let's take a look at the new. In the last decade or two, three new written genres have emerged: email, the web page, and instant messaging now form a significant slice of writing practice in the United States and at least email and the web page are gaining importance around the globe as well. In addition, the mobile phone is now a major factor influencing spoken communication. Watching these new genres arise and evolve is like being present at the birth of stars: we have the unusual opportunity to observe these linguistic genres spin off from older ways of doing things with words, starting out as one sort of communication practice and winding up as something completely different, developing their own conventions of style and usage, of appropriateness and correctness, of grammaticality and acceptability.

Let's look first at email and instant messaging, and then the mobile phone.

Email started out in the emerging computer companies of the 1960s and 1970s for in-house electronic memos. In addition, programmers sent email to one another to pass the time while their programs were compiling—much as telegraphers in the early days of electronic communication sent personal messages to one another, and played games, while they waited for paying customers. The first email users were techies, and the mainframe computer systems they sent their email on were not user-friendly. Those computers were designed for number-crunching, not word-processing. Even programmers didn't program on the machines: they wrote out their code on pads of paper—and they probably used no. 2 pencils to write with. Line editors were cumbersome to work with, and initially computer keyboards only allowed working in one case, upper or lower.

This technology was so unforgiving that only a few diehards saw the possibilities that computers offered writers. Many of the early computer writers were a ragged and persistent gang, and as a result, in the early days of email, a frontier mystique developed around computer writing: it wasn't something for the faint of heart. Because correcting text was so difficult, and perhaps also because programmers wanted to give the impression that they had more important things to do than submit to the niceties of writing conventional prose, emailers were lawless—at least when it came to observing the laws of spelling, grammar, and usage that constrain writers using conventional technologies. They typed their email quickly, without concern for form or style: it was their version of shooting from the hip. They wore incorrectness as a badge of authority. They keyed their messages in lower case. They rejected linguistic conventionality and wrapped themselves in the mantle of Thoreau.

But as it is with all communication, an initially chaotic system began to self-organize. Plus, the early chaos of email may have been more myth than reality. Anecdotal evidence supports a claim that there was plenty of concern for linguistic correctness when computer writing was young. And even those writers of emails who openly derided the schoolmarm approach to grammar developed conventions early on. For one thing, writers were using computers to send conventional messages—memos, reports, notices of meetings—at the same time that what I will call the "desperado email" was emerging. But even among the lawless ones on the electronic frontier, a sense of appropriateness in communication style soon emerged. Early norms may have been few, but the community of computer writers banded together to express outrage for someone who inadvertently violated an unspoken norm. If you wrote in caps by mistake, you were accused of "shouting." If you corrected someone's spelling or usage, you were scorned for insisting on bourgeois civility. If you showed yourself unfamiliar with the community's standards by being too formal, or too careless, or just a tad inappropriate, you were flamed or shunned. Even the electronic frontier had its rough justice.

As with the early days of writing itself, digital literacy was limited to a 20 class of scribes, or programmers, who had mastered the steep learning curve of the technology and who could, if necessary, mediate the literacy technology for the uninitiated. For digital writing to spread beyond this small group of adepts a number of things had to happen: the practice had to become easier to learn (both the hardware and the software needed to be made more writer-friendly); and computers had to become less expensive if more people were to have access to them.

In fact both of these things started to happen, first with the success of the personal computer in the early 1980s. Then in the later 1980s, graphical user interfaces and black-on-white screens allowed for text display approximating an actual typed or printed document. This, combined with significantly lower costs, led more people both to be able to afford the machine and to see that it could allow them to produce the kinds of documents they were already used to producing.

As more people adopted the technology, they brought with them their conventional concerns. The new converts to digital writing, like typists and pen-men before them, wanted to know how to do it right: how to write a business letter; how to write a report; how to write a personal letter, and they brought their concern for this medieval *ars dictaminis*,[6] as updated for the modern office, to the newly emerging genres of email and newsgroups. The electronic frontier was suddenly becoming settled and urbanized, and there arose a sometimes not-so-subtle distinction between newcomers and old-timers. The old-timers clung to their lawlessness as a badge of authority. They were there first, after all: they invented the wheel. Newcomers asked silly questions like, "Should an email have a greeting?" And newcomers to the discourse show an inordinate fondness for spell-checking.

Soon manuals on correct electronic communication, or netiquette, began to surface. There are numerous on-line lists of do's and don'ts for email. The traditional etiquette books—the Emily Posts and Miss Manners' Guides, also began to include directions for appropriate emailing. Even the digital-chic chronicler of the computer revolution, *Wired Magazine*, known for its free-wheeling writing style, came up with its own email rulebook, in which the editor discusses such matters as whether *email* should be capitalized, hyphenated or printed solid, whether *email* can be a verb and a count noun as well as a mass noun, and the correct plural for *computer mouse*. One sure sign that conventionality has come into play once and for all, that the electronic frontier is finally becoming civilized, is the appearance of chapters on electronic communication in every major college writing textbook.

THE CHARGE AGAINST EMAIL

While it is heralded by its proponents as the best thing since sliced bread, technology also seems often to generate suspicion. Critics of email view it as a leading force in the inevitable decline and fall of the English language.

Located somewhere between the traditional letter and the phone call, 25 email continues to carve out its own communication space. True, there are junk emails that replicate conventional technology's junk mail. And there are

---

6. **ars dictaminis** the art of letter writing, a subfield of medieval European rhetoric, which gave rise to manuals providing examples of various kinds of model letters (e.g., how a student should write to his dad for money and how the letter should be altered if it is likely that the old man has heard about his son's propensity for wasting it).

email confidence schemes that are as intrusive as
the soliciting phone calls timed to coincide with dinner. Email seems private but is in fact very public: it
is discoverable in court, and if you use email at
work, it is the property of your employer, who may
spy on your email as well as your phone calls at will.

But the main charge against email is that it is
too informal. By 'too informal' critics tend to mean
that, despite the prevalence of usage guides,
emailers do not evince enough concern for spelling and usage. They use too
many shortcuts: acronyms like IMHO or BTW, and emoticons. There's too
much slang. In short, the language of Shakespeare, Addison and Steele,[7] and
Hemingway gets no respect from emailers. And emoticons have become our
newest punctuation marks.

Of course emails vary in their degree of formality, and in their observance of stylistic niceties, the way any text may. The speed of email, compared to the post office, may take some getting used to. And so perhaps the
most common complaint of emailers themselves doesn't concern error or
slang, it's the experience many of us have had of sending off an email before
we are really ready. It may be an angry email, or an incomplete one. Or we
may have sent it to the wrong recipient. Of course this can and does happen
with conventional written text, and it certainly continues to happen with spoken language. But the "oops" quotient of email seems particularly high, even
for experienced users of the genre.

Nonetheless email has made inroads in our communication practice.
Once you start down the email path, there's no going back. See what happens when the computers go down in an office. People don't immediately
switch over to the phone, or walk down the corridor for a chat. Initially, at
least, they sit around staring at their screens, wondering how they're going
to get anything done today.

INSTANT MESSAGING

Instant messaging [IM] is an even newer genre than email, popular with college students as well as the teen and pre-teen set. It differs from email in
that it is a real-time exchange, a digital conversation among two or more se-

---

7. **Joseph Addison and Sir Richard Steele** editors of the daily London periodicals *The Tatler*
(1709–1711) and *The Spectator* (1711–1712), which helped spread the intellectual ideas of the
times.

lected participants, the so-called "buddy list," that seems to thrive on short turns, rapid turn-taking, with participants dropping in and out of the conversation with regularity. I have observed IM, though only briefly, and participated in one or two IM exchanges, just to see what it was like. I am no expert, as my children will readily attest. And I stopped dabbling because IM does not at the moment fit my own communication needs.

Inexpert as I am, let me make a few claims that may not be altogether supportable, but are at least worth exploring. As email becomes conventionalized, IM takes its place as the new trend-setter, at least in an American context, and IM jargon (LOL, BRB, TTFN)[8] has elbowed its way into public consciousness. There is clearly some age-grading associated with IM. While it is normal for adults to email one another, it is less usual for them to IM. My nineteen-year-old daughter refused to believe I was IM-ing her at college in Boston. "Who is this, really?" she asked, suspiciously, and she made me identify myself by answering a question to which only she and I would know the answer (I actually got it wrong on the first try, because I misunderstood what aspect of the question she wanted answered, and IM lacked the contextual flexibility for us to quickly determine that I had misunderstood her).

From what I can tell by looking at transcripts of IM sessions among the seventh-grade set, IM is mostly phatic communication.[9] "I'm here. Are you there?" "I'm here." "Silly joke, silly joke." "Acronym, acronym." "G2G."[10] "TTFN." If Monty Python were still going strong, they'd surely do an IM skit.

Is this new? Not entirely. Acronyms have abounded for some time in pre-teen written communication, especially among girls: SWAK and JMJ[11] are two quite different yet common acronyms I saw regularly thirty years ago when I began teaching. And phatic dialogue played an important part in the 1950s Paddy Chayefsky play and movie, "Marty," where Ernest Borgnine and his friend got great mileage out of deathless lines like, "What dya wanna do, Marty?" "I dunno, whadda you wanna do?"

---

8. **LOL** laughing out loud; **BRB** be right back. **TTFN** ta ta for now; **BTW** what does it mean if you have to read the glosses for these acronyms?

9. **phatic communication** refers to interactions that do not exchange to new information but rather to establish and maintain a positive, friendly connection among conversation partners. Greetings, for example, are phatic.

10. **G2G** got to go.

11. **SWAK** sealed with a kiss. **JMJ** Jesus, Mary, Joseph. According to a Catholic sister in her mid-seventies, a friend of ours, "In my day, we were taught to place the JMJ at the top of our school papers to offer the effort to the honor of the Holy Family . . . also with the hope we would get the right answers!"

It hasn't taken long for complaints about IM's effect on the language to surface. These tend to replicate the complaints against email, though there seems to be a strong objection to IM acronyms as they make their way from the digital context into the realm of student writing. An article in the *New York Times* reports that teachers are finding IM jargon seamlessly embedded in such middle- and high-school genres as the book report and the term paper. Students claim to be surprised when teachers tell them that the language of IM is not appropriate for the school context, although it is certainly not unusual for novice writers to make all sorts of moves that their audience finds contextually inappropriate. Yesterday I even saw a car on campus with a license plate that said TTFN.

IM is more than a written conference call, with images and sounds to accompany its staccato exchanges. It is already thriving beyond the teen set in offices everywhere: it provides an easier switch than email does between on-screen work and chatting with a friend, since the IM screen can remain open alongside the spreadsheet or word processing document. It seems safe to predict that IM will develop more fully just as email has done, and that it too, while remaining reasonably informal, will develop rules and conventions of the kind every speech community seems to form.

CELL PHONES

IM, even when only two buddies converse, seems to be private discourse 35 carried on in a public electronic space. Both email and Instant Messaging are skewing our ideas of public and private language. But cell phones warp the contexts of public and private even more noticeably. Consider these scenarios:

- In a crowded gate area at O'Hare Airport in Chicago, a man who looks like he's been sleeping in his clothes marches up and down amidst the clumps of weary passengers huddled with their luggage. There's a scowl on his face and his arms saw the air as he talks loudly and angrily to himself. Terrorist? Psychotic off his meds? Neither, actually: he's a frustrated business traveler talking on his hands-free cell phone, squeezing in some work while he waits for his long-delayed flight to board.

- At a Scottsdale, Arizona, movie theater, where I have gone to escape the 100-degree evening heat in June, a slide comes on the screen between the ads and the previews asking patrons to turn off their cell phones. At least twenty people in the audience respond to this request by rummaging noisily for their phones and making one last call before the show starts. The sound track of the movie turns out to be so loud that the management's request to power down the phones seems superfluous.

- It's the first day of my "Literacy and Technology" class at the University of Illinois, and just as I begin my soliloquy on how the new technologies are changing the ways we communicate, a tinkling melody emanates from a backpack. Without any embarrassment, a student digs out her phone, answers the call, carries on a short conversation, then hangs up. I say, pointedly, "As I was saying . . . ," though only some of the students see the irony: what just happened was exactly the point I was trying to make, that mobile telephony changes conditions for more people than just the caller and the called. Subsequent in-class phone calls are less well-timed to coincide with the syllabus. Despite my requests that students turn their phones off before coming into the room—requests there was no need to make only a semester earlier—it takes the class a while to get into the habit. Then one day my own phone rings while I am teaching. I answer the call, have a short, embarrassed conversation while the class giggles and strains to hear what I am whispering, then go back to teaching. We have no more interruptions that semester, but I notice that students now turn their phones back on even before they close their books and stow them away—the traditional signal to the instructor that my fifty minutes is up. And as the students leave class many of them are already deep in conversation with someone who commands their attention more than I could ever hope to.

- And finally, this one: I'm driving down a busy Chicago street when a man driving a silver Mercedes while talking on his cell phone pulls out of a parking lot and into my path. I slam on the brakes of my humble blue Corolla, narrowly avoiding his expensive bumper, and reflexively I show my annoyance by honking the horn. In turn, he shows his annoyance at having his conversation so rudely interrupted by raising aloft the hand in which he holds his phone, its antenna extended in a high-tech gesture of obscenity. In astonishment and glee my daughter cries out, "Hey, dad, that guy just gave you the phone." The occupants of our car dissolve in laughter, and a new family idiom is born: to give someone the phone.

Cell phones have come a long way in a few short years. In 1994, when I went to that movie in Scottsdale, perhaps 10 million Americans had cell phones. Today more than 100 million Americans have them, and some people are giving up their land phones entirely. They are changing both the nature of telephone interaction and the way people behave in public.

Cell phones are ringing everywhere. I've heard phones go off at weddings, bar mitzvahs, and funerals; at restaurants (of course), in bathrooms, and in idyllic outdoor settings. One day, as I was strolling across a California campus where I was giving a lecture, I heard a cell phone chime. Pavlov[12] would have smiled as twenty nearby students immediately rummaged in their backpacks to see if the call was for them. It's not just students who do this. Last month I was talking at a reception to a group of deans and department heads, when the muffled ring of a phone interrupted us. Then began the inevitable writhing dance as these grown men and women searched pockets and purses to determine whose elusive phone was ringing. Several phones emerged and presbyopic eyes held them at arm's length, squinting to examine the caller ID screen. Eventually the lucky winner waved his phone in the air, then moved aside to take the call. We are constrained to suddenly become private when our phone rings in public.

More and more I see people walking together in an animated group, but each person is talking on a phone to someone else. At least I presume they're talking to someone else. There is, after all, that scene in the movie "Clueless" where Cher strolls alongside her best friend, Dionne, and they are chattering to one another on their cell phones.

Before cell phones, people in a group could talk to one another face to face, and people alone could give full attention to their immediate surroundings: looking at the scenery, driving the car, perusing the menu, observing the *comédie humaine*. Now the cell phone connects us across space, freeing us from our local context just as the land phone did when it first came on the scene.

Cell phones used in public can create an instant audience, albeit a sometimes unwilling one. This morning at the local coffee bar, a woman came in already talking loudly on her phone, and while she was ordering her latte she took a second call and switched deftly between her two callers and the barrista, at times involving all three in what seemed to be a single conversation. But the rest of us in the coffee line were also auditors, for talking on a cell phone seems to bring out an emotive voice. People bare half a conversation to an audience of strangers, a conversation that is sometimes un-

---

12. **Ivan Pavlov (1849–1936)** Russian psychologist who researched conditioned reflexes. His best-known experiment involved teaching a dog that had salivated at the sight of food to salivate at the sound of a bell.

comfortably personal for those within earshot, though it is even more often boring (who cares what your mother ate for lunch?) or simply distracting (I can't hear the person I'm with because the cell phone talker is so loud). Even the dean who moved aside to take his call felt obliged to return to the group when he was done and tell us what the call was about.

But some mobile callers remain uncomfortable with the public nature of cell phone use. One student says she is so reluctant to conduct even the blandest phone conversation in front of strangers that she not only whispers into the phone, she also tries to minimize her physical profile, hunching over the phone, turning away from others, covering her mouth as she talks. But to her chagrin, she concludes, this privacy behavior only serves to draw more attention to the fact that she's walking down the street, talking on the phone. And curiously, she feels little of the same discomfort when talking on her home phone, even a cordless one, when others are in the room, perhaps because whispering seems more natural with the older phone technology. 40

But when telephones first came on the scene, in the 1880s, whispering was not an option. Neither was privacy. Phones were rare, and when households or businesses got their first phones, they were placed in a central location: a first-floor hallway or a front desk or counter. Speaking on the telephone meant there was no place to hide, and it took some time before extensions became available that allowed callers to retreat into bedrooms or back offices, or phone cords became long enough for teenagers to haul the phone into a closet or bathroom for privacy. Not only bystanders listened in to phone calls. Telephone operators were required to check in on conversations to determine whether the line was still in use, since the connection was not automatically broken when a caller hung up the phone. But soon enough operators took on the role of conversation monitors, occasionally threatening to suspend the phone privileges of callers who used vulgar language and profanity. Privacy was further compromised in rural areas by party lines, where members of other households on the same phone line could eavesdrop.

Early telephone technology was poor by today's standards, too. Voice reproduction was so unnatural, and line noise so common, that in many cases speakers had to shout or speak very loudly in order to be heard. And speakers shouted as well in response to the room noise that occasionally made it hard for them to hear their callers. This same attempt to overcome background noise from traffic, machinery, and other talkers nearby, may lie behind the tendency of cell phone users to speak more loudly on the phone than they would to someone who is right next to them.

CONCLUSIONS

New technologies of communication often get their big break by duplicating older ones. When writing emerged in the ancient Mediterranean as an inventory device, it was useful to merchants. But once someone realized that writing could duplicate speech, there was no turning back. Cabinet makers invented the wood pencil in the sixteenth century to mark measurements in wood without gouging the wood. Once someone realized they were perfect portable writing and drawing instruments, freeing writers from their dependence on the inkwell, pencils became the first laptops. Computers began life as number crunchers (the name *computer* was first used to refer to human beings doing repetitive computations). They still crunch numbers, it's true, but most of us now depend on our computers as writing tools, not calculators.

Our communication practices have been permanently altered by electronic technologies, and that should surprise no one, nor should it be the cause of lamentation. The computer allows more people to become authors, if by authors we mean any writer who sends a creation out into the world of readers. By doing that, the computer allows more authorial languages to claim public space and authority they might not otherwise have had.

But at the same time, as authorship and linguistic prominence shift from older technologies to the computer, this democratization of the public word reinforces the divide between those who have computers and those who don't, and it further distances those who have literacy from those who don't.

But even as we worry about access to computers, equating that, perhaps mistakenly, with access to literacy, the technology is moving in new ways that may cause us once again to rethink what we mean by literacy, and to re-evaluate the interactions of language practice and technology. Already mobile phones are becoming more computer-like, and there is some chance that computers will become more like telephones. If the next big development in the digital world is the perfection of speech to text software, then writers will no longer key in their texts, they'll speak them, and their words will magically appear on screen.

If this actually works, and it's probably still a long time coming, it will signal a change in writing practice: we will all be dictating our text to our computers. More important, it will mark a change in our thinking about literacy. Computers can already turn text to speech efficiently enough to eliminate our dependence on the visual processing of text. Link speech to text with text to speech and you eliminate the middle terms: writing and reading could conceivably be reconfigured in such a way that they become an invisible part of the communication.

At the very least, this will cause traditionalists to lament the decline in the keyboarding skills of the young. But in fact the implications of speech to text for reconfiguring literacy are staggering. However there's no need to see the library going the way of the 8-track tape, or the quill pen. Even though my cell phone can receive email messages, for now speech to text still belongs in the realm of science fiction, like cold fusion or, dare I say, machine translation?

about the text

1. Make a list of the parallels Baron draws between earlier writing technologies and more recent ones. To what extent do you think these parallels are valid? How do they make the point that the introduction of new technology gives rise to certain predictable consequences?

2. Baron discusses the globalizing effect of the new technologies, but he also asserts (in paragraph 2) that these technologies often produce "a surprising reinforcement of the local." What does that phrase mean? What evidence does Baron give to support his assertion? What does he mean when he talks about imposition "from the top" and empowerment "at the bottom" (paragraph 3)?

3. Baron wrote this essay as a conference address, to be delivered to a live audience (notice the bracketed text in paragraph 6, "hold up pencil"). What other evidence can you find that Baron meant for his audience to hear, rather than read? Explain your choices. How would the text be different if he'd meant for it to be read? In what ways is reading aloud a technology?

on language use

4. Are IM customs and conventions the same for all IMers? Are yours identical to or different from those of your friends and other peers? What might you be able to tell about people from their IM styles?

5. As new language technologies appear, others become obsolete. (For example, one of the authors remembers that a standard item on her sixth-grade school supplies list was a bottle of blue ink and a fountain pen.) What language technologies that you've grown up with might become obsolete in your lifetime—and why? What might replace them?

6. What plural do you use to refer to more than one computer mouse—"mice"? "mouses"? Browse on the Web to see what you find and poll your friends and relatives on their preferences. Is there any age pattern to the responses? Gender pattern? How might you explain the preferences that you encounter? Using the *mouse/mice/mouses* example, hypothesize about what happens to words when they take on new meanings.

7. Baron speculates about speech-to-text technologies, mentioning that in the future we may simply speak our ideas into a computer

rather than typing them (paragraph 48). Are you looking forward to such a day? Do you think you will be able to express yourself more easily by speaking instead of by writing? Why or why not? What might you miss about typing or handwriting? Discuss your ideas with one or two classmates.

---

for writing

8. Anyone attending college in the early twenty-first century has witnessed tremendous changes in everyday communication. Write an essay in which you discuss your use (or non-use) of email, IMing, and cell phones, and describe how your daily habits have been changed or shaped by these technologies. Have you made friends you might not have if it weren't for these technologies? Why or why not? Have they changed your relations with parents or siblings? If you don't use email or IM, and never use or call a cell phone, how is your life different from the lives of those who do? Is it less complicated? more complicated? more stressful? less stressful? Give specific examples.

9. Interview someone much older or younger than you to learn about technologies of the word in his or her life. Which technologies does your interviewee prefer to use? Why? Are there technologies the person avoids? Why? How do his or her practices compare with yours? Write an essay about what you discover.

Jennifer 8. Lee *is a science and technology writer for the* New York Times, *where this article appeared on September 19, 2002. (By the way, 8 is her middle name. Google "Jennifer 8. Lee middle name" to find out more about it.) This article examines IMing, demonstrating how it influences the practice of writing even in schools, the institutions assigned the task of teaching and upholding the standard form of the language.*

The title of this article is a play on a famous line from seventeenth-century French philosopher René Descartes, who wrote, "I think, therefore I am," a crucial claim in his Meditations on the First Philosophy: In Which the Existence of God and the Distinction Between Mind and Body are Demonstrated *(1641). Lee's title suggests that the written language innovations resulting from new technologies such as IMing are not always welcomed in classrooms even as her allusion to Descartes reminds us that language practices—how members of various groups actually use language—are related to questions of identity and, in some sense, of existence.*

JENNIFER 8. LEE

I Think, Therefore IM

Text Shortcuts Invade Schoolwork, and Teachers Are Not Amused

EACH SEPTEMBER Jacqueline Harding prepares a classroom presentation on the common writing mistakes she sees in her students' work.

Ms. Harding, an eighth-grade English teacher at Viking Middle School in Guernee, Ill., scribbles the words that have plagued generations of schoolchildren across her whiteboard:

There. Their. They're.

Your. You're.

To. Too. Two.

Its. It's.

This September, she has added a new list: u, r, ur, b4, wuz, cuz, 2.

When she asked her students how many of them used shortcuts like these in their writing. Ms. Harding said, she was not surprised when most of them raised their hands. This, after all, is their online lingua franca: English adapted for the spitfire conversational style of Internet instant messaging.

Ms. Harding, who has seen such shortcuts creep into student papers over 5 the last two years, said she gave her students a warning: "If I see this in your assignments, I will take points off."

"Kids should know the difference," said Ms. Harding who decided to address this issue head-on this year. "They should know where to draw the line between formal writing and conversational writing."

As more and more teenagers socialize online, middle school and high school teachers like Ms. Harding are increasingly seeing a breezy form of Internet English jump from e-mail into schoolwork. To their dismay, teachers say that papers are being written with shortened words, improper capitalization and punctuation, and characters like &, $ and @.

Teachers have deducted points, drawn red circles and tsk-tsked at their classes. Yet the errant forms continue. "It stops being funny after you repeat yourself a couple of times," Ms. Harding said.

But teenagers, whose social life can rely as much these days on text communication as the spoken word, say that they use instant-messaging shorthand without thinking about it. They write to one another as much as they write in school, or more.

"You are so used to abbreviating things, you just start doing it uncon- 10 sciously on schoolwork and reports and other things," said Eve Bracker, 15, a student at Montclair High School in New Jersey.

Ms. Bracker once handed in a midterm exam riddled with instant-messaging shorthand. "I had an hour to write an essay on Romeo and Juliet," she said. "I just wanted to finish before my time was up. I was writing fast and carelessly. I spelled 'you' 'u.'" She got a C.

Even terms that cannot be expressed verbally are making their way into papers. Melanie Weaver was stunned by some of the term papers she received from a 10th-grade class she recently taught as part of an internship. "They would be trying to make a point in a paper, they would put a smiley face in the end," said Ms. Weaver, who teaches at Alvernia College in Reading, Pa. "If they were presenting an argument and they needed to present an opposite view, they would put a frown."

As Trisha Fogarty, a sixth-grade teacher at Houlton Southside School in Houlton, Maine, puts it, today's students are "Generation Text."

Almost 60 percent of the online population under age 17 uses instant messaging, according to Nielsen/NetRatings. In addition to cellphone text messaging, Weblogs and e-mail, it has become a popular means of flirting, setting up dates, asking for help with homework and keeping in contact with distant friends. The abbreviations are a natural outgrowth of this rapid-fire style of communication.

"They have a social life that centers around typed communication," said   15
Judith S. Donath, a professor at the Massachusetts Institute of Technology's Media Lab who has studied electronic communication. "They have a writing style that has been featured in a teenage social millieu."

Some teachers see the creeping abbreviations as part of a continuing assault of technology on formal written English. Others take it more lightly, saying that it is just part of the larger arc of language evolution.

"To them it's not wrong," said Ms. Harding, who is 28. "It's acceptable because it's in their culture. It's hard enough to teach them the art of formal writing. Now we've got to overcome this new instant-messaging language."

Ms. Harding noted that in some cases the shorthand isn't even shorter. "I understand 'cuz.' but what's with the 'wuz'? It's the same amount of letters as 'was,' so what's the point?" she said.

Deborah Bova, who teaches eighth-grade English at Raymond Park Middle School in Indianapolis, thought her eyesight was failing several years ago when she saw the sentence "B4 we perform, ppl have 2 practice" on a student assignment.

"I thought, 'My God, what is this?'" Ms. Bova said. "Have they lost their   20
minds?"

The student was summoned to the board to translate the sentence into standard English; "Before we perform, people have to practice." She realized that the students thought she was out of touch. "It was like 'Get with it, Bova,'" she said.

Ms. Bova had a student type up a reference list of translations for common instant-messaging expressions. She posted a copy on the bulletin board by her desk and took another one home to use while grading.

Students are sometimes unrepentant.

"They were astonished when I began to point these things out to them," said Henry Assetto, a social studies teacher at Twin Valley High School in Elverson, Pa. "Because I am a history teacher, they did not think a history teacher would be checking up on their grammar or their spelling," said Mr. Asseto, who has been teaching for 34 years.

But Montana Hodgen, 16, another Montclair student, said she was so ac-   25
customed to instant-messaging abbreviations that she often read right past them. She proofread a paper last year only to get it returned with the messaging abbreviations circled in red.

"I was so used to reading what my friends wrote to me on Instant Messenger that I didn't even realize that there was something wrong," she said. She said her ability to separate formal and informal English declined the more she used instant messages. "Three years ago, if I had seen that, I would have been 'What is that?'"

The spelling checker doesn't always help either, students say. For one. Microsoft Word's squiggly red spell-check lines don't appear beneath single letters and numbers such as u, r, c, 2 and 4. Nor do they catch words which have numbers in them such as "18r" and "b4" by default.

Teenagers have essentially developed an unconscious "accent" in their typing. Professor Donath said. "They have gotten facile at typing and they are not paying attention."

Teenagers have long pushed the boundaries of spoken language, introducing words that then become passé with adult adoption. Now teenagers are taking charge and pushing the boundaries of written language. For them, expressions like "oic" (oh I see), "nm" (not much), "jk" (just kidding) and "lol" (laughing out loud), "brb" (be right back), "ttyl" (talk to you later) are as standard as conventional English.

"There is no official English language," said Jesse Sheidlower, the North 30 American editor of the *Oxford English Dictionary*. "Language is spread not because anyone dictates any one thing to happen. The decisions are made by the language and the people who use the language."

Some teachers find the new writing style alarming. "First of all, it's very rude, and it's very careless," said Lois Moran, a middle school English teacher at St. Nicholas School in Jersey City.

"They should be careful to write properly and not to put these little codes in that they are in such a habit of writing to each other," said Ms. Moran, who has lectured her eighth-grade class on such mistakes.

Others say that the instant-messaging style might simply be a fad, something that students will grow out of. Or they see it as an opportunity to teach students about the evolution of language.

"I turn it into a very positive teachable moment for kids in the class," said Erika V. Karres, an assistant professor at the University of North Carolina at Chapel Hill who trains student teachers. She shows students how English has evolved since Shakespeare's time. "Imagine Langston Hughes's writing in quick texting instead of 'Langston writing,'" she said. "It makes teaching and learning so exciting."

Other teachers encourage students to use messaging shorthand to spark 35 their thinking processes. "When my children are writing first drafts. I don't care how they spell anything, as long as they are writing," said Ms. Fogarty, the sixth-grade teacher from Houlton, Maine. "If this lingo gets their thoughts and ideas onto paper quicker, the more power to them." But during editing and revising, she expects her students to switch to standard English.

Ms. Bova shares the view that instant-messaging language can help free up their creativity. With the help of students, she does not even need the cheat sheet to read the shorthand anymore.

"I think it's a plus," she said "and I would say that with a + sign."

---

about the text

1. What criticisms do people level against IM-ing text shortcuts? Why? How does this new technology complicate the challenges students face in mastering the "standard" English required and rewarded at school?

2. Why do you think middle-school English teacher Lois Moran perceives IM style as "very rude" (paragraph 31)? What assumptions must she be making about the nature or purpose of written language? What does using or not using standardized spelling have to do with etiquette? Do you agree with her? Why or why not?

3. U.S. newspaper articles generally avoid taking explicit positions on the issues. Still, a journalist's point of view often comes through. Do you think Lee disapproves of the use of IM conventions in student writing? Why or why not? Give evidence from the article to support your answer.

on language use

4. Lee describes the writing practices of students who use IM conventions and abbreviations in their academic work. Think about your own recent papers. Have you used any of the conventions that Lee describes? Why or why not? If so, how did your instructor respond? How aware are you of the differences between formal writing and writing for social purposes? To what degree do you try to keep this distinction in mind as you write or edit schoolwork?

for writing

5. Take a paragraph of Lee's article and "translate" it into IM abbreviations. Is it possible? Why or why not?

6. Do you and your friends have your own IM abbreviations that others might not understand? What are they and how did they develop? What might the motivation be for *kewl*, or *wuz*, which use the same number of keystrokes as *cool* or *was*? Write a brief dictionary of the abbreviations that you use, giving their meanings and suggesting when it may or may not be appropriate to use them.

7. Do you agree with instructors who believe that "the instant-messaging style might simply be a fad, something that students will grow out of" (paragraph 33). Why or why not? Do you think students *should* "grow out of" IM writing conventions, or do you think that formal writing should expand to accommodate new conventions? For example, r u surprised 2 find sthg like this n ur txtbk? y or y not? Write an essay in which you take a position on the use of IM conventions in formal writing. Consider issues such as audience (for example, do you want your formal writing to be understandable to people other than your peers?) and topic.

ur2Kewl, Romeo

These three cartoons all comment on the relationship between technology and language use.

Zits, by Jim Borgman and Jerry Scott, is a comic strip about fifteen-year-old aspiring rock musician Jeremy Duncan and his friends and family, appears in more than a thousand newspapers. This selection was published in 2003.

Bill Amend's comic strip **FoxTrot**, which appears in dozens of daily newspapers, focuses on the Fox family, especially high school junior Peter, freshman Paige, and Jason, age ten, who spends his life wired. This strip is from 2002.

Roz Chast's cartoons are published frequently in the New Yorker and also in The Sciences and Harvard Business Review. The New Yorker, where this cartoon appeared in February 2002, describes itself as a weekly magazine that "reports and reflects on the world at large with insight, intelligence and authority."

about the texts

1. Why is the *Zits* cartoon funny? How believable is it? Why? Can you imagine a time or situation in which such a thing could happen?

2. Did you find the *FoxTrot* cartoon funny? Why or why not? Can you explain its humor?

3. Why would a cartoon about the IMs of Romeo and Juliet likely appeal to the audience of the *New Yorker*? What couple might have been chosen for a similar cartoon in a teen or entertainment magazine? Why? Would such cartoons be as humorous as this one is? Why or why not?

on language use

4. In what ways do each of the cartoons illustrate themes discussed in the selections by Baron and Lee? For example, how does the exchange between Paige and Jason in *FoxTrot* parody a teacher-student interaction? How does this cartoon illustrate the conflicts between informal writing and the standards teachers use to judge writing?

5. Both the *FoxTrot* cartoon and the one from the *New Yorker* show typical IM writing, geared toward maximum efficiency and minimum keystrokes. Words are represented by a single character—a letter or sometimes a number—common phrases are reduced to initial letters, and capitalization and some punctuation are eliminated. Still, each includes commas. Make note of two or three commas in an IM conversation. Use your usage manual's section on commas as a model, and write guidelines for the use of each of the commas in your conversation. (If you copy parts of the usage manual, be sure to provide appropriate citations.)

on writing

6. *Romeo and Juliet* was of course intended to be performed. Chast's version presents a different kind of dialogue between Romeo and Juliet. With a partner, try using Chast's IM version as a script and read it aloud. Which lines are easy to say, which are difficult, and why? What does this performance let you infer about the differences between spoken language and written language? Is writing simply a system for transcribing speech, as some scholars have claimed? Why or why not? Write an essay, stating your position clearly and presenting a thorough and detailed argument; feel free to provide examples of other kinds of written texts to support your position.

7. Imagine that you witnessed the scene depicted in the *Zits* cartoon. Rewrite it as a story in prose form, giving as much descriptive detail as necessary. How do the two genres—prose narration and cartoon—differ? What are the strengths and weaknesses of each?

Katie Hafner *is a technology writer whose work has appeared in the* New York Times, Business Week, Esquire, *and* Wired; *she is also the author of* Where Wizards Stay Up Late; The Origins of The Internet *(1998, with Matthew Lyon). She has been writing about technology since 1983 . . . the year after the smiley face was born.*

The smiley face in Hafner's 2002 New York Times *article raises questions about what the existence of such a symbol teaches us about the nature of writing and of communication ;-).*

KATIE HAFNER

Happy Birthday :-) to You

A Smiley Face Turns 20

Twenty years ago today, Scott E. Fahlman, a computer scientist at Carnegie Mellon University, posted an electronic message on a university bulletin board system suggesting that a colon, a minus sign and a parenthesis be used to convey a joking tone.

Dr. Fahlman's brief post was almost an aside, made in the midst of a discussion about something else. But his idea caught on, and the typed smiley face and its many variants, known as emoticons, are now fixtures online.

For years Dr. Fahlman, now a researcher at I.B.M., thought that his post, stored on a form of magnetic tape that is now obsolete, had disappeared. But this year some colleagues embarked on a dig through Carnegie Mellon's digital archives in the hope of unearthing the original post. Last week, after months of detective work, they succeeded. The post was a simple one, even briefer than he remembered.

I propose that the following character sequence for joke markers:

:-)

Read it sideways. Actually, it is probably more economical to mark things that are NOT jokes, given current trends. For this, use :-(

The recovery effort was 5 initiated by Mike Jones, a research scientist at Microsoft who worked at Carnegie Mellon when the post was made. Dr. Jones asked people he knew on the university's technical support staff to sift through piles of old backup tapes.

Jeff Baird, supervisor of Unix engineering for the School of Computer Science at Carnegie Mellon, and a handful of colleagues rose to the challenge. Eventually they tracked down the correct magnetic tapes and a corresponding tape drive, decoded the old formats and searched for the right character strings to find the actual posts.

Why expend all the time and effort? "It was an interesting part of departmental history," said Mr. Baird, who estimated that he spent an accumulated five days on the quest.

He said he had other motives, too. "We're archiving these tapes off-site, and we were curious to see if we could still read them," he said. "A lot of them are deteriorating, and it was approaching now or never."

Such diligent sleuthing notwithstanding, it is doubtful that Dr. Fahlman was the first to come up with a typographical means of denoting emotion online. In 1979, for instance, Kevin Mackenzie, a member of a discussion group on the Arpanet, the precursor to the Internet, made a similar suggestion.

"What he did was certainly 10 an emoticon," Dr. Fahlman said of Mr. Mackenzie, who seems to have disappeared from the computer scene. "As far as I know, I'm the first one who did colon, minus, paren. And he didn't have the turn-your-head-sideways idea." Dr. Fahlman added that Mr. Mackenzie's suggestion failed to catch on as his did.

News of the unearthing of Dr. Fahlman's post prompted a spirited discussion at Slashdot .org, a site that bills itself as "News for Nerds." One comment questioned the benefits of emoticons altogether.

"Once upon a time, people could communicate emotions effectively simply through the tone of their writing," wrote a Slashdot reader under the name KnifeEdge. "Now that people have apparently lost this ability, they use a crude text representation of a facial expression.

This is not an improvement."

Dr. Fahlman is no stranger to such criticism. By way of rejoinder, his personal Web site includes a 1973 quotation that he attributes to Vladimir Nabokov.

When an interviewer asked 15 Nabokov how he ranked himself among great writers, Dr. Fahlman said, the writer replied, "I often think there should exist a special typographical sign for a smile—some sort of concave mark, a supine round bracket, which I would now like to trace in reply to your question."

---

about the text

1. If you were born after 1975, the yellow smiley face symbol and the smiley face emoticon have probably always been a part of your life. Were you surprised to learn that the :-) is only twenty years old? Why or why not?

2. Hafner cites a Slashdot reader named KnifeEdge who says that the emoticons are a crude substitute for the ability to convey emotion with the tone of one's writing. If we assume that many writers have the skills to convey quite clearly the tone they intend, why would they not do so when writing on a computer? Why might they prefer typographic conventions like smiley faces?

3. Hafner concludes the article with a 1973 quotation from Russian-born novelist Vladimir Nabokov in which he says that he would like to answer a question by using "a special typographical sign for a smile" (paragraph 14). Why might Nabokov have wished to use a smiley face rather than give a verbal response? Why do you think Hafner used this quotation to conclude her article?

on language use

4. Why have emoticons developed, and why are they so popular? What functions do they serve for you and your friends both within and outside the context of email?

5. Research has shown that female wait staff in restaurants and bars who draw smiley faces on their checks (often along with "Thank you" or "Have a great day") receive larger tips than those who do not. The opposite is true, however, for male wait staff: the

male smiley-face drawers receive lower tips. Why might this be the case?

---

for writing

---

6. Think about your own use (or non-use) of emoticons. How do you use them in your writing? Which emoticons do you use most? For what purpose—to add emphasis? to clarify meanings or intentions? to maintain good contact as you might do with a nod or a smile in f-2-f conversation? How do you decide when and with whom to use emoticons? Write an essay describing and analyzing the functions and meanings of emoticons in your writing or in the things that you read. Make as detailed a description as possible; then look for patterns in the usage. Draw conclusions from the patterns that you find.

7. Emoticons express emotion, something that is universally experienced. You may think,

then, that emoticons would be the same in all parts of the wired world that use the Roman alphabet, but, in fact, they're not. Here, for example, are three common Japanese emoticons:

(^ ^)

\(^o^)/

(-_-) zzz

What do you think they represent? (The answer is at the end of this page). Were you able to see the faces right away? Why or why not? What differences do you notice between these emoticons and the sideways ones more commonly used in the United States? Write an essay comparing and contrasting Japanese and U.S. smiley styles. What expressions are possible in the Japanese orientation that aren't possible with sideways faces? What expressions or gestures are easier with a sideways orientation?

(BTW, the Japanese emoticons represent smiling, happy, WOW!, and Good night.)

Amy's mom on the phone

Amy Borkowsky, a stand-up comic and former advertising executive, has been saving answering machine messages from her mother for more than ten years and in 2002 compiled a book and CD of them. This selection is the transcript of a May 2002 interview with Borkowsky from Morning Edition on *National Public Radio*; sound clips from her mother's messages are interspersed throughout the interview.

For all of the ways that answering machines have aided and simplified our lives, they've added new complications as well. We can convey and receive information fairly promptly, and fulfill social obligations without having to converse directly with someone. However, we may receive unwanted messages, and it may now be more difficult to "get away from it all." As you read and listen, try to imagine the context in which the messages left by Amy's mother are not entirely unwelcome, but rather from part of a generally comfortable and complex relationship between the two women.

Amy's Answering Machine

A Collection of Irritatingly Funny Messages from Mom

Bob Edwards, host: Amy Borkowsky is a stand-up comic who lives in New York.

Ms. Amy Borkowsky: How are you? Nice to meet you.

Edwards: And this is Amy's mother.

(Soundbite of answering machine message)

(Soundbite of beep)

Amy's Mother: Hi, Amila. It's me, honey. Maybe I could come up for a little while, like for a few months maybe?

Edwards: For more than 10 years, Amy Borkowsky has been collecting phone 5 messages from her mother, whom she identifies only as "Mom." The funniest and warmest of those messages have been compiled in a CD and a book titled "Amy's Answering Machine."

Ms. Borkowsky: The mothers, like her peers, love it because they get to use the CD and the book as evidence. Like, 'You see, compared to Amy's mom, I'm really not that bad.'

(Soundbite of answering machine message)

(Soundbite of beep)

Amy's Mother: Amila, I hope you're on your way home. I just heard on the weather; there's a big storm headed for New York. On the weather map, they had snowflakes the size of bagels. So if you have to go out, wrap a scarf around your face to protect it because, you know, there was that man who climbed Mt. Everest and lost his entire nose. OK, honey? Bye-bye.

Edwards: She's always been like this, right?

Ms. Borkowsky: Oh, yes. My mother has always been overprotective. The difference is, it's appropriate when you're like two years old and your mother's asking you if you need to go potty. That's appropriate. But once you, like, hit 30, it's really not necessary.

(Soundbite of answering machine message)

(Soundbite of beep)

Amy's Mother: Hi, Amila. I just was watching the news, and I heard about that little girl who was alone in an apartment for nine days without food. Honey, please, be sure you have what to eat in the fridge, 'cause last time you came to visit, you looked like Olive Oyl. OK, honey. Bye-bye. 10

Edwards: When did you realize she was funny?

Ms. Borkowsky: I'm still waiting to realize that. Other people seem to get a kick out of her. I think it's always easier to laugh at somebody else's mother.

Edwards: Well, this had to be exasperating once.

Ms. Borkowsky: Oh, yeah. Now I'm torn, because part of me, of course, is still frustrated, and another part of me thinks, 'OK. Here comes volume two.'

(Soundbite of answering machine message)

(Soundbite of beep)

Amy's Mother: Yeah, Amila, hi, it's me. I meant to tell you so you don't set off the metal detector at the airport, make sure you don't wear an underwire

bra. A lady on the bus said it happened to a woman she knew, and she   15
claims they frisked her for four hours. Even if she's exaggerating and it
was only two, that's a long time to have a stranger surveying your land.
So just for one day, you may even want to consider going braless. Love
you. Bye.

Ms. Borkowsky: That actually happened. I was going to a fund-raiser in, I
think it was Omaha, and the alarm went off. And they asked me—the
guy said, 'Are you wearing an underwire bra?' And actually, I was, so
sometimes she's right, as much as I hate to admit it.

Edwards: She's afraid of you catching things.

(Soundbite of answering machine message)

(Soundbite of beep)

Amy's Mother: Hello, Amila. I don't know if you heard the latest on the portable stereos, but they're saying that the foam earpiece on the headphones is a prime breeding ground for bacteria. So if you still insist on
walking around with the headphones on, you may want to take an
antibiotic. OK, hon? Bye.

Ms. Borkowsky: She saw some health-watch story that the bacteria that
causes gum disease can be transmitted through saliva, so she says, 'So
if you're planning on kissing any new guys, before you get too involved,
you should just casually ask them if they have gingivitis.' Now how do
you do that casually, you know? It's like, 'So do you have any hobbies or
any inflamed gums?'

(Soundbite of answering machine message)

(Soundbite of beep)

Amy's Mother: Hi, Amila. In *People* magazine, there's an article on a single
Jewish guy who owns a restaurant in Fairbanks, Alaska, and he's now in
New York looking for a wife. You know, my friend Muriel saw the same ar-   20
ticle, so you better hurry up and contact him before her daughter does. At
least if he's from Alaska, you figure he knows how to pick out a fresh
salmon. Call me.

Edwards: What happens when she actually gets you on the phone?

Ms. Borkowsky: Well, when she gets me on the phone, and that does happen
sometimes—you know, I do love her even though she drives me crazy—

and sometimes we actually do talk, but I've found that the only way to get her off the phone in a reasonable amount of time is to tell her that I'm busy with something she would absolutely have to approve of. You know, like, 'Look, Mom, I would love to talk, but I was just getting ready for my date tonight with the single doctor. So can we talk another time?' 'No, no, no, Mom, tomorrow's no good. I'm going to be busy all day eating roughage.'

(Soundbite of answering machine message)

(Soundbite of beep)

Amy's Mother: Yeah, hello, Amila. They just said on TV, 'It's 10 PM, do you know where your children are?' And I'm thinking, 'I don't know,' so I figured I'd call you . . . (unintelligible). Call me when you get this message, honey, OK? Bye-bye.

(Soundbite of beep)

Michael: Hi, Amy, it's Michael. It's like 11:30-something, I think. I just got woken up. Your mom actually called me and wanted to know where you are.

(Soundbite of beep)

Alison: Amy, it's Alison. I just got home. I have seven messages on my machine from your mother.

(Soundbite of beep)

25

Andrew: Hi, Amy. Yeah, it's Andrew. I just got a call from your mom. She wanted to know if you were spending the night at my house. I told her we broke up four years ago.

Ms. Borkowsky: My mother calls me on an average day about three times, and these are long-distance calls. So another problem, you know, is the cost of making a long-distance call, which I really feel is way too low.

Edwards: You may never want a child because of this, huh? I don't know.

Ms. Borkowsky: Well, if I ever had a child, I'm sure that I would worry about them, but my hope would be that I would be able to just forward my mother's calls to my child and cut out the middleman.

Edwards: Comedienne Amy Borkowsky. Her mom's phone messages are featured in a book and CD titled "Amy's Answering Machine." And you can hear more messages from Amy's mom and learn about the history of answering machines on the Web site npr.org.

This is MORNING EDITION from NPR News. I'm Bob Edwards.

(Soundbite of answering machine message)

Amy's Mother: (Singing) How old are you now? How old are you now? Better hurry and find a husband before your ovaries shut down.

All right, that's just a little creativity for my birthday girl. I love you, sweetie.

---

about the text

1. Why are Amy's mother's messages funny? Does Amy's mother intend to be funny? Why or why not? Why do you think she might call and leave her daughter such messages?

2. Amy's mother leaves several messages daily, mainly with unwelcome advice. Might her advice be different if she and Amy were having actual conversations, either on the phone or face to face? Why or why not? What differences might you expect? How are Amy's mother's messages typical of the messages you've heard or left? How are they different?

3. What would Borkowsky and her mother's relationship be like if there were no answering machines? How does this technology help them to maintain their relationship?

on language use

4. Amy's mother seems to call more often when Borkowsky isn't home than when she is. Why might "Mom" want to do that? When do you hope to leave a message for someone rather than speak directly with him or her? Why? When do you screen calls? Why? Is screening calls ever unfair or wrong or impolite?

5. Amy's mother's messages generally end with the same two phrases—"OK honey? Bye-bye." What are the functions of each of those two phrases? Do you do the same things in the messages you leave? Try leaving two or three messages in the next few days without any closing phrases at all. Does it feel peculiar or difficult to do so? Why or why not? Did the people you called comment about your messages? Compare your responses with one or two classmates. Why are closing phrases necessary? How do they compare with conventional ways of concluding face-to-face conversations? Why?

for writing

6. Some people leave long chatty messages on answering machines while others simply hang up. Where do you fall on this continuum? Record the details of the messages that you leave over a few days. Write an essay in which you describe your approach to leaving, or not leaving, messages. You might consider these criteria: topic, length, rate of speech, and self-consciousness. Do you say things in messages that you would likely not say in person? Why? Explain.

Why Not Everyone Likes PowerPoint

Unless you're Rip Van Winkle, you've likely sat through more than your share of Power-Point presentations; odds are you've created some of them. If you haven't, don't worry. You will before graduating, especially if you're majoring in disciplines such as business, communications, or engineering that prepares students for the workplace. Here, we present two essays that evaluate the likely effects of PowerPoint on how we communicate—and how we think. Although Geoffrey Nunberg doesn't claim that PowerPoint means the decline of Western civilization, he is quick to point out some of its (potential) pitfalls. Citing NASA's investigation of the Columbia shuttle disaster as evidence, Clive Thompson is blunter: PowerPoint makes you dumb.

Nunberg is a consulting professor of linguistics at Stanford University and chair of the Usage Panel for the American Heritage Dictionary. The author of several books, most recently The Way We Talk Now *(2001) and* The Future of the Book *(1996), he regularly is featured on the NPR program* Fresh Air *and publishes commentaries in the* New York Times. **The Trouble with PowerPoint** *originally appeared in the business magazine* Fortune, *in December 1999.*

Clive Thompson writes on technology for the New York Times, Wired, *and* Newsday. *In 2002, he was a Knight Science-Journalism Fellow at MIT.* **PowerPoint Makes You Dumb** *originally appeared in the* New York Times *in 2003.*

GEOFFREY NUNBERG

The Trouble with PowerPoint

SLIDES RULE

You've got to hand it to Scott McNealy—he never misses an opportunity to try to stick it to Bill Gates. A couple of years ago the Sun Microsystems CEO went so far as to try to ban the use of PowerPoint at Sun, claiming that employees were wasting colossal amounts of time using the Microsoft software to prepare slides.

It was a dramatic gesture, but this is one tide that isn't about to roll back on command. PowerPoint and other presentation software are de rigueur[1] now wherever business people meet to communicate . . . well, I was about to say "face to face," but that isn't quite accurate when everybody's staring at the screen. The technology has even created a new unit of measure for meting out access to senior management. It used to be that you got ten minutes of a CEO's time; now you get three slides to make your pitch.

The ability to prepare a slide presentation has become an indispensable corporate survival skill. Rank novices can start with the templates that come with the software—"Reporting Progress" (Kandinsky[2]-style blue and red rectangles) or "Communicating Bad News" (a suggestive shade of brown). But most managers have come to realize that slides are too important to pick off the rack. So managers have come up to speed—remarkably quickly.

Corporate types whose interest in media aesthetics was once limited to watching Siskel and Ebert have now become adept at discussing the use of arcane filmic effects like builds, dissolves, and wipes. Or if you're too busy or too old to learn those new tricks, you can use the postmodern ploy of appropriation—a strategy favored by senior managers. Employees with a portfolio of good slides can find themselves as much in demand as a kid with a Nolan Ryan rookie card.

What is the effect of all this? Some say the presentation software explosion is part of a general decline in public speaking—as Stanford professor of communications Cliff Nass puts it, "Try to imagine the 'I have a dream' 5

---

1. *de rigueur* indispensable, compulsory, required (French).

2. **Wassily Kandinsky (1866–1944)** Russian-born abstract painter whose work often features bright colors and geometric shapes.

speech in PowerPoint." But then, it isn't as if public speaking was exactly flourishing in pre-PowerPoint corporations. And you have to give the benefit of the doubt to any technology that promises to make the average corporate speech a bit less numbing.

What's troubling is the way that slides have begun to take on a life of their own, as if they no longer needed talking heads to speak for them. No one asks for a memo or report anymore; now it's just "Send me your slides." Conferences post the slides of their speakers' talks; professors post the slides of their lectures; the clergy post slides of their sermons on the Web.

Making sense of such slides in isolation can be like trying to reconstruct the social life of Pompeii[3] from the graffiti its inhabitants left behind. But that hasn't stopped the format from spreading to other genres, like the Web. The slide aesthetic has even made inroads in the book, the last bastion of connected prose. The other day I went to the business section of a local bookstore and started opening books at random. I had to do this twelve times before I came to two facing pages of text that were uninterrupted by a subhead, illustration, figure, sidebar, or some other graphic distraction.

And like the book and other communications technologies of the past, this one is having its effects on the structure of thought itself. The more PowerPoint presentations you prepare, the more the world seems to package itself into slide-sized chunks, broken down into bullet items or grouped in geometric patterns that have come to have almost talismanic force. A friend of mine who works for a large Silicon Valley company maintains that no proposal can win management buy-in until it has been reduced to three items placed along the sides of a triangle.

You could think of all this as the New Illumination. In many ways we've become the most visual culture since the High Middle Ages. Still, we probably don't want to toss out all the achievements of the age of print. When you move from connected text to bullet items you leave some useful communicative tools behind—verbs, for example. And as lively as a good slide show can be, some ideas are better absorbed in a more leisurely, considered way, with the aid of older technologies like an armchair and a good reading light.

---

3. **Pompeii** a large Italian city that was completely destroyed by the volcano Mt. Vesuvius in 79 C.E. Because of the speed with which the eruption occurred, much of the city was preserved in ash, providing us one of the best archeological examples of daily urban Roman life of that period.

CLIVE THOMPSON

PowerPoint Makes You Dumb

I N AUGUST, the *Columbia* Accident Investigation Board at NASA released Volume 1 of its report on why the space shuttle crashed. As expected, the ship's foam insulation was the main cause of the disaster. But the board also fingered another unusual culprit: PowerPoint, Microsoft's well-known "slideware" program.

NASA, the board argued, had become too reliant on presenting complex information via PowerPoint, instead of by means of traditional ink-and-paper technical reports. When NASA engineers assessed possible wing damage during the mission, they presented the findings in a confusing PowerPoint slide—so crammed with nested bullet points and irregular short forms that it was nearly impossible to untangle. "It is easy to understand how a senior manager might read this PowerPoint slide and not realize that it addresses a life-threatening situation," the board sternly noted.

PowerPoint is the world's most popular tool for presenting information. There are 400 million copies in circulation, and almost no corporate decision takes place without it. But what if PowerPoint is actually making us stupider?

This year, Edward Tufte—the famous theorist of information presentation—made precisely that argument in a blistering screed[1] called *The Cognitive Style of PowerPoint*. In his slim 28-page pamphlet, Tufte claimed that Microsoft's ubiquitous software forces people to mutilate data beyond comprehension. For example, the low resolution of a PowerPoint slide means that it usually contains only about 40 words, or barely eight seconds of reading. PowerPoint also encourages users to rely on bulleted lists, a "faux analytical" technique, Tufte wrote, that dodges the speaker's responsibility to tie his information together. And perhaps worst of all is how PowerPoint renders charts. Charts in newspapers like the *Wall Street Journal* contain up to 120 elements on average, allowing readers to compare large groupings of data. But, as Tufte found, PowerPoint users typically produce charts with only 12 elements. Ultimately, Tufte concluded, PowerPoint is infused with "an attitude of commercialism that turns everything into a sales pitch."

Microsoft officials, of course, beg to differ. Simon Marks, the product manager for PowerPoint, counters that Tufte is a fan of "information density," 5

---

1. **screed** a harangue, a piece of writing that criticizes some subject, often tediously.

shoving tons of data at an audience. You could do that with PowerPoint, he says, but it's a matter of choice. "If people were told they were going to have to sit through an incredibly dense presentation," he adds, "they wouldn't want it." And PowerPoint still has fans in the highest corridors of power: Colin Powell used a slideware presentation in February when he made his case to the United Nations that Iraq possessed weapons of mass destruction.

Of course, given that the weapons still haven't been found, maybe Tufte is onto something. Perhaps PowerPoint is uniquely suited to our modern age of obfuscation—where manipulating facts is as important as presenting them clearly. If you have nothing to say, maybe you need just the right tool to help you not say it.

about the texts

1. In writing for a business audience, Nunberg criticizes the use of PowerPoint in business presentations. Might he feel the same way about academic presentations (class lectures, student presentations, etc.)? Why or why not? How might he alter his argument for an academic audience? What evidence would he likely present?

2. Nunberg quotes a Stanford professor who asks people to "try to imagine that 'I have a dream' speech in PowerPoint" (paragraph 5). Is that a reasonable challenge given the context of this essay? Why or why not? What similarities and differences are there between oratory such as Martin Luther King Jr.'s 1963 speech and the business presentations targeted in Nunberg's essay?

3. Thompson's essay concludes with the example of Colin Powell employing PowerPoint. How does Thompson use this example to make his final point? What is that point? To what extent do you agree with his claim? Explain your reasoning.

on language use

4. How does PowerPoint shape the ways language is used? How does it constrain what is possible? How does it offer new ways of organizing and presenting information? Why do Nunberg and Thompson claim that it may be influencing the way we represent knowledge—that is, the way we think?

5. Nunberg and Thompson aren't alone in their dislike of PowerPoint. Edward Tufte, a professor at Yale University, who has written critically about the influence of PowerPoint on information design and presentation. Go to Tufte's Web site at <edwardtufte.com/tufte/powerpoint>, the cartooned photo that you see of Soviet troops marching before a statue of Stalin illustrates an essay which is critical of PowerPoint. Analyze the cartoon and its message. What is Tufte saying about PowerPoint? How does he use visual elements to make his argument? What do Stalin and his army have to do with PowerPoint? Why might Tufte have chosen this image to illustrate his ideas?

6. Go to <norvig.com/Gettysburg> and explore the parody PowerPoint presentation given there. What are the challenges of distilling prose into slide form? What is gained or lost? Choose another famous text, make your own PowerPoint presentation of it, and show it in class. Did any of the presentations improve on the original text? Why or why not?

| for writing |

7. You've probably seen a few PowerPoint presentations in your classes. Do you find them helpful? Interesting? Have they made learning easier? Why or why not? Is there a difference between using them to introduce new material and using them to review or summarize familiar material? Jot down your impressions of PowerPoint presentations. List their negative and positive characteristics. Write a letter to a faculty committee on classroom technology in which you assess the learning value of PowerPoint presentations in your classes. Evaluate PowerPoint as an instructional tool and make recommendations about when it should (or should not) be used.

Technologies and Religious Practices

••

In these articles, journalists Yilu Zhao and Debra Nussbaum Cohen remind us of the ways in which technology becomes an integral part of the daily religious practices for believers of many faiths. In **Loss of Net Halts an Online Ritual**, *Zhao focuses on how Jewish seminary students' loss of Internet access led them to reflect on the meaning of ritual practices before Yom Kippur, and also on how computer technology often discourages us from communicating with others face to face or by telephone.* **Hot-Synching with a Heavenly Presence** *explains the ways that members of religious communities are using electronic technologies such as personal digital assistants (PDAs) to assist them in practicing their faith. Both Zhao and Cohen have won awards for their journalism, the former for her work on education and the latter for her writings on Jewish identity and spirituality.*

These articles originally appeared in the New York Times; Zhao's article in October 2001, only a few weeks after September 11, and Cohen's article in February 2002. As you read, consider how technology of any kind comes to be a natural part of our daily lives; those of us who use a particular technology soon take it for granted, acting as if it has always been part of human life.

••

YILU ZHAO

Loss of Net Halts an Online Ritual

For Neil Tow, a 23-year-old student at the Jewish Theological Seminary in Morningside Heights, the Internet serves a religious function. Asking acquaintances and friends for forgiveness before Yom Kippur as a way to atone for sins committed against people is an age-old Jewish practice. Mr. Tow and many of his fellow students gave the practice a modern twist by asking for forgiveness through group e-mail messages.

Until this year, that is. Because of the recent terrorist attacks, the company that provided the university's Internet access had to be evacuated and its system shut down. Students and teachers have been unable to log into their e-mail accounts or gain access to the Web through the school's server since Sept. 11.

With the school's Internet connection went Mr. Tow's hope of asking a large number of people for forgiveness

quickly at no cost. He is one of many students to use e-mail for the ritual.

"I used to send out those mass e-mails, which said, 'If I have hurt any of you, I ask for your forgiveness,'" said Mr. Tow, who is studying at the rabbinical school at the university. "It was a good way for someone on a student budget like me to connect with people. It was quick."

So this year, Mr. Tow 5 bought cards—actual paper

ones—and sent them the old-fashioned way, through the mail. "This year, I probably have reached far fewer people than I otherwise would have," he said.

Some of Mr. Tow's schoolmates said that the loss of service was a good thing.

"Asking for forgiveness should be a little hard," said Ethan Linden, a 24-year-old rabbinical student. "It's better this way." Mr. Linden said that in

den said. "It forces us not to be lazy."

Teachers at the school are finding the deprivation similarly refreshing. "After the attack, even the school's internal e-mail system between teachers was down," said Marianna Mott Newirth, the assistant director of media relations at the university. "It forced the professors to go to each other's office and talk in person."

Ann Lapidus Lerner, who 10

cere," Ms. Lerner said. "If someone asks you for forgiveness three times and you don't give it to them, it's not right."

And that situation is exactly what Mr. Linden fears. "There may be people who have asked for forgiveness from me through e-mail and are waiting in limbo for my forgiveness," said Mr. Linden, who hasn't been able to check his In box since Sept. 11. "I may be holding them up for a good judgment."

Mr. Linden knows of at least one e-mail message he would have liked very much to read. It was the letter sent by the dean of the rabbinical school at the seminary soon after the collapse of the twin towers.

Sending e-mail messages before Yom Kippur hits a snag.

previous years he had sent out many individual e-mail messages (as opposed to group messages) asking for forgiveness, but that he had to communicate by phone or in person this year.

"This is something we should do in person," Mr. Lin-

teaches Jewish literature, said that having to live without e-mail complicated the ancient ritual.

"People are supposed to give forgiveness to anyone who asks for it unless they feel the person who has asked for it is not sin-

"It was a great idea, and e-mailing was how you could reach everybody," Mr. Linden said. "There was no other clear, easy way. People would have liked some guidance from the dean, but we couldn't get it."

DEBRA NUSSBAUM COHEN

Hot-Synching with a Heavenly Presence

Derek May is an active member of Fellowship Bible Church in McKinney, Tex., and a devoted user of his hand-held computer, a Handspring Visor.

Mr. May, who bought the Visor two Christmases ago, takes notes with it during the pastor's sermon and records coming events from the church bulletin. When people in his Bible study group ask for prayers for someone in need, he jots down the requests so he doesn't forget. He uses the search function to find specific verses in the King James Bible that he downloaded from a Christian Web site that caters to palmtop users, www.olivetree.com.

And that's not to mention passing along Scripture by infrared. A program called Eternity Gospel Tract can be downloaded at a site created by Mr. May (www.palmstogether .com) and used to beam biblical verses and prayers from one palmtop to another in much the way business people exchange virtual business cards.

"If nothing else," Mr. May said, "it helps me to share my faith a little bit easier."

A growing number of peo- 5 ple are finding that pocket-size computers are useful for religious purposes, from saying a virtual rosary to relaxing with a virtual Zen garden while using the palmtop's stylus to rake images of digital sand.

"Religious tradition and modern technology are not antithetical," said Randall Balmer, a professor of American religion at Barnard College. "People think that religion is a kind of quaint illusion and that it makes no room for technology or modernity. This certainly belies that."

Hundreds of religious software applications for hand-held devices, many of them free, can be downloaded from Web sites created by programmers with

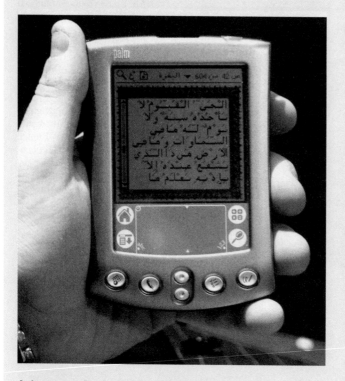

Information Appliances International hopes that its Arabic palmtop software taps into the Muslim market.

sectarian interests and from more general sites like that of Palm Inc. (<palm.com>) and <palmgear.com>. Among the most popular downloads at PalmGear.com is Bible-Reader (more than 30,000 downloads), a program from Olive Tree that offers a wealth of options for searching text and customizing the display screen.

The Bible can be downloaded in many languages. Roman Catholics may want to use the Saint a Day program, while Muslims can consult an Arabic dictionary, a Ramadan timetable or the Prophet Mohammad's last sermon. Mormons can download the teachings of their church's founder, Joseph Smith.

The Lubavitch Hasidim's forthcoming Web site www. palmtorah.org will present a selection of downloadable texts for palmtops, including Torah commentary from rabbis and philosophers as distant as the medieval sage Maimonides and as recent as Menachem Mendel Schneerson, grand rabbi of the Lubavitch Hasidic movement, who died in 1994.

"Our embrace of technology 10 goes back to the understanding that everything created in this world was created to serve Hashem," or God, said Rabbi Zalman Shmotkin, director of www.chabadonline.com, another site founded by the movement.

Ed Kountz, a mobile technologies analyst with Tower-Group, a research and consulting firm in Needham, Mass., describes the use of palmtops as "just a step further in the process of democratizing access to religious information."

"It's easier to carry a P.D.A. [Personal Digital Assistant] than three or four religious texts," he said. "The image of the religious individual carrying a dog-eared Bible is changing with the times."

For Muslims like David Kearns, a convert, the handheld can even deliver the muezzin's call to prayer. Mr. Kearns has set his Sony Clié to beep one minute before it is time to pray. A palmtop program that he created reports the correct time for the prayer ritual, which is pegged to daybreak, noon, afternoon, sunset and last light, wherever the worshiper is.

"If you're planning your day ahead of time, you want to know when that is—especially in the United States, where we don't have mosques every 10 feet to tell us when to pray," said Mr. Kearns, who works for a Web site developer in Washington.

Along with a few Nintendo- 15 type games and the Washington Capitals hockey schedule, Mr. Kearns has loaded the Koran in English onto his Clié. When he prays on Friday, the Muslim holy day, at a mosque at Georgetown University, "they'll have maybe three Korans translated into English and they're all taken," he said. "My Arabic is very poor, and this makes it convenient not to have to carry a translation around."

Information Appliances International [I.A.I.] of Falls Church, Va., developed a system that enables users of Palm-based devices to function in Arabic—including right-to-left text entry, a Graffiti-type program and observance of the Islamic calendar.

I.A.I.'s president and chief executive, Ayad Sleiman, a Lebanese-born Muslim who said he did not consider himself religious, said that the company tapped into a market of observant Muslims hungry for technological tools. I.A.I. has even developed a kind of virtual compass for Palm OS users, Sala Times, which enables them to face Mecca when they pray.

For Jews, the Web site Pilot Yid.com <pilotyid.com> offers downloads of hundreds of Palm-compatible programs, from lists of kosher restaurants to selections from the Talmud. The site's creator, Ari Engel, said that Jewish calendar programs were among the most popular downloads. Most of them sync with the secular calendar already on the organizer to help users anticipate scheduling problems.

"When someone wants to set up a meeting, I don't want it to conflict with a Jewish holiday, so I check it on my Palm," Mr. Engel said.

He said he realized how use- 20 ful palmtops could be while studying in the library as a student at Yeshiva University in Manhattan. At evening prayer time, at least 10 men would congregate to form the required quorum. With few prayer books handy, most would pull out their hand-held organizers.

Mr. Engel began by scanning daily prayers and blessings after meals—things that observant Jews usually carry on laminated paper in their wallets—into a Palm-compatible format and posting them on the Web.

Today his site offers over 200 programs and texts, and 7,000 people have signed up to receive e-mail notification when something new is added. PilotYid also provides links to free programs and shareware based on non-Palm operating systems.

For users with less customary religious interests or enthusiasms, the Software Connection area of Palm Inc.'s Web site offers a Hindu Vedic astrology program, a free program outlining the tenets of China's Falun Gong spiritual movement, and software called Tarot2Go.

Scott Koon, creator of the program Pocket Zendo, available at <amsoftw.tripod.com/idl2.htm>, described it as being "like having a little meditation hall, complete with master, in your pocket." Users determine the timing for a deep-breathing routine in advance, and hand-held beeps cue them to breathe in or out.

Not every devotee of the 25 hand-held organizer considers it an enhancement of the religious experience.

Sister Mary Boys, a nun and a professor of practical theology at Union Theological Seminary in Manhattan, has been using a palmtop for more than a year, but only for secular purposes like keeping track of appointments and phone numbers.

"When I pray I don't want to sit with a computer, which I do enough during the day," she said. "I'm a real book person. I like to hold the little pages in my hands, thank you very much."

about the texts

1. How did the people interviewed by Yilo Zhao and Debra Nussbaum Cohen use technology in practicing their faith? How have these uses of technology given rise to new uses of spoken or written language?

2. According to those interviewed for Zhao's and Cohen's articles, what are the advantages and disadvantages of using new technologies in one's spiritual practice?

on language use

3. For what functions or for what purposes do you use a PDA? How did people accomplish tasks before they used these technologies? Or did they? Do you prefer the new technology? How does it differ from earlier technologies?

for writing

4. These articles invite us to think about how members of religious communities approach their practices in similar ways. Based on these articles and your examination of Web sites devoted to sharing or selling religious products for PDA users, write an essay in which you compare and contrast how members of different religious faiths (including some with which you are not already familiar) use PDAs.

5. For many of us, email has become the preferred medium for personal communication. Is email always appropriate? Would you use email to deliver especially good or bad news? How do you draw the line between what is and is not appropriate for email? What are your criteria? Write an essay in which you argue for the appropriate email limits, using criteria that you establish.

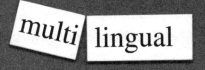

even though English is the dominant language in the United States and the official one in some jurisdictions, many Americans speak another language (or languages) at least some of the time. In the 2000 census, nearly 1 in 5 Americans reported speaking a language other than English at home. The readings in this chapter give you some insight into what it means to be multilingual, how languages and language choice become matters of identity for individuals and groups, and what roles language plays in being or becoming American.

The opening selections provide background for understanding the discussions of specific languages and language communities in the remainder of the chapter. Hyon B. Shin and Rosalind Bruno, demographers for the U.S. Census, report on the results of the 2000 census with regard to language use and the ability to speak English, and Janny Scott compares the number and percentage of foreign-born in the United States in 2000 and in decades past. Not surprisingly, the foreign-born and their children are likely to speak languages other than English. Of course, languages other than English have been spoken in what is today the United States since long before speakers of English arrived; these languages include the Native American languages, Hawaiian, and Spanish. Immigrants across the centuries have brought their languages with them, and some of these languages have fared better than others. Many have influenced and continue to influence American English even as English has influenced them.

Later in the chapter, three groups of readings treat some of the languages that make up the American linguistic mosaic. If you live life in two or more languages, this chapter may give you new perspective on your life experience. If you speak only English, these readings may give you insight into the life and languages of many of your classmates.

HYON B. SHIN AND ROSALIND BRUNO

Census 2000

Language Use and English-Speaking Ability in the USA

In this excerpt from a report produced by the 2000 U.S. Census Bureau, two demographers, Hyon B. Shin and Rosalind Bruno, offer an overview and analysis of data about the presence of languages other than English in the United States. As you'll see, the Census Bureau does not collect information on speakers of other languages because of an interest in sociolinguistics or multilingualism; rather, it collects the data for other specific purposes. Try to discern what these purposes are as you read as well as how these purposes influence what data are collected and how they are analyzed.

THE ABILITY TO COMMUNICATE WITH GOVERNMENT and private service providers, schools, businesses, emergency personnel, and many other people in the United States depends greatly on the ability to speak English.[1] In Census 2000, as in the two previous censuses, the U.S. Census Bureau asked people aged five and over if they spoke a language other than English at home. Among the 262.4 million people aged five and over, 47.0 million (18 percent) spoke a language other than English at home.

This report, part of a series that presents population and housing data collected in Census 2000, presents data on language spoken at home and the ability to speak English of people aged five and over. It describes population distributions and characteristics for the United States, including regions, states, countries, and selected places with populations of 100,000 or more.

The questions illustrated in Figure 1 were asked in the census in 1980, 1990, and 2000. Various questions on language were asked in the censuses from 1890 to 1970, including a question on "mother tongue" (the language spoken in the person's home when he or she was a child).

The first language question in Census 2000 asked respondents whether they spoke a language other than English at home. Those who responded "Yes" to Question 11a were asked what language they spoke. The write-in answers to Question 11b (specific language spoken) were optically scanned and coded. Although linguists recognize several thousand languages in the world, the coding

---

1. The text of this report discusses data for the United States, including the 50 states and the District of Columbia. Data for the Commonwealth of Puerto Rico are shown in Table 2 and Figure 5.

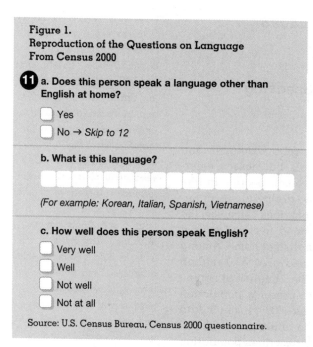

Figure 1.
Reproduction of the Questions on Language From Census 2000

11 **a. Does this person speak a language other than English at home?**

☐ Yes

☐ No → *Skip to 12*

b. What is this language?

☐☐☐☐☐☐☐☐☐☐☐☐☐☐☐☐☐☐☐☐

(For example: Korean, Italian, Spanish, Vietnamese)

c. How well does this person speak English?

☐ Very well

☐ Well

☐ Not well

☐ Not at all

Source: U.S. Census Bureau, Census 2000 questionnaire.

operation used by the Census Bureau put the reported languages into about 380 categories of single languages or languages families.[2]

For people who answered "Yes" to Question 11a, Question 11c asked respondents to indicate how well they spoke English. Respondents who said they spoke English "Very well" were considered to have no difficulty with English. Those who indicated they spoke English "Well," "Not well," or "Not at all" were considered to have difficulty with English—identified also as people who spoke English less than "Very well."

THE NUMBER AND PERCENTAGE OF PEOPLE IN THE UNITED STATES WHO SPOKE A LANGUAGE OTHER THAN ENGLISH AT HOME INCREASED BETWEEN 1990 AND 2000.

In 2000, 18 percent of the total population aged 5 and over, or 47.0 million people, reported they spoke a language other than English at home.[3] These figures were up from 14 percent (31.8 million) in 1990 and 11 percent (23.1 million) in 1980. The number of people who spoke a language other than English at home grew by 38 percent in the 1980s and by 47 percent in the 1990s. While the population aged 5 and over grew by one-fourth from 1980 to 2000, the number who spoke a language other than English at home more than doubled.

---

2. More detailed information on languages and language coding can be found in "Summary File 3: 2000 Census of Population and Housing Technical Documentation" Issued December 2002 <census.gov/prod/cen2000/doc/sf3.pdf>.

3. The estimates in this report are based on responses from a sample of the population. As with all surveys, estimates may vary from the actual values because of sampling variation or other factors. All statements made in this report have undergone statistical testing and are significant at the 90-percent confidence level unless otherwise noted.

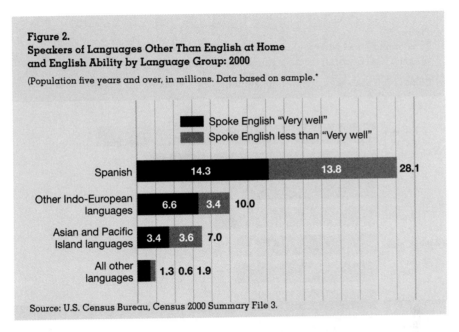

Figure 2.
Speakers of Languages Other Than English at Home and English Ability by Language Group: 2000
(Population five years and over, in millions. Data based on sample.*)

Spoke English "Very well"
Spoke English less than "Very well"

Spanish — 14.3 | 13.8 | 28.1
Other Indo-European languages — 6.6 | 3.4 | 10.0
Asian and Pacific Island languages — 3.4 | 3.6 | 7.0
All other languages — 1.3 | 0.6 | 1.9

Source: U.S. Census Bureau, Census 2000 Summary File 3.

In 2000, most people who spoke a language other than English at home reported they spoke English "Very well" (55 percent or 25.6 million people). When they are combined with those who spoke only English at home, 92 percent of the population aged five and over had no difficulty speaking English. The proportion of the population aged five and over who spoke English less than "Very well" grew from 4.8 percent in 1980, to 6.1 percent in 1990, and to 8.1 percent in 2000.

In Figure 2, the number of speakers of the four major language groups (Spanish, Other Indo-European languages, Asian and Pacific Island languages, and All other languages) is shown by how well they spoke English. Spanish was the largest of the four major language groups, and just over half of the 28.1 million Spanish speakers spoke English "Very well."

Other Indo-European language speakers composed the second largest group, with 10.0 million speakers, almost two-thirds of whom spoke English "Very well." Slightly less than half of the 7.0 million Asian and Pacific Island-

* For information on confidentiality protection, nonsampling error, sampling error, and definitions in all figures and tables, see <census.gov/prod/cen2000/doc/sf3.pdf>.

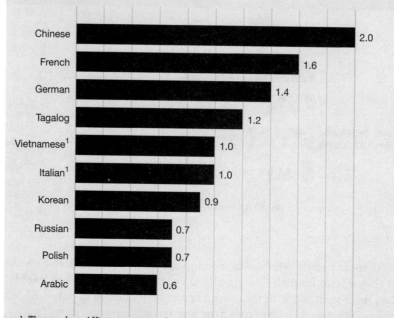

Figure 3.
Ten Languages Most Frequently Spoken at Home
Other Than English and Spanish: 2000

(Population five years and over, in millions. Data based on sample.)

Language	Speakers (millions)
Chinese	2.0
French	1.6
German	1.4
Tagalog	1.2
Vietnamese[1]	1.0
Italian[1]	1.0
Korean	0.9
Russian	0.7
Polish	0.7
Arabic	0.6

1. The number of Vietnamese speakers and the number of Italian speakers were not statistically different from one another.

Note: The estimates in this figure vary from actual values due to sampling errors. As a result, the number of speakers of some languages shown in this figure may not be statistically different from the number of speakers of languages not shown in this figure.

Source: U.S. Census Bureau, Census 2000 Summary File 3.

language speakers spoke English "Very well" (3.4 million). Of the 1.9 million people who composed the All other language category, 1.3 million spoke English "Very well."

After English and Spanish, Chinese was the language most commonly spoken at home (2.0 million speakers), followed by French (1.6 million speakers) and German (1.4 million speakers, see Figure 3). Reflecting historical

Table 1. Twenty Languages Most Frequently Spoken at Home by English Ability for the Population Five Years and Over: 1990 and 2000

(Data based on sample.)

Language spoken at home	1990		2000					
				Number of speakers				
				Total	English-speaking ability			
	Rank	Number of speakers	Rank	Total	Very well	Well	Not well	Not at all
United States	(X)	230,445,777	(X)	262,375,152	(X)	(X)	(X)	(X)
English only	(X)	198,600,798	(X)	215,423,557	(X)	(X)	(X)	(X)
Total non-English	(X)	31,844,979	(X)	46,951,595	25,631,188	10,333,556	7,620,719	3,366,132
Spanish	1	17,339,172	1	28,101,052	14,349,796	5,819,408	5,130,400	2,801,448
Chinese	5	1,249,213	2	2,022,143	855,689	595,331	408,597	162,526
French	2	1,702,176	3	1,643,838	1,228,800	269,458	138,002	7,578
German	3	1,547,099	4	1,382,613	1,078,997	219,362	79,535	4,719
Tagalog	6	843,251	5	1,224,241	827,559	311,465	79,721	5,496
Vietnamese[1]	9	507,069	6	1,009,627	342,594	340,062	270,950	56,021
Italian[1]	4	1,308,648	7	1,008,370	701,220	195,901	99,270	11,979
Korean	8	626,478	8	894,063	361,166	268,477	228,392	36,028
Russian	15	241,798	9	706,242	304,891	209,057	148,671	43,623
Polish	7	723,483	10	667,414	387,694	167,233	95,032	17,455
Arabic	13	355,150	11	614,582	403,397	140,057	58,595	12,533
Portuguese[2]	10	429,860	12	564,630	320,443	125,464	90,412	28,311
Japanese[2]	11	427,657	13	477,997	241,707	146,613	84,018	5,659
French Creole	19	187,658	14	453,368	245,857	121,913	70,961	14,637
Greek	12	388,260	15	365,436	262,851	65,023	33,346	4,216
Hindi[3]	14	331,484	16	317,057	245,192	51,929	16,682	3,254
Persian	18	201,865	17	312,085	198,041	70,909	32,959	10,176
Urdu[3]	(NA)	(NA)	18	262,900	180,018	56,736	20,817	5,329
Gujarathi	26	102,418	19	235,988	155,011	50,637	22,522	7,818
Armenian	20	149,694	20	202,708	108,554	48,469	31,868	13,817
All other languages	(X)	3,182,546	(X)	4,485,241	2,831,711	1,060,052	479,969	113,509

NA Not available.   X Not applicable.
1. In 2000, the number of Vietnamese speakers and the number of Italian speakers were not statistically different from one another.
2. In 1990, the number of Portuguese speakers and the number of Japanese speakers were not statistically different from one another.
3. In 1990, Hindi included those who spoke Urdu.
Note: The estimates in this table vary from actual values due to sampling errors. As a result, the number of speakers of some languages shown in this table may not be statistically different from the number of speakers of languages not shown in this table.
Source: U.S. Census Bureau, Census 2000 Summary File 3.

Table 2. Language Use and English-Speaking Ability for the Population Five Years and Over for the United States, Regions, and States and for Puerto Rico: 1990 and 2000

(Data based on sample.)

Area	1990			2000					1990 and 2000 percent change in "Spoke a language other than English at home"
	Population 5 years and over	Spoke a language other than English at home	Percent	Population 5 years and over	Spoke a language other than English at home	Percent	Spoke English less than "Very well"	Percent	
United States	230,445,777	31,844,979	13.8	262,375,152	46,951,595	17.9	21,320,407	8.1	47.4
Region									
Northeast	47,319,352	7,824,285	16.5	50,224,209	10,057,312	20.0	4,390,538	8.7	28.5
Midwest	55,272,756	3,920,660	7.1	60,054,144	5,623,538	9.4	2,398,120	4.0	43.4
South	79,248,852	8,669,631	10.9	93,431,879	14,007,396	15.0	6,149,756	6.6	61.6
West	48,604,817	11,430,403	23.5	58,664,920	17,263,330	29.4	8,381,993	14.3	51.0
State									
Alabama	3,759,802	107,866	2.9	4,152,278	162,483	3.9	63,917	1.5	50.6
Alaska	495,425	60,165	12.1	579,740	82,758	14.3	39,842	5.3	37.6
Arizona	3,374,806	700,287	20.8	4,752,724	1,229,237	25.9	539,937	11.4	75.5
Arkansas	2,186,665	60,781	2.8	2,492,205	123,755	5.0	57,709	2.3	103.6
California	27,383,547	8,619,334	31.5	31,416,629	12,401,756	39.5	6,277,779	20.0	43.9
Colorado	3,042,986	320,631	10.5	4,006,285	604,019	15.1	267,504	6.7	88.4
Connecticut	3,060,000	466,175	15.2	3,184,514	583,913	18.3	234,799	7.4	25.3
Delaware	617,720	42,327	6.9	732,378	69,533	9.5	28,380	3.9	64.3
District of Columbia ..	570,284	71,348	12.5	539,658	90,417	16.8	38,236	7.1	26.7
Florida	12,095,284	2,098,315	17.3	15,043,603	3,473,864	23.1	1,554,865	10.3	65.6
Georgia	5,984,188	284,546	4.8	7,594,476	751,438	9.9	374,251	4.9	164.1
Hawaii	1,026,209	254,724	24.8	1,134,351	302,125	26.6	143,505	12.7	18.6
Idaho	926,703	58,995	6.4	1,196,793	111,879	9.3	46,539	3.9	89.6
Illinois	10,585,838	1,499,112	14.2	11,547,505	2,220,719	19.2	1,054,722	9.1	48.1
Indiana	5,146,160	245,826	4.8	5,657,818	362,082	6.4	143,427	2.5	47.3
Iowa	2,583,526	100,391	3.9	2,738,499	160,022	5.8	68,108	2.5	59.4
Kansas	2,289,615	131,604	5.7	2,500,360	218,655	8.7	98,207	3.9	66.1
Kentucky	3,434,955	86,482	2.5	3,776,230	148,473	3.9	58,871	1.6	71.7
Louisiana	3,886,353	391,994	10.1	4,153,367	382,364	9.2	116,907	2.8	-2.5
Maine	1,142,122	105,441	9.2	1,204,164	94,966	7.8	24,063	2.0	-10.9
Maryland	4,425,285	395,051	8.9	4,945,043	622,714	12.6	246,287	5.0	57.6
Massachusetts	5,605,751	852,228	15.2	5,954,249	1,115,570	18.7	459,073	7.7	30.9
Michigan	8,594,737	569,807	6.6	9,268,782	781,381	8.4	294,606	3.2	37.1
Minnesota	4,038,361	227,161	5.6	4,591,491	389,988	8.5	167,511	3.6	71.7
Mississippi	2,378,805	66,516	2.8	2,641,453	95,522	3.6	36,059	1.4	43.6
Missouri	4,748,704	178,210	3.8	5,226,022	264,281	5.1	103,019	2.0	48.3
Montana	740,218	37,020	5.0	847,362	44,331	5.2	12,663	1.5	19.7
Nebraska	1,458,904	69,872	4.8	1,594,700	125,654	7.9	57,772	3.6	79.8
Nevada	1,110,450	146,152	13.2	1,853,720	427,972	23.1	207,687	11.2	192.8
New Hampshire	1,024,621	88,796	8.7	1,160,340	96,088	8.3	28,073	2.4	8.2
New Jersey	7,200,696	1,406,148	19.5	7,856,268	2,001,690	25.5	873,088	11.1	42.4
New Mexico	1,390,048	493,999	35.5	1,689,911	616,964	36.5	201,055	11.9	24.9

Table 2. (cont.) Language Use and English-Speaking Ability for the Population Five Years and Over for the United States, Regions, and States and for Puerto Rico: 1990 and 2000

(Data based on sample.)

Area	1990			2000					1990 and 2000 percent change in "Spoke a language other than English at home"
	Population 5 years and over	Spoke a language other than English at home	Percent	Population 5 years and over	Spoke a language other than English at home	Percent	Spoke English less than "Very well"	Percent	
New York	16,743,048	3,908,720	23.3	17,749,110	4,962,921	28.0	2,310,256	13.0	27.0
North Carolina	6,172,301	240,866	3.9	7,513,165	603,517	8.0	297,858	4.0	150.6
North Dakota	590,839	46,897	7.9	603,106	37,976	6.3	11,003	1.8	−19.0
Ohio	10,063,212	546,148	5.4	10,599,968	648,493	6.1	234,459	2.2	18.7
Oklahoma	2,921,755	145,798	5.0	3,215,719	238,532	7.4	98,990	3.1	63.6
Oregon	2,640,482	191,710	7.3	3,199,323	388,669	12.1	188,958	5.9	102.7
Pennsylvania	11,085,170	806,876	7.3	11,555,538	972,484	8.4	368,257	3.2	20.5
Rhode Island	936,423	159,492	17.0	985,184	196,624	20.0	83,624	8.5	23.3
South Carolina	3,231,539	113,163	3.5	3,748,669	196,429	5.2	82,279	2.2	73.6
South Dakota	641,226	41,994	6.5	703,820	45,575	6.5	16,376	2.3	(NS)
Tennessee	4,544,743	131,550	2.9	5,315,920	256,516	4.8	108,265	2.0	95.0
Texas	15,605,822	3,970,304	25.4	19,241,518	6,010,753	31.2	2,669,603	13.9	51.4
Utah	1,553,351	120,404	7.8	2,023,875	253,249	12.5	105,691	5.2	110.3
Vermont	521,521	30,409	5.8	574,842	34,075	5.9	9,305	1.6	(NS)
Virginia	5,746,419	418,521	7.3	6,619,266	735,191	11.1	303,729	4.6	75.7
Washington	4,501,879	403,173	9.0	5,501,398	770,886	14.0	350,914	6.4	91.2
West Virginia	1,686,932	44,203	2.6	1,706,931	45,895	2.7	13,550	0.8	3.8
Wisconsin	4,531,134	263,638	5.8	5,022,073	368,712	7.3	148,910	3.0	39.9
Wyoming	418,713	23,809	5.7	462,809	29,485	6.4	8,919	1.9	23.8
Puerto Rico	3,522,037	(NA)	(NA)	3,515,228	3,008,567	85.6	2,527,156	71.9	(NA)

NA Not available. NS Not statistically different from zero at the 90-percent confidence level.
Source: U.S. Census Bureau, Census 2000 Summary File 3 and 19909 Census Summary Tape File 3.

patterns of immigration, the numbers of Italian, Polish, and German speakers fell between 1990 and 2000, while the number of speakers of many other languages increased.

Spanish speakers grew by about 60 percent and Spanish continued to be the non-English language most frequently spoken at home in the United States. The Chinese language, however, jumped from the fifth to the second most widely spoken non-English language, as the number of Chinese speakers rose from 1.2 to 2.0 million people (see Table 1).[4] The number of Vietnamese

4. The changes in ranks between 1990 and 2000 have not been tested and may not be statistically significant.

FOUR MAJOR LANGUAGE GROUPS

Spanish includes those who speak Ladino.

Other Indo-European languages include most languages of Europe and the Indic languages of India. These include the Germanic languages, such as German, Yiddish, and Dutch; the Scandinavian languages, such as Swedish and Norwegian; the Romance languages, such as French, Italian, and Portuguese; the Slavic languages, such as Russian, Polish, and Serbo-Croatian; the Indic languages, such as Hindi, Gujarathi, Punjabi, and Urdu; Celtic languages; Greek; Baltic languages; and Iranian languages.

Asian and Pacific Island languages include Chinese; Korean; Japanese; Vietnamese; Hmong; Khmer; Lao; Thai; Tagalog or Pilipino; the Dravidian languages of India, such as Telegu, Tamil, and Malayalam; and other languages of Asia and the Pacific, including the Philippine, Polynesian, and Micronesian languages.

All other languages include Uralic languages, such as Hungarian; the Semitic languages, such as Arabic and Hebrew; languages of Africa; native North American languages, including the American Indian and Alaska native languages; and some indigenous languages of Central and South America.[*]

---

[*] Languages you've never heard of? For information on the world's languages, visit *Ethnologue:*

speakers doubled over the decade, from about 507,000 speakers to just over 1 million speakers.

Of the 20 non-English languages most frequently spoken at home shown in Table 1, the largest proportional increase was for Russian speak-ers, who nearly tripled from 242,000 to 706,000. The second largest increase was for French Creole speakers (the language group that includes Haitian Creoles), whose numbers more than doubled from 188,000 to 453,000.

THE GEOGRAPHIC DISTRIBUTION OF PEOPLE WHO SPOKE A LANGUAGE OTHER THAN ENGLISH AT HOME

This section discusses the geographic distribution of the population aged five and over who stated in Census 2000 that they spoke a language other than English at home.

Table 3. Language Spoken at Home for the Population 5 Years and Over Who Spoke a Language Other Than English at Home for the United States and Regions: 1990 and 2000

(Data based on sample.)

Area	Spanish			Other Indo-European languages			Asian and Pacific Island languages			All other languages		
	1990	2000	Percent change	1990	2000	Percent change	1990	2000	Percent change	1990	2000	Percent change
United States ...	17,345,064	28,101,052	62.0	8,790,133	10,017,989	14.0	4,471,621	6,960,065	55.6	1,238,161	1,872,489	51.2
Region												
Northeast	3,133,043	4,492,168	43.4	3,547,154	3,778,958	6.5	845,442	1,348,621	59.5	298,646	437,584	46.5
Midwest	1,400,651	2,623,391	87.3	1,821,772	1,861,729	2.2	459,524	760,107	65.4	238,713	378,311	58.5
South	5,815,486	9,908,653	70.4	1,909,179	2,390,266	25.2	715,235	1,277,618	78.6	229,731	430,859	87.5
West	6,995,884	11,076,840	58.3	1,512,028	1,987,036	31.4	2,451,420	3,573,719	45.8	471,071	625,735	32.8

Source: U.S. Census Bureau, Census 2000 Summary File 3 and 1990 Census Summary Tape File 3.

THE WEST HAD THE GREATEST NUMBER AND PROPORTION OF NON-ENGLISH-LANGUAGE SPEAKERS.[5]

People who spoke languages other than English at home were not distributed equally across or within regions in 2000.[6] While the West had only slightly more than one-fifth of the U.S. population aged five and over, it was home to more than one-third (37 percent) of all non-English-language speakers, the highest proportion of any region (see Table 2). Within regions, the

---

5. Hereafter, this report uses the term "non-English-language speakers" to refer to people who spoke a language other than English at home, regardless of their ability to speak English (see Table 1).

6. The Northeast region includes the states of Connecticut, Maine, Massachusetts, New Hampshire, New Jersey, New York, Pennsylvania, Rhode Island, and Vermont. The Midwest region includes the states of Illinois, Indiana, Iowa, Kansas, Michigan, Minnesota, Missouri, Nebraska, North Dakota, Ohio, South Dakota, and Wisconsin. The South region includes the states of Alabama, Arkansas, Delaware, Florida, Georgia, Kentucky, Louisiana, Maryland, Mississippi, North Carolina, Oklahoma, South Carolina, Tennessee, Texas, Virginia, West Virginia, and the District of Columbia, a state equivalent. The West region includes the states of Alaska, Arizona, California, Colorado, Hawaii, Idaho, Montana, Nevada, New Mexico, Oregon, Utah, Washington, and Wyoming.

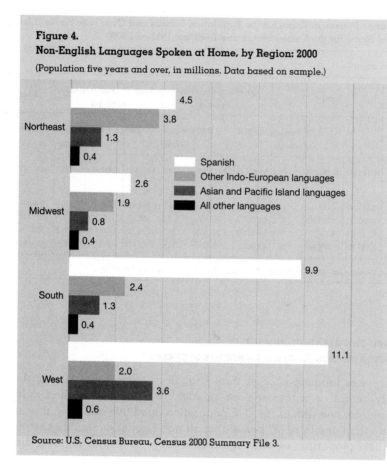

Figure 4.
Non-English Languages Spoken at Home, by Region: 2000
(Population five years and over, in millions. Data based on sample.)

Northeast
- Spanish: 4.5
- Other Indo-European languages: 3.8
- Asian and Pacific Island languages: 1.3
- All other languages: 0.4

Midwest
- Spanish: 2.6
- Other Indo-European languages: 1.9
- Asian and Pacific Island languages: 0.8
- All other languages: 0.4

South
- Spanish: 9.9
- Other Indo-European languages: 2.4
- Asian and Pacific Island languages: 1.3
- All other languages: 0.4

West
- Spanish: 11.1
- Other Indo-European languages: 2.0
- Asian and Pacific Island languages: 3.6
- All other languages: 0.6

Source: U.S. Census Bureau, Census 2000 Summary File 3.

proportion who spoke a non-English language at home was 29 percent in the West, 20 percent in the Northeast, 15 percent in the South, and only 9 percent in the Midwest.

Reflecting the higher proportion of speakers of non-English languages in the West, people in that region were more likely than those in the other regions to have difficulty with English. In 2000, 14 percent of all people aged five and over in the West spoke English less than "Very well"—compared with 9 percent in the Northeast, 7 percent in the South, and 4 percent in the Midwest.

Figure 4 Illustrates the prevalence of the four major non-English-language groups spoken in each region. Spanish was spoken more than any other language group in all regions. The West and the South combined had about three times the number of Spanish speakers (21.0 million) as the Northeast and the Midwest combined (7.1 million). In the Northeast and the Midwest, Spanish speakers composed slightly less than half of all non-English-language speakers, while in the South and the West, they represented around two-thirds (71 percent and 64 percent, respectively), in large part because of the geographic proximity to Mexico and other Spanish-speaking countries. In the Northeast, the Midwest, and the South, speakers of Other Indo-European languages made up the second largest non-English-language speaking group, while in the West, the second largest group was speakers of Asian and Pacific Island languages. Half of Asian and Pacific Island-language speakers lived in the West in 2000.

Table 3 shows the change in the number of speakers of Spanish, Other Indo-European languages, Asian and Pacific Island languages, and All other languages between 1990 and 2000. The largest percentage increase of Spanish speakers was in the Midwest. Asian and Pacific Island-language speakers increased most rapidly in the South and the Midwest. Although the number of Spanish speakers grew in all regions, more than three-fourths of that growth was in the West and the South. The number of Asian and Pacific Island-language speakers grew substantially in all regions, with the greatest numerical increase in the West, which was home to more than half of all Asian and Pacific Island-language speakers in both years.

MORE THAN ONE-QUARTER OF THE POPULATION IN SEVEN STATES SPOKE A LANGUAGE OTHER THAN ENGLISH AT HOME IN 2000.

California had the largest percentage of non-English-language speakers (39 percent), followed by New Mexico (37 percent), Texas (31 percent), New York (28 percent), Hawaii (27 percent), Arizona, and New Jersey (each about 26 percent, see Table 2). The five states with fewer than 5 percent of the population who spoke a language other than English at home were all in the South—Tennessee (4.8 percent), Alabama and Kentucky (each 3.9 percent), Mississippi (3.6 percent), and West Virginia (2.7 percent).

Eight states had over 1 million non-English-language speakers in 2000, led by California (12.4 million) with more than twice the number of any other state. Texas had the second largest number of non-English-language speakers (6.0 million), followed by New York (5.0 million), Florida (3.5 million), Illinois (2.2 million), New Jersey (2.0 million), Arizona (1.2 million), and Massachusetts (1.1 million).

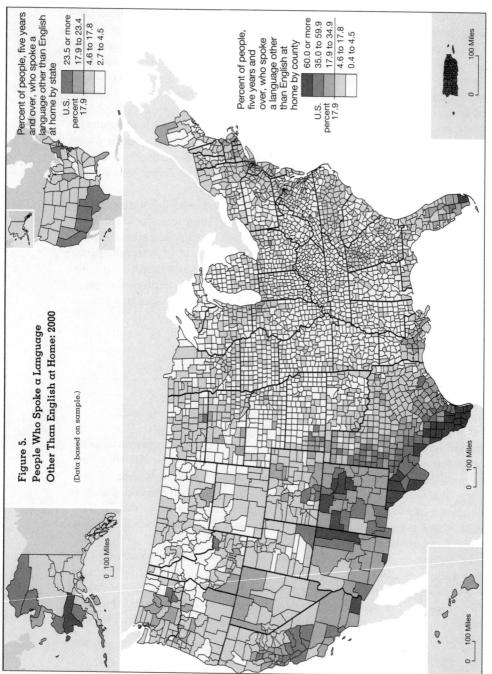

Figure 5.
People Who Spoke a Language Other Than English at Home: 2000

(Data based on sample.)

Percent of people, five years and over, who spoke a language other than English at home by state

U.S. percent 17.9

- 23.5 or more
- 17.9 to 23.4
- 4.6 to 17.8
- 2.7 to 4.5

Percent of people, five years and over, who spoke a language other than English at home by county

U.S. percent 17.9

- 60.0 or more
- 35.0 to 59.9
- 17.9 to 34.9
- 4.6 to 17.8
- 0.4 to 4.5

0   100 Miles

Source: U.S. Census Bureau, Census 2000 Summary File 3. American FactFinder at <factfinder.census.gov> provides census data and mapping tools.

During the 1990s, California surpassed New Mexico as the state with the 20 largest proportion of non-English-language speakers. While the proportion of non-English-language speakers in New Mexico increased slightly from 36 percent to 37 percent, the proportion in California jumped from 31 percent to 39 percent.

The number of non-English-language speakers at least doubled in six states from 1990 to 2000. The largest percentage increase occurred in Nevada, where the number increased by 193 percent. Nevada also had the highest rate of population increase during the decade. Georgia's non-English-language-speaking residents increased by 164 percent, followed by North Carolina (151 percent), Utah (110 percent), Arkansas (104 percent), and Oregon (103 percent).[7]

Since 1990, the proportion of people who spoke a language other than English at home decreased in three states. North Dakota had the largest decrease (19 percent), followed by Maine (11 percent) and Louisiana (2 percent). These three states also had low rates of population growth from 1990 to 2000.

COUNTIES WITH A LARGE PROPORTION OF THE POPULATION WHO SPOKE A LANGUAGE OTHER THAN ENGLISH AT HOME WERE CONCENTRATED IN BORDER STATES.

Figure 5 illustrates the high proportions of people who spoke a language other than English at home in 2000 in the states that border Mexico, the Pacific Ocean, or the Atlantic Ocean. Some of these "border states" were entry points for many immigrants.

In 2000, in about 1 percent of the 3,141 counties in the United States, more than 60 percent of the population spoke a language other than English at home. In seven counties, more than 80 percent of the population spoke a non-English language at home—Maverick, Webb, Starr, Kenedy, Zavala, Presidio, and Hidalgo—all in Texas. All but one of the 20 counties with the highest proportions of non-English-language speakers were located in Texas (Santa Cruz County, Arizona, being the exception).

Figure 5 shows the high proportion of non-English-language speakers 25 in counties with large cities, such as Atlanta, Chicago, Miami, and New York City. Other counties with relatively high proportions of non-English-language speakers included concentrations of people who spoke Native American languages. For example, in Bethel Census Area, Alaska, 66 percent of the population spoke a language other than English at home, and

---

7. The percentage increases between Arkansas and Utah and between Arkansas and Oregon were not statistically different from one another.

97 percent of the non-English-language speakers spoke a Native North American language. The Navajo speakers in the Navajo Nation Indian Reservation, which spanned several counties throughout Arizona, New Mexico, and Utah, accounted for a large proportion of the population who spoke a language other than English at home in these counties.

In some counties, relatively high proportions of non-English-language speakers are found in small, rural populations. For example, the proportions of non-English-language speakers were 25 percent in Logan County and 36 percent in McIntosh County in North Dakota and 33 percent in McPherson County in South Dakota.[8] In these three counties, each with a population of fewer than 4,000, German speakers were predominant among non-English-language speakers: 95.3 percent, 98.1 percent, and 99.6 percent, respectively.[9]

Among all counties, the median percentage of the population who spoke a language other than English at home was 4.6 percent.[10] The fact that the proportion was below 4.6 percent in one half of all counties, while the national average was 17.9 percent, reflects the large number of counties (primarily non-metropolitan counties in the Midwest and the South) with relatively small populations and with low proportions of non-English-language speakers.

Figure 5 illustrates the low proportions of non-English-language speakers in many counties in the South and the Midwest, including Alabama, Arkansas, Iowa, Kentucky, Michigan, Mississippi, Missouri, Tennessee, West Virginia, and Wisconsin. In West Virginia, all but two of the fifty-five counties had a proportion of non-English-language speakers below 4.6 percent.

★   ★   ★

---

8. The proportions of non-English-language speakers in McIntosh County, North Dakota, and McPherson County, South Dakota, were not statistically different from each other.

9. The proportions of German speakers among non-English-language speakers in Logan County and McIntosh County, North Dakota, were not statistically different from each other.

10. The median percentage is a point estimate based on a sample.

ABOUT CENSUS 2000

WHY CENSUS 2000 ASKED ABOUT LANGUAGE USE AND ENGLISH-SPEAKING ABILITY

The question on language use and English-speaking ability provides government agencies with information for programs that serve the needs of people who have difficulty speaking English. Under the Voting Rights Act, information about language ability is needed to meet statutory requirements for making voting materials available in minority languages.

The Bilingual Education Program uses data on language to allocate 30 grants to school districts for children with limited English proficiency. These data also are needed for local agencies developing services for the elderly under the Older Americans Act.

about the text

1. This report contains a great deal of information about the number of people who speak languages other than English in the United States. Which parts of this report did you find surprising? Why?

2. What is the logic of asking census questions of any kind about languages other than English in the U.S. census? What other data about these languages and their speakers might be beneficial? Why?

3. The language data in the U.S. census are self-reported; someone in the household reports for everyone living there. What are the advantages and disadvantages of self-report data?

4. Census data are often used both by those who argue that the United States should declare English its official language and by those who are against such an action. Find data in the report that could be used to advance each argument, and explain how they would be useful.

on language use

5. Examine Table 2 and Figure 5, finding the place(s) where you are from and/or the place where you attend school. In each of these places, what is the percentage of people who spoke a language other than English at home in 2000? How did this percentage change between 1990 and 2000? Are these results surprising to you? Why or why not?

6. Figure 2 shows one way of displaying the data on which this section of the report is based. What are the benefits of this figure compared with the prose account of the same data? Why?

7. Has the number of speakers of other languages where you live increased, decreased, or remained the same during your lifetime? Have the languages spoken changed? The origins of the speakers? If so, why do you think these changes have occurred?

for writing

8. Visit the language section of the Census 2000 Web site (you can access that link through <wwnorton.com/write/language>). See what you can learn about your home community and state or the community where you now live. You may want to explore how the presence of languages other than English changed between 1990 and 2000, or how a language spoken by your ancestors has fared, whether locally or nationally. Use the data you access to write a report about the status of a language other than English found in the United States today.

9. Find a different figure or table about languages other than English from the Census 2000 Web site. Write a summary of it, following Shin and Bruno's model in this report.

Using data from the 2000 Census, Janny Scott, who has written for the New York Times
since 1994, gives historical context for recent immigration to the United States. In this February 7, 2002, article from the Times she not only provides facts and figures about immigration but also explores what the significance of immigration may be for the country as a
whole. As you read, think about the consequences of the situation she describes for bi-
and multilingualism in the past, present, and future of the United States.

JANNY SCOTT

Foreign Born in U.S. at Record High

The number of foreign-born residents and children of immigrants in the United States has reached the highest level in history, according to a Census Bureau report released yesterday. It found that the number had leapt to 56 million from 34 million in the last three decades.

Mexico accounted for more than a quarter of all the foreign-born residents, the bureau's analysis of data from its March 2000 Current Population Survey showed. That share is the largest any country has held since the 1890 census, when about 30 percent of the country's foreign-born population was from Germany.

The study found that, on average, foreign-born residents were much more likely than native Americans to live in or around a handful of big cities. They were almost equally likely to be in the labor force. But foreign-born residents earned less and were less likely to have health insurance than native Americans.

While the number of foreign-born residents and their children is higher than ever, their percentage in the population is not. In the 1910 census, that group made up 35 percent of the population, compared with 20 percent in 2000, a spokesman for the Census Bureau said.

The report brings together 5 data on the age, sex and birthplaces of the foreign born, their education levels, jobs and earnings. In doing so, it makes clear the near impossibility of generalizing about immigrants and the immigrant experience.

For example, while only 33.8 percent of residents over age 25 and born in Mexico had completed high school, 95 percent of those born in Africa had. While the median household income for those born in Latin America was $29,338, it was $51,363 for those from Asia, well above that of native Americans.

The proportion of married couples with children under 18 ranged from 35 percent for residents born in Europe to 73.4 percent for those from Latin America. The proportion of naturalized citizens varied widely, from 52 percent of those born in Europe to 21.1 percent of those born in Central America.

"The big question is how the second generation is going to do," said Nancy Foner, a professor of anthropology at the State University of New York at Purchase and the author of *From Ellis Island to JFK: New York's Two Great Waves of Immigration* (Yale, 2000). "And how the presence of large proportions of Asians, Latinos and black immigrants are changing Americans' notions of race."

The Census Bureau study found that the foreign-born population was heavily concentrated in California, New York, Florida, Texas, New Jersey and Illinois; those six states accounted for

70.4 percent of the total. Nearly 55 percent lived in the nine metropolitan areas with populations of five million or more.

California led the nation with the highest percentage of foreign-born residents with 25.9 percent, followed by New York State with 19.6. The metropolitan areas with the largest percentage of foreign-born populations were Los Angeles with 29.6 percent and New York with 22.8.

In New York City, said John H. Mollenkopf, a demographer at the City University of New York, 43 percent of the residents are foreign born and another 9.2 percent are the children of two foreign-born parents. In 1900, Professor Mollenkopf said, only 23 percent of New Yorkers had native-born parents.

The Census Bureau's report put at 55.9 million the number of people of so-called foreign stock, which includes 28.4 million foreign born, 14.8 million native born with two foreign-born parents, and 12.7 million of mixed parentage. That group is likely to grow, in part because the proportion of births to foreign-born women rose to 20.2 percent in 1999 from 6 percent of all births in 1970, the report said.

While the median ages of the foreign-born and native populations barely differed, foreign-born residents fell disproportionately between the ages of 25 and 54. The percentage of foreign-born residents in that age group was 58.7, compared with 41.7 percent of native Americans.

"In some ways, it has complemented the baby boom," Dianne Schmidley, a Census Bureau statistician and author of the report, said of the rise of the foreign born. "Every discussion you hear about the baby boom and the effect of the baby boom—all that has been made greater by the addition of those young adults."

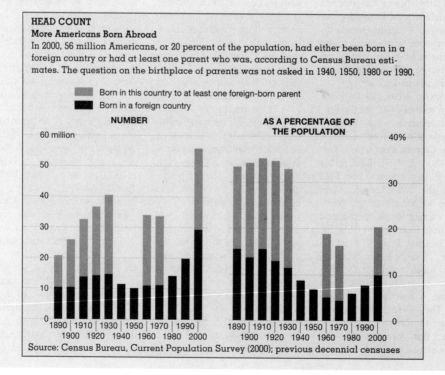

HEAD COUNT

More Americans Born Abroad

In 2000, 56 million Americans, or 20 percent of the population, had either been born in a foreign country or had at least one parent who was, according to Census Bureau estimates. The question on the birthplace of parents was not asked in 1940, 1950, 1980 or 1990.

Born in this country to at least one foreign-born parent
Born in a foreign country

Source: Census Bureau, Current Population Survey (2000); previous decennial censuses

about the text

1. Scott's argument is informative: her goal is to give readers of the *Times* information about immigration from several perspectives. Make a list of the generalizations she makes and the evidence she cites for them. What consequences might these generalizations have for bi- or multilingualism in the United States? Why?

2. This article presents visual information in the two Head Count bar graphs. What do we learn from each chart? From the two charts together? Why is it important to have both kinds of historical information to understand immigration? To understand bi- or multilingualism in the United States?

3. At the Head Count caption notes, the Census Bureau did not ask about the birthplace of parents in 1940, 1950, 1980, or 1990. What challenges does this omission present for students of immigration? Of American multilingualism?

on language use

4. What evidence can you find in your community of the trends in this article? What consequences do these trends have for language spoken there? Some things to consider might be ethnic restaurants with foreign names or signs, grocery stores that carry products labeled in languages other than English, or radio and television programs in other languages. If you are from a community where there have always been large numbers of speakers of other languages, have those languages changed over the past decade? How?

5. English speakers commonly borrow words from other languages, especially for new phenomena. We can see this process at work in American English with ethnic foods brought to the United States by immigrants. List all the terms you know for foods that originated in another language and culture. Why would we expect to borrow words for foods from other languages? How would English—and our lives—be different if we hadn't borrowed these words and come to appreciate the foods they name?

for writing

6. Using the Internet, find information from the 2000 Census about immigration to your hometown and state. Write an essay describing the demographic changes in your hometown or state during the 1990s and speculate on the consequences these changes have had for the situation there.

7. Using the Internet, find information from the 2000 Census about immigration involving speakers of a specific language. Study the available data to determine where speakers of this language have tended to settle, the effects of their arrival on the local community where this language was already spoken (if there was such a community), and the effects of their arrival on the larger, English-speaking community. You may also wish to investigate what might have attracted immigrants to the area during the 1990s. Write a report about your findings.

spanish *en* los estados unidos

All the readings in this group deal with Spanish, the second most widely spoken language in the United States and at least in the Southwest, one spoken here since the sixteenth century. Texts by Marjorie Agosín, Myriam Marquez, and Sandra Cisneros comment on what it means to be bilingual and to use both Spanish and English in daily life. Interestingly, the two languages connote different things for each of these writers (or, more accurately, for Agosín, Marquez, and the protagonist in one of Cisneros's stories). The sociolinguist Ana Celia Zentella examines Spanglish, the Spanish-English codeswitching of the sort many bilinguals engage in. (The title of this group of readings, "Spanish *en los Estados Unidos*," is an example of codeswitching, the use of two or more languages in a single speech exchange.) As Zentella demonstrates, such switching is systematic in terms of its structure and function—a claim that may well shock those who see it as a bastardization of the languages involved. Cartoons by Greg Evans, creator of *Luann*, and Hector Cantú and Carlos Castellanos, creators of *Baldo*, illustrate how speakers of English and Spanish use codeswitching strategically, sometimes to communicate things that neither language alone can express. (Yes, things are sometimes lost in translation.) Finally, a news article by Diane Smith demonstrates that while immigrants come to the United States expecting to use English, they sometimes find that learning Spanish is useful or even necessary as they seek to survive and flourish in their new home. As you explore these readings, see what aspects of Spanish *en los Estados Unidos* affect the linguistic practices and communities that you know.

MARJORIE AGOSÍN

Always Living in Spanish

RECOVERING THE FAMILIAR, THROUGH LANGUAGE

Marjorie Agosín *is a professor of Spanish at Wellesley College in Wellesley, Massachusetts, and an award-winning writer and human-rights activist. She grew up in Chile, where her grandparents moved early in the twentieth century when Jews faced increasing persecution in parts of Europe. Her family moved to the United States after General Augusto Pinochet took over the Chilean government in 1973. In* **Always Living in Spanish***, an essay which was translated by Celeste Kostopulos-Cooperman in* Poets & Writers *in 1999, Agosín explains why she, as a political exile, "writes only in Spanish and lives in translation." Her poem* **English***, translated by Monica Bruno, appeared alongside the essay and explains why she ultimately finds English insufficient as a tool for communicating the things that matter most to her.*

I N THE EVENINGS in the northern hemisphere, I repeat the ancient ritual that I observed as a child in the southern hemisphere: going out while the night is still warm and trying to recognize the stars as it begins to grow dark silently. In the sky of my country, Chile, that long and wide stretch of land that the poets blessed and dictators abused, I could easily name the stars: the three Marías, the Southern Cross, and the three Lilies, names of beloved and courageous women.

But here in the United States, where I have lived since I was a young girl, the solitude of exile makes me feel that so little is mine, that not even the sky has the same constellations, the trees and the fauna the same names or sounds, or the rubbish the same smell. How does one recover the familiar? How does one name the unfamiliar? How can one be another or live in a foreign language? These are the dilemmas of one who writes in Spanish and lives in translation.

Since my earliest childhood in Chile I lived with the tempos and the melodies of a multiplicity of tongues: German, Yiddish,[1] Russian, Turkish, and many Latin songs. Because everyone was from somewhere else, my relatives laughed, sang, and fought in a Babylon of languages. Spanish was reserved for matters of extreme seriousness, for commercial transactions, or for illnesses,

---

1. **Yiddish** a Germanic language, much influenced by Hebrew and Aramaic and written in the Hebrew alphabet. Spoken by the Ashkenazi Jews, who lived in Central and Eastern Europe, and their descendants, including those who came to the Americas.

but everyone's mother tongue was always associated with the memory of spaces inhabited in the past: the shtetl,[2] the flowering and vast Vienna avenues, the minarets of Turkey, and the Ladino[3] whispers of Toledo. When my paternal grandmother sang old songs in Turkish, her voice and body assumed the passion of one who was there in the city of Istanbul, gazing by turns toward the west and the east.

Destiny and the always ambiguous nature of history continued my family's enforced migration, and because of it I, too, became one who had to live and speak in translation. The disappearances, torture, and clandestine deaths in my country in the early seventies drove us to the United States, that other America that looked with suspicion at those who did not speak English and especially those who came from the supposedly uncivilized regions of Latin America. I had left a dangerous place that was my home, only to arrive in a dangerous place that was not: a high school in the small town of Athens, Georgia, where my poor English and my accent were the cause of ridicule and insult. The only way I could recover my usurped country and my Chilean childhood was by continuing to write in Spanish, the same way my grandparents had sung in their own tongues in diasporic[4] sites.

The new and learned English language did not fit with the visceral emotions and themes that my poetry contained, but by writing in Spanish I could recover fragrances, spoken rhythms, and the passion of my own identity. Daily I felt the need to translate myself for the strangers living all around me, to tell them why we were in Georgia, why we are different, why we had fled, why my accent was so thick, and why I did not look Hispanic. Only at night, writing poems in Spanish, could I return to my senses, and soothe my own sorrow over what I had left behind.

This is how I became a Chilean poet who wrote in Spanish and lived in the southern United States. And then, one day, a poem of mine was translated and published in the English language. Finally, for the first time since I had left Chile, I felt I didn't have to explain myself. My poem, expressed in another language, spoke for itself . . . and for me.

---

2. **shtetl** a small Jewish village or town in Eastern Europe, from the Yiddish word meaning "little town."

3. **Ladino** a nearly extinct Romance language, based on archaic Spanish and brought from Spain by Jews expelled during the Inquisition; spoken by Sephardic Jews, who ultimately settled in the Balkans, North Africa, and the Middle East.

4. **diasporic** relating to a diaspora, or dispersion of a group of people across a large geographic area.

Sometimes the austere sounds of English help me bear the solitude of knowing that I am foreign and so far away from those about whom I write. I must admit I would like more opportunities to read in Spanish to people whose language and culture is also mine, to join in our common heritage and in the feast of our sounds. I would also like readers of English to understand the beauty of the spoken word in Spanish, that constant flow of oxytonic and paraoxytonic syllables (*Vérde qué té quiéro vérde*),[5] the joy of writing—of dancing—in another language. I believe that many exiles share the unresolvable torment of not being able to live in the language of their childhood.

I miss that undulating and sensuous language of mine, those baroque descriptions, the sense of being and feeling that Spanish gives me. It is perhaps for this reason that I have chosen and will always choose to write in Spanish. Nothing else from my childhood world remains. My country seems to be frozen in gestures of silence and oblivion. My relatives have died, and I have grown up not knowing a young generation of cousins and nieces and nephews. Many of my friends were disappeared, others were tortured, and the most fortunate, like me, became guardians of memory. For us, to write in Spanish is to always be in active pursuit of memory. I seek to recapture a world lost to me on that sorrowful afternoon when the blue electric sky and the Andean cordillera[6] bade me farewell. On that, my last Chilean day, I carried under my arm my innocence recorded in a little blue notebook I kept even then. Gradually that diary filled with memoranda, poems written in free verse, descriptions of dreams and of the thresholds of my house surrounded by cherry trees and gardenias. To write in Spanish is for me a gesture of survival. And because of translation, my memory has now become a part of the memory of many others.

Translators are not traitors, as the proverb says, but rather splendid friends in this great human community of language.

---

5. **oxytonic** with main stress on the final or only syllable of a word. **paroxytonic** with main stress on the next-to-last syllable of a word. ***Vérde qué té quiéro vérde*** "Green. How I want you green," the opening line of a poem by Federico García Lorca, illustrating oxytonic and paroxytonic stress.

6. **cordillera** mountain ranges consisting of parallel chains of peaks.

English

I discovered that English
is too skinny,
functional,
precise,
too correct,   5
meaning
only one thing.
Too much wrath,
too many lawyers and sinister policemen,
too many deans at schools for small females,   10
in the Anglo-Saxon language.

II
In contrast Spanish
has so many words to say come with me friend,
make love to me on
the *césped*, the *grama*, the *pasto*.[1]   15
Let's go party,[2]
at dusk, at night, at sunset.
Spanish
loves
the unpredictable, it is   20
dementia,
all windmills[3] and velvet.

---

1. All three words mean *grass* in English [Translator's note].

2. The Spanish version of this poem uses two phrases which mean *to party: de juerga* and *de fiesta* [Translator's note].

3. **windmills** an allusion to Don Quijote, who tilted at windmills on his old nag, imagining them to be giants. Quijote is the hero of Miguel de Cervantes's comic and satiric seventeenth-century novel of the same name. In the book, Quijote (also spelled Quixote), having read too many courtly romances, goes off to find adventure. Quijote's name and the adjective "quixotic" are used for someone who, inspired by high (but often false) ideals, pursues an impossible project or task. See the reference to Quijote in line 33.

III
Spanish
is simple and baroque,
a palace of nobles and beggars,   25
it fills itself with silences and the breaths of dragonflies.
Neruda's[4] verses
saying "I could write the saddest verses
tonight,"
or Federico[5] swimming underwater through the greenest of greens.   30

IV
Spanish
is Don Quijote maneuvering,
Violeta Parra[6] grateful
spicy, tasty, fragrant   35
the rumba, the salsa, the cha-cha.
There are so many words
to say
naive dreamers
and impostors.   40
There are so many languages in our
language: Quechua, Aymará, Rosas chilensis, Spanglish.[7]

V
I love the imperfections of
Spanish,

---

4. **(Pablo) Neruda** pen name of the Nobel Prize–winning Chilean poet, politician, and diplomat (1904–1973), whom many consider the finest Latin American poet of the twentieth century.

5. **Federico García Lorca** Spanish poet and playwright (1898–1936); a sympathizer with leftist causes and a homosexual, Lorca was executed by a Nationalist firing squad early in the Spanish Civil War under mysterious circumstances.

6. **Violeta Parra** Chilean folksinger (1917–1967) most often associated with "La Nueva Canción," a style of Chilean and Latin American popular music influenced by folk traditions. Her best-known song is perhaps "Gracias à la Vida" ("Thanks to life").

7. **Quechua** the language of the former Inca Empire and the major indigenous language of the central Andes today. **Aymará** a major indigenous language of Bolivia. **Rosas chilensis** Latin species name for a rose indigenous to Chile. **Spanglish** popular label for the practice of switching between Spanish and English within conversation or sentences as many bilingual Hispanics do when they speak with other bilinguals.

the language takes shape in my hand: 45
the sound of drums and waves,
the Caribbean in the radiant foam of the sun,
are delirious upon my lips.
English has fallen short for me,
it signifies business,   50
law
and inhibition,
never the crazy, clandestine,
clairvoyance of
love.

about the texts

1. Why does Agosín write only in Spanish? How does she relate using Spanish to her Jewish ancestry?

2. What sort of experiences did Agosín have while trying to learn English? How did Spanish represent a source of strength and consolation to her when she was learning English? How typical do you think her experiences are?

3. How does Agosín use two very different genres, the essay and poetry, to express similar sentiments? What advantages and limitations does each genre have? Why?

on language use

4. What do Spanish and English each represent for Agosín? Why? Most people have attachments like those Agosín describes to some language, language variety (e.g., a regional, social, or ethnic dialect), or language practice (e.g., codeswitching, hearing prayers recited in a particular language). Describe one such attachment you have.

5. What does English represent for you? Do you think it should signify the same thing to all its users? Why or why not?

6. Agosín's family has a multilingual history. How far back do you have to go to find multilingualism in your family? What was its source? What led to its disappearance?

for writing

7. Part of the power of Agosín's texts comes from the ways she links language and her decision to write in Spanish to many histories: her own, her family's, and the exiled Jewish people's. How does each of her languages contribute to these histories? Consider how she uses English and Spanish in her life and write an essay analyzing what it means for her to "recover . . . the familiar, through language" (paragraph 2). As you prepare to write, it may be useful to consider what Agosín might feel if she were forced to use English to narrate her life, and that of her family.

8. Judaism has been linked to many languages, including Hebrew, Yiddish, and Ladino. Choose one of the world's major religions and research the languages with which it has been linked and why. Write an essay about what you discover.

MYRIAM MARQUEZ

Why and When We Speak Spanish in Public

Myriam Marquez *writes for the* Orlando Sentinel, *and her columns are syndicated nationally. In this opinion piece, from the July 1999* Austin American Statesman, *Marquez explains why she, a Cuban American who grew up in Miami, and her family use Spanish in public, often within earshot of people who don't speak the language.*

WHEN I'M SHOPPING with my mother or standing in line with my stepdad to order fast food or any-where else we might be together, we're going to speak to one another in Spanish.

That may appear rude to those who don't understand Spanish and overhear us in public places.

Those around us may get the impression that we're talking about them. They may wonder why we would in-sist on speaking in a foreign tongue, especially if they knew that my family has lived in the United States for 40 years and that my parents do understand English and speak it, albeit with difficulty and a heavy accent.

Let me explain why we haven't adopted English as our official family language. For me and most of the bilin-gual people I know, it's a matter of respect for our parents and comfort in our cultural roots.

It's not meant to be rude to others. It's not meant to 5 alienate anyone or to Balkanize America.

It's certainly not meant to be un-American—what con-stitutes an "American" being defined by English speakers from North America.

Being an American has very little to do with what language we use during our free time in a free country. From its inception, this country was careful not to pro-mote a government-mandated official language.

We understand that English is the common language of this country and the one most often heard in international-business circles from Peru to Norway. We know that, to get ahead here, one must learn English.

But that ought not mean that somehow we must stop speaking in our native tongue whenever we're in a public area, as if we were ashamed of who we are, where we're from. As if talking in Spanish—or any other language, for that matter—is some sort of litmus test used to gauge American patriotism.

Throughout this nation's history, most immigrants—whether from 10 Poland or Finland or Italy or wherever else—kept their language through the first generation and, often, the second. I suspect that they spoke among themselves in their native tongue—in public. Pennsylvania even provided voting ballots written in German during much of the 1800s for those who weren't fluent in English.

In this century, Latin American immigrants and others have fought for this country in U.S.-led wars. They have participated fully in this nation's democracy by voting, holding political office and paying taxes. And they have watched their children and grandchildren become so "American" that they resist speaking in Spanish.

You know what's rude?

When there are two or more people who are bilingual and another person who speaks only English and the bilingual folks all of a sudden start speaking Spanish, which effectively leaves out the English-only speaker. I don't tolerate that.

One thing's for sure. If I'm ever in a public place with my mom or dad and bump into an acquaintance who doesn't speak Spanish, I will switch to English and introduce that person to my parents. They will respond in English, and do so with respect.

about the text

1. How does Marquez explain and justify why she (and other immigrants) continue to speak languages other than English in public? What fear does she acknowledge on the part of monolingual English speakers? How does she respond?

2. What values does Marquez appeal to when she explains why she speaks Spanish in public? Why might she focus on these values when writing about a potentially divisive topic for an audience that is likely not bilingual?

3. The last three paragraphs of this essay represent a clear shift in tone and emphasis. What is their purpose? Do the final paragraphs contribute to or detract from the essay's overall effect? Explain.

on language use

4. Marquez discusses links between language choice and perceptions of politeness or rudeness. How are politeness and rudeness linked to language—and its audience—in your home community? Many people, for example, use certain language with their peers that they would not use in front of their parents. Why might this be so?

5. Marquez observes that many English-speaking Americans think that people speaking another language in their presence *must* be talking about them. What might be the source of this belief?

for writing

6. Marquez argues that "being an American has very little to do with what language we use during our free time in a free country" (paragraph 7). Write an essay in which you agree or disagree with her claim. Before you start, you may find it useful to investigate the history of language legislation in the United States.

7. Write an essay in which you define and evaluate the appropriateness of speaking languages other than English in public in the United States. Marquez notes that for her and many Americans, public space is not an English-only environment, but she acknowledges that there are limits to what is polite or appropriate. In your essay, draw on Marquez's terms to define public space with respect to language use and then evaluate Marquez's characterization of that space, based on your own values and experiences.

SANDRA CISNEROS

Excerpt from *"Bien Pretty"*

Born in Chicago, Sandra Cisneros is a Mexican American writer who now lives in San Antonio. Her first major work was The House on Mango Street (1983), and her most recent novel is Caramelo (2002). She received a MacArthur Foundation fellowship in 1995. In this selection from Woman Hollering Creek and Other Stories (1991), Cisneros helps readers understand how bilingual people experience the languages they know.

I'D NEVER MADE LOVE in Spanish before. I mean not with anyone whose *first* language was Spanish. There was crazy Graham, the anarchist labor organizer who'd taught me to eat jalapeños and swear like a truck mechanic, but he was Welsh and had learned his Spanish running guns to Bolivia.

And Eddie, sure. But Eddie and I were products of our American education. Anything tender always came off sounding like the subtitles to a Buñuel film.[1]

But Flavio. When Flavio accidentally hammered his thumb, he never yelled "Ouch!" He said *"¡Ay!"* The true test of a native Spanish speaker.

¡Ay! To make love in Spanish, in a manner as intricate and devout as la Alhambra.[2] To have a lover sigh *mi vida, mi preciosa, mi chiquitita,* and whisper things in that language crooned to babies, that language murmured by grandmothers, those words that smelled like your house, like flour tortillas, and the inside of your daddy's hat, like everyone talking in the kitchen at the same time, or sleeping with the windows open, like sneaking cashews from the crumpled quarter-pound bag Mama always hid in her lingerie drawer after she went shopping with Daddy at the Sears.

That language. That sweep of palm leaves and 5 fringed shawls. That startled fluttering, like the heart of a

---

1. **Luis Buñuel** Spanish filmmaker (1900–1983), best known for his work in commercial films in Mexico. His first and most famous film, *Un Chien Andalou* (1929), is considered a surrealist classic.

2. **la Alhambra** fortress and palace built between 1238 and 1358 on a plateau above Granada, Spain; it was home to the Moorish rulers, Muslims who controlled the area at the time. It is considered a masterpiece of Moorish architecture.

goldfinch or a fan. Nothing sounded dirty or hurtful or corny. How could I think of making love in English again? English with its starched r's and g's. English with its crisp linen syllables. English crunchy as apples, resilient and stiff as sailcloth.

But Spanish whirred like silk, rolled and puckered and hissed. I held Flavio close to me, in the mouth of my heart, inside my wrists.

Incredible happiness. A sigh unfurled of its own accord, a groan heaved out from my chest so rusty and full of dust it frightened me. I was crying. It surprised us both.

"My soul, did I hurt you?" Flavio said in that other language.

I managed to bunch my mouth into a knot and shake my head "no" just as the next wave of sobs began. Flavio rocked me, and cooed, and rocked me. *Ya, ya, ya.* There, there, there.

I wanted to say so many things, but all I could think of was a line I'd read   10
in the letters of Georgia O'Keeffe[3] years ago and had forgotten until then. Flavio . . . did you ever feel like flowers?

---

3. **Georgia O'Keeffe** American painter (1887–1986) best known for her semi-abstract landscapes and large paintings of flowers in vivid colors.

about the text

1. The languages Cisneros's narrator knows are associated with different worlds of experience. What do Spanish and English respectively connote for the narrator in Cisneros's text? Where and how would the narrator have learned such connotations?

2. Cisneros's narrator claims that she and Eddie were "products of our American education" (paragraph 2) and were thus unable to use Spanish convincingly in some situations. What does she mean by this claim?

3. Myriam Marquez writes about the use of Spanish in public in "Why and When We Speak Spanish in Public" (p. 207), and Cisneros, in contrast, writes about the use of Spanish in the most private of contexts. What do Marquez and Cisneros agree about? Explain.

on language use

4. Bilingual writers often codeswitch between the languages they know. In this selection, there are simple noun phrases like "la Alhambra" (paragraph 4) which we can understand even if we know no Spanish. There are also phrases like "Ya, ya, ya" (paragraph 9), which are followed immediately by the English equivalent. But there are also phrases like *mi vida, mi preciosa, mi chiquitita* (paragraph 4), which go untranslated. (In fact, these phrases translate literally as "my life, my precious (one), my dearest little (one)" — terms of endearment that native speakers of English wouldn't normally use, but which are perfectly normal among speakers of Spanish.) Why might a writer purposely write words readers may not be able to understand? Why would such a strategy be especially effective when talking about intimacies? (For

more on the ways writers use codeswitching in their work, go to this book's website.)

5. Cisneros's narrator comments that subtitles to films in other languages often sound unnatural, reminding us that different languages get used in different ways and for different purposes. Consider a subtitled movie you have seen, or some other occurrence of translated language, and explain why some situations can't be translated easily or well.

for writing

6. Most people have an emotional attachment to certain languages or language varieties, most often ones they associate with childhood. Compose a text in which you explore and define the meaning of some language or language variety — a regional, social, or ethnic variety of English, for example — that has significance for you. Your text can be an essay or a sketch like Cisneros's (though you needn't write about anything so intimate as love-making!). Be sure to help readers — both those who know the language variety about which you write and those who don't — understand its meanings and significance for you.

7. As the selections by Agosín, Marquez, and Cisneros make clear, Spanish means something different to everyone who speaks it. These writers also assert that for many Hispanics, to lose Spanish would be to lose some fundamental part of their identity as individuals and as members of various larger groups. Using these texts, personal experience, and/or discussions you have had with people who speak more than one language, write an essay in which you define the role of language(s) in the creation of individual and group identities.

ANA CELIA ZENTELLA

The Hows and Whys of "Spanglish"

This selection comes from Ana Celia Zentella's book Growing Up Bilingual: Puerto Rican Children in New York (1997), which won the 1998 Book Prize of the British Association of Applied Linguistics and the 1999 Book Award of the Association of Latina and Latino Anthropologists of the American Anthropology Association. The book is based on several years of ethnographic research, involving long-term participant observation, in el bloque in El Barrio, a Puerto Rican neighborhood in New York City. Zentella is currently a professor in the Department of Ethnic Studies at the University of California, San Diego. In this selection, she describes the social functions of switching between Spanish and English for el bloque's children.

O**N THE STREET** and at home, multiple activities and channels of information in English and Spanish enveloped the children of *el bloque*. Radio, TV, telephone, juke box, older and younger siblings, adults' conversations—all in two languages—crowded in on the children's activities, talk, and daydreams. As Paca, Isabel, Lolita, Blanca, and Elli added their voices to those of their community, they made choices as active agents constructing their own social identities in ways that simultaneously reflected and resisted their position as members of an ethno-linguistic minority. Of particular significance was their choice of English or Spanish or both languages together, and the ways in which they used them.

All native speakers demonstrate a tacit cultural knowledge of how to speak their language appropriately in different speech situations, in keeping with their community's "ways of speaking" (Hymes 1974). Whereas monolinguals adjust by switching phonological, grammatical, and discourse features within one linguistic code, bilinguals alternate between the languages in their linguistic repertoire as well. Children in bilingual speech communities acquire two grammars and the rules for communicative competence which prescribe not only when and where each language may be used, but also whether and how the two languages may be woven together in a single utterance.

Uriel Weinreich's contention that "the ideal bilingual switches from one language to the other according to the appropriate changes in the speech situation (interlocutors, topic, etc.), but not in unchanged speech situations, and certainly not within a single sentence" (1968: 73) has not been borne out as universal. In some bilingual communities, including immigrant communities in the United

States like *el bloque*, codes are switched by the same speaker in the same setting. Gumperz defines a code switch as "the juxtaposition within the same speech exchange of passages belonging to two different grammatical systems or subsystems" (1982: 59). Code switches can occur at the boundary of complete sentences (inter-sententially), as in 1 or within sentence boundaries (intra-sententially), as in 2:

1. *Si, pero le hablo en español.*
   ("Yes, but I talk to her in Spanish.")
   When I don't know something I'll talk to her in English.

2. You know they walk *que ellas se comen el* aisle *completo.*
   ("in such a way that they take up the whole") aisle

Code switching is characteristic of many parts of the world where two or more speech communities live in close contact, but often it is misunderstood. Sometimes code switching is confused with the historically recurrent process of word borrowing. For example, English loans like *londri* ("laundry"), *lonchar* ("to lunch"), *biles* ("bills"), *el bloque* ("the block") regularly appear in the Spanish of monolinguals in New York City, and they have been adapted phonologically and morpho-syntactically to such an extent that members of the second generation think they belong to the Spanish lexicon (Acosta-Belén 1975; Zentella 1981). Because other non-adapted words like "aisle" in 2 above may be on their way to becoming similarly integrated, it is not always easy to distinguish loans from code switches, and some researchers believe "that efforts to distinguish codeswitching, codemixing and borrowing are doomed" (Eastman 1992; 1).[1] In this study, popular loans that appear in monolingual speech (like *londri*, etc., above) are not counted as code switches. In any case, as this chapter makes clear, most of the children's code switches were not single words.

More serious than confusing code switching with loans is the charge 5 that code switching represents language deterioration and/or the creation of a new language—called Tex-Mex or "Spanglish" in US Latino communities, Japlish, Chinglish, etc. in others. The pejorative connotations of these labels

---

1. The difficulties of untangling the competing terminology in code switching studies noted by Baker (1980) continue, with the added problem of determining their punctuation, e.g., Torres (1992) uses "code-mixing" for what I call code switching and "code-switching" for what I call language alternation. Myers-Scotton's definition refers to the phenomenon as one word—"codeswitching involves at least two languages used in the same conversation" (1992: 19)—and all her examples fall under what I call code switching [Zentella's note].

reflect negative evaluations of the linguistic and/or intellectual abilities of those who code switch:

> Speakers of the non-defined mixture of Spanish and/or English are judged as "different," or "sloppy" speakers of Spanish and/or English, and are often labelled verbally deprived, alingual, or deficient bilinguals because supposedly they do not have the ability to speak either English or Spanish well (Acosta-Belén 1975: 151).

To counteract such charges and the "hate literature campaign being conducted against the Spanish spoken by our New York City Puerto Rican community," Milán (1982: 202–203) urged that "both the researchers studying contemporary Puerto Rican speech in New York City and the practitioners striving for an equal educational opportunity for the city's Puerto Rican population make a truly concerted effort to avoid using the term 'Spanglish'." He favored "New York City Spanish" as less "misleading" and "more scientifically sound" (ibid). My initial support for Milán's position was based on similar concerns—and members of *el bloque* did not use the term anyway—but it has been modified by the recognition that more NYPRs (New York Puerto Ricans) are referring to "Spanglish" as a positive way of identifying their switching. Just as the African American community transformed "Black" into a proud racial designation in the 1960s, members of the second and third generations of NYPRs are rehabilitating "Spanglish," along with their unembarassed adoption of "Nuyorican" as an identity label.

This chapter presents quantified evidence that the young have reason to be proud of their ability to switch languages. Their communication in English, or Spanish, or both, responds to complex social and linguistic variables and demonstrates a skill that challenges Weinreich's definition of an "ideal bilingual." I begin by presenting a framework that encompasses both language alternation, that is, when a speaker changes languages for a change in addressees or a new turn at speaking, and code switching, a change in languages that occurs within a speaker's turn with no change in addressee, and then I indicate how language alternation sets the stage for code switching.

ANALYZING LANGUAGE CHOICES

Repeated observations of various networks in similar situations revealed community patterns of choice in who spoke what to whom, and when to change languages. In the process of acquiring those patterns and adapting them to their reality, children made their own contributions to *el bloque's* linguistic and cultural norms. At any given moment numerous factors combined to determine a bilingual's choice of one language or another, but for the sake of analysis, it was necessary to tease them apart. I found it helpful to separate what could be observed, what must be interpreted as having been in the knowledge of the speaker, and what could be analyzed with precision in their individual utterances.

The "observables" of the interaction in *el bloque* included the physical setting as well as the linguistic and social identities of the participants, principally speakers and those they were addressing as well as other listeners. The particular location and the people involved existed together outside the specific stretch of time, but the specific mix of the components on the occasion in question, and the language which preceded the moment of choice helped determine the children's choice of language(s). This part of the interaction is, in a catch phrase, "on the spot."

In the heads of the speakers is the shared knowledge of how to manage conversations, how to achieve intentions in verbal interaction, and how to show respect for the social values of the community, the status of the interactants, and the symbolic value of the languages. Both choice of language and of switches between languages are made in anticipation of some outcome of each selection. Moreover, speakers not only anticipate an outcome and select among appropriate means for achieving the desired end, they also monitor the responses of the person(s) they are speaking to in relation to the anticipated outcome. They can alter their language choices or vary the style and purpose of the discourse accordingly, and offer a substitute for a previously made choice. This social and linguistic knowledge is built up over years of participating in interactional activities in their cultural setting. "In the head" factors are not meant to be psychological or cognitive processes, but communicative knowledge not directly observable in each speech situation.

The third set of factors is more linguistic, more anchored in the structure 10 of the languages themselves and in the individual's knowledge of the languages. I call these, for the purpose of symmetry with the first two categories, what is "out of the mouth," the rubric for what influences a speaker to produce a particular word or expression in one language or the other, including lexical limitations and syntactic constraints. The analysis of this third category—the grammar of "Spanglish"—is the topic of the next chapter.

* * *

ON THE SPOT

The most important on the spot observables that guided children's language choices were the linguistic proficiency of the person to whom they were speaking (also called "hearer," "addressee," or "interlocutor"[2]), and the language requirements of the setting. The children of el *bloque* were most responsive to the dominant language of their addressee, in accordance with a general norm that they speak the language that was spoken to them, if possible.

COMMUNITY NORMS AND LANGUAGE ALTERNATION

The role of code switching as an in-group phenomenon has its origin in community expectations regarding the language that children should choose for addressing others. Parents were very clear about their conviction that children should speak the language their addressee could understand best. When asked whether or not there were any times when the children should speak only English or Spanish, parents were nearly unanimous in stressing the presence of monolinguals as the determining factor. Locales were mentioned only as corollaries, that is, some teachers and students at school might be English monolinguals; mothers and other Spanish-monolingual relatives were at home. Activities or topics were never mentioned in relation to either language; any task or discussion could be carried out in either Spanish or English, depending on the language proficiency of participants.

Since most families consisted of caretakers who spoke and understood more Spanish than English and children who spoke and understood more English than Spanish, children changed languages every time they addressed elders in Spanish and siblings in English. Language alternation for a change of addressees such as the following was commonplace:

[Context: Lolita (eight years old) pushes Timmy (five years old) off her bike, and Timmy tells the adults nearby.]

L to T:	Get off, Timmy, get off.
T to adults:	*Ella me dió* ("She hit me.")
L to T:	*¡Porque TU me diste!* ("Because YOU hit me!")

---

2. **interlocutor** the person with whom one is speaking.

T to L:	Liar!
Adult to L:	¿*Por qué*—[interrupted by L] ("Why?")
L to adult:	*Porque él me dió por eso.* ("Because he hit me, that's why.")
	El siempre me está dando cuando me ve.
	("He's always hitting me whenever he sees me.")

Lolita and Timmy always spoke English to each other and did so in this exchange, except when Lolita addressed him in Spanish for the adults' benefit: "*¡Porque TU me diste!*" Both she and Timmy had the ability to speak entirely in English or Spanish throughout the incident, but they alternated languages in accordance with the language dominance of those they were addressing. Such alternations were most likely to go from English into Spanish at turn points in the conversation when children interrupted their activities to speak to older community members. Rapidly alternating languages to accommodate people who were dominant in one language or the other accustomed the children to juxtapose the distinct phonology, morphology, syntax, and lexicon of Spanish and English with ease. In families with members of two or more generations, this process begins in infancy.

Most of the Spanish monolingual adults on the block who provided regular opportunity for inter-turn changes from English to Spanish were women, either recent migrants or older homemakers. They included a few men who had limited contact with the children. *Don Luís,* in his seventies, spent long hours sitting with Armando and the other domino players. The use of *Don* before his name was a reflection of his respected senior status; he was the only block resident so honored. The elderly man did not speak fluent English although he had lived in New York City for twenty years.[3] He complained bitterly about young Latino social workers who he believed lied when they denied being able to speak Spanish. Because the selection of English for *Don Luís* would have constituted a clear lack of *respeto* ("respect"), children who were not confident of their Spanish ability avoided him. Those who had to approach the domino-players frequently, like Armando's daughter Lolita, always spoke to *Don Luís* in Spanish.

＊　＊　＊

---

3. The only people likely to remain monolingual after ten or more years in the United States are those who migrate in middle age or older and never achieve regular employment, like *Don Luís* [Zentella's note].

IN THE HEAD: COMMUNICATIONAL FACTORS

Alternations at turn points helped pave the way for intra-turn code switches. [15] Knowledge of how to manage a conversation—the factors "in the head"— enabled children to employ code switching for greater communicative power and social bonding.

CONVERSATIONAL STRATEGIES

The smooth integration of switches in NYPR bilinguals' speech led Poplack and Sankoff (1988: 1,176) to conclude that "it could be said to function as a *mode* of interaction similar to monolingual language use . . . and no special rhetorical effect is accomplished thereby." They contrast this with other communities, for example, French-English bilinguals in Ottawa-Hull, Canada, in which "the use of virtually every switch serves a rhetorical purpose" (ibid: 1,177), presumably because they "flag" their switches with pauses and other hesitation phenomena. Yet, *el bloque*'s switching suggests that while hesitation phenomena may provide a salient rhetorical flourish, a smooth switch does not necessarily mean a non-purposeful switch. Even young bilinguals who were still learning both languages usually did not interrupt their flow of speech or otherwise call attention to their switches. They switched not only because it was the community "mode"—switching undoubtedly was a hallmark of community membership—but also because they shared with peers and adults "in the head" knowledge of how to use switching for particular communicative purposes.

Code switching performed important conversational work for the children, only some of which was an extension of the functions of language alternation at turn boundaries. As they went about co-constructing an NYPR identity with other community members, they used code switching to accomplish at least 22 conversational strategies, including and beyond those noted in previous research. Three major categories distinguished themselves: Footing, Clarification, and Crutch-like code mixes. [Only the discussion of footing is included here.]

FOOTING

Goffman's concept of Footing provides the principle that underlies a broad variety of switches: "A change in footing implies a change in the alignment we take up to ourselves and others present as expressed in the way we manage the production or reception of an utterance" (Goffman 1979; 5). The children of el *bloque* used code switching primarily to signal a change in footing, via two approaches; they switched languages to underscore or highlight the re-alignment they intended (Realignment), or to control their interlocutor's behavior (Appeal/Control). Among the eight Realignment strategies for example, a change in the speaker's role—from speaker to quoter of another's speech, from friend to protector, or from narrator to evaluator of the narration—could be accompanied by a code switch. Also, children sometimes interrupted themselves with a switch to check for approval, attention, or the interlocutor's knowledge of what they were about to refer to. If children asked a question and then answered it themselves, their answer might be in the other language, mirroring the opposition of interrogative and declarative stances. In this instance, switching allowed the children to keep control over their turn, with a shift in language indicating momentary departure and re-alignment.

A shift in topic represented the most popular type of change in Footing; switches that re-directed listeners' attention away from the topic at hand amounted to 27 percent of the category. The leading role played by code switching for topic shifts within a bilingual's turn at speaking was a logical extension of the community practice of alternating languages for different interlocutors, which was often linked to a shift in topic. For topic shifts and seven other changes which constituted the Realignment sub-category of Footing, children shifted away from their initial focus or role, and the code switch served to highlight the re-alignment.

Quantification helped underscore the variable nature of code switching, [20] for example, not every attempt to realign a conversation was accompanied by a switch because switching was optional, not obligatory. The name of each conversational strategy is followed by the number (n) of occurrences in the data and the proportion the strategy represents in the corpus of strategic switches (803). The following examples are only some of the ways in which code switching carried out communicative functions in the everyday talk of el *bloque's* children:

REALIGNMENT

1. *Topic shift* (n = 73, 9 percent)
   The speaker marks a shift in topic with a shift in language, with no consistent link between topic and language.
   Example: "*Vamos a preguntarle.* It's raining!"
         ("Let's go ask her.")

2. *Quotations, direct and indirect* (n = 70, 9 percent)
   The speaker recalls speech and reports it directly or indirectly, not necessarily in the language used by the person quoted.
   Example: "*El me dijo, 'Call the police!' pero yo dije,*"
   ("He told me")   ("but I said")
   "*No voy a llamar la policia nada.*"
   ("I'm not going to call the police nothin'.")

3. *Declarative/question shift* (n = 29, 4 percent)
   The language shift accompanies a shift into or out of a question.
   Example: "I wiggle my fingers, *¿qué más?*" ("what else?")

4. *Future referent check and/or bracket* (n = 27, 3 percent)
   The speaker makes an aside, marked by a shift in language, to make sure that the listener knows her next referent.
   Example: "*Le dió con irse para*—you know Lucy?—
   ("She up and decided to go to—)
   para la casa del papá de Lucy."
   (—"to Lucy's father's house.")

5. *Checking* (n = 19, 2 percent)
   The shift seeks the listeners' opinion or approval, usually in the form of a tag.
   Example: "*Porque estamos en huelga de gasolina,* right?"
   ("Because we are in a gas strike")

6. *Role shift* (n = 17, 2 percent)
   The speaker shifts languages as s/he shifts role from actor to narrator or interviewer, for mothering, etc.
   Example: Interviewer [speaking into the recorder's microphone]
   "*My-mi nombre es Lourdes.* Now we're going to my sister."[4]
   ("My name is Lourdes.")

7. *Rhetorical ask and answer* (n = 16, 2 percent)
   The speaker asks a question and immediately follows it with the answer, in the opposite language.
   Example: "You know what my cousins do [to cockroaches]?
   Los agarran por las patitas y los ponen en la estufa paras achicharrarlas.
   (They grab them by their little legs, and they put them on the stove to burn them to a crisp.")

---

4. In this example, Lolita assumed the role of her mother as interviewer and then moved toward her sister to interview her [Zentella's note].

8. *Narrative frame break*—*evaluation or coda*[5] (n = 10, 1 percent)
The speaker departs from the narrative frame to evaluate some aspect of the story, or to deliver the punch line, or ending.
Example: "Charlie tried to push Gina in and, *bendito*, Kitty fell on her head.
[*bendito* is a Puerto Rican lament, literally 'blessed']
Y eso es lo que le pasa a los presentados como tú.
(And that's what happens to busybodies like you.")

Realignment strategies were employed in nearly one-third (32 percent) of the switches identified by strategy. This category was more varied and prevalent than others, except for Clarification, which included the most favored strategy.

APPEAL AND/OR CONTROL

Appeal and/or Control switches are a sub-type of Footing, but they deserve separate consideration because they sought to direct the addressee's behavior by means of imperatives tinged with threats or entreaties. Often, they were accompanied by appropriate changes in intonation and other signs of aggravation or mitigation.

1. *Aggravating requests* (n = 37, 5 percent)
The switch intensifies/reinforces a command.
Example: "*Ella tiene*—shut up! Lemme tell you!"
("She has—")

2. *Mitigating requests* (n = 26, 3 percent)
The switch softens a command.
Example: "Victoria Jenine go over there! *Jennie vete para alla.*"
("Jennie go over there.")

3. *Attention attraction* (n = 17, 2 percent)
The language shift calls for the attention of the listener.
Example: "*Este se está llenando,* lookit, Ana."
("This one is filling up.")

The low proportion of Appeal and/or Control switches (10 percent) may be due to community inhibitions against children's importuning more than to

---

5. Following Labov (1972), the evaluation departs from the sequential telling of the narrative to comment, and the coda is the final wrap-up or clincher of the narrative [Zentella's note].

acknowledge their lack of centrality. Early studies of code switching singled out their significance in adult speech; Gumperz (1976) cited examples of attention attraction in four language groups around the world. Valdés (1981) was the first to point out the role of switching for the aggravation and mitigation of requests. Members of *el bloque* acknowledged their use of these strategies when they cited "getting mad" as a reason for switching languages.

LANGUAGE KNOWLEDGE AND LANGUAGE CHOICE

A similar number of switches into English (837/1,685) and Spanish (848/1,685) was the most telling illustration of the children's interweaving of their two worlds.[6] Smooth bilingual transitions exploited the opposition between the status embodied in the language of the dominant group and the solidarity embodied in the language of their less powerful community, blurring the boundaries between them. A closer look at the data revealed that some of the distinctions in the patterns of English and Spanish switches corresponded to individual differences in language proficiency. More significant, English maintained its powerful associations in some ways but in others the symbolic values traditionally attached to it and to Spanish were being challenged.

Table 5.2 Language choice and knowledge of switches

	English (%)		Spanish (%)		Totals
1 Known	75	(629	74	(629)	1,258
2 No evidence	19	(157)	16	(159)	316
3 Not known	4.5	(38)	2	(19)	57
4 Lapse	1.5	(13)	5	(41)	54
	100	(837)	100	(848)	1,685

---

6. Researchers who determine a base language and count another language segment inserted into the base language as one switch would count "I love *las montañas* in Puerto Rico" as one switch, an approach which generates less symmetry than mine (see note 7). I count it as two because the speaker could have continued in Spanish but chose to switch back to English before the prepositional phrase, and that option is obscured by the previous method. The difficulties involved in quantifying code switches are discussed in Zentella 1990 [Zentella's note].

The great majority of the switches in both languages were part of the children's bilingual repertoire (see Table 5.2). The girls knew the English for 74 percent of their Spanish switches, and they knew the Spanish for 75 percent of their English switches. For the switches for which there was no evidence as to whether the child knew how to say it in the other language, there was only a 3 percent difference—in favor of English switches. Twice as many of the (few) switches which the children did not know how to say in the other language were in English and three times as many of the switches that stood in for momentary lapses were in Spanish. Despite the paucity of examples, these figures hint at a weaker command of Spanish and a dependence on English vocabulary, a pattern which was corroborated by ethnographic data and children's self-reports. These exceptions aside, there was an extraordinary parity between English and Spanish in 93 percent of the switches (1,574/1,685).

INDIVIDUAL SPANISH/ENGLISH PREFERENCES

The rate of switches into English (49.7 percent) and Spanish (50.3 percent) for the five girls as a group was nearly equal, but the combined group figures averaged out a slight weighting in the direction of the dominant language of each speaker (Table 5.3).

The girls were all born, raised, and educated in *El Barrio*, and whatever their proficiency in Spanish, they became more English dominant as they got older, which showed up in their code switching choices. There was a progression from the youngest and most Spanish dominant, Paca, who favored Spanish switches by 10 percent, to the oldest, Elli, an English-dominant bilingual who favored English switches by 4 percent, although the differences

Table 5.3 Individual differences in language of the switch

	Dominance	Age*	English (%)	Spanish (%)	(n)
Paca	(Spanish Dominant)	7	45	55	281
Isabel	(Spanish Bilingual)	9	49	51	424
Lolita	(English Bilingual)	10	52	48	630
Blanca	(English Bilingual)	10	49.8	50.2	205
Elli	(English Bilingual)	13	51	49	145
Total (n)			840	845	1,685

*age in December 1980

were not statistically significant. The almost equivalent Spanish-English rates of all except the youngest echoed similar findings in studies of older Puerto Rican bilinguals (Marlos and Zentella 1978, Poplack 1980).[7]

LANGUAGE, POWER, AND STRATEGIES

English enjoyed symbolic domination because of its power on international, national, and local levels. Whereas English was the language of an independent and wealthy United States, spread by its technologically superior media and spoken by its first class citizens, Spanish was the language of a dependent and impoverished Puerto Rico, and of its second class citizens.[8] Beyond *el bloque*, English was the language of widest applicability. As the children grew, so did the number of their activities beyond the confines of the block—for shopping, education, sports, parties, and movies—activities which required English and enhanced its status. The most affluent people the children saw or met spoke English. Some of them also spoke Spanish, like I did, and not everyone who spoke English was well off, like the African Americans in their neighborhood, but all the Spanish monolinguals they knew were poor: the newcomers from Puerto Rico invariably were the neediest families on the block.

Unexpectedly, the traditional associations between Spanish and English and their symbolic values did not result in predictable patterns of language-linked strategies. Despite the connection of English to the powerful public domain and of Spanish to poor in-group members and intimate settings, there was no consistent coupling of specific topics with either Spanish or English. Children moved from debating the national gas strike or the Skylab rocket in Spanish to discussing their experiences in Puerto Rico or at home in English. The colonial past of Puerto Rico had introduced the instability and ambiva-

---

7. In this study and the one conducted by Marlos and Zentella (1978) on Puerto Rican adolescents in Philadelphia, a similar coding system may account for the similarity in results, i.e., a Spanish constituent bounded on each side by one in English, or the reverse, e.g., ESE/SES, was counted as two switches (see note 6). It seems that Poplack (1980) counted ESE type utterances as one switch into Spanish in her study of *El Barrio* adults, but she did not specify. That disparate methods had the same results attests to a widespread U.S. Puerto Rican preference, in different age groups and cities, for using English and Spanish code switches to an equivalent degree [Zentella's note].

8. Puerto Ricans were not granted citizenship until 1917, 19 years after U.S. occupation began, when the United States needed soldiers for World War I (only citizens could be drafted). Also, the U.S. Supreme Court determines which parts of the U.S. Constitution apply to Puerto Rico [Zentella's note].

lence in language associations that is the consequence of the imposition of the imperial power's linguistic and cultural models. The socio-economic reality of *el bloque* heightened them. For second generation NYPRs, the conventional symbolic values of Spanish (the intimate "we" language of solidarity), and English (the outsider "they" language of power) were being challenged as English engulfed an increasing number of domains and activities. In every setting, including home, school-age children usually spoke English to each other, thus weakening the connection between Spanish and Puerto Rican culture, and threatening to edge out Spanish altogether. The prevalent pattern for Spanish exchanges was one or two sentences. The pressures in school to conform to English and the lack of insistence on communicating in Spanish at home augured language loss; code switching seemed to be the vehicle for the vestigial remnants of the children's Spanish. Yet their knowledge of how to say more than 90 percent of what they switched in either language proved that they did not need to switch as much as they did, and called attention to the persistence of code switching and its significance for the community. Of particular interest was the nature of the bond between Spanish or English and specific conversational strategies.

★ ★ ★

CONCLUSION

Contrary to the attitude of those who label Puerto Rican code switching "Spanglish" in the belief that a chaotic mixture is being invented, English-Spanish switching is a creative style of bilingual communication that accomplishes important cultural and conversational work. Ethnographic and quantitative analyses of the switching done by *el bloque*'s school-girl network revealed that it is neither "an individualistic whim—merely stylistic and largely non-functional—or a pre-programmed community routine" (Auer 1984: 7). Code switching is, fundamentally, a conversational activity via which speakers negotiate meaning with each other, like *salsa* dancers responding smoothly to each other's intricate steps and turns. Among *el bloque*'s children, the construction of an NYPR bilingual identity was facilitated by switches that responded to parts of the micro context that were "on the spot" observables such as setting and speakers, and reflected "in the head" knowledge of how to manage conversations. Of particular importance were conversational strategies that allowed speakers to realign their footing, to clarify or emphasize their messages, and to control their interlocutors. Children manipulated conversational strategies in two languages in keeping with *el bloque* norms, the communicative objectives of the moment, individual styles, and the unequal positions of the majority and minority language groups in the national economy.

★ ★ ★

On the periphery of a prestigious English monolingual world and the periphery of a stigmatized Spanish monolingual world, *el bloque's* children lived on the border of the "borderlands" alluded to by Anzaldúa (1987), unwilling to relinquish their foothold in either. Their code switching was a way of saying that they belonged to both worlds, and should not be forced to give up one for the other. Switches into Spanish were attempts to touch home base, a resistance to being engulfed by English. As one 16-year-old male explained it, "Sometimes I'm talking a long time in English and then I remember I'm Puerto Rican, lemme say something in Spanglish." "Spanglish" moved them to the center of their bilingual world, which they continued to create and define in every interaction. Every time they said something in one language when they might just as easily have said it in the other, they were re-connecting with people, occasions, settings, and power configurations from their history of past interactions, and imprinting their own "act of identity" (Le Page and Tabouret-Keller 1985) on that history. In the process, they called upon their knowledge of how to exploit the similarities in two sets of grammatical rules to accomplish rule-governed code switching, challenging the view that their code switching, or "Spanglish," was a chaotic jumble.

REFERENCES

Anzaldúa, G. C. (1987). *Borderlands/la frontera: The new mestiza.* San Francisco: Spinsters/Aunt Lute.

Acosta-Belén, E. (1975). Spanglish: A case of languages in contact. In M. Burt & H. Dulay (Eds.), *New directions in second language learning, teaching and bilingual education* (pp. 151–158). Washington, DC: TESOL.

Auer, P. (1984). *Bilingual conversation.* Amsterdam: John Benjamins.

Baker, O. (1980). Categories of code switching in Hispanic communities: Untangling the terminology (Sociolinguistic Working Paper No. 76). Austin, TX: Southwest Educational Development Laboratory.

Eastman, C. (Ed.). (1992). Codeswitching as an urban language contact phenomenon. *Journal of Multilingual and Multicultural Development, 13*(1/2), 1–17.

Goffman, E. (1979) Footing. *Semiotica, 25,* 1–29.

Gumperz, J. J. (1976). The sociolinguistic significance of conversational code-switching (Working Papers No. 46). Berkeley: University of California.

Gumperz, J. J. (1982). *Discourse strategies.* Cambridgeshire: Cambridge University Press.

Hymes, D. H. (1974). *Foundations in sociolinguistics: An ethnographic approach.* Philadelphia: University of Pennsylvania Press.

Labov, W. (1972). *Sociolinguistic patterns.* Philadelphia: University of Pennsylvania Press.

LePage, R. B., & Tabouret-Keller, A. (1985). *Acts of identity: Creole-based approaches to language and ethnicity.* Cambridge: Cambridge University Press.

Marlos, L., Zentella, A. C. (1978). A quantified analysis of code switching by four Philadelphia Puerto Rican adolescents. *University of Pennsylvania Review of Linguistics, 3,* 46–57.

Milán, W. (1982). Spanish in the inner city: Puerto Rican speech in New York. In J. A. Fishman & G. Keller (Eds.), *Bilingual education for Hispanic students in the United States* (pp. 191–206). New York: Columbia University, Teachers' College Press.

Myers-Scotton, C. (1992). Comparing codeswitching and borrowing. In C. Eastman (Ed.), *Code switching* [Special issue]. *Journal of Multilingual and Multicultural Development, 13*(1/2), 19–39.

Poplack, S. (1980). Sometimes I'll start a sentence in Spanish y *termino en español:* Toward a typology of code switching. *Linguistics, 18,* 581–616.

Poplack, S., & Sankoff, D. (1988). Code-switching. In U. Ammon, N. Dittmar, & K. J. Mattheier (Eds.), *Sociolinguistics: An international handbook of language and society.* Berlin: Walter de Gruyter.

Torres, L. (1992). Code-mixing as a narrative strategy in a bilingual community. *World Englishes, 11*(2/3), 183–193.

Valdés, G. (1981). Code switching as a deliberate verbal strategy: A micro-analysis of direct and indirect requests among Chicano bilingual speakers. In R. P. Durán (Ed.), *Latino language and communicative behavior* (pp. 95–108). Norwood, NJ: Ablex Press.

Weinreich, U. (1968). *Languages in contact.* The Hague: Mounton. (Original work published 1953)

Zentella, A. C. (1981). Language variety among Puerto Ricans. In C. F. Ferguson & S. B. Heath (Eds.), *Language in the USA* (pp. 218–238). London: Cambridge University Press.

Zentella, A. C. (1990). Integrating qualitative and quantitative methods in the study of bilingual code switching. *Annals of the New York Academy of Sciences: The uses of linguistics, 583,* 75–92.

1. Zentella says she disagrees with two sorts of comments that have been made about bilinguals: first, the sort of comments made by Uriel Weinreich that the "ideal bilingual" doesn't switch languages with a single sentence (paragraph 3) and, second, the popular notions that bilinguals who codeswitch are doing harm to the languages they speak and that they don't necessarily speak those languages well (paragraph 5). What evidence does Zentella offer against these views? How successful is she in arguing against them? Why?

2. Zentella distinguishes three kinds of factors that influence the behavior of bilingual codeswitchers: "on the spot," "in the head," and "out of the mouth." What do they mean? Why are these distinctions useful to students of bilingualism?

3. What evidence does Zentella provide that codeswitching relates to the creation of identities in bilingual communities? What sorts of identities do codeswitchers create? How?

on language use

4. Codeswitching is especially noticeable to those who don't speak one of the languages involved in the switching, yet even monolinguals engage in style shifting, moving from one style or variety of their language to another (for example, when a minister or politician who is speaking Standard English switches to a regional or ethnic dialect for humor or to make a point). When do you shift styles? Why?

for writing

5. Imagine that someone has written to an on-line chat room you frequent, complaining about the language practices of bilinguals where he or she lives. The complainer argues that when the bilinguals mix their two languages, they show that they do not speak either language well and that they will never be able to separate their languages. Write a rebuttal in which you explain that the complainer does not understand basic facts about how bilingualism works, drawing on Zentella's selection for evidence.

6. A challenge of research writing is summarizing lengthy arguments of the sort that Zentella makes here. In about 300 words, write a summary of this selection that you might be able to draw on if you were writing a research paper on bilingualism or codeswitching.

Greg Evans is the creator of **Luann**, a syndicated comic strip that focuses on adolescence through the adventures of Luann, her friends, her classmates who are anything but friends, and her family. In this selection, Miguel, a high-school exchange student from a Spanish-speaking country, and Luann are having a conversation until Tiffany arrives. Note how Evans uses codeswitching for humorous ends so that even monolingual speakers of English can understand what is going on.

Hector Cantú's and Carlos Castellanos's **Baldo** focuses on a Hispanic family—Baldo, his sister, his dad, and an elderly aunt who lives with them. Cantú is the writer for the series, and Castellanos, the illustrator. Here, we feature two selections. The first comic strip mocks the status of Spanish in the United States while the second one demonstrates codeswitching as a resource for creating verbal art. (We include a Spanish-language version of the second strip to demonstrate what is lost in translation.) As you study these comic strips, consider how comics in general—a marginal genre in many ways—offer evidence of the issues that society at large finds problematic.

Em-push-a-los! an artful combination of English *push* and Spanish *empujalos* "shove them" (note the phonetic similarity between English *push* and Spanish *-puj-*). Likely the closest Spanish verb to "push back" is *rechazar* "to repel, drive back, rebuff," which, like many of its English meanings, has formal or learned connotations and would be inappropriate in this context.

Atras "back."

Ru-ra nonsense sounds (like English "Rah-Rah, Sis-boom-bah"). **Túmbalos** "knock them down." **¡Duro, duro!** "hard, hard." **Zam, pam, pam** onomatopoeic sounds (of someone getting knocked down).

Esta gente no sabe apreciar el espíritu de solidaridad. "These guys don't know how to ap-

about the texts

1. How does Greg Evans combine English and Spanish in his comic strip so that even monolingual speakers of English can understand everything that is going on?

2. In the *Baldo* strip about bilingual telemarketers, why must Baldo's dad "resist [the] phony allure of bilingual telemarketers"? What does this strip tell us about the status of Spanish in the United States? Explain.

3. In the *Baldo* strip about school spirit, how do Cantú and Castellanos employ codeswitching? What sorts of cultural knowledge must one have to understand the strip? Why?

on language use

4. It's almost certain that Greg Evans does not speak Spanish well. Miguel says Luann looks "*muy fantástico*," instead of "*muy fantástica*," what he should have said according to the rules for gender agreement in Spanish. (Had Luann or Tiffany told Miguel that *he* looked fantastic, the correct form would have been *fantástico*.) A native speaker of Spanish would never make such an error. Evans's error can also be used to support the claim that what is usually termed Spanglish is not a new language but a linguistic practice with complex rules for combining the two languages, using the grammatical rules of each language. Why and how?

5. Study the two versions of the *Baldo* comic strip about school spirit carefully. How do they compare? (The monolingual version of the cheers is "Push 'em back, Push 'em back, Way back.") How does the strip combine English and Spanish to convey more than can be communicated in either language separately?

for writing

6. Analyze several *Baldo* strips <ucomics.com/baldo>; for evidence of codeswitching. Write an essay in which you analyze how the characters combine the two languages and their purposes for doing so. If you don't have experience with Spanish or a language other than English, you can work with a classmate who does. In writing your paper, be sure to provide glosses for readers who may not understand some of the language in the strip. Be sure to include the strips you discuss.

7. Though comic strips are intended to be humorous, they function as a mirror of social issues, including attitudes about language. Choose any comic strip and study it for what it reveals about attitudes toward language. (For instance, the character Cathy from the eponymous strip speaks in exclamations!) Look for comics using the language of people who are not middle-class, who are not white, or who are from an area widely believed to have a unique accent. Write an essay in which you present your findings. Be sure to include the strips you discuss.

In this article, which ran in the Fort Worth Star Telegram in April 2002, staff writer Diane Smith discusses a situation that many Americans might find surprising: immigrants to the United States often find that learning Spanish is as valuable as or even more valuable than learning English. As you read, seek to discover why this might be true.

DIANE SMITH

Newcomers Confront Language Melting Pot

Sabina Celebic's Spanish words tumble out effortlessly as she lists the names of her favorite Mexican actors.

In English, the 17-year-old explains how her childhood memories are tarnished by the reality of war. And in her native Bosnian, she talks to her parents.

"I can switch back and forth —English, Bosnian and Spanish," Celebic said, her voice filling with pride. "People are like, 'Wow, that's so impressive.'"

Celebic's family came to Dallas as refugees. She said their aim was to build a better future in the United States after war destroyed their homeland. Many refugees and immigrants who arrive in North Texas come with the understanding that they will have to work hard, save money and learn English.

But survival in their new surroundings often means learning some Spanish, too.

"You learn to talk like the 5 people around you. The people that you meet on a day-to-day basis," said Keith Walters, a professor at the University of Texas who studies multilingualism in the United States.

Because refugees and Latin American immigrants often lack English skills, they end up in entry-level jobs such as cleaning, factory work or construction work, said Anne Marie Weiss-Armush, founder of Dallas International, a nonprofit coalition of more than 1,400 international and ethnic organizations in North Texas.

"They don't have much interaction with English-speakers because the people in those jobs are Latinos," she said.

Historically, Texas has attracted hundreds of thousands of immigrants from Mexico, but it has also drawn immigrants from other countries.

During the past decade, waves of people fleeing wars, natural disasters and poverty have moved to the state, drawn by family and economic opportunities. Africans, Eastern Europeans and Asians have moved here along with a continuing influx of Latin Americans who want to start anew.

These diverse cultures met, 10 and the result is a rich international exchange every day at work, in school and in immigrant neighborhoods. It enables Celebic to speak with friends who were born in Mexico City, while allowing a Somalian woman to communicate with her Latin American co-workers at an airport eatery.

Anab Ibrahim, 25, picked up Spanish on the job at Dallas/ Fort Worth Airport.

Sabina Celebic, 17, of Dallas, concentrates on homework. She has been learning Spanish in addition to English since coming to Texas.

"I just talked to my employees. They just teach me," the Euless resident said.

Ibrahim slips from Somalian to Spanish with little prompting.

"*¿Cómo estas, amiga?* (How are you, friend?)," said a Somalian friend.

"*Bien. Bien* (Fine. Fine)," she responded with a chuckle. "It is very important to learn Spanish 15 in Texas," Ibrahim said in Somali through an interpreter.

Zonia Velasco, an immigrant from the Philippines, took some Spanish classes in her homeland. But the physical therapist decided to brush up on the language when she moved to Texas to better serve patients. Often they were her teachers.

"We are very globalized," she said.

Spanish-language news and television help supplement lessons for some people. Celebic watches Spanish soap operas and listens to Shakira, a well-known Colombian singer.

At North Dallas High School where Celebic is a sophomore, cultural exchange is the norm. There, Mexican students talk about soccer with those who played the sport in Africa.

And learning Spanish is al- 20 most a subconscious endeavor, said Rhadames Solano, Celebic's Spanish teacher. He said attending classes alongside Salvadorians, Asians and Bosnians can offer "a great opportunity to be trilingual."

Even Solano is making that attempt.

"My target is Vietnamese, but it is so tough," he said.

about the text

1. Do you think most Americans would be surprised by this article? Were you? Why or why not?

2. Bilingualism in the United States is often tied to social class and mobility. As best you can, describe those complex relationships. How do they help account for the generally negative attitudes many Americans have toward other languages, especially Spanish?

on language use

3. Which languages other than English are widely spoken where you live or study? What is the likelihood that immigrants in your area will have to learn not only English but another language as well? What would that language be? Why?

4. Smith does not say that immigrants to any country, especially those who come for economic reasons, generally expect that they will have to make changes to adapt to their new country. Additionally, she does not point out that in most parts of the world, people do not find the idea of learning a new language—or languages—alarming. (Recall that most of the world's inhabitants are bilingual or multilingual and that bilingualism or multilingualism can be found in many communities and countries around the world.) Why does she leave these facts out? What helps account for the fact that Americans usually do not think of learning another language as an opportunity?

for writing

5. This article reminds us that there is no single American experience, whether for immigrants or for those whose ancestors have been here for centuries. Interview two immigrants to the United States who did not arrive here speaking English. Ask them how they learned the language, what motivations they had for learning it, and what challenges it presented. Try to interview at least one person who is not a student. If you immigrated to the United States and learned English here, you may write about your own experience, but interview at least one other person. Whoever you interview, be sure to identify the person using a pseudonym in order to maintain his or her anonymity (unless you're writing about yourself). In your essay, describe those experiences in all their complexity.

6. Investigate your school's resources for helping adults learn English as a foreign or second language. Look for information on programs that prepare adult students to do academic work and those that prepare immigrants or foreign workers for other types of work. As part of this assignment, you may wish to interview a few of the students themselves, as well as the people who organize or teach in these programs, in order to learn about what support, if any, is available for these adult students. If your school has no such resources, investigate whether there is a need for such programs in your area. Write an essay reporting your findings.

a host of other tongues

The next group of readings in this chapter considers a small number of the many other languages found in the United States today. In some cases, the selections demonstrate how these languages have influenced American English or how English has shaped them. Other selections look at these languages from the perspectives of identity or loss. We begin by looking at the linguistic legacy of Eastern European Jewish immigrants to this country. Clyde Haberman examines the influence of Yiddish on American English, and a page from Dr. Seuss shows us that the Cat in the Hat sometimes speaks Yiddish. The next set of readings addresses some of the languages that Asian immigrants have brought here. Amy Tan writes about all her Englishes and how many of them have been influenced by the Chinese spoken in her home when she was growing up. The selection from Lan Cao's novel *Monkey Bridge* offers a fictional account of the language in Vietnamese immigrant families and the ways that children, because of their language-learning abilities, often become linguistic and cultural translators for their parents. Hien Nguyen, responding to Cao, describes his own experiences translating for his mother. Finally, Monileak Ourng, an exchange student from France whose parents emigrated there from Cambodia, compares and contrasts her experiences with those of an American-born friend whose parents had likewise fled Cambodia, exploring the complex links between language and identity among first-generation immigrants. For each of these readings, think about what the languages—both from the old and from the new countries—have to do with the identities of the people who use them.

This selection focuses on Yiddish, a language that has played an important role in the history of American English and in Jewish communities around the world. A Germanic language that has borrowed many words from Hebrew, Aramaic, Slavic, and Romance languages, Yiddish is currently spoken by some 5 million Jews around the world, all of whom trace their roots to Eastern Europe. In **The Oys of Yiddish (Ignore at Your Peril),** *which appeared in the New York Times in October 2000, Clyde Haberman discusses the influence of Yiddish on American English. As implied by Haberman, Yiddish is not widely spoken today in the United States. Although many Jewish immigrants to the United States from Eastern Europe in the early twentieth century spoke this language, they quickly gave it up as a response to the great pressures on all immigrants to assimilate, pressures further fueled by anti-Semitism, both in their homelands and in the United States. Thus, the majority of American speakers of Yiddish learned the language as children, but are now elderly and have not spoken it for years.*

We also include here a page from **Di Kats der Payats,** *literally "The Clowning Cat," which is the Yiddish version of The Cat in the Hat, by Dr. Seuss and translated by Zackary Sholem Berger. It's an example of the process of reclaiming Yiddish that some younger Jewish Americans are now engaged in. One aspect of reclaiming the language is the desire for consumer goods, in this case, a children's book, in* mame-loshen, *the native language.*

CLYDE HABERMAN

The Oys of Yiddish (Ignore at Your Peril)

WHAT A *NOODGE!* She made me *shlep* to the theater for tickets to a *schmaltzy* play. While I waited, this *nudnik* kept *kibitzing*. I don't mean to *kvetch*, but his *schmoozing* was annoying. His *shtick* made me so *meshuga*, I walked away. But I tripped. Sometimes, I can be a *klutz.*

The funny thing is that, however inelegant that paragraph may be, you probably understood it. If you are a New Yorker, you may even have thought that every word was standard English. That's pretty solid evidence of how a fair amount of Yiddish, the language of European Jews, has become mainstream in America, land of the free and home of the *bagel.*

Here is another sign. Few eyebrows were raised when Hillary Rodham Clinton and Representative Rick A. Lazio, rivals for a New York Senate seat and without a Jewish bone in their bodies, both tossed out *chutzpah* in a recent debate. They took for granted that a national television audience would know they meant gall.

Ah, but there is a pitfall that can leave the unwary messed up—*farpotshket*, if you will. The Yiddish that Americans tend to know (most Jews included) consists of only a word here, a word there, and often those words are exceedingly vulgar. Yet clueless speakers casually toss them out all the time, and now and then they land in hot water.

Former senator Alfonse M. D'Amato of New York learned his lesson during his 1998 re-election campaign when he tried to be a *shtarker*, a big shot, before a Jewish audience. He dismissed his opponent, Charles E. Schumer, with a Yiddish word commonly used by New Yorkers to call someone a jerk. Most of them have no idea that the word means penis and is so coarse that it won't be printed here. No doubt Mr. D'Amato lost the election for many reasons. But he didn't help himself by behaving like a *shmo* (a cleaned-up version of another popular Yiddish word for jerk that also means penis).

"People can get into trouble when they think they know more than they do—what's surprising?" said Samuel Norich, publisher of *The Forward*, a venerable Yiddish newspaper in New York that also has English and Russian editions.

Call it, with apologies to the late lexicographer Leo Rosten, the Oys of Yiddish.[1]

A few years ago, lawyers in a Boston case called the other side's court papers "*dreck*." They thought they were simply saying "junk." But in Yiddish, *dreck* means excrement. The judge, not amused, gave them a *klop in kop*. If you prefer, he read them the riot act.

Americans in places where the Jewish influence has been great often refer blithely to the rear end as the *tochis*, having no inkling that this word, too, is vulgar. They will say something is worth *bubkes*—nothing—unaware that the word derives from Yiddish for goat droppings. They will call a crotchety old man an *alter kocker*, blind to the fact that it means old defecator. (And that is a sanitized translation; just try saying it in front of your *bubbe*.)

On the flip side, some innocent words have come to assume sexual meaning. *Shtup* means to push or to press, but it has also become a way to say fornicate.

Why do such problems arise?

---

1. **The Oys of Yiddish** a pun on the title of Leo Rosten's book *The Joys of Yiddish*. "Oy" is a Yiddish exclamation of surprise or disbelief.

Partly it is because Yiddish in the post-Holocaust era is hardly a thriving language, despite enjoying a small revival on college campuses and remaining the *mame-loshen*, or mother tongue, of many Hasidic Jews. In the absence of natural growth, the language fell into the hands of Hollywood and the Borscht Belt[2]—treated far too often, Mr. Norich says, as just "a bunch of curse words."

Lost in the popular culture is memory of Yiddish as the language of "a vast body of literature," says Aaron Lansky, president of the National Yiddish Book Center in Amherst, Massachusetts. A similar lament comes from Ruth R. Wisse, a Harvard professor of Yiddish and comparative literature. "Unfortunately," she says, "what people associate Yiddish with is *kitsch* and poverty and a part of the Jewish culture that ultimately doesn't have to be taken seriously."

She has a point. Sometimes, all it takes to get a laugh is to put a Yiddish 15 "sh" in front of a word. That shushing sound has "formidable phonetic power," Mr. Rosten once observed in his best fancy-shmancy language.

Not everyone bemoans Yiddish's joke potential. Rabbi Moshe Waldoks of Brookline, Massachusetts, who co-edited "The Big Book of Jewish Humor," admires Yiddish's "earthy realism" and calls it the perfect light vehicle to "deflate pomposity."

Mr. Lansky understands that sentiment, even if he feels that Yiddish doesn't get the respect it deserves. "Look, I don't want to get too heavy-handed," he says. "You want to make a joke? *Gezintahayt.*" Go in health.

---

2. **Borscht Belt** nickname for an area in the Catskill Mountains, northwest of New York City, where summer resorts were popular with Jewish families early in the twentieth century. The entertainment at these resorts often included comedy routines that were performed at least partially in Yiddish. The name comes from *borscht*, a Russian soup made of beets, which was popular among Jewish immigrants and their families.

"Te, te! Nisht gedayget!
Nisht gezorgt!" makht di kats.
"A kunts iz nisht shlekht,"
Makht di Kats der Payats.

‫„טע, טע! נישט געדאַגהט!‬
‫ניטש געזאָרגט!" מאַכט די קאַץ.‬
‫„אַ קונץ איז נישט שלעכט",‬
‫מאַכט די קאַץ דער פּאַיאַץ.‬

Some Yiddish Borrowings in American English

Here's a list of the Yiddish-origin words in Haberman's article. As is often the case with words borrowed from languages that do not use the Roman alphabet, some words have multiple spellings. How many words do you know? How many do you use? Why would some Americans but not others be likely to know and use these words?

alter kocker crotchety old man.

bagel hard, ring-shaped bread roll.

bubbe, bobe, bubbeh grandmother.

bubkes (something) worthless.

chutzpah gall or impudence.

dreck trash, rubbish.

farpotshket messed up.

gezintahayt, gesundheit: literally, "health," said to someone who sneezes.

kibitz interfere in a meddling way (e.g., looking over someone's shoulder and offering advice while s/he is playing cards).

kitsch art that is sentimental yet pretentious.

klop in kop a knock on the head.

klutz someone who is clumsy and inept, physically or interactionally.

kvetch a whiner or complainer; to whine or complain.

mame-loshen (sometimes written as one word), mother tongue, especially Yiddish.

meshuga crazy.

noodge a bore, a person who nags or pesters.

nudnik an oaf or foolish person.

schlep, shlep to carry or drag something, generally something that is heavy and unnecessary.

schmaltzy, shmaltzy sentimental or corny (literally, chicken fat).

schmooze engage in intimate conversation, gossip, chat.

shmo an idiot, a fool.

shtarker big shot.

shtick originally, a stage routine; now broadened to area of interest.

shtup push, press, copulate.

tochis, tochus the backside or buttocks (source of English "tush").

about the texts

1. Which words of Yiddish origin in the article did you already know? Which can you figure out from context, even if they are not familiar?

2. Haberman claims that your ability to understand the opening paragraph of his article depends on where you live in North America. Why?

3. What does Ruth Wisse mean when she says that "what people associate Yiddish with is kitsch and poverty and a part of Jewish culture that ultimately doesn't have to be taken seriously" (paragraph 13)? Many would argue that American society generally treats immigrant cultures in this way. Can you find evidence for such a claim in language or popular culture (for example, in movies, cartoons, television, or advertisements)?

on language use

4. Words that have been borrowed from Yiddish to English have often changed meanings, a common consequence of language contact and borrowing. Give several examples from this article, comparing the original meaning with the meaning in English. Note that in many cases, the English meaning has been "bleached" so that a vulgar meaning in Yiddish has an emotionally loaded, but far less charged, meaning in English. Why might borrowing work this way?

5. Haberman notes that Hillary Rodham Clinton and Rick Lazio, neither of whom is Jewish, both used the word "chutzpah" during their debate for a New York senate seat. Why might they have used this word in that context? What risks do speakers run when using terms or expressions that belong to a group of which they are not members?

6. The ad for the Yiddish translation of *The Cat in the Hat* notes that it will contain transliteration of the Yiddish text in Roman script (in addition to the Hebrew alphabet). Why would the creator of this book likely include the transliteration? What functions might the transliteration serve, and for whom?

for writing

7. Yiddish is associated with a group of people who share a religion and culture that have suffered discrimination; when Yiddish came to the United States, its use began to decline under the assimilationist pressure immigrants felt early in the twentieth century. Investigate how Yiddish came into being, how it spread, or why its use has declined in the United States. Write an essay about what you discover, focusing on the effect of social factors on the nature and life of languages.

8. Choose a language other than Yiddish and investigate words English has borrowed from it. Focus in particular on which words have been borrowed, the semantic domains of the words (e.g., medical, religious, or culinary terms), and the likely path of borrowing (e.g., did immigrants bring the words with them, as was the case in the United States? Did educated people make a point of using the words to show they knew a particular language, as was the case in the Renaissance? Did the words come into English at a time when speakers of English were conquered, as was the case after the Battle of Hastings in 1066?). Write an essay in which you present your findings.

9. Speakers of Yiddish are not the only group participating in an ethnic revival. Choose another group and investigate it, focusing on what role, if any, language plays in this revival. Language learning may range from individuals making an effort to learn some of their heritage language to efforts that result in the heritage language being introduced into the school curriculum, as has been done by speakers of Cajun French in Louisiana.

AMY TAN

Mother Tongue

I AM NOT A SCHOLAR of English or literature. I cannot give you much more than personal opinions on the English language and its variations in this country or others.

I am a writer. And by that definition, I am someone who has always loved language. I am fascinated by language in daily life. I spend a great deal of my time thinking about the power of language—the way it can evoke an emotion, a visual image, a complex idea, or a simple truth. Language is the tool of my trade. And I use them all —all the Englishes I grew up with.

Recently, I was made keenly aware of the different Englishes I do use. I was giving a talk to a large group of people, the same talk I had already given to half a dozen other groups. The nature of the talk was about my writing, my life, and my book, *The Joy Luck Club*. The talk was going along well enough, until I remembered one major difference that made the whole talk sound wrong. My mother was in the room. And it was perhaps the first time she had heard me give a lengthy speech—using the kind of English I have never used with her. I was saying things like, "The intersection of memory upon imagination" and "There is an aspect of my fiction that relates to thus-and-thus"—a speech filled with carefully wrought grammatical phrases, burdened, it suddenly seemed to me, with nominalized forms, past perfect tenses, conditional phrases—all the forms of standard English that I had learned in school and through books, the forms of English I did not use at home with my mother.

Just last week, I was walking down the street with my mother, and I again found myself conscious of the English I was using, the English I do use with her. We were talking about the price of new and used furniture and I heard myself saying this: "Not waste money that way." My husband was with us as well, and he didn't notice any switch in my English. And then I realized why. It's because over

Amy Tan *is best known for her novels* The Joy Luck Club *(1989),* The Kitchen God's Wife *(1991), and* The Bonesetter's Daughter *(2001). She often writes of the relationships between Chinese American daughters and their mothers, and her work is praised for its realistic and sensitive rendering of dialogue. During adolescence, Tan lost her father and her brother to brain tumors. That was perhaps one reason her mother hoped she would become a neurosurgeon, but instead Tan studied English, at San Jose State. This selection is the text of a talk Tan gave as part of a panel entitled "Englishes: Whose English Is It Anyway?" at a symposium on language in San Francisco in 1989. As you read, try to imagine Tan delivering this speech. Also reflect on the ways in which American English is what it is because of the many people who, like Tan's mother, have not spoken it natively but have come to claim it as their own.*

the twenty years we've been together I've often used that same kind of English with him, and sometimes he even uses it with me. It has become our language of intimacy, a different sort of English that relates to family talk, the language I grew up with.

So you'll have some idea of what this family talk I heard sounds like, I'll quote what my mother said during a recent conversation which I videotaped and then transcribed. During this conversation, my mother was talking about a political gangster in Shanghai who had the same last name as her family's, Du, and how the gangster in his early years wanted to be adopted by her family which was rich by comparison. Later, the gangster became more powerful, far richer than my mother's family, and one day showed up at my mother's wedding to pay his respects. Here's what she said in part:

"Du Yusong having business like fruit stand. Like off the street kind. He is Du like Du Zong—but not Tsung-ming Island people. The local people call putong, the river east side, he belong to that side local people. That man want to ask Du Zong father take him in like become own family. Du Zong father wasn't look down on him, but didn't take seriously, until that man big like become mafia. Now important person, very hard to inviting him. Chinese way, came only to show respect, don't stay for dinner. Respect for making big celebration, he shows up. Mean gives lots of respect. Chinese custom. Chinese social life that way. If too important won't have to stay too long. He come to my wedding. I didn't see, I heard it. I gone to boy's side, they have YMCA dinner. Chinese age I was 19."

You should know that my mother's expressive command of English belies how much she actually understands. She reads the *Forbes* report, listens to Wall Street Week, converses daily with her stockbroker, reads all of Shirley MacLaine's books with ease—all kinds of things I can't begin to understand. Yet some of my friends tell me they understand fifty percent of what my mother says. Some say they understand eighty to ninety percent. Some say they understand none of it, as if she were speaking pure Chinese. But to me, my mother's English is perfectly clear, perfectly natural. It's my mother tongue. Her language, as I hear it, is vivid, direct, full of observation and imagery. That was the language that helped shape the way I saw things, expressed things, made sense of the world.

Lately, I've been giving more thought to the kind of English my mother speaks. Like others, I have described it to people as "broken" or "fractured" English. But I wince when I say that. It has always bothered me that I can think of no way to describe it other than "broken," as if it were damaged and needed to be fixed, as if it lacked a certain wholeness and soundness. I've heard other terms used, "limited English," for example. But they seem just as bad, as if everything is limited, including people's perception of the limited English speaker.

I know this for a fact, because when I was growing up, my mother's "limited" English limited my perception of her. I was ashamed of her English. I believed that her English reflected the quality of what she had to say. That is, because she expressed them imperfectly her thoughts were imperfect. And I had plenty of empirical evidence to support me: the fact that people in department stores, at banks, and at restaurants did not take her seriously, did not give her good service, pretended not to understand her, or even acted as if they did not hear her.

My mother has long realized the limitations of her English as well. When I was fifteen, she used to have me call people on the phone to pretend I was she. In this guise, I was forced to ask for information or even to complain and yell at people who had been rude to her. One time it was a call to her stockbroker in New York. She had cashed out her small portfolio and it just so happened we were going to go to New York the next week, our very first trip outside California. I had to get on the phone and say in an adolescent voice that was not very convincing. "This is Mrs. Tan." 10

And my mother was standing in the back whispering loudly, "Why he don't send me check, already two weeks late. So mad he lie to me, losing me money."

And then I said in perfect English. "Yes, I'm getting rather concerned. You had agreed to send the check two weeks ago, but it hasn't arrived."

Then she began to talk more loudly, "What he want, I come to New York tell him front of his boss, you cheating me?" And I was trying to calm her down, make her be quiet, while telling the stockbroker, "I can't tolerate any more excuses. If I don't receive the check immediately, I am going to have to speak to your manager when I'm in New York next week." And sure enough, the following week there we were in front of this astonished stockbroker, and I was sitting there red-faced and quiet, and my mother, the real Mrs. Tan, was shouting at his boss in her impeccable broken English.

We used a similar routine just five days ago, for a situation that was far less humorous. My mother had gone to the hospital for an appointment, to find out about a benign brain tumor a CAT scan had revealed a month ago. She said she had spoken very good English, her best English, no mistakes. Still, she said, the hospital did not apologize when they said they had lost the CAT scan and she had come for nothing. She said they did not seem to have any sympathy when she told them she was anxious to know the exact diagnosis since her husband and son had both died of brain tumors. She said they would not give her any more information until the next time and she would have to make another appointment for that. So she said she would not leave until the doctor called her daughter. She wouldn't budge. And when the doctor finally called her daughter, me, who spoke in perfect English—lo and behold—we had assurances the CAT scan would be found, promises that a conference call on Monday would be held, and apologies for any suffering my mother had gone through for a most regrettable mistake.

I think my mother's English almost had an effect on limiting my possibil- 15 ities in life as well. Sociologists and linguists probably will tell you that a person's developing language skills are more influenced by peers. But I do think that the language spoken in the family, especially in immigrant families which are more insular, plays a large role in shaping the language of the child. And I believe that it affected my results on achievement tests, IQ tests, and the SAT. While my English skills were never judged as poor, compared to math, English could not be considered my strong suit. In grade school, I did moderately well, getting perhaps Bs, sometimes B⁺s in English, and scoring perhaps in the sixtieth or seventieth percentile on achievement tests. But those scores were not good enough to override the opinion that my true abilities lay in math and science, because in those areas I achieved As and scored in the ninetieth percentile or higher.

This was understandable. Math is precise; there is only one correct answer. Whereas, for me at least, the answers on English tests were always a judgment call, a matter of opinion and personal experience. Those tests were constructed around items like fill-in-the-blank sentence completion, such as "Even though Tom was _____, Mary thought he was _____." And the correct answer always seemed to be the most bland combinations of thoughts, for example, "Even though Tom was shy, Mary thought he was charming," with the grammatical structure "even though" limiting the correct answer to some sort of semantic opposites, so you wouldn't get answers like "Even though Tom was foolish, Mary thought he was ridiculous." Well, according to my mother, there were very few limitations as to what Tom could have been, and what Mary might have thought of him. So I never did well on tests like that.

The same was true with word analogies, pairs of words, in which you were supposed to find some sort of logical, semantic relationship—for example, "sunset" is to "nightfall" as _____ is to _____. And here, you would be presented with a list of four possible pairs, one of which showed the same kind of relationship: "red" is to "stoplight," "bus" is to "arrival," "chills" is to "fever," "yawn" is to "boring." Well, I could never think that way. I knew what the tests were asking, but I could not block out of my mind the images already created by the first pair, "sunset is to nightfall"—and I would see a burst of colors against a darkening sky, the moon rising, the lowering of a curtain of stars. And all the other pairs of words—red, bus, stoplight, boring —just threw up a mass of confusing images, making it impossible for me to sort out something as logical as saying: "A sunset precedes nightfall" is the same as "a chill precedes a fever." The only way I would have gotten that answer right would have been to imagine an associative situation, for example, my being disobedient and staying out past sunset, catching a chill at night, which turns into feverish pneumonia as punishment, which indeed did happen to me.

I have been thinking about all this lately, about my mother's English, about achievement tests. Because lately I've been asked, as a writer, why there are not more Asian-Americans represented in American literature. Why are there few Asian-Americans enrolled in creative writing programs? Why do so many Chinese students go into engineering? Well, these are broad sociological questions I can't begin to answer. But I have noticed in surveys—in fact, just last week—that Asian students, as a whole, always do significantly better on math achievement tests than in English. And this makes me think that there are other Asian-American students whose English spoken in the home might also be described as "broken" or "limited." And perhaps they also have teachers who are steering them away from writing and into math and science, which is what happened to me.

Fortunately, I happen to be rebellious in nature, and enjoy the challenge of disproving assumptions made about me. I became an English major my first year in college after being enrolled as pre-med. I started writing non-fiction as a freelancer the week after I was told by my former boss that writing was my worst skill and I should hone my talents toward account management.

But it wasn't until 1985 that I finally began to write fiction. And at first I wrote using what I thought to be wittily crafted sentences, sentences that would finally prove I had mastery over the English language. Here's an example from the first draft of a story that later made its way into *The Joy Luck Club*, but without this line: "That was my mental quandary in its nascent state." A terrible line, which I can barely pronounce.

Fortunately, for reasons I won't get into today, I later decided I should envision a reader for the stories I would write. And the reader I decided upon was my mother, because these were stories about mothers. So with this reader in mind—and in fact, she did read my early drafts—I began to write stories using all the Englishes I grew up with: the English I spoke to my mother, which for lack of a better term, might be described as "simple"; the English she used with me, which for lack of a better term might be described as "broken"; my translation of her Chinese, which could certainly be described as "watered down"; and what I imagined to be her translation of her Chinese if she could speak in perfect English, her internal language, and for that I sought to preserve the essence, but not either an English or a Chinese structure. I wanted to capture what language ability tests can never reveal: her intent, her passion, her imagery, the rhythms of her speech and the nature of her thoughts.

Apart from what any critic had to say about my writing, I knew I had succeeded where it counted when my mother finished reading my book, and gave me her verdict: "So easy to read."

about the text

1. How have Tan's attitudes toward her mother's English changed over the years? Why? Have you had similar experiences with your attitudes toward your parents' or other relatives' ways of using language? When?

2. Why is Tan suspicious of language ability tests? What are her specific complaints? What evidence does she offer for them? Do you agree or disagree with her argument? Why?

on language use

3. Part of the power of Tan's prose (and argument) lies in the artful way in which she uses language. Select several passages that you find especially effective and be prepared to explain why you like them.

4. Tan's text was written to be read aloud by the author herself. How does the text reflect this fact? How would hearing her deliver this paper be different from the experience you had reading it silently? How might it have been different if it were written to be read silently, as you read it?

5. Tan writes sympathetically about a group of people who often receive little sympathy, nonnative speakers of English. How does she achieve this effect? Why, in your opin-

ion, do nonnative speakers of English not receive much sympathy from native speakers of the language? Do you think the situation might be different if more Americans had the experience of living in a non-English-speaking country or spent more time studying other languages? Explain.

for writing

6. What does Tan mean when she says that she uses "all the Englishes [she] grew up with" (paragraph 2)? What are these Englishes? What problems does she have in giving them labels? Do you agree with Tan's implied argument that we should use all our Englishes proudly? Write an essay in which you evaluate Tan's position. To prepare for this assignment, think about your own Englishes and how you use and feel about them.

7. Tan writes about the ways in which matters of language create and divide families across generational lines. While such divisions are often especially clear in immigrant families, they are also present in nonimmigrant families where everyone speaks English. Write about such a division in your own family or that of someone you know. What do such divisions teach us about families? About generational differences? About language?

Lan Cao is a professor at the Marshall-Wythe School of Law at the College of William and Mary. She is also the author of Monkey Bridge (1997), the novel from which **Keeper of the Word** comes. (A monkey bridge is a spindly bamboo bridge used by Vietnamese peasants.) The novel recounts the experiences of a young woman who, like Lan Cao, fled the Vietnam War in 1975 and came to the United States. Some of the incidents Cao describes are recounted frequently in the writing of immigrants who came to the United States as children: specifically, the ways in which the transition from home country to the United States and the child's ability to learn English quickly force the child to become a caretaker for the family, robbing the parents of their authority and the child of her or his innocence and childhood.

At this point in the novel, the adolescent narrator and her mother have moved to the United States, leaving the girl's maternal grandfather—their only living relative—in Vietnam. The girl had arrived before her mother and stayed with Uncle Michael and Aunt Mary, an American colonel and his wife, whom her family had befriended while he was in Vietnam. As becomes clear, the narrator's mother understands very little English while her daughter has become quite fluent. As you read, try to put yourself in the narrator's situation. For some readers, it will be an all-too-familiar one; for others, it may be almost unimaginable.

In response to this excerpt from Cao's novel, Hien Nguyen wrote **Memories** in a course on bilingualism in 2002 at the University of Texas at Austin, where he majored in electrical engineering.

LAN CAO

Keeper of the Word

with a response by Hien Nguyen

I DISCOVERED SOON AFTER MY ARRIVAL in Falls Church that everything, even the simple business of shopping the American way, unsettled my mother's nerves. From the outside, it had been an ordinary building that held no promises or threats beyond four walls anchored to a concrete parking lot. But inside, the A&P brimmed with unexpected abundance. Built-in metal stands overflowed with giant oranges and grapefruits meticulously arranged into a pyramid. Columns of canned vegetables and fruits stood among multiple shelves as people well rehearsed to the demands of modern shopping meandered through the fluorescent aisles. I remembered the sharp chilled air against my face, the way the hydraulic door made a sucking sound as it closed behind.

My first week in Connecticut with Uncle Michael and Aunt Mary, I thought Aunt Mary was a genius shopper. She appeared to have the sixth sense of a bat and could identify, record, and register every item on sale. She was skilled in the art of coupon shopping—in the American version of Vietnamese haggling, the civil and acceptable mode of getting the customers to think they had gotten a good deal.

The day after I arrived in Farmington, Aunt Mary navigated the cart—and me—through aisles, numbered and categorized, crammed with jars and cardboard boxes, and plucked from them the precise product to match the coupons she carried. I had been astonished that day that the wide range of choices did not disrupt her plan. We had a schedule, I discovered, which Aunt Mary mapped out on a yellow pad, and which we followed, checking off item after item. She called it the science of shopping, the ability to resist the temptations of dazzling packaging. By the time we were through, our cart would be filled to the rim with cans of Coke, the kinds with flip-up caps that made can openers obsolete, in family-size cartons. We had chicken and meat sealed in tight, odorless packages, priced and weighed. We had fruits so beautifully polished and waxed they looked artificial. And for me, we had mangoes and papayas that were still hard and green but which Aunt Mary had handed to me like rare jewels from a now extinct land.

But my mother did not appreciate the exacting orderliness of the A&P. She could not give in to the precision of previously weighed and packaged food, the bloodlessness of beef slabs in translucent wrappers, the absence of carcasses and pigs' heads. In Saigon, we had only outdoor markets. "Sky markets," they were called, vast, prosperous expanses in the middle of the city where barrels of live crabs and yellow carps and booths of ducks and geese would be stacked side by side with cardboard stands of expensive silk fabric from Hong Kong. It was always noisy there—a voluptuous mix of animal and human sounds that the air itself had assimilated and held. The sharp acrid smell of gutters choked by the monsoon rain. The unambiguous odor of dried horse dung that lingered in the atmosphere, partially camouflaged by the fat, heavy scent of guavas and bananas.

My mother knew the vendors and even the shoppers by name and would take me from stall to stall to expose me to her skills. They were all addicted to each other's oddities. My mother would feign indifference and they would inevitably call out to her. She would heed their call and they would immediately retreat into sudden apathy. They knew my mother's slick bargaining skills, and she, in turn, knew how to navigate with grace through their extravagant prices and rehearsed huffiness. Theirs had been a mating dance, a match of wills.

Toward the center of the market, a man with a spotted boa constrictor coiled around his neck stood and watched day after day over an unruly hodgepodge of hand-dyed cotton shirts, handkerchiefs, and swatches of white muslin; funerals were big business in Vietnam. To the side, in giant paper bags slit with round openings, were canaries and hummingbirds which my mother bought, one hundred at a time, and freed, one by one, into our garden; it was a good deed designed to generate positive karma for the family. My mother, like the country itself, was obsessed with karma. In fact, the Vietnamese word for "please," as in "could you please," means literally "to make good karma." "Could you please pass the butter" becomes "Please make good karma and pass me the butter." My mother would cup each bird in her hand and set it on my head. It was her way of immersing me in a wellspring of karmic charm, and in that swift moment of delight when the bird's wings spread over my head as it contemplated flight, I believed life itself was utterly beautiful and blessed.

Every morning, we drifted from stack to stack, vendor to vendor. There were no road maps to follow—tables full of black market Prell and Colgate were pocketed among vegetable stands one day and jars of medicinal herbs the next. The market was randomly organized, and only the mighty and experienced like my mother could navigate its patternless paths.

But with a sense of neither drama nor calamity, my mother's ability to navigate and decipher simply became undone in our new life. She preferred the improvisation of haggling to the conventional certainty of discount coupons, the primordial messiness and fishmongers' stink of the open-air market to the aroma-free order of individually wrapped fillets.

Now, a mere three and a half years or so after her last call to the sky market, the dreadful truth was simply this: we were going through life in reverse, and I was the one who would help my mother through the hard scrutiny of ordinary suburban life. I would have to forgo the luxury of adolescent experiments and temper tantrums, so that I could scoop my mother out of harm's way and give her sanctuary. Now, when we stepped into the exterior world, I was the one who told my mother what was acceptable or unacceptable behavior.

All children of immigrant parents have experienced these moments. 10 When it first occurs, when the parent first reveals the behavior of a child, is a defining moment. Of course, all children eventually watch their parents' astonishing return to the vulnerability of childhood, but for us the process begins much earlier than expected.

"We don't have to pay the moment we decide to buy the pork. We can put as much as we want in the cart and pay only once, at the checkout counter."

It took a few moments' hesitation for my mother to succumb to the peculiarity of my explanation.

And even though I hesitated to take on the responsibility, I had no other choice. It was not a simple process, the manner in which my mother relinquished motherhood. The shift in status occurred not just in the world but in the safety of our home as well, and it became most obvious when we entered the realm of language. I was like Kiki, my pet bird in Saigon, tongue untwisted and sloughed of its rough and thick exterior. According to my mother, feeding the bird crushed red peppers had caused it to shed its tongue in successive layers and allowed it to speak the language of humans.

Every morning during that month of February 1975, while my mother paced the streets of Saigon and witnessed the country's preparation for imminent defeat, I followed Aunt Mary around the house, collecting words like a beggar gathering rain with an earthen pan. She opened her mouth, and out came a constellation of gorgeous sounds. Each word she uttered was a round stone, with the smoothness of something that had been rubbed and polished by the waves of a warm summer beach. She could swim straight through her syllables. On days when we studied together, I almost convinced myself that we would continue that way forever, playing with the movement of sound itself. I would listen as she tried to inspire me into replicating the "th" sound with the seductive powers of her voice. "Slip the tip of your tongue between your front teeth and pull it back real quick," she would coax and coax. Together, she and I sketched the English language, its curious cadence and rhythm, into the receptive Farmington landscape. Only with Aunt Mary and Uncle Michael could I give myself an inheritance my parents never gave me: the gift of language. The story of English was nothing less than the poetry of sound and motion. To this day, Aunt Mary's voice remains my standard for perfection.

My superior English meant that, unlike my mother and Mrs. Bay, I knew the difference between "cough" and "enough," "bough" and "through," "trough" and "thorough," "dough" and "fought." Once I made it past the fourth or fifth week in Connecticut, the new language Uncle Michael and Aunt Mary were teaching me began gathering momentum, like tumbleweed in a storm. This was my realization: we have only to let one thing go—the language we think in, or the composition of our dream, the grass roots clinging underneath its rocks—and all at once everything goes. It had astonished me, the ease with which continents shift and planets change course, the casual way in which the earth goes about shedding the laborious folds of its memories. Suddenly, out of that difficult space between here and there, English revealed itself to me with the ease of thread unspooled. I began to understand the levity and weight of its sentences. First base, second base, home run. New terminologies were not difficult to master, and gradually the possibility of perfection began edging its way into my life. How did those numerous Chinatowns and Little Italys sustain the will to maintain a distance, the desire to inhabit the edge and margin of American life? A mere eight weeks into Farmington, and the American Dream was exerting a sly but seductive pull.

By the time I left Farmington to be with my mother, I had already created for myself a different, more sacred tongue. Khe Sanh, the Tet Offensive, the Ho Chi Minh Trail[1]—a history as imperfect as my once obviously imperfect English—these were things that had rushed me into the American melting pot. And when I saw my mother again, I was no longer the same person she used to know. Inside my new tongue, my real tongue, was an astonishing new power. For my mother and her Vietnamese neighbors, I became the keeper of the word, the only one with access to the light-world. Like Adam, I had the God-given right to name all the fowls of the air and all the beasts of the field.

The right to name, I quickly discovered, also meant the right to stand guard over language and the right to claim unadulterated authority. Here was a language with an ocean's quiet mystery, and it would be up to me to render its vastness comprehensible to the newcomers around me. My language skill, my ability to decipher the nuances of American life, was what held us firmly in place, night after night, in our Falls Church living room. The ease with which I could fabricate wholly new plot lines from TV made the temptation to invent especially difficult to resist.

And since my mother couldn't understand half of what anyone was saying, television watching, for me, was translating and more. This, roughly, was how things went in our living room:

---

1. **Khe Sanh** a remote U.S. Marine base in Vietnam. On January 21, 1968, North Vietnamese troops launched an attack on Khe Sanh, starting a brutal 77-day battle. **Tet Offensive** a surprise attack on over a hundred South Vietnamese cities and towns by North Vietnamese troops during a truce declared to celebrate Tet, the Vietnamese New Year, in 1968. Although the offensive cost the North Vietnamese, it simultaneously cost the United States because it reduced the American public's willingness to continue fighting the war. **Ho Chi Minh Trail** a complex network of roads, paths, and jungle trails from North Vietnam through Laos and Cambodia to South Vietnam. The North used the trail throughout the war for transporting supplies and troops to the South. Ho Chi Minh (1890–1969) was president of North Vietnam from 1845 until 1969. He led the longest and costliest war against colonialism of the last century, first against the French and later the American presence in the Vietnamese peninsula.

The Bionic Woman had just finished rescuing a young girl, approximately my age, from drowning in a lake where she'd gone swimming against her mother's wishes. Once out of harm's way, Jaime made the girl promise she'd be more careful next time and listen to her mother.

Translation: the Bionic Woman rescued the girl from drowning in the lake, but commended her for her magnificent deeds, since the girl had heroically jumped into the water to rescue a prized police dog.

"Where's the dog?" my mother would ask. "I don't see him."　　20

"He's not there anymore, they took him to the vet right away. Remember?" I sighed deeply.

"Oh," my mother said. "It's strange. Strong girl, Bionic Woman."

The dog that I convinced her existed on the television screen was no more confusing than the many small reversals in logic and the new identities we experienced her first few months in America.

"I can take you in this aisle," a store clerk offered as she unlocked a new register to accommodate the long line of customers. She gestured us to "come over here" with an upturned index finger, a disdainful hook we Vietnamese use to summon dogs and other domestic creatures. My mother did not understand the ambiguity of American hand gestures. In Vietnam, we said "Come here" to humans differently, with our palm up and all four fingers waved in unison—the way people over here waved goodbye. A typical Vietnamese signal beckoning someone to "come here" would prompt, in the United States, a "goodbye," a response completely opposite from the one desired.

"Even the store clerks look down on us," my mother grumbled as we　25 walked home. This was a truth I was only beginning to realize: it was not the enormous or momentous event, but the gradual suggestion of irrevocable and protracted change that threw us off balance and made us know in no uncertain terms that we would not be returning to the familiarity of our former lives.

It was, in many ways, a lesson in what was required to sustain a new identity: it all had to do with being able to adopt a different posture, to reach deep enough into the folds of the earth to relocate one's roots and bend one's body in a new direction, pretending at the same time that the world was the same now as it had been the day before. I strove for the ability to realign my eyes, to shift with a shifting world and convince both myself and the rest of the world into thinking that, if the earth moved and I moved along with it, that motion, however agitated, would be undetectable. The process, which was as surprising as a river reversing course and flowing upstream, was easier said than done.

HIEN NGUYEN

Memories

AFTER READING THIS STORY, I found that many memories of my child-hood came rushing back. When I was a young child, my mother was very weak in the English language. Even after she had been here for more than fifteen years, she could hardly carry on a decent English conversation. As a result, I served as her translator while I was growing up. Out of my siblings, I had the best grasp of the Vietnamese language. The challenges were enormous. Since I was so young, I didn't know many words in English, which would result in me not being able to translate that particular word into Vietnamese. Not only did this frustrate her, but it also definitely frustrated me. I had to be there for her whether we were at the store, church, or movies or on the streets. My mother loved to talk, and her limited English forced her to repeat elementary sentences on a regular basis. She did how-ever, master filler words. Her favorite was "you know." I must admit, during the start of my translation days, I was often embarrassed to be speaking a foreign language around people who did not speak my language. This was most true when I had to translate words for her around my friends. Even though most people were amazed by my ability, I felt lower than them be-cause I was held back by my mother. As I got older, I felt a sense of pride whenever I translated for my mother. I felt proud because I knew that she was so grateful that I was there. I felt proud because I was slowly mastering two languages at the same time. My mother passed away over a year ago, and I still remember translating for her during her last days. Never had my Vietnamese meant so much. I was the only link between what her American friends said to her and what she said to them during her final hours. I knew that she appreciated how I was there from the beginning to the end. I often feel sad that I can no longer do this service for her. I often miss trying to find the right Vietnamese word to replace the English word I just heard. I'm just happy that I got a chance to do this for her and will never forget how much this service has affected me.

about the texts

1. What is your initial response to this selection from Cao's novel?

2. What is Cao's argument about the relationship between language and immigrant families? What evidence does she offer? How does her own use of language help convey her ideas?

3. How does Nguyen's response to Cao's selection help you think about language issues in immigrant families?

4. What are the consequences for immigrant family life in the United States when children speak more English than their parents? How does language become a source of power for the child that might disrupt the traditional patterns of family life?

on language use

5. If you've traveled abroad, you've quickly learned that simple gestures don't always mean the same thing in all cultures. Gestures that are vulgar in the United States may be acceptable elsewhere, and vice versa. Talk to three people who have lived outside the United States, asking them to discuss what they learned about gestures and gesturing across cultures.

6. Nguyen's response to Cao's selection offers insight into the challenges translators face, especially when they are children translating for adults. What are these specific linguistic and social challenges?

for writing

7. Like many immigrant children, Cao lost much of her native language—Vietnamese—and French, another language once widely spoken in Vietnam. The decline in her ability to use these languages hurt her relationship with her parents. As she has commented, "The more educated I became, the more separate I was from my parents. I think that is a very immigrant story." Many native speakers of English report similar situations: the more educated they become, the less they fit into their parents' world. Is such separation a necessary consequence of education for speakers of English in the United States? Are there ways to prevent it? Are there benefits of doing so? Should such efforts be made? Who should make those efforts? Why? Write an essay in which you respond to these questions.

8. Cao reminds us of the challenges that adult immigrants often face. Learning a new language can be very difficult if one has little education to begin with, if one's native language is different from English, or if one has to work and has little time to study. Also, in adjusting to a new culture, immigrants find that "common sense" often doesn't apply. Interview two people who came to the United States as adults and ask them what their transition was like. Write an essay about what you learn.

MONILEAK OURNG

Negotiating Identity

"W HEN I WAS A KID, my mom used to sing Taiwanese lullabies to me. Since then, I have always associated Taiwanese with my mom and with lullabies . . . Taiwanese lullabies."

Lying on her bed in her house in Stevensville, Maryland, on a summer night of the year 1999, Koeun was talking to me of her Taiwanese mother for the first time since we knew each other. Sitting on the mattress, which I was using as my bed during my stay at her home, I was listening to her confession thoroughly. As she was staring at the ceiling, talking slowly, I was under the impression that she had forgotten about my very presence in her room. She was speaking in the same way one speaks to a psychiatrist in his or her consulting room. Then, she suddenly came back to real life, looked at the alarm clock that was on her night stand: it was 2 in the morning. "OK, it's late," she said, and she turned off the light.

In the darkness of that summer night, I realized that there was a part of Koeun which made her completely different from me.

As a girl raised in a Cambodian family with no Chinese connections whatsoever, I'd always thought the Chinese language sounded rude. It was the language of the shopkeepers in the Chinese grocery stores in Lyon and Paris, the language of the butcher speaking in his native language to his colleague while he was cutting a big piece of meat for my mother, with his huge knife and his apron stained with blood. But to Koeun, Taiwanese was the language of the past, the language of her childhood. It was the language that reminded her of the time when her mother was still her father's wife. When morning came, Koeun did not mention the discussion we had the preceding night. She was the girl I had always known—a girl more Cambodian than Chinese at home, with the same passive competence in Cambodian as me, and out-

Monileak Ourng *wrote this essay in a course on bilingualism at the University of Texas at Austin in 2002. At the time, she was an exchange student from France, majoring in English. Although she grew up in a household where Cambodian was spoken, French is her dominant language. In this essay, she compares some of her experiences growing up in France with the experiences of an American friend, also the daughter of a Cambodian father. As you'll note, Ourng might be said "to write with an accent"—her word choice and manner of expression reveal that English is not her first language. Yet her argument is crystal clear: our relationship with our linguistic heritage is complex and influences our behavior and sense of self in complex ways.*

257

side the home, more American than Cambodian, talking with an American accent that one day encouraged me to study in the United States rather than in Britain, closer to my home.

Koeun's complex linguistic background, which seems to make us so alike but at the same time so different, together with the important part she came to play in my English linguistic heritage, was the reason I decided to choose her as the subject of my investigation. Our relationship leads me to ask several questions: what are the ways in which our linguistic heritage influences our behavior? What do our languages mean to us? Is there a language which we mostly identify ourselves with? Do we feel like we are being torn between these different languages and therefore between these different cultures? Is multilingualism an advantage or a drawback? Finally, is it possible to come up with a generalization about the influence of linguistic heritage on the behavior of second-generation immigrants like Koeun and me, or does linguistic heritage influence each individual differently, according to the languages he or she speaks and the place he or she lives?

Just before the war broke out in Cambodia in 1975, Koeun's father, Mr. O. Kop, who is also my father's best friend, was given the opportunity to study in the United States. Wishing to get an American degree, he left his wife with their two daughters in Cambodia, promising that he would come back after he had finished his studies. But there would be no coming back and no reunion. In the midst of war, he was given the news that his wife had been killed by the Khmer Rouge and that his two daughters were left motherless. Worried to the utmost for his two kids and shattered by the loss of a wife he cherished, he went through a period of deep depression, which he would only get over thanks to a Taiwanese woman he met. He finally decided to marry her, and a daughter was born from this union. They called her Koeun —a Cambodian name that seemed to foreshadow the fact that her Taiwanese mother would never play an important role in her life.

Koeun was born in 1982. In that year, and after seven years of separation, Koeun's father managed to track down his two daughters left in Cambodia and to bring them to the United States. But it was hard for his two Cambodian daughters to admit that their father could live with another woman, a woman, moreover, who was not Cambodian, a woman who did not even speak the same language as them. In situations such as this one, where a father did not go through what his daughters went through, it was easy for the children to reproach their father for being a coward. No doubt the two girls assumed that while they were in Cambodia, fighting to survive in a country at war and while their mother was being massacred, their father was abroad flirting with another woman. Tensions rapidly rose within the family, and three years after the two daughters arrived in the United States, the couple divorced.

From what Koeun told me, I understood that her mother had felt alienated from the day her half sisters arrived. One way they made her feel she was not a member of the family was by speaking Cambodian all the time.

Up to the age of five, Koeun had a perfectly healthy relationship with Taiwanese. She could see her mother from time to time during weekends and with her, she could speak Taiwanese and understand the lullabies her mother sang to her in that Chinese dialect. But when she was five, two years after the divorce, her father fell seriously ill. While he was fixing his car, he suddenly had a stroke from which he would never recover; from that moment on, he was paralyzed on the right side of his body. During the days he spent at hospital, Koeun went to live at Auntie's, a good friend of the family. It was during these days spent at Auntie's house that she lost her Chinese skills. One day, she was so worried for her father that she went to pray in the bathroom in Auntie's house. It was a prayer said in Taiwanese, her very last words said in that language. The little girl that she was felt that the reason why her father had fallen ill and had been hospitalized was her mother. Consequently, Koeun unconsciously repressed everything that was related to her mother, and Taiwanese was among these things.

Today, Koeun has made up with her mother. She understands that her 10 mother was not to blame for her father's sickness. She also gets along with her half sisters quite well. However, she still struggles with her Taiwanese identity from time to time. Because she is living in an environment that is mainly Cambodian, she always feels she must forget about her Chinese identity, so as to more be like the other members of her family when with them. During the day, she tries to *attenuate* her Taiwanese traits. "Only at night could I return to my senses," Marjorie Agosín wrote. That is how things go with Koeun: only at night can she remember her mother's pleasant voice singing Taiwanese lullabies to her.

My father has another friend in Philadelphia. He was also an officer and, just like Koeun's father, he went to study in the United States before the war broke out in Cambodia, leaving his wife and their two sons there. His wife was also killed by the Khmer Rouge while he was in the United States, and he too managed to bring his two sons in the United States afterwards. He also married another woman, a Filipina, but, unlike Koeun's father, did not divorce. I went to visit him during that summer spent at Koeun's home. "I don't speak your language," his Filipino wife told me as soon as I introduced myself. She was smoking a cigarette, perhaps a sign that she felt some kind of nervousness. "Almost the same story," I told myself. Same feeling of exclusion. How can one be part of a social network[1] if one cannot speak the language its members use?

My family did not have to deal with such situations. For my parents, my sister, my brother, and myself, there has been no linguistic heritage other than Cambodian and French, and because there was nobody among us with a different linguistic heritage, there has been no tension. Cambodian and French have lived together peacefully within my family, with Cambodian as the private language and French as the public language. But what if a person with a different linguistic heritage had come in our family and had disrupted the harmony of the social network? It seems that there would have been the same reactions as in the other families I have described. Indeed, the examples of Koeun's and the friend of my father are strong evidence that a person's linguistic heritage in one language can be a real source of conflict if this language is not the language of that person's social network. This different language can be rejected by members of the social network, as Koeun's mother was, or repressed by the person him- or herself, who senses that the only way to be a part of the social network is to stop speaking this language. On this matter, there is yet one similarity between these different families that is worth pointing out since such attitudes undeniably throw light on the reason why second-generation immigrants such as Koeun and me have eventually stopped speaking our native languages: to be part of the larger social network that makes up the European or American society in which we are living and because this social network has made us feel that our different linguistic heritage is not *acceptable*.

At one point, I asked Koeun which language she most identifies herself with. Had anyone happened to ask me this question, I would have hesitated, saying "Yes, it is true that I cannot speak Cambodian and that I speak French in my everyday life but, on the other hand, Cambodian means so many different and important things to me." Koeun did not hesitate. Her reply was categorical: "English." She justified her answer by saying that the language could not be Cambodian because she felt too different from her half sisters, not only in the way she spoke but also in the way she behaved and the way she thought. "*They* identify themselves with Cambodian. *My dad* identifies himself with Cambodian. I don't." As for Taiwanese, how could she relate to it when people in Taiwan regarded her only as an American girl? "So, this

---

1. **social network** an individual and all of his or her social contacts; social scientists interested in how "peer pressure" works often analyze the structure and strength of social networks among people of different backgrounds.

means that it is English that brings more positive connotations to you," I said to her. "Not really," she replied. "Sure, English is the language I speak with my friends when I'm on the campus of my university, showing me that I'm perfectly integrated in American society but, sometimes, I'm tired of English, of speaking it so well. My dad always wants me to do everything for him because of that." A complex identity was being enacted in a way that could not be clearer. English was what made her the brilliant college sophomore that she was, while on the other hand, turning her family into one with a *filiarchal* family structure.[2] When I compare myself with Koeun, I know that her father relies on her much more than my parents rely on me; how could it be any other way in a one-parent family whose parent, moreover, suffers from a stroke? "But it's okay now, I'm in college," she says. "At least, during the week, I can get some kind of independence."

Thinking about Koeun's need for independence, I could not help wondering about my own situation. Why did I decide to come to the United States? Was it only because I wanted to learn about the American school system, as I used to say to my mother? Deep within my heart, I know that one of the main reasons to leave my home for an entire year was the need to escape from this filiarchal responsibility for a while. As I am writing these lines, I still remember my mother asking for help understanding some administrative form and telling myself, "At least I won't have to do that next year." I know that my mother still cannot really understand why I decided to live so far from home for an entire year, and I know that I undertook this adventure against her will, even if she did not tell me that openly. But I am also sure that it was necessary for both of us. My French linguistic heritage was weighing heavier and heavier on me, and there was no way I could identify myself with my Cambodian linguistic heritage. I needed to stand back a bit to try to understand what these different languages, these different cultures mean to me.

Just like Koeun, who understood she could not relate to Taiwanese during the time she spent in Taiwan, I discovered from my trip to Cambodia last year that people there saw me as nothing but a French girl. Indeed, I will never forget what a guard at the entrance of Angkor Watt temple said to me because I had not paid the forty dollars that tourists are supposed to pay: 15

---

2. **filiarchal family structure** a family structure in which children hold the authority (in contrast to a patriarchal structure, where fathers hold the power, or matriarchal structure, where mothers hold it). In immigrant families, children sometimes come to have a kind of authority or power—and responsibility—that they generally do not have in their native countries.

"You're not Cambodian." How did he end up saying such a thing? How did he know I was "not" from Cambodia? It may have been because of my French accent when I tried to answer him in Cambodian, or it may have been the way I walked or the way I was dressed; however, whether it be this or that, I know that people there regard me as a French or even an American person, a person from the Western world, but for sure not a Cambodian. In the country where I was born, there was no way I could pass unnoticed: people there simply knew that I did not belong in that country. This is the main thing that I learned from my trip to Cambodia. At the beginning, I found it hard to accept this idea, but I now understand that this is how things go. Yes, now I have managed to accept this idea that I will always be regarded as an outsider in my own country and that it has to do with the influence of my French cultural heritage on my behavior.

The difficulty for persons with a linguistic background other than the one of the social network of the majority is to get this different linguistic background accepted by the larger social network; there is also the difficulty of reconciling those different aspects of their identity and knowing exactly where they belong and the complexity, finally, of their roles within the family structure. These are among the many other ways in which the linguistic heritage of bilinguals and multilinguals influence their behaviors and their lives. However, growing up in a bilingual and bicultural environment such as the one Koeun and I have been raised in does not represent only drawbacks, contrary to what it may appear at first sight. Indeed, if one manages to take advantage of this situation, one can really profit from a multicultural background.

When Koeun went to Taiwan last year, she went there for a special purpose: to perform traditional Cambodian dance. When she informed me about it by email last year, I thought that it was a simply wonderful way to link those different aspects of her identity—Taiwanese, Cambodian, and American—as well as to take advantage of them. Koeun has been performing traditional Cambodian dance since she was four and during the summer I spent at her home, I had the chance to see her dance. She performed in Washington, D.C., on Independence Day, and I remember how impressed I was by her performance and by the suppleness with which she danced. She was also a cheerleader in her high school at that time, and no doubt her suppleness resulted from her cheerleading exercises. One day, she showed me some movements from a traditional Cambodian dance, but she had the original idea to mix them with some cheerleading movements. What resulted was a mix of movements from completely different types of dances that was surprisingly beautiful. The conclusion I drew is that Koeun's multicultural background undeniably influences her behavior, but her strength is this: rather than seeing it as a drawback, she has managed to accept the various influences in her life and to use them to her advantage.

All my life I have known that I need to take advantage of my bilingual background in French and Cambodian. In high school, I took advantage of it by doing volunteer work in my home town in Lyon, helping kids of immigrant families who encountered great difficulty in school and especially in their dealings with the French language. I could easily understand their situation because I had been in the same situation myself and, at the same time, I could offer them the hope that they had a chance to succeed as well. Indeed, I remember how hard my first days of school in France were. I was a very shy kid who had always been very close to her mother. Thus, up to the age of three, I did not really bother talking to anybody else outside my home. But, at the age of three, I suddenly had to go to pre-school in France,[3] and I realized that people there did not speak the same language that I spoke. I thus had to adjust to this new language, French, and fortunately managed to do it. From this day on, I was under the impression that I would always be able to adjust to another language. That is one reason why I did not fear the possibility of studying in the United States for a year. I knew that I would be able to adjust to English because I knew that this is what my multilingual and multicultural background has given me: the possibility to adjust to another language and, therefore, to another culture, in any kind of situation, and with all kinds of people and cultures.

Researching the influence of linguistic heritage on people's behavior has thus showed me that even within the family domain, someone's linguistic heritage influences the way that person perceives the linguistic heritage of anyone else who enters that family. If such a situation happens even within the domain of the family, we get a better understanding of what is likely to happen on a larger scale, especially when we think of the attitudes and opinions that purists tend to have towards immigrants and their fear of seeing the language of the dominant culture "contaminated" by the language of those bilingual immigrants. It also helps me get a better understanding

---

3. **pre-school in France** There are no bilingual programs in France; hence, even in pre-school, students who do not speak French at home must operate in that language. In the United States, such programs are sometimes called immersion or sink-or-swim programs.

of the reason why the presidential elections in France[4] have turned out as they have: fear of the "Other," of difference, fear which manifests itself through linguistic discrimination towards the "Other" as well as through racist attitudes.

And yet, even though our linguistic heritages vary, we can notice strong similarities in the ways in which this linguistic heritage influences people's behavior. The comparison between Koeun's situation and mine represents strong evidence for this claim since despite the difference between our respective linguistic heritages and our respective cultural backgrounds, we are basically going through the same kinds of experience. This may be the reason why it is so crucial to respect the "Other": because the "Other" and the difference that he or she embodies is, after all, not so different from what we are ourselves.

This is also the reason why I can now come to the conclusion that the way we both feel towards our linguistic heritage—that is, an awareness of our complex identities but at the same time, a rising sense of ethnic pride, is what characterizes many second-generation immigrants, and this generalization applies whether they live in the United States or in France or elsewhere. These are the ways in which our linguistic heritage influences our behaviors and our lives, making us the persons that we are today, a mix of different cultures and different identities, full of contradictions and questions, while at the same time being nothing more than human beings trying our best to remain truthful to what we are and who wish, more than anything else, to make the most of it.

---

4. **presidential elections in France** an allusion to the French presidential primaries in 2002, when a far-right, anti-immigration candidate did especially well at the polls, surprising many people in France and around the world.

about the text

1. Ourng's essay discusses the identity of second-generation immigrants (that is, the native-born children of people who came to the United States or another country) who visit the land of their ancestors. If we take her examples as typical, what do such children find there? How does this situation complicate their construction of a coherent identity?

2. What conclusions does Ourng draw about the intersection of language and identity for second-generation immigrants? How clearly does her evidence support these conclusions?

on language

3. English has become a global language, and one of the consequences for native speakers will be understanding that most speakers of our language are not native speakers—and might not use English exactly as we do. Ourng is just such a speaker of English. Her language and style of argumentation are clear and easy to understand, yet it is evident that English is not her first or strongest language. How should native speakers of English respond to this situation? What adjustments will native speakers likely have to make as the ways of using English around the world become increasingly varied?

4. Ourng contends that the children of immigrants construct their identities through and against the languages of their parents and the society in which they were born. Choose several of the selections in this chapter, analyze what they say about language and identity, and use these analyses as evidence for or against Ourng's claim.

for writing

5. How do the languages or language varieties used in your family influence how you understand yourself as a person? Write an essay in which you explore this question.

6. As this selection makes clear, France and the United States treat questions of immigration and immigrant languages very differently. Investigate the nature of these differences and their origins and write an essay about them.

america's first languages

We end our look at America's multilingualism with the languages that have been here the longest, those spoken by the land's original residents. When Europeans arrived in what is today the United States, there were likely some 300 languages indigenous to the area. Today, about 175 of them survive, but only 20 of these are still being learned natively by children. About 30 indigenous languages are spoken by parents and elders but not children, whereas some 70 are spoken by elders only—and of these, 55 have fewer than 10 remaining speakers.

Much of the loss of indigenous languages can be traced to missionary efforts, which often forced Indians to give up their language as part of converting to Christianity. Later, the Bureau of Indian Affairs, which until the 1930s educated Native American children from different groups in boarding schools, prohibited the use of languages other than English. Removing children from their home communities meant that they did not grow up with the language—or with native ways of doing things—and in fact, Indian children were severely punished for speaking their native language. Many native children left these schools unable to fit into either their home communities or white communities but having learned well that they should be ashamed of their native language and background. Only in the past few decades have native groups regained control of their schools and begun preserving and revitalizing their languages. These news articles tell of efforts to hold on to and pass on native heritage through language.

In a 2003 article from the Palm Springs *Desert Sun*, Doug Abrahms discusses the revitalization of the Luiseño language. Next, in an article from the *Green Bay News-Chronicle* in Wisconsin, Monique Balas details the work of Maria Hinton, an Oneida Nation elder whose native name means "She Remembers." Finally, in a June 2003 article, Dorreen Yellow Bird, who writes for the *Grand Forks Herald* in North Dakota, and is a member of the Sahnish (Arikara) tribe, discusses the efforts of her people to document and revitalize their language.

DOUG ABRAHMS

Tribes Struggle to Keep Languages Alive

As population ages, the spoken word of Indian ancestors is beginning to die off

WASHINGTON — The Pechanga Band of Luiseño Indians had to hire an outside linguist last year to help preschoolers learn the Luiseño language because the only native speakers left in the tribe were in their 70s and 80s.

We can't use them as resources because they're too frail," said Gary DuBois, director of the Temecula tribe's cultural resources program."We're running against time."

The Pechangas are spending $200,000 from their casino profits to fund a preschool language-immersion program that they plan to expand into kindergarten, and perhaps to later grades. Fewer than 10 of the tribe's 1,500 members speak Luiseño.

The Pechangas' situation is typical for California tribes, said Leanne Hinton, chairwoman of the University of

California at Berkeley linguistics department. More than 85 native languages were once spoken in the Golden State. Today, 35 languages have no native speakers and each of the other 50 are only spoken by a handful, she said.

"Here in California we have 5 50 languages . . . almost all of them are spoken by people over 60," Hinton said. "As soon as the kids stop speaking it, essentially it's a dead language."

Many American Indians and educators worry that tribes throughout the nation are in a race against time to save their languages—a vital part of American Indian culture—before they die off with tribal elders. Consider:

A 1997 study by the Mississippi Band of Choctaw Indians found 3 percent of children under 6 could speak the language.

Only an estimated 2,000 Ojibwes, or Chippewas, out of

more than 100,000 in the United States speak the language.

About 80 percent of the nation's 175 existing Indian languages will disappear in the next generation if nothing is done because the vast majority of speakers are older than 60, according to one study.

But tribes are taking steps to 10 revive their languages, with the help of funds from gambling or the government. Some tribes are spending their casino profits on preschools where children are immersed in their native tongue. And Senator Daniel Inouye, D-Hawaii, has sponsored a bill to provide more funds to language-immersion schools.

Language revitalization programs started in the 1970s in Hawaii, where the Aha Pūnanan Leo[1] language organization brought together preschoolers with island elders. The children then were moved into language-immersion schools. Members of the first senior class, who speak both Hawaiian and English, graduated in 1999.

FEDERAL FUNDS COULD HELP
Inouye's bill would provide roughly $10 million a year to help fund private school efforts to teach Indian languages

---

1. **Aha Pūnanan Leo** language revitalization organization in Hawaii. Its motto is "e Ola Ka Ōlelo Hawaii," which means, "The Hawaiian language shall live." Modeled on successful programs begun by the Māori in New Zealand, the schools teach in Hawaiian. "Pūnanan Leo" is Hawaiian for "nest of voices," or language nest.

and provide money for teacher training. Inouye has introduced similar legislation in previous congressional sessions that failed to pass.

Congress passed legislation in the early 1990s that funded language revitalization programs but these short-term grants leave programs in a constant hunt for funds, said Mary Hermes, an education professor at the University of Minnesota in Duluth. She also is a board member and parent at the Waadookodaading Ojibwe language-immersion school in Hayward, Wisconsin.

American Indians blame the government for eradicating their languages by pushing them off their lands, removing children to English-speaking boarding schools, and barring them from talking in school in their native tongue. Governments in New Zealand and Canada have acknowledged their roles in eradicating native languages and have provided funding to tribes, Hermes said.

"It is really the responsibility of the government that we're in this situation," Hermes said. "We're not asking for money because of the harm suffered. We're asking for efforts to revitalize our language."

REASONS TO SAVE LANGUAGES

Cindy LaMarr heads Capitol Area Indian Resources, a non-profit group in Sacramento that offers cultural and academic programs for area Indian youth. She believes bringing back the languages that American Indians have used for centuries to pass on their culture and history will give Indian children more confidence and a better education. LaMarr, president-elect of the National Indian Education Association, said few studies have been done on the relatively new language-immersion schools to back up her belief.

"To me, it's pretty much a no-brainer: If you feel good about your culture and identity, then you will feel better about yourself," LaMarr said. Her parents were taken from the Pit River reservation in northern California to boarding schools in Riverside and Carson City, Nevada.

"Language is essential to the continuance of our cultural and spiritual traditions and is an ac-knowledgment of our gift from the great creator," she said.

TORRES MARTINEZ IN THERMAL

California Indian groups might seek legislation to help fund language-immersion schools, she said, because the state's tribes have so few native speakers left.

Some California tribes have started master-apprentice programs where a native speaker teaches an instructor who then can teach classes. But those programs can be difficult, even when you're learning the language from your mother.

Faith Morreo, language program coordinator at the Torres Martinez tribe in Thermal, was part of a group that met with her mom, Tina, several times a week to learn Cahuilla. But it was difficult fitting the classes into daily life, Morreo said.

"We started out with a big group," she said, "but we got burned out."

The Torres Martinez tribe, which has 14 native speakers among its 600 members, hopes to start a day-care center next fall that will include some teaching of Cahuilla, she said.

MONIQUE BALAS

She Remembers So Others Can Learn

One of the Last Native-Speaking Elders Takes a Look Back

Her Oneida name is "She Remembers."

A more fitting name for Oneida Nation elder Maria Hinton would be hard to find, for it is thanks to Hinton that the Oneidas can remember, too: Their stories, their language, their culture.

One of only 20 remaining native-speaking elders in the Oneida Nation ("Maybe less, maybe less," she mused as she thought about those who have since passed), Hinton, 93, spoke recently about what it means to learn those things that need to be remembered.

"Oneida language is culture. It's just our way," she said. "It all goes together. You don't say, 'I'm teaching your culture,' you're teaching the language. That's the way I feel."

Prim but with plenty of 5 spunk, the Oneida matriarch was raised by her grandmother and didn't learn English until she was 10. "She remembers" were the instructional words Hinton's grandmother would say when Hinton was supposed to be learning.

"When I was growing up, and my grandmother used to teach me things, she didn't say, 'Now, this is culture, now this is the language.' She just taught me."

So it was an odd twist of fate that Hinton would be named "She Remembers" in Canada, at the age of 46.

Over the next 40 years, Hinton would grow into that name and make it her own.

When a movement in the 1970s for Oneidas to get back in touch with their linguistic roots starting from the elementary-school level, Hinton would find herself being asked to help.

"Because my brother and I 10 were native speakers, well, then they put their attention on us," Hinton said.

So in 1973, at the age of 63, the former teacher thought nothing of going back to school to pursue her bachelor's degree in linguistics through the University of Wisconsin System (she spent two years in Milwaukee before coming to Green Bay to receive her degree in 1979).

That's how she ended up becoming one of the founders and first teachers at the Oneida Nation Turtle Elementary School, one of 185 Bureau of Indian Affairs–funded schools nationwide that integrate native American language and culture into the primary school curriculum, said Sheri Mousseau, school administrator of the Oneida Nation School System.

When they opened the

school in 1980, Hinton taught language and culture to kindergartners and spent some time teaching middle-schoolers as well; the Turtle School serves children from kindergarten through eighth grade. Hinton also spent time as a language curriculum developer at the school, where she taught the Oneida language to teachers.

"A lot of us look to her as a role model and mentor," said Mousseau, who taught special education in the classroom next to Hinton's and has known her for more than 20 years.

"With her determination and 15 willingness to mentor, to unconditionally provide support for anyone who wanted to learn, it's like the passion that a teacher has for a classroom, she had that passion for teaching her craft, teaching her language, the Oneida language."

Hinton's ability to remember was a key reason why she, along with her late brother, Amos Christjohn, was a natural person to ask when the Oneida Grants Office offered $18,000 for the compilation of an Oneida dictionary.

The dictionary is one of the Oneida's most tangible representations to keep the language alive and a valuable tool for linguists.

Hinton and Christjohn both worked daily over the course of two years to put the book together. Now sold at the Turtle School, the reference work is requested nationally and as far away as Russia.

In addition to the dictionary, Hinton has also put together several translations of Oneida short stories and is currently working on another. But for now, she has other concerns to keep her occupied.

Her 30-year-old great-grandson (she has 22 great-grandchildren) is expected to be coming back from Iraq later this month. He has been deployed there with the U.S. Army for nearly two years and Hinton is planning a big home-[20] coming celebration at her home.

Although she wishes he weren't in the military, she said he wants to be there to help people who are less fortunate than he is.

"It makes you feel good to think he has that attitude," Hinton said.

DORREEN YELLOW BIRD

Keeping the Flame of a Language Alive

Indian people throughout the nation are losing their languages at an alarming rate. This means the culture of the 540-plus tribes may be lost forever.

In Indian country, some say this is well and good. We should all speak one common language. That will build stronger relationships with mainstream society, they say.

Dr. Douglas Parks, an anthropologist at Indiana University in Bloomington, Indiana, like most Native people, disagrees. With Parks' help, the Sahnish (Arikara) and Lakota Sioux languages are being studied and documented for preservation at the American Indian Research Institute that Parks founded.

I had to giggle at my audacity when I called Parks about the institute. I was sure he remembered me as one of those Sahnish women who gave him a hard time several years ago when he visited White Shield, North Dakota. He laughed about the incident, so I think he's over it.

My excuse is that when uni-[5] versity types study our people — this bug with the pin through her midsection gets a little cranky. I remember that meeting with him because I fumbled with Sahnish words and Parks broke into fluent Sahnish. Here was a Sahnistaaka (white man) who could speak the language better than most Arikara. It was a scary realization that we'd lost so much.

Parks' program, however, is a stone in a path to reclaiming our laws, songs, cures, wisdom and prayers. He has several books, language tapes and is working with the White Shield school on a language program for their curriculum.

It is important that our Native languages don't disappear because they are a different way of thinking. Sometimes a Sahnish word or sentence cannot be translated into English.

In addition, if the language is no longer spoken, many of the cultural elements specific to a group are lost, Parks said. It stands for and sums up the entire economy, religion, health care system, and philosophy. There is very little in the culture that does not require language. Part of who we are would disappear with the language.

While I was home this weekend, the family gathered for a graduation celebration. The day after the celebration, we all sat over breakfast and talked about the grandson who prayed and sang in Sahnish at the graduation celebration. My aunt and mother cried while he sang and talked. It was a long time since they had heard the young people speak the language.

Then my aunt told this story 10 about her sister Dorothy, who is my mother. Years ago, my aunt said, when her mother and her mother's two sisters were alive, they came to visit my mother, Dorothy. Mary, one of the elder aunts who used crutches all of her life because of a childhood accident, had a good sense of humor although sometimes it was a little off-color. But then, all those old people were pretty frank. Well, my aunt said, "Your grandmas Mary, Daisy and Philomene were all seated in a room in the basement of the house. Your mother came running down the stairs and said in Sahnish to Grandma

Mary, "Quick, look out the window." All three women's heads turned toward her, rather than toward the window. The women uttered a long drawn out, Myyyy.

With a smile, Grandma Mary asked my mother, "Do you know what you just said to me?" "You just told me in Sahnish to put my (derriere) out the window." She added, "the window is too small for my (derriere.)" Grandma Mary was not a slim woman.

When my aunt finished telling this story, my other aunts smiled and nodded in agreement. The Sahnish language isn't easy to learn, and is even harder to get the correct pronunciation. In fact, they didn't all learn the language either, because some of their elders had laughed at their Sahnish pronunciations.

One of my relatives from Spirit Lake tries to teach us Sahnish. I usually write it in English phonetically, then I can remember it. He told one of his students that he (the student) spoke Sahnish with a Norwegian accent. Yes, it is hard to rid ourselves of our non-Sahnish accents, we agreed.

I first heard my nephew

speak the language in a ceremony. It was dark, but I knew it was him because I recognized the language and some of the words. It was as if the grandfathers were speaking to us. I cried like my aunt and mother when I heard the sounds and I remembered my grandmother.

There is an awakening 15 among the Sahnish people about the language. When our parents were young, they knew the language, but were influenced by the non-Indian teachings that said they were better off to leave the language and culture behind. "You live in the white world, so forget the old ways," they were told.

It must have been the prayers of the elders that give the Sahnish incentive and tenaciousness to keep words on our tongues. Today we have records, computer programs and books of the language and slowly, speakers are rising from the books and tapes.

We prayed that day that the tears of the elders would nourish the sounds and words of the Sahnish people and these words would grow into tall and great understandings of our culture and people.

about the texts

1. Based on these texts, what challenges do the native peoples of the United States face as they seek to document, preserve, and pass on their languages?

2. What do speakers of these languages believe will be lost if the languages disappear? What do they believe are the benefits of maintaining and revitalizing the languages for their tribes? Why? Give examples.

3. According to those who were interviewed for these articles, how are language and culture related? Why?

on language use

4. Many Americans who speak only English believe that nothing is lost if a group loses its language. (The children and grandchildren of immigrants who were forced to give up their language often cite the case of their relatives, sometimes forgetting it seems, that the languages spoken by their parents or grandparents are still spoken somewhere else in the world.) Why do Americans attach little importance to the maintenance and preservation of languages other than English within our borders? Do you think we should be concerned? Why or why not?

5. Americans who speak more than one language are often made to feel ashamed or embarrassed because they do—except when the second language is seen as an asset in a globalized economy. Why do you think this is the case? What factors encourage Americans to enforce monolingualism? Do you think we should be concerned? Why or why not?

for writing

6. The potential loss of indigenous languages is an issue all over the world. Should those of us who do not speak these languages be worried that they are disappearing? Why or why not? Does a shrinking number of languages threaten humans in the same way that a decline in biodiversity does? Write an essay in which you argue for or against language preservation, considering the possible consequences of language death for speakers and non-speakers.

7. Investigate the efforts of an indigenous group in the United States to maintain, preserve, or revitalize its language. If you live near a tribe, you may want to contact its members directly. Or, consult research on language revitalization and look for articles about the tribe online. A good place to start is the Web site of the National Association of Tribal Historic Preservation Officers, <nathpo.org>. Write an essay about what you learn.

chapter 5

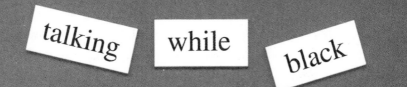

african american language in the united states

the most controversial variety of American English is the one known variously as African American Vernacular English, Black English, and Ebonics. Debates about Ebonics engulfed the country from 1996 to 1998, generating books, editorials, bar-stool arguments, and living-room discussions. Yet today, Americans may not be any closer to understanding what Black English is and isn't or nearer to appreciating its contributions to our national culture than we were. Would all Americans agree on a definition of Black English? Do all African Americans—or only African Americans—use it? What is its history? Its future? How do its speakers feel about it? Why, in a society valuing empirical knowledge, hasn't a linguistic approach to Black English received serious attention? To help answer these questions, this chapter presents many views of Black English—from the personal to the scientific, from the historical to the very here-and-now.

We begin with three approaches to the question of what Black English is: Patricia Smith's narrative of her mother's view of her own speech and, by extension, her very self; the linguist John Rickford's description of the history and grammar of Black English; and a Jump Start comic strip. Next, David D. Troutt looks at the social implications of language varieties. Next comes an article by Michael Erard on linguistic profiling. Think you can identify race and ethnicity from just a voice? Take the ABC News Linguistic Profiling Quiz to find out. Next, John Baugh's and June Jordan's essays explore the relationships speakers have with the language varieties in their repertoires.

We end with an ad demonstrating the strength of feelings Ebonics evokes. In it, as in life, we need to analyze the picture and read the fine print, remembering that words are more than the sum of their meanings even as a language variety is more than the sum of its words.

PATRICIA SMITH

Talking Wrong

Patricia Smith, *born in Chicago, is a performance artist, journalist, and poet. She is the author of several collections of poetry, including* Life According to Motown *(1993), and co-author of* Africans in America *(1999), a companion volume to the PBS television series of the same name. Smith has won the National Poetry Slam individual championship four times. This selection was originally published in* Ms. *magazine in December 2000.*

A N ANXIOUS IMMIGRANT AT **64**, my mother says she is learning English. After pulling Sears Best cinnamon stockings to a roll beneath her knees and sitting that Baptist ski slope of a hat on her head, she rides the rattling El train to a steel spire in downtown Chicago, pulls back her gulp as the glass elevator hurtles upward, and comes to sit at a gleaming oak table across from a pinstriped benevolent white angel who has dedicated two hours a week to straightening the black, twisted tongues of the afflicted. It is this woman's job to scrape the moist infection of Aliceville, Alabama, from my mother's throat.

"I want to talk right before I die," Mama says, "Want to stop saying *ain't* and *I done been*, like I don't have no sense. I done lived too long to be stupid, acting like I just got off the boat."

My mother has never been on a boat.

But 50 years ago, a million of her, clutching strapped cloth suitcases and peppery fried chicken in waxed bags, stepped off the buses at the Greyhound depot in Chicago, eagerly brushing the stubborn red dust from their shoes.

"We're North now," they said in their southern 5 tongues, as if those three words were vessels big enough to hold all those dreams with bulging seams.

My mother's northern dreams were simple, but huge. She thought it a modern miracle to live in a box stacked upon other boxes, a tenement apartment where every surface smelled of Lysol and effort, and plump roaches, cross-eyed with spray, dropped dizzily from the ceiling into our food, our beds. Mama's huge dream required starch-stiff pinafores. Orlon sweaters with embroidered roses, and A-line skirts in the color of winter. There had to be a tavern on the corner with a jukebox where men begged forgiveness in gravel voices and a comfortable stool by the door where Mama could sit and look like a Christian who was just leaving.

She needed a job that didn't involve soil or branches, in a factory where she could work in a straight line with other women, no talking allowed, their heads heavy and drooping with dreams. And within walking distance of wherever she lived, there had to be a Baptist Church where she could pull on the pure white gloves of service and wail to the rafters when she felt the hot, icy hand of the Holy Ghost pressing insistently at the small of her back. Yes, Jesus had to be there after all. He had blessed her journey so far, quickened her step, stroked her free of the Delta. She was his child, building herself anew here in the North where the burning of her hair was a ritual and she'd given up wearing pants because the Lord reckoned she should.

Her dreams for the most part realized, my mother now busies herself preparing for burial, stashing away money to pay for her own coffin, not wanting to bother me, as she says, "with that nonsense." She sternly relates the story of the dutiful daughter who neglected details, so her dead mother's body was sent to church #1 while everyone waited to mourn in church #2, and if that happened, "Chile, I'd be so embarrassed." No mother, I think, you would be so dead, but I don't say that out loud, because Annie Pearl Smith is not a fan of humor.

I know that she doesn't believe that men ever landed on the moon—that the whole thing was staged in a desert in Arizona because "American folks are stupid that way and always will be."

I know she had a hysterectomy and never told me.

I know that her motto was "Always be respectful of white folks."

But I never knew that the way she spoke was ever a problem for anyone. Especially her.

My mother's voice: It's like cornbread, buttery and full of places for heat to hide. When she is angry, it curls into a fist and punches straight out. When she is scared, it gathers strength and turns practical, matter-of-fact. Like when she is calling her daughter to say. "They found your father this morning, someone shot him and he is very dead."

She cannot sing, not a lick, not at all. When she tries, her voice cracks and collapses and loses all acquaintance with a key, and every Sunday morning in church, of course, my mother's voice is the loudest, wild, and unleashed and creaking toward glory. I don't think the Lord is allowed to cover His ears.

When my mama talks, the sound is flat and broad and wild with unexpected flowers, like fields in Alabama. Her rap is peppered with *ain't gots* and *don't have nones* and *I done beens* and *she be's* and *he be's* the way mine is when we are sweet color among coloreds and don't have to worry about being graded. I see no shame in this.

But one of my mother's leftover dreams is not to meet Sidney Poitier or travel to Jamaica, it's to wash history from her throat, to talk like a woman who got some sense and future, to talk English instead of talking wrong.

Talking wrong.

I pick up the phone these days and my mother is on the other end, precisely using her new mouth. I always counted on her to rip a hole in my carefully crafted cocoon, to talk to me one colored girl to another, to warm me up with double negatives. It hurts to hear the measured effort, which conjures a picture of the two of her on the Greyhound bus headed for the Windy City from Alabama—my southern mother in one seat, her sweet mouth sewn shut, and my northern mother in the other, dreaming of perfection and heading for hell.

---

about the text

1. What image does the first sentence of Smith's narrative evoke? What rhetorical effect does she hope to achieve by beginning her essay with such an image? Is she successful? Why or why not?

2. Without ever explicitly stating it, Smith expresses a strong sense of cultural pride in the variety of English that we are calling African American English. Cite three examples from the text that demonstrate pride in Smith's mother's speech.

on language use

3. Your speech reflects where you grew up, your social background, and other aspects of your life experience. Evaluate your own speech. What do you like best about it? Why? What do you like least? Why?

4. Have you ever had a strong emotional response—pride or embarrassment, for example—to the speech of a family member? What was your response and why? Have your feelings toward this particular person's speech changed over time? Why or why not? Discuss your experiences and answers with a classmate. How are your experiences similar or different? Why?

for writing

5. Smith employs metaphors of heat and warmth to describe speech. Select a relative or acquaintance of your parents' generation or older, and write a description of the person's speech, using sensory images other than sound. Then write a paragraph about the process of writing this description. Why did you select the images that you used? Does your description successfully capture the important features of your subject's speech? Why or why not?

6. Reread paragraph 4. With that single sentence, Smith describes and invokes a whole chapter of twentieth-century American history. What does a reader need to know in order to appreciate the information in that sentence? Write an essay analyzing the sentence. How does each word and phrase contribute to the history that Smith invokes and the portrait she creates of her mother?

John Rickford *is a professor of
linguistics and director of the
Center for African American
Studies at Stanford University.
A native speaker of Guyanese
Creole, Rickford has written
extensively on African
Americans and language. His
2002 book,* Spoken Soul:
The Story of Black English, *co-written with his son Russell
Rickford, won a National Book
Award. This essay originally
appeared in* Discover *magazine in 1997, one year
after the school board in Oakland, California, announced
a policy about Ebonics that
intensified an already long-
running controversy. You have
no doubt heard or read about
that debate, and perhaps
participated in it, but you have
not likely approached it as
Rickford does—from the point
of view of linguistics.*

JOHN RICKFORD

Suite for Ebony and Phonics

To JAMES BALDWIN, writing in 1979, it was "this passion, this skill . . . this incredible music." Toni Morrison, two years later, was impressed by its "five
present tenses" and felt that "the worst of all possible
things that could happen would be to lose that language."
What these novelists were talking about was Ebonics, the
informal speech of many African Americans, which rock-
eted to public attention a year ago this month after the
Oakland School Board approved a resolution recognizing
it as the primary language of African American students.

The reaction of most people across the country—in
the media, at holiday gatherings, and on electronic bulletin boards—was overwhelmingly negative. In the flash
flood of e-mail on America Online, Ebonics was described
as "lazy English," "bastardized English," "poor grammar,"
and "fractured slang." Oakland's decision to recognize
Ebonics and use it to facilitate mastery of Standard English also elicited superlatives of negativity: "ridiculous,
ludicrous," "VERY, VERY, STUPID," "a terrible mistake."

However, linguists—who study the sounds, words,
and grammars of languages and dialects—though less
rhapsodic about Ebonics than the novelists, were much
more positive than the general public. Last January, at the
annual meeting of the Linguistic Society of America, my
colleagues and I unanimously approved a resolution describing Ebonics as "systematic and rule-governed like
all natural speech varieties." Moreover, we agreed that
the Oakland resolution was "linguistically and pedagog-
ically sound."

Why do we linguists see the issue so differently from
most other people? A founding principle of our science is
that we describe *how* people talk; we don't judge
how language should or should not be used. A second

principle is that all languages, if they have enough speakers, have dialects —regional or social varieties that develop when people are separated by geographic or social barriers. And a third principle, vital for understanding linguists' reactions to the Ebonics controversy, is that all languages and dialects are systematic and rule-governed. Every human language and dialect that we have studied to date—and we have studied thousands—obeys distinct rules of grammar and pronunciation.

What this means, first of all, is that Ebonics is not slang. Slang refers just 5 to a small set of new and usually short-lived words in the vocabulary of a dialect or language. Although Ebonics certainly has slang words—such as *chillin* ("relaxing") or *homey* ("close friend"), to pick two that have found wide dissemination by the media—its linguistic identity is described by distinctive patterns of pronunciation and grammar.

But is Ebonics a different language from English or a different dialect of English? Linguists tend to sidestep such questions, noting that the answers can depend on historical and political considerations. For instance, spoken Cantonese and Mandarin are mutually unintelligible, but they are usually regarded as "dialects" of Chinese because their speakers use the same writing system and see themselves as part of a common Chinese tradition. By contrast, although Norwegian and Swedish are so similar that their speakers can generally understand each other, they are usually regarded as different languages because their speakers are citizens of different countries. As for Ebonics, most linguists agree that Ebonics is more of a dialect of English than a separate language, because it shares many words and other features with other informal varieties of American English. And its speakers can easily communicate with speakers of other American English dialects.

Yet Ebonics is one of the most distinctive varieties of American English, differing from Standard English—the educated standard—in several ways. Consider, for instance, its verb tenses and aspects. ("Tense" refers to *when* an event occurs, "aspect" to *how* it occurs, whether habitual or ongoing.) When Toni Morrison referred to the "five present tenses" of Ebonics, she probably had usages like these—each one different from Standard English—in mind:

1. He runnin. ("He is running.")

2. He be runnin. ("He is usually running.")

3. He be steady runnin. ("He is usually running in an intensive, sustained manner.")

4. He bin runnin. ("He has been running.")

5. He BIN runnin. ("He has been running for a long time and still is.")

In Standard English, the distinction between habitual or nonhabitual events can be expressed only with adverbs like "usually." Of course, there are also simple present tense forms, such as "he runs," for habitual events, but they do not carry the meaning of an ongoing action, because they lack the "-ing" suffix. Note too that "bin" in example 4 is unstressed, while "BIN" in example 5 is stressed. The former can usually be understood by non-Ebonics speakers as equivalent to "has been" with the "has" deleted, but the stressed BIN form can be badly misunderstood. Years ago, I presented the Ebonics sentence "She BIN married" to 25 whites and 25 African Americans from various parts of the United States and asked them if they understood the speaker to be still married or not. While 23 of the African Americans said yes, only 8 of the whites gave the correct answer. (In real life a misunderstanding like this could be disastrous!)

Word pronunciation is another distinctive aspect of dialects, and the regularity of these differences can be very subtle. Most of the "rules" we follow when speaking Standard English are obeyed unconsciously. Take for instance English plurals. Although grammar books tell us that we add "s" to a word to form a regular English plural, as in "cats" and "dogs," that's true only for writing. In speech, what we actually add in the case of "cat" is an s sound; in the case of "dog" we add z. The difference is that s is voiceless, with the vocal cords spread apart, while z is voiced,[1] with the vocal cords held closely together and noisily vibrating.

Now, how do you know whether to add s or z to form a plural when you're speaking? Easy. If the word ends in a voiceless consonant, like "t," add voiceless s. If the word ends in a voiced consonant, like "g," add voiced z. Since all vowels are voiced, if the word ends in a vowel, like "tree," add z. Because we spell both plural endings with "s," we're not aware that English speakers make this systematic difference every day, and I'll bet your English teacher never told you about voiced and voiceless plurals. But you follow the "rules" for using them anyway, and anyone who doesn't—for instance, someone who says "bookz"—strikes an English speaker as sounding funny.

One reason people might regard Ebonics as "lazy English" is its tendency to omit consonants at the ends of words—especially if they come after another consonant, as in "tes(t)" and "han(d)." But if one were just being lazy

10

---

1. **voiced/voiceless** one of the features that linguists use for describing the sounds of a language. In English, for example, all vowels are voiced, and consonants can be either voiced or voiceless. Place your fingers lightly on the front of your throat and say "sue" and "zoo." Can you feel that your throat vibrates more on "zoo"? Sounds that vibrate in your throat are called "voiced," and those that don't are called "voiceless."

or cussed or both, why not also leave out the final consonant in a word like "pant"? This is not permitted in Ebonics; the "rules" of the dialect do not allow the deletion of the second consonant at the end of a word unless both consonants are either voiceless, as with "st," or voiced, as with "nd." In the case of "pant," the final "t" is voiceless, but the preceding "n" is voiced, so the consonants are both spoken. In short, the manner in which Ebonics differs from Standard English is highly ordered; it is no more lazy English than Italian is lazy Latin. Only by carefully analyzing each dialect can we appreciate the complex rules that native speakers follow effortlessly and unconsciously in their daily lives.

Who speaks Ebonics? If we made a list of all the ways in which the pronunciation and grammar of Ebonics differ from Standard English, we probably couldn't find anyone who always uses all of them. While its features are found most commonly among African Americans (*Ebonics* is itself derived from "ebony" and "phonics," meaning "black sounds"), not all African Americans speak it. The features of Ebonics, especially the distinctive tenses, are more common among working-class than among middle-class speakers, among adolescents than among the middle-aged, and informal contexts (a conversation on the street) rather than formal ones (a sermon at church) or writing.

The genesis of Ebonics lies in the distinctive cultural background and relative isolation of African Americans, which originated in the slaveholding South. But contemporary social networks, too, influence who uses Ebonics. For example, lawyers and doctors and their families are more likely to have more contact with Standard English speakers—in schools, work, and neighborhoods—than do blue-collar workers and the unemployed. Language can also be used to reinforce a sense of community. Working-class speakers, and adolescents in particular, often embrace Ebonics features as markers of African American identity, while middle-class speakers (in public at least) tend to eschew them.

Some Ebonics features are shared with other vernacular varieties of English, especially Southern white dialects, many of which have been influenced by the heavy concentration of African Americans in the South. And a lot of African American slang has "crossed over" to white and other ethnic groups. Expressions like "givin five" (slapping palms in agreement or congratulation) and "Whassup?" are so widespread in American culture that many people don't realize they originated in the African American community. Older, nonslang words have also originated in imported African words. *Tote*, for example, comes from the Kikongo word for "carry," *tota*, and *hip* comes from the Wolof word *hipi*, to "be aware." However, some of the distinctive verb forms in Ebonics—he run, he be runnin, he BIN runnin—are rarer or nonexistent in white vernaculars.

How did Ebonics arise? The Oakland School Board's proposal alluded to 15 the Niger-Congo roots of Ebonics, but the extent of that contribution is not at all clear. What we do know is that the ancestors of most African Americans came to this country as slaves. They first arrived in Jamestown in 1619, and a steady stream continued to arrive until at least 1808, when the slave trade ended, at least officially. Like the forebears of many other Americans, these waves of African "immigrants" spoke languages other than English. Their languages were from the Niger-Congo language family, especially the West Atlantic, Mande, and Kwa subgroups spoken from Senegal and Gambia to the Cameroons, and the Bantu subgroup spoken farther south. Arriving in an American milieu in which English was dominant, the slaves learned English. But how quickly and completely they did so and with how much influence from their African languages are matters of dispute among linguists.

The Afrocentric view is that most of the distinctive features of Ebonics represent imports from Africa. As West African slaves acquired English, they restructured it according to the patterns of Niger-Congo languages. In this view, Ebonics simplifies consonant clusters at the ends of words and doesn't use linking verbs like "is" and "are"—as in for example, "he happy"—because these features are generally absent from Niger-Congo languages. Verbal forms like habitual "be" and BIN, referring to a remote past, it is argued, crop up in Ebonics because these kinds of tenses occur in Niger-Congo languages.

Most Afrocentrists, however, don't cite a particular West African language source. Languages in the Niger-Congo family vary enormously, and some historically significant Niger-Congo languages don't show these forms. For instance, while Yoruba, a major language for many West Africans sold into slavery, does indeed lack a linking verb like "is" for some adjectival constructions, it has another linking verb for other adjectives. And it has *six* other linking verbs for nonadjectival constructions, where English would use "is" or "are." Moreover, features like dropping final consonants can be found in some vernaculars in England that had little or no West African influence. Although many linguists acknowledge continuing African influences in some Ebonics and American English words, they want more proof of its influence on Ebonics pronunciation and grammar.

A second view, the Eurocentric—or dialectologist—view, is that African slaves learned English from white settlers, and that they did so relatively quickly and successfully, retaining little trace of their African linguistic heritage. Vernacular, or non-Standard features of Ebonics, including omitting final consonants and habitual "be," are seen as imports from dialects spoken by colonial English, Irish, or Scotch-Irish settlers, many of whom were indentured servants. Or they may be features that emerged in the twentieth century, after African Americans became more isolated in urban ghettos. (Use of habitual "be," for example, is more common in urban than in rural areas.) However, as with Afrocentric arguments, we still don't have enough historical details to settle the question. Crucial Ebonics features, such as the absence of linking "is," appear to be rare or nonexistent in these early settler dialects, so they're unlikely to have been the source. Furthermore, although the scenario posited by this view is possible, it seems unlikely. Yes, African American slaves and whites sometimes worked alongside each other in households and fields. And yes, the number of African slaves was so low, especially in the early colonial period, that distinctive African American dialects may not have formed. But the assumption that slaves rapidly and successfully acquired the dialects of the whites around them requires a rosier view of their relationship than the historical record and contemporary evidence suggest.

A third view, the creolist view, is that many African slaves, in acquiring English, developed a pidgin language—a simplified fusion of English and African languages—from which Ebonics evolved. Native to none of its speakers, a pidgin is a mixed language, incorporating elements of its users' native languages but with less complex grammar and fewer words than either parent language. A pidgin language emerges to facilitate communication between speakers who do not share a language; it becomes a creole language when it takes root and becomes the primary tongue among its users. This often occurs among the children of pidgin speakers—the vocabulary of the language expands, and the simple grammar is fleshed out. But the creole still remains simpler in some aspects than the original languages. Most creoles, for instance, don't use suffixes to mark tense ("he walked"), plurals ("boys"), or possession ("John's house").

Creole languages are particularly common on the islands of the [20] Caribbean and the Pacific, where large plantations brought together huge groups of slaves or indentured laborers. The native languages of these workers were radically different from the native tongues of the small groups of European colonizers and settlers, and under such conditions, with minimal access to European speakers, new, restructured varieties like Haitian Creole French and Jamaican Creole English arose. These languages do show African influence, as the Afrocentric theory would predict, but their speakers may have simplified existing patterns in African languages by eliminating more complex alternatives, like the seven linking verbs of Yoruba I mentioned earlier.

Within the United States African Americans speak one well-established English creole, Gullah. It is spoken on the Sea Islands off the coast of South Carolina and Georgia, where African Americans at one time constituted 80 to 90 percent of the local population in places. When I researched one of the South Carolina Sea Islands some years ago, I recorded the following creole sentences. They sound much like Caribbean Creole English today:

1. E.M. run an gone to Suzie house. ("E. M. went running to Suzie's house.")

2. But I does go to see people when they sick. ("But I usually go to see people when they are sick.")

3. De mill bin to Bluffton dem time. ("The mill was in Bluffton in those days.")

Note the creole traits: the first sentence lacks the past tense and the possessive form; the second sentence lacks the linking verb "are" and includes the habitual "does"; the last sentence uses unstressed "bin" for past tense and "dem time" to refer to a plural without using an s.

What about creole origins for Ebonics? Creole speech might have been introduced to the American colonies through the large numbers of slaves imported from the colonies of Jamaica and Barbados where creoles were common. In these regions the percentage of Africans ran from 65 to 90 percent. And some slaves who came directly from Africa may have brought with them pidgins or creoles that developed around West African trading forts. It's also possible that some creole varieties—apart from well-known cases like Gullah—might have developed on American soil.

This would have been less likely in the northern colonies, where blacks were a very small percentage of the population. But blacks were much more concentrated in the South, making up 61 percent of the population in South Carolina and 40 percent overall in the South. Observations by travelers and commentators in the eighteenth and nineteenth centuries record creole-like features in African American speech. Even today, certain features of Ebonics, like the absence of the linking verbs "is" and "are," are widespread in Gullah and Caribbean English creoles but rare or nonexistent in British dialects.

My own view is that the creolist hypothesis incorporates the strengths of the other hypotheses and avoids their weaknesses. But we linguists may never be able to settle that particular issue one way or another. What we can settle on is the unique identity of Ebonics as an English dialect. 25

So what does all this scholarship have to do with the Oakland School Board's proposal? Some readers might be fuming that it's one thing to identify Ebonics as a dialect and quite another to promote its usage. Don't linguists realize that nonstandard dialects are stigmatized in the larger society, and that Ebonics speakers who cannot shift to Standard English are less likely to do well in school and on the job front? Well, yes. The resolution we put forward last January in fact stated that "there are benefits in acquiring Standard English." But there is experimental evidence both from the United States and Europe that mastering the standard language might be easier if the differences in the student vernacular and Standard English were made explicit rather than entirely ignored.

To give only one example: At Aurora University, outside Chicago, inner-city African American students were taught by an approach that contrasted Standard English and Ebonics features through explicit instruction and drills. After eleven weeks, this group showed a 59 percent reduction in their use of Ebonics features in their Standard English writing. But a control group taught by conventional methods showed an 8.5 percent increase in such features.

This is the technique the Oakland School Board was promoting in its resolution last December. The approach is not new; it is part of the 16-year-old Standard English Proficiency Program, which is being used in some 300 California schools. Since the media uproar over its original proposal, the Oakland School Board has clarified its intent: the point is not to teach Ebonics as a distinct language but to use it as a tool to increase mastery of Standard English among Ebonics speakers. The support of linguists for this approach may strike nonlinguists as unorthodox, but that is where our principles—and the evidence—lead us.

about the text

1. According to Rickford, how do linguists look at language? Why? How does their perspective differ from that of the general public?

2. What three theories of the origins of Ebonics does Rickford discuss? What does he see as the strengths and weaknesses of each? How persuasive is Rickford? Do you agree with his acceptance of the creolist view, given the evidence he offers? If not, why not? Do you think Rickford assumes you will agree? How can you tell?

on language use

3. Select two or three minutes from a rap song, comedy routine, or other presentation of verbal art that is performed in Ebonics, and transcribe it exactly as you hear it. Do you find any of the features that Rickford describes? If so, which ones? Provide a detailed description, giving examples of words or sentences. Share your results with one or two classmates. Did you arrive at similar results? Why or why not?

4. Rickford mentions Gullah, a creole language spoken in coastal South Carolina and Georgia. Locate one of the Gullah stories told by Aunt Pearlie-Sue at www.know itall.org/gullahtales/tales/index.html>. Then, listen to the story once or twice without reading the print version on the screen. Which of the features of Gullah described by Rickford do you hear in the story? Transcribe (as you hear them, not as they are printed on the screen) two sentences with *bin*. Choose two more interesting sentences and discuss their features with two or three classmates. What observations can you make about pronouns in Gullah? Is Rickford's description accurate? Why or why not?

for writing

5. Write an essay responding to the final sentence of Rickford's essay. You can agree with him, disagree, or both—but make sure you provide reasons and evidence for your stance.

6. In paragraph 4, Rickford asks why "linguists see the issue [of Ebonics] so differently from most other people." Why, indeed, doesn't the general public perceive language use and language varieties as linguists do? Write a letter to Rickford responding to his question, based on the information he gives. You might try suggesting to him some ways in which linguists could make their ideas more available to the general public.

Jump Start

Jump Start is a cartoon about an African American couple with two small children. In addition to depicting their family life, the cartoon often focuses on the workday experiences of Joe, a police officer, and Marcy, a nurse. Jump Start appears daily in over 250 newspapers. Robb Armstrong, one of the few syndicated African American cartoonists in the United States, is from Philadelphia and has been writing and drawing Jump Start for ten years. He is also very active in youth organizations and travels throughout the country as a motivational speaker. As you read this strip, first published in 1993, think about the cultural assumptions a reader has to make in order to "get" it.

about the text

1. Marcy responds to the patient's statement by saying that she is "fluent in slang." Indeed, the patient's utterance could have been a slang expression. Do you think Marcy (and Armstrong) really intend to refer to slang, or did Marcy actually mean African American English? Why or why not? Do you think the general reading audience would interpret the patient's statement as slang or as an ordinary utterance in African American English? Why? Present evidence to support your conclusions.

2. Can you read all or part of what the patient says? How does the style of lettering in the utterance contribute to the meaning of the comic strip? How would you describe the lettering to someone who has not seen it? Why might Armstrong have chosen to draw the letters as he did?

3. When Marcy's coworker looks for a bilingual nurse, Marcy immediately assumes that she needs someone who speaks Spanish. Why? Is Marcy's response unexpected? Why or why not? Marcy then wonders whether the patient speaks French. How realistic is this second guess, and why?

on language use

4. What is the implication of the other nurse's statement that the patient "speaks no English"? What might John Rickford, author of "Suite for Ebony and Phonics" (p. 278), say about Armstrong's text? Why? Provide evidence from Rickford's essay to support your answer.

for writing

5. Think of a phrase you and your friends use frequently, and write, draw, or type the phrase in letters that evoke the meaning. Consider design elements such as size, color, punctuation, letter shape, letter style (serif, sans-serif, italic, upper case, lower case, etc.) or special effects such as icicles or flames. Share your creation with three or four classmates, describing what you did and why. Do your group members see the relationship between the phrase and your presentation of the phrase? Why or why not?

6. Do you think this *Jump Start* strip portrays African American English in a derogatory way? Why or why not? Write an essay responding to this question, providing evidence from the cartoon to support your conclusions.

DAVID D. TROUTT

Defining Who We Are in Society

David D. Troutt *is a professor of law at the Rutgers School of Law at Newark. His recent publications include law reviews that analyze economic development in American ghetto areas and essays on race, law, and society in the* New York Times, *the* Washington Post, *and other major newspapers. He is also the author of a collection of short stories,* The Monkey Suit *(1998), based on several famous legal cases dealing with African Americans. This essay originally appeared in the* Los Angeles Times *in January 1997.*

WHEN PASSING A CONTROVERSIAL RESOLUTION to help black schoolchildren learn standard English through Ebonics, the speech patterns many use at home, the Oakland School District reminded the nation of what language means to us. It is our very beginning. Once we as toddlers are given the gift of the communicating self, we can forever discover, learn and expand in a world of common symbols.

Perhaps nothing defines us more than our linguistic skills; nothing determines as much about where we can and cannot go. How we talk may be the first—and last—clue about our intelligence and whether we're trusted or feared, heard or ignored, admitted or excluded.

But we treat our fluency like property. Depending where we are, our ability to speak in certain ways entitles us to access, membership and social riches, such as employment or popularity. As a culture, the greatest benefits go to those who write and speak in standard English, ways identified by most of us as "white," specifically middle-class white.

But participating in the benefits of communication doesn't require being white. It only requires that people around us—wherever we are—understand what we're saying. Ebonics merely validates the distinctive talk among people on a margin far from the majority's view of competence and invites them in. It recognizes that a voice developed amid inequality does not bespeak inferiority.

The problem with Ebonics is not that it will teach 5 children what they already know, which, as critics point out, would be silly. The problem is that its public acceptance might throw into question claims of ownership to intelligence and belonging. After all, Ebonics is not as much the language of blackness as it is the only dialect of persistently poor, racially segregated people—the so-called black underclass. It is the dumbness against which all smartness is measured. But if we reached consensus that Ebonics is a real linguistic system born of difference whose use in schools may facilitate inclusion for children of the excluded, we must deal frankly with the exclusion itself.

Ebonics therefore becomes a troubling measure of separation. For many whites, it measures the contradictions of colorblind convictions. For many blacks, Ebonics measures the complications of assimilation and the resiliency of shame.

The ridicule and disparagement on talk radio confirm why an Ebonics program makes sense. Many whites have used the issue as an opportunity to vent racist jokes ordinarily kept underground or in sports bars. Others invoke it in order to restrict black cultural influences, such as banning rap music or canceling TV shows in which black characters use slang.

Meanwhile, more serious mainstream criticism sees the colorblind vision of the republic at stake. Suddenly interested in the achievement of poor black schoolchildren, pundits, federal officials and policymakers unanimously condemn Ebonics for lowering standards. Inadvertently echoing English-only advocacy, they argue that Oakland's resolution would replace children's individuality with militant group identification and promote black "separatism." The Standard English language, they say, belongs to all of us.

Such hypocrisy is hard to beat. Of course, language, like intelligence, is no group's personal property. But despite the well-meaning ring of colorblind ideals, you cannot demand sameness of language while perpetuating segregated education. Privately, any master of the language will admit, the best thing you can do for your kids is get them into schools with the tiniest percentage of (poor) blacks. Thus, it is no coincidence that the public school districts experimenting with Ebonics have long been abandoned by white parents. In fact, many public schools are funded by property taxes, making direct the connection between residential and education segregation. This separatism is quite normal. It is how social advantages are reproduced. But you can't enjoy them at a distance and demand conformity, too.

Since the Supreme Court declared separate-but-equal school facilities unconstitutional in Brown vs. Board of Education,[1] most urban school districts have become more, not less, segregated. Moreover, as wealth and resources develop the suburbs, the residential segregation that accompanies 10

---

1. **Brown vs. Board of Education** landmark 1954 Supreme Court decision that declared segregated schooling unconstitutional and put an end to the doctrine of "separate but equal."

separate schooling has produced a degree of racial isolation among inner-city blacks that approaches complete homogeneity.

To be sure, the Oakland resolution's description of Ebonics as a "primary" language was unfortunate. Such a language would not be English, and non-English cannot be criticized for being "bad English." It is enough that Ebonics has a distinct lexicon and grammatical rules that are spoken exclusively by some blacks. It then qualifies as a reliable measurement of the gulf between many poor blacks and the middle-class world where Standard English is spoken.

Recognition of this fact by sociolinguists and its application in school settings are at least three decades old. In addition to Los Angeles and Oakland, schools in Michigan, Texas and New York use what scholars call Black English Vernacular (BEV) as a teaching tool. The principle is hardly new: Begin teaching from where students are and bridge the familiar with the untried.

Another principle at work, however, is assimilation. If Ebonics measures distance, it also measures a closeness more successful blacks have to mainstream culture. Formally educated blacks who use both Standard English and Ebonics depending on social context, or "code switching," remain close to two worlds that seem at odds with each other. For white co-workers, they may introduce black English idioms into common parlance. Among less-assimilated family and friends, they may be ostracized for "talking white." As a result, they often both bemoan and boast of their bidialectalism. It is a mark of cross-cultural identification, involving a complicated mix of pride, achievement and lingering shame.

Jesse Jackson illustrated this when he immediately denounced the Oakland resolution as an "unacceptable surrender," then, soon after, changed his mind. His first reaction honored a long, revolutionary tradition of black educators teaching Standard English to children at a time when white institutions and hate groups forcibly and deliberately denied us the written and spoken language. Much of the NAACP's legacy—including the Brown decision—was built on such demands for access. It is not surprising, then, that its current director, Kweisi Mfume, denounced Ebonics by resurrecting the memory of Frederick Douglass,[2] the freed slave who taught himself to read five languages.

---

2. **Frederick Douglass (1818–1895)** African American orator, autobiographer, abolitionist, and journalist, considered by many to have been the most significant African American writer and speaker of the nineteenth century.

The Reverend
Jesse Jackson

Secretary of State
Condoleezza Rice

Rapper Jay-Z

Jackson inherits that tradition of civil-rights leadership. He understands 15
how the social benefits of assimilation come primarily through language acquisition. Surely, he also recognizes a deep-seated shame many blacks feel
at the persistent inability of less-advantaged blacks to cross over and speak
both tongues. The public and institutional denigration of black speech patterns for so long contributes to an undeniable sense of stigma against which
blacks from a variety of class backgrounds still struggle.

But in his second reaction, Jackson must have resolved that Ebonics does
not dignify some shameful difference. If done right, it should validate, then
transcend difference. This reaction also enjoys a long tradition in black culture, as illustrated by the diverse work of writers such as Zora Neale Hurston
and Amiri Baraka.[3] Many wrote powerfully in Standard English, only to return at times to black dialect and write just as beautifully there.

Although Ebonics may prove valuable in teaching underperforming
black children Standard English, implementing Ebonics programs probably
shouldn't be confused with bilingualism. This would create potential competition for scarce funds between blacks and students for whom English is not
a primary language. Hopefully, we will find a better way than pitting outsiders against outsiders. There are important differences in the experience of
a Guatemalan or Vietnamese third-grader, who returns from school to immigrant parents. The stigma may not result from associating her language with
ignorance, but the unkindness is just as real.

Instead, the Ebonics debate should heighten our appreciation of differences among us, as well as the special difficulties faced by students on the
margins, who, along with their families, are trying, against long odds, to
belong.

---

3. **Zora Neale Hurston (1891–1960)** African American writer and anthropologist who wrote
novels, including *Their Eyes Were Watching God*, and short stories as well as book-length
folklore and anthropological studies of African American, Haitian, and Jamaican cultures.
Amiri Baraka (1934–) African American writer, political activist, and theater director. His
earlier works were published under the name LeRoi Jones.

about the text

1. Troutt begins by asserting that our language, perhaps more than anything else about us, defines our identity. What evidence does he offer to support such a strong assertion?

2. Troutt states that a "voice developed amid inequality does not bespeak inferiority" (paragraph 4). What does this statement mean? Paraphrase the statement and explain it within the context of this essay.

3. Why does Troutt compare black children and their families to immigrant children and their families? Is the comparison valid? Why or why not? Is it effective in supporting his argument? Why or why not?

4. According to this essay, how were the responses of African Americans and whites to the Ebonics controversy different? What were the origins and consequences of these differences? What evidence does Troutt offer to support his position? How does he use the example of Jesse Jackson to demonstrate the attitude of many African Americans toward Ebonics?

on language use

5. Do you agree with the suggestion that racist jokes are often heard in sports bars (paragraph 7)? How do you think Troutt is defining sports bars? Why might he have chosen to associate sports bars with racist attitudes? Is the association accurate? Fair? Why or why not?

6. Troutt asserts that language "determines . . . where we can and cannot go" (paragraph 2). What does he mean? Think about an experience in which your linguistic skills enabled you to do something that you

wouldn't otherwise have been able to do, or about an experience in which your lack of a particular linguistic skill prevented you from doing something that you wanted to do. All of us, regardless of who we are or how linguistically skilled, have had both of these experiences. (If you need some ideas to stimulate your thinking, look ahead to the next section on linguistic profiling.) Discuss your experiences with two or three classmates. Do you agree with Troutt's assertion? Why or why not?

for writing

7. This essay and Patricia Smith's narrative in this chapter ("Talking Wrong," p. 275) raise many of the same points, although in very different ways. Find one argument made (explicitly or implied) by both Troutt and Smith and write an essay summarizing each writer's arguments and comparing how they make their point. How do they go about convincing readers to accept their position? (Who, by the way, are their audiences?)

8. Troutt argues that American society is not exactly honest about "standard" English. All agree that "the greatest benefits go to those who write and speak in standard English," but, according to Troutt, these "ways [of using language are] identified by most of us as 'white,' specifically middle-class white." At the same time, "[t]he standard English language, they say, belongs to all of us." Does standard English belong to everyone? To what extent is it linked implicitly or explicitly to class and ethnicity (and perhaps other axes of social difference like region or gender)? Write an essay in which you explore the ownership of standard English.

The phenomenon of racial
profiling has been prominent
in the news, but linguistic
profiling, a similar social
occurrence, may not be as
well known. The term refers to
racial discrimination based
solely on a person's speech. In
this selection, the Texas-based
author Michael Erard reports
on a legal case involving
linguistic profiling practices in
apartment rentals (the case is
still pending as we go to
press). Erard's work has
appeared in the New York
Times, Salon, Rolling Stone,
and the Atlantic Monthly. This
report was published in 2002
in Legal Affairs, which describes itself as "the magazine
at the intersection of law and
life." As you read, think about
the kinds of judgments you
routinely make on the basis of
a person's speech.

MICHAEL ERARD

Can You Be Discriminated Against Because of the Way You Speak?

IN APRIL 2001, a Californian named James Johnson began to suspect that the owners of an apartment he
wanted to rent in the San Francisco Bay Area were ignoring his phone calls because he was African-American.
Johnson hadn't met the landlords in person or told them
about his race. But he had spoken to them by telephone,
and he assumed that they could identify his race from the
way he spoke. So he sued, alleging racial discrimination.

In *Johnson v. Jensen*, which will be heard in upcoming
months in the U.S. District Court for Northern California,
the defendants will likely argue that they had no idea
Johnson was black. Having only heard Johnson's voice,
they couldn't have discriminated against him on the basis of his race. Race, after all, is something one sees, not
hears.

Or is it? John Baugh, an African-American linguist at
Stanford University, is on Johnson's side. In *Johnson v.
Jensen*, he will provide expert testimony to support the
claim that people can often identify a speaker's race from
speech alone. In recent years, Baugh has emerged as one
of the leading experts on the intersection of race and language, largely as a result of his research into this sort of
"linguistic profiling," a term he coined.

Johnson's case offers a potential breakthrough in discrimination law. No judge has yet recognized linguistic
profiling as a distinct form of racial discrimination, and
many lawyers feel that an official ruling would have a
significant effect on future litigation. Shanna L. Smith, the
president of the nonprofit National Fair Housing Alliance,

predicts that if the concept of linguistic profiling is vindicated in court, the number of housing complaints will rise significantly.

For skeptics, this is not promising news. John McWhorter, an African- 5 American linguist at the University of California at Berkeley and the author of *Losing the Race: Self-Sabotage in Black America,* argues that linguistic profiling is a phenomenon largely dreamed up by civil rights crusaders desperate for fresh battlefields. "We're at a point in this country where great progress is being made in race relations," he says. "There's still racism, but naked discrimination is a thing of the past. So if you're going to look for racism, it's going to get more and more subtle." He worries that Baugh is exaggerating the problem: "No one before 1964 was running around complaining about linguistic profiling, because it was a marginal issue. It still is."

In 2002, however, James Johnson and others think there's something to complain about. The practical question is: Can they prove it in court?

At a linguistics conference last April at the University of Texas at Austin, Baugh spoke about the topic of linguistic profiling. In the course of his talk, without warning, he switched seamlessly from the Standard English dialect he had been speaking to Black English and then to Chicano English. The scholarly audience, accustomed to his "professional voice," burst out laughing. Baugh learned to speak all three dialects fluently while growing up in the inner cities of Philadelphia and Los Angeles, where he was raised by well-educated parents. In his first book, *Black Street Speech* (1983), he recalls hearing his mother talk on the telephone: "As I grew older," he writes, "it became fairly easy to tell if Mom was talking to someone black or someone white, based on her speech alone."

Baugh became seriously interested in this phenomenon in 1987, when he was 38 and looking for a place to live in an affluent suburban section of Palo Alto, California. Using his professional voice, he phoned landlords and consistently received appointments. But when the landlords met him in person, he says, things quickly changed. "That's when I was told the apartment was no longer available," he recalls, "or there had been some mistake." He decided to conduct an experiment, making a large number of phone calls to landlords in the Bay Area, varying the calls among his three dialects. As he predicted, when he spoke in Standard English he set up far more appointments in predominantly white areas than when he spoke in his other dialects.

Over the next ten years, this type of telephone audit became a standard way for social scientists to gauge patterns of housing discrimination. In 2001, using similar techniques, Douglas Massey and Garvey Lundy, two sociologists at the University of Pennsylvania, published a study about access to rental housing in Philadelphia and found significant disparities. Around that time, Baugh began thinking about how such cases might be handled in a courtroom. Without hard scientific evidence, he figured, plaintiffs in housing discrimination cases would be at a loss to defend their intuition that their race had been identified over the phone. "From a legal standpoint," he says, "that's real problematic. Any defense attorney can say, Why are these Black English speakers? And a plaintiff doesn't have anything to say about that, except that they *sound* more black."

In response, Baugh has made a systematic study of people's ability to 10
recognize dialects, often using recordings of his own voice in experiments. In 1997, he and two fellow linguists played recordings of a variety of his speech samples to a group of 421 university students: Eighty-four percent identified his Black English as such, 86 percent recognized his Standard English, and 91 percent identified his Chicano English. "To my chagrin," Baugh quipped to the audience at the Austin conference, "my Black English is judged to be one of the least authentic styles." From a scientific standpoint, though, the significant fact was that all the rates of identification were high. Even when listeners were played recordings of Baugh saying nothing but "hello" in his three dialects, an astonishing 72 percent of them accurately identified the dialect in question. Results like these suggested that linguistic profiling was possible—and could be proved in court.

But does linguistic profiling really need a scientific defense? The novelty of Baugh's involvement has created a stir of excitement around Johnson's case, but in truth courts have long acknowledged that race can be identified by speech—at least in a variety of criminal cases. In the 1912 case *Rhea v. State*, the Supreme Court of Arkansas upheld a murder conviction that hinged on testimony from a witness who said he had heard a "cultured" white voice shout in a crowd. Lawyers for the convicted murderer W. S. Rhea argued that the testimony should have been inadmissible, but the Arkansas justices ruled otherwise. "It is not a mere matter of opinion," the court wrote, "[that] one [can] . . . recognize and know the difference between the voices of persons of different nationalities, and between that of a white man and a negro."

More recently, in the 1999 case *Clifford v. Kentucky*, the Kentucky Supreme Court upheld the drug conviction of a black man named Charles Clifford on similar grounds. In that case, an undercover narcotics detective had purchased drugs from Clifford and secretly transmitted their conversation via microphone to a police surveillance team. The resulting recording was inaudible, but a police officer who had monitored the surveillance equipment testified that he had heard a black man's voice make the sale.

Since Clifford was the only black man in the room with the undercover detective, he was convicted.

In upholding the conviction, the Kentucky Supreme Court argued that a witness who testifies about the racial characteristics of a speaker's voice is no less credible than a witness who testifies on other matters of human experience: the height of a suspect; the speed at which a car was traveling; the smell of gasoline. "We perceive no reason," the court ruled, "why a witness could not likewise identify a voice being that of a particular race or nationality, so long as the witness is personally familiar with the general characteristics, accents, or speech patterns of the race or nationality in question."

If racial identification by voice has been acknowledged in murder and drug cases, why hasn't it played a more conspicuous role in housing discrimination cases? Baugh worries that the reason may be simple racial bias: In criminal and drug cases, where blacks are disproportionately defendants, courts have allowed the notion of racial identification by voice; in housing discrimination cases, where blacks are disproportionately plaintiffs, racial identification by voice has not been ruled on. The imbalance works to the disadvantage of blacks in both situations.

Some fair-housing experts, however, have a less cynical explanation for 15 the imbalance. Linguistic profiling has not been addressed in fair-housing cases, they argue, because by and large the notion of linguistic profiling hasn't been needed. Connie Chamberlin, the president of Housing Opportunities Made Equal (HOME), one of the most successful fair-housing organizations in the country, notes that her organization has been winning cases for years without the help of scholars like Baugh. When HOME receives a complaint, she explains, it typically begins by placing telephone calls to the landlord in question.

More effectively, though, HOME also sends teams of "testers" to visit the landlord in person and inquire about housing availability. The testers are pairs of people who differ in race, but who present nearly identical career paths, income, and marital status. In court, they testify on the contrasting ways in which they were treated (or mistreated). As a result, there isn't necessarily a need for fair-housing cases to be decided solely on voice evidence. James Johnson's lawsuit, for instance, also contains testimony from testers who visited the landlord he contacted, and is therefore winnable without engaging the issue of linguistic profiling.

Chamberlin concedes, however, that voice evidence has an impact in typical cases—albeit in subtle ways. Fair-housing lawyers often play tape recordings to juries of the phone calls made by prospective tenants. But since the tapes provide only one form of evidence among others introduced, the lawyers don't need to instruct the jury to draw conclusions about racial identification—though jurors surely do so as a matter of course. "It's our experience," Chamberlin explains, "that when juries are confronted with taped evidence, they have no difficulty deciding what the housing provider would have known on the phone. There isn't a need to be as technical as linguistic profiling makes it appear." Stephen Dane, a Toledo-based lawyer who has litigated housing discrimination cases for 15 years, concurs: "In my mind, you don't need an expert to tell a jury that you can tell race by voice. I think everybody knows that."

Even if housing discrimination suits have been won for years without the assistance of scientific studies like Baugh's, some fair-housing advocates think that a firm legal precedent acknowledging linguistic profiling can't do any harm, and will only make litigation easier. As the linguist Dennis Preston argues, "We need a judicial decision that says we don't have to test this more than once." Still, practitioners like Chamberlin and Dane remain cautious about Baugh's high-profile involvement. "More power to him if he wants to strengthen the general understanding of the validity of linguistic profiling," Chamberlin says. "But if the precedent becomes that you can't prove a fair-housing case without an expert, that's doing us no favors."

Evidence of linguistic profiling may eventually be forced to take center stage, however, as interactions between buyers and sellers occur increasingly on the telephone. Many insurance and home mortgage companies, for instance, conduct negotiations and transactions entirely by phone. Shanna L. Smith of the National Fair Housing Alliance has urged such companies to hire linguists to train their employees so they'll be aware of inferences they draw from a speaker's voice. "I say to the big companies," she explains, "that this training helps if you have a class-action lawsuit, since you can diminish or eliminate the damages. If it's just an individual employee discriminating, you can't punish the company, just the employee."

For his part, Baugh anticipates that a favorable ruling on linguistic pro- [20] filing would help serve the cause of a range of non–Standard English speakers, not just blacks. "One thing I didn't expect when I started this," he says, "is that linguistic profiling affects the deaf, and it extends to sexual orientation as well. It's much bigger than racial profiling." As for McWhorter's argument that linguistic profiling is being blown out of proportion, Baugh is dismissive. McWhorter's point that linguistic profiling wasn't discussed in 1964 is irrelevant, Baugh argues, since the notion of racial profiling didn't exist then either. Ironically, he adds, the increasing economic and social parity of blacks and whites that McWhorter celebrates has been a factor in the emergence of linguistic profiling cases. "The Mr. Johnsons of the world," Baugh says, "now have the money, now have the credit, and they're saying enough is enough."

about the text

1. Summarize Erard's argument. Do you agree with his conclusions? Why or why not?

2. Three of the people Erard interviewed argue that fair-housing cases should not need "experts" or scientific studies in court. Given the value our society places on science and empirical research, are their arguments persuasive? Why or why not?

3. How might David Troutt, author of "Defining Who We Are in Society" in this chapter (p. 289), respond to the issues raised in Erard's report? Would he be more likely to agree with John Baugh, who argues that a court ruling on linguistic profiling would diminish housing discrimination, or would he side with John McWhorter, who believes that Baugh is exaggerating the problem? Present examples from Troutt's essay to support your argument.

4. Erard describes an early experiment conducted by John Baugh, who speaks three varieties of English with native proficiency. What are the advantages and disadvantages of having only one speaker in the experiment? Do you consider Baugh's research effective? Why or why not?

on language use

5. Have you ever consciously altered your voice on the telephone for a specific reason? For example, to sound older? younger? to present another gender? another cultural or regional background? Were you successful? If not, why not? Describe your experiences and your motives with two or three classmates. How does your discussion reinforce or challenge your ideas about linguistic profiling?

6. John Baugh asserts that linguistic profiling is "much bigger than racial profiling" and that its effects extend to other social categories (paragraph 20). What can you tell about a person from speech alone? Age? Gender? Height? Cultural background? Weight? Regional background? Level of schooling? Religion? Sexual orientation? Political inclination? What is it about speech that lets you tell these things? How reliable are your guesses? Discuss your responses to these questions with two or three classmates.

for writing

7. Erard describes the opposing arguments made by two African American linguists, John McWhorter and John Baugh. (You might take a look at the essay by Baugh, "Linguistic Pride and Racial Prejudice," in this chapter [p. 302], and the one by McWhorter, "Missing the Nose on Our Face: Pronouns and the Feminist Revolution," in chapter 6 [p. 376].) Which position do you agree with? Write an essay in which you argue for one of the two positions.

8. As this book goes to print, the ruling on the Johnson case is expected very soon. Other linguistic profiling cases have also gone to court. Research the Johnson case and one or two other similar cases. Imagine that you are a journalist and write your report as an in-depth feature article for the Sunday edition of your local newspaper.

<abcNEWS.com>

Linguistic Profiling

A Quiz

• •

When you get phone calls from telemarketers, do you pay attention to the person who's calling? What, if anything, can you tell about the caller from just a voice? In the past few years, some researchers refer to linguistic profiling *(a term which parallels racial profiling) as the ways that we can and do assign race or ethnicity to disembodied voices. But these researchers aren't concerned about innocent cases like the one above; they investigate possible cases of discrimination in the housing market where an apartment's availability seems to depend on the accent of the person who calls, rather than her or his ability to pay.*

We invite you to take the Web-based quiz that accompanied a December 2001 ABC World News Tonight segment on linguistic profiling. Go to <www.norton.com/write/language>, click on the profiling quiz link, and score yourself (if you need to take a second guess, play the sound clip again). The quiz is programmed to accept the following choices (not case-sensitive):

> *African-American* or *black*
> *Caucasian* or *white*
> *Indian (Asian)*
> *Hispanic* or *Latino(a)*
> *Middle Eastern* or *Arab*
> *Caribbean*

What does it mean if you get all the answers right—or all of them wrong? Perhaps we can't help but make these or other distinctions based on ethnicity, sex, age, region of origin or residence, or even sexual orientation. But what do we do once the assessments—right or wrong—are made?

• •

1. How many of the ten voices were you able to identify correctly on the first try? Which (if any) were surprises? Why? Compare your responses with those of two or three classmates. What do you find? How might you account for the differences and similarities among your answers? Were there any "tricky" items in the quiz?

2. Some of the people whose voices are in the quiz were reading a script of "Mary Had a Little Lamb," while others were reciting from memory. How might that have influenced your responses? The designers of the quiz likely chose that nursery rhyme because it would be familiar to a wide variety of people. Who might not be familiar with "Mary Had a Little Lamb"? Why not? Can you think of another short text that a greater range of people would know from memory? What might be the implications of your choice? Whom might your choice exclude?

on language use

3. Do the ten voices in the quiz represent an adequate sample of the U.S. population? Why or why not? Do you think they should have? Why or why not? Were the ten voices sufficient to demonstrate the phenomenon of linguistic profiling? Why or why not? Work with a partner and design a different ten-item quiz that attempts to show the type of linguistic profiling that can result in illegal discrimination (you don't have to record any voices, just describe the ideal sample you would choose).

4. Think about the categories of "race" that the quiz accepts as right answers. Are the categories parallel? Are they adequate? Why or why not? (You will probably not find them inclusive of all possibilities, but the quiz doesn't claim to be all-inclusive.)

for writing

5. This quiz accompanied a news report on linguistic profiling (including one of the same cases that was described by Michael Erard in "Can You Be Discriminated Against Because of the Way You Speak?" [p. 294]. How well does the quiz demonstrate the phenomenon of linguistic profiling and the problems it presents? Write an essay evaluating the quiz as a tool for demonstrating the problems of linguistic profiling. First determine the characteristics of a good quiz for this subject. You may want to consider the types of questions, as well as which voices should be included or excluded. Next, consider how well the ABC News quiz meets your criteria. In your essay, explain your criteria and discuss whether the ABC News quiz does or does not satisfy them.

John Baugh *is a professor of education and linguistics at Stanford University. He has written extensively on African American English and on linguistic issues in education and society (see Michael Erard's essay "Can You Be Discriminated Against Because of the Way You Speak?" in this chapter [p. 294] for more information on Baugh's work) and serves on the advisory committees of the* Merriam-Webster's Collegiate Dictionary *and the* American Heritage College Dictionary. *He is the author of* Black Street Speech *(1983) and* Out of the Mouths of Slaves: African-American Language and Education Malpractice *(1999). This selection, from the opening chapter of Baugh's book* Beyond Ebonics: Linguistic Pride and Racial Prejudice *(2000) examines recent episodes of the Ebonics controversy.*

JOHN BAUGH

Linguistic Pride and Racial Prejudice

LABELS PERTAINING to American slave descendants have undergone considerable change over the decades since our forebears were freed. W. E. B. Du Bois observed that racial classifications can be misleading, particularly if those classifications are detested. In 1928 Du Bois spoke of these matters in response to Roland A. Barton, a high school student, and Barton's advocacy of the change from "Negro" to "colored."

> Do not at the outset of your career make the all too common error of mistaking names for things. Names are only conventional signs for identifying things. Things are the reality that counts. If a thing is despised, either because of ignorance or because it is despicable, you will not alter matters by changing its name. If men despise Negroes, they will not despise them less if Negroes are called "colored" or "Afro-American." (Du Bois 96–97)

Du Bois's sage advice holds true for the Ebonics controversy as well. If the vernacular speech of urban or rural slave descendants is devalued, modified nomenclature will not increase its worth in the eyes of those who hold black speech—or African Americans—in low regard. Many who criticized Ebonics did not do so merely because they objected to the term; they scoffed at Ebonics as an attempt to legitimize "bad English" in the name of politically correct linguistic enlightenment. Detractors often claimed to be offended, resentful, or worse.

On the other hand, Ebonics advocates were elated by efforts to elevate its stature, because they had never equated black speech with "improper English," and they embraced "Ebonics" as a term that could offer linguistic legitimacy and enhance cultural pride among American slave descendants.

Were this tale one of mere labels it might be brief, but Ebonics was first used nearly a quarter of a century ago by African American scholars who objected to "black English." The scholars met at a 1973 conference, "Cognitive and Language Development of the Black Child," hosted by Robert Williams (who coined the term "Ebonics"). In an editorial titled "Ebonics as a Bridge to Standard English," Williams stated, "We met to define our language" ("Ebonics"). Here is the way the conversation went on January 26, 1973:

> ROBERT WILLIAMS: We need to define what we speak. We need to give a clear definition of our language.
> ERNIE SMITH: If you notice, every language in the world represents a nation or a nationality. What we are speaking has continuity not only in the United States, but outside the United States and all the way back to the mother country. We need to get the term completely off the English scale and start calling it what it really represents.
> ROBERT WILLIAMS: Let me make a point here. Language is a process of communication. But we need to deal with the root of our language. What about Ebo? Ebo linguistics? Ebolingual? Ebo Phonics? Ebonics? Let's define our language as Ebonics.
> THE GROUP: That sounds good.
> ROBERT WILLIAMS: I am talking about an ebony language. We know that ebony means black and that phonics refers to speech sounds or the science of sound. Thus, we are really talking about the science of black speech sounds or language. ("Ebonics" 14)

From a linguistic point of view, Ebonics—as originally constituted—refers to a complex mixture of European and African languages born of the African slave trade. How, then, did this original definition become transformed? How did it come to focus more narrowly on the speech of U.S. slave descendants—and are slave descendants in Brazil, the Dominican Republic, or Haiti to be included or excluded from Ebonics? Stated in other terms, does Ebonics refer to one language or to more than one language?

Within the United States a portion of this answer is ideological, because the federal government has never formally acknowledged that slave descendants represent a "language minority population" (see Baugh). Therein lies part of the motivation to declare that "Ebonics is not a dialect of English," and that "limited English proficient (LEP) African American pupils are equally entitled to be provided bilingual education and English as a second language programs to address their LEP needs" (Smith, "What Is Black English?" 58).

Although considerable time has elapsed since Oakland educators [5] passed their controversial Ebonics resolution, many of the linguistic and educational problems they articulated have yet to be resolved. These educational impediments are still with us, as American students from all walks of life have been shown to be less well prepared than the vast majority of students from other advanced industrialized countries.

It would be myopic and wrongheaded to pursue educational reforms for African American students in a social vacuum, and I will attempt to consider broader educational implications as we contemplate ways to increase linguistic tolerance among all Americans. But in this instance, those larger educational goals derive from the Ebonics debate that focuses exclusively on the linguistic behavior of African Americans.

Readers presumably seek an informed yet dispassionate survey of Ebonics, but it would be misleading to suggest that I approach this topic with complete linguistic objectivity. Although I bring more than twenty years of linguistic analyses to this subject, I spent my early childhood in inner-city communities where standard English is rare, and those experiences have shaped my life and professional work in ways that defy disengaged objectivity. Thus, this topic is one that remains deeply personal.

To a certain extent, my experiences were similar to those of fellow black students who attended overcrowded, underfunded, inner-city schools. However, unlike many of my childhood peers, I had the advantage of being raised by well-educated parents who were activists on my behalf at school and who strongly encouraged the academic importance of standard English.

Despite the obvious benefits of living in a home with well-educated parents who vigilantly stressed the importance of "proper English," I was also surrounded by friends and neighbors who did not exhibit or prize these linguistic virtues. One of the episodes my parents often recount—an incident I simply don't recall—demonstrated just how firmly I had embraced their steadfast advocacy of standard English.

When I was three or four, one of the older Sisters from our church paid a 10 social call on my parents. Seeing me, she exclaimed, "You sho' is a fine young man." To which I was said to reply, "Are! You are a fine young man." My parents retell the story emphasizing both their pride and embarrassment —after all, I was using standard English, which they valued, but my comment could also be interpreted as a sign of precocious impertinence and disrespect for my elders. Fortunately for all of us their friend was undaunted and unfazed; she simply said, "You sho' is."

Beside such episodes lie the earliest linguistic recollections that were sculpted by numerous social encounters with others in the black neighborhoods of Philadelphia where we lived. Back then, during the 1950s, I knew nothing of the distinction between blue-collar and white-collar jobs, but my parents were younger than many of our neighbors, and we were one of a few families that owned a car. The apparent economic abyss between those who rely exclusively on public transportation and those who own their own cars was one of the first sociological distinctions I recall, and I came to this realization long before attending school.

There were early signs of racial and linguistic differentiation as well. For example, I routinely observed that my mother would speak differently to various people on the telephone. She would typically answer any incoming call with a neutral "Hello," and then her speech would shift; if she responded formally—typically to a white person—her speech would become more standard, and if she spoke to a black person, her speech would sound more natural and relaxed. Even her body language would change during the phone calls; her posture during the formal calls was far more rigid and tense than was the case when she would speak to friends or relatives, and her facial expressions would likewise reflect these differences. Again, these were some of my earliest memories of linguistic observations, and I lacked the experience, knowledge, or understanding to fully comprehend the significance of her linguistic modifications.

Beyond the sanctuary of our home, the social and linguistic performances I observed were wildly diverse, spanning the loud antics of hip teens who lived in the neighborhood in contrast to the prim speech of older gracious Sisters at church, which ritually reinforced mainstream social, linguistic, and family virtues. Language was often mentioned in these hallowed gatherings; elders chided those with foul mouths and vile language who held forth beyond the sanctuary of the good God-loving folk who attended church. In my youthful mind I extended this linguistic parable; those who spoke "good English" were supposed to be emulated; those who spoke "bad English" were not.

At a young age, then, I received mixed messages about language; some were overt, advocating that I "speak properly" and avoid "bad language," whereas others were more subtle, reflected by the hippest Sisters and Brothers who emphatically rejected "white speech." I was perplexed. On what basis should I develop my personal sense of linguistic pride, and how would it relate to the looming "racial prejudice" that older peers told me existed in "white" neighborhoods? Because my parents worked in professional contexts, they had much more contact with whites than did most of our other neighbors, who had few social contacts beyond our African American community. My parents were mindful of racial prejudice, but they were equally concerned that I not be consumed by racial paranoia, especially so early in life. Long before racial equality became a highly visible national concern, they sought to instill in me the color-blind ethos that is our national creed; they taught me and my siblings that all people are created equal, and that it was our collective good fortune to live in a country with *the potential* of providing liberty and justice for all. Their love and wisdom initially shielded us from the burdens of racial bigotry, and as we grew older they gradually began to prepare us to withstand the barbs of antagonistic racial hostilities.

Their color-blind mythology was never truly challenged in my youth be- 15 cause few white students were enrolled at the inner-city elementary schools I attended. Thus most of my classmates and I weren't constantly reminded of racial divisions or potential white versus nonwhite conflicts, although the vast majority of our teachers were white. Like my parents and the elders at church, these teachers strongly endorsed standard English, and, thanks to the diligent efforts of my mother, I was able to improve my reading even though many of my teachers did little to encourage or fully develop my full academic potential.

Were it not for my parents' love and educational intervention I could have easily been counted among the millions of African American students who never achieved standard English proficiency. But I faced an added socio-linguistic paradox; I didn't want to sound "lame" (see Labov), and, as I had observed "on the corner," most of the "cool brothers" could "talk"—and those who exhibited urban eloquence never did so in standard English. What, then, was I to do? Should I use standard English, to the exclusion of African-American vernacular speech norms, and risk ridicule or social rejection from my black peers? Or, should I resist my parents' standard English advocacy and suffer the domestic consequences of open linguistic rebellion at home? I gradually began to compromise, employing nonstandard speech among my friends while using standard English (to the best of my ability) in church and at home. I confess that my linguistic behavior at school fluctuated greatly. Bad grades were not tolerated in the Baugh household, yet—not wanting to appear either lame or too eager to "act white" (see Fordham and Ogbu)—I became a linguistic chameleon, seeking to avoid speech that would call attention to itself, depending on my immediate circumstances. I felt as though I were trapped in a cultural vise consisting of two opposing linguistic barricades with each side offering situationally dependent rewards or sanctions.

It is also important to acknowledge that my linguistic circumstances changed drastically in 1958. My father had accepted a job in Los Angeles, and we moved from a black neighborhood to one that was in racial transition. Upon arriving in Los Angeles I encountered a strange new world with neighbors who were learning English as a second language. I vividly recall my own racist reactions of linguistic superiority as I listened to them struggle to use English—a "superiority" I tried to exploit in attempts to gain favor among my new African American neighbors and classmates.

Having grown up as a "baby boomer" in black neighborhoods in Philadelphia, my African American male friends and I would play military "war games" against classical American foes. In essence, we considered any enemy of John Wayne's to be our enemy. After all, we had all been weaned on westerns and World War II movies that tended to reinforce some unfortunate racist stereotypes and hypotheses that I projected on many of my new "foreign" California neighbors.

My immediate reaction of racist skepticism was met in turn by cautious curiosity from the almond-eyed children who stopped playing with their hula hoops just long enough to stare at me, "the new kid." Without fully understanding my emotions at the time, I experienced my own burgeoning racism, which was continually reinforced each time I heard a "funny accent."

A few weeks after we arrived in Los Angeles it was time for school and 20 not only was I the new kid in my class, but I was "fresh meat" for the local bullies, who promptly shattered any false hopes I had about making new friends. However, because of my misplaced youthful sense of cultural and linguistic superiority, combined with my lack of experience or tolerance of people who were unfamiliar (i.e., people who were not black), I only considered the prospect of making new black friends.

I was not only insensitive to many of my fellow classmates who were learning English as a new language, I was also occasionally cruel. I found their speech awkward, and their funny accents served as a source of considerable linguistic amusement. In an effort to endear myself to my fellow African Americans I began to mimic the speech of nonblack students who were struggling to learn English; these racist antics were rather pitiful displays that I hoped would impress my fellow black classmates, most of whom remained quite unimpressed. Rather than change tactics, I opted to turn up the volume, which led to some personal confrontations—many centered around language and my misguided sense of linguistic superiority.

My presumptuous sense of linguistic grandeur resulted mainly from the considerable value Mom and Dad placed on the importance of standard English and speaking properly, and at home I did my best to conform to their linguistic preferences. But away from home my youthful quest to become "cool" at the expense of other minority students was unfortunate, and just as shameful as any distasteful form of racial bigotry. In retrospect I can now admit to myself, and others, that I was somewhat "lame"; but because I aspired to be "hip," I concluded that the road from nerdiness to greater popularity (particularly with my black peers) could be paved with linguistic and racial insults against other minority students whose English proficiency was inferior to mine. Each day young verbal warriors would gather in the schoolyard, exchanging taunts, jeers, and various insults before an audience of onlookers who would take considerable delight at the spectacle of this, generally, bloodless sport. Girls were often among the best combatants or instigators — and some girls were clearly superior, with the eloquence and timing to devastate any and all comers who were foolish enough to engage them in verbal or physical battle.

Lacking the skill to face off against the best among the schoolyard verbal gladiators, I sought less challenging linguistic prey on which to hone my —less than adequate—oral dueling skills. One incident in particular provided a personal epiphany that shaped my future as a linguist.

The verbal insults that were daily ritual displays at our school conformed to certain routines. Teachers and school administrators hoped we would play organized games before school and at recess, and they typically provided jump ropes, basketballs, tetherballs, and kick balls for this purpose. Inevitably, during the course of a game or some other hostile encounter, two or more students would begin hurling insults, which typically began with the phrase, "Yo' Mama. . . ." This utterance rarely resulted in an immediate fight, although there were noteworthy exceptions. The more common response would be, "Don't be talking' 'bout my Mama, 'cause yo' Mama done . . ." At that point a group of spectators would inevitably surround the joust, and upon any such gathering then ever greater numbers of students would drop whatever they were doing to watch any escalating confrontation. Students often had the luxury of choosing among several conflicts.

On the day in question I happened to be drawn into the center of the ring. My adversary, Carlos, was considerably larger than I, but English was quite new to him, which magnified my skewed sense of linguistic superiority. We were having an honest disagreement about the game we were playing until he withheld the ball, which stopped play altogether.

JB: C'mon, man, give me the ball.
C: I'll give the ball to yo' Mama, punk.
JB: My Mama ain't got nothin' to do with this, man, just give me the damn ball!

The confrontation escalated, becoming louder and more vulgar, and Carlos turned up the insults in his best rendition of a vulgar urban vernacular, claiming that my mother had excessively large breasts. I, of course, took considerable umbrage and responded in kind, with equally distasteful comments about his mother and her sexual proclivities. In the process I not only insulted his mother but mimicked his Latino accent, which infuriated him even more.

At that time I was relatively small—and quite small in comparison to Carlos. To my physical detriment, Carlos decided it was time to stop talking and start fighting, and he began to give me the "ass whippin'" he and his fellow Latinos and Latinas felt I deserved—and they may have been right. I knew that my linguistic mockery was cruel, but I was too young to fully comprehend their anger, nor did I really care at the time. I wish I could say that I held my own during the fight, but that would be a lie. Carlos was a far more skilled fighter than I, and—although I kept spewing verbal insults—I beat a fairly hasty retreat to the relative safety of our classroom, where the teacher, a middle-aged white man, overheard me "badmouthing" Carlos.

TEACHER: John: Stop it.
JB: Hey man! He's hitting me. I ain't doing nothing.
TEACHER: You're making fun of him.
JB: Yeah, but he's hitting me, I'm just talking.
TEACHER: But you're making fun of the way he talks, so stop it.
JB: (*shucking and jiving in my best rendition of exaggerated standard English*) I'm very sorry, I didn't realize I was doing anything wrong.
TEACHER: Now, John, why don't you speak that way all of the time and improve yourself?

The teacher failed to realize what my black peers sensed immediately; namely, my rendition of standard English was an overt attempt to mock the teacher and standard English with one blow. He assumed I was being contrite—not sarcastic, and his statement regarding my linguistic self-improvement was intended to reinforce the virtues of speaking standard English, which had little linguistic usefulness or value among the African American peer group I so desperately wanted to impress.

It was at that moment that my personal linguistic epiphany occurred: When I was insulting Carlos—by mimicking his dialect—the teacher interpreted it as an authentic linguistic affront, but when I attempted to sarcastically insult the teacher—through my exaggerated rendition of standard English—he concluded that I was being apologetic, deferential, or perhaps both.

Much like the fabled one-eyed man in the land of the blind, I felt an absolute sense of linguistic superiority over my classmates for whom English was not native. Not only were they learning English as a new language, they were also doing so in ways that placed them at considerable linguistic disadvantage in the ritualized verbal bouts that consumed so much of our youthful recreational activity.

The talent I possessed, to mimic the nonstandard dialects of my peers, was not initially developed for the educational and scholarly causes I have come to endorse as a professional linguist, but that mimicry provided early exposure to the combinations of racial prejudice and linguistic pride—or shame—that lie at the heart of the Ebonics controversy.

I share these observations, in part, because readers should be fully 30 aware of my early childish sense of linguistic superiority over my classmates and neighbors who were learning English as a new language, along with my racist reactions to their speech. In a real sense my uninformed negative response to learners of English as a second language was similar in nature to many of those who chastise African American vernacular speech norms. Having previously straddled the fence between linguistic dexterity and racial bigotry, I saw both sides of these issues long before Williams and his associates created the term "Ebonics." Smitherman speaks eloquently of her own linguistic trauma at the hands of speech pathologists who equated her black speech with cognitive disabilities, and Smith describes the linguistic contexts in which he took great pride in his capacity to employ vernacular African American speech at the same time that he repudiated "white speech" ("Ebonics"). Even conservative African American pundits who lament affirmative action speak at length about their personal sense of linguistic shame.

It is against this backdrop of linguistic devaluation that Ebonics was born. During those early years, when Ebonics was first introduced, it was nurtured in racially segregated contexts that offered limited exposure beyond the community of African American scholars who embraced the term and celebrated its Afrocentric conceptualization (Tolliver-Weddington).

That racially sheltered incubation was shattered when Oakland educators, at the behest of the Oakland African American Educational Task Force, chose to adopt Ebonics as the official language of their students of African descent, but the content of the resolutions adopting Ebonics evoked a firestorm of controversy. The wording of their original resolution proved to be so controversial that they eventually retracted much of its content, producing a substantially revised resolution that attempted to deflect the anger and angst that Ebonics critics directed at the Oakland school board.

Although many legislators and parents continue to express strong support for more "school choice" along with simultaneous advocacy of greater local authority over school decisions; many balked when Oakland's local school officials demonstrated such choice by choosing Ebonics. Government officials at every level, from local school boards and municipalities to various state legislators, as well as members of Congress and the secretary of education, rejected Ebonics. Politicians of every political persuasion detected the pervasive sense of public outrage against Ebonics, and a flurry of legislative activities to banish Ebonics were spawned shortly after the media had lost interest in the topic.

But much of the legislative effort to drive a spike through the heart of Ebonics was so broad, or so poorly worded, that many of these anti-Ebonics bills fizzled. In retrospect it is clear that the vast majority of politicians were eager to drop this controversial and racially evocative topic in favor of other pressing business. Once Oakland educators had abandoned Ebonics there was little justification to pursue the matter. One African American legislator noted that passing laws to abolish educational programs based on Ebonics would be akin to passing laws to banish liquor sales in churches; they would be superfluous.

Still other reasons that Ebonics legislation failed were related to com- 35 peting definitions of the term. Due largely to its ideological origin, Ebonics has come to mean different things to different people. Professional linguists did not begin to use the term until after Oakland's resolution (O'Neil), and even when some did, typically they were unaware of its origin—or the fact that Williams and his colleagues had defined Ebonics quite differently from the most common interpretation in the United States ("Ebonics").

The combination of the media spotlight, race, language, education, and politically correct dogma soon leapt beyond the political realm and became fodder for comedians, pundits, and editorial cartoonists, and "bonics" soon became a productive suffix[1] as off-color Ebonics jokes began to flourish. Daytime and late-night talk shows began to lampoon Ebonics and those who continued to champion its educational utility. Some of those reactions were racist, providing bigots with a license to engage in the type of overtly racist rhetoric that was far more common during the bygone era of blatant racial segregation. But many African Americans mocked Ebonics too, including Maya Angelou, Bill Cosby, and Kweisi Mfume, among others. It would therefore be simplistic and wrong to paint Ebonics supporters or detractors in contrastive racial terms.

Of considerable relevance to this debate are some qualitative results from a national linguistic survey completed shortly after the Oakland school board passed its infamous Ebonics resolution. That survey attempted to determine what groups favored or disfavored Ebonics and why. The results of the survey—which include observations that African Americans who en-

---

1. **productive suffix:** the ordinary word "productive" is also a technical term in linguistics, used to describe a word segment that combines easily to form other words (a Google search of "*bonics" will demonstrate Baugh's point very clearly).

dorse Ebonics tend to reject racial integration—have prompted me to promote linguistic tolerance in our national quest for racial reconciliation. Blacks who dislike Ebonics tend to value racial integration. Slave descendants who favor Ebonics were also in favor of racially segregated schools, as long as those schools are fully funded and free to adopt an Afrocentric curriculum. African American Ebonics detractors, for the most part, disfavor the prospect of racially segregated schools.

Ironically, the national dialogue on race has sidestepped the Ebonics controversy, but few other topics that have captured global attention on a comparable scale have more to do with the linguistic and educational themes that are central to America's struggle toward racial reconciliation. Ebonics, by virtue of its African American classification and Oakland's efforts to adopt it for educational purposes, lies at the vortex of public education and national race relations. Until such time as leaders in positions of political authority have the collective courage, vision, and wisdom to redress the linguistic legacy of American slavery within the context of providing equal educational opportunities to all children, we will never be able to fully overcome our long history of race-based inequality.

Works Cited

Baugh, John. "Linguistics, Education, and the Law: Educational Reform for African-American Language Minority Students." *African American English: Structure, History, and Use.* Ed. Salikoko Mufwene, John Rickford, Guy Bailey, and John Baugh. London: Routledge, 1998: 282–301.

Du Bois, W. E. B. "The Name 'Negro.'" *The Crisis* 35 (1928): 96–97.

Fordham, Signithia, and John Ogbu. "Black Students' School Success: Coping with the Burden of 'Acting White.'" *The Urban Review* 8.3 (1986): 176–206.

Labov, William. *Language in the Inner City: Studies in the Black English Vernacular.* Philadelphia: U of Pennsylvania Press, 1972.

O'Neil, Wayne. "If Ebonics Isn't a Language, Then Tell Me, What Is?" *The Real Ebonics Debate: Power, Language, and the Education of African American Children.* Ed. Theresa Perry and Lisa Delpit. Boston: Beacon, 1998: 38–48.

Smith, Ernie. "Ebonics: A Case History." *Ebonics: The True Language of Black Folks.* Ed. R. Williams. St. Louis: Williams, 1975: 77–85.

———. "What Is Black English, What Is Ebonics?" *The Real Ebonics Debate: Power, Language, and the Education of African-American Children.* Ed. Theresa Perry and Lisa Delpit. Boston: Beacon, 1998: 49–58.

Smitherman, Geneva. *Talkin' and Testifyin': The Language of Black America.* Boston: Houghton, 1978.

Tolliver-Weddington, Gloria, ed. *Ebonics (Black English): Implications for Education.* Spec. issue of *Journal of Black Studies* 9.4 (1979).

Williams, Robert, ed. *Ebonics: The True Language of Black Folks.* St. Louis: Williams, 1975.

———. "Ebonics as a Bridge to Standard English." *St. Louis Post-Dispatch* 28 Jan. 1997: A14.

about the text

1. Baugh argues that linguistic issues are at the very core of persistent race-based inequality. What, exactly, is he urging education policymakers to do? Do you agree? Why or why not?

2. Notice how Baugh combines personal narrative with scholarly argument. How does the personal narrative support his scholarly argument—and how does the argument enhance his personal narrative? Do you think the combination is effective? Why or why not?

on language use

3. Baugh recounts an episode from his early childhood in which he quotes "an older Sister" from church (paragraph 10). Is it important that Baugh wrote the woman's statement with non-standard spelling? Why or why not? In what other formal writing situations might it be appropriate to use non-standard spelling? Whose speech is likely (or not likely) to be represented with non-standard spelling?

4. Have you ever witnessed linguistic taunting like Baugh describes? Have you ever teased someone about their speech or been teased about some feature of yours? Describe linguistic tauntings experience where you were perpetrator, object, or witness. Try to remember what you felt and thought, and share your experiences with two or three classmates. On the basis of that discussion, recommend guidelines for school authorities to deal with linguistic taunting.

for writing

5. What are your earliest linguistic observations? Baugh's observations relate to circumstances of his background—his being African American, of a family with relatively high status in his community, and receiving explicit instruction in standard English grammar. What life circumstances are relevant to your earliest observations? Write an essay in which you describe an early linguistic memory and explain what may have primed you to make your observation. Discuss the ways in which your observation and/or its social context have influenced your life.

6. In paragraph 27, Baugh describes the "personal linguistic epiphany" he had from observing that the teacher interpreted Baugh's mimicking Carlos's speech as insulting, but interpreted his "exaggerated rendition of standard English" as praiseworthy. He leaves it to the readers, however, to infer the precise ramifications of the experience. Based on what you have learned about Baugh from his essay, what did he understand, at that moment, about the teacher? About standard English? About himself? Use Baugh's experiences and conclusions to write an essay explaining the perceived superiority of standard English. Don't argue your own position, but rather explain a social phenomenon in its historical context.

JUNE JORDAN

Nobody Mean More to Me Than You, and the Future Life of Willie Jordan

June Jordan *was a professor of English at the State University of New York at Stony Brook in 1985 when she wrote this essay. Jordan explains that the title phrase, "Nobody mean more to me than you," is a Black English aphorism crafted by Monica Morris, a junior at S.U.N.Y. at Stony Brook, October 1984. The essay anticipates much of the linguistic scholarship on black English and predates the Ebonics controversy in 1996– 1997. Jordan was the author of more than twenty-five books of poetry, essays, fiction, plays, and children's stories. Her first novel,* His Own Where *(1971), was nominated for the National Book Award. Jordan died of breast cancer in 2002. This essay originally appeared as the opening chapter of* Moving Towards Home: Political Essays *(1989).*

BLACK ENGLISH is not exactly a linguistic buffalo; as children, most of the thirty-five million Afro-Americans living here depend on this language for our discovery of the world. But then we approach our maturity inside a larger social body that will not support our efforts to become anything other than the clones of those who are neither our mothers nor our fathers. We begin to grow up in a house where every true mirror shows us the face of somebody who does not belong there, whose walk and whose talk will never look or sound "right," because that house was meant to shelter a family that is alien and hostile to us. As we learn our way around this environment, either we hide our original word habits, or we completely surrender our own voice, hoping to please those who will never respect anyone different from themselves: Black English is not exactly a linguistic buffalo, but we should understand its status as an endangered species, as a perishing, irreplaceable system of community intelligence, or we should expect its extinction, and, along with that, the extinguishing of much that constitutes our own proud, and singular identity.

What we casually call "English," less and less defers to England and its "gentlemen." "English" is no longer a specific matter of geography or an element of class privilege; more than thirty-three countries use this tool as a means of "international communication."[1] Countries

---

1. *English Is Spreading, but What Is English?* A presentation by Professor S. N. Sridahr, Dept. of Linguistics, S.U.N.Y. at Stony Brook, April 9, 1985; Dean's Conversation among the Disciplines [Jordan's note].

as disparate as Zimbabwe and Malaysia, or Israel and Uganda, use it as their non-native currency of convenience. Obviously, this tool, this "English," cannot function inside thirty-three discrete societies on the basis of rules and values absolutely determined somewhere else, in a thirty-fourth other country, for example.

In addition to that staggering congeries of non-native users of English, there are five countries, or 333,746,000 people, for whom this thing called "English" serves as a native tongue.[2] Approximately ten percent of these native speakers of "English" are Afro-American citizens of the U.S.A. I cite these numbers and varieties of human beings dependent on "English" in order, quickly, to suggest how strange and how tenuous is any concept of "Standard English." Obviously, numerous forms of English now operate inside a natural, an uncontrollable, continuum of development. I would suppose "the standard" for English in Malaysia is not the same as "the standard" in Zimbabwe. I know that standard forms of English for Black people in this country do not copy that of whites. And, in fact, the structural differences between these two kinds of English have intensified, becoming more Black, or less white, despite the expected homogenizing effects of television[3] and other mass media.

Nonetheless, white standards of English persist, supreme and unquestioned, in these United States. Despite our multilingual population, and despite the deepening Black and white cleavage within that conglomerate, white standards control our official and popular judgments of verbal proficiency and correct, or incorrect, language skills, including speech. In contrast to India, where at least fourteen languages co-exist as legitimate Indian languages, in contrast to Nicaragua, where all citizens are legally entitled to formal school instruction in their regional or tribal languages, compulsory education in America compels accommodation to exclusively white forms of "English." White English, in America, is "Standard English."

This story begins two years ago, I was teaching a new course, "In Search of ⁵ the Invisible Black Woman," and my rather large class seemed evenly divided between young Black women and men. Five or six white students also sat in attendance. With unexpected speed and enthusiasm we had moved through historical narratives of the nineteenth century to literature by and about Black women, in the twentieth. I had assigned the first forty pages of

---

2. Ibid [Jordan's note].

3. The *New York Times*, March 15, 1985, Section One, p. 14: Report on study by Linguistics at the University of Pennsylvania. [Jordan's note].

Alice Walker's *The Color Purple*, and I came, eagerly, to class that morning:
"So!" I exclaimed, aloud. "What did you think? How did you like it?"
The students studied their hands, or the floor. There was no response.
The tense, resistant feeling in the room fairly astounded me.
At last, one student, a young woman still not meeting my eyes, muttered
something in my direction:
"What did you say?" I prompted her.
"Why she have them talk so funny. It don't sound right." 　　　　　　10
"You mean the language?"
Another student lifted his head: "It don't look right, neither. I couldn't
hardly read it."
At this, several students dumped on the book. Just about unanimously,
their criticisms targeted the language. I listened to what they wanted to say
and silently marveled at the similarities between their casual speech patterns and Alice Walker's written version of Black English.
But I decided against pointing to these identical traits of syntax; I
wanted not to make them self-conscious about their own spoken language—
not while they clearly felt it was "wrong." Instead I decided to swallow my
astonishment. Here was a negative Black reaction to a prize-winning accomplishment of Black literature that white readers across the country had selected as a best seller. Black rejection was aimed at the one irreducibly Black
element of Walker's work: the language—Celie's Black English. I wrote the
opening lines of *The Color Purple* on the blackboard and asked the students
to help me translate these sentences into Standard English:

> *You better not never tell nobody but God. It'd kill your mammy.*
> Dear God,
>
> I am fourteen years old. I have always been a good girl. Maybe
> you can give me a sign letting me know what is happening to me.
>
> Last spring after Little Lucious come I heard them fussing. He
> was pulling on her arm. She say it too soon, Fonso. I aint well. Fi-
> nally he leave her alone. A week go by, he pulling on her arm again.
> She say, Naw, I ain't gonna. Can't you see I'm already half dead, an
> all of the children.[4]

Our process of translation exploded with hilarity and even hysterical,
shocked laughter: The Black writer, Alice Walker, knew what she was doing!
If rudimentary criteria for good fiction includes the manipulation of language so that the syntax and diction of sentences will tell you the identity of

---

4. Alice Walker, *The Color Purple*, p. 11, Harcourt Brace, N.Y. [Jordan's note].

speakers, the probable age and sex and class of speakers, and even the locale—urban/rural/southern/western—then Walker had written, perfectly. This is the translation into Standard English that our class produced:

> *Absolutely, one should never confide in anybody besides God. Your secrets could prove devastating to your mother.*
>
> Dear God,
> I am fourteen years old, I have always been good. But now, could you help me to understand what is happening to me?
> Last spring, after my little brother, Lucious, was born, I heard my parents fighting. My father kept pulling at my mother's arm. But she told him, "It's too soon for sex, Alfonso. I am still not feeling well." Finally, my father left her alone. A week went by, and he began bothering my mother, again. Pulling her arm. She told him, "No, I won't! Can't you see I'm already exhausted from all of these children?"

(Our favorite line was "It's too soon for sex, Alphonso.") 15

Once we could stop laughing, once we could stop our exponentially wild improvisations on the theme of Translated Black English, the students pushed me to explain their own negative first reactions to their spoken language on the printed page. I thought it was probably akin to the shock of seeing yourself in a photograph for the first time. Most of the students had never before seen a written facsimile of the way they talk. None of the students had ever learned how to read and write their own verbal system of communication: Black English. Alternatively, this fact began to baffle or else bemuse and then infuriate my students. Why not? Was it too late? Could they learn how to do it, now? And, ultimately, the final test question, the one testing my sincerity: Could I teach them? Because I had never taught anyone Black English and, as far as I knew, no one, anywhere in the United States, had ever offered such a course, the best I could say was "I'll try."

He looked like a wrestler.

He sat dead center in the packed room and, every time our eyes met, he quickly nodded his head as though anxious to reassure, and encourage, me.

Short, with strikingly broad shoulders and long arms, he spoke with a surprisingly high, soft voice that matched the soft bright movement of his eyes. His name was Willie Jordan. He would have seemed even more unlikely in the context of Contemporary Women's Poetry, except that ten or twelve other Black men were taking the course, as well. Still, Willie was conspicuous. His extreme fitness, the muscular density of his presence underscored the riveted, gentle attention that he gave to anything anyone said. Generally, he did not join the loud and rowdy dialogue flying back and forth, but there could be no doubt about his interest in our discussions. And, when he stood to present an argument he'd prepared, overnight, that nervous smile of his vanished and an irregular stammering replaced it, as he spoke with visceral sincerity, word by word.

That was how I met Willie Jordan. It was in between "In Search of the In- 20 visible Black Woman" and "The Art of Black English." I was waiting for Departmental approval and I supposed that Willie might be, so to speak, killing time until he, too, could study Black English. But Willie really did want to explore Contemporary Women's poetry and, to that end, volunteered for extra research and never missed a class.

Towards the end of that semester, Willie approached me for an independent study project on South Africa. It would commence the next semester. I thought Willie's writing needed the kind of improvement only intense practice will yield. I knew his intelligence was outstanding. But he'd wholeheartedly opted for "Standard English" at a rather late age, and the results were stilted and frequently polysyllabic, simply for the sake of having more syllables. Willie's unnatural formality of language seemed to me consistent with the formality of his research into South African apartheid. As he projected his studies, he would have little time, indeed, for newspapers. Instead, more than 90 percent of his research would mean saturation in strictly historical, if not archival, material. I was certainly interested. It would be tricky to guide him into a more confident and spontaneous relationship both with language and apartheid. It was going to be wonderful to see what happened when he could catch up with himself, entirely, and talk back to the world.

September, 1984: Breezy fall weather and much excitement! My class, "The Art of Black English," was full to the limit of the fire laws. And, in Independent Study, Willie Jordan showed up, weekly, fifteen minutes early for each of our sessions. I was pretty happy to be teaching, altogether!

I remember an early class when a young brother, replete with his ever present pork-pie hat, raised his hand and then told us that most of what he'd heard was "all right" except it was "too clean." "The brothers on the street," he continued, "they mix it up more. Like 'fuck' and 'motherfuck.' Or like 'shit.'" He waited, I waited. Then all of us laughed a good while, and we got into a brawl about "correct" and "realistic" Black English that led to Rule 1.

Rule 1: *Black English is about a whole lot more than mothafuckin.*

As a criterion, we decided, "realistic" could take you anywhere you want 25 to go. Artful places. Angry places. Eloquent and sweetalkin places. Polemical places. Church. And the local Bar & Grill. We were checking out a language, not a mood or a scene or one guy's forgettable mouthing off.

It was hard. For most of the students, learning Black English required a fallback to patterns and rhythms of speech that many of their parents had beaten out of them. I mean *beaten*. And, in a majority of cases, correct Black English could be achieved only by striving for *incorrect* Standard English, something they were still pushing at, quite uncertainly. This state of affairs led to Rule 2.

Rule 2: *If it's wrong in Standard English it's probably right in Black English, or, at least, you're hot.*

It was hard. Roommates and family members ridiculed their studies, or remained incredulous, "You *studying* that shit? At school?" But we were beginning to feel the companionship of pioneers. And we decided that we needed another rule that would establish each one of us as equally important to our success. This was Rule 3.

Rule 3: *If it don't sound like something that come out somebody mouth then it don't sound right. If it don't sound right then it ain't hardly right. Period.*

This rule produced two weeks of compositions in which the students ag-   30
onizingly tried to spell the sound of the Black English sentence they wanted to convey. But Black English is, preeminently, an oral/spoken means of communication. *And spelling don't talk.* So we needed Rule 4.

Rule 4: *Forget about the spelling. Let the syntax carry you.*

Once we arrived at Rule 4 we started to fly because syntax,[5] the structure of an idea, leads you to the world view of the speaker and reveals her values. The syntax of a sentence equals the structure of your consciousness. If we insisted that the language of Black English adheres to a distinctive Black syntax, then we were postulating a profound difference between white and Black people, *per se*. Was it a difference to prize or to obliterate?

There are three qualities of Black English—the presence of life, voice, and clarity—that testify to a distinctive Black value system that we became excited about and self-consciously tried to maintain.

1. Black English has been produced by a pre-technocratic, if not antitechnological, culture. More, our culture has been constantly threatened by annihilation or, at least, the swallowed blurring of assimilation. Therefore, our language is a system constructed by people constantly needing to insist that we exist, that we are present. Our language devolves from a culture that abhors all abstraction, or anything tending to obscure or delete the fact of the human being who is here and now/the truth of the person who is speaking or listening. Consequently, *there is no passive voice construction possible*

---

5. **syntax** in this context, both the linear order of words in a sentence and the pattern of relationships between words in a sentence.

in Black English. For example, you cannot say, "Black English is being eliminated." You must say, instead, "White people eliminating Black English." The assumption of the presence of life governs all of Black English. Therefore, overwhelmingly, *all action takes place in the language of the present indicative.* And every sentence assumes the living and active participation of at least two human beings, the speaker and the listener.

2. A primary consequence of the person-centered values of Black English is the delivery of voice. If you speak or write Black English, your ideas will necessarily possess that otherwise elusive attribute, *voice.* 35

3. One main benefit following from the person-centered values of Black English is that of *clarity.* If your idea, your sentence, assumes the presence of at least two living and active people, you will make it understandable because the motivation behind every sentence is the wish to say something real to somebody real.

As the weeks piled up, translation from Standard English into Black English or vice versa occupied a hefty part of our course work.

Standard English (hereafter S.E.): "In considering the idea of studying Black English those questioned suggested — "

(What's the subject? Where's the person? Is anybody alive in there, in that idea?)

Black English (hereafter B.E.): "I been asking people what you think about somebody studying Black English and they answer me like this."

But there were interesting limits. You cannot "translate" instances of Standard English preoccupied with abstraction or with nothing/nobody evidently alive, into Black English. That would warp the language into uses antithetical to the guiding perspective of its community of users. Rather you must first change those Standard English sentences, themselves, into ideas consistent with the person-centered assumptions of Black English.

GUIDELINES FOR BLACK ENGLISH

1. Minimal number of words for every idea: This is the source for the aphoristic and/or poetic force of the language; eliminate every possible word.

2. Clarity: If the sentence is not clear it's not Black English.

3. Eliminate use of the verb *to be* whenever possible. This leads to the deployment of more descriptive and, therefore, more precise verbs. 40

4. Use *be* or *been* only when you want to describe a chronic, ongoing state of things.

> He *be* at the office, by 9. (He is always at the office by 9.)
> He *been* with her since forever.

5. Zero copula: Always eliminate the verb *to be* whenever it would combine with another verb in Standard English.

> S.E.: She is going out with him.
> B.E.: She going out with him.

6. Eliminate *do* as in:

> S.E.: What do you think? What do you want?
> B.E.: What you think? What you want?

Rules number 3, 4, 5, and 6 provide for the use of the minimal number of verbs per idea and, therefore, greater accuracy in the choice of verb.

7. In general, if you wish to say something really positive, try to formulate 45 the idea using emphatic negative structure.

> S.E.: He's fabulous.
> B.E.: He bad.

8. Use double or triple negatives for dramatic emphasis.

> S.E.: Tina Turner sings out of this world.
> B.E.: Ain nobody sing like Tina.

9. Never use the -*ed* suffix to indicate the past tense of a verb.

> S.E.: She closed the door.
> B.E.: She close the door. Or, she have close the door.

10. Regardless of international verb time, only use the third person singular, present indicative, for use of the verb *to have*, as an auxiliary.

> S.E.: He had his wallet then he lost it.
> B.E.: He have him wallet then he lost it.
> S.E.: He had seen that movie.
> B.E.: We seen that movie. Or, we have see that movie.

11. Observe a minimal inflection of verbs. Particularly, never change from the first person singular forms to the third person singular.

> S.E.: Present Tense Forms: He goes to the store.
> B.E.: He go to the store.
> S.E.: Past Tense Forms: He went to the store.

B.E.: He go to the store. Or, he gone to the store. Or, he been to the store.

12. The possessive case scarcely ever appears in Black English. Never use an apostrophe ('s) construction. If you wander into a possessive case component of an idea, then keep logically consistent: ours, his, theirs, mines. But, most likely, if you bump into such a component, you have wandered outside the underlying world-view of Black English. 50

 S.E.: He will take their car tomorrow.
 B.E.: He taking they car tomorrow.

13. Plurality: Logical consistency, continued: If the modifier indicates plurality then the noun remains in the singular case.

 S.E.: He ate twelve doughnuts.
 B.E.: He eat twelve doughnut.
 S.E.: She has many books.
 B.E.: She have many book.

14. Listen for, or invent, special Black English forms of the past tense, such as: "He losted it. That what she felted." If they are clear and readily understood, then use them.

15. Do not hesitate to play with words, sometimes inventing them: e.g. "astropotomous" means huge like a hippo plus astronomical and, therefore, signifies real big.

16. In Black English, unless you keenly want to underscore the past tense nature of an action, stay in the present tense and rely on the overall context of your ideas for the conveyance of time and sequence.

17. Never use the suffix -ly form of an adverb in Black English. 55

 S.E.: The rain came down rather quickly.
 B.E.: The rain come down pretty quick.

18. Never use the indefinite article an in Black English.

 S.E.: He wanted to ride an elephant.
 B.E.: He want to ride him a elephant.

19. Invariant syntax: in correct Black English it is possible to formulate an imperative, an interrogative, and a simple declarative idea with the same syntax:

 B.E.: You going to the store?

 You going to the store.
 You going to the store!

Where was Willie Jordan? We'd reached the mid-term of the semester. Students had formulated Black English guidelines, by consensus, and they were now writing with remarkable beauty, purpose, and enjoyment:

I ain hardly speakin for everybody but myself so understan that. — Kim Parks

Samples from student writings:

Janie have a great big ole hole inside her. Tea Cake the only thing that fit that hole . . .
    That pear tree beautiful to Janie, especial when bees fiddlin with the blossomin pear there growing large and lovely. But personal speakin, the love she get from staring at that tree ain the love what starin back at her in them relationship. (Monica Morris)

Love is a big theme in, *They Eye Was Watching God.* Love show people new corners inside theyself. It pull out good stuff and stuff back bad stuff . . . Joe worship the doing uh his own hand and need other people to worship him too. But he ain't think about Janie that she a person and ought to live like anybody common do. Queen life not for Janie. (Monica Morris)

In both life and writin, Black womens have varietous experience of love that be cold like a iceberg or fiery like a inferno. Passion got for the other partner involve, man or woman, seem as shallow, ankle-deep water or the most profoundest abyss. (Constance Evans)

Family love another bond that ain't never break under no pressure. (Constance Evans)

You know it really cold / When the friend you / Always get out the fire / Act like they don't know you / When you in the heat. (Constance Evans)

Big classroom discussion bout love at this time. I never take no class where us have any long arguin for and against for two or three day. New to me and great. I find the class time talkin a million time more interestin than detail bout the book. (Kathy Esseks)

As these examples suggest, Black English no longer limited the students, in any way. In fact, one of them, Philip Garfield, would shortly "translate" a pivotal scene from Ibsen's *Doll's House,* as his final term paper.

NORA: I didn't gived no shit. I thinked you a asshole back then, too, you make it so hard for me save mines husband life.
KROGSTAD: Girl, it clear you ain't any idea what you done. You done exact what I once done, and I losed my reputation over it.

NORA: You asks me believe you once act brave save you wife life?
KROGSTAD: Law care less why you done it.
NORA: Law must suck.
KROGSTAD: Suck or no, if I wants, judge screw you wid dis paper.
NORA: No way, man. (Philip Garfield)

But where was Willie? Compulsively punctual, and always thoroughly [60] prepared with neatly typed compositions, he had disappeared. He failed to show up for our regularly scheduled conference, and I received neither a note nor a phone call of explanation. A whole week went by. I wondered if Willie had finally been captured by the extremely current happenings in South Africa: passage of a new constitution that did not enfranchise the Black majority, and militant Black South African reaction to that affront. I wondered if he'd been hurt, somewhere. I wondered if the serious workload of weekly readings and writings had overwhelmed him and changed his mind about independent study. Where was Willie Jordan?

One week after the first conference that Willie missed, he called: "Hello, Professor Jordan? This is Willie. I'm sorry I wasn't there last week. But something has come up and I'm pretty upset. I'm sorry but I really can't deal right now."

I asked Willie to drop by my office and just let me see that he was okay. He agreed to do that. When I saw him I knew something hideous had happened. Something had hurt him and scared him to the marrow. He was all agitated and stammering and terse and incoherent. At last, his sadly jumbled account let me surmise, as follows: Brooklyn police had murdered his unarmed, twenty-five-year-old brother, Reggie Jordan. Neither Willie nor his elderly parents knew what to do about it. Nobody from the press was interested. His folks had no money. Police ran his family around and around, to no point. And Reggie was really dead. And Willie wanted to fight, but he felt helpless.

With Willie's permission I began to try to secure legal counsel for the Jordan family. Unfortunately Black victims of police violence are truly numerous while the resources available to prosecute their killers are truly scarce. A friend of mine at the Center for Constitutional Rights estimated that just the preparatory costs for bringing the cops into court normally approaches $180,000. Unless the execution of Reggie Jordan became a major community cause for organizing, and protest, his murder would simply become a statistical item.

Again, with Willie's permission, I contacted every newspaper and media person I could think of. But the William Bastone feature article in *The Village Voice* was the only result from that canvassing.

Again, with Willie's permission, I presented the case to my class in Black 65
English. We had talked about the politics of language. We had talked about
love and sex and child abuse and men and women. But the murder of Reggie
Jordan broke like a hurricane across the room.

There are few "issues" as endemic to Black life as police violence. Most
of the students knew and respected and liked Jordan. Many of them came
from the very neighborhood where the murder had occurred. All of the students had known somebody close to them who had been killed by police, or
had known frightening moments of gratuitous confrontation with the cops.
They wanted to do everything at once to avenge death. Number One: They
decided to compose personal statements of condolence to Willie Jordan and
his family written in Black English. Number Two: They decided to compose
individual messages to the police, in Black English. These should be prefaced by an explanatory paragraph composed by the entire group. Number
Three: These individual messages, with their lead paragraph, should be sent
to *Newsday*.

The morning after we agreed on these objectives, one of the young
women students appeared with an unidentified visitor, who sat through the
class, smiling in a peculiar, comfortable way.

Now we had to make more tactical decisions. Because we wanted the
messages published, and because we thought it imperative that our outrage
be known by the police, the tactical question was this: Should the opening,
group paragraph be written in Black English or Standard English?

I have seldom been privy to a discussion with so much heart at the dead
heat of it. I will never forget the eloquence, the sudden haltings of speech,
the fierce struggle against tears, the furious throwaway, and useless explo-
sions that this question elicited.

That one question contained several others, each of them extraordinarily 70
painful to even contemplate. How best to serve the memory of Reggie Jordan?
Should we use the language of the killers—Standard English—in order to
make our ideas acceptable to those controlling the killers? But wouldn't what
we had to say be rejected, summarily, if we said it in our own language, the
language of the victim, Reggie Jordan? But if we sought to express ourselves
by abandoning our language wouldn't that mean our suicide on top of Reggie's murder? But if we expressed ourselves in our own language wouldn't
that be suicidal to the wish to communicate with those who, evidently, did
not give a damn about us/Reggie/police violence in the Black community?

At the end of one of the longest, most difficult hours of my own life, the
students voted, unanimously, to preface their individual messages with a
paragraph composed in the language of Reggie Jordan. "*At least we don't*

give up nothing else. At least we stick to the truth: Be who we been. And stay all the way with Reggie."

It was heartbreaking to proceed, from that point. Everyone in the room realized that our decision in favor of Black English had doomed our writings, even as the distinctive reality of our Black lives always has doomed our efforts to "be who we been" in this country.

I went to the blackboard and took down this paragraph, dictated by the class:

. . . YOU COPS!
WE THE BROTHER AND SISTER OF WILLIE JORDAN, A FELLOW STONY BROOK STU-
DENT WHO THE BROTHER OF THE DEAD REGGIE JORDAN. REGGIE, LIKE MANY
BROTHER AND SISTER, HE A VICTIM OF BRUTAL RACIST POLICE, OCTOBER 25, 1984.
US APPALL, FED UP, BECAUSE THAT ANOTHER SENSELESS DEATH WHAT OCCUR IN
OUR COMMUNITY. THIS WHAT WE FEEL, THIS, FROM OUR HEART, FOR WE AIN'T
STAYIN' SILENT NO MORE.

With the completion of this introduction, nobody said anything. I asked for comments. At this invitation, the unidentified visitor, a young Black man, ceaselessly smiling, raised his hand. He was, it so happens, a rookie cop. He had just joined the force in September and, he said he thought he should clarify a few things. So he came forward and sprawled easily into a posture of barroom, or fireside, nostalgia:

"See," Officer Charles enlightened us, "most times when you out on the 75 street and something come down you do one of two things. Over-react or under-react. Now, if you under-react then you can get yourself kilt. And if you over-react then maybe you kill somebody. Fortunately it's about nine times out of ten and you will over-react. So the brother got kilt. And I'm sorry about that, believe me. But what you have to understand is what kilt him: Over-reaction. That's all. Now you talk about Black people and white police but see, now, I'm a cop myself. And (big smile) I'm Black. And just a couple months ago I was on the other side. But see it's the same for me. You a cop, you the ultimate authority: the Ultimate Authority. And you on the street, most of the time you can only do one of two things: over-react or under-react. That's all it is with the brother. Over-reaction. Didn't have nothing to do with race."

That morning Officer Charles had the good fortune to escape without being boiled alive. But barely. And I remember the pride of his smile when I read about the fate of Black policemen and other collaborators, in South Africa. I remember him, and I remember the shock and palpable feeling of shame that filled the room. It was as though that foolish, and deadly, young man had just relieved himself of his foolish, and deadly, explanation, face to face with the grief of Reggie Jordan's father and Reggie Jordan's mother. Class ended quietly. I copied the paragraph from the blackboard, collected the individual messages and left to type them up.

Newsday rejected the piece.

The Village Voice could not find room in their "Letters" section to print the individual messages from the students to the police.

None of the TV news reporters picked up the story.

Nobody raised $180,000 to prosecute the murder of Reggie Jordan.   80

Reggie Jordan is really dead.

I asked Willie Jordan to write an essay pulling together everything important to him from that semester. He was still deeply beside himself with frustration and amazement and loss. This is what he wrote, unedited, and in its entirety:

> Throughout the course of this semester I have been researching the effects of oppression and exploitation along racial lines in South Africa and its neighboring countries. I have become aware of South African police brutalization of native Africans beyond the extent of the law, even though the laws themselves are catalyst affliction upon Black men, women, and children. Many Africans die each year as a result of the deliberate use of police force to protect the white power structure.
>
> Social control agents in South Africa, such as policemen, are also used to force compliance among citizens through both overt and covert tactics. It is not uncommon to find bold-faced coercion and cold-blooded killings of Blacks by South African police for undetermined and/or inadequate reasons. Perhaps the truth is that the only reasons for this heinous treatment of Blacks rests in racial differences. We should also understand that what is conveyed through the media is not always accurate and may sometimes by construed as the tip of the iceberg at best.
>
> I recently received a painful reminder that racism, poverty, and the abuse of power are global problems which are by no means unique to South Africa. On October 25, 1984, at approximately 3:00 P.M. my brother, Mr. Reginald Jordan, was shot and killed by two New York City policemen from the 75th precinct in the East New York section of Brooklyn. His life ended at the age of twenty-five. Even up to this current point in time the Police Department has failed to provide my family, which consists of five brothers, eight sisters, and two parents, with a plausible reason for Reggie's death. Out of the many stories that were given to my family by the Police Department, not one of them seems to hold water. In fact, I honestly believe that the

Police Department's assessment of my brother's murder is nothing short of ABSOLUTE BULLSHIT, and thus far no evidence had been produced to alter perception of the situation.

Furthermore, I believe that one of three cases may have occurred in this incident. First, Reggie's death may have been the desired outcome of the police officer's action, in which case the killing was premeditated. Or, it was a case of mistaken identity, which clarifies the fact that the two officers who killed my brother and their commanding parties are all grossly incompetent. Or, both of the above cases are correct, i.e., Reggie's murderers intended to kill him and the Police Department behaved insubordinately.

Part of the argument of the officers who shot Reggie was that he had attacked one of them and took his gun. This was their major claim. They also said that only one of them had actually shot Reggie. The facts, however, speak for themselves. According to the Death Certificate and autopsy report, Reggie was shot eight times from point-blank range. The Doctor who performed the autopsy told me himself that two bullets entered the side of my brother's head, four bullets were sprayed into his back, and two bullets struck him in the back of his legs. It is obvious that unnecessary force was used by the police and that it is extremely difficult to shoot someone in his back when he is attacking or approaching you.

After experiencing a situation like this and researching South Africa I believe that to a large degree, justice may only exist as rhetoric. I find it difficult to talk of true justice when the oppression of my people both at home and abroad attests to the fact that inequality and injustice are serious problems whereby Blacks and Third World people are perpetually short-changed by society. Something has to be done about the way in which this world is set up. Although it is a difficult task, we do have the power to make a change.

– Willie J. Jordan, Jr.
EGL 487, Section 58, November 14, 1984

It is my privilege to dedicate this book to the future life of Willie J. Jordan, Jr.
August 8, 1985

about the text

1. How does Jordan call into question the concept of standard English? What information does she present? What devices and imagery does she use? Is her argument effective? Why or why not?

2. How does Jordan's grammatical description of black English compare with that of John Rickford (in "Suite for Ebony and Phonics," p. 278)? Which features are similar? Which are different?

3. Jordan's essay covers much ground—black English with regard to standard English, her students' reaction to *The Color Purple*, the black English that she worked out with her students, her student Willie Jordan and her relationship with him, the murder of Reggie Jordan and the response of her class, the visit to her class by the rookie police officer, and the essay written by Willie Jordan. What does each of these elements contribute to her argument as a whole? Why do you think she included Willie Jordan's essay in its entirety? How would her argument have been different if she hadn't?

on language use

4. Reread Jordan's description of her students' reaction to *The Color Purple*. Select another passage written in black English from the novel (there are several found easily on the Web). Work with two or three classmates to translate your passage to formal standard written English. How does the new version

sound compared to the original? Were your group's reactions similar to those of Jordan's students? Why or why not? What would have been lost if Walker had written the entire novel in standard English?

5. Jordan claims that black English is "person-centered," immediate, and "assumes the presence of at least two living and active people" (paragraph 36). How does her description relate to the idea that face-to-face conversation in general is distinct from written language? What does the written/spoken distinction have to do with Jordan's observation that "White English, in America, is 'Standard English'" (paragraph 4)?

for writing

6. Jordan's students were forced to make a difficult choice about which language variety to use in their letters to the police. How did you feel when you read this passage? What might you have contributed to the discussion if you had been there? Would your response have been clear and unambivalent? In a page or two, describe your reaction to Jordan's description, and present at least two of the ways you might have considered the decision if you had been there.

7. What new understanding of black English have you gained from reading Jordan's essay? Write an essay explaining the grammatical patterns and social features of black English to an audience who knows little or nothing about the subject.

This ad, sponsored originally by an organization in Atlanta, ran in a number of newspapers in 1997 and 1998, during the height of the national controversy surrounding the Oakland School Board's 1996 resolution on Ebonics. The ad and its designers won a national advertising industry award in 1998, and the New York Times gave it a full page free of charge. A poster version of the ad was produced and requested by schools in several states. Study the ad, paying attention to both the textual message (reprinted below) and the design elements that contribute to the overall message.

I Has a Dream.

Does this bother you? It should. We've spent over 400 years fighting for the right to have a voice. Is this how we'll use it? More importantly, is this how we'll teach our children to use it? If we expect more of them, we must not throw our hands in the air and agree with those who say our children cannot be taught. By now, you've probably heard about Ebonics (aka, Black English). And if you think it's become a controversy because white America doesn't want us messing with their precious language, don't. White America couldn't care less what we do to segregate ourselves.

The fact is language is power. And we can't take that power away from our children with Ebonics. Would Dr. Martin Luther king, Malcolm X and all the others who paid the price of obtaining our voice with the currency of their lives embrace this? If you haven't used your voice lately, consider this an invitation.

Speak out against Ebonics.

I HAS A DREAM.

Does this bother you? It should. We've spent over 400 years fighting for the right to have a voice. Is this how we'll use it? More importantly, is this how we'll teach our children to use it? If we expect more of them, we must not throw our hands in the air and agree with those who say our children cannot be taught. By now, you've probably heard about Ebonics (aka, black English). And if you think it's become a controversy because white America doesn't want us messing with their precious language, don't. White America couldn't care less what we do to segregate ourselves.

The fact is language is power. And we can't take that power away from our children with Ebonics. Would Dr. Martin Luther King, Malcom X and all the others who paid the price of obtaining our voice with the currency of their lives embrace this? If you haven't used your voice lately, consider this an invitation.

SPEAK OUT AGAINST
EBONICS
This message brought to you by Atlanta's Black Professionals.

about the text

1. Who is the African American man standing with his back to us meant to evoke? What is the allusion in the caption "I has a dream"? Why is the allusion especially powerful?

2. What audience does this ad consciously address? Whom else does it invoke as readers, in part with its pronouns? (Clue: Who are "you," "we," and "their" in this text?)

3. Why might the *New York Times* have offered to run the ad at no charge? How does that fact help you understand more about the Ebonics controversy of the late 1990s?

on language use

4. Is the phrase "I has a dream" a well-formed sentence in Ebonics? Consult John Rickford's and June Jordan's grammatical descriptions of the language variety (in this chapter, pp. 277–285; 314–328) to determine your response. Provide appropriate evidence from one or both readings to support your decision.

5. You have no doubt heard recordings of Martin Luther King Jr.'s speeches. Would you say that his speech is distinctly African American? Would you characterize his speech as black English or Ebonics? Why or why not? What implications do your responses to the first two questions have for the nature of the speech variety known as black English or Ebonics? What implications do your responses have for the message conveyed by the ad?

for writing

6. How do the design elements of the ad (photo, large type, overall composition, overall visual impact) contribute to its overall meaning? Write an essay in which you analyze these design elements and discuss how each contributes to the message of the ad.

7. David Troutt ("Defining Who We Are in Society," p. 289) or John Rickford ("Suite for Ebony and Phonics," p. 278) would probably consider this ad overly simplistic in its representation of Ebonics and the controversies surrounding it. Write an essay about the specific ways in which Troutt or Rickford would criticize this ad. Use evidence from their pieces to support your assertions.

chapter 6

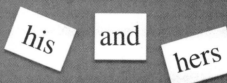

his and hers

language and gender

"**W**omen are from earth, men are from earth. Deal with it." So proclaimed a bumper sticker we saw recently. How, exactly, do we deal with it? Is there more to it than simply replacing words like "fireman" with "firefighter" or changing the generic use of "he" to "he or she"? Given how much attention has been drawn to the differences between women's and men's communication styles, would it be possible for each of us to understand and accommodate the other's style? If we did, would it be enough? To what extent do we use language to construct our genders? Does language use perpetuate sexism? Can changes in language use reduce or eliminate sexism? In this chapter, we go beyond Venus and Mars to explore other ways of talking about gender, gender in language, and how we use language and talk to become the gendered individuals that we are.

Is gender something we are or something we do? Would it develop naturally, or is it something we learn? Newborn girls and boys don't behave differently; they're all simply babies. Yet, from birth, they are spoken to differently and are subjected to different sets of expectations about their verbal behaviors. How does gender identity differentiation occur, and what is the role of language in the process? As the readings in the chapter show, language plays a central role in the ways that we come to know ourselves and others as boys and girls, women and men.

Do the basic grammatical features in languages contribute to the separate (and not equal) social positions for men and women speakers? What innovations in language use have emerged to promote equal treatment of women and men? The grammatical structure of each language lends itself to different solutions. English speakers, say "Someone left their book on the table," when the unidentified person's gender doesn't matter. In Spanish, which has gendered nouns and adjectives, "two male friends" is dos amigos, and "two female friends" dos amigas, with a as the last vowel; what happens when there is one male and one female friend? The grammatically correct form is dos amigos, essentially erasing the woman. The gender-equalizing form, however, is dos amig@s, efficiently combining the o and the a.

We begin the chapter with two examinations of language use in gender socialization. Lynda Willer presents a detailed analysis of birth congratulation cards, followed by Penelope Eckert and Sally McConnell-Ginet's essay discussing gender reference in languages. Some, like Finnish, have a third-person pronoun equivalent to English he or she that does not distinguish gender. French, on the other hand, has gendered adjectives, so speakers must identify their own gender in simple statements like "I am happy"— je suis heureux for males, je suis heureuse for females. How might grammatical features contribute to the ways that speakers think about the importance of gender in everyday life?

How easily could you alter your speech to sound convincingly like the other gender? In a National Public Radio report, Linda Wertheimer and Cathy Duchamp describe voice feminization training for male-to-female transsexuals. Next comes a Bizarro cartoon presenting a scene of gender reversal in a stereotypically male linguistic activity—making catcalls at passersby. Do cars have gender? The next selections—a New Yorker cartoon and a postcard of a graffitied billboard—play on Anglo-phones' widespread cultural custom of referring to cars as "she."

Are all women "girls"? Whom does the term describe? Darryl Mc-Grath addresses the apparent resurgence of this volatile word. We return to the question of pronouns in an essay by John McWhorter, in which he argues in favor of the use of singular "they." In the final selection, we take a look at three usage manuals to see what rules and advice they offer about pronouns—and to see the language changing before our very eyes.

Together, the readings in this chapter demonstrate that issues of language and gender are about more than communication styles and non-sexist words. Whether it's sugar and spice or snails and puppy dog tails, language is very much what we are all made of.

It is perhaps fitting to begin a chapter on gender and language with an analysis of baby cards. If you've ever shopped for a baby card, you may have noticed that the baby's gender is an important feature; almost all such cards are gender-specific. This report was originally published in the academic journal Women and Language *in April 2001. The author, Lynda R. Willer, researches gender and organizational communication at Purdue University Calumet. Willer presents here a detailed, scholarly analysis of the content of 300 cards.*

LYNDA R. WILLER

Welcome to Your World, Baby

INTRODUCTION

"Congratulations on your new bundle of joy." "Welcome to the bouncing baby boy." "Welcome to the sweet angelic baby girl." A friend has just had a baby and you want to send a greeting card acknowledging the event. As you examine card after card at the local greeting card store, you realize you need to negotiate the greeting card industry's social construction of gender. Amid pinks and blues, sugar & spice and snakes & snails, and angelic behavior and roughhousing, a definite message of what having a girl baby means and what having a boy baby means is being delivered (whether you want to support that message or not). A question can be raised concerning the impact of these greeting card messages on the fostering and perpetuating of sex role identities.

THE GREETING CARD INDUSTRY AND GREETING CARDS AS MESSAGE COMMUNICATORS

The greeting card industry is an industry worth more than seven billion dollars a year. Additionally, over 90 percent of the consumers of greeting cards are women. As a result, greeting cards have great communication potential, particularly for women and about issues related to gender. As a form of mass communication, greeting cards are used [primarily by women] to "maintain, reinforce and reestablish social, particularly familial, relationships."

* * *

SEX ROLE IDENTITY

One of the first questions asked by family and friends upon the arrival of a baby is answered by the message "it's a boy" or "it's a girl." With that simple announcement begins a process of socialization into a "gendered" world. Children are influenced through the socialization processes of family and friends. Mothers and fathers frequently have different expectations for daughters and sons. They communicate differently in the family and they have different ways in which they are responsible for sex role acquisition. Thus, as Bate and Bowker (1997) explain, "Once a baby's sex has been announced, other messages will be sent and received that concern that first announcement of biological sex into gender-related expectations" (p. 209).

We make these announcements through birth announcements and we acknowledge this announcement with a congratulatory greeting card. And with the message of "it's a boy/girl," and subsequent congratulatory messages, messages of perceptions of gender and "appropriate" sex role behaviors are sent.

The assignment of sex roles can begin with birth as adults send and re- 5 ceive messages about the attributes they perceive the infant possesses. Adults both perceive they should, and in many cases actually do, communicate differently with children depending on the gender of the child. That communication difference may start earlier than believed as we foster the difference through communication expressed in the birth congratulation greeting card. "Gender symbols and expectations emerge early in the family system. . . . The baby as topic of conversation receives a large amount of language and nonverbal behavior based on others' connotations for the labels 'boy' and 'girl' " (Bate & Bowker, 1997, p. 218).

Williams and Best (1982) propose that from birth it is clear that male and female babies are treated differently. This difference can be illustrated through the use of language to describe babies. Words such as loving, cute, sweet are often used to describe female babies while male infants are more likely to be described with words such as strong, solid, independent. Thus, the language used in birth congratulation cards can be examined to illustrate the reflection of these perceived gender differences. As a result, the following research question is raised:

Research Question 1: What are the differences in language usage in boy-specified birth congratulation greeting cards, girl-specified birth congratulation greeting cards, and no gender-specified birth congratulation greeting cards?

Differences between male and female infants are also communicated nonverbally.

The ritual of assigning gender-specific colors of pink and blue helps perpetuate the gender identity issue of difference. Further, when the objects/symbols are attached to either male babies or female babies, support for sex role differences is communicated—from the pink cap given to girl babies in a hospital to the way the baby's room is decorated, to the way the baby is clothed, to the toys selected for play. Thus, birth congratulation cards can be examined for the nonverbal messages that are sent that may perpetuate perceived gender differences. As a result, a second research question can be asked:

Research Question 2: What are the differences in nonverbal communication usage in boy-specified birth congratulation greeting cards, girl-specified birth congratulation greeting cards, and non gender-specified birth congratulation greeting cards?   10

METHOD

THE CARDS

Three hundred "Welcome Baby" greeting cards were examined. A convenience sample[1] was collected by visiting ten card stores and choosing 10 boy-identified cards, 10 girl-identified cards and 10 non-gender-specific cards at each store. The manufacturers of each card were identified and a manipulation check was performed to make sure a variety of manufacturers were represented. The following greeting card manufacturers were identified: Carlton (20,22,17), Simply Said: Bjorkman Brothers (1,0,0), Gibson (20,17,17), Forget Me Not (6,8,17), Mahogany (3,0,10), Hallmark (26,20,8), Ambassador (15,21,6), Card Factory Outlet (8,6,22), Life as We Know It (0,1,1), Creative Papers (0,5,0) and Kinka (0,0,3). The numbers in parentheses represent the number of boy-identified cards, girl-identified cards and non-gender specific cards, respectively. Carlton and Hallmark account for 70 percent of the greeting card market (Sheikh, 1999). This selection represents a cross-section of greeting card manufacturers who stock retail greeting card stores as well as other retailers who sell greeting cards; from Hallmark, the manufacturer with the largest share of the greeting card market to the small, specialty manu-

---

1. **convenience sample** one that is easily available, in contrast to a random sample, where every card within a category has an equal chance of being chosen.

facturers. All cards were available in stores located in a midwestern metropolitan area.

THE CATEGORIES

The cards were categorized first based on gender specification. Did the card welcome a baby boy, a baby girl or was the card non-gender-specific? One hundred cards in each of these categories were identified. Previous research has failed to use the non-gender-specified card as an informal control group. Including the non-gender-specified cards in this analysis will presumably highlight the anticipated differences between cards intended for girl babies and cards intended for boy babies.

Each card was examined for its outside greeting, its inside greeting, its outside colors and symbols, and its inside colors and symbols. Within these categories, more specific categories were created utilizing a coding scheme identified by Bridges (1993). For the outside and inside greetings, several items were examined. The number of words used in the greeting was calculated. The quality of the message was assessed (was the message serious, humorous or offer nothing but congratulations). The style of the message was identified (was the verse in rhyme or prose). And the specific word choice was analyzed for whether it was a physical or nonphysical descriptor, for what emotion or experience the word/phrase represented and for whether a gender-specific interest was identified.

In examining the nonverbal message sent via these greeting cards, the colors represented both on the front and inside of the card were identified. Additionally, what the pictures represented were separated into categories of toys, animals and objects (such as baby items, hearts, flowers, moon, stars and clothing) and what type of scene (active or passive) was depicted. Bridges' (1993) work in this area did not examine this quantity of cards and did not use non-gender-specific cards as a comparison baseline. Further, Bridges' focus was on the psychological versus the communicative function of these messages.

RESULTS

In general, the results might be identified as what one might, unfortunately, 15 expect. In many instances there are differences between girl-identified cards and boy-identified cards. This paper establishes a 10 percent frequency difference as a difference that had some meaning. At the same time, other results not meeting those criteria but providing interesting or unexpected information are also provided. The discussion will primarily focus on the differences between boy/girl-identified cards, utilizing the non-gender-specified cards as an informal control group to highlight some of the verbal and nonverbal issues being raised.

RESEARCH QUESTION #1

Research question #1 dealt with the verbal characteristics of greeting cards and how gender differences might be illustrated. The general categories of outside (front) of card text, and inside card text were identified. The cards were analyzed by looking at the number of words, the style of the message, the message quality, physical/nonphysical word descriptions of the baby, and words used to express emotion and experiences about the birth of a child.

Number of Words, Message Style and Message Quality. All three main types of birth congratulation cards contained similar numbers of words. Girl cards averaged 38.3 words, boy cards averaged 37.1 words and non-gender-specified cards averaged 31 words. The messages of non-gender-specified cards were more likely (68%) than both girl (56%) and boy (38%) cards to be in a prose style. Additionally, the messages of girl cards were more likely than boy cards to be in prose style. Boy cards were more likely to be in rhyme instead of prose and more likely to be in rhyme than both girl and non-gender-specified cards. Boy was rhymed frequently with "joy" or son with "fun" while the only rhyme matched with the word "girl" was "whirl" and "twirl." At least 80 percent of each of the types of cards was likely to have a message that was serious rather than funny or one that just provided congratulations.

Word Descriptors. The analysis also looked at specific word usage concerning descriptions of the baby. One category of words concerned physical characteristics of the baby. The words "little," "tiny" or "small" appeared more frequently in girl cards (46%) or non-gender-specified cards (45%) than boy cards (34%). Furthermore, "tiny" and "small" were only used to describe girl babies or a non-gender-specified baby. Girl babies were also more likely to be described as "cute" or "beautiful" than boys or the non-gender-specified baby. However, this difference did not meet the 10% difference criterion. Although there was a wide variety of words used to describe non-physical characteristics of a baby, three were used most frequently: "sweet," "precious" and "dear." Girl babies were much more likely to be described as "sweet" (27%) or "precious/dear" (29%) than boy babies. The non-gender-specified babies approached a similarity with girl babies with the words "precious" or "dear" and similarity with boy babies with the word "sweet." Although not providing a statistical difference, it is interesting to look at words that were used to describe girls but not boys and to describe boys but not girls. Examples of words used to describe girl babies but not boy babies were: "delicate," "irresistible," "trusting," "gentle," "warm," "innocent," "soft," and "giggly." Examples of words used to describe boy babies but not girl babies were: "bold," "brave," "tough," "important," "busy," "alarming," "noisy," "bright," "healthy" and "fine." Further, boy babies were much more likely to have active words describing them such as "doer," "rascal," "scamp," "crawler," "grower," "teaser," "walker," "player" and "talker."

Emotions/Experiences. The content of the messages of the cards was also examined for what emotions or experiences were presented. Love (40%) and joy (21%) were the most expressed emotions in the girl baby cards. Love (29%), joy (47%) and happiness (29%) were the most expressed emotions in the boy baby cards. And yet, love was more frequently expressed concerning girl babies and joy and happiness were more frequently expressed regarding boy babies. Thus, there was a difference between the girl baby and boy baby cards on these expressions of emotions. Other emotions expressed concerning girls were fun/laughter and happiness, while pride and fun/laughter were also expressed about boys. Love (34%), happiness (30%), and joy (22%) were also the predominant emotions expressed in the non-gender-specified cards. Also interesting was the difference between non-gender-specified cards and boy and girl cards regarding the expression of being blessed (13% to 3% and 4% for girl cards and boy cards, respectively). This implies that the more religious birth congratulation cards may more frequently not be gender specific.

An additional analysis looked at terms that seemed to present a gender- 20 specific interest. Although not significant, there were birth congratulation cards for girls that identified a girl as a shopper, as a phone talker, as clothing conscious, as an enchanting spell binder, as a secret keeper, as a heart and scene stealer, as needing security, as "daddy's prize." Additionally, there were birth congratulation cards for boys that identified a boy as a champion, as a prince, as a blue dresser, as an explorer, as first class male, as a skipper/mate, as someone who would change the world, as a main event.

RESEARCH QUESTION #2

Research question #2 dealt with the nonverbal aspects of birth congratulation greeting cards. In order to accomplish this analysis the cards were each examined for the images they presented through pictures and symbols and for the color usage on the cards.

Toys. The toys pictured on the cards were identified. The single most-represented toy for both girls and boys and in non-gender-specified cards was blocks. However, the toy appeared more frequently in cards about boys (29%) than cards about girls (14%). All three types of cards pictured balls on the cards without meaningful difference. However, if you combine toy balls with sporting balls and other sporting equipment such as mitts, bats and helmets, there was a meaningful difference between what is shown on boy cards (42%) and girl cards (14%) and non-gender-specified cards (6%). In fact, cards for girl babies and cards that had no gender specification had no other types of balls or other sporting equipment.

The item pictured second most on boy cards was a boat (24%). Both girl and non-gender-specified cards had only one card each with a picture of a boat. And if you add to boats other toys that represent forms of transportation such as trains, planes, cars, trucks and wagons, the frequency of pictures increased immensely for boy cards to sixty-eight, while the girl cards and the non-gender-specified cards only increased from 1 percent each to 2 and 3 percent, respectively.

One of the surprising results came from the unmet expectations about pictures of dolls. While certainly more girl cards than boy cards (or non-gender-specified cards) had a picture of a doll, only 11 percent of the cards included a picture of a doll (boy cards and nongender specified cards contained only one picture of a doll each).

Animals. Bears (both Teddy bears and real bears) were the most frequently represented animal on all three types of cards. In fact, there were no frequency differences among the cards in the three most pictured animals: bears, rabbits and ducks.

Objects. There were several differences specifically between the boy cards and the girl cards identified concerning visual representation of specific objects. For example, three times as many girl cards (30%) as boy cards (9%) and two times as many girl cards as non-gender-specified cards (15%) had hearts pictured on the cards. A similar comparison between girl cards and boy cards is true as well for pictures of flowers (27% to 1%) and rattles (27% to 15%). Boy cards were more likely to have pictures of sky items (clouds, moons, stars, suns) than girl cards (25% to 15%). If baby-related items such as bottles, bibs, pins, mobiles, pacifiers, blankets/quilts, and rattles are combined, both girl cards (64%) and non-gender-specified cards (69%) are more likely to have such items pictured than boy cards (49%).

In the clothing department, dresses were more likely to be pictured on girl cards (11%) than on boy cards (0) as were bows (21% on girl cards and no boy cards had a bow). Similarly, nine cards for girls had lace on them while only one boy card and one non-gender-specified card had lace on them. However, when it came to a specific outfit such as a cowboy outfit, a sailor suit, a uniform, overalls, a ballet costume, boy cards (18%) were more likely to have such an outfit pictured than girl cards (7%).

Scenes. The scene pictured on the card was also interpreted as either being "active" (the baby was doing something on his/her own such as walking or crawling) or "passive" (the baby was seen as sleeping, sitting in his/her crib, being held, etc.). Given gender stereotype and sex role identity research, as one might expect, on boy cards babies were pictured doing something active in 51 percent of the cards compared to 18 percent and 16 percent on girl cards and non-gender-specified cards, respectively). Conversely, on girl cards and non-gender-specified cards, babies were pictured doing something passive in 49 percent and 43 percent of the cards, respectively, as compared to 23 percent of the cards where a baby was pictured doing something passive on a boy card.

Colors. Finally, the colors used on the cards were identified. Colors were identified on the front (outside) of the cards, on the inside of the card and for color of the writing on the inside of the card (where frequently the majority of the message is). The results of this analysis are what might typically be expected. Boy cards utilized dark blue (77%) and yellow (74%) most frequently. Girl cards utilized pink (92%) and yellow (40%) most frequently. non-gender-specified cards used yellow (68%), red (51%), and light blue (50%) most frequently. On the inside of the cards, dark blue is used more frequently on boy cards (34 to 0 when compared with girl cards) with pink being used on girl cards (34 to 2 when compared to boy cards). Black was the most frequently used color for the writing on all types of cards although 32% of boy cards also used dark blue for the writing.

DISCUSSION

This paper presents the results of a content analysis of birth congratulations 30 greeting cards. It is argued that greeting cards represent a means of sending intentional or unintentional messages about gender roles. This study sought to examine messages of gender expectations in birth congratulation cards. Three hundred cards were analyzed of which 100 each were cards designated for boy babies, cards designated for girl babies and cards not designated for either gender. The results suggest that "gendered" messages are being sent and are consistent with previous research in sex role identity and socialization. Further, the results are consistent with past research on the communicative value of greeting card messages. In spite of (or perhaps because of) living in the '90's, the same stereotypical messages about gender are being sent and received as have been perceived in the past. The message of expected differences between boys and girls is communicated. Additionally, the message of appropriate behaviors for each of the sexes is communicated. Thus, the greeting card industry reflects (or perhaps infects) society's perceptions of what girl babies are and what boy babies are and what they do depending on their gender. And while the babies are not doing the actual receiving of the message, they are going to be the recipients of these perpetuated gender expectations via family, friends and the mass media.

Language usage organizes our perceptions of gender. Further, we can examine language usage to evaluate these gendered messages. And so in this study, we see differences in the message style of birth congratulation cards, differences in words used to describe physical characteristics of boy babies and girl babies, as well as differences in words used to describe non-physical differences. Further, there are some differences in the emotions expressed about girl babies and boy babies.

Previous research has indicated ways in which we can communicate gender differences nonverbally through, for example, color usage and the attachment of specific symbols or objects only to girls or only to boys. Thus, nonverbal differences are also identified in the current study. There are differences in the type of toys pictured as well as some of the objects identified such as hearts, flowers and baby-related items. Additionally, what babies are observed doing, in cards that portray such behavior, appears to be different depending upon whether it is a girl card or a boy card since girls are observed as being more passive and boys as being more active. In fact, boys are frequently seen doing things (playing sports) or playing with toys (elaborate train sets) that are inappropriate for a newborn child. Babies on girl

cards and non-gender-specified cards seem to be doing age-appropriate behaviors such as sleeping in a crib and being held by an adult. Finally, the
colors used on the cards appear to further delineate the pink-blue dichotomy
based on gender.

As with many research projects, limitations can be identified in this
study as well. The sample selection was a convenience sample. And while a
large number of cards were selected and several card companies were used
to create a cross-section of examples and to identify a minimum of 100 cards
per category, this sample did not mirror the market shares of the card companies utilized. Thus, caution should be used when attempting to generalize
beyond the sample studied.

A second limitation may be the geographical usage of the Midwest. It
may be possible that card selection and availability is different in other
parts of the country and in different types of stores selling greeting cards.

Further research is needed in this area. Several issues remain to be ex- 35
amined. Obviously, the current study could be replicated with a representative random sample. Another intriguing area of research would be to flesh
out the results of the non-gender-specified cards. In many of the categories
studied the results relating to the non-gender-specified cards were similar to
the results of the girl cards. It is interesting to contemplate that those buyers
wanting not to send a gendered message are actually forced into sending either a religious message or one that approximates the message sent to welcome little girls.

This study implies that greeting cards are another source of gender messages. They continue to communicate stereotypical messages about gender
expectations. The limited choices for card buyers suggest societal expectations at play in the market research. The selection of a gender-free card, or a
card that identifies biological gender without stereotypical trappings about
what one gender or the other is or should be, becomes a challenge for anyone sensitive to the impact of continuing to communicate these "gendered"
messages. And when lack of choice prevails, those of us concerned with such
issues need to voice these concerns to greeting card companies. And when
all else fails, with greeting card software available, we can make our own
cards and welcome these babies into the world without the stereotypical
trappings of gender expectations.

REFERENCES

Bate, B., & Bowker, J. (1997). *Communication and the sexes.* Prospect Heights, IL:
Waveland Press.

Bridges, J. S. (1993). Pink or blue: Gender stereotypic perceptions of infants as conveyed by birth congratulations cards. *Psychology of Women Quarterly, 17*, 193–205.

Sheikh, F. (1999, Sept. 13). Ad spend soars for greeting cards. *Marketing, 104,* p. 2.

Williams, J. E., & Best, D. L. (1982). *Measuring sex stereotypes: A thirty nation study*. Beverly Hills, CA: Sage.

about the text

1. Who is Willer's intended audience? What does she assume about its prior knowledge and beliefs?
2. In nearly all of the categories measured, the gender-unspecified cards more closely resembled the girl cards than the boy cards. How might you account for that difference?

on language use

3. Imagine receiving a birth announcement from a friend or relative that didn't mention the baby's gender. How would you react? How long might you wait before you asked about the baby's gender? Would you be comfortable not knowing? Why or why not?
4. To be consistent, Willer analyzed equal numbers of boy, girl, and gender-unspecified baby cards. But are they equally available? With a classmate visit three stores that have a large selection of greeting cards (try not to use different locations of the same chain store). Count the number of baby cards in each category — boy, girl, and unspecified. Are the proportions fairly equal or are there many more or fewer of one category? Did you find cards that differ from Willer's description — girl cards with pictures of trucks or boy cards with the words "sweet" or "precious?" Compare and discuss your findings with those of your classmates.

5. Willer reports that boy cards are more likely to rhyme than girl cards, which in turn are more likely to rhyme than gender-unspecified cards. What does she suggest accounts for the difference? Why might the unspecified cards be least likely to rhyme? Work with two or three classmates and compose rhymes for unspecified baby cards.
6. If you speak another language and have access to greeting cards in that language, make an informal survey of the baby cards you find. In what ways are they similar to the cards Willer describes? In what ways different? Report your results to the class.

for writing

7. How might Willer's report be changed for publication as a feature article in a Sunday newspaper? What might need to be added or deleted for a more general audience? Imagine that you are a journalist; write an audience-grabbing introductory paragraph for an article reporting on Willer's results.
8. How would you like to see gender treated in baby cards? Even if you are generally happy with such cards, you may have some ideas about how they might be more interesting. Write a letter to a card company in which you suggest ideas for changes in baby cards; back up your suggestions with reasons and examples.

**PENELOPE ECKERT
AND SALLY MCCONNELL-GINET**

Learning to Be Gendered

DICHOTOMOUS BEGINNINGS:
IT'S A BOY! IT'S A GIRL!

In the famous words of Simone de Beauvoir,[1] "Women are not born, they are made." The same is true of men. The making of a man or a woman is a never-ending process that begins before birth—from the moment someone begins to wonder if the pending child will be a boy or a girl. And the ritual announcement at birth that it is in fact one or the other instantly transforms an "it" into a "he" or a "she" (Butler 1993), standardly assigning it to a lifetime as a male or as a female.[2] This attribution is further made public and lasting through the linguistic event of naming. To name a baby *Mary* is to do something that makes it easy for a wide range of English speakers to maintain the initial "girl" attribution. In English-speaking societies, not all names are sex-exclusive (e.g., *Chris, Kim, Pat*), and sometimes names change their gender classification. For example, *Evelyn* was available as a male name in Britain long after it had become an exclusively female name in America, and *Whitney*, once exclusively a surname or a male first name in America, is now bestowed on baby girls. In some times and places, the state or religious institutions disallow sex-ambiguous given names. Finland, for example, has lists of legitimate female and legitimate

This selection from a 2003 book, Language and Gender, by Penelope Eckert and Sally McConnell-Ginet, *takes a detailed look at gender socialization in the first days and years of a baby's life. Eckert is a linguistics professor and director of the women's studies program at Stanford University; she is the author of* Linguistic Variation as Social Practice *(2000) and* Jocks and Burnouts: Social Categories and Identity in High School *(1989).* McConnell-Ginet *is a professor of linguistics at Cornell University; in addition to publications in formal semantics, she has written several works on language and gender together with Eckert. This selection examines everyday behavior so ordinary that we barely notice it; as you read, think about how many times in the last month you have done or said something that Eckert and McConnell-Ginet describe.*

---

1. **Simone de Beauvoir (1908–1986)** French philosopher, novelist, and social analyst. De Beauvoir's 1953 book, *The Second Sex*, explores women's need for independence.

2. Nowadays, with the possibility of having this information before birth, wanting to know in advance or not wanting to know can become ideologically charged. Either way, the sex of the child is frequently as great a preoccupation as its health. [Eckert & McConnell-Ginet's note]

male names that must be consulted before the baby's name becomes official. Thus the dichotomy of male and female is the ground upon which we build selves from the moment of birth. These early linguistic acts set up a baby for life, launching a gradual process of learning to be a boy or a girl, a man or a woman, and to see all others as boys or girls, men or women as well. There are currently no other legitimate ways to think about ourselves and others—and we will be expected to pattern all kinds of things about ourselves as a function of that initial dichotomy. In the beginning, adults will do the child's gender work, treating it as a boy or as a girl, and interpreting its every move as that of a boy or of a girl. Then over the years, the child will learn to take over its part of the process, doing its own gender work and learning to support the gender work of others. The first thing people want to know about a baby is its sex, and convention provides a myriad of props to reduce the necessity of asking—and it becomes more and more important, as the child develops, not to have to ask. At birth, many hospital nurseries provide pink caps for girls and blue caps for boys, or in other ways provide some visual sign of the sex that has been attributed to the baby. While this may seem quite natural to members of the society, in fact this color coding points out no difference that has any bearing on the medical treatment of the infants. Go into a store in the United States to buy a present for a newborn baby, and you will immediately be asked "boy or girl?" If the reply is "I don't know" or, worse, "I don't care," sales personnel are often perplexed. Overalls for a girl may be OK (though they are "best" if pink or flowered or in some other way marked as "feminine"), but gender liberalism goes only so far. You are unlikely to buy overalls with vehicles printed on them for a girl, and even more reluctant to buy a frilly dress with puffed sleeves or pink flowered overalls for a boy. And if you're buying clothing for a baby whose sex you do not know, sales people are likely to counsel you to stick with something that's plain yellow or green or white. Colors are so integral to our way of thinking about gender that gender attributions have bled into our view of the colors, so that people tend to believe that pink is a more "delicate" color than blue. This is a prime example of the naturalization of what is in fact an arbitrary sign. In America in the late nineteenth and early twentieth centuries, Anne Fausto-Sterling (2000) reports, blue was favored for girls and bright pink for boys.

If gender flowed naturally from sex, one might expect the world to sit back and simply allow the baby to become male or female. But in fact, sex determination sets the stage for a lifelong process of gendering, as the child becomes, and learns how to be, male or female. Names and clothing are just a small part of the symbolic resources used to support a consistent ongoing gender attribution even when children are clothed. That we can speak of a child growing up *as a girl* or *as a boy* suggests that initial sex attribution is far more than just a simple observation of a physical characteristic. *Being a girl* or *being a boy* is not a stable state but an ongoing accomplishment, something that is actively *done* both by the individual so categorized and by those who interact with it in the various communities to which it belongs. The newborn initially depends on others to *do* its gender, and they come through in many different ways, not just as individuals but as part of socially structured communities that link individuals to social institutions and cultural ideologies. It is perhaps at this early life stage that it is clearest that gender is a collaborative affair—that one must learn to perform as a male or a female, and that these performances require support from one's surroundings.

Indeed, we do not know how to interact with another human being (or often members of other species), or how to judge them and talk about them, unless we can attribute a gender to them. Gender is so deeply engrained in our social practice, in our understanding of ourselves and of others, that we almost cannot put one foot in front of the other without taking gender into consideration. Although most of us rarely notice this overtly in everyday life, most of our interactions are colored by our performance of our own gender, and by our attribution of gender to others.

From infancy, male and female children are interpreted differently, and interacted with differently. Experimental evidence suggests that adults' perceptions of babies are affected by their beliefs about the babies' sex. Condry and Condry (1976) found that adults watching a film of a crying infant were more likely to hear the cry as angry if they believed the infant was a boy, and as plaintive or fearful if they believed the infant was a girl. In a similar experiment, adults judged a 24-hour-old baby as bigger if they believed it to be a boy, and finer-featured if they believed it to be a girl (Rubin, Provenzano and Luria 1974). Such judgments then enter into the way people interact with infants and small children. People handle infants more gently when they believe them to be female, more playfully when they believe them to be male.

And they talk to them differently. Parents use more diminutives (*kitty,* 5 *doggie*) when speaking to girls than to boys (Gleason et al. 1994), they use more inner state words (*happy, sad*) when speaking to girls (Ely et al. 1995). They use more direct prohibitives (*don't do that!*) and more emphatic prohibitives (*no! no! no!*) to boys than to girls (Bellinger and Gleason 1982). Perhaps, one might suggest, the boys need more prohibitions because they tend to misbehave more than the girls. But Bellinger and Gleason found this pattern to be independent of the actual nature of the children's activity, suggesting that the adults and their beliefs about sex difference are far more important here than the children's behavior.

With differential treatment, boys and girls eventually learn to *be* different. Apparently, male and female infants cry the same amount (Maccoby and Jacklin 1974), but as they mature, boys cry less and less. There is some evidence that this difference emerges primarily from differential adult response to the crying. Qualitative differences in behavior come about in the same way. A study of thirteen-month-old children in day care (Fagot *et al.* 1985) showed that teachers responded to girls when they talked, babbled, or gestured, while they responded to boys when they whined, screamed, or demanded physical attention. Nine to eleven months later, the same girls talked more than the boys, and the boys whined, screamed, and demanded attention more than the girls. Children's eventual behavior, which seems to look at least statistically different across the sexes, is the product of adults' differential responses to ways of acting that are in many (possibly most) cases very similar indeed. The kids do indeed learn to "do" gender for themselves, to produce sex-differentiated behavior—although even with considerable differential treatment they do not end up with dichotomizing behavioral patterns.

Voice, which we have already mentioned, provides a dramatic example of children's coming to perform gender. At the ages of four to five years, in spite of their identical vocal apparatus, girls and boys begin to differentiate the fundamental frequency of their speaking voice. Boys tend to round and extend their lips, lengthening the vocal tract, whereas girls are tending to spread their lips (with smiles, for example), shortening the vocal tract. Girls are raising their pitches, boys lowering theirs. It may well be that adults are more likely to speak to girls in a high-pitched voice. It may be that they reward boys and girls for differential voice productions. It may also be that children simply observe this difference in older people, or that their differential participation in games (for example play-acting) calls for different voice productions. Elaine Andersen (1990, pp. 24–25), for example, shows that children use high pitch when using baby talk or "teacher register" in role play. Some children speak as the other sex is expected to and thus, as with other aspects of doing gender, there is not a perfect dichotomization in voice pitch (even among adults, some voices are not consistently classified). Nonetheless, there is a striking production of mostly different pitched voices from essentially similar vocal equipment.

There is considerable debate among scholars about the extent to which adults actually do treat boys and girls differently, and many note that the similarities far outweigh the differences. Research on early gender development—in fact the research in general on gender differences—is almost exclusively done by psychologists. As a result, the research it reports on largely involves observations of behavior in limited settings—whether in a laboratory or in the home or the preschool. Since these studies focus on limited settings and types of interaction and do not follow children through a normal day, they quite possibly miss the cumulative effects of small differences across many different situations. Small differences here and there are probably enough for children to learn what it means in their community to be male or female.

The significance of the small difference can be appreciated from another perspective. The psychological literature tends to treat children as objects rather than subjects. Those studying children have tended to treat others—parents, other adults, peers—as the primary socializing agents. Only relatively recently have investigators begun to explore children's own active strategies for figuring out the social world. Eleanor Maccoby (2002) emphasizes that children have a very clear knowledge of their gender (that is, of whether they are classified as male or female) by the time they are three years old. Given this knowledge, it is not at all clear how much differential treatment children need to learn how to do their designated gender. What they mainly need is the message that male and female are supposed to be different, and that message is everywhere around them.

It has become increasingly clear that children play a very active role 10 in their own development. From the moment they see themselves as social beings, they begin to focus on the enterprise of "growing up." And to some extent, they probably experience many of the gendered developmental dynamics we discuss here not so much as gender-appropriate, but as *grown-up*. The greatest taboo is being "a baby," but the developmental imperative is gendered. Being grown-up, leaving babyhood, means very different things for boys than it does for girls. And the fact that growing up involves gender differentiation is encoded in the words of assessment with which progress is monitored—kids do not behave as good or bad people, but as *good boys* or *good girls*, and they develop into *big boys* and *big girls*.[3] In other words, they do not have the option of growing into just people, but into boys or girls. This does not mean that they see what they're doing in strictly gendered terms. It is probable that when boys and girls alter the fundamental frequency of

---

3. Thorne (1993) and others have observed teachers urging children to act like "big boys and girls." Very rarely is a child told "don't act like a baby—you're a big kid now." [Eckert & McConnell-Ginet's note]

their voices they are not trying to sound like *girls* or like *boys*, but that they are aspiring for some quality that is itself gendered—cuteness, authority. And the child's aspiration is not simply a matter of reasoning, but a matter of desire—a projection of the self into desired forms of participation in the social world. Desire is a tremendous force in projecting oneself into the future —in the continual remaking of the self that constitutes growing up.

Until about the age of two, boys and girls exhibit the same play behaviors. After that age, play in boys' and girls' groups begins to diverge as they come to select different toys and engage in different activities, and children begin to monitor play, imposing sanctions on gender-inappropriate play. Much is made of the fact that boys become more agonistic than girls, and many attribute this to hormonal and even evolutionary differences (see Maccoby 2000 for a brief review of these various perspectives). But whatever the workings of biology may be, it is clear that this divergence is supported and exaggerated by the social system. As children get older, their play habits are monitored and differentiated, first by adults, and eventually by peers. Parents of small children have been shown to reward their children's choice of gender-appropriate toys (trucks for boys, dolls for girls) (Langlois and Downs 1980). And while parents' support of their children's gendered behavior is not always and certainly not simply a conscious effort at gender socialization, their behavior is probably more powerful than they think. Even parents who strive for gender equality, and who believe that they do not constrain their children's behavior along gender lines, have been observed in experimental situations to do just that.

*   *   *

GENDERIZING DISCOURSE: CATEGORY IMPERIALISM

Many discursive practices presuppose the pervasive relevance of gender categorizations. We say that discourse is genderized when messages about gender categorizations are superimposed on the basic content of the discourse. Genderizing discursive practices can involve particular linguistic resources—gendered pronouns, grammatical gender agreement, genderizing affixes and other gender-marked lexical items.

Genderizing discourse does not always, however, depend on linguistic conventions but may involve such matters as journalistic norms to mention the nondefault sex in some field. Stories about a woman murderer or child molester or politician will, for example, use the word *woman* far more than parallel stories use the word *man*. There are many cases where users can choose gendered or nongendered terms. The teacher can say "good morning, kids" or "good morning, students" or the discourse can be genderized: "good morning, girls and boys." Some years ago, philosopher Elizabeth Beardsley (1981) argued that referential genderization—cases where sex distinctions seem to be forced, whether or not they are relevant—problematically encourages gender inequities by making gender categorizations appear to be relevant where morally they ought not to be.

PRONOUNS

Many communities of practice take establishing and conveying a (consistent) gender attribution for everyone to be of fundamental importance. In English-using communities, for example, gendered pronouns make it difficult indeed to talk about anyone other than oneself without presupposing a gender attribution. The late Sarah Caudwell (a pen name) wrote several novels featuring a protagonist whose gender she never discloses. How did she pull this off? Well, the character's first name is Hilary, used for both sexes, and Hilary relates the stories in the first person, using *I*, which is completely gender-neutral, for self-reference. Others refer to Hilary using that name or some generic description like "my friend," or address Hilary using the second-person *you*, which is also gender-neutral.[4]

Some languages do mark gender in the first- or second-person pronouns. 15 Japanese, for example, has a fairly large array of first-person pronouns, a number of which are gender-marked, as are a number of the second-person pronouns (for speaker and addressee). Interestingly, a considerable number of female Japanese high-school students have now adopted the practice of referring to themselves as *boku*, which is the first-person form boys are expected to use in self-reference and which is also used in reference to very young boys being addressed. Naoko Ogawa and Janet Shibamoto Smith (1997) examined address as well as first- and third-person references used in a documentary film by two gay men in a committed relationship, finding that the two men labeled themselves and the other in much the same ways as do the canonical husband and wife of a traditional Japanese heterosexual marriage.

Pronouns are most often gendered in the third person. As we have already noted, singular English third-person pronouns typically presuppose

---

4. See Livia (2001) for much interesting discussion of literary uses of pronouns to convey gender messages, and in many cases to challenge standard gender categories. [Eckert & McConnell-Ginet's note]

gender attributions to their (actual or potential) referents. To refer to specific individual human beings pronominally, *it* is seldom used and then it is used either insultingly, to convey that the referent is not conforming properly to gender norms, or in reference to very young babies. Even in reference to babies, *it* can be seen as dehumanizing. In July 2000 the American Academy of Pediatrics cautioned doctors not to use *it* to speak of a baby born with ambiguous genitalia but instead to speak to parents of "your baby" or "your child." This injunction came in the context of a more general reconsideration of the long-standing assumption that all babies should very quickly be assigned to one sex or the other, often with surgery to make genital appearance conform more closely with the assigned sex or with prescriptions for hormonal or other treatment to produce bodies that conform more closely with the polarized sexing assumed by English third-person singular pronouns. "X" is a 1970s story about a child who was going through the early years with everyone but the parents and the doctor who delivered it ignorant of its sex. It is not insignificant that "Baby X" is so dubbed and not given a personal name; it's much easier to repeat "Baby X" or "X" or even to use an *it* than it would be if we had a proper name for the child (Gould [1972] 1983).

Gender attributions conveyed by the pronouns *he* and *she* are explicit, but they are nonetheless backgrounded, presented as taken for granted. Somewhere around the twelfth or thirteenth century, the masculine form (*hē*) and the feminine form (*hēo*) began frequently to sound alike because the unstressed final vowel of the feminine form was often just dropped. Had that change simply proceeded in the same way that many similar shifts did, we might now have a single third-person singular personal pronoun, presumably pronounced like modern *he*. In that case, we would have found it easy to talk about Baby X, whose sex we did not know or someone whose sex we did not want to reveal. Some English speakers, however, apparently did not want to lose obligatory genderizing of third-person pronominal reference. The actual history is unclear but one hypothesis is that they began using the word *scho*, ancestor of modern *she*, as a substitute for *hēo*. The suggestion is that this form was imported into English from one of the Scandinavian languages then spoken in the British Isles. The etymology of *she* is still disputed. Whether or not English speakers did import a precursor for *she* from another language, it is clear that there was something more going on than standard phonetic developments, which would have left us with a single third-person pronoun for humans. However it actually happened, it must have been the importance of genderizing to then current discursive practices among English speakers that drove this change in the pronominal system.

English does now have a nongendered pronoun for human referents, namely *they*. Prescriptive grammars restrict *they* to plural contexts, but it has long been used in singular generic contexts of the kind we discuss below in the section on generalizing. But what about nongeneric contexts? Increasingly, we find *they* used when sex is unknown or the speaker wants to avoid genderizing. "Someone called but they didn't leave their name" or "A friend of mine claimed they had met the Beatles." Second-person pronouns in English once distinguished plural from singular, but the originally plural form *you* is now virtually the only choice, even if the addressee is a single individual. It would not be surprising, therefore, if *they* were also to become more widely used in singular contexts.

With definite antecedents like *my teacher* or *the photographer, they* is still infrequent even colloquially. Definiteness seems to make genderizing of subsequent references hard to avoid. "My teacher promised they would write me a letter of recommendation" still sounds as if the teacher were going to enlist others in the letter writing, and "The photographer forgot to bring their tripod" suggests the tripod is not the photographer's individual property. Still, there are some cases like this where *they* does link to a definite singular antecedent, and such degenderizing may well be spreading. With proper names, however, *they* is still virtually unheard. Discursive practice among English speakers does not yet support interpreting "Chris said they are having their birthday party tomorrow" as Chris's having said that she or he was going to have her or his birthday party tomorrow. Of course there are some nongenderizing options: "My teacher promised to write me a letter of recommendation" or "The photographer forgot to bring the tripod" or "Chris claimed to be having a birthday party tomorrow."

Such alternatives simply eliminate pronouns, but pronoun elimination is not always so easy. Genderizing definite pronominal references is still predominant in the discursive practice of most English speakers though it may begin to wane as more and more speakers use *they* for singular deictic—i.e., "pointing"—references. "What do they think they're doing?" seems unremarkable when one is pointing to a single individual scaling a high rooftop in the distance or referring to a violinist producing unpleasant sounds in the adjacent room. But if used of a bearded individual dressed in high heels and wearing a long dress, earrings and lipstick, it might seem to suggest that the referent is somehow trying to "pass" (and not succeeding), is "really" male though apparently engaging in a feminine self-presentation. Referring to young babies, no matter what their genital appearance, as *they*, might begin to move us nearer to a stage where there are real live options to presuppos- 20 ing gender attribution in English singular third-person reference. Already, many health professionals now routinely use *they* to refer to people in the process of sex/gender change.

Many languages do not mark gender in third-person pronouns. Finnish is one such language. The singular third-person pronoun *hän* can translate either *she* or *he*, and in many contexts where English would require a pronoun Finnish (like many other so-called pro-drop languages[5] allows its omission. Interestingly, however, in a number of contexts where English speakers would use a singular third-person pronoun, Finnish speakers often choose a gendered noun—for example *tyttö*, which glosses as 'girl.' Thus though third-person pronouns do not force genderization in Finnish, third-person reference is often genderized anyway.

In spoken Mandarin Chinese, there is no gender distinction for third-person pronouns, although writing now does make such a distinction. In transcribing speech, however, there are often no grounds for using *he* rather than *she* (or vice versa) to translate a third-person pronoun into English, and some linguists do now use *he or she* or something similar. For a long time, however, *he* was routinely used, even in contexts where the English form implied maleness and the Chinese being translated did not.

Gender (dis)agreement

The first-person pronoun in French is not itself gendered, but adjectives agree with it according to the ascribed sex of its referent, the speaker. The effect, of course, is to genderize first-person discourse. A French-speaking girl, for example, learns to say "je suis heureuse" to express her happiness, whereas a boy learns to say "je suis heureux." Saying *heureuse* rather than *heureux* is one way that one constructs oneself as a girl or a woman, not a boy or a man. The "agreeing" forms impute a sex to the referent of *je*, even though that first-person pronoun does not itself carry grammatical gender. One cannot avoid self-attributions of gender using French first-person discourse as Sarah Caudwell's Hilary could in the English first person. When people talk about themselves in French (or any of a number of other languages with grammatical gender), they must frequently superimpose the message "I am female" or the message "I am male."

---

5. **pro-drop languages** languages such as Finnish or Spanish that do not require an explicit subject. In these languages, the subject can be determined by prefixes or suffixes on the verb. English allows subjectless constructions in very limited and informal contexts, as in the often-parodied advertising slogan "Got milk?"

At the same time, this gender agreement morphology can be a communicative resource for challenging permanent dichotomous gender assignments. Anna Livia (1997) shows that a first-person narrator in French can play with gender (dis)agreement possibilities to present the self sometimes as female, sometimes as male. She offers examples of transsexuals as well as others resisting conventional gender arrangements by exploiting gender-bending possibilities offered by French grammatical gender. The Hindi-speaking hijras[6] of India use not only gendered pronouns but also gender agreement markers to speak of themselves and others strategically as female or male, according to the situation. Grammatical gender, thus, can be a resource for challenging standard gender binarism.

What happens in a language with gender agreement when plurals are 25 used or a choice that (usually) indicates sex must be made when the referent's sex is unknown? In the Indo-European languages like French and Hindi, the "rule" is to use the masculine in such cases. Again, there is the possibility of playing with this "rule" to express challenges to the dominant gender order. But there is a strong tendency in languages with grammatical gender for the masculine forms to function as defaults. In his extensive discussion of grammatical gender in languages around the world. Corbett (1991) notes this tendency. At the same time, he notes some exceptions to it, languages where females are (linguistically) the default humans and males the special case. Among others, he mentions the Nilotic language Maasai, Iroquoian languages in general, and Seneca in particular, and the Arawakan language Goajiro (spoken by people in the Guajira peninsula in South America). In Goajiro, one gender is used for nouns referring to male humans and a very few other nouns (e.g., the words for "sun" and "thumb"), whereas most nouns are in the other gender. This nonmasculine gender includes nouns referring to female humans as well as nouns referring to nonhuman animals, inanimates, and most everything else; it is used whenever sex is not known (Corbett pp. 220–221). Unfortunately, we cannot provide any information on the social gender practices in which these (relatively rare) "marked masculine" gender systems have entered into communicative practices. In addition, Corbett notes that some languages offer an alternative to either masculine or feminine agreement in cases where sex is unknown: the Polish neuter, for example, is sometimes used much like the English singular *they* to avoid signaling either femaleness or maleness. In Archi, a Northeast Cau-

---

6. **hijras** a category of men in India who dress as women, often take male partners, and sometimes undergo castration or penectomy. They play an important role in Indian society as performers at celebrations.

casian language with four genders, two of which are used for human males and human females respectively, one of the other two genders (which normally is used mostly for abstracts) can be used for agreement with nouns like *child* or *thief* if the sex of (potential) referents is unknown, unimportant, or undetermined.

REFERENCES

Andersen, E. S. 1990. *Speaking with style: The sociolinguistic skills of children.* London: Routledge.

Beardsley, E. 1981. Degenderization. In Vetterling-Braggin (ed.), *Sexist language: A modern philosophical analysis.* Totowa, NJ: Littlefield, Adams.

Bellinger, D., & Gleason, J. B. 1982. Sex differences in parental directives to young children. *Journal of Sex Roles, 8,* 1123–1139.

Butler, J. 1993. *Bodies that matter: On the discursive limits of sex.* New York: Routledge.

Condry, J., and Condry, S. 1976. Sex differences: a study in the eye of the beholder. *Child Development, 47,* 812–819.

Corbett, G. 1991. *Gender.* Cambridge Textbooks in Linguistics. Cambridge and New York: Cambridge University Press.

Ely, R., Gleason, J. B, Narasimhan, B., & McCabe, A. 1995. Family talk about talk: Mothers lead the way. *Discourse Processes, 9* (2), 201–218.

Fagot, B. I., Hagan, R., Leinbach, M. D., & Kronsberg, S. 1985. Differential reactions to assertive and communicative acts of toddler boys and girls. *Child Development, 56,* 1499–1505.

Fausto-Sterling, A. 2000. *Sexing the body: Gender politics and the construction of sexuality.* New York: Basic Books.

Gleason, J. B., Perlmann, R. Y., Ely, D., & Evans, D. 1994. The baby talk register: Parents' use of diminutives. In J. L. Sokolov & C. E. Snow (eds.), *Handbook of research in language development using CHILDES* (pp. 50–76). Hillsdale, NJ: Erlbaum.

Gould, L. 1983. X: A fabulous child's story. In L. C. Pogrebin (ed.), *Stories for free children.* New York: McGraw-Hill.

Langlois, J. H., & Downs, A. C. 1980. Mothers, fathers, and peers as socialization agents of sex-typed play behaviors in young children. *Child Development, 62,* 1217–1247.

Livia, A. 1997. Disloyal to masculine identity: Linguistic gender and liminal identity in French. In Livia & Hall (eds.), *Queerly phrased: Language, gen-*

der and sexuality (pp. 349–368). Oxford and New York: Oxford University Press.

2001. *Pronoun envy: Literary uses of linguistic gender*. Studies in Language and Gender. Oxford and New York: Oxford University Press.

Maccoby, E. 2000. Perspectives on gender development. *International Journal of Behavioural Development*, 24(4), 398–406.

2002. The intersection of "nature" and socialization in childhood gender development. In C. VonHoften & P. Blackman (eds.), *Psychology at the turn of the millennium*, Vol. II, *Social, developmental, and clinical perspectives* (pp. 37–52). Hove: Psychology Press.

Maccoby, E. E., and Jacklin, C. N. 1974. *The psychology of sex differences*. Stanford, CA: Stanford University Press.

Ogawa, N., & Smith, J. S. 1997. The gendering of the gay male sex class in Japan: A case study based on "Rasen no Sobyo." In Livia & Hall (eds.), *Queerly phrased: Language, gender and sexuality* (pp. 402–415). Oxford and New York: Oxford University Press.

Rubin, J. Z., Provenzano, F. J., & Luria, Z. 1974. The eye of the beholder: Parents' view on sex of newborns. *American Journal of Orthopsychiatry*, 44, 512–519.

Thorne, B. 1993. *Gender play*. New Brunswick, NJ: Rutgers University Press.

---

about the text

1. Why, according to Eckert and McConnell-Ginet, do people not "sit back and simply allow the baby to become male or female" (paragraph 2)? Do you think the authors advocate such a means of child-rearing? Why or why not?

2. Eckert and McConnell-Ginet are very careful about gender references in their own writing. They don't use the generic "he" to refer to both males and females, and they manage to avoid the sometimes awkward "he or she." Read their essay carefully and note the ways in which they handle generic references. What do they do? Is it effective? Is it smooth? Why or why not?

---

on language use

3. What do Eckert and McConnell-Ginet mean by the phrase "gender work" (paragraph 1)? What things have you done today that could be classified as gender work? What aspects of your life are strongly influenced by gender work? Is there any part of your life that is untouched? Why or why not?

4. The authors suggest that any sales clerk would likely be "perplexed" if you stated that you didn't know or care about the gender of the baby you were buying a gift for. Test their hypothesis. Go to a store with a classmate and ask for information or help in buying a baby gift. If the clerk asks the gender of the baby, say that you don't care or it

doesn't matter to you. Pay attention to the response; take notes once you've left the store so that you can remember all the details. Discuss your results with your classmates.

5. What behavior or attitude might prompt you to call a child a "good boy"? A "good girl"? A "good kid"? Work in groups of three, with each member making a list of the qualities or criteria for one of those categories. Then, compare your lists. How is a "good kid" different from either a "good girl" or a "good boy"?

6. Eckert and McConnell-Ginet discuss how English discourse is automatically gendered any time third-person pronouns are used. How long could you go in conversations without using gendered references? Try it for one day. Avoid third-person singular pronouns by using singular "they." Instead of saying "girlfriend" or "boyfriend," use an ungendered term like "sweetheart"; use "spouse" instead of "husband" or "wife," "sib" instead of "sister" or "brother," etc. Discuss your experience with two or three classmates. What terms were most successful for you? When was it difficult to avoid gender references? Why? How did you feel about the experience? Were your conversation partners confused? Why or why not?

---

for writing

7. Read Lynda Willer's essay on baby cards, "Welcome to Your World, Baby," in this chapter, and make a similar survey of ten or twelve birthday cards for four- and five-year-olds (It is not necessary to purchase the cards; you can take notes in the store. It may be helpful to work in pairs to collect your data). Are there any that are ungendered? How are the girls' cards and the boys' cards different? Some of the cards in this category are directed at the kids themselves, while some are intended mainly for the parents. What gender differences do you find between those two broad categories? Write a report on your results, focusing mainly on the linguistic elements of the cards—the words themselves and the visual effect of the lettering. You may also want to talk about the colors and images; draw ideas from Willer's essay about what elements to look for.

8. Many parents choose to find out the gender of a baby before it is born. How might this practice affect the "gender work" that parents do in the first days or weeks of a baby's life, or even before it's born? Write an essay in which you explore how knowing a baby's gender before it arrives could affect the "gender work" done on its behalf.

LINDA WERTHEIMER AND CATHY DUCHAMP
ALL THINGS CONSIDERED

How to Sound More Feminine

F ROM NPR NEWS, it's ALL THINGS CONSIDERED. I'm Linda Wertheimer. The voice is one of the most defining human characteristics. Voice gives instant recognition to family members, friends; certainly film stars.

(Soundbite of movie)

Ms. Marilyn Monroe: Oh, Josephine just imagine, me, Sugar Kowalczyk from Sandusky, Ohio, on a millionaire's yacht. If my mother could only see me now.

Wertheimer: But what makes a voice like Marilyn Monroe's female? That question is an important one for transgender people. The number of transgender people living in America is difficult to gauge, but it ranges from as few as 10,000 to more than 25,000 people. For many of them, voice is a concern as they redefine themselves by changing gender. From member station KUOW in Seattle, Cathy Duchamp reports on a voice therapy program designed to help men becoming women to sound more feminine.

* * *

Duchamp: Voice feminization therapy. A handful of speech pathologists nationwide specialize in the field, including Michelle Mordaunt, who runs the program for transgender women here at the University of Washington.

How are women's and men's voices different? Is it only a matter of higher or lower pitch? This selection explores the gendering of the voice. In this report produced for the National Public Radio program All Things Considered *in 2001, Cathy Duchamp speaks with voice therapists and transgendered individuals to examine the process of acquiring a feminine voice. As you read, try to imagine the sound of each voice. Listen to the NPR report on our website <wwnorton.com/write/language>.* *

---

*The transcript you are reading has been edited for length.

Ms. Michelle Mordaunt (*speech pathologist*): A lot of transgender people will ₅ change the way they look; they can change the way they walk; they can change the way they wear their hair, their makeup. But they need to be able to communicate. And if you look like a woman, act like a woman, but don't have the voice to go with it, it's detrimental to the whole transition process.

Duchamp: Mordaunt is not necessarily aiming for the ultimate feminine voice. The goal is an ambiguous voice that, when combined with walk, hair and wardrobe, creates a total female package. Changing the voice is relatively easy for female-to-male transsexuals. That's because testosterone injections, which help grow facial hair, also thicken the vocal cords, automatically lowering pitch. But estrogen injections in men, which help to create breasts, do not raise pitch, leaving the transition from male to female incomplete. In fact, a masculine voice can often betray. It's happened to Judy Osborn.

* * *

Ms. Osborn: I'll be talking with a guy on a street corner about the weather or something like that, waiting for a bus and all of a sudden my voice slips to a place where one syllable is detectable as kind of having a guy voice underneath it. And you see this look of horror on somebody's face. It's almost like you fooled them, and you have. And there's no further communication possible. It's very sad when that happens.

Duchamp: The transgender community emerged in the US in the 1970s. It includes people who change their sexual identity with or without sex reassignment surgery. But it took 20 years to develop formal voice therapy programs, in part because compared to hormone injections and sex change surgery, there's no easy procedure for changing the voice.

This is Kurt Everett Eckhardt, an audio diary of a trip to Europe eight years ago.

Mr. Kurt Everett Eckhardt: OK. May the 20th, Kurty turns 41 years old. And ₁₀ we're waiting to catch a bus to go down to the Sea-Tac International Airport.

Duchamp: Four years after that trip, Kurt became Katherine. Throughout the transition she kept her job as a bus driver in Seattle.

Ms. Katherine Eckhardt: Next stop, West Lake Station, 35th and Pine Street, downtown retail shopping court . . .

Duchamp: Following a year and a half of voice therapy, Eckhardt feels comfortable announcing stops over the loudspeaker. But she says voice was the hardest part of the gender transition.

Ms. Eckhardt: It was scary. I was terrified that people were going to stop—you know, just say, "Stop that. Just stop doing that." (Laughs) And like anything, it's a learned process. So the initial focus was on the business of pitch. And so I kept trying to drive my pitch up higher, and then it would get into that range to where it sounded ridiculous. You know, it sounded ridiculous to me. Yeah, it was a real challenge.

Duchamp: Eckhardt says the hard work begins in the lab, where each component of the voice is isolated, then adjusted. Pitch is the main one, but there's also intonation, intensity and resonance, how and where the sound of the voice reverberates. Men tend to resonate in the chest; women's voices tend to resonate in the throat or face. Equally important, says speech pathologist Michelle Mordaunt, is nonverbal communication. 15

Ms. Mordaunt: A female has more facial expression, tends to smile more, which is a technique that a lot of transgender clients come in with, grinning from ear to ear, which is not always appropriate given what they're saying.

Duchamp: Mordaunt breaks bad habits, then gradually she brings the different components of voice back together with one ultimate goal.

Ms. Mordaunt: They need to be able to do this on the street when the bus goes by, in a library, in a bar, at a concert. They need to be able to use this voice in multiple locations and have the comfort level with it.

Duchamp: Mordaunt says that comfort level usually comes after six to nine months of sessions and practice. But mastery may never come. Julie Barkmeyer is the voice specialty director of the American Speech-Language-Hearing Association. She says the male physical structure limits the ability to change the voice completely.

Ms. Julie Barkmeyer (*American Speech-Language-Hearing Association*): Most 20 of what they are facing as far as the battle goes has to do with the fact that the—the cavity size of their throat and of the oral cavity really isn't going to change. That's the one thing we cannot change, and it does always give them some kind of an element of being a male. In addition, even if we were able to get them to elevate their pitch and to speak with more of a feminized voice, other giveaways are when they start to laugh or if they cough or even when they cry, the voice tends to go down to the lower pitch and reveal that they have a more masculine sounding voice. So that's a challenge that they cannot overcome.

Duchamp: An alternative to voice therapy is surgery where the vocal cords are stretched to raise pitch. The procedure is considered risky; the results, mixed. But voice feminization therapy is not risk-free either. Barkmeyer acknowledges driving the pitch too high can result in chronic pain and tension in the vocal cords. Also, there is little research on what works and what doesn't, nor are there standards of practice for voice therapists to follow. Still, in Katherine Eckhardt's case, she believes the therapy has revealed the true self within.

Ms. Eckhardt: It feels as though the prison doors have been opened and I've walked out into the sunshine. Life happens to me and I get to participate in it in a way that I never was able to before. I mean, I'm here. I wasn't here before. I was very far back there. And now I get to participate in my life.

about the text

1. After you've read the selection, try to imagine how the featured voices might sound and then listen to the audio clip at <wwnorton.com/write/language>. Were you surprised by any of the voices? Which ones? Why? Did Judy Osborn and Katherine Eckhardt sound like ordinary women to you? Why or why not? If you had heard their voices without knowing any of their personal history, would you have suspected that they weren't lifelong females? Why or why not?

on language use

2. Can you always correctly distinguish gender from a telephone or radio voice? Have you ever made a gender-identification error or been the subject of one? How did it happen? How did you feel—embarrassed? amused? annoyed? confused? How do you think the other person felt?

3. Is the gender marking of a person's voice a simple matter of pitch? Reporter Cathy Duchamp suggests that female-to-male transgendered persons have no problem in masculinizing their voices because testosterone injections lower their pitch, implying that female voices involve more than pitch, but male voices don't. What other factors help make a deep voice sound feminine or a high voice sound masculine? How? Discuss these questions with two or three classmates and report your ideas to the class.

4. Do you ever consciously make your voice sound more feminine or more masculine? How? When? Why? Would you say your efforts have been effective? How do you know? Under what circumstances might a man want to sound more masculine? More feminine? Under what circumstances might a woman want to sound more feminine? More masculine? Give examples.

5. Try to imitate Britney Spears's or Marilyn Monroe's voice. What features of your own voice do you have to alter? Then imitate Elvis Presley's or Arnold Schwarzenegger's voice. What features do you have to alter? How well did you do each imitation? What parts did you have trouble with?

for writing

6. Duchamp notes that speech pathologist Michelle Mordaunt's goal for clients is not "the ultimate feminine voice," but rather "an ambiguous voice that, when combined with walk, hair, and wardrobe, creates a total female package" (paragraph 6). What, exactly, might a "total female package" be? For example, many cartoon males—Bugs Bunny, Mickey Mouse, SpongeBob SquarePants—have voices that are high-pitched but not feminine. Why not? How is Michelle Mordaunt's work similar to the gender work described in Eckert and McConnell-Ginet's essay, "Learning to be Gendered"? How is it different? Write an essay in which you describe how gender work is accomplished with voice. Consider both masculine and feminine voices in your description.

7. As you passed from childhood to adulthood, you may have consciously trained your voice or played with voice qualities in order to sound more womanly, manly, or adult. Perhaps you tried to sound more like (or less like) a parent or other relative. You may have wanted the change to be permanent or only for a specific occasion. If you ever experimented with voice to shape your adult self, write a personal narrative describing what you did, how you did it, and why. How successful were you in achieving the desired effect? Looking back, how do you feel now about your efforts?

Dan Piraro's Bizarro appears in more than 200 newspapers in the United States, Canada, and parts of Europe, Asia, and South America. The cartoon won the National Cartoonist Society's award for Best Cartoon Panel of the Year in 2000, 2001, and 2002. Piraro's solo stand-up comedy act, the Bizarro Bologna Show, won an award at the 2002 New York International Fringe Festival. The cartoon reproduced here first appeared in 1999; in it, Piraro puts a new twist on the stereotypical construction worker catcall.

DAN PIRARO

Bizarro

1. If you look just at the drawing and not at the speech balloons, what would you guess the women might be saying? Why? (You might try covering the words and asking a few other people to guess what's being said.) Is your imagined version funnier than the original cartoon? Why or why not?

2. The handwriting in each of the speech balloons is slightly different. What purpose does that serve in the cartoon? What do the style and shape of the letters tell you about the voice or tone of each speaker? Which speaker has the most feminine voice? The most masculine voice? The highest pitch? The lowest? How do you know? What elements of the lettering provide clues? Read Linda Wertheimer and Cathy Duchamp's selection in this chapter, "How to Sound More Feminine." Does that text help you answer these questions?

on language use

3. The women in the cartoon are not commenting on the man's body in the way that male construction workers stereotypically do when women walk past them. Might their comments still be considered offensive by the man? By anyone? Why or why not? Would the cartoon be as funny if the women were remarking on the man's physical characteristics the way that some men do to women? Why or why not?

4. A crew of all female construction workers is still somewhat implausible, at least in the United States, but is the scenario realistic in any other ways? How? Have you ever heard women publicly direct these kinds of remarks to man they don't know? Have you ever heard men do something similar?

5. The catcalls in the cartoon are not typical— that's partly why it's funny. Catcalls usually have to do with physical appearance and often contain subtle or overt sexual innuendo. Have you ever had catcalls directed at you? How have they made you feel? Compare your answers with those of your classmates. How do the women's responses differ from the men's? Are the responses or the gender patterns surprising? Why or why not?

for writing

6. Would this cartoon be plausible if the women were wearing business suits? Why or why not? How might its meaning be different? Why? How might it be different if the man were wearing a UPS uniform, perhaps, or electrician's overalls? Why? How might it be different if the cartoon were set on the beach and all of the people were in bathing suits? Why? Keeping your answers to these questions in mind, write an essay in which you analyze how each element of the cartoon—setting, posture, attire, words—contributes to its overall argument. Provide examples from your "what-if" scenarios to support your thesis.

Guys, Cars, and Language

In the United States, cars are more than just a mode of transportation. They are status symbols, identity markers, mobile ads, friends, sports equipment, toys, and more. In advertisements, on calendars, and elsewhere, automobile photos are often saturated with sexual innuendo, with shiny cars sometimes even adorned with scantily clad women in alluring poses. The man who cares more about his car than about his wife is a cliché of American humor, spending his weekends in his driveway waxing, and polishing, the object of his affection. Many of us talk to our cars; some of us refer to our cars as "she."

The two images here play on the identification of women with cars and cars with women. The first is a cartoon by **Peter Steiner** that appeared in The New Yorker in 1995. Steiner's cartoons also ran in the New York Times, the Washington Post, among others. The second image is a 1979 postcard by **Jill Posener** of a billboard advertising Fiats in England. The ad text draws an analogy between the sporty Fiat and women; a graffiti artist used the same analogy to criticize the original message.

"If I were a car, you could find the words."

1. In the cartoon, we are dropped into what is clearly the middle of a conversation. What might the man have said to elicit the woman's statement? How do you know? What visual and linguistic clues can you use to construct the scenario?

2. Some of the details of the cartoon are background and make only a minor contribution to the meaning of the whole. For example, the fact that the painting on the wall is a sailboat probably doesn't have a great deal of significance. (Or does it? Boats, after all, are traditionally referred to as "she.") The ornateness of the frame, on the other hand, may indicate something about the atmosphere of the restaurant, which could, in turn, be an important clue to the occasion. What are the important details of the drawing? What implications can you draw from them? How do they contribute to the meaning of the cartoon as a whole?

3. The cartoon and the ad both use the "car as woman, woman as car" analogy, and in both cases, the women respond in anger. What is each woman angry about? Are they angry about the same thing? Why or why not? With two or three classmates, compare what each woman responds to and explain the similarities and differences. Use specific examples from the images to support your explanation.

on language use

4. In #3, we made the assumption that the graffiti artist was a woman. Is that, in fact, a safe assumption? Why or why not? Are there any clues—handwriting perhaps—that might reveal the gender of the graffitist? Sleuth out this question with two or three classmates.

5. What, exactly, does Fiat imply by making the analogy between cars and women? In other words, what is the ad's message? Could the same analogy be used to deliver the same message in a less offensive manner? How? Work with one or two classmates to describe or sketch out a possible billboard.

6. Our understanding of sexist language and behavior has improved in the years since the Fiat billboard, though some would say that we have a way to go before women and men enjoy equal status and opportunities. Can you imagine seeing a billboard or magazine ad today that makes a humorous reference to "bottom pinching"? If so, where? Whose bottom would be being pinched? What might such an ad say or look like? If not, why not?

for writing

7. Why might the Fiat ad designers have chosen to use the word "lady" and not "woman," "chick," or "girl"? What are the connotative differences among those terms? How might the ad have been different if one of the other terms were used? Do some research to find out if the connotations of any of these words have changed since 1979, the year the billboard appeared. Write an essay answering these questions and reporting on the results of your research.

8. Find an example of sexist language in a public setting—on a billboard or TV commercial or in a store display; in a newspaper, catalog, or magazine. Write an analysis of why you think it is sexist. Is the sexism deliberate or unintentional? How do you know? How could you revise the language to remove the sexism? Include a description of the item in question and provide a photo or a copy, if possible.

DARRYL MCGRATH

The Return of Girl

• •

Darryl McGrath *is a journalist based in Albany, New York, who writes for various publications on issues of politics, reproductive health, and child welfare. In this selection, she writes about the spread of the word "girl" to refer to adult women. This essay was originally published in October 2002 in the Web-based periodical* Women's News; *its motto is "bridging the gender gap every day." In the essay, McGrath describes and analyzes an ordinary phenomenon that you almost certainly hear every day; as you read, think about whether the uses of "girl" that you see and hear are in any way remarkable.*

• •

T HE WORD "GIRL"—which feminists railed against a generation ago as a demeaning and offensive term for women—is making a comeback.

Embraced by the media and advertising, "girl" is popping up everywhere: in fashion catalogs, newspaper articles, advertisements on Web sites and television, and everyday conversation.

Feminists are taking note, and not all of them are pleased. The hard-fought battle to get American society to stop saying "girl" and start saying "woman" when referring to females in their late teens or older is still a fresh memory for veterans of the consciousness-raising 1970s.

" 'Girl' is an infantilizing term for women," says Sherryl Kleinman, a sociology professor at the University of North Carolina at Chapel Hill. "This becomes clearest when the doctor uses it to refer to his assistant or secretary, even if she is 50 years old: 'Talk to the girl up front.' I have heard this numerous times in the recent past."

She is likely to hear it many times more, because examples of "girl" suddenly abound. 5

SELLING IS ALL ABOUT THE GIRL

The John Frieda hair products company promises that "golden girls rule" in a magazine advertisement for its "Sheer Blonde," shampoo and conditioner. The voiceover in a promotion for an upcoming episode of the NBC television show *Watching Ellie* says that the lead character in the series "promised the necklace to one girl, but gave it to another." An announcer giving a sports update on ESPN Radio tells listeners that "two girls" in the Women's National Basketball Association have been suspended for fighting.

A student's advertisement for a roommate posted on a State University of New York campus reads, "Girls are okay to move in (as long as you don't make the place too . . . girlie)?" In an online advertisement for its personal greeting service, the home page for the Yahoo! Internet search engine asks, "Looking for a girl who likes to make waves?" And the spring catalog for the J. Crew clothing company tells readers that wearing a dress is "a girl thing." That wasn't what designer Diane vonFurstenberg told her customers 30 years ago when she marketed her wrap dress with the slogan, "Feel like a woman, wear a dress!"

THE *NEW YORK TIMES* CALLS A CABINET SECRETARY THE 'GO-TO GIRL'

Users of "girl" are unapologetic, saying no offense is intended. *The New York Times Manual of Style and Usage*, the paper's guide to printed propriety, declares that "girl" should be reserved for "the very young," but "girl" has slipped into frequent use in the paper's Sunday Styles and fashion sections—where it sometimes appears on the same page as an article using "woman"—and it also has started to appear in the paper's news sections.

In the "Our Towns" Metro section column of the July 14 Sunday *Times*, writer Matthew Purdy pondered why former New Jersey governor and current Environmental Protection Agency Administrator Christine Todd Whitman has been the target of so much criticism lately.

"Pick a problem that needs a villain . . . and she's the go-to girl," Purdy 10 wrote.

Kathy Park, a *Times* spokeswoman, says "girl" is a purely subjective style choice, and that the *Times* stylebook allows for flexibility.

"The haste and deadline pressure are the cause of most deviations from our style," Park says. "In occasional instances, writers may choose to substitute their own ear or judgment."

J. Crew has used "girl" in editorial copy for quite a while, says Thomas Cochill, a copywriter at the clothing company.

"Rather than using it to target a specific demographic, or imply a specific age group, we believe it conveys an attitude that transcends age, a sensibility that our customers identify with," Cochill says. "We use the word 'girl' to communicate a mood that is feminine, with the qualities of a youthful spirit of independence, enthusiasm, individuality, and confidence."

HAS FEMINISM ACHIEVED ITS GOALS?

"Girl" may have re-emerged "perhaps because many people believe that 15
feminism has achieved what it set out to do," says Robin Lakoff, a linguistics
professor and Guggenheim fellow at the University of California at Berkeley.

Lakoff also theorizes that "feminism itself has become an object of
scorn for many women, especially younger ones, who don't know their history."

Ann Ciasullo, a lecturer in English at the University of Oregon, sees a
"kind of watered-down feminism that goes along with the use of 'girl' and
'girl power.'"

"It seems to be a kind of depoliticization of feminism," says Ciasullo.
She sees the use of the word by advertisers as yet another reinforcement of
the message that women should strive to look sexual and youthful.

Whatever its intended use, "girl" has a complicated history in English,
fraught with nuance and controversy, noted Lakoff and other language-
watchers. It has long been accepted in certain professions and settings, but
only if used in the proper context, or by people who have gained the right to
use it. And even then, it's difficult for everyone to be happy with its use.

For example, "girl" has always been accepted in the modeling industry 20
as a term for women models. Lakoff notes that the word takes on a bizarre
overtone, however, upon a closer examination of how models are treated.

"Models themselves are infantilized: They wear clothing sizes normal
for 6-year-olds, they are treated like children, ordered around," Lakoff says.

AMONG AFRICAN AMERICANS, 'GIRL' DENOTES INCLUSION

"Girl" has been long been a part of Black English, but in a specialized way
that has little to do with the feminist movement, says James Peterson,
a social linguist who is now a doctoral candidate at the University of Pennsylvania.

Among many black women, "girl" is a sign of inclusion and acceptance
among friends, Peterson notes. The word remains offensive, however, if used
by whites toward black women, or if directed at black women "by anyone
outside their immediate speech community," Peterson says.

Some younger women have embraced "girl" as a hip, edgy term identified with a movement known as Third Wave feminism. In the book, *MANI-
FESTA: Young Women, Feminism, and the Future*, co-authors Jennifer

Baumgardner and Amy Richards examine how Third Wave feminism can be a choice for young women who can't identify with the battles fought during the suffrage movement and the feminism of the 1970s.

"I think it's both a generational reaction and an age reaction," says 25 Richards, explaining why younger women might find "girl" acceptable. "I think 'girl' has a certain freedom. I know that my own usage of the word 'girl' is among girlfriends. It's very fun. If I'm having a business dinner, I'm not going to say, 'I'm going out with these girls.' There are moments when it's still derogatory. The real issue is context."

In keeping with that philosophy, the organizers of an annual gathering of Southern feminist women known as the Southern Girls Convention deliberately uses "girls" in its title.

"We are all about the reclamation of the word girl; taking it back and consequently helping to take away its negative connotation," reads an explanation on the convention's Web site. Organizers also thought the Convention would have attracted a different audience, with less of an activist bent, had it been named the Southern Women's Convention. The gathering features workshops on a range of progressive topics such as body image, sexuality, sexual orientation, and reproductive health.

MEN AND GIRLS

The problem with defining "girl" as acceptable in specific settings and contexts however, is that others cannot be expected to respect those boundaries, says Jackson Katz, an author and nationally recognized expert on the prevention of gender-based violence.

"My biggest concern is the use of the word by men and how it perpetuates sexist attitudes by men," says Katz, who has conducted training sessions on preventing gender-related violence at universities and military bases in the United States and abroad.

"It's not about Amy Richards reclaiming this word," Katz says. "What 30 are men thinking about when they use this word? I think some of what is called Third Wave feminism is an accommodation of how things have not changed."

about the text

1. McGrath does not explicitly state her opinion of the use of "girl." What elements of the essay may reveal her point of view? Does she approve or disapprove? Provide specific examples to support your choice.

2. McGrath concludes the essay with a quotation from author Jackson Katz, who says, "some of what is called Third Wave Feminism is an accommodation of how things have not changed" (paragraph 30). What does Katz's statement mean? What are the "things" that "have not changed"? What is Third Wave Feminism? (You will probably need to do some research in order to answer this part.) Why might McGrath have concluded her essay with Katz's quotation?

on language use

3. As McGrath notes, the word "girl" has different connotations and is used differently in African American communities than among the U.S. population in general. Compare the communities you are familiar with. In any of those communities, is "girl" used differently than it is in the general population? Provide a detailed description, with examples.

4. If you are under thirty, "girl" likely has very different connotations for you than it does for people a generation older than you. Survey three to five people of your same gender who are at least twenty years your senior, and three to five more who are about your age. Ask them to list the connotations of "girl" and to tell you when they might use the word. Compare all your responses; do you find any age-based patterns? If so, what are they? Combine your results with those of your classmates to increase your data. What patterns emerge? What can you infer from these results? Are there any surprises?

5. It is very likely that the women and men in your class have different opinions about the word "girl" and the appropriateness of its use. Work together with classmates to devise a short questionnaire, and poll the class. What kinds of patterns emerge? What can you infer from your results? Are there any surprises?

for writing

6. If you were talking with a friend, would you refer to your own mother as a "girl"? Why or why not? What about other mothers — your friend's mother, your sweetheart's mother, any woman of an older generation? How would the context matter? Under what circumstances might it be acceptable to refer to women of an older generation as "girl"? Experiment with different scenarios. Write an essay exploring your ideas and feelings about the word "girl." Discuss who you think should or should not use the word, who it can or can't apply to, and under what circumstances its usage may or may not be appropriate. Provide detailed examples to illustrate your opinion.

7. According to linguist Robin Lakoff, "girl" has re-emerged because "many people believe that feminism has achieved what it set out to do" (paragraph 15). What did feminism set out to do? What are some of the goals that are generally recognized? Have those goals been met? Write an essay taking a position on these questions. Provide details and examples to support your position.

We know that language use can reflect sexism, but how deeply ingrained in the language are sexist practices? This selection brings up the question of sexism —and efforts to eliminate it—in the pronoun system of English, specifically the usage of "they" and "them" as third-person singular pronouns. John McWhorter is a professor of linguistics at the University of California at Berkeley; his 2002 book, The Power of Babel, deals with language change and dialects. The selection here is a chapter from his 1998 book, Word on the Street: Debunking the Myth of "Pure" Standard English.

JOHN MCWHORTER

Missing the Nose on Our Face

Pronouns and the Feminist Revolution

HERE ARE THREE SENTENCES of ordinary English:

> Ask one of the musicians whether they lost a page of this score.
>
> Somebody left their book here.
>
> If a student asks for an extension, tell them no.

Thoroughly everyday pieces of English, no? And yet as unobjectionable as those mundane little utterances may seem, according to the rules of classroom grammar, they are considered wrong. *To wit*, what we are often told is that the use of *they, them*, or *their* to refer to single persons is a mistake because *they, them* and *their* are plural words.

Yet the question is what singular pronoun we are supposed to use here. Instead of the offending plural plural pronouns, we have often been told by many official sources that it is better to use *he, him*, or *his*:

> Ask one of the musicians whether he lost a page of this score.
>
> Somebody left his book here.
>
> If a student asks for an extension, tell him no.

This, however, does not sit quite right with many of us, especially in light of the profound change in the roles of women in Western societies over the past several decades. Using *he, him* and *his* seems to imply that musicians, students, and, well, somebodies of the world are all men, or at least so often men that the occasional females are just so much static.

In older grammars, pundits often actually came right out and said that men were higher than women in the cosmic order of things, as in an admonition from 1500s to "let us keep a natural order, and set the man before the woman for maners Sake," since after all, "the worthier is preferred and set before." Even by the 1700s, however, this was beginning to seem a rather bald thing to put down in black and white (if not to think), and the party line became that *he* was intended as gender-neutral, since English has no pronoun that was originally gender-neutral.

This is nonsense. To decree a pronoun gender-neutral in a book has no effect on how we link language to basic meanings, and for all of us, a sentence like *Somebody left his book here* calls up the image of a boy or man leaving the book. As a matter of fact, applying the sentence to the image of a girl or woman leaving the book seems downright inappropriate because of the obvious male connotation of *he*, whatever Robert Lowth and Lindley Murray[1] say. This becomes particularly clear when we narrow the male-female assembly to two: *Margaret Thatcher and Ronald Reagan each angered much of his constituency*—whatever you think of the Iron Butterfly,[2] let's face it, this is a clunker.

In any case, a bad odor has grown around this gender-neutral feint of late, as the feminist revolution has led a call to eliminate words and expressions from the language that promote the conception that the levers of power in society are the province of men. The commitment that has substituted *police officer* for *policeman* and *chairperson* for *chairman* has led in the pronoun department to a long overdue rethinking of the gender-neural pronoun issue. One of the most popular suggestions has been to use *he or she*, both in speech and in writing. This construction becomes more prevalent with every year:

Ask one of the musicians whether he or she lost a page of this score.

Somebody left his or her book here.

If a student asks for an extension, tell him or her no.

He or she is founded upon good intentions, but ultimately it will not do. For one thing, the man is still first. Why not *she or he*? But then, two wrongs

---

1. **Robert Lowth and Lindley Murray** eighteenth-century grammarians of English. Lowth's *A Short Introduction to English Grammar* (1762) and Murray's *English Grammar* (1795) are considered instrumental in establishing many of the rules of English usage that are still followed today.

2. **Iron Butterfly** slightly derisive nickname of former British Prime Minister Margaret Thatcher, so named for the stern conservatism she brought to her administration.

don't make a right—why should women be first either? If one argues that this would redress millennia of oppression, one might ask how we would decide exactly when the oppression had been redressed, and besides, *then* what would we do?

Moreover, as a look at the above sentences shows, *he or she* is a construction of inherently limited domain. Conscious and forced, it could never go beyond writing and formal speech. There is not a single language out of the over 5,000 on earth in which people spontaneously refer to unisex subjects as "he or she" in conversation, including English. It's one thing to use this in a paper (albeit with that nagging Why-should-men-come-first? problem), lecture, speech, or announcement. However, imagine anyone using *he or she* chewing on a mouthful of pizza while watching a football game on the tube. When we are rattling along in real time in the real world, our concern, while we juggle shopping bags and avoid offending and fix our hair, is the subject we are addressing. A cooked construction like *he or she* is not a piece of spontaneous language, but a statement of allegiance to gender-neutral speech. As laudable as this is, to genuflect to an allegiance to a broad sociopolitical position in the middle of a casual discussion of anything else is no more natural than to genuflect to any number of other noble issues outside of our topic, such as concern with injustice or love of our children. In other words, *he or she* is strictly conscious, whereas spoken language is inherently unconscious, like breathing, or walking without falling. What this means is that if our response to the *they* issue is to decree that *he or she* is the proper form, then while we have applied a Band-aid to formal speech, we are meanwhile leaving casual speech with the same old *they* that grammarians make us feel guilty about.

One variation on this theme, particularly hip lately, is to switch between *he/him/his* and *she/her/her* in alternate sentences. This one, however, is as hopelessly conscious as *he or she*. Doing this takes a kind of close attention to one's text flow that is virtually impossible outside of writing or careful, planned speech, such as lectures. Once again, there is no language on earth in which people spontaneously alternate their pronouns like this, and there's a reason. This switching also has this disadvantage: Whether spoken or written, each particular use of the male or female pronoun calls up an image of that particular gender, which is both awkward and ends up calling attention to itself instead of to the content of the utterance. To say *he*, especially to audiences familiar with the problems with the gender-neutral fallacy, gives the little jolt of seeming sociologically unsavory; when the speaker or writer corrects this by saying *she* a while later, this usage is distracting as well because after all, women aren't the only ones referred to either. To say *she* first still creates this problem, and even when *he* is used second, it still creates the jolt, especially if the reference to *she* occurred a while ago. In any case, because of the heavy self-monitoring required, this kind of self-conscious alternation is unlikely to ever go beyond a tiny segment of society with a particularly strong interest in demonstrating their commitment to gender-neutral speech.

Of course, some might say that I lack imagination in declaring that *he or she* and the switching are alien to spontaneous speech, and that our goal ought to be to change the very nature of spontaneous speech for the future. I am the last one to dismiss idealism, but there are times when it is best described as quixotic. In that vein, we must ask how realistic it is to imagine, say, children using *he or she* or switching pronouns between sentences. Like *Billy and I went to the store* and *whom*, these devices are the kind of thing only learnable as artificial second layers. They will always flake away with two drinks, laughter, or even simple social comfort.

Then there is *s/he*, which is a complete disaster. This one makes no pre-tense of being intended for spoken language; it is as unpronounceable as the glyph that the artist formerly known as Prince adopted. Even in writing, how-ever, just look at it—it's too darned ugly to be used as frequently as a pro-noun has to be. Imagine great literature splattered with *s/he*'s! 10

Why are we stuck with all of these awkward little concoctions for written English while condemned to "misusing" *they* in spoken English? The source of the problem here is that there happens to have been no originally singular gender-neutral pronoun in English. Many, many languages do not distin-guish between males and females with their third person pronouns. For ex-ample, the Finnish pronoun *hän* can refer to either a man or a woman, which is why Finns new to English often mistakenly refer to a woman as *he*. This lack has even led some people to try to work up their own gender-neutral pro-noun to bestow on English, but to date, proposals like *hesh, hirm, co, et, E, ho, mon, ne, po,* and *thon* have had distinctly marginal impact on English (yes, people actually have suggested that these be used!). It's not that it's impossi-ble to introduce new words into a language, of course: words like *humongous* and *zillion* do not descend nobly from ancient roots, but were instead made up and somehow hung on. However, around the world, languages are much more resistant to accepting new words, made up or foreign, which are as central to their grammar as pronouns are. It can happen: none other than *they, them,* and *their* were actually taken from Scandinavian after Danes in-vaded Britain—the originals were the now impossible-looking *hi, heo,* and *hira*. Yet it is still a sometime thing, and even these pronouns entered the language gradually, without any individual commanding that it be so. It is all but impossible for such things to catch on when the introducer is a sole person brandishing a pamphlet.

"The entire question is unlikely to be resolved in the near future" intones the latest edition of the *American Heritage Dictionary*, after a fine capsule summary of the *they/he/she* or *she/s/he* conundrum. The fact is, however, that the issue has been brilliantly resolved for several centuries, if only our grammarians would wake up and realize that language is a lava lamp and not a clockworks. English has long offered a very simple solution that could neatly apply to both casual and formal speech, sail over the problems of whether men or women are to go first, and spare us the drain on the mental battery of parlor tricks like switching between sentences. Notice that in the last paragraph, I said that English has no *originally* singular gender-neutral pronoun. It does, however, have a *presently* singular gender-neutral pronoun, and that is none other than the *they*, which all of us use in this function all of the time despite the frowns of prescriptivists.

We are told that because it is a plural pronoun, *they* must not be used to refer to single persons because it "doesn't make sense." However, the fact is that today, *they* is indeed both a singular and a plural pronoun, as indicated by the fact that all English speakers use it so. *They* is singular as well as plural for the simple reason that the language has changed and made it so. The idea that *they* is only a plural pronoun is an illusion based on the fallacy of treating the English of one thousand years ago as if it was somehow hallowed, rather than just one arbitrary stage of an endless evolution over time.

I say that we know *they* can be singular because people use it that way so regularly, but it is tempting to suppose that English speakers may have just gotten lazy and infected each other with a bad habit. But once again, we gain perspective on this by looking at languages elsewhere. The French pronoun *vous* began as the plural *you*, originally used with people of the highest rank with the implication that they were such awesome personages that they were more like two people, rather like a person today might facetiously refer to themselves as "we" to connote a certain aristocracy. (Note the use of *themselves* in that last sentence—does it really look like a mistake?) Over time, *vous* came to be used to refer to single people as a mark of respect, and gradually percolated down to indicating respect for ordinary people of authority or even just one's elders. Thus today, within the first month of French instruction we learn that single persons are referred to as *vous* when we are conveying respect (*Comment allez-vous?*), and no one in France or elsewhere considers this to "not make sense"—it happened, and it just is.

In the same month we are also taught that "we" is *nous*, as in *Nous prenons du café chaque matin*, "We drink coffee every morning." However, 15 once we get to France, one of the first things we learn about French as it is actually spoken casually is that "we" is usually rendered with the singular gender-neutral pronoun *on. On prend du café chaque matin* has not exclusively meant "one drinks coffee every morning" for centuries, and is so commonly used to mean "we," and not just "in the streets" but even among educated folk, that mastering spoken French usually entails unlearning the *nous* that textbooks emphasize. Again, the claim that this "doesn't make sense" would be meaningless—it wouldn't have eons ago when *on* still only meant "one," but it has long since acquired this new meaning, to no one's objection.

Things are even more far out in Italian, where the polite form of "you" is *lei,* which also means "she"! Thus *lei parla* means both "she speaks" and "you speak." The reason for this is that centuries ago, noble women were addressed as "she," and this percolated down first to women in ordinary society, and then spread even to men! Things are similar even in the plural—to address two people respectfully one uses *loro,* the word which is also used for "they." One would search in vain for any Italian newspaper editorial where someone complained that these usages don't make sense. They wouldn't have made sense 1,500 years ago when these changes had yet to occur, but this is today, when these changes have taken place. These usages create no confusion and thus make perfect sense.

And then we return to English and recall once again that our own *you* began as plural, with *thou* being the original second-person singular form. As we saw, there were once indignant grammarians who decried the use of *you* in the singular as illogical. Today, however, *thou* is now relegated to the Bible and jocular imitations of archaic speech, while *you* is both plural and singular. None of us have any sense of singular *you* as in any way wrong or sloppy; and the fact that it used to be a plural word only is something we only learn about in books like this one. In other words, the use of *you* changed over time, and now, whatever its original use happened to be, it has had a new one longer than anyone can now remember.

Language change is ever thus. In the beginning a word has one meaning or use. Then as the meaning or use begins to change, prescriptivist grammarians call the new form sloppy and wrong. This sort of thing cannot stop the language from changing because nothing can. Instead it just creates a situation where people use the new form casually when Aunt Lucy isn't looking but avoid it in formal speech. Eventually, the new form becomes so prevalent that it starts popping up even in formal language (*whole nother*); the grammarians give up and jump on the latest new forms (*Hopefully, she'll come*); and before long no one, grammarian or civilian, even remembers that

382 ☐ Chapter 6: His and Hers

the now accepted form was even ever considered a problem (singular *you*). The old criticisms, the trees felled to provide the paper on which they were written, and the insecurity they sowed in millions of people—all of it served no more purpose than throwing salt over our shoulder to ward off bad luck.

In this light, our modern grammarians' discomfort with singular *they* is nothing but this comical intermediate stage in an inevitable change, as misguided and futile as the old grumbles about singular *you*. As much as we might like pronouns to stick to their little corners and hone to a perfect model where there is one form for each person/number combination with no overlaps, the fact is that very few languages ever maintain things this way, and if they do, it's by accident. We have to be told by Aunt Lucy that *they* "cannot" refer to one person, and the reason this never occurs to us until we are told is because in Modern English, *they* indeed *can* refer to one person. That's why we use it that way and are understood when we do. We are no more wrong in allowing *they*, *them*, and *their* to change in this way than the French speakers were who started saying *on prend du café* or the Italians who started calling their monsignors *lei*; or the Middle English speakers who started saying *Charles, you have to do it* instead of *Charles, thou hast to do it*; or the horselike mammals who started developing longer necks on their way to evolving into giraffes. Like life forms, languages are always changing. We would no more expect one to be the way it used to be than we would expect whales to still be bearlike critters bumbling around the seashore. (Yes, this is what whales began as!) Most importantly, language change goes the whole nine yards—nothing in it is exempt, not sounds, not word order, not word meanings, and certainly not good old pronouns.

Thus English has already taken care of the unisex pronoun issue—we don't need *he or she*, *s/he*, "Look-Ma-I'm-politically-correct" switching, *co*, *hesh*, or *thon*; because we have *they*. The *they* case is particularly exasperating in that singular *they* has been available to English speakers for several centuries. The only thing keeping us from taking advantage of it has been the power of the prescriptivist hoax, starting with Lowth and Murray's inevitable whacks at it back in the 1700s. The next time someone tells you that *they* must be used only to refer to plural things, ask *them* to explain why it is okay to use *you* in the singular or what's wrong with the sentence *Comment allez-vous, Guillaume?*, and see what *they* come up with.

1. According to McWhorter, certain phrases "will always flake away with two drinks, laughter, or even simple social comfort" (paragraph 9). What does he mean? Do you agree? Why or why not?

2. Why does McWhorter compare criticisms of language change with the practice of throwing salt over one's shoulder (paragraph 18)? What is he trying to accomplish with the comparison? Do you think it's effective? Why or why not?

3. Would you say that McWhorter is a feminist? Why or why not? Present examples from his essay to support your conclusions. (You'll need to define exactly what you mean by "feminist" before you address the question.)

4. Do you use "they" as singular? Do your friends and classmates? Pay attention to conversations that you have or hear for three days, and listen for instances of singular "they." Make note of any that you hear, including the whole sentence (or two, if necessary), where it appeared, who said it, and to whom. In what kinds of conversations did you most often hear singular "they"—between friends or peers? in a professor's lecture? talking with a parent or professor? on TV or radio? Were you surprised by what you found? Why or why not? Compare your results with those of your classmates.

5. In paragraph 11, McWhorter implies that all languages have pronouns that mark gender. Examine the pronoun system of a lan-

guage other than English—a language that you or someone you know speaks, one that you study, or one that you can find out about from a dictionary or textbook. What distinctions are made in the pronoun system with regard to males and females? Humans and animals? Singular and plural? Other distinctions? Compare your findings with those of three or four classmates.

6. McWhorter argues that the phrase "he or she" is conscious and awkward. Is it a natural phrase for you? What has been your experience with it?

7. How do you feel about McWhorter's criticisms of grammar rules? Tickled? nervous? offended? encouraged? Discuss your responses with two or three classmates. Your discussion may stimulate you to notice many different kinds of responses to McWhorter's ideas.

8. Have English pronouns changed? Research the word "she" or "thou" and write a report on its history in the language. In the case of "she," when did it appear and why? In the case of "thou," when did it disappear and why?

9. Do you agree with McWhorter that singular "they" is a reasonable way to make English usage more gender-inclusive? Why or why not? Is there a better solution? What would it be and why is it better? Do you agree that generic "he" is worth changing? Why or why not? Write an essay agreeing or disagreeing with McWhorter, presenting reasons for your position.

Sexist Pronouns and Usage Guides

· ·

What do writing handbooks and publication manuals have to say about gender and language? We include here guidelines on gender and sexist language from two popular college handbooks and a social sciences publication manual. **The Everyday Writer,** *by Andrea Lunsford, a professor at Stanford University, was published in 2001.* **The Scott Foresman Handbook for Writers,** *by Maxine Hairston and John Ruszkiewicz, both affiliated with the University of Texas at Austin, was published in 2003. Both books are widely used by students studying composition at college and universities throughout the United States. The* **Publication Manual of the American Psychological Association** *is a standard reference in the social sciences. All these books are revised regularly to keep up with changes in language use.*

Handbooks and usage manuals help establish and maintain the rules of appropriate language use; they are the reference sources that writers consult when they are unsure or when they are seeking suggestions for improving their work. As such, these books may serve as the arbiters of disagreements and gatekeepers of change. How do these books navigate social change, language change, and the maintenance of rules and standards for appropriate written English? You have probably consulted such books many times, but you have likely not sat down to read one as you might read a novel or magazine. Approach each of the following guidelines as having a story to tell about the generic use of "he." As you read, consider whether they give the same reasons and solutions for eliminating the generic "he."

· ·

ANDREA LUNSFORD

from *The Everyday Writer*

Consider Assumptions about Gender

Powerful and often invisible gender-related elements of language affect our thinking and our behavior. At one time, for instance, speakers always labeled a woman who worked as a doctor a *woman doctor* or any man who worked as a nurse a *male nurse*, as if to say, "they're exceptions." Equally problematic was the traditional use of *man* and *mankind* to refer to people of both sexes and the use of *he, him, his,* and *himself* to refer to people of unknown sex. Because such usage ignores half the human race, it hardly helps a writer build common ground.

Sexist language, those words and phrases that stereotype or ignore members of either sex or that unnecessarily call attention to gender, can usually be revised fairly easily. There are several alternatives to using masculine pronouns to refer to persons of unknown sex. One option is to recast the sentence using plural forms.

▶ *Lawyers* — A lawyer must pass the bar exam before *they* he can begin to practice.

Another option is to substitute pairs of pronouns such as *he or she, him or her,* and so on.

▶ A lawyer must pass the bar exam before he *or she* can begin to practice.

Yet another way to revise the sentence is to eliminate the pronouns.

▶ A lawyer must pass the bar exam before *beginning* he can begin to practice.

INSTEAD OF	TRY USING
anchorman, anchorwoman	anchor
businessman	businessperson, business executive
chairman, chairwoman	chair, chairperson
congressman	member of Congress, representative
mailman	mail carrier
male nurse	nurse
man, mankind	humans, human beings, humanity, the human race, humankind
manpower	workers, personnel
mothering	parenting
policeman, policewoman	police officer
salesman	salesperson, sales associate
woman engineer	engineer

Editing for Sexist Language

- Have you used *man* or *men* or words containing one of them to refer to people who may be female? If so, consider substituting another word —instead of *fireman*, for instance, try *firefighter*.

- If you have mentioned someone's gender, is it necessary to do so? If you identify someone as a female architect, for example, do you (or would you) refer to someone else as a *male architect*? Unless gender and related matters—looks, clothes, parenthood—are relevant to your point, leave them unmentioned.

- Do you use any occupational stereotypes? Watch for the use of female pronouns for nurses and male ones for engineers, for example.

- Do you use language that patronizes either sex? Do you refer to a wife as *the little woman*, for instance, or to a husband as *her old man*?

- Have you used *he, him, his*, or *himself* to refer to people who may be female?

- Have you overused *he and she, him and her*, and so on? Frequent use of these pronoun pairs can irritate readers.

MAXINE HAIRSTON AND JOHN RUSZKIEWICZ

from *The Scott Foresman Handbook for Writers*

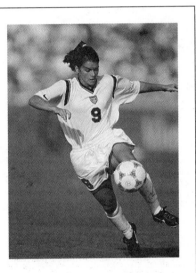

Thirty years ago, Americans were just beginning to see what female athletes could accomplish when given the chance. Today, women such as soccer superstar Mia Hamm garner as much attention for their athletic prowess as their male counterparts.

No matter who their audience may be, responsible writers avoid language that stigmatizes or demeans particular groups. Language that attributes to individuals negative associations based on gender, race or ethnicity, religion, profession, or class is always out of place in public writing.

Avoid sexist language. Over the past four decades, women's activists have made most of us more aware of how profoundly language shapes attitudes and reinforces traditional gender roles. Twenty-five years ago, when the typical writer consistently referred to doctors, scientists, inventors, and artists as "he" and to secretaries, nurses, teachers, and receptionists as "she," youngsters got strong messages about which professions they were expected to choose. You seldom see such ingrained bias today in reputable newspapers, books, and magazines—

most readers find such bias offensive. To keep sexist blunders out of your writing, consider these guidelines.

- **Avoid using *he* and *him* as all-purpose pronouns to refer to people in general.**

WHY WRITE . . .	WHEN YOU COULD WRITE . . .
Every executive expects *his* bonus.	Every executive expects a bonus.
	Executives expect *their* bonuses.
	Every executive expects *his* or *her* bonus.

- **Guard against using the word *man* as a catchall term to refer to all people or all members of a group.** Instead use *people* as a general term, or refer to a specific occupation or role: *worker, parent, voter.*

WHY WRITE . . .	WHEN YOU COULD WRITE . . .
the *man* who wants to be an astronaut	*anyone* who wants to be an astronaut
men who do their own auto repairs	*car owners* who do their own repairs

- **Watch out for assumptions that professions or roles are primarily for men or for women.** Don't write "A senator will improve *his* chances of election by going back home frequently" or "A nurse usually enjoys *her* profession." Also be careful not to slip into hidden assumptions by writing "woman doctor" or "woman engineer," thereby suggesting one wouldn't expect to find women in those professions.

WHY WRITE . . .	WHEN YOU COULD WRITE . . .
men who hope to become scholarship athletes	*young people* who hope to become scholarship athletes
stay-home *mothers*	stay-home *parents*

police*man*	police officer
mail*man*	mail carrier/letter carrier
cleaning *woman*	custodian/janitor
business*men*	business executives

- **When possible, find out what name a married woman wants to go by and honor that choice.** Here are the possibilities.

woman's first and last names	Olga Perez
woman's first and last names + husband's last name	Olga Perez Marciano
woman's first name + hyphenated last name	Olga Perez-Marciano
woman's first name + husband's last name	Olga Marciano
title + husband's full name	Mrs. Ralph Marciano

Some traditionalists may find this array of choices complicated and unnecessary; to many women, however, the distinctions are important. Many women, single or married, prefer the title *Ms.* to *Miss* or *Mrs.* When you're not sure, *Ms.* is the best choice.

- **Watch out for between-the-lines implications that men and women behave in stereotypical ways.** Don't suggest that women are generally talkative and overly emotional or that most men are sportsminded and sloppy. Avoid sexist descriptions such as "a slim blonde" or "a petite brunette" unless you make the same kind of comments about men. Finally, the generic term *woman* (or *women*) is more appropriate than *lady* or *girl*, which many women find patronizing.

from the *Publication Manual of the American Psychological Association*

GUIDELINES TO REDUCE BIAS IN LANGUAGE

As a publisher, APA accepts authors' word choices unless those choices are inaccurate, unclear, or ungrammatical. As an organization, APA is committed both to science and to the fair treatment of individuals and groups, and this policy requires authors of APA publications to avoid perpetuating demeaning attitudes and biased assumptions about people in their writing. Constructions that might imply bias against persons on the basis of gender, sexual orientation, racial or ethnic group, disability, or age should be avoided. Scientific writing should be free of implied or irrelevant evaluation of the group or groups being studied.

Long-standing cultural practice can exert a powerful influence over even the most conscientious author. Just as you have learned to check what you write for spelling, grammar, and wordiness, practice reading over your work for bias. You can test your writing for implied evaluation by reading it while (a) substituting your own group for the group or groups you are discussing or (b) imagining you are a member of the group you are discussing. If you feel excluded or offended, your material needs further revision. Another suggestion is to ask people from that group to read your material and give you candid feedback.

What follows is a set of guidelines, followed in turn by discussions of specific issues that affect particular groups. These are not rigid rules. You may find that some attempts to follow the guidelines result in wordiness or clumsy prose. As always, good judgment is required. If your writing reflects respect for your participants and your readers, and if you write with appropriate specificity and precision, you will be contributing to the goal of accurate, unbiased communication.

* * *

GENDER

Avoid ambiguity in sex identity or sex role by choosing nouns, pronouns, and adjectives that specifically describe your participants. Sexist bias can occur when pronouns are used carelessly, as when the masculine pronoun *he* is used to refer to both sexes or when the masculine or feminine pronoun is used exclusively to define roles by sex (e.g., "the nurse . . . *she*"). The use of *man* as a generic noun or as an ending for an occupational title (e.g., *policeman*) can be ambiguous and may imply incorrectly that all persons in the group are male. Be clear about whether you mean one sex or both sexes.

To avoid stereotypes, use caution when providing examples:

> To illustrate this idea, *an American boy's* potential for becoming a football player might be an aggregate of strength, running speed, balance, fearlessness, and resistance to injury. [The manuscript was revised to *a child's.*]

There are many alternatives to the generic *he*, including rephrasing (e.g., from "When an individual conducts this kind of self-appraisal, *he* is a much stronger person" to "When an individual conducts this kind of self-appraisal, that person is much stronger" or "This kind of self-appraisal makes an individual much stronger"), using plural nouns or plural pronouns (e.g., from "A therapist who is too much like *his* client can lose *his* objectivity" to "Therapists who are too much like *their* clients can lose *their* objectivity"), replacing the pronoun with an article (e.g., from "A researcher must apply for *his* grant by September 1" to "A researcher must apply for *the* grant by September 1"), and dropping the pronoun (e.g., from "The researcher must avoid letting *his* own biases and expectations" to "The researcher must avoid letting biases and expectations"). Replacing *he* with *he or she* or *she or he* should be done sparingly because the repetition can become tiresome. Combination forms such as *he/she* or *(s)he* are awkward and distracting. Alternating between *he* and *she* also may be distracting and is not ideal; doing so implies that *he* or *she* can in fact be generic, which is not the case. Use of either pronoun unavoidably suggests that specific gender to the reader.

about the texts

1. What recommendations do the three books make for avoiding generic "he"? If you are using a writers' handbook or manual in your class, consult it as well. Do they all present the same solutions? How might you explain any differences that you find?

2. Lunsford's handbook and the APA manual give different reasons for why it's important to avoid generic "he." What are they? Why might these books emphasize different reasons? (Hint: Think about what kind of writing each is concerned with.)

3. What might John McWhorter say about each of the texts presented here? Present evidence from his essay "Missing the Nose on Our Face: Pronouns and the Feminist Revolution" to support your ideas.

on language use

4. Do you avoid generic "he" in your writing? Why or why not? What is your preferred way to do so? Why? Do you consciously avoid any of the alternatives to generic "he"? Why?

5. Language innovations and new words often originate with young people. Have you and your friends devised other manners of gender reference and/or gender inclusion? What are they? (For example, whom might you address as "dude"? "guys"?) Do you think your usages might catch on with other speakers? Why or why not?

6. Usage manuals are generally more concerned with written language than with spoken language. In what ways is your everyday spoken language different from your academic writing? In what ways has your spoken language been influenced by the grammar rules you have learned?

Brainstorm possible responses to these questions with two or three classmates.

7. Is there a usage manual for rap or hip-hop? If there were, what might it say? What would happen to the genres, their artists, and the significance of music if such a manual did exist? Is it hard to conceive of such a manual? Why or why not?

for writing

8. Hairston and Ruszkiewicz mention the singular "they" as a possible alternative to generic *he*, although they point out that not everyone finds that alternative acceptable. Look at the most recent handbooks you can find (check the Web) and, if you haven't already done so, read John McWhorter's essay "Missing the Nose on Our Face: Pronouns and the Feminist Revolution," in this chapter. Do you think we are seeing the beginning of change? Why or why not? Write an essay in which you speculate on the possible future of singular "they." Do you think it will be acceptable in the next ten years? twenty? fifty? Why or why not?

9. Spanish, French, German, and other European languages have official academies that establish rules for grammar and spelling. How are the rules for English established? How, if at all, do they change? Research these two questions and write an essay about whether English, with its system of establishing and maintaining rules for appropriate usage, is more responsive to social change than the languages with formal academies. What recommendations might you make for changing the ways in which English rules are established or changed? Write an essay responding to these questions.

chapter 7

language in deaf communities

american Sign Language (ASL) is the third most used language in the United States—and yet hearing people know little (or often nothing) about it. Two common misconceptions: that it is merely English signed, and that signers around the world use a single language. In fact, ASL is more closely related to the sign language used in France than to that used in England (because Deaf education in the United States was influenced by Deaf education in France, as you'll learn in Andrew Solomon's essay in this chapter). If signers from around the world have an easier time understanding one another than hearing people do, it is not because there is a universal sign language but likely because signs often resemble the things they represent more than the words of spoken languages can. Signers also use all the available resources they have, including facial expression, movement, and gesture, to communicate in ways even the most animated hearing people do not. If hearing people know little about ASL, they tend to know even less about deafness as a physiological condition. And few are aware that there's a difference between deaf and Deaf: deaf people are those who cannot hear, whereas Deaf people are those who cannot hear and who take deafness and ASL to be essential parts of their identity. In our writing, we've used Deaf as the default term except when we're referring to a clearly physiological condition or to a time in the past when no such distinction was made. Go to this book's Web site at <wwnorton.com/write/language> for a more detailed explanation of the Deaf/deaf distinction.

In this chapter's first reading, Carol Padden and Tom Humphries write about how children who cannot hear learn what it means to be Deaf in a hearing world and how they make sense of their experiences. Then, the ASL Fingerspelling Dictionary Web site introduces you to fingerspelling, an important but small part of ASL. Matthew Moore and Linda Levitan go on to offer Deaf answers to hearing people's questions about deafness, from their collection For Hearing People Only. Next, Greg Evans, the cartoonist who creates Luann, reminds us that ignorance about deafness and insensitivity to Deaf people often go hand in hand. In his lengthy essay from The New York Times Magazine, here divided into three parts, Andrew Solomon offers an account of what he learned from the Deaf about the complexity of their own communities. His essay is a meditation on the meaning and significance of difference in American society. The chapter concludes with Brenda Jo Brueggemann's poem to Alexander Graham Bell, who is known to Deaf people not just as the inventor of the telephone but also as a strong proponent of oralism, the philosophy that advocates educating those who cannot hear by forcing them to speak and to speechread with the goal of integrating them into the hearing community. As these readings make clear, learning to speak when one cannot hear and to speechread (even if one can hear) are challenging tasks. A corollary of oralism is that sign language—the form of language Deaf people have traditionally used and one that all can easily learn—must be suppressed. The irony is that Bell's mother and wife were unable to hear and that the teaching method he advocated turned out to be the one that robbed Deaf people of the one language accessible to all of them—and to hearing people as well.

As the readings in this chapter demonstrate, for the Deaf, language has everything to do with identity.

In this chapter of their book
Deaf in America: Voices from
a Culture (1988), Carol Padden
and Tom Humphries, both of
whom are Deaf, explain how
children who are born deaf or
become deaf early in life
come to understand and appreciate what it means to be
deaf in an overwhelmingly
hearing world. As they note in
their introduction, "the traditional way of writing about
Deaf people is to focus on the
fact of their condition—that
they do not hear—and to interpret all other aspects of
their lives as a consequence
of this fact." They seek, instead, to convey "far more interesting facets of Deaf
people's lives": "the lives they
live, their art and performances, their everyday talk,
their shared myths, and the
lessons they teach one another." Padden and
Humphries, who are wife and
husband, teach in the department of communication at the
University of California, San
Diego. They have also published two textbooks to help
hearing people learn American Sign Language.

CAROL PADDEN AND TOM HUMPHRIES

Learning to Be Deaf

WHEN WE COLLECTED A STORE OF REMINISCENCES from Deaf adults about their childhoods, many told how as young children they discovered that they could not hear sound or speech. For example, in a story that appears in a videotaped version of a stage production by the National Theatre of the Deaf, Dorothy Miles recalls how, after a long childhood illness, she discovers that she can no longer hear her own voice. These are the expected anecdotes, those which confirm the popular wisdom about deafness—that it is the experience of not hearing. But we also came across stories that, although they were about discovering deafness, seemed only remotely connected to the fact of loss of hearing. One such example came from an interview Carol conducted with two sisters, one five and the other seven years old, as part of a study on language learning in the home. Both girls are Deaf, as are their parents. After an afternoon of tests and conversation, the younger girl, Vicki, brought a toy for Carol to inspect:

> *Vicki:* My friend Michael gave it to me.
> *Helen:* Michael's her boyfriend. (giggles)
> *Vicki:* Michael is not! Anyway Michael is Deaf.
> *Helen:* No! Michael is hearing!
> *Vicki:* (confused, but not convinced) Michael is Deaf!
> *Helen:* You're wrong! I know! Michael is hearing.
> *Carol:* Well, which is he? Deaf or hearing?
> *Vicki:* (pauses) I don't know.
> *Carol:* What do you think?
> *Vicki:* Both! Michael is Deaf and hearing!

The solution was immensely satisfying to Vicki, but her older sister was aghast. No one is ever both Deaf and hearing at the same time. One is either Deaf or hearing. But Vicki had become attached to her explanation. After repeatedly telling Vicki that her solution would not work,

Helen threw up her hands in exasperation and complained to their parents. The adults, of course, found the girls' argument yet another amusing example of the marvelously inventive logic of children.

Let us look closer at the conversation. Vicki believes that her friend Michael is Deaf. And she evidently considers this fact a notable one, since she mentions it when she presents her toy to Carol. She has learned that, in the world of her parents and their friends, when one wishes to say something of note about someone, terms like "Deaf" and "hearing" are obligatory. Even at age five, she knows that in conversations about people one needs to refer to the person's status. This conversation would have continued unremarkably except for the fact that Vicki was wrong about Michael.

What apparently has impressed Vicki about Michael is that he uses signs. To her, hearing people do not use signed language and therefore lack ways to make themselves understood. To her, Michael's ability to converse with her in her language is sufficient evidence that he is Deaf. But the older child knows better: there are characteristics other than signing that determine whether someone is really Deaf.

Children are astute observers of the world—they are often "wrong" for ₅ the most interesting reasons and "right" for reasons we never expect. This quality makes them revealing theorists. As we see in Vicki's case, a child's insight can be useful for bringing out hidden definitions for a supposedly straightforward word like "deaf."

When Vicki reaches her older sister's age, she will be able to identify other elusive but important properties from which one can deduce whether a person is Deaf. At age seven, Helen can detect subtle differences in movement contours between native or very fluent signers and those who have learned the language relatively recently; she knows that inexperienced signers often distort circular movements or add wrong movements to signs. She also watches how the person mouths while signing; skilled signers mouth along with signs in characteristic ways, and unskilled signers mouth in yet another recognizable style. And she is better able than Vicki to decipher the meanings of signs; a wrong choice of sign in a sentence might tip her off to the signer's true status. Hearing children of Deaf parents sometimes confuse her if they sign as well as their parents, but this is a mistake even her own parents might make. And Helen has also learned that another of Michael's characteristics is his ability to hear.

One might expect that characteristics other than signing would be important in distinguishing Deaf from hearing persons: the ability or the inability to speak, or even the ability or inability to hear sound. But these seem irrelevant to Vicki. There may be an easy explanation for this: Deaf children cannot hear, thus perhaps they do not appreciate the ability of others to perceive sound.

We think this explanation is too simple. We do not believe that Vicki's conception of the world simply lacks an "auditory" sense and that her view of the world is consequently limited to what remains. Instead, we believe her "error" is typical of young children her age who are forming hypotheses about how the world works. Vicki's error is an attempt to formulate an analysis of the world within the set of assumptions and ideas to which she has been exposed. The assumptions and ideas in this case involve her family's ways of determining the status of visitors, such as whether Michael is Deaf or hearing. A hearing child would have an equally restricted range of possible guesses about the world, based on the beliefs shared by the family. For example, white middle-class children understand that black people have some distinctive physical characteristic, but they are sometimes confused about who is to be called "black"; we know one young child who refers to all dark-haired men as black.

Sam Supalla once described to us his childhood friendship with a hearing girl who lived next door. As Sam's story went, he had never lacked for playmates; he was born into a Deaf family with several Deaf older brothers. As his interests turned to the world outside his family, he noticed a girl next door who seemed to be about his age. After a few tentative encounters, they became friends. She was a satisfactory playmate, but there was the problem of her "strangeness." He could not talk with her as he could with his older brothers and his parents. She seemed to have extreme difficulty understanding even the simplest or crudest gestures. After a few futile attempts to converse, he gave up and instead pointed when he wanted something, or simply dragged her along with him if he wanted to go somewhere. He wondered what strange affliction his friend had, but since they had developed a way to interact with each other, he was content to accommodate to her peculiar needs.

One day, Sam remembers vividly, he finally understood that his friend was indeed odd. They were playing in her home, when suddenly her mother walked up to them and animatedly began to move her mouth. As if by magic, the girl picked up a dollhouse and moved it to another place. Sam was mystified and went home to ask his mother about exactly what kind of affliction the girl next door had. His mother explained that she was HEARING and because of this did not know how to SIGN; instead she and her mother TALK, they move their mouths to communicate with each other. Sam then asked if this 10 girl and her family were the only ones "like that." His mother explained that no, in fact, nearly everyone else was like the neighbors. It was his own family that was unusual. It was a memorable moment for Sam. He remembers thinking how curious the girl next door was, and if she was HEARING, how curious HEARING people were.

When Sam discovers that the girl next door is hearing, he learns something about "others." Those who live around him and his family are now to be called "hearing." The world is larger than he previously thought, but his view of himself is intact. He has learned that there are "others" living in his neighborhood, but he has not yet learned that others have different ways of thinking. Perhaps others are now more prominent in his world, and his thoughts about the world now have to acknowledge that they exist in some relation to himself, but it does not occur to him that these others might define him and his family by some characteristic they lack.

In fact, in almost all the stories of childhood we have heard from Deaf children of Deaf families, hearing people were "curious" and "strange" but mostly were part of the background. The children's world was large enough with family and friends that the existence of "others" was not disruptive. At the age when children begin to reflect on the world, we see an interesting positioning of the self with respect to "others," people like Sam's playmate and her mother. Sam has not yet understood that the outside world considers him and his family to have an "affliction"; to him, immersed in the world of his family, it is the neighbors who lack the ability to communicate.

But before long, the world of others inevitably intrudes. We can see children learning about the minds of others in stories Deaf adults tell about their childhoods. A Deaf friend of ours, Howard, a prominent member of his community, made a revealing comment to a mixed audience of hearing and Deaf people. All members of his family—his parents and brother as well as aunts and uncles—are Deaf. He told the audience that he had spent his early childhood among Deaf people but that when he was six his world changed: his parents took him to a school for Deaf children. "Would you believe," he said, pausing expertly for effect, "I never knew I was deaf until I first entered school?"

Howard's comment caused the intended stir in the audience, but it was clear to us that some people thought it meant that Howard first became aware of his audiological deficiency when he was six—that he had never realized before that he could not hear sounds. But this was not his meaning at all.

Howard certainly knew what "deaf" meant. The sign DEAF was part of his   15
everyday vocabulary; he would refer to DEAF people whenever he needed to
talk about family and friends, in much the same way as Vicki mentioned that
Michael was DEAF. When Howard arrived at school, he found that teachers
used the same sign he used for himself at home, DEAF. But it did not take him
long to detect a subtle difference in the ways they used the sign.

The child uses DEAF to mean "us," but he meets others for whom DEAF
means "them, not like us." He thinks DEAF means "friends who behave as expected," but to others it means "a remarkable condition." At home he has
taken signing for granted as an activity hardly worth noticing, but he will
learn at school that it is something to be talked about and commented on.
Depending on what school a child attends, he may be forbidden to use
signed language in the presence of his teachers. He will then have to learn
how to carry out familiar activities within new boundaries, to learn new social contexts for his language. Skills he learned at home, such as to tell stories with detail about people and events, are not likely to be rewarded by
teachers who do not know the language. His language will be subordinated
to other activities considered more important, notably learning how to "use
his hearing," and to "speak" (Erting 1985b).

The metaphor of affliction, as it is used to describe deaf children, represents a displacement from the expected, that is, from the hearing child.
Howard and Sam were used to a certain mode of exchange at home, certain
ways in which Deaf friends and family acknowledge each other. But the
alien organization of the school, from its hierarchical structure and its employment of hearing people to its insistence on speech, makes plain to the
child that an entirely different set of assumptions is in force. Even the familiar—adults in his school whom he recognizes as DEAF—do not and cannot
behave in the same ways they do in his community; their roles must change
in the face of the demands of an institution that largely belongs to others
(Erting 1985a).

The child "discovers" deafness. Now deafness becomes a prominent fact
in his life, a term around which people's behavior changes. People around
him have debates about deafness, and lines are sharply drawn between people depending on what position they take on the subject. He has never
thought about himself as having a certain quality, but now it becomes something to discuss. Even his language has ceased to be just a means of interacting with others and has become an object: people are either "against"
signed language or "for" signed language. In the stories we have collected
from Deaf children of Deaf parents, the same pattern emerges over and over:
"deafness" is "discovered" late and in the context of these layers of meaning.

It is not surprising that the school is often the setting for this kind of discovery. School is not the only place where Deaf children meet others, of course, but the realization that others have different ways of thinking, and that these ways of thinking are influential in the school, is forced upon them when they arrive.

Bernard Bragg, in a personal story about his Deaf mother, represents in 20 spatial terms the vast distance between the home and the world of others. We have translated this story from a videotaped record of the National Theatre of the Deaf's original production *My Third Eye* (1973):

> I asked again where we were going but she gave no reply. For the first time I began to feel a sense of fear and foreboding. I stole glances at her face, but it was immobile and her eyes were fixed on an unseen place somewhere ahead. We rode for a long time, and then we stopped and found ourselves in front of an enormous building. . . . We walked into the building, and once inside I was immediately struck by a medicinal, institutional smell. This did not look like a hospital, or like any other building I had seen before. My mother bent down, turned me toward her, and said: "This is where you will get all your education. You will live here for a while. Don't worry, I will see you again later." Then she couldn't seem to say any more, she hugged me quickly, gave me a kiss, and then, inexplicably, left.[1]

The spotlight dims and Bragg disappears in the darkness. The audience feels a brief but powerful sense of loss. For generations of Deaf people who have left home for school, this story evokes intense images of encountering more than just an unknown place. Bragg chooses powerful triggers: his mother's unusual inarticulateness, the looming size of the school building, the cavernous halls, and the sharpest image of all, the unfamiliar, faintly threatening institutional smell. The smell wraps around him, frightening him, and when he reaches for his mother she is gone. Her parting words, about education and school, are hardly comforting.

Deaf children in hearing families face an equally unusual and complementary dilemma. Compare Howard's and Sam's stories with that of Tony, a child of hearing family who learns that, as a result of medical treatment of childhood diseases, he has become deaf at age six.

> I don't remember any one moment when I thought to myself, "I can't hear." Rather it was slowly assimilating a combination of different

---

1. Translated by the authors [Padden's and Humphries' note].

things. I had been ill for a long time. I remember the repeated visits
to the doctor, until finally somehow I sensed a permanence to what
had been happening to me. I remember my parents worrying about
me, and at some point everyone seemed concerned about my illness.
It was at that point I felt changed, and when I thought about how I
was changed, my thought was: "I'm the only one like this."

When this child referred to himself as "deaf," he meant an intensely individual and personal condition. The illness had affected him and no one
else in his family. There were no others like himself:

I had a second cousin who was deaf but I decided I wasn't like her at
all. She used her hands, she signed. I wasn't like her—I talked and I
was like everyone else, except I couldn't hear. There wasn't anyone
else in my hometown who was deaf, except I guess for this woman
down the road we called "mute," who lived with her sister. She didn't
talk and she and her sister had this private home sign language
they used with each other. I wasn't any of them.

For Tony, being deaf meant being set apart from his family and friends;
he was "deaf" and had had an "illness." In contrast, Sam, the Deaf child of
Deaf parents, thought of being "Deaf" not as a consequence of some event,
but simply as a given. For Sam, "Deaf" was not a term used to refer to him
personally, but was just a normal way of describing himself and everyone he
knew.

Another child of hearing parents, Jim, told us that his hearing loss was
not diagnosed until he was almost seven years old (his "difficulties" were attributed to other causes). He remembered that as a child, "I thought everyone
lipread. But it always puzzled me that others seemed to lipread better than I
could." Later, when his loss was discovered, he began to wear a hearing aid,
and his new teachers taught him another way of describing the difference
between himself and others. He was told that the difference didn't have to do
with lipreading ability; it had to do with his not being able to hear.

In contrast to Vicki and Helen, who watch people's signing abilities, Jim
was attentive to mouthing behaviors of the people around him, who did not
sign. As a very young child he was probably not aware that he was "lipreading," but he knew oral behaviors were important in social exchanges.

As an exercise contrasting Sam and Howard's world with that of Tony
and Jim, let us imagine under what sorts of dependencies or conditions certain behaviors follow others in Deaf and hearing families. In Deaf families,
people signal one another by touching or by making a movement into another's visual range. Making a small vibration on a table or the floor is also

possible, and for some people in certain ranges, one can call loudly. After one person acknowledges the other, they begin to interact in other ways. They look at each other, and they use signs.

But in a hearing family, the types of behaviors used to signal one another are different. One person can move his mouth and cause another person's behavior to change. And they do not even have to be visible to each other; someone can move his mouth and make another person come into the room. Once one person acknowledges the other, they alternate moving mouths. Sometimes they look at each other, but sometimes they do not.

We can imagine that Jim, a deaf child whose hearing family did not even realize he was deaf, must have noticed "strange" dependencies between events and behaviors. One behavior would suddenly be provoked, and it would not be clear to the young boy what the stimulus was. Imagine Jim sitting in a room near a door. Suddenly his mother appears, walking purposefully to the door. She opens the door, and there is a visitor waiting on the doorstep. But if the child opens the door at another time, odds are that no visitor will be there. How does the child, who does not hear the doorbell, understand what the stimulus is for the odd behavior of opening a door and finding someone standing there? We can only guess. We know only that Jim assumed other people had powers not yet discernible to him, such as better lipreading skills.

_·_-·_-·_-·_-·_

Jim's story and the other stories we have recounted are about how children learn the significant arrangements of their worlds. Jim's theory about other people's lipreading powers is not a bad one; it is consistent with our point that his hypotheses follow from the set of assumptions held by his family about how to conduct one's life. What Jim's and the other cases have in common is that being able or unable to hear does not emerge as significant in itself; instead it takes on significance in the context of other sets of meaning to which the child has been exposed.

As a final example to drive home this point, we turn to the story of Joe, 30 the youngest child of a Deaf family on a farm in the heart of Indiana. Joe told us, "I never knew I was hearing until I was six. I never suspected in any way that I was different from my parents and siblings."

It seems ludicrous to imagine a hearing child who does not know he can hear. Is a child like this unresponsive to sounds? Are we to imagine a hearing child who discovers sound at the age of six? Of course not. Joe did know about sound. He responded to sounds, and his conception of the world included sound. But in the flow of everyday life he had no cause to think about sound in anything but an incidental way. He probably thought about it as often and as consciously as children reflect on the fact that they have feet.

The key part of his comment lies in the sentence "I never suspected I was in any way different from my parents and siblings." This is not a case of pretended deafness; Joe did not fail to hear, but simply understood sound in a way he could reconcile with the experiences of his family. We can imagine a range of phenomena in this child's world that have double but compatible interpretations: a spoon falls and makes a sound as it hits the floor. Someone picks it up, not simply because it made a sound but because it slipped from view. The farmer goes out to milk the cows not only because they make noises, but because it is daybreak, the time set aside for milking. A door slams, air rushes into the room, and objects on the table rattle and wobble. Many sounds coincide with nonauditory events, to which Joe would have seen his parents responding. His parents' world gave him no reason to identify sound as a primary cause of events.

One might ask how a hearing child would understand a sound that had no corresponding nonauditory event. What if the door slammed in another room and his family did not respond? Would he not see this as odd, or even as a contradiction? We might imagine a moment when the child is startled by a loud noise, looks at his family, and is puzzled by their lack of response. But the child does not yet have a basis for being "puzzled." He does not have an alternative explanation. The most striking observation hearing children of Deaf parents make about their early years is that it never occurs to them until they are older that there is anything unusual about their abilities. For young children immersed in the world of their families, there is not yet space for contradictions.

These stories by adults about their childhood memories reveal a rare perspective on the question of how the world comes to mean what it does. The conventional belief is that there are certain immutable events, such as sound, that do not need translation and can be known directly. But Joe's story reminds us that very little is not filtered through the larger pattern of everyday life. Sound is not an entity that is free of interpretation, but something that emerges within a system of knowledge. One does not merely "hear" thunder, but also must assimilate its place in relation to all other activity of the world, how to react to it, how to talk about it, how to know its relationship to other sounds. For both Deaf and hearing people, sound finds its place against the larger pattern of everyday life.

— — — — — — —

Up to this point we have been vague in our references to the "patterns of everyday life" or "sets of assumptions and ideas about the world" to which we say the children have been exposed. Before explaining what we mean by these references, we should make clear what we do not mean. We are not referring to the children's behavior as "adjustments" that they make in order to "cope" with extraordinary features of their lives, such as the inability to hear. We do not see Vicki's, Howard's or Sam's everyday signing activity with their families as an adjustment to not hearing, nor do we see their sign language as a compensation for the fact that they do not hear. "Adjustments" are what take place later in Deaf children's lives, when they arrive at school and find that their home practices are different from those of the new environment. They are startled to encounter a different set of beliefs, and must adjust to them. They must learn an alternative definition for "deaf," and new ways of interacting with the adults in their schools.

Instead, what we have been referring to are the more basic patterns of interpretation that lead Sam to ask him mother about the curious people next door, or that keep a child like Joe, who hears, from realizing he is different in any way from his Deaf family. A simple characterization of these behaviors in terms of "deafness" is not helpful, for stories like those of Sam and Joe are not unusual if compared to the way *all* children learn about the world.

Our explanation of this phenomenon is influenced by the work of theorists such as Clifford Geertz (1973), who characterizes the human being as an "unfinished animal" dependent on worlds of significant symbols. In Geertz's terms, the special condition of human beings is that their behaviors are guided by, indeed are dependent on, the presence of significant arrangements of symbols, which he calls "culture." The human capacity for culture appears over an astonishing range of specific symbol systems or "cultures." Each culture prescribes "a set of control mechanisms—plans, recipes, rules, instructions . . . for the governing of behavior" (1973:44).

By definition, cultures are highly specific systems that both explain things and constrain how things can be known. Sam wondered why the girl next door behaved so strangely. His mother offered a sensible explanation: the girl had some significantly different feature that led her to behave unlike us. Sam found this explanation completely sensible. And conversely, cultures limit the capacity to know. Howard never knew he was "deaf" until he started school; his family life did not prepare him for the odd definitions of "deaf" he would later encounter. His is not a story about failing to understand the meaning of deafness, but a story of cultural difference.

This concept of culture also explains Joe's supposedly naive ideas about himself. Joe should retrieve a fork that has fallen to the floor because eating utensils that disappear from the table should be placed back on the table; the fact that they make a sound when they fall is incidental. In Jim's hearing family, forks that fall to the floor and make a sharp noise upon contact require a look in the direction of the noise, followed by retrieval of the fork. We do not know what Jim's beliefs about sound are, but from his comments about lipreading we can deduce that he has correctly understood another significant feature in his family's everyday patterns—the role of speaking. His idea that the rest of his family have superior lipreading skills follows from his knowledge that in his family's culture interaction is crucially based on speaking.

We have used these particular examples to highlight a central point. The stories tell us not about "childish" or "naive" views of the world, but rather about the unfolding of the human symbolic capacity. Children spend their time learning what things are supposed to mean and how to think about relationships between events. As children living in the world of their caretakers, they are powerfully guided by the conventions of their culture. From the stories we have included here, we see the different ways the "recipes" and "instructions" of their worlds guide the perceptions and theories of children like Vicki, Joe, and Jim. 40

But here we want to focus on the similarities between the early experiences of Vicki, Helen, Sam, Howard, and Joe. There are recurrent themes that underlie their stories, a foundation of meaning that does not exist by coincidence, nor by the presence of a common physical condition. What unites their cases is the fact that each has gained access to a certain cultural history, the culture of Deaf people in America.

REFERENCES

Erting, C. (1985a). Cultural conflict in a school for deaf children. *Anthropology and Education Quarterly, 16,* 225–243.

Erting, C. (1985b). Sociocultural dimensions of deaf education: Belief systems and communicative interaction. *Sign Language Studies, 47,* 111–125.

Geertz, C. (1973). *Interpretation of culture.* New York: Basic Books.

National Theatre of the Deaf (Producer). (1973). *My third eye* [Video].

about the text

1. What do Padden and Humphries mean when they note that Deaf people learn at an early age that "one needs to refer to [a] person's status" when talking about that person (paragraph 3)? What sorts of statuses might they be referring to? Why?

2. What various and sometimes contradictory meanings does the term "Deaf" have for people who are Deaf? Why? What specifically do Padden and Humphries have in mind when they write of the "metaphor" of "affliction" that surrounds deafness for hearing people (paragraph 17)?

3. Padden and Humphries emphasize that the interpretation of sounds like thunder or speech, or gestures like waving or signing, makes sense only within "systems of knowledge" (paragraph 34). What different systems of knowledge do Deaf and hearing people have? What about the systems of knowledge that the hearing children of Deaf parents have? How do these systems develop? Why? In what ways is each system logical?

4. How do Padden and Humphries define "adjustments" (paragraph 35)? Why? What relationships exist between adjustments and culture? Which comes first? Why?

on language use

5. If you are a hearing person, how did you come to be aware that you can hear? If you do not know, consider why not. If you are Deaf or your hearing status has changed during your lifetime, how did you learn that you are deaf or become aware that your hearing status was changing?

6. What specific strategies do Padden and Humphries use to avoid what they term the "traditional way of writing about Deaf people"? How effective are these strategies? To what extent is the authors' perspective novel to you? Why?

for writing

7. While this essay focuses on how Deaf people learn that they are different from hearing people, all of us have had the experience of realizing that we—or our families—are somehow different from those around us and that the difference matters. Write an essay in which you recount such an experience, reflecting on what you learned from it.

8. Padden and Humphries conclude their selection by talking about culture. Write an essay in which you explain an often misunderstood aspect of your native culture to an outsider, providing examples from your own experience.

The American Sign Language Fingerspelling Site

<where.com/scott.net/asl/>

Fingerspelling is an important part of American Sign Language. Signers generally use it to spell unfamiliar words, names, and some English words. Fluent signers, however, do not use fingerspelling a great deal, and it is important to appreciate that it is not the same thing as sign language. (Imagine how tedious spoken language would be if you had to spell everything you wanted to say!) On the other hand, fingerspelling is a useful skill for nonsigners to know because it facilitates basic, if clumsy, conversation with Deaf people who do not speechread. Go to <where.com/scott.net/asl/>. If you already know how to fingerspell, go straight to the quiz. If not, take a few minutes to practice the alphabet and learn how to fingerspell your name. You may then wish to try the quiz.

Can't All Deaf People Read Lips?
and Other Common Questions

••

The first selection, **Questions & Answers from Deaf Life***, comes from "For Hearing People Only," a column in the monthly magazine* Deaf Life *that answers questions submitted by hearing readers. Many of these questions have been collected in* For Hearing People Only: Answers to Some of the Most Commonly Asked Questions about the Deaf Community, Its Culture, and the "Deaf Reality" *(1993). Matthew S. Moore and Linda Levitan are the editors of* Deaf Life.*

We also include a cartoon from **Luann***, a syndicated comic strip by Greg Evans. In this strip, Tiffany insults Aaron's girlfriend, who is Deaf. Notice how Evans is able to show how Tiffany, Aaron, and his girlfriend sound as they speak.*

••

MATTHEW S. MOORE AND LINDA LEVITAN

Questions & Answers from *Deaf Life*

I've been working with a Deaf man for 20 years. He's an excellent lip-reader. Recently I met his friend, who uses sign language. I tried to communicate with him and couldn't. I was shocked. Can't all Deaf people read lips?

A: One of the most common "Hearing" misconceptions is that all deaf people have this magic ability to "read lips." All too often, the first question a hearing person asks a new deaf acquaintance is, "Can you read my lips?" (Note: This is the one question *all* deaf people can undoubtedly speechread!) Even if the answer is "yes," the hearing person will often exaggerate his or her mouth movements and talk abnormally slowly, which of course makes communication that much more difficult. If the answer is "no," the deaf person may be perceived as a poor sport and/or a nitwit, and whatever potential there was for communication will be totally nullified. ("Huh? How can she say no? She answered my question correctly, didn't she? Is she playing games?")

Lipreading involves a high proportion of guesswork and "instant mental replay." Only some 30% of all spoken sounds are visible on the lips. Many sounds, like "b," "p," and "m," are virtually impossible to distinguish by watching the mouth. And what about homonyms (homophones)—"blue" and "blew"? They look *and* sound identical! Moreover, everyone makes sounds a bit differently; everybody's voice and articulation are different. A stranger, whose speech patterns are unfamiliar to the lipreader, presents a more formidable challenge than members of the household or close friends. All this means that even a skilled lipreader must rely to some extent on guesswork to understand what's being said, using the context to fill in the inevitable gaps.

Anyway, 'lip-reading' is a misnomer. A more accurate term is *speechreading*. Speechreaders don't just look at the mouth; they read the entire face: the eyes, the way the eyebrows tilt or the brows knot when certain words are emphasized. They note changes in expression, shoulder shrugs, posture, gestures. They also note any props the speaker is carrying; their surroundings. Picking up these *associational cues* is an art in itself. It requires a high degree of attention. It can be exhausting.

Everybody (hearing as well as deaf) makes use of some degree of speechreading at times. For deaf people, it's a survival skill. Even so, some consider speechreading skill an inborn ability, like dancing. Many deaf people never become very proficient at it. If all else fails, hearing people should forget the "rubberlipping" and try the old standby, pencil and paper.

Speechreading protocol: a few words of advice

Nothing creates so much anxiety in Deaf-Hearing relations, it seems, as the   5
fateful first encounter. A few suggestions to make it a bit easier for all those involved:

1. **Facial Topography:** Many deaf people who are skilled speechreaders have difficulty "reading" men who have full or unkempt beards and/ or thick, sweeping mustaches. Men and women who don't remove sunglasses or doff hats that overshadow their faces also create difficulty for deaf readers. People who nervously shield their mouths with their hands while talking or who take frequent furtive glances to the side, breaking eye contact, drive us crazy. It's best to remain relaxed, focused, and clear as possible.

2. **Popping the Question:** If you run into a deaf person (and we're assuming that you don't know sign language or fingerspelling, which is the case with the majority of hearing folks), ask politely, in as natural a way as possible, "Can you read my lips?" or "Can you speechread me?" Don't over-enunciate (exaggerate) your question. You don't *have* to point to your lips (but most hearing people do this instinctively); if you do, do it discreetly—don't ham it up, repeatedly jabbing at the air in front of your mouth. You're not auditioning for a third-rate sit-com; you're trying to communicate.

3. **What Comes Next:** If the deaf reader shakes her/his head or says "No," be friendly. Don't shrug, throw up your hands in dismay, or mumble, "Sorry." And whatever you do, *don't* walk away. Try to establish some common ground. Get a pen and paper. Use a restaurant napkin. Scratch letters on your vertically upended palm. (Don't bother "writing" letters in the air, however—this *never* works well.) If you want to badly enough, you and your deaf reader will think of *something.* Human beings are a pretty in-genious species. Two persons who have a language barrier and *really* want to communicate will usually find a way.

Do Deaf people ever wish they were hearing?

A: Yes, primarily because they are disgusted with having to deal with the 10 constant bullshit they get from the hearing world—restrictions, discrim-ination, *can't* this, *can't* that. *And* the peculiar brand of bullshit found in the Deaf community—the gossip, the backstabbing.

Do Deaf people suffer from sensory deprivation? Most don't. Surpris-ingly, many born-deaf people don't "miss" sound, music, and spoken con-versation anywhere near as much as hearing people think they do. They don't find themselves missing what they never had. (Similarly, many people who are born blind or early-blinded, when asked if they don't miss the beauties of the visual world, colors, rainbows, and sunsets, have said that they can't miss something they've never experienced.) Late-deafened[1] people are a different matter entirely. They've lost an integral aspect of their lives they've taken for granted (as do hearing people), and their feelings of loss and pain should never be denigrated. Born-deaf adults, as a rule, tend to be well-adjusted, with a positive view of them-selves as Deaf people. They see themselves as whole persons, *not* broken

---

1. **late-deafened** becoming deaf later in life, generally as an adult, after one has learned a spoken language and been a member of hearing culture.

ears, *not* defective hearing machines, *not* deprived of "normalcy." If they don't miss the beauties of music, it's because they have other things going on in their heads and their lives that keep them occupied.

Occasionally, hearing people tell us how much they "envy" the supposed peace and quiet which (they imagine) deaf people experience in their "silent world." An understandable but patronizing sentiment. Our lives are filled with hubbub and noise—visual noise—and we're discriminated against. (We pay a pretty high price for that "peace and quiet.")

A good number of Deaf people don't see the spoken word as the supreme unit of communication. Their early experiences with speech may not be pleasant or productive. They have a fully developed, subtle, and expressive means of communication—sign language—which suits their needs perfectly. Sometimes they feel a bit sorry for hearing people who can't sign. Signing adds visual zip to one's life—why would *anyone* want to be without it?

One of the worst things about being deaf is the isolation we experience—which has nothing to do with the quality of our residual hearing and much to do with the quality of social attitudes. A problem frequently experienced by oral and mainstreamed deaf children is the absence of deaf adult mentors (a.k.a. "role models"). A number of these deaf children honestly believe that they're going to become hearing when they grow up. Since they're surrounded by hearing teachers, therapists, counselors, and staffers, and since their families and all other adults they meet are hearing, they logically assume that there are no deaf adults in the world, and therefore, once they reach adulthood, they too will be hearing. This is one reason why so many mainstreamed deaf children have "difficulties adjusting." It simply underscores the vital need to bring successful deaf/Deaf adults into these children's lives.

Anyone who has grown up in the Deaf community knows that Deaf people can be unbelievably vicious to other Deaf people—especially those whose only crime is to be "different," to aspire to something which is not the "norm," to cherish a "hearing" ambition, and to succeed in it. Deaf people trashing other Deaf people is a shameful fact of life for many of us. It originates in jealousy. Instead of encouragement and support, achievers get sneers. Instead of appreciation (let alone admiration), backstabbing. Instead of understanding, hostility. Add this to the "Hearing" discrimination and incomprehension they are already battling, and you have a pretty heavy burden, one that can be intolerable. Thus, a number of Deaf people have to deal—simultaneously—with bullshit from both Hearing and Deaf communities. Small wonder that some creative Deaf people who have labored diligently to increase understanding and acceptance of Deaf culture in the hearing world, find themselves wishing they were hearing—as a quick solution to an endlessly exasperating problem. Given this double inheritance, who *wouldn't* wish to be free from it?

What bothers a Deaf person the most about hearing people?

A: What bothers me most is when hearing people think they are complimenting you when they remark, "You are smart for a deaf person," "You did very well for a deaf person," "You speak so well for a deaf person" . . . and other variations of the same. Hearing people never compare hearing people this way. This remark automatically shows the false assumption in our society that deaf people are usually inept, not smart, or not on par with hearing people.

D. S.
Northampton, Massachusetts

A: As a congenitally deaf physician, I have a pet peeve concerning many of my colleagues who constantly use expressions such as "deaf and dumb," "weird speech pattern," "deaf-mute," "talks with gestures," etc.

I take pains to respond to each physician guilty of such entries on medical/surgical charts and/or records and explain that the above-mentioned comments are, at the least, very rude.

I am offering this example if you can use it. If nothing else, it makes *me* feel better.

F. H., M.D.
Fremont, California

A: I can think of many things that are frustrating and irritating, yet I can 20 take them in stride. However, the one thing that upsets me the most is when I am in a group of people, whether friends or family, and a story or joke is told that I cannot understand or has not been interpreted. I ask "What did you just say?" only to be told "I'll tell you later," with a wave of the hand serving as the only acknowledgment. This not only frustrates me, it makes me feel isolated. This is one of the primary reasons I prefer to be with other deaf people, and those hearing who know ASL and are willing to ensure that all present, deaf or hearing, can be full participants in the group. I have talked with other deaf in my area, and they agree this is also very frustrating. The key here, I think, is to be aware of those around you.

D. E.
Davis, California

A: What bothers me the most about hearing people is when they are speaking to you and you tell them that you did not understand and mention that you are deaf/hearing-impaired. They would respond with an "Oh, I am so sorry" and start to speak louder and very slow (very articulate). It makes it harder for me to understand them. It would help if they just spoke normally and did not raise their voice. It would also help if those people were educated about the different kinds of disabilities and how to handle any kind of situations with the handicapped people.

E. M. S.
Newbury Park, California

A: Easy . . . meeting a hearing person and having their first question be, "Do you speechread?" (of course, expecting me to get that through speechreading). I usually answer "A little," sometimes answer "No," and once answered "I try not to!" (An absurd answer to an absurd question.) It angers me that the attitude is that communication is *my* problem. Without delving too deep—the reason I resist admitting this "speechguessing" ability is that on the occasions before I learned better, I would answer "Yes" and from then on, they expected 100%, a feat I am not capable of under the best circumstances.

Maybe my next answer should be, "Do you sign?" (in sign only!!)

E. K.
Houston, Texas

1. Why is the term "speechreading" more accurate than "lipreading"? Why, in your opinion, are the strategies described for effective interactions between a hearing person and a Deaf person not intuitive to hearing people?

2. How does the *Deaf Life* column characterize the attitudes of hearing people toward Deaf people and deafness? The attitudes of Deaf people toward one another?

3. To what extent is the information here new to you? What assumptions must one make for this information to seem obvious, like "common sense"?

4. Which of the topics discussed by Matthews and Levitan are played out in the *Luann* cartoon strip? Why, according to Matthews and Levitan, is Tiffany's behavior offensive to Deaf people?

on language use

5. What typographical conventions does Greg Evans use to illustrate how the characters in this *Luann* strip sound? What do the periods between words in the first and second frames of the cartoon represent? Based on this strip, what attitude do you have toward Tiffany? Aaron? His girlfriend?

6. Talking about being different is never simple, especially when one belongs to a minority group and is talking to a member of the majority. What strategies do Matthews and Levitan use in their answers, and how successful are they?

for writing

7. Are you a member of a group that is sometimes misunderstood or mischaracterized — whether the mistake relates to something about who you are, where you grew up, where you worship (or don't), or who your friends are? What "dumb" or insensitive question do you most resent? Why? Write a response to this question, explaining how you see your situation.

8. Although Deaf people who are skilled speechreaders have usually had special training, you can get some idea of how challenging their task is. Watch one of your favorite TV programs with the sound and closed captioning off. As you watch, make notes about the things you can understand and those you can't. You'll want to write the notes during the commercials — your eyes will need to be *glued* to the set at all other times.) Write an essay in which you describe the experience of trying to speechread. Which parts of the program do you believe you understood? Why? What clues, linguistic or nonlinguistic, helped you? Which parts of the program escaped you? Why? (You also may wish to evaluate some of the *Deaf Life* comments about speechreading.) Why are some kinds of interactions easier to understand than others?

In this 1994 article from The New York Times Magazine, Andrew Solomon seeks to explain the complexities of Deaf culture to hearing readers while posing difficult questions about society's need for people to conform. Solomon is the author of The Irony Tower: Soviet Artists in a Time of Glasnost (1991) and A Stone Boat (1994), a novel about a young concert pianist's relationship to his dying mother, his sexuality, and his nationality. His most recent book is The Noonday Demon: An Atlas of Depression, which chronicles his own struggles with depression in pragmatic, social, cultural, political, and historical terms. It won the National Book Award and was a finalist for the Pulitzer Prize. Solomon is currently at work on a new book, My Nearest and Dearest Enemy: Traumatized Families and Difficult Love, which looks at how families love against the odds and focuses in part on Deaf children of hearing parents. He also writes for The New Yorker and Art Forum.

ANDREW SOLOMON

Defiantly Deaf

The protests at the Lexington Center, which includes New York's oldest Deaf school, are an important stage in the Deaf struggle for civil rights, and on April 25, the first day of student demonstrations, I ask an African-American from the 11th grade whether she has also demonstrated for race rights. "I'm too busy being Deaf right now," she signs. "My two older brothers aren't Deaf, so they're taking care of being black. Maybe if I have time I'll get to that later."

A Deaf woman standing nearby throws in a question for my benefit: "If you could change being Deaf or being black, which would you do?" The student looks confused, and is suddenly shy. Her signing gets smaller, as though she doesn't want everyone to see it. "Both are hard," she signs back. Another student intercedes. "I am black and Deaf and proud and I don't want to be white or hearing or different in any way from who I am." Her signs are pretty big and clear. The first student repeats the sign "proud"— her thumb, pointing in, rises up her chest—and then suddenly they are overcome with giggles and go back to join the picket line.

This principle is still new to me, but it has been brewing in the Deaf community for some time: while some deaf people feel cut off from the hearing world, or disabled, for others, being Deaf is a culture and a source of pride. ("Deaf" denotes culture, as distinct from "deaf," which is used to describe a pathology.) A steadily increasing number of deaf people have said that they would not choose to be hearing. To them, the word "cure" —indeed the whole notion of deafness as pathology—is anathema.[1]

---

1. **anathema** something cursed or detested.

My guide here is Jackie Roth, one of the protest's organizers—a Lexington alumna, an actress and an advocate with a practice in cross-cultural sensitivity training for hearing people. Charismatic, self-assured and sharp, she has excellent oral skills and lipreads well. She speaks and signs simultaneously, which has made her a natural for communicating with the hearing world, and, therefore, an object of suspicion among the Deaf (a position made more difficult by the fact that she has, like many influential Deaf leaders, a hearing spouse). She is unyieldingly ambitious.

"I'm Deaf of Deaf," she says. "I've always said that I'd get to the top and open as many doors as I could for the whole Deaf community. Every deaf child should know he can do anything except hear." Since 90 percent of deaf children are born to hearing parents, Deaf of Deaf carries a certain exclusivity and prestige: Deaf of Deaf have usually grown up understanding from an early age the issues that other deaf people may not take on until much later in life. "My father was a dreamer. If he hadn't been deaf, he would have done big things. His family was so ashamed of his being deaf. My mom was a pragmatist, but my father used to say I could do anything. If I said I wanted to be a singer, he never said, 'Deaf girls can't.' He just told me to sing."

With time, I will learn how unusual such attitudes are. "When I mentioned a deaf dentist to my deaf mother," the superintendent of Lexington, which is located in Jackson Heights, Queens, tells me, "she said, 'How good a dentist can he be if he's deaf?'" A powerful sense of self is, for most empowered Deaf, a product of the last 10 years. "My dad worked his whole life in a factory, printing," Jackie says. "It's one of those traditional deaf trades. The machines are so loud you can't talk anyway; if you're already deaf you won't sue when you lose hearing from the noise. Dad had to settle for that. It was the 40's, about as low a time as there was for being deaf in America. He told me never to settle." In Deaf culture, everyone begins with family and school history, then leads back to the topic at hand; it's part of the structure of intimacy I will encounter here. "Lexington isn't going to settle either," says Jackie.

An hour after I meet the two proud students, I attend a meeting between the nine-member core committee that organized this protest and the chief executive of the school. Jackie opens. "We do not accept the process by which a new C.E.O. has been named this week to the Lexington Center for the Deaf," she says. "We would like him to resign, and for a new search process to take place." Every detail of the baroquely complex search process is called into question. They want to oust the new chief executive, R. Max Gould, who would oversee the component institutions of the Lexington Center. Most would like to replace him with a Deaf candidate, but whether the

Deaf students demonstrate for more Deaf teachers and administrators at the Lexington Center in Queens.

new chief executive is Deaf or not, they want him to be approved by the Deaf community.

The center's director of public affairs says that the protests will peter out soon, that students just want an excuse to miss classes, but that is not my impression. "There are no Deaf role models at Lexington," Jackie tells members of the press four days later as the marches continue. Her signs, like her voice, are impatient, quick, funny and fluid. "Few Deaf teachers and even fewer Deaf administrators." The protesters—mostly Lexington students—watch closely. Some are wearing big placards: "The Board Can Hear but They Are Deaf to Us" and "Board Who Can Hear Don't Listen. Those Who Can't Hear Do Listen." Some are wearing "Deaf Pride" T-shirts or buttons. Individuals climb a low wall so everyone can see their rallying cheers, and the crowd chants back to them, many hands moving in repeating patterns.

The faculty representatives to the core committee—Maureen Woods, Jeff Bravin and Janie Moran—are especially vigilant. "Do you think the protest will work?" I ask. Maureen's signing is methodical and impressive. "There is no choice," she says. "It must work." Jeff interrupts. "The pressure has been building, maybe since the school was founded in 1864. Now it's exploding, and nothing can stop it."

A few days later, at another protest, Jeff and his grandmother chat con-   10
genially. "My father and my grandfather went to Lexington," Jeff says. "I am Deaf of Deaf of Deaf. We're ready to take what should be ours." Jeff is 25, a member of the "rubella[2] bulge." In the early 60's, a rubella epidemic resulted in a very high incidence of deaf children, and they have made up most of the leadership of the Deaf Pride movement.

Concurrent with these protests, Jackie is giving a performance in the New York Deaf Theater's adaptation of "The Swan." The play describes how a deaf woman of great passion (Jackie) leaves her hearing lover and finds true love with the Swan, who enables her imagination. The lover uses signed English as he speaks; the Swan begins with no language but learns perfect American Sign Language (ASL), the language of the American Deaf, which has its own syntax. Signed English, the use of word signs in English-language word order, is not actually a language at all; cumbersome and slower-paced, it is often used when hearing and deaf people interact. For Jackie's character, love is a liberation from the limitations of hearing culture. As her language, which had suffered the cramp and limitation of her lover's English-oriented signing, opens up into the bodily richness of the Swan's pure ASL, she discovers her Deaf self and becomes free.

"I didn't learn real ASL until college," says Jackie, "and what a spreading of the wings it was when it happened! Lexington's tradition of arrogant oral-ism—they've got a lot to make up for." That Jackie should take so strong a stand against oralism—a philosophy that the deaf should learn to speak like hearing people—is striking, since she is an oral "success story," a woman who can carry on a spoken conversation with little apparent diffi-culty, who could, if she wanted to, pretty much pass for hearing and who is sometimes dismissed by Deaf purists as "not really Deaf." When Lexington was founded as the first great bastion of oralism in America, it was the ide-alist wish of hearing people to teach the deaf to speak and read lips so they could function in the "real world" from which they had been excluded. How that dream went horribly wrong is the grand tragedy against which modern Deaf culture has constructed itself.

---

2. **rubella** German measles; women who have rubella while pregnant often give birth to deaf children.

WORDS, WORDS, WORDS

The story of the Deaf is the history of Deaf education, and is recounted in Harlan Lane's "When the Mind Hears," then analyzed in his "Mask of Benevolence." These are the seminal texts of the Deaf movement. In sixteenth-century Spain, for example, only those who had given confession were allowed to inherit property or title, so inbred noble families undertook the oral education of their deaf children. But it was more than 200 years before the Abbé de l'Epée pursued a vocation among the poor deaf of Paris, learned their manual language and used it to teach written French, so freeing the deaf from their prison of illiteracy and isolation.

In 1815, the Rev. Thomas Gallaudet of Connecticut traveled to the institute founded by de l'Epée in Paris, and persuaded Laurent Clerc, a teacher, to accompany him to America to establish a school in Hartford in 1817. A golden age for the American deaf followed. Clerc's French sign language mixed with indigenous American signs and a dialect used on Martha's Vineyard (where there was much hereditary deafness) to form American Sign Language. Deaf people wrote books, entered public life, achieved. Gallaudet College was founded to provide the highest advanced education to the deaf and is still the world's only Deaf university.

In "Seeing Voices," Oliver Sacks suggests that once the deaf were seen   15
to function so broadly, it was natural that they should be asked to speak. Alexander Graham Bell led the oralist movement, which culminated with the dread Congress of Milan in 1880 and an edict to ban the use of sign. The insistence on teaching English only (which prevailed until the 1980's; "I got my hands rapped if I signed," Jackie recalls) served not to raise deaf literacy, but to lower it.

Forbidding sign turned children not toward spoken English, but away from language. "We felt retarded," Jackie says. "Everything depended on one completely boring skill, and we were all bad at it. Some bright kids who didn't have that talent just became dropouts." Even those who developed pronunciation lost out. "History lessons," Jackie says. "We spent two weeks learning to say 'guillotine' and that was what we learned about the French Revolution. Then you go out and say 'guillotine' to someone with your deaf voice, and they haven't the slightest idea what you're talking about—usually they can't tell what you're trying to pronounce when you say 'Coke' at McDonald's."

Learning was supposed to happen through lip reading, a remarkably inexact science; most lip movements are associated with more than one sound, and the lip reader must guess and intuit in order to make sense of what is being said. "Pat, mat, bat," Jackie mouthed. "Now, did I say the same word three times or did I say three different words?" For someone who already speaks English—someone deafened postlingually[3]—the technique can be developed, but for someone with limited English, it is an excruciating endeavor. "Socially or in secret," Jackie says, "we always signed. No theory could kill our language."

Though at least 30 percent of deafness is genetic, more than 90 percent of deaf children are born to hearing parents. So most deaf children enter families that neither understand nor know their situation. They must identify in their peer group; they are first exposed to Deaf ways in school. When you meet a deaf person, his school is a primary mode of self-identification; it's usually told after his name but before his job. "Lexington" and "Gallaudet" were among the first signs I learned.

The Deaf debates are all language debates. "When I communicate in ASL, my native language," M. J. Bienvenu, a political activist, said to me, "I am living my culture. I don't define myself in terms of 'not hearing' or of 'not' anything else." A founder of the Bicultural Center (a sort of Deaf think tank), M. J. is gracious, but also famously terrifying: brilliant, striking-looking and self-possessed, with signing so swift, crisp and perfectly controlled that she seems to be rearranging the air in front of her into a more acceptable shape. Deaf of Deaf, with Deaf sisters, she manifests, like many other activists, a pleasure in American Sign Language that only poets feel for English. "When our language was acknowledged," she says, "we gained our freedom." In her hands "freedom"—clenched hands are crossed before the body, then swing apart and face out—is like an explosion.

The fact that ASL is a full (though not written) language, with a logical internal grammar and the capacity to express anything that can be expressed verbally, eluded scholars until William Stokoe published his ground-breaking "Sign Language Structure" in 1960. This became the basis for the Deaf activism of which Lexington's is the most recent example. "To establish the validity of ASL," Stokoe says, "we had to spend a long time dwelling on how it resembles spoken language. Now that the validity of ASL has been accepted, we can concentrate on what's interesting—how the life perceptions and experiences of a native ASL-user will differ from the perceptions and experiences of hearing people." Or, as M. J. put it, "There are many things that I can experience for which you have no equivalent." 20

---

3. **postlingually** after learning to talk.

Perception of ASL uses the language center of the brain more than the visual-emotion center. Deaf children show no predisposition to spoken language; they respond intuitively to sign, and acquire it exactly as hearing children acquire spoken languages. During the critical period for language acquisition—at its height between 18 and 36 months, dwindling around 12 years—the mind can internalize the principles of grammar and signification.[4] This paves the way for human thought. (There is no rich abstraction without words.)

Once you have learned one language, you can go on, at any age, to learn more or other languages. Spoken-written language can readily be taught to the Deaf as a second language. But to bring up deaf children without sign models is terribly dangerous. Though some remarkable ones acquire English through lip reading and residual hearing with constant attention, more often deaf children without exposure to sign bypass the key age for language acquisition without really acquiring any language at all. Once that happens, they frequently fail to develop full cognitive skills; they may suffer permanently from what has been described as a preventable form of mental retardation.

Helen Keller famously observed that being blind cuts people off from things, while being deaf cuts people off from other people. Poor communication skills result in psychosis; the National Institutes of Health had a workshop this June on the link between poor hearing (nonsigners) and violence.

Deaf of Deaf learn sign as a first language at home and are often surprised to discover that other systems of communication are used elsewhere. For the deaf children of hearing parents, school is often the place where they first encounter sign. It is not just social or intellectual stimulation that school may provide; when it is the beginning of language, school is the first awakening of the mind. As I slide deeper into Deaf culture by way of the Lexington protests, I see how a language has defined a system of thought—and I begin to imagine what M. J. may be able to experience that I may not.

---

4. **signification** meaning.

about the text

1. Whose voices do we first hear in Solomon's essay? Where are they located (literally)? Why might Solomon have chosen to begin the article at the Lexington Center for the Deaf?
2. How does Solomon describe education for the Deaf in the United States? What role has oralism played? Why? What are some consequences of oralism for many deaf people? Why?
3. What images of deaf people does Solomon present? How do they compare or contrast with representations of deaf people that you have encountered elsewhere?

on language use

4. How does Solomon describe signers and ASL? Some linguists who study sign language might claim that Solomon's description is overly simplistic and even romantic, and that it ignores the fact that sign language is not *just* making visual pictures of objects found in the real world. Which aspects of Solomon's description would linguists criticize? (It is worth remembering that most signers don't think of themselves as being poetic any more than most speakers of French think of themselves as being romantic.)

for writing

5. Investigate the arguments for and against oralism, either as a component or as a sole focus of education for Deaf people. As you look for information, pay special attention to the sources you find and how they are positioned: Are the authors hearing or Deaf? What assumptions do they make about deafness and the Deaf in society? Write an essay about your findings, summarizing the debates about oralism and arguing for the role it might play in Deaf education.
6. Do some research on Deaf education, especially residential schools. Write an essay in which you explain the role residential schools played in the past and the concerns some Deaf people currently have about the decline in number of residential schools.

part 2

THE BEST TIME TO BE DEAF

On Monday, May 2, the demonstrators go to the Queens Borough President's 25 office. It is a beautiful, sunny day, and the demonstration, though still in deadly earnest, has that air of festivity that clings to anything for which people are skipping work or school. Jackie Roth is holding forth, and so are a variety of distinguished Deaf leaders. And Greg Hlibok, a leader of the Deaf President Now movement, is expected.

In March 1988, Gallaudet University, the center of American Deaf culture, announced the appointment of a new president. Students had rallied for the school to have its first Deaf president, but the chairman, remarking that "the deaf are not yet ready to function in the hearing world," announced that a hearing candidate had been selected.

In the following week, the Deaf community as a political force came abruptly into its own. The movement that had begun with Stokoe's validation of ASL took its next great leap forward. The Deaf President Now movement made it clear that the Deaf community was able to function at any level it chose. In a week, they closed down the university, won substantial coverage in the media and staged a march on the Capitol with 2,500 supporters. The chairman resigned, and her place was taken by Jeff Bravin's father, Phil Bravin (who is also on the Lexington board). The board immediately named the first Deaf president of Gallaudet, I. King Jordan. Late-deafened in a motorcycle accident at 21, King Jordan is the most unaffectedly bicultural person I have met; against all the predictions of the hearing world, he has proved a remarkable leader while vastly increasing the school's endowment.

Deaf President Now is Lexington's inspiration. At the Borough President's office, Hlibok is electrifying. An articulate signer can build up a picture in front of himself, and the iconic content of ASL provides much of its immediacy and power. Like M. J., Hlibok takes over a substantial block of space in front of himself when he signs. He says that the Lexington board members are like adults playing with a doll house, moving deaf students like dolls. He seems to create the house in the air; by the time he has finished, you can see it and the interfering arms of the board reaching into it. It is as if his fingers have left trails of light behind them that hold the pictures he is drawing. His wrists snap sharply with conviction, and his hands open and close as if they might eventually stop in the shape of fists. The students cheer, many of them by raising their hands over their heads and waving them, fingers splayed, in Deaf applause.

In the midst of the Lexington fracas, Max Gould, the newly appointed chief executive, resigns. There are waves of astonishment. Gould claims that his appointment has been muddying the real issues facing Lexington. Seizing the air of opportunity, a board member proposes Phil Bravin as board president, and the incumbent withdraws. The Gallaudet scenario has repeated itself. Many Deaf people, when they are very excited, make loud sounds, often at very high or very low pitches, wordless exclamations of delight. In the halls of Lexington, students cheer, almost incredulous that their actions could have been fruitful, and anyone hearing is transfixed by the sound.

"It was a real sense of déjà vu,"[5] Phil Bravin would say to me one after- 30 noon a few months later. "It was so much like Gallaudet all over again, and it showed that that victory was just the beginning. It was also the best thing that could have happened to those students, no matter how many classes they missed during the protests. You can't learn civil rights from a textbook. Some of them came from families that said, 'You're deaf; don't shoot too high.' Now they know better."

At Lexington graduation, a week later, Hlibok is the speaker. In the midst of a hackneyed, boring speech, he says, rather casually, "From the time God made earth until today, this is probably the best time to be Deaf." At a victory celebration the next day, Jeff Bravin says, "We'll be running our own show now." Jackie Roth says: "It's all great. But the battle's not over." And indeed, within a month a new saga will begin over the appointment of a principal for J.H.S. 47, New York City's only public school for the deaf; once more, the Deaf will be excluded from the selection process.

SAVE THE CHILDREN

"Mainstreaming" (or "inclusion")—"the backlash," as M. J. Bienvenu calls it —is making schools ever more the locus of Deaf struggles. The Americans with Disabilities Act, in an attempt to give full educational benefits to people once shunted into second-rate special schools, has recommended that schools be made more fully accessible. Public law 94-142 maintains that everyone who can use ordinary schools should do so. For the deaf, often physically unable to learn the mainstream's means of communication, this is the worst disaster since the Congress of Milan. "Children from Spanish-

---

5. **déjà vu** literally, "already seen," a French expression used to describe the illusion that one has already observed or experienced something that is currently taking place.

speaking homes may learn English at school as a second language," says M. J. "Children from nonsigning homes who are taught only in English at school may never learn language at all." The Clinton administration has not been receptive to calls for separate Deaf schools. "It is a terrible abuse," says Oscar Cohen, Lexington's superintendent. Jackie Roth says, "It makes me sick with rage."

"There are some children who can function well in mainstream schools," says Robert Davila, an assistant secretary of Education under George H. W. Bush and a leader of the Hispanic Deaf community. "They need help from supportive families, special abilities, good language of some kind and constant individual help from teachers. Many children, even if they overcome the incredible obstacles, will be so lonely there. The Deaf school where I went was my salvation."

According to the Rowley decision, which upheld a school district's refusal to provide interpreter services to a deaf girl on grounds that she was passing, it is the obligation of the schools into which children are mainstreamed to give "sufficient" education rather than to "maximize" those students' potential. Their social welfare is not a concern.

Once considered the vanguard of Deaf separatism, M. J. Bienvenu's Bicultural Center now focuses on cooperation; it laid the groundwork for the Bi-Bi (bilingual, bicultural) movement in education, which is the Deaf community's answer to mainstreaming and an alternative to the trend in Deaf education for "total communication." 35

"Total communication" means speaking and signing at once, and it's difficult to do. Non-ASL signed languages, predicated on oral syntax as they are, are sometimes nearly incomprehensible. And the structures of English and ASL are completely different; you can no more speak English while signing in ASL than you can speak English while writing Chinese. In English, words are used in sequence; ASL often uses words simultaneously, or amalgamates them into composite signs. So in ASL, one gesture could mean "He moved from the East Coast to the West Coast." If you sign "he," then "moved," then "from" and so on, logic disappears; a visual grammar conveyed sequentially is "unnatural" and counterintutitive.

In Bi-Bi, children are encouraged to develop sign as a "natural" first language; written English is taught as a second language, and many students seem to excel at it, running close to their hearing counterparts. (It should be noted that, on average, deaf high-school graduates have a fourth-grade reading level.) The technique is gaining: Eddy Laird, superintendent of the Indiana School for the Deaf, has been one of the first to institute Bi-Bi on a full scale. It has also been used at the schools on the Gallaudet campus.

Spoken English is taught but not emphasized within the Bi-Bi system. The system's successes are astonishing, and yet the lack of spoken language is a real disability. It is striking that many of the most extreme anti-oralists themselves have and use excellent oral skills. "They're incredibly useful, and anyone who can learn them should," Jackie Roth acknowledged. "I happen to have a skill there, and it's been invaluable for me. But speech can't be taught at the cost of human growth. Balance!"

A 'FAMILY' GATHERING

Fresh from Lexington, I go to England to meet leaders of the British Deaf community. Word of the protests has reached them through the Deaf media (a broad range of local and international newspapers, newsletters, special television programs, fax and E-mail), but in Britain there has been no equivalent of Gallaudet's Deaf President Now; the situation I describe seems inconceivable. "We're 40 years behind," says Doug Alker, the only Deaf executive at the Royal National Institute for the Deaf (which the Deaf call Really Not Interested in the Deaf). "Most deaf people in Britain see themselves as victims." Hearing people often make the mistake of assuming that sign is a universal language, but there are almost as many signed as spoken languages. American Sign Language is related to French sign (because of Laurent Clerc), but British sign is extremely different.

I also visit the famed Deaf Scottish musician Evelyn Glennie, who can feel the trembling of the separate instruments of an orchestra, can modulate her voice's timbre with real beauty, can even understand words through vibration. Her solo percussion performances astonish. "If I had a deaf child," she says, "I would teach him by holding him against my body all the time, so he could feel the vibrations of my speech. I would lie with his hands on my throat, hold him against my heart, lay him on the piano so he could learn about sound and music from the air. With a hearing child, I'd do the same. Your ears are just one of a multitude of ways of experiencing sound."

Back in the United States, I attend the biennial National Association of the Deaf convention, which takes place this year in Knoxville, Tenn., with almost 2,000 Deaf participants. At Lexington, I saw Deaf people stand up to the hearing world. I learned how a TTY (a telephone-cum-typewriter device for the Deaf) works, met pet dogs who understood sign, talked about mainstreaming and oralism and the integrity of visual language. I became accustomed to doorbells that flashed lights instead of ringing. But none of this could have prepared me for the immersion that is the NAD convention, where the brightest, most politicized, most committed Deaf gather for political focus and social exchange. The association has been the center of Deaf self-realization and power since it was founded in 1880. There, it is not a question of whether the hearing will accept the existence of Deaf culture, but of whether Deaf culture will accept the hearing.

I arrive the night of the president's reception. There are 1,000 people in the grand ballroom of the Hyatt Regency, the lights turned up because these people are unable to communicate in darkness. The crowd is nearly soundless; you hear the claps that are part of the articulation of ASL, the clicks and puffing noises the deaf make when they sign, and occasionally their big uncontrolled laughter. People greet each other as if they have been waiting forever for these encounters—the Deaf community is close, closed and affectionate.

Deaf people touch each other far more than the hearing, and everyone here hugs friends. I see demonstrators I got to know at Lexington and people I talked to only in formal interviews; here at the NAD, there are no barriers and boundaries, and I, too, find myself hugging people as if I have known them forever. Yet I must be careful of the difference between a friendly and a forward embrace; how you touch communicates a world of meaning in Deaf circles. I must be careful of looking abstractedly at people signing; they will think I am eavesdropping. I do not know any of the etiquette of these new circumstances. "Good luck with the culture shock," more than one person says to me, and I get many helpful hints.

As I look across the room it seems as if some strange human sea is breaking into waves and glinting in the light, as thousands of hands move at stunning speed, describing a spatial grammar with sharply individual voices and accents. The association is host to the Miss Deaf America pageant, and the young beauties, dressed to the nines and sporting their state sashes, are objects of considerable attention. "Look how beautifully she expresses herself," says someone, pointing to one contestant, and then, of another: "Can you believe that blurry Southern signing? I didn't think anyone really signed like that!" (Regional variations of sign can be dangerous: the sign that in New York slang means "cake" in some Southern states means "sanitary napkin," which led to considerable confusion at mealtimes; my own poor articulation led me to invite someone not to have "lunch," but to have "a lesbian.")

The luminaries of the Deaf world—activists, actors, professors—mix 45 comfortably with the beauty queens. I am one of perhaps a dozen hearing people at this party. I will soon come to understand better how factionalized the Deaf community is. (M. J. Bienvenu and Jackie Roth and Greg Hlibok, for example, do not seem to like each other, though "all the factions always pull

Contestants in the Miss Deaf America pageant

together when necessary," M. J. reassures.) I will hear of the crab theory (if one crab is strong enough to climb out of the barrel, the others pull him back down; Deaf people use this metaphor to describe their community all the time), and I will see how petty ideology has split a community that once stood firmly united. Nonetheless, the basic fact of Deaf culture remains. I have heard Deaf people talk about how their "family" is the Deaf community. Rejected in so many instances by parents with whom they cannot communicate, united by their struggle with a world that is seldom understanding of them, they have formed inviolable bonds of love of a kind that are rare in hearing culture. At the National Association of the Deaf, they are unmistakable. Disconcerting though it may sound, it is impossible, here, not to wish you were Deaf. I had known that Deaf culture existed, but I had not guessed how heady it is.

The association members are a tiny minority, less than 10 percent of the nation's Deaf; most deaf people are what the Deaf call "grass roots." The week after the convention, the national Deaf bowling championships in Baltimore will attract a much larger crowd, people who go to Deaf clubs, play cards and work in blue-collar jobs. Below them in the Deaf status structure are the peddlers (the Deaf word for the mendicants who "sell" cards with the manual alphabet on subways—the established Deaf community tried as early as the 40's to get them off the streets); on Lexington Avenue around 103d

Street in New York, some homeless deaf were living on the roof of a building. "Those people also," says Jackie Roth, "whatever they have lost, have this connectedness in their own Deaf communities. It comes with the territory, so long as they are not isolated from other Deaf people."

During the following week, I will do dozens of interviews, struggling to pick up the subtleties of ASL accent that betray so much of the meaning of what people are saying. I will discuss the Deaf travel industry with Aaron Rudner, of Deafstar Travel, who started this business going, and with Joyce Brubaker, of Deaf Joy Travel, who is organizing the first Deaf gay cruise. I will watch videos of eloquent signers telling stories. I will attend seminars on ASL usage, on AIDS, on domestic violence. I will talk to Alan Barwiolek, who founded the New York Deaf Theater, about the difference between plays translated for the Deaf and Deaf plays. I will see Deaf comedians. (Ken Glickman, a.k.a. Professor Glick: "Deaf and dumb? No, I'm deaf and bright. You must be hearing and dumb or you wouldn't have asked me that. You think I'm hearing-impaired? I think you're deaf-impaired, and I can sell you, cheap, a deafing aid. This ball of cotton wool can help any profoundly hearing person who needs it. Put one in each ear and we'll be making a start. My blind dates are always deaf dates. You ever been on a deaf date? You go out with someone and then you never hear from her again.") Over dinner, Bernard Bragg will do his lyrical signed translations of William Blake while his pasta gets cold. (Signers can talk with their mouths full, but they can't easily cut up their food and talk at once.)

Gary Mowl, head of the ASL department at National Technical Institute of the Deaf, has come to the conference with his children. He often corrects their grammar and usage in ASL The importance of having a correct language—"Gallaudet ASL," an answer to standard English—has only recently been recognized. "People ask why you need to teach ASL to native signers. Why do English-speaking students study English?" I think of the sign used by the Deaf gangs of Harlem and the East Village, which is completely incomprehensible to an ASL-user.

Late one night, I am watching captioned television with Deaf friends. "When I was little, before captioning came in," one says, "we used to watch TV as a family. It was great. We would compare notes on what we saw and propose our own versions of the plot. Later, if we saw other Deaf friends who had seen the same show, we would all discuss what we thought had happened. We would construct personalities and events from our guesswork and imaginations; it was practice for the guesswork and humor we need to interpret the world. We laughed so much, and it brought us so close together." He stops for a moment, and we both look back at the television with its neatly typed messages. "Of course having captions on the news is great, but—this is so boring by comparison to the old days."

I get into a lot of conversation about interpreters: the shortage of compe- 50 tent interpreters is appalling. There is always competition between CODA (Children of Deaf Adults; refers only to hearing people) professional inter- preters and non-CODA ones. The complexities and ambivalences of CODA- Deaf relations, humorously but knowingly conveyed by Lou Ann Walker in "A Loss for Words," are a big part of Deaf culture. (I have the good fortune to work with a CODA named Marie Taccogna, a gifted interpreter who trans- lates both language and culture.) At public meetings, there are often inter- preters who are "doing some kind of a dance," says Rob Roth, who is at the National Association of the Deaf to represent AT&T, "which is lovely as inter- pretive performance but conveys no information in a language I speak. Hear- ing people love their picturesque eloquence."

A New York City court recently refused to get a new interpreter for a plaintiff who couldn't understand the trial as it was interpreted to her. There are lawsuits pending involving Beth Israel and New York University hospi- tals for failure to provide interpreting services. Early this year, Leah Hager Cohen—daughter of Oscar Cohen—published an eloquent book, "Train Go Sorry," which follows the careers of a few students at Lexington, and through a stunningly empathetic examination of their stories and her own creates a brilliant narrative of Deaf culture. One of the most moving passages in that book describes the death of Leah Cohen's grandfather. Oscar tried to stay in the hospital to interpret for his father, but was prevented on grounds that the hospital had an interpreter. The interpreter was in fact off duty for the week- end, and Oscar's father died without being able to communicate with his doctors, without knowing what was happening to him or where he was go- ing, without being consulted about his own treatments.

On Thursday, there is a College Bowl involving Gallaudet, the National Technical Institute of the Deaf and California State University at Northridge. I am impressed by the questions (I cannot answer more than half), and I re- member how, 20 years ago, the deaf were generally held to be somewhat re- tarded. Friday night is Miss Deaf America. For the talent section, two girls do monologues about AIDS. There is some signed poetry, some signed music. The National Deaf Dance Theater, whose members pick up the nuance of mu- sic through its vibrations, do a dramatic stage piece, and Bob Daniels, a partly deaf performer, does a dance and sign number to "With You on My Arm" from "La Cage Aux Folles." The emcees are Bernard Bragg (who could, tonight, be Bert Parks) and Mary Beth Barber (who was Miss Deaf America in 1980). For the onstage interview, each of the semifinalists is asked how she feels about doctors' attempts to cure the deaf. "If someone's unhappy with be-ing deaf and he wants to change it, that's up to him," says Genie Gertz, Miss Deaf New York, succinctly. "I wouldn't ever change it. Why would I?" I am in the cheering section for Genie, the beautiful daughter of Russian Jewish par-ents who came to this country from Leningrad when she was 8. In an elo-quently rendered monologue written for the talent section, she tells the story of her parents' struggle against Communism, and of the freedom everyone found in the United States—which included, for her, the move from being a social misfit to being Deaf and proud. I have made endless jokes about the Miss Deaf America Contest and yet in reality it's surprisingly moving. It is such a striking idea, such a radical one, that you can be Deaf and glamorous.

The V.I.P. party after the gentle, radiant Miss Deaf Maryland has won is back in the grand ballroom at the Hyatt. I am talking to Alec Naiman, whom I first met at Lexington. A world traveler, he was one of the pilots in this year's Deaf fly-in at the Knoxville airport. We are discussing a trip he made to China. "I met some Deaf Chinese people my first day, and went to stay with them. Deaf people never need hotels; you can always stay with other Deaf people. We spoke different signed languages, but we could make ourselves understood. Though we came from different countries, Deaf culture held us together. By the end of the evening we'd talked about Deaf life in China, and about Chinese politics, and we'd understood each other linguistically and culturally." I nod. "No hearing American could do that in China," he says. "So who's disabled then?"

At 2:30, I still have not left. I remember that one Deaf sociologist is writ-ing a thesis on Deaf goodbyes. Until the 1960's, deaf people had no means of communication except letters, telegrams or personal appearances. If you wanted to organize dinner with a friend, you had to go to his house; you could take two days just inviting people to a party. Saying goodbye was never easy; you would suddenly remember whatever you had forgotten to tell, and, knowing it would be some time before you could make contact again, you would keep saying goodbye, and you would keep on not leaving. "It's a Deaf party," people had said to me of more than one event. "It'll go on forever." And so this evening, it is impossible to tear yourself away. People are even more physical, more flirtatious than usual. Upstairs there is danc-ing to loud, pulsing music whose beat goes right along the floor and up your legs. No matter how great the noise, you can dance and sign—the blurring edge between what bodies say to each other as bodies and what they say to each other with words. I finally tear myself away near 4. But I am of the im-pression that some people will never leave, that the sun will rise and set be-fore that intense, exuberant conversation will draw to a close.

about the text

1. Why do many deaf people in America believe that "this is probably the best time to be Deaf" (paragraph 31)? How does Solomon's discussion of the situation in England confirm such a claim?

2. What sort of culture shock does Solomon experience at the NAD conference? How does his description of NAD reinforce the idea that for its members, the issue is whether Deaf culture will accept the hearing?

3. Solomon comments that "it is impossible [at the NAD conference] not to wish you were Deaf" (paragraph 45). How appropriate is such a claim? Why? How would you react, for example, if, in describing the annual meeting of the National Association of Black Journalists, someone who wasn't African American claimed that she or he wished to be black? Or that she or he wished to be a journalist? Or if a minority journalist covering a meeting of a white supremacist organization, seeing the strong bond between the members, commented that he or she wished to be white? Are these scenarios comparable? Why or why not?

4. How does this section of the article complicate the description of the Deaf community that Solomon is offering readers? How do the new information and topics contribute to your understanding of the Deaf community?

on language use

5. Make a list of all the comments that the signers in Solomon's article make about language. (For example, "Look how beautifully she expresses herself" [paragraph 44].) In what ways are Deaf communities like hearing communities when it comes to attitudes about language and language variation?

6. What generalizations can you make about the challenges interpreters face in moving from ASL to spoken English or spoken English to ASL? What does Solomon mean when he claims that Marie Taccogna "translates both language and culture" (paragraph 49)?

for writing

7. This article was written in 1994, during the Clinton administration. Research the policies of the last four presidential administrations toward education for the Deaf and the reasons for their supporting these policies. Did they, for example, support mainstreaming? What was their policy with respect to residential schools? How has the Americans with Disabilities Act (Public law 94-142) affected deaf education in the United States? Write an essay reporting on the effects of this act.

8. Solomon discusses several technologies that have made it easier for the Deaf to communicate and to understand television broadcasts. Investigate the ways that technology continues to improve communication among the Deaf, especially with regard to Web cameras and the Internet.

$$\boxed{\text{part } 3}$$

Finding the Cure, Fighting the Cure

How to reconcile this Deaf experience with the rest of the world? Should it be 55 reconciled at all? M. J. Bienvenu has been one of the most vocal and articulate opponents of the language of disability. "I am Deaf," she says to me in Knoxville, drawing out the sign for "Deaf," the index finger moving from chin to ear, as though she is tracing a broad smile. "To see myself as Deaf is as much of a choice as it is for me to be a lesbian. I have identified with my culture, taken a public stand, made myself a figure within this community." Considerably gentler now than in her extremist heyday in the early 80's, she acknowledges that "for some deaf people, being deaf is a disability. Those who learn forced English while being denied sign emerge semilingual[6] rather than bilingual, and they are disabled people. But for the rest of us, it is no more a disability than being Japanese would be."

This is tricky territory. If being deaf is not a disability, then deaf people should not be protected under the Americans with Disabilities Act. It should not be legally required (as it is) that interpreters be provided in hospitals and other public service venues, that a relay operator be available on all telephone exchanges, that all televisions include the chip for caption access. It should not be necessary for the state to provide for separate schools. Deaf people should not be eligible for Social Security Disability Insurance (which they often claim). Those who say that being deaf is not a disability open themselves up to a lot of trouble.

Few words provoke a more passionate response in deaf people than "cochlear implant." Approved in 1985, cochlear implants are the closest thing to a "cure" for deafness. A tiny chip is surgically implanted in the inner ear and connected to a magnet just under the skin, which attracts another magnet in a transmitter attached behind the ear. A wire leads from that to a "speech processor" you can clip to your belt. The processor converts sound into electrical impulses and sends them to the implant, which conveys them to the brain, where they are processed as sound would be. The result is an approximation of hearing.

Supporters say implants allow people to overcome a terrible disability, giving those who would be marginalized access to normal life. Opponents complain, first, of the limitations of the implant itself: that it is dangerous,

---

6. **semilingual** having mastered no language.

deforming and ineffectual; that it makes people un-deaf without making them hearing. They object also to the very idea of trying to cure the deaf. Paddy Ladd, a British Deaf scholar, calls implants "The Final Solution." The problem is worsened by the fact that the implants are most effective when put in children at about age 2. ("Like the Nazis," says M. J., "they seem to enjoy experimenting on little children.")

Decisions about implanting are therefore usually made by parents, most often by hearing parents (though *Hearing Health* magazine published an anecdote of a 90-year-old deaf mother who tried to browbeat her 70-year-old son into getting implants). This feeds into an ongoing debate about who the "parents" of deaf children are—their biological progenitors or the Deaf community.

Cochlear implants are not very dangerous. Surgical complications are 60 unusual, though several surgeons scoffed at the Cochlear Corporation's assertion that the surgery is "comparable to a tonsillectomy"; some people have suffered disfiguring facial paralysis that appears to be connected to the surgery. The implant has been around for only about 30 years, but so far they have not caused the complications that have resulted from other placements of foreign material in the body. (Deaf activists talk about the horrors of silicone implants and pacemakers.) The implant interferes with certain diagnostic tests (magnetic resonance imaging, etc.), but the electronic stimulation the implant creates appears to have a positive effect on the nerve tissue that surrounds it. Having a wire coming out of your neck can make you look like an extra from a bad "Star Trek" episode, but it is possible to grow hair so the wire is generally hidden. Much National Association of the Deaf propaganda about the danger of implants is alarmist; some of it is positively inaccurate.

The question of the effectiveness of the implants is more complicated. Cochlear implants are sometimes very effective, often somewhat effective and sometimes practically useless. A late-deafened[7] adult who "regained" his hearing with an implant said it made everyone sound like R2D2 with laryngitis. For late-deafened people, however, implants can be a godsend; the approximation of sound they provide is sufficient for people already functional in spoken language to understand much of what they hear. Lord Ashley, the Member of Parliament who has been one of Britain's most inspired campaigners for civil rights, was deafened 20 years ago and now has implants; he spoke on the phone with apparent ease, and said that he has no

---

7. **late-deafened** becoming deaf later in life, generally as an adult, after one has learned a spoken language and been a full-fledged member of hearing culture.

trouble speaking to people he knows, one on one, though he might have difficulty with a new voice or with a busy conversation.

Prelingual deaf adults who have the implants often find them ineffective
or just irritating; whether this is because they are unaccustomed to interpreting sound and would find that difficult even if they were given perfect hearing is unclear. For small children, there have been mixed results. The F.D.A.
failed to set language acquisition as one of the criteria for approval. Almost
all children with implants have some "useful" perception of sound, but the
sound they receive is often too garbled for them to interpret it as language,
and so some fall into that frightening category of the cognitively retarded
who develop no real language. The Cochlear Corporation can provide the
statistics to show that many implanted children learn more and better oral
language, but "more and better" is not really enough, especially if this is to
be your sole mode of communication forever.

The problem—in practical terms—is that parents too often want to believe that the implants make their children hearing, which they do not do.
Implants are not a cure; to treat them as a cure is a dire mistake. The children who receive them are often not given any special Deaf education. Dr.
Robert Ruben, an ear-nose-and-throat specialist at Montefiore Hospital in the
Bronx, said: "If I had a deaf child, I would implant one ear, leaving the other
free in case cures develop that require an intact inner ear. I would bring up
that child bilingually. Parents could phase out sign later on if they wanted,
but it should not be abandoned until it becomes clear that the child can develop satisfactory oral language. The worst mistake is for parents to neglect
the one most important thing—that language of any kind, no matter what
kind, must somehow be got into the child soon enough." There are also miracle stories of children for whom the implant has been peerless, but they are
unusual and unpredictable.

The implant destroys all residual hearing a child might have. Though
accurate hearing tests can be done on infants, it is impossible to determine
how well those children might use their residual hearing. Anyone with a
hearing loss over 90 decibels is classified as "profoundly deaf." I met people
with a 50-decibel hearing loss who could understand me only with interpretation or lip reading; Jackie Roth is categorized as "profoundly deaf," but I
could talk to her as I would to a hearing person. "I don't know," she says to
me. "I just get a lot when people speak to me." Hearing loss is measured as
an average of loss in various registers, so someone with a 100-decibel loss
could have good perception for very high frequency sound—and most
sounds operate at many frequencies. Further, detection of sound and dis-

crimination of sound are two separate abilities. Some people can discriminate sound well beyond their ability to detect it. So deciding which children
are so deaf that they need implants is not easy, because by the time you can
detect discriminatory abilities, it is too late for the implants to be the basis of
primary language acquisition.

Cochlear implants remind me, more than anything else, of sex-change 65
surgery. Are transsexuals really members of their chosen sex? Well, they
look like that other sex, take on the roles of that other sex and so on, but they
do not have all those internal workings of the other sex, and cannot create
children in the organic fashion of members of the chosen sex. Cochlear implants do not allow you to hear, but rather to do something that looks like
hearing. They give you a process that is (sometimes) rich in information and
(usually) free of music. They make the hearing world easier, but they do not
give you hearing. What they give you has value, so long as you know in advance what that is.

While the implant debate rages, doctors are searching for more sophisticated and effective cures for the deaf. There are many kinds of deafness, but
most come from the loss of the auditory hair cells in the cochlea. These cells,
which receive sound in a form in which it can be conveyed along nerve pathways to the brain, are produced in the first three months of the embryonic
period and are then incapable of regenerating. Once you lose them, conventional wisdom has always had it, they're gone. In the early 1980's, Jeffrey Corwin, working with sharks in Hawaii, noticed that adult sharks have larger
ears than baby sharks—larger in their number of hair cells. This indicated
that it is possible for hair cells to be produced by vertebrates in a postfetal
state; and subsequent research demonstrated that fish can produce hair cells
throughout life, even to replace hair cells that have been lost. A few years
later, Douglas Cotanche discovered that baby chicks whose hair cells were
partly destroyed regenerated hair cells; observable lesions of the inner ear
simply disappeared. When deafened chicks were tested, it was confirmed
that they had recovered hearing.

This blew away the notion that hair cells cannot regenerate. In 1992, researchers in Jeffrey Corwin's lab fed retinoic acid to pregnant mice, and the
result was that the mice were born with extra hair cells. Building on this, a
few scientists began work to see what effect retinoic acid might have on the
inner ear of mammals past the usual prenatal stage for developing sensory
cells, and in April 1993, a team of researchers working under the supervision
of Robert Ruben published an article in *Science* in which they described
their unprecedented success at causing the regrowth of hair cells by treating

excised portions of the damaged inner ear of an adolescent rat with retinoic acid and calf serum. It is possible to kill the hair cells of mammals after birth and then get them to regrow.

It has not yet been possible to stimulate this growth in a live animal, but, according to Dr. Ruben, successful *in vivo*[8] work is just around the corner. "I would hope to see trials in humans by the end of the century," he said. If it were possible to cause regrowth of cochlear hair cells in human beings, almost all deafness could be treated. Since most deafness is degenerative (those born deaf have lost the cells *in utero;*[9] almost no fetus exists that doesn't develop the cells at some stage), the question would be whether the new hair cells would remain alive in the inner ear, or whether they would die off again as their predecessor cells had done. There can be no question, however, that if hair regeneration were possible, there would be treatments for many deaf people. "From the time God made earth until today, this is probably the best time to be Deaf," Greg Hilbok said; and yet this is also the moment when the Deaf population is dwindling as it has never done before. Even now, deafness is defined as a "low-incidence disability"; there are 20 million deaf or hard-of-hearing people in the United States, but the profoundly deaf population is only about 2 million. Even without cutting-edge research, the control of childhood diseases is shrinking that population. As it gets better and better to be deaf, it also gets rarer and rarer.

MAKING THE IRREGULAR REGULAR

What to say, then, of the cries of genocide, the resistance to the whole idea of curing the deaf? I have heard of a couple who opted for an abortion when they heard that their child was hearing, so strong a view did they hold on the superiority of Deaf ways. But I also met many Deaf individuals who objected to the way that the Deaf leadership (focused around the National Association of the Deaf) has presumed to speak for all the deaf people of America. There were plenty who said that being deaf is of course a disability, and that anything you could do about it would be welcome. They were righteously indignant at the thought of a politically correct group suggesting that their problems weren't problems. I also met people who subscribed to the old deaf self-hatred, who were ashamed and saddened when they gave birth to deaf children, who felt that they had always been second-class people and that

---

8. *in vivo* within a living organism (Latin).

9. *in utero* in the uterus, before birth (Latin).

they could never be anything more if they were deaf. Their unhappy voices cannot be forgotten; in some ways, it doesn't matter whether M. J. Bienvenu "cures" them of their ignorance or Dr. Ruben "cures" their ears, but they are out there in numbers and need help from someone.

Most hearing people respond to cries of genocide with an arrogant 70 shrug. Of course if you can help deaf people you should help them. Give them hearing. Let them escape from their prison of silence. The triumph at Lexington this year coincided with the Stonewall[10] 25th anniversary celebrations in New York, and one could not help being struck by the parallels. Here were thousands of people converging on New York to celebrate an identity that, 25 years ago, was described not as an identity, but as an illness. Unlike other minority groups, gay men and women are members of a culture that does not include their parents; most are born to parents who would have liked them to be born otherwise. In a procreative society, their condition has been described as a handicap. Twenty-five years ago, before the principle of gay rights had been broadly articulated, few people questioned that it was right and fit to try to cure homosexuality—a terrible misfortune despite which (rather than because of which) some people managed to function at a high level.

Lewis Merkin is an actor and playwright, co-author of a remarkably moving play, "Language of Love," which the New York Deaf Theater will open in December [1994]. It is "the personal odyssey of a Deaf gay man." Born to grass-roots deaf parents in Philadelphia, with very good residual hearing, he grew up between the Deaf and hearing communities. "I could fit in almost well enough in the hearing community, almost well enough to pass," he said. "When I was about 18, I had to sort of come out of the closet as a Deaf person. I had to admit how much I couldn't hear, and to recognize that I would always speak with an 'accent.' I stopped going to parties and pretending I could follow everything going on. I stopped struggling against something I would never be able to change." Within a few years, Merkin had grown fully into a Deaf identity, and he became an actor, appearing in the role of Orin in "Children of a Lesser God" on Broadway.

He describes the parallel journeys of gay and Deaf identity. "When I was growing up, I looked around at these grass-roots deaf people, who were marginal, unimportant, not part of society, completely dependent on others, with

10. **Stonewall** a gay bar in Greenwich Village, New York City, where, on June 28, 1969, a riot ensued when the police tried to issue a warrant charging that liquor was being served without the proper license. This resistance to law enforcement, which lasted four days, is seen as the beginning of the modern gay rights movement in America.

no education, people who saw themselves as second-rate. And I recoiled. I thought, that's not me, and I felt sick at the thought that I was deaf. It took a long time for me to understand what it meant to be Deaf, what a world was open to me. When I first began to think about being gay, I saw limp-wristed drag queens and guys in leather hanging out on street corners, and again I thought, that's not me, and I hated the idea of being gay. And it was only with time that I came into a real gay identity."

The Deaf community is riddled with prejudice; deaf people tend to be conservative, and can be very intolerant of minorities or of other handicaps. Deaf parents are no happier about gay offspring than are hearing parents — though, interestingly, the incidence of gayness within the Deaf community is perhaps 15 percent higher than in the hearing world. There is a kinship between the groups. It has been suggested that as many as 90 percent of hearing-Deaf marriages end in divorce, but the majority of successful Deaf-gay relationships appear to be between Deaf and hearing individuals. "What we have experienced is so similar," M. J. told me. "If you are deaf, you know almost exactly what it is like to be gay, and vice versa."

Some opponents of the implants have demanded that young children not be implanted, and have proposed that people choose when they are 18 whether to have the implants or not. But if you are 18 and asked to make a choice, you are choosing not simply between being deaf and being hearing, but between the culture you have known and the culture you have never known. By then it is too late; your experience of the world has been defined by being Deaf, and to give it up is to reject who you have become. It lacks dignity: it is an admission of inadequacy, a discarding of your self.

It's hard to have children who are different from you. If gayness could be 75 detected in infancy and easily "corrected," then many parents would happily pay through the ears for the surgery. "In a world full of childhood cures," said Rob Roth, "I would be neither Deaf nor gay. That doesn't make me feel bad about myself, but I know it's true." Many gay men and lesbians would have been glad, at 8 or 10 or 12 or 14, to become "normal," even if, a few years later, they had grown into selves defined by the experience of gayness. Most Deaf children of hearing parents have had periods of rejecting their Deaf identity. Twenty-five years ago, the arguments for curing gayness seemed as unarguable as the arguments for curing the Deaf seem to be now. When and how did the shift from the pathological to the cultural view of gayness take place? How did we get from hormone injections and electroshock to gay soldiers and domestic partnership?

It is tempting, in the end, to say there is no such thing as a disability. Equally, one might admit that almost everything is a disability. There are as many arguments for correcting everything as there are for correcting nothing. Perhaps it would be most accurate to say that "disability" and "culture" are really matters of degree. Being Deaf is a disability and a culture in modern America; so is being gay; so is being black; so is being female; so even, increasingly, is being a straight white male. So is being paraplegic, or having Down syndrome. What is at issue is which things are so "cultural" that you wouldn't think of "curing" them, and which things are so "disabling" that you must "cure" them—and the reality is that for some people each of these experiences is primarily a disability experience while for others it is primarily a cultural one. Some blacks are handicapped by blackness; some who are gay are handicapped by gayness; some paraplegics thrive on the care they receive and would be lost if their mobility were returned. Some deaf people are better off deaf and some would be better off hearing. Some could perhaps be both: "I would never want to move away from my Deaf identity," Jackie Roth said. "But if I could have full hearing, without complications, I would like to have it."

There is something eerie and sinister about the image of a world sanitized of irregularity; there is a terrifying point when good works become fascistic control. If therapists who set out to "cure" gayness had succeeded, and succeeded fast, there would probably never have been a gay civil rights movement, and we would have lost all the singular contributions to the mainstream that an acknowledged gay culture has provided. The National Association of the Deaf convention demonstrates amply that the Deaf have as much of a culture as anyone. There is a race going on. Running on one team are the doctors who will make the deaf hear. They are humanitarian miracle workers, and they are bringing something very valuable to the many nonhearing individuals who would like to know sound and to speak. On the other team are the exponents of Deaf culture. They are visionary idealists who are trying to preserve a remarkable and seductive community.

If Deaf culture can be made as visible, important and proud as gay culture now is before the cure is perfected, then perhaps the accomplishments of the rubella bulge activists will allow for a long history of Deaf culture. Perhaps, like the search for a cure to gayness, the search for a cure for the deaf will be dropped by respectable institutions—which would be both a bad and a good thing. If the cure comes before the search for it is obviated, then virtually all hearing parents and many grass-roots deaf parents will cure their children, and the tremendous accomplishments that have followed the Gallaudet uprising will be the conclusion rather than the beginning of a story. Then the history recounted in this article will be as poignant and remote as a tale of Babylon. This, too, would be both a bad and a good thing. As genetic engineering progresses, we may be able to cure everything, and how we will decide which good and which bad we prefer will be increasingly important.

"Our situation also bears on yours, on the whole world's," M. J. Bienvenu said, her signs almost mockingly urgent. I think she is right. This race may be a good indicator for how we value difference altogether.

about the text

1. How does Solomon introduce and deal with the issue of cochlear implants? How "fairly" does Solomon evaluate them? Why do you think so? At one point, Solomon draws an analogy between cochlear implants and sex-change surgery. How appropriate and/or accurate do you think this analogy is? Explain.

2. How does Solomon conclude this article? What do you think were his purposes in concluding it in this way? How effective do you think Solomon's arguments are?

on language use

3. Consider how Solomon begins and ends his article. Who is the first person that we see and hear (p. 416)? Who is the last (p. 442)? Why might he have chosen to use these individuals, and their words, as he has? What do they contribute to the overall structure of the article?

4. How does Solomon use the metaphor of "curing"? How does he demonstrate the complicated nature of debates about who or what needs to be cured and how?

for writing

5. Write an essay in which you evaluate the appropriateness of one of Solomon's two analogies—the comparison of cochlear implants with a sex-change operation, or of being Deaf and being gay or lesbian. What are the strengths of the analogy? What are its limitations?

6. Write an essay in which you argue for or against the idea that it is the hearing community, not the Deaf, who need to be cured.

7. Solomon raises profound questions about the nature of disability (and ability), on the one hand, and of difference and diversity, on the other hand. When does difference become disability, and what, if anything, might be done about it? Write an essay in which you take a position on these issues.

BRENDA JO BRUEGGEMANN

Call to A. G. Bell

Got a quarter
so I call you up on the telephone
ring-ring-ring
but only your wife and mother are home,
so no one answers.   5
You out charting and graphing
marriages and progeny
of the deaf,
while only your wife and mother
—deaf—   10
are home. (ringed in)

So I leave a message
after the beep—
but actually,
it's before the beep because   15
the beep
I cannot hear.

So, you miss
half of it.

I start again.   20
This time, I mouth the message—
so you can lipread.
But you don't get it,
can't tell my b's from my p's,
my f's from my v's.   25

So I try again
slowing . . . down . . .
emph-a-siz-ing
each
W-O-R-D,   30
my face contorted, clownlike.
Still,
that won't do.
(What are you, dumb?)

No doubt you know that Alexander Graham Bell invented the telephone. What you may not know is that he was a staunch advocate for oralism—teaching deaf people to talk so that they could fit into the hearing world, rather than encouraging them to learn and use sign language. Many Deaf people find oralism frustrating and inefficient. This poem comes from Brenda Jo Brueggemann's 1999 book, Lend Me Your Ear: Rhetorical Constructions of Deafness. Brueggemann, who identifies herself as "hard of hearing"—and thus marginal in both the hearing and the Deaf worlds—points out that Bell believed in eugenics, the branch of science devoted to creating "superior" offspring. He sought to demonstrate that permitting deaf people to intermarry was bad because it would result in more deaf people. Ironically, both Bell's mother and his wife were deaf. Brueggemann is a professor of rhetoric and composition and the head of the disability studies program at Ohio State University. As you read, use the knowledge you've gained from the other readings in this chapter to help you understand the humor—and irony—in this poem.

I try signing,   35
hands across space
in your face,
but you are horrified
by the spectacle of my body
moving   40
beyond speech,
and you avert your eyes.

Too late.
I have burned your retina,
salt-pillared[1] you,   45
left you speechless.
And oh, the time is up,
message too long.
(It's taken 120 years to
get this call through.)   50
Sorry.

No, wait—
I'll fax you the facts;
I'll send a video,
documentary of my life,   55
caption and all,
interpreter on standby;
or perhaps TTY or relay service;[2]
an e-mail even,
coming through.   60
Let's "talk."

But oh—
now that I've gotten my medium,
I've forgotten my message.

---

1. **salt-pillared** an allusion to Genesis 19:26, where Lot's wife is turned into a pillar of salt because she looked back at the cities of Sodom and Gomorrah, which were being destroyed by God.

2. **TTY** a teletypewriter or teletype machine, which enables people to communicate by typing their message. **relay service** a system whereby a hearing person interacts with a Deaf person with the help of a relay operator who conveys each party's message to the other by typing the hearing person's words into a TTY for the Deaf person and reading aloud the Deaf person's message to the hearing person.

Alexander Graham Bell and his wife, Mabel Hubbard Bell, at their home in Nova Scotia, circa 1918.

---

about the text

1. In what ways is Brueggemann mocking Bell and his beliefs? Which aspects of the poem show her attitude toward him? How effective is her critique? Why?

2. What are the advantages and disadvantages of oralism for the Deaf? for the hearing? Is support for oralism on the part of the hearing a sign of benevolence or of nonacceptance? Why? In what ways does oralism permit hearing people to avoid dealing with the complex situation of the Deaf in society?

3. The closing lines of the poem are a play on an aphorism attributed to media critic Marshall McLuhan, "The medium is the message." What might this statement mean? What does it mean in Brueggemann's poem?

on language use

4. Which of Brueggemann's words or images invoke language, sounds, hearing, or deafness? How does Brueggemann juxtapose these words and images to construct her argument?

5. In what ways is this poem ironically humorous? Which aspects of the poem contribute to its humor?

for writing

6. Write an essay in which you evaluate the effectiveness of Brueggemann's poem, paying special attention to the situation itself (a phone call from someone who is hard of hearing to Alexander Graham Bell, who is long dead), the images and language, and the message.

7. Brueggemann's poem reflects the frustration and anger that many Deaf people feel about oralism and efforts to force them to be (or appear to be) something they are not: hearing. Similar sentiments are expressed in other readings in this chapter, many of which have sought to explain deafness from the perspective of the Deaf. What responsibilities do both the Deaf and the hearing have to themselves and one another in living together in an overwhelmingly hearing world? Write an essay in which you explore this question, giving some thought to the ways in which the Deaf are and are not like other marginalized groups in American society.

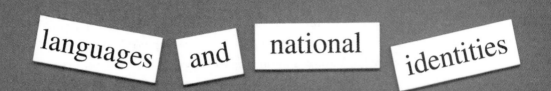

languages and national identities

Of the many ways that we identify ourselves as citizens of nations, language is one of the most fundamental. What's language got to do with it? A lot. Language is almost always considered a defining feature of nationhood, the reason many national and local governments, including some in the United States, have enacted laws to control the language use of their citizens and residents. Until recently, for example, the nearly three million Kurds who live in Turkey were prohibited from giving their children Kurdish names. Some countries even try to govern a language itself, as France does, for example, by prohibiting the introduction of English words into French.

In addition, a name may have very different meanings in different places, and sometimes multiple names can refer to the same thing—depending on whom you ask. An Arkansawyer (the name used by some people from Arkansas) who was working in Central America, for example, was "horrified" to be referred to there as a "Yankee" simply because he was from the United States. In the United States, the river that forms the border with Mexico is called the Rio Grande, but on the other side of that same river, its name is the Rio Bravo. What might account for the two different names? This chapter examines several such aspects of language use and how they contribute to the ways that nations and communities are known by their members and by others.

We begin in two regions of Canada, where language issues are often in the news. In Quebec, DeNeen Brown reports on French speakers' efforts to maintain the status of their language despite the national dominance of English. And in Nunavut, Andrew Duffy writes about Inuktitut, an indigenous language whose speakers are attempting not only to maintain the status of their language but also to ensure its very survival. Next, two readings examine the ongoing debate in the United States about the use of Native American names for sports teams—Andrea Woo's report of a 2002 Sports Illustrated opinion poll and Mike Wise's account of recent arguments at the University of Illinois about its mascot, Chief Illiniwek.

We have seen regions in which one language is replaced by another because of shifts in population and social conditions, but what happens in places where politics and history motivate a major change in a language's writing system? Hugh Pope describes the case of Azeri, the language spoken for centuries in the former Soviet republic of Azerbaijan and historically written in the Cyrillic (Russian) alphabet until it shifted to the Roman alphabet after Azerbaijan became independent. Next, David W. Chen reports on an issue of written language and national identity within the United States, where publishers of some Chinese-language newspapers have changed the orientation of the writing from the traditional top-to-bottom columns to lines of left-to-right type.

The next readings examine the movement to give English official status in the United States. How important is English to our national identity? Is the language secure and stable? Should it be protected by federal legislation? The first pair of readings advocates an "official" English: the website of the organization ProEnglish provides language statistics from the 1990 census, and the political analyst John Miller raises similar points in an essay from the journal of a conservative think tank. The linguist Dennis Baron, with tongue in cheek, takes an even stronger stand, arguing that English would be best protected by banning it altogether. Still another view is offered by the cartoonist Tom Tomorrow. We conclude the chapter with an essay in three parts by the linguist Geoffrey Nunberg, which presents an overview of the Official English question and places it in a global and historical context.

The language(s) we speak automatically give us access to specific cultural knowledge and customs and guarantee us membership in — what? We hope that the readings in this chapter provide some tools and information for exploring that question and for helping you think about how language does — and doesn't — contribute to our identities as members of particular nations, regions, and ethnicities, however we may imagine them.

Language and the Law: Two Cases from Canada

The following two articles relate attempts by a Canadian province and a Canadian territory to protect their ethnic identities with legislation about language use. Quebec and Nunavut both passed laws designed to protect their local languages from the encroachment of other languages, principally English. **Quebec "Tongue Troopers" Defend French**, was written by the Canadian bureau chief of the Washington Post, DeNeen Brown, in April 2001. She reports on a 1993 law in Quebec mandating that all public signs either be completely in French or include French with lettering twice the size of that in any other language used. The second article, **Nunavut Wants Quebec-Style Sign Law**, is from the territory of Nunavut, a name meaning "our land" in Inuktitut, the language of the Inuit people who live there. Chartered as a territory in 1999, Nunavut is located in the northern-most part of central Canada. Written by the journalist Andrew Duffy for the Ottawa Citizen in January 2002, this article reports on a proposed Nunavut law, similar to Quebec's law regarding French, that would promote and protect the Inuktitut language. As you read, think about the similarities and differences between each perception of the threat posed by English.

DENEEN BROWN

Quebec "Tongue Troopers" Defend French

An anonymous informant tipped the Quebec government. Then a stranger appeared, taking photographs. Soon, a letter came, fining Bob Rice. The 60-year-old plumber was then convicted at a trial he did not attend. His tractor and truck were confiscated and put up for auction.

All the while, Rice stood by, not quite sure what he had done wrong, his lawyer recounts—the letter, informing Rice of the infraction and an impending trial, was in French, which Rice does not speak. He tossed it. Rice's offense: A sign that read "BOB'S PLUMBING SERVICE & FARM SUPPLIES."

It was nailed onto a metal shed 240 feet off the public road in the small town of Venosta, Quebec, Rice said. The Quebec government deemed that Rice had violated a law requiring small commercial signs to include French, with the French letters at least twice the size of those of any other language on them. The law has been in effect since 1993, and the government enforces it strictly.

Rice depicts himself as an unwitting victim of a fight he doesn't understand. "I think it's kind of ridiculous," he said. "We are still in Canada."

The language police, 5 "tongue troopers," as they are called, are sometimes seen walking down the streets of Montreal, whipping out tape measures to make sure French on signs is of legal size. Owners of signs that aren't in compliance are fined by an organization called the Commission for the Protection of the French Language.

Guy Dumas, a Quebec associate deputy minister who is responsible for language policy, said this and other laws regulating language in Quebec are necessary to save a culture and language that are in a minority in North America. "The weight of French speakers in Canada is decreasing year by year," he said in an interview. "In 1950, the French population in Canada was 30 percent. In 1996, the last census, it was 24 percent."

"We are surrounded by a sea of Anglophones, the media weight of English, the cultural weight of English," he said. "It is important to maintain French culture, not in a folkloric way, but in the capacity of being able to service everyone in everyday activities: going to the store and being able to work in your language."

The laws and enforcement methods infuriate some Quebecers, notably those who aren't of French descent. "They operate on anonymous sources," says Keith Henderson, leader of the Equality Party in Quebec, which is fighting the law. "If you are a French nationalist, you can go and launch an anonymous complaint. It's like a covert operation. . . . The language regime is Stalinist in this province."

Mike King, a Montreal journalist, sees historical roots. "It goes back to when the French lost to the British" in 1759, he said. "The British let the French keep the culture. So they act like they didn't lose. To them it is just a technicality they lost the war."

The language laws have 10 been applied to American Express stickers on restaurant doors and to packages of matzo balls that were stopped at the border because they displayed English and Hebrew but no French.

Many shops with English names try to meet the letter of the law by putting a "Le" in front of the name. Example: Le Bargain Shop. Kentucky Fried Chicken changed its name, though, to Poulet Frit Kentucky.

The original version of the sign law, better known as Bill 101, barred all languages other than French on outdoor commercial signs. The law was amended in 1993, after the U.N. Human Rights Committee intervened, calling it a human rights violation. The new law requires that French be "markedly predominant." Bilingualism is tolerated on smaller signs, but anything as big as a sign on the side of a bus or a billboard must be entirely French.

Brent Tyler, a civil rights lawyer in Montreal, explains the law as "the phenomenon of linguistic insecurity" in Quebec. People go along with it because of an innate Canadian respect for authority, he suggests: "In Canada, we still have the queen on our money."

It's not only the authorities who enforce Frenchness. The battle is also being fought on the streets by minor terrorists.

Last fall, three coffee shops owned by a chain called Second Cup were firebombed. Earlier, a group calling itself the French Self-Defense Brigade warned that the cafes in the trendy Plateau Mont Royal district of Montreal would become targets because they violated "linguistic purity." A communiqué sent to newspapers warned that the Second Cup was "in the line of fire."

The bombings caused minor damage and no injuries. The Quebec government condemned the bombings. Doug Hurley, commander of the Property Crime Division of the Montreal Urban Community Police Service, said the police were treating the bombings as serious. "One of the bombs didn't go off, but it was right under a gas main. . . . Anybody who lays a bomb, I would call him fanatical."

Tyler and Henderson say small companies seem to suffer the brunt of the language laws, known collectively as the French language charter. In recent years, he has defended a couple accused of violating language that says: "Consumers of goods or services have the right to be informed or served in French."

The two corner-store owners were fined because a customer complained they did not speak enough French to sell beer and milk. The owners were ordered to take French courses or hire a bilingual employee. The owners, Marie Sia and Rene Sia, immigrants from the Philippines, said they could afford to do neither. So they closed shop.

In a cafe in the heart of Montreal, the city that is ground zero in this conflict, a man in a green beret sits in a gray high-back chair. His legs are crossed. He is reading a novel called "*Noël sur Ganymède.*"[1]

Outside the snow is falling, dusting Avenue du Mont-Royal. A campaign poster for Bloc Quebecois leader Gilles Duceppe clings to the top of a pole. Across the street is Aldo, Centre de Liquidation. A bus with a poster of a smiling prime minister rolls by. The sign on the bus is in French.

But two pay phones outside the cafe bear the name "Bell."

Everywhere French dominates English. But the English is still present, as if taunting the language police.

---

1. ***Noël sur Ganymède*** French title of Isaac Asimov's 1942 *Christmas on Ganymede*, in which Santa Claus visits Ganymede, the largest moon of Jupiter. Both names—Ganymede and Jupiter—originate in classical mythology.

ANDREW DUFFY

Nunavut Wants Quebec-Style Sign Law

Nunavut's language commissioner wants to introduce a Quebec-style sign law to ensure Inuktitut remains the dominant language in the northern territory.

Under the proposal, presented to Nunavut legislators earlier this month by Language Commissioner Eva Aariak, all business signs, posters and commercial advertising would have to be in Inuktitut.

Other languages would be permitted on signs as long as the lettering was not more prominent.

"In order for a language to survive and to have an impact on the public, it has to be visible in your environment," Ms. Aariak told a Nunavut government committee reviewing the territory's Official Languages Act. "One way of addressing that is through business signs and public signs." The proposed law would also guarantee Inuit students the right to be educated in their native language and would prevent employers from discriminating against unilingual Inuktitut-speakers— unless they can show that English is essential to a job.

Members of Nunavut's language committee have agreed to review Ms. Aariak's proposal.

They intend to make a recommendation to the legislative assembly after about four months of public consultation.

If it adopts a sign law, Nunavut will be wading into the kind of language politics that have long been an incendiary feature of life and government in Quebec.

Under Quebec's existing language laws, French lettering must be more prominent on outdoor signs. The law has survived several court challenges, most recently in April 2000 when a Quebec Superior Court judge ruled an antique store in Sutton, Que., could not post a sign with English and French letters of the same size.

In Nunavut, Inuktitut has come under pressure, particularly in the territory's capital, Iqaluit.

Iqaluit has enjoyed a building and population boom since the territory came into existence in April 1999. More than $75 million worth of development has transformed the city into a modern capital, but that building boom has also drawn Canadians from across the country and increased the prominence of English and French.

About 60 percent of Iqaluit's population remains Inuit, but many of the city's business signs are in English only.

Such is the case with Mary's Movie Club, the video rental store owned by Denis Cote. But Mr. Cote is among those who do not see anything wrong with fledgling attempts to protect the territory's dominant language.

"I'm from Quebec, so I'm used to this," he said in a telephone interview yesterday. "If I have to comply with a new sign, I will comply. It's not a big deal."

Suzanne Laliberte, manager of the Baffin Hair and Tanning Studio, came to Iqaluit from Montreal nine years ago. Her business offers customers service in three languages—Inuktitut, English and French—and already boasts a bilingual sign.

Ms. Laliberte said the language issue in Nunavut has created little tension between Inuktitut and non-Inuktitut speakers. "There is still tension here between English and French, but besides that, no, there's nothing," she said, adding: "English and French, the problems follow us everywhere."

Nunavut now has an Official Languages Act that recognizes Inuktitut, but the legislation does not govern its use in the private sector. The act applies only to the legislative assembly, court system and government, all of which guarantee services are available in Inuktitut.

Nunavut's Language Commissioner considers the legislation too limited. "Inuktitut is in need of special measures that will protect and strengthen its status and use in Nunavut," said Ms. Aariak, who called for the creation of an Inuktitut Protection Act.

Many Inuit elders now speak only Inuktitut while their grandchildren speak more and more English because of the influences of satellite television and English schooling.

Inuit students in Nunavut study Inuktitut from kindergarten to Grade 3. But English is the primary language of instruction from Grades 4 to 12, largely because not enough Inuit teachers have been trained to instruct the higher grades.

While the Nunavut govern- 20 ment has committed itself to extending the use of Inuktitut in schools, the proposed Protection Act would enshrine that process in law.

As a language, Inuktitut is still evolving. Inuktitut was for hundreds of years an entirely oral language and efforts to put it on paper began only a century ago. It means spellings and meanings of many Inuktitut words are still in dispute.

Inuktitut is written today with letters of the alphabet and with a system of a syllabics originally developed by Anglican missionaries for the Cree and later adapted for the Inuit. A dictionary with definitive spellings and translations is under development.

about the texts

1. What is Brown's attitude toward the Quebec "Tongue Troopers"? How do you know? Cite evidence from the reading to support your conclusion.

2. In the title and opening sentence of Duffy's article, we see that Nunavut has a language commissioner. What does that fact tell you about Nunavut's linguistic (and political) situation?

3. Duffy quotes Suzanne Laliberte, who says that there is little tension in her town between Inuktitut and non-Inuktitut speakers, but that "there is still tension between English and French" (paragraph 15). How would you account for the difference?

4. Brown concludes her article by presenting a café scene from everyday life in Montreal. Work with one or two classmates to explore how this scene ironically underscores Brown's views.

on language use

5. What is your response to each of the language situations described? Are you more sympathetic to one than the other—and if so, which one and why?

6. Inuktitut is a language only recently written down, and Duffy says it is "still evolving" (paragraph 21). What does that phrase imply about Inuktitut? about writing in general? Is English also "still evolving"? French? Other languages? Explain.

for writing

7. In what ways are the perceived threats to French and Inuktitut similar or different? Do you think legislative solutions can achieve the desired effects? Why or why not? What are the likely effects for speakers of these languages? for non-speakers? for the identity of each group in general? Write an essay comparing and contrasting the two situations.

Native American Images as Team Icons

These selections present two perspectives on the use of Native American team names and mascots in the United States. In recent years, there have been many organized movements pressing for changes in the names of the Washington Redskins, the Atlanta Braves, the University of North Dakota Fighting Sioux, and several other teams. The NCAA has encouraged schools to change objectionable names but so far has stopped short of requiring that they do so.

The first reading, **Polls Apart: A Survey**, is by Andrea Woo, a writer for Sports Illustrated, where this survey appeared in March 2002. **The Squabbling Illini: Rallying Cries Lead to a Rift**, by Mike Wise, a sports writer at the Washington Post, reports on the ongoing debates at the University of Illinois at Urbana-Champaign about their mascot (or symbol, depending on whom you ask), Chief Illiniwek. Wise was formerly on the staff of the New York Times, where this report was published in December 2003.

Although most Native American activists and tribal leaders consider Indian team names and mascots offensive, neither Native Americans in general nor a cross section of U.S. sports fans agree. That is one of the findings of a poll conducted for *SI* by the Peter Harris Research Group. The pollsters interviewed 351 Native Americans (217 living on reservations and 134 living off) and 743 fans. Their responses were weighted according to U.S. census figures for age, race and gender, and for distribution of Native Americans on and off reservations. With a margin of error of ±4%, 83 percent of the Indians said the professional teams should not drop using Indian nicknames, mascots or symbols, and 79 percent of the fans agreed with them. Surprisingly, there is a greater divergence of opinion between Native Americans who live on reservations and those who don't. Sixty-seven percent of Indians on reservations do not object to the use of Indian images, against 87 percent of the those off the reservations. When pollsters asked about the Washington Redskins, they found no great resentment toward the name. Instead, they again found agreement between Native Americans and fans (69 percent of the former and 74 percent of the latter do not object to the name), and less agreement between Indians on and off reservations (57 percent and 72 percent, respectively). Other results appear in the boxes that follow. ——Andrea Woo

Asked whether the use of Native American team names and mascots contributes to discrimination against Indians, respondents said:

	TOTAL FANS%	TOTAL INDIANS%	INDIANS LIVING ON/OFF RESERVATION	
			ON%	OFF%
Contributes to discrimination	12	23	45	17
Does not contribute	88	75	53	81
Undecided	0	2	2	2

Asked what they thought of the tomahawk chop at Atlanta Braves games, respondents said:

	TOTAL FANS%	TOTAL INDIANS%	INDIANS LIVING ON/OFF RESERVATION	
			ON%	OFF%
Like it	28	28	11	33
Find it objectionable	21	23	39	18
Don't Care	51	48	46	49
Undecided	0	1	4	0

Asked their opinions of team nicknames derived from other ethnic groups—Celtics, Fighting Irish, Ragin' Cajuns, Flying Dutchmen—respondents said:

	TOTAL FANS%	TOTAL INDIANS%	INDIANS LIVING ON/OFF RESERVATION	
			ON%	OFF%
Like them	49	25	16	27
Find it objectionable	4	12	14	12
Don't Care	47	62	68	60
Undecided	0	1	2	1

Source: Peter Harris Research Group, Inc.

MIKE WISE

The Squabbling Illini

Rallying Cries Lead to Rift

The history books say the last Indian tribe in Illinois was forcibly relocated to Kansas and then Oklahoma early in the nineteenth century.

But there is one Indian left, according to members of the Honor the Chief Society: Chief Illiniwek.

Of course, the chief is not a typical Indian, and he is not even a real one. He is a student dressed in Hollywood-style regalia, created seventy-seven years ago by an assistant band director at the University of Illinois. He dances at half-time of football and basketball games.

A debate over whether mascots with Indian themes are offensive or harmless has played out on college campuses and at professional stadiums for more than two decades. But there is something singular here, a fierce loyalty to a student in war paint that makes the hair stand on grown men's forearms. The passions aroused by the chief also make the great-great-granddaughter of Sitting Bull, a junior at Illinois, fear for her safety.

The catalyst for the debate 5 was a proposal last month by Dr. Frances Carroll, a new member of the university's board of trustees, to have Chief Illiniwek "honorably retired." She set aside her proposal after her support on the board eroded unexpectedly, but she intends to raise it again in March.

The proposal has divided the board and the university along political and, at times, racial lines. A symbol of pride to many students and alumni, Chief Illiniwek can at the same time be a hurtful reminder to American Indians of their mistreatment, of the misappropriation of their culture.

The chief's presence at football and basketball games flies in the face of a national trend. In 1970, more than 3,000 American athletic programs referred to American Indians in nicknames, logos or mascots, according to the Morning Star Institute, a Native American organization. Today, there are fewer than 1,100. At a time when American Indians are reclaiming their heritage, the use of Indian mascots and nicknames has ceased at all but a handful of major universities.

At Illinois, though, the forces of change have met strong resistance. Roger Huddleston, a local home builder and the president of the Honor the Chief Society, calls Carroll's proposal the "November ambush at the O.K. Corral."

"Chief Illiniwek is part of my geographic heritage," he said. "For anyone to dismiss that because I'm Caucasian, that's racist."

WHOSE SYMBOL IS IT?

John Gadaut, a lawyer in Cham- 10 paign, said he had spent more than $5,000 on keep-the-chief billboards and buttons.

"I'm a Native American," said Gadaut, who is white. "I was born and bred in Illinois. The chief means something to me, too. People keep saying we have a mascot. No, we have a symbol."

But those who think it is time to do away with the chief note that the symbol for the past three years, and for almost all of the past eight decades, has been portrayed by a white college student.

More than 800 faculty members have signed petitions, contending that the mascot interferes with fulfilling an academic mission, diversity. Nancy Cantor, the chancellor of the university's Champaign-Urbana campus, supports doing away with the mascot.

Carroll said: "It's time for it

to be put to bed. It's tough, but we have to do it."

Their success is still very much in doubt, with well-financed boosters and alumni determined to keep the chief.

"It's got all the subtexts," said Lawrence C. Eppley, the chairman of the board of trustees. On one side, he said, are "the people who see themselves as the do-goodie white person."

"On the other, you got the old, bad white people from the Midwest who can't change with the times," he said. "This is about the chief, of course, but it's partly about the tail end of the p.c. backlash of the 90's. When you start throwing the word racist around, the other side becomes firmly entrenched."

Genevieve Tenoso, an anthropology major who is a seventh-generation descendant of Sitting Bull, the legendary Hunkpapa leader, experienced a dose of the rolling emotions when she ran into a group of students demonstrating on behalf of the chief under the banner "The Illini Nation."

"I think I said, 'Look, now they've got their own tribe,'" she said. "And a guy told me if I didn't shut up he was going to pop me in the lip."

"Who knew," she said, "that this would be the issue on campus to get people to resort to a threat of violence?"

THE BATTLE BEGINS

The movement to abolish American Indian nicknames began in the 1960's in Indian communities and on several college campuses. Oklahoma's "Little Red" was the first nickname to be retired, in 1970. Stanford and Dartmouth soon followed, dropping Indians from their team names.

The movement to do away with the nicknames and mascots appeared to have won a key battle in 1999, when a panel in the United States Patent and Trademark Office ruled that Redskins was a disparaging moniker and violated federal law. Six trademarks involving the Washington Redskins were revoked.

Last month, federal District Court Judge Colleen Kollar-Kotelly overturned that ruling. Suzan Harjo, one of six plaintiffs in the case, said they had appealed.

At Illinois, Charlene Teters, a member of the Spokane Nation, took her children to a football game in the late 1980's and decided to do something about Chief Illiniwek.

Soon after, Teters, a graduate student at the time, started holding up a handmade placard outside the stadium that read "American Indians are people, not mascots." News accounts of her protest spurred the movement.

"When you see a community erode your child's self-esteem, you act," said Teters, now an artist and professor at the Institute of American Indian Art in Santa Fe, N.M. When she arrived at Illinois, a campus sorority was still holding a Miss Illini Squaw contest.

"I felt then we needed to kill the fake Indian," Teters said. "They say, 'We're doing it to honor Native Americans and the history of the state.' But it just seems like misplaced atonement, especially when they want to dictate the boundaries of that atonement."

Ever since, the chief's three-minute halftime performance has divided the university, sometimes along political lines.

Carroll, the trustee seeking to retire the mascot, is an African-American former schoolteacher with Democratic leanings who grew up and still lives on the South Side of Chicago. Carroll insisted that her motivation had nothing to do with being an African-American woman and everything to do with "being a human being."

Marge Sodemann, one of two voting trustees on the university's ten-member board who adamantly defend the chief, is a staunch Republican from the prairie. The license plate on her sedan reads "GOP Lady."

"The chief stands for the values, trust and honor of everything that went on in the past," Sodemann said. "It's not a racist mascot. Everything he's done is honorable. The people here really dote on him."

More than 200 students, including dozens of members of the marching band, held an all-night vigil in support of the mascot before the board meeting Nov. 13. The day of the meeting, other students demonstrated in favor of retiring the chief. And during the public board meeting, some white students sang Indian songs and performed tomahawk chops.

PROPOSAL MUST WAIT

Carroll needs six of the board's ten votes to retire the chief. At the eleventh hour, she said, at least two trustees waffled in their support, so she shelved the proposal until March.

Anti-chief factions contend that wealthy alumni have long pressured Illinois governors to maintain the mascot, and they say that governors, through channels, have pressured their appointees on the university's board. Governor Rod R. Blagojevich has said that the decision is a university matter.

While her fellow trustees were aware of Carroll's passion for the issue, they did not know the ancestry of the woman for whom she is named. Frances Graves, Carroll's grandmother, was a Creek Indian from York, Ala. Carroll brought a photo of Graves, a light-skinned woman with straight hair who was wearing a cloth hat and a collared, white powdery sweater, to an interview at the university's Chicago campus.

"I haven't really told anyone about that, just didn't see the need," Carroll said. "They always said she was full-blooded, but I'm not really sure.

"Anyhow, I never thought about it, being a black woman sticking up for the American Indian or doing this for my grandmother. I just thought about doing what's right."

Chief Illiniwek was created in 1926 by the university's assistant band director, Lester Luetwiler.

The chief's first appearance came during a game against Penn; he offered a peace pipe to a mascot of William Penn.

Red Grange[1] was the Illini star then, and many alumni associated the Galloping Ghost with the advent of the chief era. An icon was born.

Matt Veronie, a white graduate student with spiked, gelled hair and neatly ironed khaki pants, is the current chief. (An assistant chief sometimes fills in for him.) At games, Veronie's cheeks are painted Illini orange and blue. He wears a matching feathered war bonnet and Lakota-made buckskin; at halftime, he dances and leaps with a solemn countenance. He wonders about all the fuss.

"I think what I'm doing is a good thing," he said.

After graduating next semester, he said he would work to do "whatever I can to help people to see the chief tradition in the way I see it, for the good that it is, for the respect that it deserves."

"It would be very tough to see the chief go right now," he said.

The pull of the mascot for many people involves tradition, the lure of Illini athletics and college memories.

"I can still remember the first time I saw the chief in law school," said Gadaut, the lawyer from Champaign. "The hair stood right up on my arms. It's my whole heritage in front of me. Hey, these people can be my heritage even though this guy's skin is not my color."

He dismissed Carroll and other opponents of the chief as "leftist social engineers."

The people who want to retire the mascot note that virtually every major American Indian organization has long called for the elimination of sportsbased Indian references, as has nearly every civil rights and national church organization.

American Indians have rarely been heard in the dispute over the chief, but several members of the university who are American Indians talked about it one afternoon at the Native American House on campus.

"The chief is symptomatic of how American society coopts the Indian identity and simultaneously romanticizes and denigrates that identity," said John McKinn, a Maricopa from

---

1. **Red Grange (1903–1991)** football halfback, considered by some to have been the greatest halfback ever. Nicknamed the "Galloping Ghost," he played for the University of Illinois and the Chicago Bears.

the Gila River Indian Community who is assistant director of the Native American House. "Pseudo-spiritual dances are passed off as authentic. It just dismisses who we are."

Tenoso, the great, great granddaughter of Sitting Bull, described herself as a "reluctant activist."

"I wanted to ignore it and join the Native American club to learn to make fry bread and go to powwow," she said. "But I looked up on the wall at a fan shop and saw the chief head on a seat cushion. Then I went online and noticed one of the new items for sale is a chief bathroom scale and a little two-piece toddler set that said, 'Love Me and Love My Chief.' I was pulled in."

RATIONALE FOR RETAINING CHIEF

Eppley, the chairman of the board of trustees, acknowledged that he was uncomfortable with the rationale for retaining the chief.

"A lot of people see it as the dancing rabbi or the black minstrel," Eppley said. "Logically and historically, it is really tough to build a case for having it. It's likely a Boy Scout dance, at best.

"But you can't draw a 55 straight line back to that for people who like the chief. It's more complex."

Eppley said he would have voted against Carroll's resolution last month, because he thought she had rushed it onto the board's agenda.

"I do think it's a matter of when rather than if," he said, "but we have to find the right time."

Carroll, among others, isn't willing to wait much longer.

"We're in the twenty-first century in a global society," she said. "We have to be sensitive to images, thoughts, behaviors that affect other cultures—cultures that we now know we were misinformed about."

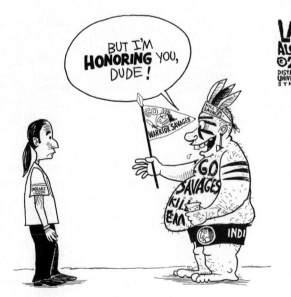

about the texts

1. Woo presents statistics from a survey that delineates three groups of people: fans, Native Americans living on a reservation, and Native Americans not living on a reservation. What other information about the respondents would you have liked to know? Why?

2. Why is it significant that *Sports Illustrated* is one of the publications supporting the use of the name "Redskins"?

3. Wise quotes the president of the Honor the Chief Society, who claims that Chief Illiniwek is part of his "geographic heritage" and that it is "racist" for anyone to dispute that claim (paragraph 9). Do you agree? Why or why not?

4. Wise presents the views of people on both sides of the Chief Illiniwek debate. Is his own position evident in the article? If so, what is it and how do you know? If not, what techniques does he use to maintain neutrality?

5. What rhetorical strategies does Woo employ to make her argument credible? How about Wise? Compare and contrast the way the two authors establish their authority. Which do you find more credible and why?

on language use

6. At the heart of this issue is the matter of propriety—who has the right to claim an ethnic name? And for what use? Does your response apply equally to all ethnic groups, or are there differences in how and by whom ethnic names might be used?

7. How have the articles by Woo and Wise influenced your thinking about the issue of ethnic mascots and team names? If there is a similar debate going on at your school, have these articles changed your mind at all?

8. Think about how many times a day you see images related to your local teams—on t-shirts, jackets, bumper stickers, or ads. How do these images contribute to the sense of community and identity of a place and its residents? (Have you ever, for example, struck up a conversation with a stranger because he or she was wearing something displaying the name of your local team?) What images, icons, and names define your hometown, and how do their various meanings influence its identity? How might the meaning of "Redskins" or "Indians" affect the community identity of Washington, D.C., or Cleveland? Discuss these questions with two or three classmates.

for writing

9. How do you feel about Chief Illiniwek? Should his image be retired? Write a letter to the University of Illinois Board of Trustees arguing your position. Support your argument with reasons and statistics from appropriate sources.

10. The name of the Boston Celtics makes an ethnic reference, but it is not usually considered offensive. Why not? Write an essay comparing the names of the Boston Celtics and the Washington Redskins. Consider the general status of the two ethnic groups named, their places in U.S. history, the connotations of the two names, the relevance of each name to the histories and cultures of the respective cities, the degree to which members of the two groups participated in creating the names and images of the respective teams, and any other factor you think is important. Then, use your comparison to argue whether you think the Washington Redskins should change their name.

Have you ever thought that the alphabet you use plays a part in your nation's identity? If you've grown up in the United States speaking English, you've probably given little thought to the alphabet at all. This article reports on the situation in Azerbaijan and other nations in Central Asia that were once part of the Soviet Union, where they have abandoned the Cyrillic alphabet imposed on them during Soviet rule—and are finding that switching alphabets is easier said than done. The article originally appeared in the Wall Street Journal *in 2000;* Hugh Pope *is that paper's bureau chief in Istanbul.*

HUGH POPE

A Soup of Alphabets Bedevils Azeri

When a shoe salesman here named Mehman Alimuradov had to move some footwear this summer, he faced an odd marketing problem.

First, few people could clearly recognize the store's sign out front, which was printed in the government-imposed Latin alphabet. But if he switched to the Russian-style alphabet most people could read, he faced possible fines from inspectors.

So the 22-year-old struck a compromise: he left the store sign alone. Above it, he hung a Russian-scripted, yellow sales banner, one provisional enough to keep inspectors off his back.

"You never know what will happen tomorrow," Alimuradov says without much thought. "This is Azerbaijan."

It's also one of the world's great alphabetical messes.

Most people here speak Az- 5 eri, so oral communication isn't a problem. Written communication is. No one can decide how to write out the Azeri language. There have been four completely different alphabets in the last 75 years, and steady replacements of various letters.

These days, at restaurants it's common to get a menu printed in Latin script (like the one you're reading right now), eat your meal, and then get the check written out in Russian-style script. Azeri newspapers don't offer much clarity. Most have Latin-scripted headlines and Russian-scripted articles. At one paper, *Azadliq*, the only recent all-Latin article was about former president Abulfez Elchibey, who made such a presentation a condition of his interview.

In the early 1990s, Azerbaijan and others celebrated their liberation from the U.S.S.R. by announcing they would junk the Cyrillic[1] alphabet that had been imposed by Soviet rule for 50 years. Azerbaijan was joined by the nations of Uzbekistan and Turkmenistan, as well as Tatarstan, which technically is still a republic of Russia. Alto-

---

1. **Cyrillic** an alphabet developed in the ninth century by St. Cyril and his brother St. Methodius, Greek monks who used it to translate liturgical texts from Greek into Slavonic. It is now used to write about fifty languages in Russia, Central Asia, and Eastern Europe, including Russian, Ukrainian, and Serbian.

gether, it has been nine years of alphabetic fits and starts.

Changing scripts isn't easy. There's logistics: think street signs and textbooks. There are philosophical issues: is it really a good idea to make it more difficult for people to read? And there are the larger realities of Central Asia: not much money, half-implemented reforms, corrupt governments, emerging ethnic rivalries and a swing back to Russia.

Take Turkmenistan. A bit larger than California, it's full of desert, natural gas and lavish government spending on projects like a revolving, gold-plated statue of the president perched atop a tower in the capital. Appropriately enough, when Turkmenistan went to a Latin script seven years ago, it briefly added three characters: the symbols for dollar, yen and pound sterling. These characters didn't simply mean dollar, yen and pound. They corresponded to certain sounds spoken by the Turkmens.

In all, the "Turkic region" 10 spreads from the Balkans to Siberia, and includes five former Soviet republics and the nation of Turkey. Each has its own spoken language, a Turkic dialect. Needless to say, life would be simpler if they all shared the same alphabet. At last count, though, the region had 21 different published scripts—in various forms of Arabic, Cyrillic and Latin.

More than 1,000 years ago, Turkic-speaking people actu-

ally wrote in a single, official script: Runic.

Then they started converting to Islam and adopted an Arabic script. The 1500s ushered in the great Asian Prince Babur, who had tough genes. His mother had descended from Genghis Khan, the great Mongol warrior, while his father had come down from Timur, the Turkic conqueror.

Prince Babur, who himself founded India's Moghul dynasty, felt the Arabic script's lack of vowels couldn't convey the rich harmonies of spoken Turkic. He tried to reform it. But Muslim clerics controlled the alphabets and blocked the prince's project.

Arabic scripts finally succumbed to revolutions and intellectual fervour. In 1926, here in the port city of Baku, the region's First Turkology Congress convened inside the expropriated palace of an oil baron to discuss the alphabet issue. In a 101-7 landslide, they picked a Latin alphabet, returning to their respective countries to spread the new gospel.

To the north, Joseph Stalin 15 was watching all this—even as much of the region was turning to communism. The Russian leader apparently liked the conversion to Latin letters, because it separated the region from Islamic countries to the south. But Stalin also wanted his own control. So, in the late 1930s, he imposed Russian-style, Cyrillic alphabets. To help drive a wedge among the

Turkic nations, he assigned unique Cyrillic characters depending on the nation. So, even though Turkic dialects had the same sounds, those sounds were written differently. These unique alphabets, in turn, further altered how people pronounced words, which further fragmented the region.

In 1992, a year after the Soviet Union collapsed, Turkey organized a modern-day alphabet congress. Academics arrived from throughout the region, and agreed on a standard 34-character, Latin alphabet—one based on Turkey's script. Everyone promised to go home and preach another Latin conversion. But few had much sway with the ex-Communist governments.

Azerbaijan, a country the size of Maine, has made the most progress—particularly given wrenching problems, like a six-year war in the mountains separating it from Armenia that displaced one-10th of its population. Many Azerbaijani kids now can read their native Azeri language in Latin. But they can't read all the Azeri literature and history printed in Russian-style Cyrillic. Their parents, meantime, can't read newly published books. In public spaces and on billboards, there's now a kaleidoscope of Cyrillic, Latin, even some Arabic.

Elsewhere, alphabet conversions have gone even more slowly. One big problem: because the Turkic states were

In public spaces and on billboards in Baku, there's a kaleidoscope of Cyrillic, Latin, even Arabic.

adopting obscure letters from well-known American computer fonts, which of course aren't part of the 34-character Latin alphabet established at the Turkey linguistic confab eight years ago.

And there's always politics, in places like Uzbekistan, a large, dusty nation whose oasis cities like Samarkand evoke the famed Silk Road[2] to China. In 1993, a nationwide committee adopted a Latin alphabet—with a goal of full conversion by 2000. Tellingly, the committee had more provincial governors than linguists. By 1995, relations soured with Turkey. Uzbekistan changed two Turkish-style consonants to English-style "ch" and "sh." And controversy remains about writing an "o" script when you're saying an "a" sound. One result of all the manipulations: when Uzbeks write "Isaac," people elsewhere read "donkey."

The new alphabet doesn't sit well with everyone. "It's so ugly. I can't bear to see it," says Mohammed Salih, Uzbekistan's opposition Erk Party leader, speaking by telephone from his exiled home in Norway. A poet, he chooses to write in Cyrillic rather than what he sees as a bastardized script.

"If we come to power," Salih says, "we'll have to modify the Latin alphabet again."

just freed of the Soviet Union, they feared a new big brother in Turkey. So, even those who went Latin did so on their own terms.

Meanwhile, businesses in the region still use Russian for conversations. So do Turkic presidents, while speaking at regional summits. For many younger people, oddly enough, Russian now is seen as cool. Recently, a young man walking through historic downtown Baku—near the confused shoe store—turned his head when

two young women walked by, not just because they were pretty, but also because their spoken Russian made them sound sophisticated. And where Russian is spoken, of course, Russian is written—which means the Cyrillic script.

Many feel that the Internet [20] will ultimately drive people to Latin scripts. But this isn't easy, either. The idiosyncratic variations on the Cyrillic alphabet that Stalin imposed aren't readily available on computers. So Turkic cybersurfers make do by

2. **Samarkand** a city in Uzbekistan, one of the oldest cities in Central Asia. Because of its location at the intersection of two important trade routes, it has been an important trade center and also has been ruled by a succession of different regimes and empires. **Silk Road** an ancient trade route that linked the empires of China and Rome.

about the text

1. What are the short- and long-term implications of writing Azeri with the Latin alphabet for Azeris as individuals? as a nation? Why? Consider educational and business possibilities, familial relations, and so on.

2. What roles has religion played in alphabet changes in the Turkic region? What roles have nationalist politics played? Do you think writing systems should ever be changed by religious or governmental authorities? Why or why not?

on language use

3. Pope's article suggests that there may be more to an alphabet than its use as symbols for written communication. What else does a writing system represent?

4. Imagine that the United States officially changed its writing system to another alphabet. How might you feel seeing the Pledge of Allegiance written in the new script?

5. What other functions does an alphabet have? For example, monogrammed letters on clothing, keychains, and jewelry may be principally decorative. Certain letters have complex meanings—X, for instance, can represent unknown quantities, obscene content, or Christianity. What other functions can you think of for the alphabet? Work with one or two classmates to think about several letters—where you see them, how they may be used, what else they may mean.

for writing

6. Coca-Cola and Pespi could both be considered quintessential American products and major symbols of U.S. culture. When U.S. citizens are traveling anywhere in the world and see or drink these sodas, they might feel a little closer to home—or would they? The photos show Coke and Diet Coke cans in Arabic and a Pespi can in Hebrew. What is your response to the cans? If you are not a reader of Arabic or Hebrew, did you immediately recognize the brands? Why or why not? If you are a reader of one or both of those languages, what was your response to the cans? Why? Freewrite and/or discuss with one of two classmates your reactions. Ask yourself what role your national or ethnic identity plays in your feelings and responses. Write an essay describing your own reactions to the photos, and discuss the possible implications of the choice of writing system for the label.

DAVID W. CHEN

Chinese Papers Really Change Direction

The world of Chinese-language newspapers in America has been turned upside down. Actually, it is just the text that has been completely flipped and reversed, although that has made for plenty of confusion all the same.

Within the last few months, the country's biggest Chinese-language dailies, all based in New York, have radically altered their printing formats. Instead of hewing to the decades-old tradition of printing the text vertically, from right side to left, the newspapers now read like their English-language counterparts with the text horizontal, from left side to right.

The newspapers also open up in reverse, so what used to be the front page is now the back page, and vice versa. And one daily paper has even abandoned traditional Chinese characters, so famously associated with ancient texts and paintings, in favor of the simplified ones that were introduced by the Beijing government in the 1950's.

Officially, the newspapers say that many practical reasons lie behind the changes. Chief among them are the ease of printing English terms like the critically important immigration law known as 2451, as well as an acknowledgment of New York's recent surge of immigrants from China, where newspapers are read horizontally, from left side to right.

But as hundreds of thou- 5 sands of readers try to reorient themselves to a fundamental daily routine, the transition so far has been uneven, producing visceral reactions to the new reading reality, one in which left is now right, horizontal is vertical and front is back. Some say that they feel liberated and are reading the newspaper for the first time in years. Others, by contrast, speculate that a political conspiracy may be afoot to court Beijing at the expense of Taipei.

Still others say that their eyes hurt from trying to read the paper.

Appreciated another way, imagine the uproar if an American paper suddenly decided that all text would be printed from right to left and that columns would run horizontally instead of vertically. Or if newspapers in Hebrew or Arabic, which read from right to left, decided to do an about-face.

"I don't like it," said Pauline Chu, who is from Taiwan and is president of the Chinese-American Parents Association in Flushing. "I don't know where to look; it's hard to tell which section to look for things you want to read. Your eyes—it's kind of exhausting."

But Ms. Chu gets no sympathy from Nan Lin, who immigrated from Fujian Province in China in 1995. For years, she was frustrated with the Chinese-language press here because she was uncomfortable with the style, and unfamiliar with many traditional characters they used.

"It was so hard to read that I didn't care whether I read the newspaper or not, which was terrible because before it was more important to read than to eat," said Ms. Lin, who works in a factory near Chinatown and also teaches the martial art of wushu. "But now, I'm very happy. I'm very happy. I'm reading the newspaper every day. This is great."

Any time a newspaper experiments with changes—be they graphic design, color photographs or new sections—complaints from readers are inevitable. But for many Chinese, the newspaper is an especially crucial and sensitive staple of life.

In Taiwan, families often subscribe to two or three newspapers. In the United States, Chinese-language newspapers, not television, provide for many the bulk of their information and the only link to current events in Asia.

For years, most people of Chinese origin in America had immigrated from Taiwan or Hong Kong after the Communist revolution in 1949, and were often anti-Communist or generally supportive of Tai-wan's long-ruling Nationalist Party. As a result, the newspapers here relied on the traditional system of complicated characters known as *fantizi* used in Taiwan and Hong Kong, and not the system of simplified characters called *jiantizi* used in post-1949 China.

Even *The People's Daily*, the official newspaper of the Chinese Communist Party, used traditional characters in its overseas edition until about five years ago. But at least the text read from left to right.

"It used to be, from left to right meant a left-wing newspaper, and pro-Communist China," said George Hua, president of the New York Association for Peaceful Unification of China.

But in recent years, there has been a surge in immigrants from China, both the highly educated and the undocumented poor. And circulation figures—hard as they are to confirm—reflect such changes, with the biggest paper, *World Journal*, which is owned by a Taiwan conglomerate, claiming a readership that is now half from Taiwan and half from China.

Three years ago, *The China Press*, which is owned by local investors and is perceived to be more pro-Beijing than the other papers switched from vertical to horizontal publishing. Some people were upset. But even more were irked, said Fan Dongsheng, the paper's president, when, in November, the paper switched from traditional to simplified characters.

"Some readers say, 'You're not respecting me, and you don't want me to read,'" said Mr. Fan, who is originally from Beijing. "Some readers also say the simplified characters are uglier."

But since that rocky start, the paper's circulation has jumped by 20 percent, attracting immigrants from China who had previously shunned newspapers in traditional formats, Mr. Fan said.

In recent months, the two biggest Chinese dailies in America, *World Journal* and *Sing Tao*, have also unveiled new format changes.

At *Sing Tao*, a healthy dose of initial reader complaints notwithstanding, newspaper executives say that they feel satisfied that they made the right decision to publish left-to-right columns. Indeed, the paper is beefing up its China coverage, with more China-related news, entertainment and sports, as well as plans to devote a half-page of news solely to Fujian Province.

For now, there are no plans to introduce simplified characters because too many readers would object, said Robin Mui, the paper's chief operating officer. "But maybe down the road, I would not guarantee that we would not change it," Mr. Mui said. "We have a lot of immigrants from mainland China, and those are our new target readers."

Still, the occasional barbs that greeted *Sing Tao* and *The China Press* were nothing compared with the reaction when *World Journal* changed formats during the Chinese New Year last month.

Some readers charged that the paper, now 26 years old, had sold out to the Communists, said Marco Liu, the paper's editor in chief. And some canceled their subscriptions, or began to look for alternatives to the daily, which claims a readership of 50,000 in the New York area and 390,000 nationwide.

But the reasons for change 25 were straightforward, Mr. Liu said. There are, for starters, technical considerations, since the paper uses computer software that is manufactured in Beijing. It is also much more convenient to incorporate English terms or numbers familiar to readers here—like, say, 9/11 or Operation Anaconda—when printing horizontally.

"We are not a Taiwanese newspaper," Mr. Liu said in an interview at the newspaper's headquarters in Whitestone, Queens. "We are not a Chinese newspaper. We want to position ourselves as an American newspaper."

Still, Mr. Liu expressed guarded optimism that readers would adapt. After all, several papers in Taiwan are now printed horizontally—especially the evening papers, which list stock prices in the Western style. The same applies to most Chinese-language Web sites, and many of the free weekly newspapers found in Chinese hubs like Flushing and Edison, N.J. And many of the paper's ads have run in left-to-right fashion for years.

Old Version:
Text reads from right to left, vertically. Paper opens at left.

New Version:
Text reads from left to right, horizontally. Paper opens at right.

1. How do national politics affect the way Chinese is written in the United States? Who prefers each orientation? Why? Is there a "correct" system? Why or why not?

2. Why does Marco Liu, the editor-in-chief of the *World Journal*, say that the paper "want[s] to position [itself] as an American newspaper" (paragraph 26)? How does horizontal orientation accommodate life in the United States for readers of Chinese? What might be the disadvantages of horizontal orientation for the publishers of the *World Journal*?

on language use

3. If English writing were to change orientation, how well do you think you would adjust? Why? Would your ease of adjustment depend on whether you supported or opposed the administration that made the change? In other words, how much would politics inform your ability to learn a new orientation, which is essentially a purely cognitive process that has nothing to do with politics?

4. As you have learned from Chen's report, Chinese-language publishing in the United States can influence the language as a whole. Should diasporic communities be able to affect how their home language changes over time, even though the speakers are geographically far from the home countries? Why or why not?

for writing

5. Visual merchandising textbooks advise merchants to arrange items on display from left to right in ascending order of price, size, or other relevant feature. What other elements of daily life in the United States follow that orientation? Try to determine, through interviews with people or Web research, whether the same is true elsewhere—do Israelis display things right to left, for example, to match the orientation of Hebrew? Write an essay describing where and how the left-to-right, top-to-bottom orientation of Latin-alphabet writing affects the shape of our daily lives. Compare your description, if possible, with what you know of life in places with differently oriented writing systems.

Here we present two arguments for making English the United States' official language. The first is **English Is Broken Here**, a 1996 article by John Miller. It originally appeared in Policy Review, a journal of the Heritage Foundation, a public policy think-tank whose mission is to "formulate and promote conservative public policies based on the principles of free enterprise, limited government, individual freedom, traditional American values, and a strong national defense." Miller also writes for the National Review, a conservative weekly magazine; his book, The Unmaking of Americans: How Multiculturalism Has Undermined the Assimilation Ethic, was published in 1998. We also include here a USA Today analysis of the Bureau's 1990 **Census language data**, compiled by ProEnglish, a nonprofit organization whose mission is to "educate the public about the need to protect English as our common language and to make it the official language of the United States." (You can access ProEnglish's Web site through <wwnorton.com/write/language>.) As you read, think about how these selections use different rhetorical formats to make similar arguments.

JOHN MILLER

English Is Broken Here

CALIFORNIA'S YUBA COUNTY is getting ready to spend $12,000 this November on election materials that nobody will use.

That's because the federal government forces local officials to print voting information in Spanish for every election.

"Bilingual ballots are an enormous waste of county resources," says Frances Fairey, Yuba County's registrar of voters.

In last March's primary election, this county north of Sacramento was forced to spend $17,411 on Spanish-language election materials. But, according to Fairey, "In my 16 years on this job, I have received only one request for Spanish literature from any of my constituents."

The biggest problem with bilingual ballots, however, is not that they go 5 unused in Yuba County, but that they are used in so many other places. Thousands of Americans are voting in foreign languages, even though naturalized citizens are required to know English. The National Asian Pacific American Legal Consortium estimates, for instance, that 31 percent of Chinese-American voters in New York City and 14 percent in San Francisco used some form of bilingual assistance in the November 1994 elections. Though these figures may be overstated, proportions anywhere near this magnitude are devastating to democracy. As Boston University president John Silber noted in congressional testimony last April, bilingual ballots "impose an unacceptable cost by degrading the very concept of the citizen to that of someone lost in a country whose public discourse is incomprehensible to him."

A nation noted for its diversity needs certain instruments of unity to keep the *pluribus* from overrunning the *unum*.[1] Our common citizenship is one such tool. Another, equally important, is the English language. It binds our multiethnic, multiracial, and multireligious society together. Not everyone need speak English all of the time, but it must be the lingua franca of civic life. Since the voting booth is one of the vital places in which citizens directly participate in democracy, it must be the official language of the election process.

Allowing voters to cast foreign-language ballots degrades the idea of citizenship

It is not, however, and political jurisdictions ranging from Yuba County to New York City can pin this mess on the perversion of voting-rights legislation. The Voting Rights Act of 1965 guaranteed blacks the right to vote in places, particularly the South, where they had been systematically blocked from electoral participation, often through the use of bogus "literacy tests." But as Manhattan Institute scholar Abigail Thernstrom has shown in her comprehensive book *Whose Votes Count?*, it did not take long for this important piece of civil rights legislation to expand in dangerous ways.

After the Act's passage in 1965, civil rights groups toiled to expand its authority. When the law came up for reauthorization in 1975, Hispanic organizations argued that English-language ballots were the equivalent of literacy tests. People whose first language was Spanish needed special protections in order to vote, they claimed, citing low turnout among Hispanics. This was sheer quackery. Literacy tests in the South were used for the fraudulent purpose of keeping blacks away from elections. Low Hispanic turnout was mainly due to the fact that so many Hispanics were not citizens and therefore ineligible to vote.

Nevertheless, Congress sided with the activists. It required bilingual ballots in any political district where "language minorities" made up at least

---

1. **pluribus/unum** Latin words from the national motto of the United States, *E pluribus unum*, which means "from the many, one." *Pluribus* means "many," and *unum* means "one."

5 percent of the total population and less than half of the district's citizens were either registered to vote or had voted in the 1972 presidential election. It also required that bilingual election materials be made available to voters in every county in which the language-minority population had an "illiteracy rate"—meaning "failure to complete the 5th grade," a trait that includes many immigrants—above the national average. Interestingly, "language minorities" were not defined by language (a cultural characteristic), but by ancestry (a genetic one). The category included only "persons who are American Indian, Asian American, Alaskan Natives, or of Spanish heritage." French Canadians living in Maine, the inhabitants of Little Italy in New York City, and the Pennsylvania Dutch received no special assistance. By the early 1990s, the foreign-language ballot provisions of federal voting-rights law applied to 68 jurisdictions in the United States.

The bilingual-ballot mandate bloated even further in 1992, when Congress said that counties with more than 10,000 residents who speak the same language and who are not proficient in English must provide bilingual voting ballots, even if their potential users make up less than 5 percent of the overall population. This applied to heavily populated areas with large numbers of non-English-speaking residents, such as Chicago, New York City, and San Francisco. To comply, New York City had to purchase new voting machinery because its old equipment did not have enough space for all the Chinese characters that the law said it must provide. Los Angeles County now offers ballots in Chinese, Japanese, Korean, Spanish, Tagalog, and Vietnamese. In the three elections between November 1993 and November 1994, the county spent more than $1.2 million to print voting materials in these foreign tongues. The Mexican American Legal Defense and Education Fund has called this "a particularly small price to pay." This "small price" could have paid for a year's tuition at UCLA for 308 Los Angeles residents.

Ballot initiatives are often worded very precisely. Will translations always convey the exact English-language meaning of every initiative? In a deliberative democracy, they must. On a 1993 New York ballot question, translators printed the Chinese character for "no" where it should have said "yes." More important, immigrant voters should not even need bilingual ballots. We have required naturalization applicants since 1907 to demonstrate English-language proficiency. In order to become citizens—and thus gain the right to vote—the foreign-born have to demonstrate the ability to speak, read, and write simple English. A handful of them are granted exemptions. Naturalization applicants who are over the age of 50 and have lived in the United States for 20 years do not have to meet the English requirement. But they only make up about 7 percent of all citizenship applicants. The other 93 percent have to pass the test. So why do we assume they lose their English skills on Election Day? Meanwhile, foreign-language voting sends one more message to immigrants that assimilation is not an important part of civil society.

A popular antidote to bilingual ballots is declaring English the official language of the United States. But that is like declaring the bald eagle its official bird—it's essentially symbolic. Many self-proclaimed official-English advocates in Congress have no intention of repealing foreign-language ballot laws or federal funding of bilingual education. When Senator Ted Stevens of Alaska opened hearings on an official-English bill last December, he proudly announced that "the bill does not affect existing laws which provide bilingual and native language instruction. Those statutes are integral parts of our national language policy." Message to civil rights activists: We're not going to change a thing.

In a speech to the 1995 American Legion convention in Indianapolis, Republican presidential candidate Bob Dole announced that "English must be recognized as America's official language." But he said nothing about bilingual ballots. As a senator in 1992, Dole voted to expand their use.

In August, the House of Representatives passed a bill that would repeal the federal government's unfunded bilingual ballot mandate by amending the Voting Rights Act. It would not deny local communities the right to print non-English voting materials, should they choose to pay for it themselves. Nor would it stop voters from taking punch cards into the election booth. No companion bill, however, has been introduced in the Senate.

There is a long tradition in the United States of ethnic newspapers— 15 often printed in languages other than English—providing political guidance to their readers in the form of sample ballots and visual aids that explain how to vote. In the absence of bilingual ballots, this practice could continue and expand. Perhaps we should also allow voters to bring a friend or relative into the booth, just as blind voters can do. The polling place would remain open to people who have trouble with English, but it also would remind them that English—or even broken English—is the common language of American democracy.

Making English Our Official Language

Languages of non-English speakers (1990 Census)

Language	Number w/ Limited English (in thousands)	Highest concentration	Percent of speakers with Limited English
1. Spanish	8,306	New Mexico	48
2. Chinese	753	Hawaii	60
3. French	476	Maine	28
4. Italian	735	New York	33
5. German	386	North Dakota	25
6. Korean	384	Hawaii	61
7. Vietnamese	321	California	63
8. Tagalog (Filipino)	287	Hawaii	34
9. Polish	268	Illinois	37
10. Japanese	224	Hawaii	52
11. Portuguese	195	Rhode Island	45
12. Russian	131	New York	54
13. Thai/Lao	128	California	62
14. Greek	122	Massachusetts	31
15. Arabic	120	Michigan	34
16. French Creole	99	Louisiana	53
17. Hindi/Urdu	97	New Jersey	29
18. Mon-Khmer (Cambodian)	93	Rhode Island	73
19. Persian	77	California	38
20. Armenian	75	California	50
21. Navaho	66	New Mexico	45
22. Miao	64	Minnesota	78
23. Yiddish	62	New York	29
24. Hungarian	52	New Jersey	35
25. "Penn." Dutch	36	Pennsylvania	43
26. Ukrainian	36	New Jersey	37
27. Gujarathi	35	New Jersey	34

Languages of non-English speakers (1990 Census) (*cont.*)

Language	Number w/ Limited English (in thousands)	Highest concentration	Percent of speakers with Limited English
28. Hebrew	34	New York	23
29. Dutch	34	Utah	24
30. Romanian	32	New York	49
31. Serbo-Croatian	28	New York	39
32. Czech	27	Nebraska	29
33. Formosan	25	California	55
34. Ilocano	23	Hawaii	56
35. Slovak	22	Pennsylvania	28
36. Panjabi (C. Asia)	18	California	36
37. Norwegian	17	North Dakota	21
38. Lithuanian	10	Illinois	30
39. Turkish	16	New Jersey	39
40. Croat	15	Illinois	34
41. Swedish	15	Minnesota	19
42. Syriac	15	Michigan	41
43. Indonesian	13	n/a	54
44. Finnish	13	Minnesota	25
45. Amharic	13	D.C.	41
46. Malayalam	13	New York	38
47. Bengali	13	New York	33
48. Kru	12	D.C.	19
49. Mandarin	12	n/a	50
50. Samoan	11	Hawaii	32

Source: ProEnglish, *USA Today* analysis of Census Bureau data. Based on Census Bureau questions allowing self-assessment. *Highest concentration* is based on the state with the highest total number of people who speak a given language as the primary home language in their household. *Percentage* is of speakers who do not speak English "very well" as a portion of people who use minority languages as a primary language in their home.

about the texts

1. How do the ProEnglish statistics make the argument that English should be the official language of the United States? Do you find the argument effective? Why or why not?

2. Miller makes no effort to sound neutral. How do his word choices contribute to his argument? Provide examples to support your conclusion.

3. Miller complains that bilingual ballots went unused in Yuba County, California, but then complains that bilingual ballots *are* used in many other parts of the country. How does the use of both complaints support his argument?

4. Was Miller's essay written for people who share his opinion or for people who are either opposed to what he asserts or undecided about the issue? How do you know?

5. Why does ProEnglish post these statistics without any explanation? What do the members of the organization want us to see? Is it an effective way to make an argument? Why or why not?

on language use

6. ProEnglish uses the term "Limited English" in its statistics. What does this term means? How is "Limited English" measured? What

information not given here would provide a more complete picture of all the languages used in the United States? Work with one or two classmates to determine how to present similar data and what information would be important to include.

7. Are Miller and ProEnglish right when they argue that the nationhood of the United States is threatened by the use of other languages within its borders? Why or why not? What might happen to the United States if its main language shifted to something other than English? Discuss your ideas with two or three classmates; then report your conclusions to the class.

for writing

8. Is English in the United States really in peril? Write an essay in which you argue that English is or isn't in danger of losing its dominance in the United States, presenting evidence for your argument.

9. What is more "devastating to democracy"— people voting in a language other than English or people *not* voting? Why? Write an essay in which you make a thorough and well-supported argument for your answer to this question.

DENNIS BARON

Don't Make English Official—Ban It Instead

Dennis Baron *is a professor of English and linguistics at the University of Illinois at Urbana-Champaign; he writes on questions of language, language laws, and language policy. His books include* The Guide to Home Language Repair *(1994),* The English-Only Question: An Official Language for Americans? *(1990), and* Grammar and Gender *(1986). In this selection, a version of which first appeared in the* Washington Post *in September 1996, he responds humorously to the official English arguments.*

ONGRESS IS CONSIDERING, and may soon pass, legislation making English the official language of the United States. Supporters of the measure say that English forms the glue that keeps America together. They deplore the dollars wasted translating English into other languages. And they fear a horde of illegal aliens adamantly refusing to acquire the most powerful language on earth.

On the other hand, opponents of official English remind us that without legislation we have managed to get over 97 percent of the residents of this country to speak the national language. No country with an official language law even comes close. Opponents also point out that today's non-English-speaking immigrants are picking up English faster than earlier generations of immigrants did, so instead of official English, they favor "English Plus," encouraging everyone to speak both English and another language.

I would like to offer a modest proposal to resolve the language impasse in Congress. Don't make English official, ban it instead.

That may sound too radical, but proposals to ban English first surfaced in the heady days after the American Revolution. Anti-British sentiment was so strong in the new United States that a few superpatriots wanted to get rid of English altogether. They suggested replacing English with Hebrew, thought by many in the eighteenth century to be the world's first language, the one spoken in the garden of Eden. French was also considered, because it was thought at the time, and especially by the French, to be the language of pure reason. And of course there was Greek, the language of Athens, the world's first democracy. It's not clear how serious any of these proposals were, though Roger Sherman[1] of Connecticut supposedly remarked that it would be better to keep English for ourselves and make the British speak Greek.

Even if the British are now our allies, there may be some benefit to banning English today. A common language can often be the cause of strife and misunderstanding. Look at Ireland and Northern Ireland, the two Koreas, or the Union and the Confederacy. Banning English would prevent that kind of divisiveness in America today.

Also, if we banned English, we wouldn't have to worry about whose English to make official: the English of England or America? of Chicago or New York? of Ross Perot or William F. Buckley?[2]

We might as well ban English, too, because no one seems to read it much lately, few can spell it, and fewer still can parse it. Even English teachers have come to rely on computer spell checkers.

Another reason to ban English: it's hardly even English anymore. English started its decline in 1066, with the unfortunate incident at Hastings.[3] Since then it has become a polyglot conglomeration of French, Latin, Italian, Scandinavian, Arabic, Sanskrit, Celtic, Yiddish and Chinese, with an occasional smiley face thrown in.

More important, we should ban English because it has become a world language. Remember what happened to all the other world languages: Latin, Greek, Indo-European? One day they're on everybody's tongue; the next day they're dead. Banning English now would save us that inevitable disappointment.

Although we shouldn't ban English without designating a replacement for it, there is no obvious candidate. The French blew their chance when they sold Louisiana. It doesn't look like the Russians are going to take over this country any time soon—they're having enough trouble taking over Russia. German, the largest minority language in the United States until recently,

---

1. **Roger Sherman (1721–1793)** attorney, astronomer, judge, signer of the Declaration of Independence, and senator from Connecticut in the First Congress.

2. **Ross Perot (b. 1930)** Texas businessman and presidential candidate in 1996 for the Reform Party; he received 8.4 percent of the popular vote. **William F. Buckley (b. 1925)** nationally syndicated conservative columnist, founder of the *National Review*; his columns appear in more than 300 U.S. newspapers.

3. **the unfortunate incident at Hastings** a reference to the defeat of England in 1066 at the Battle of Hastings by William the Conqueror of France. This was the deciding battle in the Norman Conquest, France's conquest of England, which lasted some 200 years. During this time, thousands of French words entered English and profoundly changed the language.

lost much of its prestige after two world wars. Chinese is too hard to write, especially if you're not Chinese. There's always Esperanto, a language made up a hundred years ago that is supposed to bring about world unity. We're still waiting for that. And if you took Spanish in high school you can see that it's not easy to get large numbers of people to speak another language fluently.

In the end, though, it doesn't matter what replacement language we pick, just so long as we ban English instead of making it official. Prohibiting English will do for the language what Prohibition did for liquor. Those who already use it will continue to do so, and those who don't will want to try out what has been forbidden. This negative psychology works with children. It works with speed limits. It even worked in the Garden of Eden.

---

about the text

1. Baron begins by summarizing the arguments in support of official English. Is his summary accurate? neutral? fair? Why or why not?

2. Why might Baron have called his proposal "modest"? Was the use of that adjective an effective rhetorical device? Why or why not?

3. Baron's proposal will certainly never be adopted, but is his argument effective? Why or why not?

---

on language use

4. Why does Baron call English a "polyglot conglomeration" (paragraph 8)? What does he mean by that phrase? Explain.

5. Do some research on the Web and compile a list of ten everyday English words that originated in other languages. Compare your list with those of your classmates. Which of the words surprised you? Why?

---

for writing

6. Think about whether Baron's reasons for banning English are similar to the reasons John Miller gives in his essay for making English the official language of the nation. Write an essay comparing and contrasting the underlying assumptions and reasons of the two authors, presenting examples from the texts to support your argument.

7. Baron is making his proposal in jest, but the history he refers to was no joke. Even Benjamin Franklin and some of his cohorts raised questions about which language should be spoken in the new nation. Research those debates, and then write an essay in which you report your findings and speculate on what Ben Franklin and friends might say about the official English movement of today.

ord, a cartoon of political satire, appears in approximately 150 newspapers and *he United States, including Salon, the New York Times, and the Nation. Tom Tom e of Dan Perkins, who won the 1998 Robert F. Kennedy Journalism Award for Car luded here was published in April 1996.*

THIS MODERN WORLD — by TOM TOMORROW

IF CONSERVATIVES PASS A LAW MAKING ENGLISH OUR *OFFICIAL LANGUAGE*, WILL *FOREIGN TOUR-ISTS* BE SUBJECT TO *ARREST?*

PARDONNEZ MOI, S'IL VOUS PLAÎT-- OÙ EST LE MONDE DE DIS-NEY?

HOLD IT RIGHT THERE, BAGUETTE-EATER! YOU'RE COMING WITH ME!

WILL *PIG LATIN* BE CONSIDERED A FORM OF *CIVIL DISOBEDIENCE?*

AT-WHAY EEMS-AY OO-TAY EE-BAY EE-THAY ROBLEM-PAY OFFICER-AY?

YOU'RE WALKIN' A FINE LINE, PAL.

WILL ANTI-GOVERNMENT *MILITIAS* BEGIN TO STOCKPILE *FOREIGN FILMS* AND *LANGUAGE TAPES?*

WHEN OTHER LANGUAGES ARE OUTLAWED, ONLY OUTLAWS WILL SPEAK OTHER LAN-GUAGES!

THEY'LL PRY MY BERLITZ TAPES FROM MY COLD, DEAD FIN-GERS!

ICH BIN EIN FREE-MAN!

AND ONCE THE LANGUAGE USED BY AMERICANS IN 99% OF THEIR DAILY TRANSACTIONS HAS BEEN ENSHRINED IN LAW, WILL CONGRESS WORK TO PASS OTHER, *EQUALLY NECESSARY* LEGISLATION?

I BELIEVE WE SHOULD DESIG-NATE THE SUN OUR OFFICIAL LIFE-GIVING SOURCE OF HEAT & LIGHT!

NO PROBLEM! I'LL ATTACH A RIDER TO MY MANDA-TORY BREATH-ING BILL!

SURE BEATS TRYING TO PASS A BUD-GET, DOESN'T IT?

man (panel 3) a parody of a famous statement made by President John F. Ken it to Berlin in 1963. He concluded his speech by saying, "as a free man, I take bin ein Berliner.'" Kennedy wanted to identify with the people of Berlin by sa a citizen of Berlin," but *Berliner* can also refer to a type of pastry. Some clo y said was "I am a jelly donut." You can read and hear his entire sp n/write/language>, or google the phrase to find more about the grammatical

about the text

1. Think about the details of each panel in the cartoon. Does it matter that the tourist in the first panel is French? What if he were Italian? Chinese? Pakistani? Is it important that the car in the second panel is a convertible? That the driver is white, male, and wearing a suit? What about the three fellows in the third panel—could they have been depicted in another way? What are the important features of the Congress members in the final panel? Discuss with two or three classmates how each detail contributes to the overall message of the cartoon and report your conclusions to the whole class.

2. If English were made the official language of the United States, foreign tourists would certainly not be arrested in the street, as Tom Tomorrow surely knows. What is his point? What does the cartoon suggest may happen if the official English law were to pass?

on language use

3. If foreign language study really were to become illegal or subversive, would you be more likely or less likely to want to learn another language? Why? How do national politics and current events influence your attitudes about learning (or hearing) other languages?

for writing

4. Instead of using satire and parody to make this argument, how might one make it in straightforward, nonhumorous prose? Rewrite Tomorrow's argument as it might appear on the editorial page of your local paper, including points from each of the panels.

5. Read this cartoon again and imagine that the pictures aren't there; read only the words. Does the cartoon still make sense? Are the arguments of each panel clear or not? Then reread the cartoon looking at both the pictures and the words. What do the pictures contribute to the argument? Write an essay explaining how the words and pictures function together to make a unified argument.

....

Geoffrey Nunberg *is a senior
researcher at the Center for
the Study of Language and
Information at Stanford
University and chair of the
usage panel for the American
Heritage Dictionary. The
author of several books,
including* The Way We Talk
Now *(2001) and* The Future of
the Book *(1996), he also speaks
regularly on NPR's* Fresh Air
*and writes commentaries in
the* New York Times' *"Week
in Review." This essay was
written for* Language Loyalties: A Source Book on the
Official English Controversy
*(1992), an anthology of essays,
reports, and legal documents,
including a 1753 essay by
Benjamin Franklin and a
1917 speech by Theodore
Roosevelt. It touches on many
aspects of the Official English
question—historical, legal,
educational, political, demographic, and linguistic; some
of the selections focus on
language questions and
controversies in other countries. Nunberg's essay is the
Afterword—it summarizes
and comments on many of
the texts in the anthology.*

....

GEOFFREY NUNBERG

Reimagining America

> ### part 1

NATIONS ARE "IMAGINED COMMUNITIES," in Benedict Anderson's suggestive term. "Imagined," because

> the fellow members of even the smallest nation
> will never know most of their fellow members,
> meet them, or even hear of them, yet in the minds
> of each lives the image of their communion. . . .
> Communities are to be distinguished, not by their
> falsity or genuineness, but in the style in which
> they are imagined.[1]

There are many styles of imagining national communities, out of stories of common lineage, history, religion, or
culture. But symbolically, these commonalities are often
expressed in terms of a common language, particularly in
the European traditions where the modern models of nationality were first formed. The connection between language and nation was a side effect of the introduction of
print, which made it possible to project the common experience of the members of the community as a kind of public knowledge. Language has sometimes seemed so
important as an instrument of communication that nineteenth-century nationalists came to see it as the essential
ingredient of nationhood.

But languages are not "found," like biological species
with natural limits. They are imaginings, too. A linguist
looking at the map of Europe in 1400 would have dis-
cerned no "languages" at all in the modern sense, but

---

1. Benedict R. O'G. Anderson, *Imagined Communities: Reflections
on the Origin and Spread of Nationalism* (London: Verso, 1983) 15
[Nunberg's note]. Anderson (b. 1936) is professor emeritus of government at Cornell University.

only patches of local dialects and varieties, scattered under the shadow of Latin. National languages were formed in a process of conscious creation, as a certain variety was standardized, codified, and most important, assigned a cultural value.[2] For it is not language as such that becomes a bond of national unity, but language as the emblem of a particular conception of community. The sense of common experience shared by speakers of vernacular languages like French or Polish cannot be the same as what attaches to divinely sanctioned "truth languages" like Arabic, Hebrew, or Church Latin; the first is a community of men, the second a community of God.

Even within vernacular communities, the social role of language can be imagined and reimagined in a seemingly infinite number of ways to reflect the changing conceptions of commonality that are intended to serve as the basis for nationhood. The classic example is the Italian *questione della lingua*, or "Language Question," a debate that stretches through the entire course of modern Italian history. In retrospect, the issues raised may seem obscure and trivial: should standard Italian be based on archaic Tuscan, modern Tuscan, or some amalgam of literary dialects? But the debate was really concerned with the social basis of Italian nationality—*Italianità*—that was conceived as the basis for an eventual Italian nation-state. As Gramsci wrote, speaking of Language Questions in their universal, rather than their specifically Italian manifestations: "Whenever the language question surfaces, in one way or another, it means that another series of problems is imposing itself: the formation and enlargement of the ruling class, the necessity . . . of reorganizing cultural hegemony."[3]

Not all questions about language are Language Questions. For one thing, language obviously plays a role in sorting out social and cultural distinctions that are unrelated to national identity. Conversely, the sense of national community can be shaped by other instruments. This is most apparent in multilingual nations like Switzerland and India. But even in essentially monolingual nations, the political basis of the state may be independent of the particular notion of community that the common language implies.

---

2. The process is often referred to with Heinz Kloss's term of *Ausbau*, or roughly, "extension." See Kloss, *Entwicklung Neuer Germanischer Kultursprachen* (Munich: Pohl, 1952) [Nunberg's note].

3. Antonio Gramsci, "Note sullo studio della grammatical," *Quaderni del Carcere*, ed. Valentino Gerrantano, vol. 3 (Turin, 1975) 2347 [Nunberg's note]. Gramsci (1891–1937) was an Italian political theorist and activist who founded the Italian Communist Party and served in the Italian legislature. His ideas still influence the Italian political landscape.

Britain, for example, has had a dominant standard language since the ₅
seventeenth century, at least. Yet the legitimacy of the British state has not
rested on its claim to represent a cultural order symbolized by standard English, but rather on political institutions like Parliament, the Crown, and the
body of English common law. Apart from a brief flirtation with proposals for a
language academy in the early eighteenth century (a course that Joseph
Priestley disparaged as "unsuitable to the genius of a free nation"),[4] the
British have not looked to the state for protection of the English language. It
is true that, in practice, they have had few qualms about imposing English
on colonial peoples, whether in Scotland, Ireland, or India. And beginning in
the late nineteenth century, British educators made systematic efforts to associate the study of English language and literature with nationalist ideology.[5] Symbolically, however, the political apparatus of the British state has
been kept separate from the linguistic and cultural order.

In this sense, Britain offers a marked contrast to France, where the state
has taken an active role in the preservation and promotion of the national
language since the *Académie française* was established in the seventeenth
century. It strikes the French as perfectly natural that government should
pass laws to limit the amount of airplay given to foreign-language songs;
that it should spend fully half its foreign-service budget to subsidize the
teaching of the French language abroad; or that recent spelling reforms
should have been announced at prime-ministerial press conferences. These
may seem trivial matters, but they have a larger symbolic importance. To the
extent that the legitimacy of the French state is based on an essentially cultural sense of community, its political form is flexible. France has been a liberal democracy for more than a century (apart from the Nazi occupation)[6] and
is likely to remain one. But there is little in the conception of French nationality that requires this form of government, and certainly it is imaginable

---

4. Joseph Priestley, *The Rudiments of English Grammar* (London, 1761) viii [Nunberg's note].
Priestley (1733–1804) was an Englishman who was once a Calvinist minister but whose
noncomformist ideas led to a break with the church. He believed in the perfectibility of humans. After meeting Benjamin Franklin, he became interested in science and is best known
for his work on the chemistry of gasses. He invented the carbonated beverage known to
some as "pop" and to others as "soda."

5. See Brian Doyle, *English and Englishness* (London: Routledge, 1989); Tony Crowley,
Standard English and the Politics of Language (Urbana: U of Illinois P, 1989) [Nunberg's
note].

6. **Nazi occupation** in 1940, part of France fell under Nazi control. Germany occupied and
ruled all of France from 1942 until the end of the war, in 1945.

that the Fifth Republic[7] should someday be replaced by a sixth or seventh. The history of the French nation is not, like those of Britain and the United States, identified with the history of a single political regime.

The United States inherited from Britain not just its language, but its understanding of the relation between language and national identity. Initially, there were questions: Would citizens of the new nation go on speaking "English," or develop a new "American language"? Would the state take a role in standardizing the language and, by extension, the national culture? But by the time the nation was fifty years old, Americans had come to believe that they required no national language of their own, and that American identity could rest on a common commitment to the political institutions established at the nation's founding. The state was seen as neither the representative nor the guardian of an official culture.

Like other aspects of the American experiment, however, the relation between cultural and political institutions has never been definitively resolved. It may be, as Rousseau[8] argued and as recent history seems to bear out, that no nation can successfully constitute itself around a set of purely political ideals. Certainly the American system has always presupposed a rough cultural consensus as a necessary feature of political life. For the most part, that consensus has been negotiated informally. But whenever it has appeared to be threatened from without by large-scale immigration or by the absorption of groups from different cultural backgrounds, there have been movements to bring to bear the power of the state to secure the hegemony of the majority culture, in the ostensible interest of preserving political stability. Language issues have figured in a wide variety of policy questions: immigration and naturalization, voting rights, treatment of Native Americans, statehood, civil liberties, and especially education. But only in recent years have debates over such issues given rise to a full-blown Language Question, an attempt to redefine the political basis of the American state in terms of a common culture.

---

7. **Fifth Republic** the French government has undergone several restructurings, called "Republics," since the start of the French Revolution in 1789. The present-day Republic, the Fifth, began in 1958 under the leadership of Charles de Gaulle.

8. **Jean-Jacques Rousseau (1712–1778)** French philosopher whose ideas about equality and natural rights provided the theoretical bases of the American and French revolutions.

about the text

1. What does Nunberg mean by his assertion that "[languages] are imaginings, too" (paragraph 2)? How does that statement relate to the quotation from Benedict Anderson about "imagined communities" (paragraph 1)?

2. Nunberg discusses the status of English in the early years of the United States. Why is that history important to our current situation?

3. How might advocates of the official English movement (see "Two Arguments for Official English" in this chapter) respond to Nunberg's statement that "by the time the nation was fifty years old, Americans had come to believe that they required no national language of their own, and that American identity could rest on a common commitment to the political institutions established at the nation's founding" (paragraph 7)?

on language use

4. If English were to gain official status, which English would be the official version—the English of New York? Texas? Nebraska? London? Jamaica? Bombay? How and by what criteria should the choice be made? Should there be a penalty for people speaking other varieties? Discuss these questions with two or three classmates (you don't all need to agree; just listen carefully and seriously consider one another's ideas) and report your conclusions to the whole class.

for writing

5. What does Nunberg mean when he refers to language as the "emblem of a particular conception of community" (paragraph 2)? Write an essay showing how a particular community's linguistic situation exemplifies Nunberg's statement. Use information in a selection from this chapter, or write about another community you know of. Provide examples to support your conclusions.

part 2

The Official English question is a new theme in the American political discourse. This may not be obvious, because the debate is often framed around specific programs—bilingual education is the most conspicuous example—that do not seem to differ qualitatively from other programs instituted to address the problems of minorities, whether English-speaking or not. Official English advocates have often explained their movement as a response to the "politicization" of these questions by "special interest groups" that are concerned more with promoting ethnic separatism or pork-barrelling for their own constituents than with helping language minorities. But the initial "politicization" of issues like bilingual education was part of the routine process of policy formulation, as enacted at the level of lobbying, Congressional testimony, behind-the-scenes maneuvering, litigation, and so forth. In the normal course of things, you would expect the opposition to these programs to take the form of the same kind of political activity—as indeed it has, down to the politics-as-usual accusations of personal ambition and venality.

But the opposition to these programs has not stopped with politics-as- 10
usual. It has used mass-mailing techniques to establish a national political movement, with its membership drawn from groups with no particular interest in questions of immigration or minority education. It has mounted a number of successful statewide initiatives aimed at eliminating the provision of government services in languages other than English, and it has promoted boycotts to restrict the use of foreign languages in advertising, signage, and broadcasting. And in its symbolically most ambitious effort, it has called for amending the Constitution so as to declare English the official language of the United States.

This is a response calculated to move the discussion of questions of policy into the realm of symbolic politics, with the result that it becomes difficult (and somewhat irrelevant) to debate the issues on their substantive merits. Questions about the effectiveness of bilingual education can be fairly discussed in an academic forum or a legislative hearing, but not in the popular press or in thirty-second sound bites. In a state electoral campaign, voters are in no position to evaluate the claim that the country faces a "dangerous drift toward multilingualism" on the basis of the demographic evidence, or to weigh the parallels to Canada or Belgium in the light of a familiarity with the histories of those nations. This has been an understandable source of frustration to opponents of the Official English movement, especially to scholars familiar with the American minority-language situation. As the sociologist Joshua Fishman asks: "Aren't the comparisons to Sri Lanka or India not only far-fetched and erroneous, but completely removed from the reality of the U.S.A.? . . . Why are facts so useless in this discussion?"[9]

The answer is that the debate is no longer concerned with the content or effect of particular programs, but with the symbolic importance that people have come to attach to these matters. Official English advocates admit as much when they emphasize that their real goal is to "send a message" about the role of English in American life. From this point of view, it is immaterial whether the provision of interpreters for workers compensation hearings or of foreign-language nutrition information actually constitute a "disincentive" to learning English, or whether their discontinuation would work a hardship on recent immigrants. Programs like these merely happen to be high-visibility examples of government's apparent willingness to allow the public use of languages other than English for any purpose whatsoever. In fact, one suspects that most Official English advocates are not especially concerned about specific programs per se, since they will be able to achieve their symbolic goals even if bilingual services are protected by judicial intervention or legislative inaction (as has generally been the case where Official English measures have passed). The real objective of the campaign is the "message" that it intends to send.

What actually is the message? That depends, in part, on who is listening. A number of opponents of the Official English movement have stressed its immediate significance as a reaction to the perceived "demands" of immigrant groups. It is undeniable that racism and and xenophobia have played an important role in the electoral successes of the Official English movement or that some of the movement's organizers have espoused explicitly anti-Hispanic and anti-Catholic views.

Yet this cannot be the entire story. Official English has attracted wide support among people who would not ordinarily countenance openly racist or xenophobic measures. In the 1986 California election, for example, the English-language amendment to the state constitution was adopted by fully 73 percent of the electorate, including large majorities in liberal areas like Palo Alto and Marin County. Nationally, the U.S. English organization has been able to attract approximately five times as many members as the restrictionist Federation of American Immigration Reform, which shares the

---

9. Joshua A. Fishman, "The Displaced Anxieties of Anglo-Americans," *Language Loyalties: A Source Book on the Official English Controversy*, ed. James Crawford (Chicago: U of Chicago P, 1992) 167 [Nunberg's note].

same founder and direct-mail fundraising apparatus.[10] Apparently, many people will support English Only measures who would be squeamish about directly supporting immigration restriction. Also, it is significant that many of the national politicians who have sponsored Official English legislation—Senators Huddleston of Kentucky, Burdick of North Dakota, and Symms of Idaho; Representatives Emerson of Missouri and Smith of Nebraska—come from states in which immigration is not a pressing issue and where the scapegoating of immigrants would hardly seem to be an effective way to distract constituents from their economic problems.

So the Official English movement is really sending two messages. The first is concerned specifically with members of language-minority groups, who are understandably sensitive to its xenophobic overtones. Siobhan Nicolau and Rafael Valdivieso believe that the movement is telling Hispanics: "We don't trust you—we don't like you—we don't think you can fit in—you are too different—*and there seem to be far too many of you.*"[11] Already, in states where Official English initiatives have passed, they are being interpreted as a license to discriminate on the basis of language. But long after the immediate occasion for the movement has receded—after the children of the new immigrant groups have moved into the linguistic and social mainstream and established themselves as "good Americans" like generations of immigrants before them—the legacy of the Official English movement may be felt in a changed conception of American nationality itself.

Of the various "messages," this one may be hardest to perceive. Proponents of Official English claim that they seek merely to recognize a state of affairs that has existed since the founding of the nation. After two hundred years of common-law cohabitation with English, we have simply decided to make an honest woman of her, for the sake of the children. To make the English language "official," however, is not merely to acknowledge it as the language commonly used in commerce, mass communications, and public affairs. Rather, it is to invest English with a symbolic role in national life and to endorse a cultural conception of American identity as the basis for political unity. And while the general communicative role of English in America

15

---

10. James Crawford, "What's Behind Official English?" *Language Loyalties* 172 [Nunberg's note].

11. Siobhan Nicolau and Rafael Valdivieso, "Spanish Language Shift: Educational Implications," *Language Loyalties* 317–18 [Nunberg's note]. Nicolau and Valdivieso write about various aspects of education policy, particularly with regard to Hispanic students. Nicolau has served as president of the Hispanic Policy Development Project; Valdivieso has served as executive director of the National Education Research Policy and Priorities Board.

has not changed over the past two hundred years, the cultural importance that people attach to the language has evolved considerably.

Early linguistic patriots like John Adams and Noah Webster were less concerned with the relation between the majority language and minority languages like German than with the relation between the language of Americans and the "English" from which it descended. What is significant is that the Founders viewed American political institutions not as resting on a national language or a national culture, but as giving rise to them.

★　★　★

The free institutions of the new nation would naturally lead to the formation of a new and independent culture, as symbolized by a distinct language. William Thornton made the argument in 1793, when he told Americans:

> You have corrected the dangerous doctrines of European powers, correct now the languages you have imported . . . The AMERICAN LANGUAGE will thus be as distinct as the government, free from all the follies of unphilosophical fashion, and resting upon truth as its only regulator.[12]

Thus the emergence of a distinct national language was seen to be an effect, rather than a cause, of the success of American democratic institutions.

★　★　★

The question of a national language did not emerge again until the turn of the twentieth century, when Americans found themselves confronted with the large numbers of non-English-speaking immigrants. Previously, language played a relatively minor role in nativist movements, which chiefly exploited fears that newcomers would dilute the religious and racial homogeneity of the nation. But in the first decades of this century, immigrants came to be seen as sources of political contagion. In 1919, Attorney General A. Mitchell Palmer, leader of the infamous Palmer Raids, in which more than eight thousand

---

12. *Cadmus; or, A Treatise on the Element of Written Language* (Philadelphia, 1793) v [Nunberg's note]. William Thornton (1759–1826) was a British-born architect and inventor who designed the rotunda and façade of the U.S. Capitol and developed a "universal alphabet" for representing the sounds of any language. He was the first superintendent of the U.S. Patent Office.

"radicals" were swept up and deported, could confidently assert that "fully 90 percent of Communist and anarchist agitation is traceable to aliens."[13]

One answer to the imagined threat of imported sedition was the "Americanization" campaign, a concerted effort, as John Higham writes, to "heat and stir the melting pot."[14] (The other was immigration restriction, enacted in a series of laws in the early 1920s.) The most important ingredient in the Americanization program was the effort to force immigrants to move from their native tongues to English—not just by providing English instruction, but by actively discouraging the learning and use of other languages. A Nebraska law stipulated that all public meetings be conducted in English; Oregon required foreign-language periodicals to provide an English translation of their entire contents.[15] More than thirty states mandated English as the language of instruction in all schools, public and private.

These measures were based on a particular view of the relation between language and thought, in which speaking a foreign language seemed inimical to grasping the fundamental concepts of democratic society. The Nebraska Supreme Court, in upholding a state statute barring instruction in languages other than English below the ninth grade, warned against the "baneful effects" of educating children in foreign languages, which must "naturally inculcate in them the ideas and sentiments foreign to the best interest of this country."[16]

The complement of such suspicions was a view of English as a kind of "chosen language," the bearer of Anglo-Saxon (or at least Anglo-American) ideals and institutions. English was turned into a kind of "truth language," like Arabic, Hebrew, and Church Latin, except that the truths for which it provided a unique means of expression were those of the secular religion of American democracy. At the New York State constitutional convention in 1916, during debate on an English-literacy requirement for voting, one dele-

---

13. Qtd. in David H. Bennett, *The Party of Fear: From Nativist Movements to the New Right in American History* (New York: Vintage, 1990) 193 [Nunberg's note]. The Palmer Raids were a series of raids in thirty-three U.S. cities on January 2, 1920, in which thousands of people were taken into custody; many were held for long periods without charges being filed. The raids were named after the U.S. Attorney General at the time, A. Mitchell Palmer, who attempted to justify them as a necessary defense against a Bolshevik uprising.

14. John Higham, "Crusade for Americanization," *Language Loyalties* 73 [Nunberg's note]. Higham (1920–2003) was a professor of history at Johns Hopkins University and author of many books and articles on ethnic cleansing in the United States.

15. John Higham, *Strangers in the Land: Patterns of American Nativism, 1860–1925*, 2nd ed. (New Brunswick, NJ: Rutgers UP, 1988) 260 [Nunberg's note].

16. *Meyer v. Nebraska*, 262 U.S. 390 (1923) [Nunberg's note].

gate traced the connection between English and democratic values back to the Magna Carta (a text often mentioned in this context, though it was written in Latin): "You have got to learn our language because that is the vehicle of the thought that has been handed down from the men in whose breasts first burned the fire of freedom."[17] Theodore Roosevelt sounded a similar note when he insisted that: "We must have but one flag. We must also have but one language. That must be the language of the Declaration of Independence, of Washington's Farewell Address, of Lincoln's Gettysburg speech and second inaugural."[18]

What is striking about this list is what it does not include: there is no mention of the language of Irving, Longfellow, and Emerson, much less any reference to "the language of Shakespeare," which British contemporaries would have considered obligatory. One doubts whether Webster would have approved of this list. Where are all the flowers of the literary culture that was to vindicate the American experiment in the eyes of the world? It is not that Roosevelt and his contemporaries were indifferent to literary traditions, but for them it was the political uses of English that made it an instrument of national union. The language was no longer seen as a consequence of political institutions, but as a cause of them.

This signaled a clear change in the conception of American nationality, with English as the soup stock of the melting pot. As such, Americanization was probably a more benign policy than the racially based nativism that held that immigrants were biologically incapable of adapting to American life. In the view of James J. Davis, secretary of labor under Harding and Coolidge,[19] the earlier "Nordic" immigrants were "the beaver type that built up America, whereas the newer immigrants were rat-men trying to tear it down, and obviously rat-men could never become beavers."[20] By contrast, the proponents of Americanization put the burden of transmitting values on cultural institutions, rather than on racial descent. For example, here is Ellwood P. Cubberley, dean of the Stanford University School of Education, describing the goals of the Americanization campaign:

---

17. Qtd. in Dennis Baron, *The English-Only Question: An Official Language for Americans?* (New Haven: Yale UP, 1990) 59 [Nunberg's note].

18. Theodore Roosevelt, "One Flag, One Language," *Language Loyalties* 85 [Nunberg's note].

19. Warren G. Harding (1865–1923) and Calvin Coolidge (1872–1933): U.S. presidents, Harding from 1920 until his death, and Coolidge from 1923 to 1929.

20. Qtd. in Seymour Martin Lipset and Earl Raab, *The Politics of Unreason: Right-Wing Extremism in America, 1790–1970* (New York: Harper, 1977) 142 [Nunberg's note].

Our task is to break up [immigrant] groups or settlements, to assimilate and amalgamate these people as part of our American race, and to implant in their children, as far as can be done, the Anglo-Saxon conception of righteousness, law and order, and our popular government.[21]

While this passage may strike the modern reader as smug and condescending, it is not literally racist, at least in its historical context. Cubberley obviously believed that rat-men could be turned into beavers, if only you caught them young enough.

---

21. Qtd. in James Crawford, *Bilingual Education: History, Politics, Theory, and Practice*, 2nd ed. (Los Angeles: Bilingual Educational Services, 1991) [Nunberg's note].

about the text

1. Nunberg notes that many of the sponsors of Official English legislation have little to gain in their home states by promoting the issue. What might motivate these members of Congress to support such legislation? How might they position themselves differently from members representing states with large immigrant populations?

2. Explain Nunberg's use of the metaphor of common-law cohabitation and marriage to talk about the relationship between English and the United States. Who are the "children" Nunberg refers to? Is the metaphor effective? Why or why not?

on language use

3. Read Theodore Roosevelt's quote in paragraph 22. Do you agree that English is the ideal—perhaps the only—language for expressing and understanding the fundamental concepts on which the United States was established? Would it be possible to comprehend fully the Declaration of Independence or the Gettysburg Address in a language other than English? Why or why not?

for writing

4. What does Nunberg mean when he talks about "symbolic politics" (paragraph 11) and the "symbolic importance" (paragraph 12) of particular programs, particularly bilingual education programs? How might those concepts apply to the question of Native American team names and mascots described by Andrea Woo in "Polls Apart: A Survey" and Mike Wise in "The Squabbling Illini: Rallying Cries Lead to Rift" earlier in this chapter? Write an essay analyzing Woo's and Wise's arguments in terms of "symbolic politics." Provide examples from the selections to support your conclusions.

5. James J. Davis said that immigrants of earlier times were "the beaver type that built up America, whereas the newer immigrants were rat-men trying to tear it down" (paragraph 24). How has the discourse about immigrant groups changed or remained the same? Read any immigration-related articles in your local newspaper for one week. Then, write an essay in which you compare and contrast what you've read with Davis's statement, paying attention to specific word choices and metaphors in the articles. Present examples to support your ideas.

part 3

Taken literally, the chosen-language doctrine does not stand up under 25 scrutiny. The Founders would have been distressed to be told that the truths they held to be "self-evident" could have been apprehended only by other English speakers; nothing could have been further from their own Enlightenment universalism. And there is a peculiarly American fallacy in the supposition that the meanings of words like *liberty* and *rights* are somehow immutably fixed by the structure of the language. It is the linguistic equivalent of the historical doctrine that Daniel Boorstin has described as "givenness": the belief that American values were defined at the outset by the Founders and continue to shape our institutions and experience in an uninterrupted chain, "so that our past merges indistinguishably into our present."[22]

But the doctrine did useful symbolic work. It implied that the features of the old-stock Protestant culture could be abstracted in universally accessible terms. As the hysteria of the war years and the early twenties abated and the flow of new immigrants was reduced to a trickle, the doctrine could be given a more temperate form. It was absorbed into the body of "invented traditions," of schoolroom rituals and folklore that shaped the patriotism of generations of Americans of both native-stock and immigrant backgrounds and, with it, an equally patriotic attachment to the English language itself. It has never been officially retired, and you may still encounter paeans to the political genius of English. But the conception of American nationality has been changing out from under it, and when later waves of immigration caused language issues to be raised again, the new case for a common language was made in very different terms.

The dominant theme in the rhetoric of the Official English movement is the emphasis on English as a lingua franca, the "common bond" that unites all Americans. As former Senator S. I. Hayakawa puts it, the language alone has "made a society out of the hodgepodge of nationalities, races, and colors represented in the immigrant hordes that people our nation," and has enabled Americans to draw up "the understandings and agreements that make a society possible."[23]

---

22. Daniel Boorstin, "Why a Theory Seems Needless," *Hidden History* (New York: Harper, 1987) 77 [Nunberg's note]. Boorstin (b. 1914) is a Pulitzer Prize–winning author who writes on U.S. history and politics.

23. S. I. Hayakawa, "The Case for Official English," *Language Loyalties: A Source Book on the Official English Controversy*, ed. James Crawford (Chicago: U of Chicago P, 1992) 94 [Nunberg's note]. Hayakawa (1906–1992) was a language scholar and university president

Modern official-language advocates are careful, however, to avoid the suggestion that English has any unique virtues that make it appropriate in this role as a common bond. A U.S. English publication explains: "We hold no special brief for English. If Dutch (or French, or Spanish, or German) had become our national language, we would now be enthusiastically defending Dutch." (It is hard to imagine Noah Webster or Theodore Roosevelt passing over the special genius of English so lightly.)[24] In fact, the movement often seems eager to discharge English of any cultural responsibility whatsoever. Its arguments are cast with due homage to the sanctity of pluralism. Indeed, its advocates often rest their case on the observation that the very cultural heterogeneity of modern America makes English "no longer a bond, but *the* bond between all of us," in the words of Gerda Bikales, the former executive director of U.S. English.[25] Or, as Senator Walter Huddleston argues, a common language has enabled us "to develop a stable and cohesive society that is the envy of many fractured ones, without imposing any strict standards of homogeneity."[26] Official English advocates seem to suggest that Americans need have nothing at all in common, so long as we have the means for talking about it.

Unlike the Americanizers, they no longer stress the role of English as an instrument of ideological indoctrination. The Cubans, Mexicans, Central Americans, Vietnamese, Filipinos, Chinese, Haitians, Russians, and others who have made up recent waves of arrivals are generally—and accurately—seen either as seekers after economic opportunity or as refugees from oppressive regimes of the left or right. Nor is there cause for concern that immi-

who served one term as a U.S. senator from California. He founded U.S. English, an organization in favor of official English policies, and served as its chairman until his death.

24. "Talking Points," March 1983. A U.S. English newsletter of March 1983 does observe that English is capable of "subtle nuance and great precision of meaning" and that the language has an impressively large vocabulary (but of course the same claims might be made about the language of any developed society). It notes, too, that English is the premier language of international communications, which surely would be a good reason for choosing English as a national language if we were starting the country from scratch. But what is notable is that all of these claims involve the practical utility, real or imagined, of having English as a common language. They suggest no intrinsic tie between the genius of English and our particular conception of national identity [Nunberg's note].

25. Qtd. in Joseph Leibowicz, "Official English: Another Americanization Campaign?" *Language Loyalties* 101 [Nunberg's note].

26. Qtd. in Joseph Leibowicz, "Official English: Another Americanization Campaign?" *Language Loyalties* 104 [Nunberg's note].

grants will add fuel to domestic radical movements or ignite labor unrest. At the most, they seem to many a bit too assertive about their rights and insufficiently enthusiastic about cultural assimilation. But then, the great mass of turn-of-the-century immigrants had no more interest in political questions than present-day immigrants do. What has changed is not the political nature of the new arrivals, but the way we perceive their differences from ourselves. So we might well ask: how have we changed, if our political unity can be threatened by unassimilated immigrants with whom we have no ideological differences?

Americans are no less patriotic than they were a century ago, but their sense of community is mediated in different ways. In 1900 it was unimaginable that there should be occasions at which all Americans could be present or that many Americans could acquire the sense of national identity that comes of frequent movement around the country. There were, of course, newspapers and books, but literacy was far from universal. So the burden of creating a sense of community was naturally laid on traditional institutions of schools, churches, and the like, which could ensure that experiences and ceremonies that ratified the national identity would be faithfully replicated from one locality to the next.

But the twentieth century brought means of replicating experience that required no institutional intervention, most notably the movies, radio, and television. Watching "The Cosby Show" or "NBC Nightly News," we can be assured that millions of other Americans are participating in the very same experience—laughing at the same jokes and finding the same reports noteworthy. More important, these media have the power to *show* Americans to one another, with such immediacy that we may be deceived into believing that the awareness of community can be created without any exercise of the imagination at all. Together with the extraordinary increase in geographical mobility and mass merchandising, the media create a vastly extended repertory of shared national experience: we view the same videos, eat at the same restaurant chains, visit the same theme parks, wait in the same gas lines, and so on.

The new mechanisms of national community are capable of imposing a high degree of cultural and ideological uniformity without explicit indoctrination, or indeed, without seeming to "impose" at all. This is what makes it possible for us to indulge in the rhetoric of "cherished diversity" and even to suppose that it is only our language that we have in common. But the pluralism that Official English advocates profess to cherish is the denatured ethnicity of third- and fourth-generation Americans, monolingual in English and disconnected from any real ties to the language and culture of their ancestors. For the most part, this "lifestyle" ethnicity is a matter of food, fashion, and festivals, which add a note of "colorfulness" that serves to "enrich"—and, in the course of things, to mask—the homogeneity of the values that regulate American middle-class life.

It could be argued that the very abundance of the common experience of national life makes linguistic unity superfluous. Benedict Anderson has suggested that new technologies make it possible to create a sense of community without a common language:

> Multilingual broadcasting can conjure up the imagined community to illiterates and populations with different mother tongues. (Here there are resemblances to the conjuring up of medieval Christendom through visual representations and bilingual literati.) . . . Nations can now be imagined without linguistic communality.[27]

This seems to be true in many states that have emerged in recent times—not just in Africa and Asia, but even in Switzerland, the last polity in Western Europe to have developed a modern sense of nationhood. In the United States, too, it is certainly easier for non-English-speaking immigrants to develop a sense of American identity today than at the turn of the century, thanks to national foreign-language media that reproduce many of the same images and programs as the English-language media, and to the ubiquitous apparatus of consumer culture.

Yet in America, the new mechanisms for establishing a sense of national community have only increased concerns about linguistic disunity. There are several reasons why this should be so. First, the new mechanisms depend on a voluntary participation in the public discourse rather than on explicit intervention by traditional institutions. This may explain why the Official English movement appears indifferent to the classes in Americanism and citizenship that played such an important part in the program of earlier assimilation movements. It is as if the schools can no longer make good Americans, but only give students a knowledge of English so that Americanization can happen to them in their free time. Then, too, the very homogeneity and ubiquity of the mechanisms of mass culture make departures from the cultural norm seem all the more aberrant. The presence of people who do not have access to this experience—or more to the point, who cannot be assumed to have such access—becomes increasingly intolerable. If our common values can command such widespread assent in the face of the apparent "diversity"

---

27. Benedict R. O'G. Anderson, *Imagined Communities: Reflections on the Origin and Spread of Nationalism* (London: Verso, 1983) 123 [Nunberg's note].

of European-American life, then surely it is not unreasonable to expect the members of other cultures to conform to them.

Finally, linguistic diversity is more conspicuous than it was a century 35 ago. To be aware of the large numbers of non-English speakers in 1900, it was necessary to live in or near one of their communities, whereas today it is only necessary to flip through a cable television dial, drive past a Spanish-language billboard, or (in many states) apply for a driver's license. At a best guess, there are fewer speakers of foreign languages in America now than there were then, in both absolute and relative numbers. But what matters symbolically is the widespread *impression* of linguistic diversity, particularly among people who have no actual contact with speakers of languages other than English.

Inevitably, the effect of the new mechanisms of community has been to make American identity increasingly a matter of cultural uniformity, as symbolized by linguistic uniformity, and to diminish the importance of explicit ideology. This development is partially hidden behind the rhetoric of "pluralism" and "cultural diversity," but it emerges, as repressed concerns are wont to do, in the nightmares of the Official English advocates, which are haunted by specters of separatism and civil strife. Hayakawa writes:

> For the first time in our history, our nation is faced with the possibility of the kind of linguistic division that has torn apart Canada in recent years; that has been a major feature of the unhappy history of Belgium, split into speakers of French and Flemish; that is at this very moment a bloody division between the Sinhalese and Tamil populations of Sri Lanka.[28]

Here, too, it is notable that the line of argument has no precedent in earlier nativist movements. Language conflicts were probably more common on the world scene in 1920 than they are now and certainly figured more prominently in American public consciousness during the First World War and the debate over the League of Nations. Yet the experience of other countries was rarely if ever mentioned in the Americanization campaign. Not that the possibility of a multilingual America seemed more remote then than now. Indeed, the presence of language minorities was widely (if inaccurately) perceived as an immediate threat to political stability and prompted calls for more drastic steps than anything that the contemporary Official English movement has yet proposed. For supporters of Americanization, however, international analogies were irrelevant. The point of establishing linguistic uniformity was not to preserve just any common culture, but to ensure uni-

---

28. S. I. Hayakawa, "The Case for Official English," *Language Loyalties* 99 [Nunberg's note].

versal assent to the particular ideology associated with English-language institutions. There was nothing that we had to learn about our national identity from comparisons with Alsace or Austria-Hungary; or, for that matter, from comparisons with monolingual non-English-speaking nations like France or Japan.

So why should foreign examples of language conflicts strike a responsive chord now? Not, again, because there is any actual threat to the status of English as a common language. Not even Official English advocates suggest that there is any imminent danger of separatist movements springing up in East Los Angeles or Dade County. But if the specter of civil strife is implausible, its appeal to the popular imagination is nevertheless an indication of the widespread acceptance of a changed sense of national community. If American identity is based simply on a common cultural experience, then the experience of other nations is suddenly relevant to our situation. It is notable that in the cautionary examples that Official English proponents like to invoke, particularly Canada and Belgium, the ethnic divisions are generally perceived as having no ideological significance.[29] If Quebec were to become an independent state, one assumes, it would be a liberal democracy like the rest of Canada, and like France, a secular state, despite its Catholic majority. The obvious moral is that cultural and linguistic differences alone are sufficient to divide a state—any state, including ours.

The history of American language controversies reveals a profound and troubling change in our conception of national community. For Noah Webster, the American language was a reflection of our political institutions. For Theodore Roosevelt, it was the instrument for inculcating a sense of political tradition. For proponents of the modern Official English movement, it is simply the guarantor of the cultural sameness that for them political unity seems to require. So the burden of nationality gradually shifts from political institutions to cultural commonalities, to the point where "Americanism," like "Frenchness," *Italianità* and all the rest, becomes essentially a cultural matter. Not that there is anything wrong with France, Italy, or other nations; but America was supposed to be different.

Obviously, the Official English movement is not the cause of the changed sense of nationality, but neither is it merely a symptom. As I noted at the outset, language has always done the work of symbolizing cultural categories

---

29. In point of fact, of course, the divisions in these countries owe more to long histories of social and economic inequality than to language differences per se; but few Americans are familiar with the details of Canadian or Belgian history, and these considerations are ignored when it comes to drawing the comparison to the American case [Nunberg's note].

that are in themselves too deep and inchoate to be directly expressed. Even if the official-language movement is really an "official-culture movement," it could not have been formulated in such terms. We could not very well entertain a constitutional amendment that read, "The United States shall henceforth be officially constituted around such-and-such a conception of American culture." It is only when the issues are cast in terms of language that they become amenable to direct political action, and that culture can be made an official component of American identity. The great danger is in reading the debate as literally concerned with language alone—all the more because these are relatively new themes in the American political discourse, and we have no history of Language Questions to refer to. Of course, there are real questions of language at stake in all this, but they are not *merely* questions of language; they never are.

about the text

1. According to Nunberg, how and why are arguments about language easier to make than those about culture? Do you agree?
2. Compare language issues in the United States with those in Canada or Belgium. What does Nunberg say about such comparisons? In what ways do you think the United States' situation is different from those of Canada or Belgium? Explain.

on language use

3. Speaking about the diversity of U.S. society, S. I. Hayakawa uses the phrase "immigrant hordes" (paragraph 27). What are the connotations of that phrase? What more neutral phrases can you think of?
4. Nunberg's essay was published in 1992, before email, the Web, IMing, and cell phones radically changed the way we communicate. What might Nunberg say about how these technologies modify our sense of "belonging" to the United States?

for writing

5. Puerto Rico, a United States commonwealth since 1952, is often mentioned as a candidate to become the fifty-first state. Since Spanish is the island's official language, the statehood debate often hinges on language issues. Find arguments about Puerto Rican statehood from as many perspectives as possible—pro and con, Puerto Rican and non–Puerto Rican. Carefully consider all the arguments; then write an essay in which you address how might issues of language be addressed if Puerto Rico became the fifty-first state? Consider questions of education, government, business, and any other relevant areas.
6. In speaking about present-day immigrants, Nunberg states, "What has changed is not the political nature of the new arrivals, but the way we perceive their difference from ourselves" (paragraph 29). Do you agree? Why or why not? Write an essay in which you support or oppose Nunberg's claim with examples and evidence.

chapter 9

globalizing english

i t is almost a cliché of U.S. life at the turn of the twenty-first century that English is a global language, the primary language of the Internet, of science, of commerce, and of tourism in virtually every corner of the planet. The dominance of English comes up as a tangential fact in all kinds of U.S. public discourse—in newspapers, magazines, radio call-in programs, economics textbooks. In most of these cases, global English is mentioned as a source of pride or comfort to its speakers, especially native speakers: we are encouraged to view ourselves as being, in some way, on a "winning side." Global English may even be invoked explicitly to excuse English speakers from having to exert the effort to learn another language; sooner or later, the argument goes, we'll be able to communicate with anyone, anywhere in the whole world because everyone will speak English.

How realistic is that claim? Will everyone in the world eventually speak English? And if they did, would we indeed all be able to communicate easily? What, in fact, do English speakers all over the world have in common? What might the implications be for native English speakers if the language that we cherish as a means of expressing our own cultures and identities became a resource for expressing cultures and identities very different from any found in the United States? Might there be economic consequences for native English speakers as the language spread throughout the world? And as economic opportunities consequently open for people in diverse parts of the globe, what cultural consequences might there be for those people, both individually and ethnically? The readings in this chapter address these questions, some in direct ways and others in ways that will require you to think between the lines.

The chapter begins with an essay by David Crystal that provides context for these questions. "Why a Global Language?" he asks, discussing the definition of a global language and its potential implications for both speakers and non-speakers. We include with Crystal's essay a humorous anecdote from the New York Times that calls into question Americans' claims to English.

The question of who owns English is addressed in some way in almost all the selections in the chapter. Three recent newspaper accounts deal with the use of specific varieties of English in three different nations of Asia. From Bangalore, India, Beth Duff-Brown describes the accent and cultural training that employees of Indian call centers receive in order to take customer service calls from U.S. customers of American companies. From Taiwan, Henry Chu reports on English-language schools in that country—not at all unusual, except that the students of these schools are less than three years old. And from a Korean newspaper comes a letter to the editor written by Derek Zhu, defending Konglish, a likely precursor of a local variety of English spoken in Korea. Next, Shashi Tharoor discusses questions of audience and authenticity in Indian novels written in English, addressing criticism that English is inappropriate for expressing Indian cultures and experiences. Moving westward, John Tagliabue reports on the growing use of English in European corporate affairs, to many there a practical if often distasteful policy. The chapter ends with an essay by Barbara Wallraff that revisits many of the questions that opened it: "What Global Language?"

The readings in this chapter will challenge you to take a larger view of the language in which you are reading right now, English. As you go about your daily life, possibly using English for sending instant messages, ordering merchandise over the telephone, writing papers, rapping, or any of the hundreds of activities in which the language you use comes as unconsciously as breathing, we hope you'll give some thought to what else English is doing for (and to) people all over the world. It's 10 P.M. Do you know where your language is?

David Crystal *is a linguist, writer, editor, lecturer, and broadcaster. As an honorary professor of linguistics at the University of Wales, Bangor, he writes about language for both specialists and the general public. His recent works include* Language and the Internet *(2001),* Language Death *(2000), and* Who Cares about English Usage? *(2000).* **Why a Global Language?** *is from* English as a Global Language *(2003). It looks at how languages (and their speakers) interact on the world stage—for example, in international business, diplomatic relations, and politics. Could all be conducted in only one language? If so, which one? What are some of the implications of English being the dominant world language? Will the dominance of English endure for the foreseeable future? How important is language unity to national identity?*

We have also included an entry from the **Metropolitan Diary** *a weekly column in the New York Times of "observations and poetry on life in New York." This selection, from November 11, 2002, contributed by Avram Hyman, takes up the question of who owns English with a reported conversation between a New Yorker and a British visitor.*

DAVID CRYSTAL

Why a Global Language?

WHAT MAKES A GLOBAL LANGUAGE?

Why a language becomes a global language has little to do with the number of people who speak it. It is much more to do with who those speakers are. Latin became an international language throughout the Roman Empire, but this was not because the Romans were more numerous than the peoples they subjugated. They were simply more powerful. And later, when Roman military power declined, Latin remained for a millennium as the international language of education, thanks to a different sort of power—the ecclesiastical power of Roman Catholicism.

There is the closest of links between language dominance and cultural power, and this relationship will become increasingly clear as the history of English is told. Without a strong power-base, whether political, military or economic, no language can make progress as an international medium of communication. Language has no independent existence, living in some sort of mystical space apart from the people who speak it. Language exists only in the brains and mouths and ears and hands and eyes of its users. When they succeed, on the international stage, their language succeeds. When they fail, their language fails.

This point may seem obvious, but it needs to be made at the outset, because over the years many popular and misleading beliefs have grown up about why a language should become internationally successful. It is quite common to hear people claim that a language is a paragon, on account of its perceived aesthetic qualities, clarity of expression, literary power, or religious standing. Hebrew, Greek, Latin, Arabic and French are among those which at various times have been lauded in such terms, and English is no exception. It is often suggested, for example, that there must be something inherently beautiful or logical about the structure of English, in order to explain why it is now so widely used. "It has less grammar than other languages," some have suggested. "English doesn't have a lot of endings on its words, nor do we have to remember the difference between masculine, feminine, and neuter gender, so it must be easier to learn." In 1848, a reviewer in the British periodical *The Athenaeum* wrote:

> In its easiness of grammatical construction, in its paucity of inflection, in its almost total disregard of the distinctions of gender excepting those of nature, in the simplicity and precision of its terminations and auxiliary verbs, not less than in the majesty, vigour and copiousness of its expression, our mother-tongue seems well adapted by *organization* to become the language of the world.

Such arguments are misconceived. Latin was once a major international language, despite its many inflectional endings and gender differences. French, too, has been such a language, despite its nouns being masculine or feminine; and so—at different times and places—have the heavily inflected Greek, Arabic, Spanish and Russian. Ease of learning has nothing to do with it. Children of all cultures learn to talk over more or less the same period of time, regardless of the differences in the grammar of their languages.

This is not to deny that a language may have certain properties which 5 make it internationally appealing. For example, learners sometimes comment on the "familiarity" of English vocabulary, deriving from the way English has over the centuries borrowed thousands of new words from the languages with which it has been in contact. The "welcome" given to foreign vocabulary places English in contrast to some languages (notably, French) which have tried to keep it out, and gives it a cosmopolitan character which many see as an advantage for a global language. From a lexical point of view, English is in fact more a Romance than a Germanic language.[1] And there have been comments made about other structural aspects, too, such as the absence in English grammar of a system of coding social class differences, which can make the language appear more "democratic" to those who speak a language (e.g., Javanese) that does express an intricate system of class relationships. But these supposed traits of appeal are incidental, and need to be weighed against linguistic features which would seem to be internationally much less desirable—notably, in the case of English, the many irregularities of its spelling system.

A language does not become a global language because of its intrinsic structural properties, or because of the size of its vocabulary, or because it has been a vehicle of a great literature in the past, or because it was once associated with a great culture or religion. These are all factors which can motivate someone to learn a language, of course, but none of them alone, or in combination, can ensure a language's world spread. Indeed, such factors cannot even guarantee survival as a living language—as is clear from the case of Latin, learned today as a classical language by only a scholarly and religious few. Correspondingly, inconvenient structural properties (such as awkward spelling) do not stop a language from achieving international status either.

A language becomes an international language for one chief reason: the political power of its people—especially their military power. The explanation is the same throughout history. Why did Greek become a language of international communication in the Middle East over 2000 years ago? Not because of the intellects of Plato and Aristotle: the answer lies in the swords and spears wielded by the armies of Alexander the Great. Why did Latin become known throughout Europe? Ask the legions of the Roman Empire. Why did Arabic come to be spoken so widely across northern Africa and the Middle East? Follow the spread of Islam, carried along by the force of the Moorish armies from the eighth century. Why did Spanish, Portuguese, and French find their way into the Americas, Africa and the Far East? Study the colonial policies of the Renaissance kings and queens, and the way these policies were ruthlessly implemented by armies and navies all over the known world. The history of a global language can be traced through the successful expeditions of its soldier/sailor speakers. And English has been no exception.

---

1. **Romance language** a branch of the Indo-European language family tree that includes Spanish, French, Italian, Rumanian, and Portuguese, and whose common ancestor is Latin. **Germanic language** a branch of the Indo-European language family tree that includes English, German, Dutch, Yiddish, Swedish, and Icelandic.

But international language dominance is not solely the result of military might. It may take a militarily powerful nation to establish a language, but it takes an economically powerful one to maintain and expand it. This has always been the case, but it became a particularly critical factor early in the twentieth century, with economic developments beginning to operate on a global scale, supported by the new communication technologies—telegraph, telephone, radio—and fostering the emergence of massive multinational organizations. The growth of competitive industry and business brought an explosion of international marketing and advertising. The power of the press reached unprecedented levels, soon to be surpassed by the broadcasting media, with their ability to cross national boundaries with electromagnetic ease. Technology, in the form of movies and records, fuelled new mass entertainment industries which had a worldwide impact. The drive to make progress in science and technology fostered an international intellectual and research environment which gave scholarship and further education a high profile.

Any language at the centre of such an explosion of international activity would suddenly have found itself with a global status. And English was in the right place at the right time. By the beginning of the nineteenth century, Britain had become the world's leading industrial and trading country. By the end of the century, the population of the USA (then approaching 100 million) was

larger than that of any of the countries of western Europe, and its economy was the most productive and the fastest growing in the world. British political imperialism had sent English around the globe, during the nineteenth century, so that it was "a language on which the sun never sets." During the twentieth century, this world presence was maintained and promoted, almost single-handedly, through the economic supremacy of the new American superpower. And the language behind the US dollar was English.

* * *

WHAT ARE THE DANGERS OF A GLOBAL LANGUAGE?

The benefits that would flow from the existence of a global language are con- 10
siderable; but some commentators have pointed to possible risks. Perhaps a
global language will cultivate an elite monolingual linguistic class, more
complacent and dismissive in their attitudes toward other languages. Perhaps those who have such a language at their disposal—and especially
those who have it as a mother tongue—will be more able to think and work
quickly in it, and to manipulate it to their own advantage at the expense of
those who do not have it, thus maintaining in a linguistic guise the chasm
between rich and poor. Perhaps the presence of a global language will make
people lazy about learning other languages, or reduce their opportunities to
do so. Perhaps a global language will hasten the disappearance of minority
languages, or—the ultimate threat—make *all* other languages unnecessary.
"A person needs only one language to talk to someone else," it is sometimes
argued, "and once a world language is in place, other languages will simply
die away." Linked with all this is the unpalatable face of *linguistic
triumphalism*—the danger that some people will celebrate one language's
success at the expense of others.

It is important to face up to these fears, and to recognize that they are
widely held. There is no shortage of mother-tongue English speakers who believe in an evolutionary view of language ("let the fittest survive, and if the
fittest happens to be English, then so be it") or who refer to the present global
status of the language as a "happy accident." There are many who think that
all language learning is a waste of time. And many more who see nothing
wrong with the vision that a world with just one language in it would be a
very good thing. For some, such a world would be one of unity and peace,
with all misunderstanding washed away—a widely expressed hope underlying the movements in support of a universal artificial language (such as
Esperanto).[2] For others, such a world would be a desirable return to the "innocence" that must have been present among human beings in the days before the Tower of Babel.[3]

---

2. **Esperanto** an artificial language created in 1887 by the physicist L. L. Zamenhof, who intended it to be an international second language. It is considered to be the most successful
of the many artificial languages and has approximately 100,000 speakers—all nonnative.

3. **Tower of Babel** reference to Genesis 11:1–9, in which humans, all speaking one language, begin to build a great tower that would reach the heavens. The LORD, thinking that
their cooperation would enable them to achieve any goal, made them speak different languages so that they would no longer be able to understand each other.

It is difficult to deal with anxieties which are so speculative, or, in the absence of evidence, to determine whether anything can be done to reduce or eliminate them. The last point can be quite briefly dismissed: the use of a single language by a community is no guarantee of social harmony or mutual understanding, as has been repeatedly seen in world history (e.g., the American Civil War, the Spanish Civil War, the Vietnam War, former Yugoslavia, contemporary Northern Ireland); nor does the presence of more than one language within a community necessitate civil strife, as seen in several successful examples of peaceful multilingual coexistence (e.g., Finland, Singapore, Switzerland). The other points, however, need to be taken more slowly, to appreciate the alternative perspective. The arguments are each illustrated with reference to English—but the same arguments would apply whatever language was in the running for global status.

Linguistic power   Will those who speak a global language as a mother-tongue automatically be in a position of power compared with those who have to learn it as an official or foreign language? The risk is certainly real. It is possible, for example, that scientists who do not have English as a mother-tongue will take longer to assimilate reports in English compared with their mother-tongue colleagues, and will as a consequence have less time to carry out their own creative work. It is possible that people who write up their research in languages other than English will have their work ignored by the international community. It is possible that senior managers who do not have English as a mother-tongue, and who find themselves working for English-language companies in such parts of the world as Europe or Africa, could find themselves at a disadvantage compared with their mother-tongue colleagues, especially when meetings involve the use of informal speech. There is already anecdotal evidence to suggest that these things happen.

However, if proper attention is paid to the question of language learning, the problem of disadvantage dramatically diminishes. If a global language is taught early enough, from the time that children begin their full-time education, and if it is maintained continuously and resourced well, the kind of linguistic competence that emerges in due course is a real and powerful bilingualism, indistinguishable from that found in any speaker who has encountered the language since birth. These are enormous "ifs," with costly financial implications, and it is therefore not surprising that this kind of control is currently achieved by only a minority of non-native learners of any language; but the fact that it is achievable indicates that there is nothing inevitable about the disadvantage scenario.

It is worth reflecting, at this point, on the notion that children are born $_{15}$ ready for bilingualism. Some two-thirds of the children on earth grow up in a bilingual environment, and develop competence in it. There is a naturalness with which they assimilate another language, once they are regularly exposed to it, which is the envy of adults. It is an ability that seems to die away as children reach their teens, and much academic debate has been devoted to the question of why this should be (the question of "critical periods"). There is however widespread agreement that, if we want to take the task of foreign language learning seriously, the principle has to be "the earlier the better." And when that task is taken seriously, with reference to the acquisition of a global language, the elitism argument evaporates.

Linguistic complacency Will a global language eliminate the motivation for adults to learn other languages? Here too the problem is real enough. Clear signs of linguistic complacency, common observation suggests, are already present in the archetypal British or American tourist who travels the world assuming that everyone speaks English, and that it is somehow the fault of the local people if they do not. The stereotype of an English tourist repeatedly asking a foreign waiter for tea in a loud "read my lips" voice is too near the reality to be comfortable. There seems already to be a genuine, widespread lack of motivation to learn other languages, fuelled partly by lack of money and opportunity, but also by lack of interest, and this might well be fostered by the increasing presence of English as a global language.

It is important to appreciate that we are dealing here with questions of attitude or state of mind rather than questions of ability—though it is the latter which is often cited as the explanation. "I'm no good at languages" is probably the most widely heard apology for not making any effort at all to acquire even a basic knowledge of a new language. Commonly, this self-denigration derives from an unsatisfactory language learning experience in school: the speaker is perhaps remembering a poor result in school examinations—which may reflect no more than an unsuccessful teaching approach or a not unusual breakdown in teacher-adolescent relationships. "I never got on with my French teacher" is another typical comment. But this does not stop people going on to generalize that "the British (or the Americans, etc.) are not very good at learning languages."

These days, there are clear signs of growing awareness, within English-speaking communities, of the need to break away from the traditional monolingual bias. In economically hard-pressed times, success in boosting exports and attracting foreign investment can depend on subtle factors, and sensitivity to the language spoken by a country's potential foreign partners is known to be particularly influential. At least at the levels of business and industry, many firms have begun to make fresh efforts in this direction. But at grass-roots tourist level, too, there are signs of a growing respect for other cultures, and a greater readiness to engage in language learning. Language attitudes are changing all the time, and more and more people are discovering, to their great delight, that they are not at all bad at picking up a foreign language.

In particular, statements from influential politicians and administrators are beginning to be made which are helping to foster a fresh climate of opinion about the importance of language learning. A good example is an address given to the world members' conference of the English-Speaking Union in 1996 by the former secretary-general of the Commonwealth, Sir Sridath Ramphal. His title, "World language: opportunities, challenges, responsibilities," itself contains a corrective to triumphalist thinking, and his text repeatedly argues against it:

> It is all too easy to make your way in the world linguistically with English as your mother-tongue . . . We become lazy about learning other languages. . . . We all have to make a greater effort. English may be the world language; but it is not the world's only language and if we are to be good global neighbours we shall have to be less condescending to the languages of the world—more assiduous in cultivating acquaintance with them.

It remains to be seen whether such affirmations of good will have long-term effect. In the meantime, it is salutary to read some of the comparative statistics about foreign language learning. For example, a European business survey by Grant Thornton reported in 1996 that 90 per cent of businesses in Belgium, The Netherlands, Luxembourg and Greece had an executive able to negotiate in another language, whereas only 38 per cent of British companies had someone who could do so. The UK-based Centre for Information on Language Teaching found that a third of British exporters miss opportunities because of poor language skills. And several studies have shown that English-monolingual companies are increasingly encountering language difficulties as they try to expand in those areas of the world thought to have greatest prospects of growth, such as East Asia, South America, and Eastern Europe—areas where English has traditionally had a relatively low presence. The issues are beginning to be addressed—for example, Australian schools now teach Japanese as the first foreign language, and both the USA and UK are now paying more attention to Spanish (which, in terms of mother-tongue use, is growing more rapidly than English)—but we are still a long way from a world where the economic and other arguments have universally persuaded the English-speaking nations to renounce their linguistic insularity.

Linguistic death Will the emergence of a global language hasten the disap- [20] pearance of minority languages and cause widespread language death? To answer this question, we must first establish a general perspective. The processes of language domination and loss have been known throughout linguistic history, and exist independently of the emergence of a global language. No one knows how many languages have died, since humans became able to speak, but it must be thousands. In many of these cases, the death has been caused by an ethnic group coming to be assimilated within a more dominant society, and adopting its language. The situation continues today, though the matter is being discussed with increasing urgency because of the unprecedented rate at which indigenous languages are being lost, especially in North America, Brazil, Australia, Indonesia and parts of Africa. Some estimates suggest that perhaps 80 per cent of the world's 6,000 or so living languages will die out within the next century.

If this happens, it will indeed be an intellectual and social tragedy. When a language dies, so much is lost. Especially in languages that have never been written down, or which have been written down only recently, language is the repository of the history of a people. It is their identity. Oral testimony, in the form of sagas, folktales, songs, rituals, proverbs, and many other practices, provides us with a unique view of our world and a unique canon of literature. It is their legacy to the rest of humanity. Once lost, it can never be recaptured. The argument is similar to that used in relation to the conservation of species and the environment. The conservation of languages is arguably also a priority, and it is good to see in the 1990s a number of international organizations being formed with the declared aim of recording for posterity as many endangered languages as possible.

However, the emergence of any one language as global has little to do with this unhappy state of affairs. Whether Sorbian survives in Germany or Galician in Spain has to do with the local political history of those countries, and with the regional dominance of German and Spanish respectively, and bears no immediate relationship to the standing of German or Spanish on the world stage. Nor is it easy to see how the arrival of English as a global language could directly influence the future of these or most other minority languages. An effect is likely only in those areas where English has itself come to be the dominant first language, such as in North America, Australia and the Celtic parts of the British Isles. The early history of language contact in these areas was indeed one of conquest and assimilation. But in more recent times, the emergence of English as a truly global language has, if anything, had the reverse effect—stimulating a stronger response in support of a local language than might otherwise have been the case. Movements for language rights (alongside civil rights in general) have played an important part in several countries, such as in relation to the Maori in New Zealand, the Aboriginal languages of Australia, the Indian languages of Canada and the USA, and some of the Celtic languages. Although often too late, in certain instances the decline of a language has been slowed, and occasionally (as in the case of Welsh) halted.

The existence of vigorous movements in support of linguistic minorities, commonly associated with nationalism, illustrates an important truth about the nature of language in general. The need for mutual intelligibility, which is part of the argument in favour of a global language, is only one side of the story. The other side is the need for identity—and people tend to underestimate the role of identity when they express anxieties about language injury and death. Language is a major means (some would say the chief means) of showing where we belong, and of distinguishing one social group from another, and all over the world we can see evidence of linguistic divergence rather than convergence. For decades, many people in the countries of the former Yugoslavia made use of a common language, Serbo-Croatian. But since the civil wars of the early 1990s, the Serbs have begun to refer to their language as Serbian, the Bosnians to theirs as Bosnian, and the Croats to theirs as Croatian, with each side drawing attention to the linguistic features that are distinctive. A similar situation exists in Scandinavia, where Swedish, Norwegian, and Danish are largely mutually intelligible, but are nonetheless considered to be different languages.

Arguments about the need for national or cultural identity are often seen as being opposed to those about the need for mutual intelligibility. But this is misleading. It is perfectly possible to develop a situation in which intelligibility and identity happily coexist. This situation is the familiar one of bilingualism—but a bilingualism where one of the languages within a speaker is the global language, providing access to the world community, and the other is a regional language, providing access to a local community. The two functions can be seen as complementary, responding to different needs. And it is because the functions are so different that a world of linguistic diversity can in principle continue to exist in a world united by a common language.

None of this is to deny that the emergence of a global language can influence the structure of other languages—especially by providing a fresh source of loan-words for use by these other languages. Such influences can be welcomed (in which case, people talk about their language being "varied" and "enriched") or opposed (in which case, the metaphors are those of "injury" and "death"). For example, in recent years, one of the healthiest languages, French, has tried to protect itself by law against what is widely perceived to be the malign influence of English: in official contexts, it is now illegal to use an English word where a French word already exists, even though the usage may have widespread popular support (e.g., *computer* for *ordinateur*). Purist commentators from several other countries have also expressed concern at the way in which English vocabulary—especially that of American English—has come to permeate their high streets[4] and TV programmes. The arguments are carried on with great emotional force. Even though only a tiny part of the lexicon is ever affected in this way, that is enough to arouse the wrath of the prophets of doom. (They usually forget the fact that English itself, over the centuries, has borrowed thousands of words from other languages, and constructed thousands more from the elements of other languages—including *computer*, incidentally, which derives from Latin, the mother-language of French.)

★ ★ ★

The relationship between the global spread of English and its impact on other languages attracted increasing debate during the 1990s, and the debate has continued into the new millennium. The future remains uncertain. It is impossible to make confident predictions about the way a global language will develop, simply because there has never been one before, and we do not know what long-term impact its arrival will have. It may be that a global language, once in place, becomes unremovable. Alternatively, given the close relationship between language and power, the impression of permanence may be illusory, easily affected by swings in political and economic status. There was only a suggestion of a global English a century ago. Who knows what will be in place in a century's time?

---

4. **high street** British English for main street.

AVRUM HYMAN

Metropolitan Diary

THE RECENT DIARY ACCOUNT of the Englishwoman who believed in calling people and objects by their correct names—"porter" for redcap— reminded me of a conversation along similar lines I once had with an English visitor in Manhattan.

When I referred to the front glass in the car in which we were riding as a "windshield," she advised me that in England it was more properly called a "windscreen."

Defending the Stars and Stripes, I said that our name should apply.

"After all," I proudly and chauvinistically stated, "we invented the automobile."

Upon which my visitor from England imperiously replied, "And we in- ⁵ vented the language."

about the texts

1. According to Crystal, why do some languages achieve international status? How is such status maintained? Explain, providing examples from Crystal's essay.

2. According to people who think that English is the "best" candidate for a world language, why has it achieved international status?

3. Why does Crystal believe that world language unification is not a worthwhile goal? How does he support his claim that it would be impossible for the world population to speak a single language in a mutually intelligible manner?

4. Hyman is recounting a brief conversation between two people, but he uses the word "said" only once. Much of the flavor and detail of the story are conveyed with descriptive verbs and manner adverbs. List all of the ways that Hyman presents the statements in the dialogue; what contribution does each verb and adverb make to the whole?

on language use

5. Which word do you prefer—"windshield" or "windscreen"? Can you give a reason, other than it's what you're accustomed to? Do you think you could easily switch to the other word? Use your answers as a springboard for a discussion with your classmates.

How do you think language attitudes and preferences affect the possibility of having a single, mutually intelligible language for all of the people of the world?

6. Is there more than one "right" way to spell English words? Cut and paste a page from a paper you've written into a new document. Then change the setting in your spell checker to British or Australian English. Does the program recommend any changes? Are you surprised? Why or why not?

for writing

7. Have you learned a language (or languages) not spoken in your home? Think about your experience: your age when you started learning, the formality of the learning environment, how hard/easy you found it, how well you speak the language now. Write an essay describing the experience and how it has (or has not) enhanced your life.

8. Do you think a one-language world is a good idea? Why or why not? Write an essay arguing your opinion, providing evidence (from Crystal's selection or elsewhere) to support your argument. If you support such a world, which language would you advocate and why, and how would you achieve the goal? If you don't believe in the viability and/or desirability of such a world, explain your reasons.

BETH DUFF-BROWN

Customer Service Calls Routed to India

BANGALORE, INDIA— Betty Coulter is a typical 21-year-old college grad from Illinois. She wears bell-bottom jeans and is a faithful fan of the TV shows "Friends" and "Buffy the Vampire Slayer."

Or so says Betty, if asked, while taking calls from Americans.

Her real name would be difficult for those callers to pronounce: Savitha Balasubramanyam. And if they listen closely, her Midwestern accent has a touch of South Asian exotic.

Balasubramanyam is Indian. She is a member of a booming business trend in southern India that is saving Western companies millions of dollars and earning young college graduates here their first real rupees.

When an American calls a toll-free number in the States to report a broken appliance or complain about the wrong sweater ordered from a catalog, the call is often routed through fast fiber-optic cables to a center in India.

A polite, friendly voice on the other end is eager to assist —and sounds just like the boy or girl next door, not 8000 miles away.

To get into her groove, Balasubrmanyam created an American family history: Her parents, Robert and Della Grace, are Irish immigrants who reside in Illinois. Her brother, James, is 15. Betty got her business management degree from the University of Illinois.

"A personal relationship with the customer is very important," says Balasubramanyam, who works at CustomerAsset, one of a half-dozen major call centers in Bangalore, an Indian technology hub. "It doesn't matter if I'm really Betty or Savitha. What matters is that at the end of the day I've helped the customer."

That sort of work ethic is why so many large Western companies—General Electric, British Air-ways, American Express and Ama-

516

zon.com, to name a few—have turned to India for customer service.

The agents here are edu- 10 cated, polite and speak excellent English, which is in wide use in India. Labor can be 70 percent cheaper, leading to big savings for companies that shift customer service departments from developed countries.

JOCKEYING FOR JOBS

Thousands of Indians right out of college line up for the jobs. They get months of speech training in American or British accents, depending on the client they represent. They bone up on sports terms and slang and a good dose of "Baywatch" and "Friends" to bridge the cultural divide between Bombay and Boston.

While most Americans do not aspire to work in customer service centers, young Indians see the job as the first step in a technology-related career.

"Our clients want to utilize an Indian workforce as they recognize the quality and work ethic and eagerness of our employees to improve and move up. Our U.S. clients are coming here for that. They are not coming here for cheap labor," in-

Customer service agents answer calls from the United States at CustomerAsset, one of a half-dozen major call centers in Bangalore, India. Agents get speech training in American and British accents.

sists Meena Ganesh, director of CustomerAsset.

Still, Balasubramanyam earns $213 a month on the overnight shift. She takes dozens of calls from customers of a U.S. company that she can't identify, since some clients don't want Americans knowing their calls get answered in India.

While the sum seems paltry —Indian intellectuals dub the workers here "techno coolies" who slave away in white-collar sweatshops—an average Indian earns only $450 a year.

International call centers based in India will generate $8 billion in revenue by 2008, says NASSCOM, a technology industry trade group in India. Growth is accelerating as globalization and government deregulation expand telecommunications and lower its cost in India.

"The potential is unlimited," says Prakash Gurbaxani, founder and chief executive of 24/7 customer.com, a customer service center in Bangalore whose American clients include Web sites altavista and shutterfly.com. Anticipating more business, the company's supermarket-size call center is filled with dark-screened PCs and dwarfs its 300 employees.

"We have all the ingredients here in India to make this a world-class business. As they say in the United States— it is ours to lose," says Gurbaxani.

TECH HUB IN BANGALORE

When one boards the plane in New Delhi for Bangalore, virtually every passenger is toting a laptop and sporting a T-shirt with a technology company logo. The city is awash with tech billboards and knapsack-laden geeks in a hurry.

Hundreds of thousands of computer programmers, software developers, medical transcribers and Web site designers here have left for overseas companies or work in Bangalore for them, filling a technology vacuum in the United States, Britain and other European countries.

Not everyone is keen on the latest information worker phenomenon. Labor activists and intellectuals deem call centers badly paying sweatshops, where abysmal work conditions and long hours would be illegal in the countries of the companies providing them contracts.

The critics say the "haves" are yet again making money off the "have-nots," ignoring a yawning digital divide. India's 1 billion people own only 4.3 million personal computers, 26 million fixed phones and 75 million television sets, says NASSCOM. An estimated 3.2 million use the Internet.

TREND HAS NOTABLE CRITICS

Noted Indian author Arundhati Roy, an outspoken foe of globalization, recently wrote in an article condemning the West that the adoption of American accents for jobs in call centers shows "how easily an ancient civilization can be made to abase itself completely."

"You have to change your name from Arundhati to Annie and pretend that you're an American," she says in an interview, laughing. "It's a very fascinating phenomenon . . . the other side of religious fundamentalism."

1. Duff-Brown presents several points of view in her article, some of which are in direct conflict. How does she portray each group? Is any group (or groups) portrayed particularly favorably or unfavorably? Provide evidence from the reading (i.e., word choice, sequence of information, who gets quoted) to support your conclusion.

2. Duff-Brown writes her report for an American audience that is familiar with the controversies surrounding offshore outsourcing of customer service call centers. How does she anticipate the arguments and objections of her readers? Provide specific examples.

3. The Indian author Arundhati Roy suggests that the call center phenomenon of "pretend[ing to be] an American" is "the other side of religious fundamentalism" (paragraph 24). What could she mean? Why might Duff-Brown have included that detail?

on language use

4. According to the article, the Indian call center workers receive "months of speech training in American . . . accents" (paragraph 11). Is there an "American accent"? Why or why not? Do you think any of the workers are trained in regional or ethnic varieties, such as New York or African American English? What might it mean to sound "American" if these varieties are excluded?

5. If you called a company to arrange the exchange of a sweater or the repair of your computer, what feelings would you have about the transaction if the person who took your call spoke in a dialect very different from your own? Would one variety or dialect give you more confidence about the transaction than another? Why?

6. Would you consider taking a full-time job that required you to speak convincingly in a different dialect of English? Work in groups of three or four to explore why or why not. Would it make a difference if that job paid five or ten times more than other jobs for which you were qualified? Would you be able to shift back to your "real" self easily at the end of the day? Would you want to?

for writing

7. Would you feel deceived if you found out that the friendly person who helped you track down a missing order last week was really speaking to you in an accent he or she "puts on" for their job? Would you prefer that customer service representatives speak in the way they normally speak English? Why or why not? Write an essay explaining your reasoning.

8. Imagine that you are a manager of a company that is considering outsourcing its customer service call center to India. Write a memo to your company's top executives arguing for or against outsourcing. Present evidence to support your position, using the Web to explore the experiences of other companies, cost analysis, community impact, customer impact, or other relevant topics.

This article, written by Henry Chu, a reporter at the Los Angeles Times, ran in the Austin American Statesman and other U.S. newspapers in December 2000. Chu, who was chief of the L.A. Times's Beijing bureau, is currently based in Israel. In this selection, Chu describes a growing trend in Taiwan —intensive English programs for toddlers. This social and educational phenomenon reflects another aspect of the importance of English as a global language.

HENRY CHU

Taiwan's Toddlers Learn English

TAIPEI, TAIWAN—Monica Huang is taking a crash course in English. Every weekday from 9 to 5, she and her fellow students forsake Chinese and concentrate solely on English in their private language class in downtown Taipei.

Teachers drill them on vocabulary. Textbooks and audiotapes reinforce the lessons. The students learn fast and respond well, but they look forward to their breaks—time to slurp down some milk and take out their toys: those things you do when, like Monica, you're only 3 years old.

Though still a toddler, Monica is already a veteran of the intensive language program, having been enrolled a year ago when she was barely out of diapers.

"It's for her future," Monica's mother, Hsieh Shu-huel, said firmly.

Thousands of Hsieh's peers 5 couldn't agree more. In swelling numbers, parents in Taiwan are insisting on earlier and earlier education in English for their children, convinced that fluency in the language will be key to their youngster's later success.

Immersion classes for tots —where it's all English, all the time—have zoomed in popularity and proliferated throughout the island. They don't come cheap: At the Joy American School that Monica attends, tuition is about $1,300 a semester, with an additional $300 in fees every month—a steep sum in Taiwan, where the annual per capita income averages about $12,000.

But it's worth the sacrifice, parents say, if it helps their kids compete in a world where English is increasingly the language of commerce and the Internet.

Even the Taiwanese government has hopped on the bandwagon, lowering the mandatory age for learning English in public school.

Beginning next fall, students in the fifth grade, rather than junior high, will have to start minding their Ps and Qs— literally. The government is scrambling to train 3,000 new instructors to cope with the policy shift.

"There aren't enough teach- 10 ers. If there were, we'd drop the age even further," said Fan Sun-Lu, Taiwan's deputy education minister. "The younger the better—they can learn faster."

Behind the push for early

English education is Taiwan's desire to stay competitive economically and to preserve its reputation as an international high-tech development center.

"English is an international tool," Fan said. "In an e-economy age, this kind of tool is even more important."

The emphasis is on oral skills, particularly speaking with an American accent, prized by Taiwanese parents for their youngsters. Although many teachers at the Joy American School hail from other English-speaking nations, from Britain to Australia, American terms and spellings in class are de rigueur.

By starting so early, "our kids won't be afraid to talk to foreigners," Hsieh, 39, said. "They'll find it very natural."

Like schoolchildren every- 15 where, the pupils are alternately focused and fidgety.

Teacher Arlene Nash, a Canadian, shushes her group of 3- and 4-year-old beginners, then holds up some purple plastic fruit.

"What are these?" she asks.

A slight pause ensues, followed by an chorus of enthusiastic voices: "Gwaaaaapes!"

Then everybody sits down to eat a sample of the real thing, in a classroom plastered with colorful drawings with English captions and the alphabet written in glitter.

Despite Monica's long hours 20 in class, Hsieh, 39, said she puts no pressure on her daughter.

"When they first start, the teacher uses games. The kids don't see it as pressure—they see it as fun," Hsieh said. "It's not as if at home we say, 'Memorize these words' or anything like that. Our demands aren't heavy.'"

---

about the text

1. What response do you think Chu expected from his audience? Approval? pride? alarm? sympathy? something else? Why? Provide evidence from the selection to support your ideas.

2. If Chu had been writing on the same topic for a Taiwanese newspaper, what might he have done differently? What information might he have added or deleted? Why?

3. The Taiwanese children that Chu describes are learning American terms and spellings. Why might that be important to the students and their families? Why might Chu have included that information in the article?

4. What purpose does the "Gwaaaaapes!" anecdote (paragraph 18) serve? (Hint: Begin by thinking about how and why the spelling is different from the standard 'grapes.')

on language use

5. The deputy education minister of Taiwan, Fan Sun-Lu, says that "English is an international tool" (paragraph 12). How might this attitude differ from a native English speaker's attitude toward the language? How do you perceive your native language, whatever it is? How might you use your language differently if you perceived it simply as a tool? Explain.

6. Although many U.S. children start preschool at age three, and some even younger, it is not common in the United States to enroll young children in serious academic programs. Yet we know that language learning is easier during childhood. If you wanted your children to learn a language that isn't spoken in your home, would you consider language classes like

the ones Chu describes? (Let's suppose that finances aren't an issue.) Why or why not? Explain.

---

for writing

7. Even though English is currently the dominant language of commerce and popular culture, you may still profit from knowing another language. Suppose your school planned to add a course in a new language, and it was soliciting input from students about which language they might like to study. Select a language and write a letter to the administration arguing for the development of a course in that language. What kinds of career and/or life opportunities would the study of this language provide? What kinds of literary or cultural components should be part of the program? Provide any evidence or statistics (giving credit to their sources) that help support your argument.

DEREK ZHU

Konglish: It's Not That Bad

I WAS AMUSED TO READ Elizabeth Pyon's scathing attack on the use of grammatically incorrect English—"Konglish undermines national soccer pride"—in the Weekender section of the *Korea Herald*'s June 21 edition.

As a foreigner who has lived in Seoul for over two years, I would not hesitate to agree that the standard of English in Korea needs improving. However, I feel that Pyon has been far too harsh in insisting that the use of Konglish during the World Cup undermines Korea's image. People all over the world know that English is a foreign language to Koreans and will not regard them as "less intelligent" or "lower-class" for their awkward English. I agree that it is important to teach English, or any other language, properly. However, a language is a living thing, and I do not believe that it is necessary to completely suppress the evolution of colloquial expressions in order to keep a language healthy.

Allow me to share my personal experiences with the English language. I grew up in Singapore, which has its own brand of English (called Singlish), which consists largely of English words, often mispronounced, superimposed upon a Chinese grammatical structure. Anyone who has not lived in Singapore or nearby Malaysia will generally find it impossible to understand two Singaporeans conversing in what they believe to be English.

Singlish has survived in Singapore despite the fact that in this former British colony, English is the official language and medium of instruction in schools. For over two decades, the Singapore government attempted to suppress Singlish by way of public campaigns and the banning of Singlish expressions on television and radio.

In recent years, a more enlightened government has 5 realized the cultural value of a language derivative that is homegrown and gives its people a sense of shared identity. Today, Singlish is tolerated to a limited extent on

This letter to the editor of the Korea Herald *appeared in* June 2002, following the World Cup, which was held in Korea and Japan. The Korea Herald, *published daily since 1953, describes itself as "[Korea's] number one English language newspaper." In this letter,* Derek Zhu *addresses several of the complexities of English and how it is spoken in various parts of the world. See if you can find parallels between the "Konglish" that* Zhu *describes and any "homegrown" varieties of American English that you are familiar with.*

the Singapore airwaves, much to the relief of millions of Singaporeans tired of watching local television shows where actors speak the Queen's English, unlike real Singaporeans. Singaporeans have generally become fairly comfortable switching between Singlish and English as appropriate.

When I went to college in the United States, I was exposed to words and phrases such as "Yo, wassup?" "Word to your momma," "Phat," and "That is way cool." I do not think Pyon would have objected quite so strongly to the use of American expressions such as these, despite their lack of grammatical correctness. In the two years that I have lived in Korea, I have gradually grown to understand that "service" means something free and that a "Burberry" is a coat.

Likewise, I think the messages underlying "Be the Reds" and "Korea Team Fighting" are not difficult to figure out. Konglish may make for the occasional awkward misunderstanding with foreigners, and it may slow down the pace at which Koreans learn proper English ever so slightly, but I feel that is a smaller price to pay than suppressing a part of your culture that is arguably quite charming to long-term foreign residents like myself.

By all means, teach proper English in schools and insist on its use in formal communication. But do not wholly suppress Konglish, for it is a part of what it means to be Korean. Koreans should be as proud of using it, where appropriate, as they are of the remarkable efforts of the national soccer team. Korea has performed admirably at this World Cup. I think the world will forgive us (did I say us?) a few spelling mistakes.

about the text

1. What is Zhu's argument? What reasons does he offer to convince the reader of his position? Give examples.

2. Zhu speculates that phrases such as "Yo, wassup?," "Word to your momma," and "Phat," which he calls "American expressions" (paragraph 6), would be more acceptable to critics of Konglish than Konglish itself. Do you think those phrases would be acceptable to strict grammarians here in the United States? Why or why not? What might account for differences between the Americans' and Koreans' perceptions of the phrases?

3. What is Zhu doing in the parenthetical comment "(did I say us?)" in the closing sentence of his letter? What rhetorical function does the comment serve? Do you think it is effective? Why or why not?

on language use

4. Zhu argues that local speech characteristics are positive markers of identity and community and that Konglish is "a part of what it means to be Korean" (paragraph 8). Do you speak a variety of English that is a source of pride and identity for you? Describe its distinctive features. (A good way to start is to imagine that you are traveling far from home and overhear someone speaking your own variety of English—how are you able to identify it?)

5. Google the term "Singlish" and explore some of the sites that come up to find out the basics about it. Who uses it? Where? When? Why is Singlish controversial? What are some Singlish words? How does it differ

from the English(es) that you know? With two or three classmates, discuss the information you find and whether there are any varieties of English in the United States that, like Singlish, are controversial when compared to the "standard" variety.

6. When you turn on the radio or TV, do you hear the variety of English that you speak? (Almost always? sometimes? never?) Freewrite or brainstorm with a classmate or two about how you might feel if you never heard your own variety of language spoken in the mass media (as in Zhu's description of Singaporean media in the past). Then discuss how your life and worldview might be affected if you never heard your preferred variety of English in the public media.

for writing

7. Zhu concludes his letter by saying that "the world will forgive us a few spelling mistakes" (paragraph 8). Why might Zhu have concluded by invoking "the world"? Based on his statement, how might he respond to the question "who owns English?" How would you respond? Write an essay in which you take a position on the proprietorship of English. Be sure to consider the implications of your response on the spread of English as a global language.

8. Who, if anybody, should have the power to make the rules for English? Why? Who makes the rules now? (You may need to do some research to be able to answer that question.) Given that there are many varieties of English, should the rules be interpreted to apply to all of them? Some of them? Which ones? Why? Write an essay responding to these questions, providing evidence to support your argument.

SHASHI THAROOR

••••••••••••••••••••••
Shashi Tharoor *is under-*
secretary-general for commu-
nication and public
information at the United
Nations. He is the author of
several novels, including Riot:
A Love Story *(2001) and* The
Great Indian Novel *(1991), and*
of essays on Indian history
and foreign policy. This
selection was published in
July 2001 as part of a New
York Times series on literary
themes. In it, Tharoor
discusses the audience for
his books, while taking us
deeper into questions about
the authenticity and adequacy
of global Englishes, including
his own. Is the English
language adequate to express
the life and soul of a country
where relatively few people
speak it? Is an Indian author
turning his back on his
country and compatriots by
writing in English? And,
perhaps more important, is the
English of India a legitimate
and authentic English, of
equal stature with U.S.,
Canadian, British, or
Australian English?
••••••••••••••••••••••

A Bedeviling Question in the Cadence of English

A S AN INDIAN WRITER living in New York, I find myself constantly asked a question with which my American confreres[1] never have to contend: "But whom do you write for?"

In my case the question is complicated by both geography and language. I live in the United States (because of my work at the United Nations) and write about India; and I do so in English, a language mastered, if the last census is to be believed, by only 2 percent of the Indian population. There is an unspoken accusation implicit in the question: am I not guilty of the terrible sin of inauthenticity, of writing about my country for foreigners?

This question has, for many years, bedeviled the work of the growing tribe of writers of what used to be called Indo-Anglian fiction and is now termed, more respectfully, Indian writing in English. This is ironic, because few developments in world literature have been more remarkable than the emergence, over the last two decades, of a new generation of Indian writers in English.

Beginning with Salman Rushdie's *Midnight's Children* in 1981, they have expanded the boundaries of their craft and their nation's literary heritage, enriching English with the rhythms of ancient legends and the larger-than-life complexities of another civilization, while reinventing India in the confident cadences of English prose. Of the many unintended consequences of empire, it is hard to imagine one of greater value to both colonizers and colonized.

The new Indian writers dip into a deep well of memory and experience far removed from those of their fellow   5

---

1. **confreres** fellow members of a learned profession or scientific body.

novelists in the English language. But whereas Americans or Englishmen or Australians have also set their fictions in distant lands, Indians write of India without exoticism, their insights undimmed by the dislocations of foreignness. And they do so in an English they have both learned and lived, an English of freshness and vigor, a language that is as natural to them as their quarrels at the school playground or the surreptitious notes they slipped each other in their classrooms.

Yet Indian critics still suggest that there is something artificial and un-Indian about an Indian writing in English. One critic disparagingly declared that the acid test ought to be, "Could this have been written only by an Indian?" I have never been much of a literary theoretician—I always felt that for a writer to study literature at university would be like learning about girls at medical school—but for most, though not all, of my own writing, I would answer that my works could not only have been written only by an Indian, but only by an Indian *in English.*

I write for anyone who will read me, but first of all for Indians like myself, Indians who have grown up speaking, writing, playing, wooing and quarreling in English, all over India. (No writer really chooses a language: the circumstances of his upbringing ensure that the language chooses him.)

Members of this class have entered the groves of academe and condemned themselves in terms of bitter self-reproach: one Indian scholar, Harish Trivedi, has asserted (in English) that Indian writers in that language are "cut off from the experiential mainstream and from that common cultural matrix . . . shared with writers of all other Indian languages." Dr. Trivedi metaphorically cites the fictional English-medium school in an R. K. Narayan story where the students must first rub off the sandalwood-paste caste marks from their foreheads before they enter its portals: "For this golden gate is only for the déraciné[2] to pass through, for those who have erased their antecedents."

It's an evocative image, even though I thought the secular Indian state was *supposed* to encourage the erasure of casteism from the classroom. But the more important point is that writers like myself do share a "common cultural matrix," albeit one devoid of helpfully identifying caste marks. It is one that consists of an urban upbringing and a pan-national outlook on the Indian reality. I do not think this is any less authentically "Indian" than the worldviews of writers in other Indian languages. Why should the rural peasant or the small-town schoolteacher with his sandalwood-smeared forehead

---

2. **déraciné** uprooted from one's national or social environment.

be considered more quintessentially Indian than the punning collegian or the Bombay socialite, who are as much a part of the Indian reality?

India is a vast and complex country; in Whitman's phrase, it contains 10 multitudes. I write of an India of multiple truths and multiple realities, an India that is greater than the sum of of its parts. English expresses that diversity better than any Indian language precisely because it is not rooted in any one region of my vast country. At the same time, as an Indian, I remain conscious of, and connected to, my pre-urban and non-Anglophone antecedents: my novels reflect an intellectual heritage that embraces the ancient epic the Mahabharata, the Kerala folk dance called the *ottamthullal* (of which my father was a gifted practitioner) and the Hindi B-movies of Bollywood as well as Shakespeare, Wodehouse[3] and the Beatles.

As a first-generation urbanite myself, I keep returning to the Kerala villages of my parents, in my life as in my writing. Yet I have grown up in Bombay, Calcutta and Delhi, Indian cities a thousand miles apart from one another; the mother of my children is half-Kashmiri, half-Bengali; and my own mother now lives in the southern town of Coimbatore. This may be a wider cultural matrix than the good Dr. Trivedi imagined, but it draws from a rather broad range of *Indian* experience. And English is the language that brings those various threads of my India together, the language in which my wife could speak to her mother-in-law, the language that enables a Calcuttan to function in Coimbatore, the language that serves to express the complexity of that polyphonous Indian experience better than any other language I know.

As a novelist, I believe in distracting in order to instruct — my novels are, to some degree, didactic works masquerading as entertainments. Like Molière I believe that you have to entertain in order to edify. But the entertainment, and the edification, might strike different readers differently.

My first novel, *The Great Indian Novel*, as a satirical reinvention of the Mahabharata inevitably touches Indians in a way that most foreigners will not fully appreciate. But my publishers in the West enjoyed its stories and the risks it took with narrative form. My second, *Show Business*, did extremely

---

3. **Mahabharata** called the Great Epic of India, written in Sanskrit between 300 B.C.E and 300 C.E., is also the longest epic in world literature. **Kerala** a state of India, on the southwest tip of the country. Kerala boasts of having a 100 percent literacy rate and the highest life expectancy in the country. **Bollywood** name for the thriving Indian film industry, the world's largest, based in Bombay (Bombay + Hollywood = Bollywood). **P. G. Wodehouse (1881– 1975)** English humorist and author of novels, short stories, plays, lyrics, and essays.

well with American reviewers and readers, who enjoyed the way I tried to portray the lives and stories of Bollywood as a metaphor for Indian society. With *India: From Midnight to the Millennium*, an attempt to look back at the last 50 years of India's history, I found an additional audience of Indian-Americans seeking to rediscover their roots; their interest has helped the American edition outsell the Indian one.

In my new novel, *Riot*, for the first time I have major non-Indian characters, Americans as it happens, and that is bound to influence the way the book is perceived both in the United States and in India. Inevitably the English language fundamentally affects the content of each book, but it does not determine the audience of the writer; as long as translations exist, language is a vehicle, not a destination.

Of course, there is no shame in acknowledging that English is a legacy 15 of the colonial connection, but one no less useful and valid than the railways, the telegraphs or the law courts that were also left behind by the British. Historically, English helped us find our Indian voice: that great Indian nationalist Jawaharlal Nehru wrote *The Discovery of India* in English. But the eclipse of that dreadful phrase "the Indo-Anglian novel" has occurred precisely because Indian writers have evolved well beyond the British connection to their native land.

The days when Indians wrote novels in English either to flatter or rail against their colonial masters are well behind us. Now we have Indians in India writing as naturally about themselves in English as Australians or South Africans do, and their tribe has been supplemented by India's rich diaspora in the United States, which has already produced a distinctive crop of impressive novelists, with Pulitzer Prizes and National Book Awards to their names.

Their addresses don't matter, because writers really live inside their heads and on the page, and geography is merely a circumstance. They write secure of themselves in their heritage of diversity, and they write free of the anxiety of audience, for theirs are narratives that appeal as easily to Americans as to Indians—and indeed to readers irrespective of ethnicity.

Surely that's the whole point about literature—that for a body of fiction to constitute a literature it must rise above its origins, its setting, even its language, to render accessible to a reader anywhere some insight into the human condition. Read my books and those of other Indian writers not because we're Indian, not necessarily because you are interested in India, but because they are worth reading in and of themselves. And dear reader, whoever you are, if you pick up one of my books, ask not for whom I write: I write for you.

1. Tharoor begins his essay by considering the audience of his books. Who is the audience for this *New York Times* article? How can you tell?

2. What advantages does Tharoor claim English offers to Indian writers? Cite specific passages to support your answer.

3. In addition to being a novelist and essayist, Tharoor works as under-secretary-general for communication and public information at the UN. How might that experience have contributed to his ideas in this essay?

4. The conclusion of Tharoor's essay echoes the famous passage from a sermon by the seventeenth-century English poet John Donne: "never send to know for whom the bell tolls; it tolls for thee." Ernest Hemingway borrowed from this passage to title his novel *For Whom the Bell Tolls*. To what does this passage refer? What does it mean? Why might Tharoor have chosen to conclude his essay with this evocation?

on language use

5. Tharoor mentions that he is constantly questioned about his intended audience, and he asserts that American writers/artists are not questioned about theirs. Is that necessarily true? Work with a small group to compile a list of artists and writers who have been or are likely to be asked to define their audiences (Eminem, perhaps? Queen Latifah? Ellen DeGeneres?). Once you have a list of three or more people/groups, look for what they have in common that might provoke questions about audience. Does Tharoor share this commonality? Why or why not?

for writing

6. What might Tharoor have to say about the call centers described in Beth Duff-Brown's article, "Customer Service Calls Routed to India"? What might he say to those workers who are trained to speak with American (or British) accents? To the client companies? Why do you think so? Write an essay in which you synthesize the information in the two selections and speculate on how Tharoor might respond to the phenomenon that Duff-Brown describes. Explain your reasoning and cite specific passages from both articles to support your conclusions.

7. Early in the essay, Tharoor talks about how well English expresses the flavors of Indian life and claims that his works could have been written only "by an Indian *in English*" (paragraph 6). Later, he says that "as long as translations exist, language is a vehicle, not a destination" (paragraph 14). Are these contradictory statements? Why or why not? How does Tharoor clarify his position at the end of the essay? There are other passages as well that seem to be contradictory. What are they? Write an essay pointing out any apparent contradictions and/or paradoxes in Tharoor's essay, and discuss whether he resolves them. Provide examples to support your argument.

John Tagliabue *is a Paris-based correspondent for the* New York Times, *where this selection appeared in May 2002. In it, Tagliabue shows us some ways that the European corporate world uses global English. With their history of prestige and prominence on the world stage, Europeans have now embraced English, but in carefully delineated ways.*

JOHN TAGLIABUE

In Europe, Going Global Means, Alas, English

Paris, May 18—Ludovic Timbal learned English at school and used it occasionally while studying law in Paris.

But that never prepared him for the avalanche of English he encountered after he joined a Paris law firm last year. "I want to be a business lawyer, and I realized you just cannot avoid speaking English," Mr. Timbal, 29, said in vaguely accented English.

So now Mr. Timbal attends a Paris language school and spends up to four hours several days a week drilling English conversation—"an investment in the future," he called it.

As European banks and corporations burst national boundaries and go global, many are making English the official corporate language.

Two years ago, when France, Germany and Spain merged their aerospace industries into one company, they not only gave it an English name—the European Aeronautic Defense and Space Company, or EADS—they also made English its language.

In Germany, the national postal service, Deutsche Post World Net, Increasingly uses English as its working language. Smaller companies are doing likewise. In Finland, the elevator maker Kone adopted English in the 1970s; in Italy, Merloni Elettrodomestici, a mid-size home appliance maker, did so in the mid-1990s. Management meetings at big banks like Deutsche Bank in Germany and Credit Suisse in Switzerland are routinely in English.

In part, the triumphal march of English through European business is symbolic, born of a wish to shed a parochial image and assume that of global player.

To this extent, the adoption of one language in business is probably not an indication that Europeans are abandoning their cultural identities as they have surrendered their economic nationalism and adopted a single currency.

But there are also substantive reasons to use English, which makes it easier to leverage international links and enable far-flung affiliates to communicate both with headquarters and among themselves.

Behind this choice lies a reality that unsettles some Europeans: the use of English is mainly determined by the unchallenged dominance of the United States in industry, commerce and finance.

"It is the key market in the world as a consumer; it is the center of financial markets," said Subramanian Rangan, associate professor of strategy at

531

the Insead business school outside. Paris, whose language of teaching and research is English. "So with regard to products, financing, knowledge and technology, the United States has risen to unparalleled pre-eminence in these last years, and it doesn't seem there are contenders to change that."

In Toulouse, in the south of France, English has been the official language at the aircraft manufacturer Airbus since its founding more than 30 years ago as a loose consortium of aerospace companies from France, Germany, Britain and Spain. Partly, Airbus executives say, this was because of a bad experience on an earlier project, building the Anglo-French Concorde supersonic jet: Concorde's French chief engineer, despite fluent English, refused memos from his British counterpart unless they were in French.

But the choice, also reflected American predominance in civil aviation. "Our documentation was often based on American manuals," said Barbara Kracht, the Airbus spokeswoman. "And it was complicated—you know, there's Boeing slang, G.E. slang. Pratt & Whitney slang."

In executive meetings, if a majority speak French, German or Spanish, then the majority tongue is spoken; the minutes are in English. On the factory floor, local languages prevail.

In Italy, the appliance maker Merloni adopted English in the 1990s. Merloni was a family-controlled, midsize player with a name few had heard of, competing against renowned giants like Electrolux of Sweden and Bosch-Siemens of Germany. Its chief executive at that time, Francesco Caio, believed that English would give Merloni an international image.

The company's subsequent growth cemented the role of English. In 2000, Merloni acquired Stinol, Russia's biggest refrigerator maker, and last December, Britain's Hotpoint, adding 6,600 Britons and 7,000 Russians to the work force. At both Hotpoint and Stinol, English is the language of management.

"I can't give percentages, but now many executives are not Italian—French, English, Danish, Russian and so on," said Andrea Prandi, Merloni's spokesman. "We consider ourselves a European group. For Europe, the official language is English."

Whether the use of English enables everyone to penetrate intangible cultural issues, and to communicate as closely as, say, the French have among themselves for centuries, is much less clear.

Professor Rangan of Insead suspects that the corporate use of English represents "only shallow integration."

"I doubt it's in the board room, and it's not on the factory floor," he said. "So it's a narrow sliver. It's not in labor relations, and it's not in customer relations."

But it does provide a communication tool, "much the way we use mathematics and numbers," he said.

Jussi Itavuori, a Finn who is group vice president for human resources at EADS, agrees.

"It's neither English nor American," he said. "It's some sort of operating language. It loses quite a lot of nuance."

Indeed, some would argue that English at work drives Europeans back to their native tongues.

Christine Rahard, a Frenchwoman in her 30s, manages corporate communications for the French automaker Renault, working extensively in English.

But in her home village west of Paris, friends and neighbors who increasingly feel the intrusion of English into their working lives share a kind of mild backlash, reaffirming their French roots in food and drink, everyday customs—and language.

"At the market place on a Saturday morning," she said, "you find people using old words for vegetables that everyone thought died out decades ago."

The spread of English, of course, is a gold mine for language schools. Five years ago, Wall Street Institute, where Mr. Timbal studies, had only three schools in France. Today, there are 38, six in Paris alone.

"It reflects the world we live in," said Jeremy Newman, director of Mr. Timbal's school.

Similarly pervasive is the practice of naming English speakers to top jobs at European companies.

When Myron Ullman, the 30 American executive best known in the 1990s for saving the Macy's department store chain, was hired to be chief executive of the big French-based luxury goods conglomerate LVMH Moët Hennessy Louis Vuitton, he knew his inability to speak French would not be a problem. Years earlier, the LVMH chairman, Bernard Arnault, had made English the group's official language.

Still, the chatter in the cafeteria and around the coffee machine remains in the local tongue, so not having it is recognized as a drawback.

For the time being, European banks and corporations appear set to remain linguistic hybrids, using English as their lingua franca, yet relying on local languages in telling ways. Such an arrangement appears to work against anyone who does not speak the local language.

"It's a definite disadvantage" said Horst Neller, a partner in Düsseldorf, Germany, for the executive search firm Heidrick & Struggles. "In the local language, you open your heart."

about the text

1. According to Tagliabue, why are Europeans speaking English in their work lives? What does he say are the advantages (or disadvantages) of doing so?

2. What evidence does Tagliabue provide that Europeans are adopting English in their business lives, but aren't changing their cultural identities?

3. Subramanian Rangan, professor of strategy at a business school near Paris, states that the European corporate use of English represents "only shallow integration" (paragraph 18). What does that mean? What evidence does Tagliabue give to support Rangan's claim?

on language use

4. Imagine that you work for a large company (in the United States) in which the managers speak a language other than English among themselves to make important decisions. How would you feel about that language? About its speakers, the management? Would you want to learn that language, or would you want to assert English in formal or informal work-related meetings? Why or why not? Freewrite on these questions, and compare your ideas with two or three classmates.

5. How is the situation presented by Tagliabue the same as or different from others involving global Englishes? Compare and contrast the European situation with another from this chapter.

for writing

6. The dominance of English in global commerce may seem a great stroke of luck for native English speakers, but there may be reasons for a business student to gain proficiency in another language. Write an essay in which you argue for or against the study of another language for prospective business students, supporting your points with evidence from any of the selections in this chapter. You may also want to gather additional data to back up your argument; for example, browse the job ads for executives in selected industries to see what language skills are required.

7. Although there are certainly language difficulties and challenges in Europe, they are different from the ones we face in the United States. Imagine that you are going to address (or file a written report for) a group of U.S. human resource managers. Write an essay in which you make recommendations for the resolution of language issues in their companies, using the European situation described by Tagliabue as a model (whether positive or negative). Provide concrete examples to support your recommendations.

BARBARA WALLRAFF

What Global Language?

Barbara Wallraff *is senior editor of* The Atlantic, *a monthly magazine that covers current events and debates, politics, and the arts. This two-part selection was the cover story in the November 2000 issue. In it, Wallraff looks at some of the possibilities and limitations of English as a global language. She also writes a column for the magazine that answers readers' questions about grammar and language usage. These columns have been collected in* Word Court: Wherein Verbal Virtue Is Rewarded, Crimes Against the Language Are Punished, and Poetic Justice Is Done (2000). *As you read, think about how Wallraff's ideas are influenced by her chosen role as protector and defender of the language.*

part 1

Because I am interested in what happens to the English language, over the past year or so I've been asking people, at dinner parties and professional gatherings and so on, whether they think that English is well on its way to being the global language. Typically, they look puzzled about why I would even bother to ask such an obvious question. They say firmly, Of course. Then they start talking about the Internet. We're just having a conversation, so I refrain from launching into everything I'm about to tell you. It's not that I believe they're actually wrong. But the idea of English as a global language doesn't mean what they think it does—at least, not according to people I've interviewed whose professions are bound up especially closely in what happens to the English language.

English has inarguably achieved some sort of global status. Whenever we turn on the news to find out what's happening in East Asia, or the Balkans, or Africa, or South America, or practically anyplace, local people are being interviewed and telling us about it in English. This past April the journalist Ted Anthony, in one of two articles about global English that he wrote for the Associated Press, observed, "When Pope John Paul II arrived in the Middle East last month to retrace Christ's footsteps and addressed Christians, Muslims and Jews, the pontiff spoke not Latin, not Arabic, not Hebrew, not his native Polish. He spoke in English."

Indeed, by now lists of facts about the amazing reach of our language may have begun to sound awfully familiar. Have we heard these particular facts before, or only others like them? English is the working language of the Asian trade group ASEAN. It is the de facto working

language of 98 percent of German research physicists and 83 percent of German research chemists. It is the official language of the European Central Bank, even though the bank is in Frankfurt and neither Britain nor any other predominantly English-speaking country is a member of the European Monetary Union. It is the language in which black parents in South Africa overwhelmingly wish their children to be educated. This little list of facts comes from British sources: a report, *The Future of English?*, and a follow-up newsletter that David Graddol, a language researcher at The Open University, and his consulting firm, The English Company U.K., wrote in 1997 and 1998 for the British Council, whose mission is to promote British culture worldwide; and *English as a Global Language* (1997), a book by David Crystal, who is a professor at the University of Wales.

English isn't managing to sweep all else before it—and if it ever does become the universal language, many of those who speak it won't understand one another

And yet, of course, English is not sweeping all before it, not even in the United States. According to the U.S. Bureau of the Census, ten years ago about one in seven people in this country spoke a language other than English at home—and since then the proportion of immigrants in the population has grown and grown. Ever-wider swaths of Florida, California, and the Southwest are heavily Spanish-speaking. Hispanic people make up 30 percent of the population of New York City, and a television station there that is affiliated with a Spanish-language network has been known to draw a larger daily audience than at least one of the city's English-language network affiliates. Even Sioux City, Iowa, now has a Spanish-language newspaper. According to the census, from 1980 to 1990 the number of Spanish-speakers in the United States grew by 50 percent.

Over the same decade the number of speakers of Chinese in the United States grew by 98 percent. Today approximately 2.4 million Chinese-speakers live in America, and more than four out of five of them prefer to speak Chinese at home. The rate of growth of certain other languages in the United States has been higher still. From 1980 to 1990 the number of speakers of Korean increased by 127 percent and of speakers of Vietnamese by 150 percent. Small American towns from Huntsville, Alabama, to Meriden, Connecticut, to Wausau, Wisconsin, to El Cenizo, Texas—all sites of linguistic controversy in recent years—have been alarmed to find that many new arrivals do not speak English well and some may not even see the point of going to the trouble of learning it.

How can all of this, simultaneously, be true? How can it be that English is conquering the globe if it can't even hold its own in parts of our traditionally English-speaking country?

A perhaps less familiar paradox is that the typical English-speaker's experience of the language is becoming increasingly simplified, even as English as a whole grows more complex. If these two trends are occurring, and they are, then the globalization of English will never deliver the tantalizing result we might hope for: that is, we monolingual English-speakers may never be able to communicate fluently with everyone everywhere. If we want to exchange anything beyond rudimentary messages with many of our future fellow English-speakers, we may well need help from something other than English.

The evidence strongly suggests that the range of realistic hopes and fears about the English language is narrower than some may suppose. Much discussion of what is likely to happen to English is colored, sometimes luridly, by what people dread or desire—for their children, their neighborhoods, their nations, their world. Human aspirations, of course, have a great deal to do with what comes to pass. And language is very much tied up with aspirations.

Last fall I visited David Graddol at The English Company's headquarters, in Milton Keynes, England. Graddol has a rumpled appearance somewhat at odds with the crisp publications, replete with graphs and pie charts and executive summaries, for which he is responsible. Similarly, the appearance of The English Company's offices, located in the ground-floor flat of a Victorian house and sparsely furnished with good Arts and Crafts antiques together with some flea-market stuff, is amiably out of keeping with the sophisticated, high-tech nature of the consultancy's work. Stuck on the wall above the stove, in the kitchen, were four clocks, each captioned with a big letter hand-drawn on a piece of paper: *M, K, M, A.* This was to help the staff remember what time it was in Malaysia, Kazakhstan, Mozambique, and Argentina, the four sites where officials and advisers on how to teach English throughout those countries were taking part in an online seminar moderated by The English Company.

"The main message," Graddol told me, "is that the globalization of En- 10
glish isn't going to happen the way people expect it to." He ticked off a dizzying array of eventualities that could transform the world language picture:
political alliances that have yet to be formed; the probable rise of regional
trading blocs, in such places as Asia, the Arab world, and Latin America, in
which the United States and other primarily English-speaking countries will
be little involved; the possibility that world-changing technological innovations will arise out of nations where English is little spoken: a backlash
against American values and culture in the Middle East or Asia; or the triumph of our values and culture in those places.

To understand the fundamental paradoxes of global English, though, we
should focus on two realms of possibility: demographics and technology—
yes, the Internet, but much else that's technological besides.

FIRST, SECOND, OR FOREIGN LANGUAGE

People who expect English to triumph over all other languages are sometimes surprised to learn that the world today holds three times as many native speakers of Chinese as native speakers of English. "Chinese," as
language scholars use the word, refers to a family of languages and dialects
the most widely spoken of which is Mandarin, and which share a written language although they are not all mutually intelligible when spoken. "English" refers to a family of languages and dialects the most widely spoken of
which is standard American English, and which have a common origin in
England—though not all varieties of English, either, are mutually intelligible. The versions of English used by educated speakers practically anywhere can be understood by most Americans, but pidgins, creoles, and
diverse dialects belong to the same family, and these are not always so generally intelligible. To hear for yourself how far English now ranges from what
we Americans are used to, you need only rent a video of the 1998 Scottish film
My Name Is Joe, which, though in English, comes fully subtitled.

"Native speaker" is no easier to define with any precision than "Chinese" or "English," although it means roughly what you'd think: a person
who grew up using the language as his or her first. In terms of how demographic patterns of language use are changing, native speakers are not
where the action is. And the difference between native speakers and second-
or foreign-language speakers is an important one subjectively as well as de-
mographically. The subjective distinction I mean will be painfully familiar to
anyone who, like me, spent years in school studying a foreign language and
is now barely able to summon enough of it to order dinner in a restaurant.

In any case, the numerical gap is impressive: about 1,113 million people speak Chinese as their mother tongue, whereas about 372 million speak English. And yet English is still the world's second most common native language, though it is likely to cede second place within fifty years to the South Asian linguistic group whose leading members are Hindi and Urdu. In 2050, according to a model of language use that The English Company developed and named "engco" after itself, the world will hold 1,384 million native speakers of Chinese, 556 million of Hindi and Urdu, and 508 million of English. As native languages Spanish and Arabic will be almost as common as English, with 486 million and 482 million speakers respectively. And among young people aged fifteen to twenty-four English is expected to be in fourth place, behind not only Chinese and the Hindi-Urdu languages but also Arabic, and just ahead of Spanish.

Certainly, projections of all kinds perch atop teetering stacks of assump- 15 tions. But assuming that the tallies of native languages in use today are roughly accurate, the footing for projections of who will speak what as a first language fifty years from now is relatively sturdy. That's because many of the people who will be alive in fifty years are alive now; a majority of the *parents* of people who will be here then are already here; and most people's first language is, of course, the first language of their parents.

Prod at this last idea, to see how it takes into account such things as immigration and bilingual or multilingual places, and you'll find that it is not rock-solid. By David Crystal's estimate, for example, *two thirds of the world's children grow up in bilingual environments and develop competence in two languages*—so it is an open question what the native language of a good many of those children is. Then, too, a range of population projections exists, and demographers keep tinkering with them all.

But it's undeniable that English-speakers now have lower birth rates, on average, than speakers of Hindi and Urdu and Arabic and Spanish. And the countries where these other languages are spoken are, generally, less well developed than native-English-speaking countries. In 1996, according to United Nations statistics, 21 percent of males and 38 percent of females in "less developed regions" were illiterate in every language, as were 41 and 62 percent in the "least developed countries." Nonetheless, the gains that everyone expects English to make must come because it is adopted as a second language or a foreign language by most of the people who speak it. According to "The Decline of the Native Speaker," a paper David Graddol published last year in the *AILA Review* (AILA is the French acronym for the International Association of Applied Linguistics; the review belongs to the minority of international scholarly journals that still make use of another language in addition to English), the proportion of native English-speakers in the world population can be expected to shrink over the century 1950–2050 from more than eight to less than five percent.

A few more definitions will be helpful here. "Second-language" speakers live in places where English has some sort of official or special status. In India, for instance, the national government sanctions the use of English for its business, along with fifteen indigenous languages. What proportion of India's population of a billion speaks English is hotly debated, but most sources agree it is well under five percent. All the same. India is thought to have the fourth largest population of English-speakers in the world, after the United States, the United Kingdom, and Nigeria—or the third largest if you discount speakers of Nigerian pidgin English. English is a second language for virtually everyone in India who speaks it. And obviously the United States, too, contains speakers of English as a second language—some 30 million of them in 1995, according to an estimate by David Crystal.

"Foreign-language" speakers of English live in places where English is not singled out in any formal way, and tend to learn it to communicate with people from elsewhere. Examples might be Japanese who travel abroad on business and Italians who work in tourism in their own country. The distinction between the two categories of non-native speakers is sometimes blurry. In Denmark and Sweden the overwhelming majority of children are taught English in school—does that constitute a special status?

The distinction between categories of speakers matters, in part because [20] where English is a first or second language it develops local standards and norms. India, for instance, publishes dictionaries of Indian English, whereas Denmark and Sweden tend to defer to Britain or the United States in setting standards of English pronunciation and usage. The distinction also matters in relation to how entrenched English is in a given place, and how easy that place would find it to abandon the language.

One more surprise is how speculative any estimate of the use of English as a second or a foreign language must necessarily be. How large an English vocabulary and how great a command of English grammar does a person need in order to be considered an English-speaker? Generally, even the most rigorous attempts to determine how many people speak what, including the U.S. Census, depend on self-reporting. Do those years of French in high school and college entitle us to declare ourselves bilingual? They do if we want them to. Language researchers readily admit that their statistics on second- and foreign-language use are, as Graddol put it in "The Decline of the Native Speaker," "educated guesswork."

David Crystal, in his *Cambridge Encyclopedia of the English Language* (1995), observed that only 98 million second-language speakers of English in the world could be totted up with certainty. In *English as a Global Language,* though, he argued that the true number was more nearly 350 million. Graddol put forward a variety of estimates in "The Decline of the Native Speaker," including Crystal's, and explained why each had its proponents. According to the most expansive of them, the number of second-language speakers was 518 million in 1995. From 98 million to 518 million is quite a range.

Estimates of the number of foreign-language speakers of English range more widely still. Crystal reports that these "have been as low as 100 million and as high as 1,000 million." The estimates *would* vary, because by definition foreign-language speakers live in places where English has no official or special status. They may or may not have been asked in a national census or other poll about their competence in English or other languages: they may or may not have had any formal schooling in English: their assessment of their ability to speak English may or may not be accurate.

This last point is particularly worth bearing in mind. According to recent "Eurobarometer" surveys described by Graddol, "77% of Danish adults and 75% of Swedish adults for example, say they can take part in a conversation in English." And "nearly one third of the citizens of the 13 'non English-speaking' countries in the EU 'can speak English well enough to take part in a conversation.'" However, Richard Parker, in his book *Mixed Signals: The Prospects for Global Television News* (1995), reported this about a study commissioned by Lintas, a major media buyer, in the early 1990s:

> When ad researchers recently tested 4,500 Europeans for "perceived" versus "actual" English-language skills, the results were discouraging. First, the interviewees were asked to evaluate their English-language abilities, and then to translate a series of sample English phrases or sentences. The study produced, in its own words, "sobering" results: "the number of people really fit for English-language television turned out to be less than half the expected audience." In countries such as France, Spain, and Italy, the study found, fewer than 3 percent had excellent command of English: only in small markets, such as Scandinavia and the Low Countries did the numbers even exceed 10 percent.

So the number of people in the world who speak English is unknown, 25 and how well many of them speak and understand it is questionable. No one is arguing that English is not widely spoken and taught. But the vast numbers that are often repeated—a billion English-speakers, a billion and a half —have only tenuous grounding in reality.

I have never seen any tables or charts that rank languages according to the proportions of the world's population expected to be using them as second or foreign languages ten or fifty years from now. The subject is just too hypothetical, the range of variables too great. Consider, for instance, the side effects that the breakup of the Soviet Union has had on the use of the Russian language. Now that no central authority seeks to impose Russian on school-children throughout the Soviet bloc, few countries besides Russia itself require students to learn it, and for the most part the language is less and less used. However, in places including the Caucasus, Russian continues to be valued as a lingua franca, and fluency in it remains a hallmark of an educated person.

Consider, too, the slender thread by which Canada's linguistic fate hung not long ago. In November of 1995 Quebec held a referendum to determine whether most of its citizens were in favor of independence. If 27,000 of the 4.65 million Quebeckers who voted had cast their ballots for secession rather than against, by now Canada's entire population of some 30 million people. all of them in theory bilingual, might conceivably be on the way to being largely monolingual—the nation of Quebec in French and what remained of Canada in English.

In the United States, discounting the claims that antagonists make about the other side's position, it's hard to find anyone who doesn't think it would be nice if everyone in the United States spoke English. Virtually all the impassioned debate is about whose resources should be devoted to making this happen and whether people should be encouraged to speak or discouraged from speaking other languages; too. All kinds of things have the potential to change the rate at which English as a second language is learned in the United States. Suppose that nationwide, English lessons were available free (as they already are in some parts of the country) and that employers offered workers, and schools offered parents, incentives to take them. Who can say what effect this would have?

Patterns of learning foreign languages are more volatile still. When I visited David Graddol, last fall, The English Company was reviewing materials the Chinese government had created to be used by 400,000 Chinese instructors in teaching English to millions of their compatriots. Maybe this was a step in an inexorable process of globalization—or maybe it wasn't. Plans to teach English widely in China might change if relations between our two countries took a disastrous turn. Or the tipping point could be something completely undramatic, such as the emergence of an array of Chinese-language Web sites. The information-technology expert Michael Dertouzos told me not long ago that at a conference he had attended in Taipei, the Chinese were grumbling about having to use English to take advantage of the Internet's riches.

1. What are the "fundamental paradoxes of global English" (paragraph 11) that Wallraff refers to? Summarize them in your own words.

2. What reasons does Wallraff give for the difficulty in determining the exact numbers of English speakers in the world? Are these numbers important to know? Why or why not?

3. How does Wallraff describe the linguist David Graddol and his office? What can you tell about Wallraff's general impression of Graddol and his work from her description? Provide examples from the essay to support your conclusions.

4. Wallraff asks how English can be globally dominant when "it can't even hold its own in part of our traditionally English-speaking country" (paragraph 6). What evidence does she present to support that assertion? Is it persuasive? Why or why not?

5. What is the difference between "second-language" speakers and "foreign-language" speakers? Why is this distinction important? Consider the situations described elsewhere in this chapter—in India, Taiwan, Korea, Europe, and Singapore. To which category do the speakers in these readings belong? Present evidence to support your responses. How does belonging to those categories affect the speakers' relationship to English as described in the respective accounts?

6. What is/are Wallraff's main arguments? Is she satisfied with the status of English in the world? in the United States? Cite examples from her text to support your answer.

7. Wallraff has a very personal relationship with the English language. What is your relationship to the language as a whole? If we consider languages to be living entities shaped and guided by their speakers, how do you feel about your role as a steward of English? Who is entitled to make up words or rules? Are you? Why or why not? Freewrite on these questions and share your ideas with two or three classmates. During your discussion, try to imagine yourselves in the position of those whose responses are different from your own. Write an essay describing your relationship to English as a living, changing entity and discussing your roles as a shaper and steward of the language.

$$\boxed{\text{part 2}}$$

Several languages called English

Much of what will happen to English we can only speculate about. But let's ³⁰ pursue an idea that language researchers regard as fairly well grounded: native speakers of English are already outnumbered by second-language and foreign-language speakers, and will be more heavily outnumbered as time goes on.

One obvious implication is that some proportion of the people using English for business or professional purposes around the world aren't and needn't be fluent in it. Recently I talked with Michael Henry Heim, a professor of Slavic literatures at the University of California at Los Angeles and a professional translator who has rendered into English major works by Milan Kundera and Günter Grass. By his count, he speaks "ten or so" languages. He told me flatly, "English is much easier to learn poorly and to communicate in poorly than any other language. I'm sure that if Hungary were the leader of the world. Hungarian would not be the world language. To communicate on a day-to-day basis—to order a meal, to book a room—there's no language as simple as English."

Research, though, suggests that people are likely to find a language easier or harder to learn according to how similar it is to their native tongue, in terms of things like word order, grammatical structure, and cognate words. As the researcher Terence Odlin noted in his book *Language Transfer* (1989), the duration of full-time intensive courses given to English-speaking U.S. foreign-service personnel amounts to a rough measurement of how different, in these ways, other languages are from English. Today the courses for foreign-service employees who need to learn German, Italian, French, Spanish, or Portuguese last twenty-four weeks. Those for employees learning Swahili, Indonesian, or Malay last thirty-six weeks, and for people learning languages including Hindi, Urdu, Russian, and Hungarian, forty-four weeks. Arabic, Chinese, Japanese, and Korean take eighty-eight weeks. Note that all the world's other commonest native languages except Spanish are in the groups most demanding of English-speakers. It might be reasonable to suppose that the reverse is also true—that Arabic- and Chinese-speakers find fluency in English to be more of a challenge than Spanish-speakers do.

A variety of restricted subsets of English have been developed to meet the needs of nonfluent speakers. Among these is Special English, which the Voice of America [VOA] began using in its broadcasts experimentally some forty years ago and has employed part-time ever since. Special English has a basic vocabulary of just 1,500 words (*The American Heritage Dictionary* contains some 200,000 words, and the *Oxford English Dictionary* nearly 750,000), though sometimes these words are used to define non–Special English words that VOA writers deem essential to a given story. Currently VOA uses Special English for news and features that are broadcast a half hour at a time, six times a day, seven days a week, to millions of listeners worldwide.

But restricted forms of English are usually intended for professional communities. Among the best known of these is Seaspeak, which ships' pilots around the world have used for the past dozen years or so: this is now being supplanted by SMCP, or "Standard Marine Communication Phrases," which is also derived from English but was developed by native speakers of a variety of languages. Airplane pilots and airtraffic controllers use a restricted form of English called Airspeak.

Certainly, the world's ships and airplanes are safer if those who guide them have some language in common, and restricted forms of English have no modern-day rivals for this role. The greatest danger language now seems to pose to navigation and aviation is that some pilots learn only enough English to describe routine situations, and find themselves at a loss when anything out of the ordinary happens.

Something else obviously implied by the ascendance of English as a second and a foreign language is that more and more people who speak English speak another language at least as well, and probably better. India may have the third or fourth largest number of English-speakers in the world, but English is thought to be the mother tongue of much less than one percent of the population. This is bound to affect the way the language is used locally. Browsing some English-language Web sites from India recently, I seldom had trouble understanding what was meant. I did, however, time and again come across unfamiliar words borrowed from Hindi or another indigenous Indian language. On the site called India World the buttons that a user could click on to call up various types of information were labeled "*samachar*: Personalised News," "*dhan*: Investing in India," "*khoj*: Search India," "*khel*: Indian Cricket," and so forth. When I turned to the *Afternoon Despatch & Courier* of Bombay (some of whose residents call it *Mumbai*) and called up a gossipy piece about the romantic prospects of the son of Rajiv and Sonia Gandhi, I read, "Sources disclose that before Rahul Gandhi left for London, some kind of a '*swayamvar*' was enacted at 10, Janpath with family friend Captain Satish Sharma drawing up a short list of suitable brides from affluent, well-known connected families of Uttar Pradesh."

Of course, English is renowned for its ability to absorb elements from other languages. As ever more local and national communities use English, though, they will pull language in ever more directions. Few in the world will care to look as far afield as the United States or Britain for their standards of proper English. After all, we long ago gave up looking to England—as did Indians and also Canadians, South Africans, Australians, and New Zealanders, among others. Today each of these national groups is proud to have its own idioms, and dictionaries to define them.

Most of the world's English-speaking communities can still understand one another well—though not, perhaps, perfectly. As Anne Soukhanov, a word columnist for this magazine and the American editor of the *Encarta World English Dictionary*, explained in an article titled "The King's English It Ain't," published on the Internet last year. "Some English words mean very different things, depending on your country. In South Asia, a *hotel* is a restaurant, but in Australia, a *hotel* is an establishment selling alcoholic beverages. In South Africa, a *robot* is a traffic light."

David Graddol told me about visiting China to consult on another English-curriculum project (one that had to do with teaching engineers in the steel industry) and finding a university that had chosen a Belgian company to develop lessons for it. When Graddol asked those in charge why they'd selected Belgians, of all people, to teach them English, they explained they saw it as an advantage that the Belgians, like the Chinese, are not native speakers. The Belgians, they reasoned, would be likely to have a feel both for the intricacies of learning the language in adulthood and for using it to communicate with other non-native speakers.

But by now we have strayed far beyond the relationship between demo- 40 graphics and the use of English. Technology has much to teach us too.

The Web in My Own Language

When the conversations I have with friends and acquaintances about the future of English veer immediately toward technology—especially the Internet—it's understandable. Much has been made of the Internet as an instrument for circulating English around the globe. According to one estimate that has been widely repeated over the past few years, 80 percent of what's available on the Internet is in English. Some observers, however, have recently been warning that this may have been the high-water mark. It's not that English-speakers are logging off—*au contraire*—but that other people are increasingly logging on, to search out or create content in their own languages. As the newsletter that The English Company prepared for the British Council asserted in September of 1998, "Non English speakers are the fastest growing group of new Internet users." The consensus among those who study these things is that Internet traffic in languages other than English will outstrip English-language traffic within the next few years.

There's no reason this should surprise us—particularly if we recall that there are about 372 million people in the world whose native language is English and about 5,700 million people whose native language is something else. According to the same newsletter, a recent study by Euro Marketing Associates estimated that

> nearly 44% of the world's online population now speak a language other than English at home. Although many of these Internet users are bilingual and speak English in the workplace, Euro Marketing suggests that advertisers of non-business products will more easily reach this group by using their home language. Of the 56 million people who speak languages on the Internet other than English, Spanish speakers represent nearly a quarter.

The study also estimated that 13.1 percent of all Internet users speak an Asian language at home—Japanese, for the most part. A surge in Internet use like the one that began in the United States half a dozen or so years ago is now under way in a number of other populous and relatively well-off places.

As has been widely noted, the Internet, besides being a convenient vehicle for reaching mass audiences such as, say, the citizenry of Japan or Argentina, is also well suited to bringing together the members of small groups —for example, middle-class French-speaking sub-Saharan Africans. Or a group might be those who speak a less common language: the numbers of Dutch-speakers and Finnish-speakers on the Internet are sharply up.

The Internet is capable of helping immigrants everywhere to remain proficient in their first language and also to stay current with what is going on back home. Residents in the Basque communities of Nevada and émigrés from the Côte d'Ivoire, for instance, can browse the periodicals, and even listen to the radio stations, of their homelands—much as American expatriates anywhere with an Internet connection can check the Web sites for CNN, ABC, MSNBC, and their hometown papers and radio stations.

No matter how much English-language material 45 there is on the Web, then, or even how much more English material there is than material in other languages, it is naive to assume that home computers around the world will, in effect, become the work stations of a vast English language lab. People *could* use their computers that way —just as we English-speaking Americans could enlist our

computers to help us learn Italian, Korean, or Yoruba. But, the glories of learning for its own sake aside, why would we want to do that? Aren't we delighted to be able to gather information, shop, do business, and be entertained in our own language? Why wouldn't others feel the same way? Consider, too, that many people regard high technology as something very much like a new language. Surely it's enough for a person to try to keep his or her hardware and software more or less up-to-date and running smoothly without simultaneously having to grapple with instructions or content in an actual foreign language.

Studies of global satellite television—a realm that is several years more mature than the Internet—also point to the idea that most people like new technology better when it speaks their own language. As Richard Parker wrote in *Mixed Signals*,

> Satellites can deliver programming and advertising instantaneously and simultaneously across the more than two dozen languages spoken in Western Europe, but the viewers—as repeated market research shows—want their television delivered in local tongues. Contrary to a history in which both motion pictures and early television broadcasts relied heavily on dubbing of foreign (often U.S.) programming, an affluent and culturally confident Europe now appears to be more linguistically divided than ever before.

Parker distinguishes between the "technologically feasible supply" of foreign programming and the "economically viable demand" for it, warning that we should be careful not to confuse the two. A few years ago, for example. Sweden aired a "reality-based" TV series. *Expedition: Robinson* (the word *expedition* has entered Swedish from English), and it quickly became a national obsession. But its success did not inspire American television networks to import the series: rather, they developed new shows, such as *Big Brother* and *Survivor*.

ENGLISH BY ACCIDENT

At one point in my conversation with David Graddol, he made a little sketch of something for me on a proof of his article "The Decline of the Native Speaker." The sketch was meant to remind me that technology has begun to blur the distinctions between languages in intriguing ways—and to suggest how those ways are themselves starting to overlap. Both the Internet and a range of technological applications only distantly related to it, he wanted me to see, are poised to expand what we are able to do with English.

Graddol uncapped his pen and drew a box in the broad white top margin of the page. "Text to text MT," he wrote in the box, and he said, "Of course you know about machine-translation systems," tapping the box to indicate that it was to represent them. Yes, I did: in fact, *The Atlantic* published an article about machine translation not long ago (see "Lost in Translation," by Stephen Budiansky, in the December, 1998, issue).

As the article explained, there are translation programs—Alta Vista's 50 Babel Fish among them—available for use free on the Internet. Type some English into the appropriate space on the Babel Fish Web page, or cut and paste it from another source, and choose your "destination" language— French, Portuguese, Spanish, Italian, or German. Presto! Up will pop a not entirely accurate translation of your chosen text. Or you can do this in reverse, from one of those languages—or Russian (the English-to-Russian feature is still in the works)—into English. Some professional translators use machine-translation systems as time-savers, getting the things to hack out rough texts they can then refine.

To the left of his machine-translation box Graddol drew a second box, which he labeled "Speech to text." He tapped it and said, "And you know about the voice-recognition systems that turn spoken words into written words." Yes, those, too. As it happens, I am the proud owner of a Dragon Systems program. Current versions of that and several other voice-recognition programs are reported to render speech into writing with 98 percent accuracy —not a rate that detail-oriented people are likely to find reassuring (getting two words wrong per hundred can add up), but certainly a rate that allows a user to get a point across.

Speech-to-text systems are now available for a variety of languages. Lernout & Hauspie, an industry leader that recently bought both Dragon Systems and Kurzweil Education Systems, sells products for turning British speech, as well as American, into writing, and also ones for German, Dutch, Spanish, French, Mandarin, and Cantonese.

Graddol drew a third box in the margin to the right, and labeled this box "Text to speech." He said, "And there are also machines that turn written words into spoken words." The Kurzweil reading machine, created to help the blind and visually impaired, and now capable of reading aloud in more than fifty languages, is the most advanced example in use. Simpler machines that turn computer code rather than text into speech are of course commonplace by now. We sometimes hear them when we call 411 and ask for a phone number; we hear them when we're refilling a prescription over the phone and a synthesized voice confirms our prescription number and name: we hear them on airlines' flight-information phone lines. These machines may have a vocabulary as elementary as numbers, the days of the week, and

"A.M." and "P.M." But they get the job done, and they hint at how more-complex systems might work.

Now Graddol drew lines from one box to the next. "People are starting to work on connecting all the parts," he said. "Once that happens, a lot of things will be possible."

I could, for example, speak into the microphone that came with my Dragon Systems program and have that program render what I've said in writing; instruct one of the translation programs to turn the text into French; and then use Lernout & Hauspie's French-language speech synthesizer to pronounce the computer's translation. This may strike some as a ponderous process, but surely it would be less complicated than acquiring a creditable French accent the old-fashioned way. Then, too, speech-to-writing and writing-to-speech programs may materialize on the Internet, much as the translation programs have done. In that case I will simply talk into the microphone, miraculous high-tech things will happen somewhere in the ether, and *voilà!* the computer at the restaurant L'Ami Louis, in Paris, will make my request for a reservation known to the staff, in exquisitely correct spoken or written French, and the maitre d', unwitting, will assign me a good table.

That's the theory, anyway. I have my doubts about how exquisite the actual results will be for quite some time. The interchanging of speech with writing, writing with speech, and English with other languages may, however, yield serviceable results very soon. According to a compilation of funny signs spotted around the world, published by the *Far Eastern Economic Review*, a Paris dress shop once advertised "Dresses for street walking," and a notice in a hotel elevator in the same city advised, "Please leave your values at the front desk." If we can understand the intention of these signs—as of course we can—then surely we will be able to see beyond most of the peculiarities resulting from machines involvement in language. David Graddol's neat little boxes glossed over myriad difficulties inherent in each step of linguistic interchangeability. But each of these steps is already being accomplished approximately, and implemented not just in experimental settings but in real life.

Even as software developers continue to adapt computers to our linguistic needs and wants, we are—God help us—adapting our own language to computers. For example, if I want to see the Amazon.com page about the psycholinguist Steven Pinker's book *Words and Rules* (1999), it's a complete waste of time to type into the search feature "Words and Rules, by Steven Pinker," correctly capitalized and punctuated. The computer and I will get exactly as much out of the exchange if I type "pinker rules." In effect, in this context "pinker rules" is better English than "Words and Rules, by Steven Pinker."

Where computers' processing ability and our intelligence will eventually converge is anyone's guess. As we teach ourselves, for instance, to speak in a way that will make our voice-recognition systems as productive as possible, developers are tweaking the new versions of them so that if the system misinterprets a word and we need to revise what it writes, the change will be incorporated into its database and it will never make the same mistake again.

Does this matter to the future of English? It may well. What is English, anyway? Is it the list of words and their meanings that a dictionary provides, together with all the rules about how to combine the words into sentences and paragraphs? Much more is involved than that. English is a system of communication, and highly germane to it is what or who speakers of English care to communicate with, and about what. The more we need to use English to communicate with machines—or with people whose fluency is limited or whose understanding of English does not coincide with ours—the more simplified the language will need to be.

And yet technology is expanding English, by requiring us to come up 60 with new words to describe all the possibilities it offers. Throughout the past century, according to *Twentieth Century Words* (1999), by John Ayto, technological domains—at first the likes of cars and aviation and radio, and eventually nuclear power, space, computers, and the Internet—were among the leading "lexical growth-areas." What's new of late isn't only words: we have whole new ways of combining the elements of written language. One ready example is emoticons (such as :> and :-o), which seem to have firmly established themselves in the realm of e-mail. Is *www* a word? Does one write the expression *dot com* or *.com* or what? And then there's professional jargon. In the course of exchanging ideas, global communities of astrophysicists, cardiologists, chip designers, food scientists, and systems analysts are stuffing the English language full of jargon. As science and technology grow increasingly multifarious and specialized, the jargon necessarily grows increasingly recondite: in the journal *Neurology*, for example, article titles like "Homogeneous phenotype of the gypsy limb-girdle MD with the γ sarcoglycan C283Y mutation" are run-of-the-mill. The range of English continues to expand further and further beyond any single person's ability to understand it all.

One more fact worth keeping in mind is that the relationship between science or technology and English is, essentially, accidental. It is chiefly because the United States has long been in the vanguard of much scientific and technological research, of course, that English is so widely used in these fields. If the United States were for the most part French-speaking, surely French would be the language of science and technology: there is nothing inherent in English to tie it to these fields. And if something as earthshaking as the Internet had been developed in, say, Japan, perhaps English would not now be dominant to the extent that it is. Future technology may well originate elsewhere. In the rapidly advancing field of wireless communications devices, for example, Scandinavia is already the acknowledged leader.

Here an argument is sometimes advanced that American culture furthers innovation, openness to new ideas, and so forth, and that our culture, whether by accident or not, is inseparable from the English language. But this takes us only so far. Even if the vanguards in all scientific and technological fields, everywhere in the world, used English in their work, once the fruits of their labor became known to ordinary people and began to matter to them, people would coin words in their local languages to describe these things. Theoretical physicists at international conferences may speak English among themselves, but most high school and college physics teachers use their native languages in class with their students. The Microsoft engineers who designed the Windows computer-operating system spoke English, and used English in what they created, but in the latest version, Windows Millennium, the words that users see on the screen are available in twenty-eight languages—and the spell-checker offers a choice of four varieties of English.

In sum, the globalization of English does not mean that if we who speak only English just sit back and wait, we'll soon be able to exchange ideas with anyone who has anything to say. We can't count on having much more around the world than a very basic ability to communicate. Outside certain professional fields, if English-speaking Americans hope to exchange ideas with people in a nuanced way, we may be well advised to do as people elsewhere are doing: become bilingual. This is easier said than done. If learning a second language were so simple, no doubt many more of us would have picked up Spanish or Chinese by now. It is clear, though, that the young learn languages much more readily than adults. Surely, American children who are exposed to nothing but English would benefit from being taught other languages as well.

At the same time, English is flourishing, and people here and everywhere are eager to learn it to the extent that it is practical for them to do so. It would behoove us to make learning English as easy as possible, for both children and adults, in this country and abroad.

However unwelcome this news may be to some, not even headlong technological advances mean that computers will soon be doing all the hard work of coping with other languages for us. For the foreseeable future com- 65 puters will be able to do no more than some of the relatively easy work. When it comes to subtle comprehension of our world and the other people in it, we are, as ever, on our own.

about the text

1. What recommendations regarding learning English does Wallraff make at the end of her essay? Do you agree? Why or why not?
2. Native speakers are typically considered to be the best and most knowledgeable speakers of their language. When, according to Wallraff, might it be desirable to learn English from non-native speakers? Why?

on language use

3. How do you feel as a speaker of English, a global language? Proud? indifferent? lucky? In the future for English, would you like, for example, for English to be a worldwide, mandatory school subject? for English words coined in Singapore or Kenya to spread to all English-speaking communities? Why or why not?
4. Wallraff uses the French phrase *au contraire* (paragraph 41), assuming that her readers will know. Foreign words or phrases frequently get borrowed into a language when there is no equivalent, but in this case, English, has "on the contrary." Why does Wallraff use the French phrase here? How is it different from English using the version? There are many more Spanish speakers than French speakers in the United States; why isn't *al contrario* used in similar scenarios?
5. Where have you encountered computer-generated spoken language? How do you feel interacting with a mechanical voice? Does it matter whether the program requires you to speak rather than simply punch numbers on the keypad? Why or why not?

6. Wallraff mentions the language translation programs, such as Babel Fish, that are available on the Internet and notes that the translations are "not entirely accurate" (paragraph 50). Copy a few sentences from something you've written; go to a translation page on the Web; paste in your writing to translate it into another language; and then translate the results back into English. How close are the sentences to your original version? Compare your results with those of two or three classmates. What kinds of words or phrases was the translation program least able to handle? What kinds of material, if any, came out accurately? Based on your results, what generalizations can you make about the nature of language?

for writing

7. Consider the following statement: "It is a fact that English is the dominant language in the world today. Everyone, in every country, in order to participate in the modern world, should learn English. After all, a language is just a collection of words, so how hard could it be?" Write an essay responding to this statement. Give reasons to support your argument. Wallraff's essay and the other selections in this chapter should provide you with ideas, or you might do additional research, making sure to document your sources.
8. Both this selection and David Crystal's essay "Why a Global Language?" address questions of global English. Write an essay comparing and contrasting their conclusions. How are they similar or different? Which essay is more informative? more persuasive? Why?

Glossary

AAVE (African American Vernacular English) *See* Ebonics.

affix something added to a word, usually to the beginning (PREFIX) or end (SUFFIX), that changes or alters the word's meaning; for example, with the word *lock*: *lock**s**, lock**ing**, lock**ed**, **un***lock*, **re***lock*, *lock**able**, lock**out***.

agonistic taking a competitive or oppositional position on a topic, approaching a question or topic as a matter of pros and cons. The term has its origin in Greek, where it referred to an athletic competition.

Aristotelian refers to the ideas of the Greek philosopher and scientist Aristotle (384–322 B.C.E.). Aristotle placed value on knowledge gained from the five senses—that is, empirical knowledge; Aristotle's ideas are often contrasted with those of fellow Greek philosopher, Plato, who believed that reason and discussion eventually lead to the discovery of important truths. *Contrast* PLATONIC.

ASL (American Sign Language) the principal sign language used in the United States by Deaf people and their conversation partners; it is a different language from British Sign Language and is also different from SIGNED ENGLISH.

bidialectalism the state of knowing two or more dialects of a single language. For example, people who use STANDARD ENGLISH at work and AAVE, New York English, Texas English, or any other variety with family or friends may be said to be bidialectal.

bilingualism the state of knowing two or more languages, but not necessarily using them with equal proficiency or in equal proportions. People who acquire two (or more) languages in infancy or early childhood may be considered to be native bilinguals; that is, they have two NATIVE LANGUAGES.

BVE (Black Vernacular English) *See* Ebonics.

codeswitching the use of two or more languages within a single conversation—sometimes within a single sentence. Codeswitching is performed (in speech or in writing) among bilinguals who speak the same languages. Codeswitchers intuitively know where they can, and can't, switch languages in a sentence in order to continue to make sense; also, there are complex (and usually unspoken) constraints on the social circumstances where codeswitching is and isn't appropriate. For example, codeswitching is a common practice among English/Spanish bilinguals in California, New York, or Texas; some people refer to this type of codeswitching as SPANGLISH. On the other hand, English/French bilinguals in Quebec, for a number of social reasons, are much less likely to codeswitch.

creole a type of language that is an identifiable blend of two or more languages. Creole languages develop in very specific situations of intense contact between speakers of three or more languages, one of which is politically dominant. All creoles share certain common grammatical features regardless of which languages have combined to form them, and creoles are more complex and elaborated than PIDGINS. Two examples of creole languages are Gullah, spoken in the United States, and Kreyòl, spoken in Haiti.

Deaf/deaf two words that have to do with not hearing. When written with a small *d*, deaf describes the physiological condition of not having hearing; when capitalized, the word refers to the robust culture developed by Deaf people or to its members. The principal language used in U.S. Deaf culture is ASL (AMERICAN SIGN LANGUAGE), and Deaf people believe that deafness is not pathological and that their lives are not deficient or pitiable.

descriptive grammar a description of a language as it is used by its speakers; it describes such elements as the sound inventory and sound patterns, how words and sentences are formed, and the types of verbal art and word play that speakers practice. A descriptive grammar is not concerned with what is and isn't considered correct usage. *See also* GRAMMAR and PRESCRIPTIVE GRAMMAR.

dialect a variety of a language that is spoken by some of its speakers and understood by most or all of its speakers; for example, the California English used by Buffy the Vampire Slayer or the East Coast English used by the Soprano family may not be spoken by all English speakers, but both dialects are readily understood by virtually all Americans and many other English speakers in other parts of the world. Other dialects of English include EBONICS, Texas English, South Asian (Indian) English, Australian English, and RECEIVED PRONUNCIATION, which is part of Standard English in Britain. *Contrast* LANGUAGE and REGISTER.

diminutive form of a word (most often a noun) indicating smallness of size and/or affection or endearment. Many languages have systematic ways of creating diminutive forms by adding a suffix or changing the word form in other ways. In English, for example, we may add the suffix -**y** (or -**ie**) to names (*Bob/Bobby, Tom/Tommy, Barbara/Barbie, Kate/Katie*) and other words (*duckie, doggie, baggie*). However, the use of the diminutive is relatively limited in English. In contrast, diminutives are used quite commonly in many languages, including Spanish and Arabic. In Arabic, for example, the word for dog is *kalb*; the diminutive form, *kulayb*, can be used to mean "tiny dog" (not "puppy") or something that might translate as "dear" or "beloved dog."

discursive practice refers to patterns of language use and their social functions, especially when the practice provides a meaning that is more than a literal interpretation of the words. For example, in certain circumstances the comment *"gee, it's a little warm in here, isn't it?"* may not be a simple comment on the room temperature but rather an indirect request that someone open a window or turn on a fan.

Ebonics a name used to refer to a variety of English that is spoken principally by African Americans, although not all African American people use it and it is used by some non-African Americans. Ebonics is known by various labels, including AAVE (African American Vernacular English), BVE (Black Vernacular English), Black English, and African American English. Linguists recognize that Ebonics, like all other varieties of English, is SYSTEMATIC AND RULE-GOVERNED.

English-Only movement organizations and activities with the goal of mandating that English be declared the only official language of the United States. Some of its supporters want to ensure that English is the official and only language used in government business—court proceedings, tax form instructions, driver examinations, etc. Other supporters would like to eliminate bilingual education and/or the rights of people to use languages other than English in workplaces or public space. The present-day movement is considered to have begun in the early 1980s, although English-Only legislation in the United States was enacted in some states and localities as early as the nineteenth century.

fingerspelling the alphabet expressed with positions of the hand and fingers. In ASL (American Sign Language) and other gestural systems of communication used by deaf people, proper names and technical terms or other words that do not have specific signs may be spelled out using fingerspelling.

first language the first language(s) acquired by a person; also known as NA-TIVE LANGUAGE or MOTHER TONGUE. A person who acquires more than one language from infancy or early childhood may have more than one first language.

foreign language a language (other than the native language) learned or used by a person for limited and/or specific purposes such as business transactions or reading. A foreign language is not learned with the intent of using it extensively in daily life. Contrast SECOND LANGUAGE.

gender a term referring to a social category that roughly corresponds to the physiological categories of male and female sex, but the dividing line is not as distinct. Further, as a social category, the distinguishing characteristics of gender are not universal, and they change across time and cultures. Individuals construct their own genders according to their appearance and behavior; it is possible for persons of male sex to present themselves in the world as having feminine gender, and vice versa. Sex and *gender* are often used interchangeably in informal usage but each has a precise and distinct meaning. Neither sex nor gender is a reliable predictor of a person's sexuality or sexual orientation. Contrast SEX.

gender-neutral language words or phrases that do not specify male or female gender unless there is a specific reason to do so, for example, *service technician* (not *serviceman*) or *flight attendant* (not *stewardess*). Instead of *every player should bring his bat and glove*, we may say, *every player should bring a bat and glove*.

gendered pronouns pronouns that indicate the gender of the referents; for example *she, her, he, his*. Examples of non-gendered English pronouns are *they, their, you, I*. Some languages have fewer gender-marked pronouns than English, while other languages have more.

grammar the predictable patterns and systems of sounds (or gestures), sequences or words, and assemblages of meaningful elements of any language. These patterns are also called *rules*. All languages (and dialects) have grammar, and it is this grammar that linguists study and analyze. See *also* SYSTEMATIC AND RULE-GOVERNED.

grammatical gender agreement a type of agreement system in languages, like Spanish or German, that have gendered nouns and require certain other words, such as the adjectives, verbs, or pronouns, to have gendered forms that agree with the gender of the noun. In Spanish, for example, *silla* (chair) is feminine, while *sofá* (sofa) is masculine; if you had recently bought one of each, you might refer to **la** *nueva silla y* **el** *nuevo sofá*. Other languages, like Japanese and Hebrew, distinguish the gender of the speaker, so that women and men have different words for *I* and *me*.

indigenous language a language of a people native to a particular territory, such as Navajo, Cherokee, or other Native American languages in the United States, Ojibwa or Cree in Canada, and Zapotec or Yucatec Maya in Mexico.

language (in general) a type of communication system that employs sounds and/or gestures to construct meaning. Although many animals also have communication systems—some very elaborate—language is, to the best of our current knowledge, a uniquely human enterprise. Among the characteristics that distinguish language from animal communication systems are transmission from generation to generation (rather than innate knowledge), the ability to convey information about distant places or past and future time, and the ability to lie.

language (vs. dialect) a distinction that is social and/or political rather than based on linguistic criteria. For example, Swedish and Norwegian are quite similar and mutually intelligible, yet they are considered two separate languages by their speakers, principally because they are each identified with a different country. On the other hand, Mandarin and Cantonese are considered by their speakers to be two dialects of a single language, Chinese, despite the fact that they are not mutually intelligible in their spoken forms (although they share a written form). In determining whether two systems are separate languages or dialects of the same language, linguists consider mutual intelligibility to be generally the most reliable test; only the speakers themselves, however, can make the determination.

language preservation efforts undertaken to make sure that a language does not disappear when all of its speakers begin to rely more heavily on another language for their daily lives. This is the situation of many indigenous languages of the United States, whose speakers are using English, even with their children, so that the language is not being transmitted to new generations. See also LANGUAGE REVITALIZATION.

language revitalization efforts undertaken to improve the status of a language in a community where it has traditionally been spoken and to increase the number of everyday speakers. Some programs, for example, may involve pairing elderly speakers (who may be the only people in a community who still know the language) with young people who want to learn the language of their grandparents and protect their cultural heritage. See also LANGUAGE PRESERVATION.

language rights/linguistic rights rights of individual speakers as well as of communities of speakers of any given language with regard to that language and/or others spoken in a given place. For example, a guideline published by the United Nations suggests that all children have the right to receive basic education in the language spoken in their communities. Other linguistic rights may include the right to socialize in one's language(s) of choice and the right to access primary education in the official (or dominant) language(s) of the nation or state.

linguistic determinism the controversial theory that language shapes thought, and more specifically that the language(s) spoken by an individual determines (and/or strongly influences) the content and manner of his or her possible thoughts and knowledge. Linguists continue to debate the topic, also known as the SAPIR-WHORF HYPOTHESIS.

linguistics the study and analysis of language and languages. Linguistics is concerned with many questions, such as: what does it mean to "know" a language? how do children acquire their language(s)? how do people acquire additional languages? how is language stored and processed in the brain? how do languages change over time? what features, if any, do all languages share? how do the structures of the many languages in the world differ? how are they similar? how do we use language to accomplish the work of maintaining human society? how do we use language to establish our individual and group identities?

metaphor a figurative way of comparing or understanding one thing in terms of something else, usually by saying something "is" something else. To refer, for example, to *a wave of immigrants* or *a sea of faces* emphasizes humans as a collective whole rather than as distinct individuals. All metaphors highlight certain features of the comparison and obscure others. For example, the two metaphors *dating is a game* and *dating is a dance* may be equally valid, but the first one emphasizes competition and the possibility of winning or losing while the second emphasizes the cooperative nature of the enterprise.

minority language in a given state or nation, a language spoken by a minority of residents or a language with relatively less status than another language, though it may have more actual speakers. A language may be a minority language in one country, such as Spanish or Vietnamese in the United States, and a majority, or dominant, language in others.

morphology the branch of linguistics that examines parts of words and how they can (or can't) combine to form other words. If you studied morphology, you might invent words like *awesome-icity* or *dude-itude* and analyze why your friends would understand those words easily, while other invented words like *dis-awesome* or *dude-hood* may have less success.

mother tongue the language(s) learned from infancy in the home. See *also* FIRST LANGUAGE and NATIVE LANGUAGE.

multilingualism state of knowing more than two languages. The term may be applied to individuals who use more than two languages in their lives (it is normal and customary in many places in the world—parts of Europe, Africa, and South America, for example—for the majority of the population to be multilingual). The term may also be applied to communities where more than two languages are commonly used; U.S. cities with large and diverse immigrant populations, such as New York, Chicago, or San Francisco, may be considered multilingual cities.

national language a language that is associated with a nation and whose residents are generally presumed to be speakers of that language. Its status in a given nation may or may not have been made official. For example, by legal decree, French is the national language of France; in contrast, English has no official status in the United States although it is by far the dominant language of public and private discourse in the country. A nation may have more than one national language; for example, both French and English are the national languages of Canada. See *also* OFFICIAL LANGUAGE.

native language the language(s) first learned by an individual. A person who acquires more than one language from infancy or early childhood may have more than one native language. See *also* FIRST LANGUAGE and MOTHER TONGUE.

non-standard refers to a variety or dialect of a language that differs from the standard variety and may be considered by some people to be inferior to it. Some non-standard varieties of English, for example, are various Southern Englishes (which use *y'all*) and Chicago English (with its *dis*, *dat*, and *youse*). *Contrast* STANDARD ENGLISH.

non-verbal communication meaning or intention expressed without the use of spoken or signed words. Non-verbal communication may be overt and deliberate, for example, rolling one's eyes, winking, nodding, shaking one's head, or giving a thumbs-up sign; it may also be unintentional, for example, the posture of conversation partners toward one another— facing one another or facing away, leaning toward or away from one another or crossing one's arms across the chest.

observers' paradox a phenomenon whereby people who are being observed or studied by others change or modify their words, thoughts, and actions—sometimes very blatantly and sometimes more subtly. Researchers work to minimize this effect.

official language a language whose status in a country has been officially recognized, that is, granted status by law. Countries with official languages have a variety of policies, but the existence of an official language usually means that all government business, from legislative acts to birth registrations, will be produced in that language; education may be another area conducted exclusively in the official language. See *also* NATIONAL LANGUAGE.

ontology the nature or essence of something, or the study and exploration of a thing's nature or essence.

orthography the system of correct spelling for a given language.

phatic communication exchanges of conversation intended to maintain a pleasant connection among participants rather than to convey information; comments about the weather between two people at a bus stop or on an elevator or the greeting rituals we perform (*"Hi, how are you?"*; *"Hey, what's up?"*; *"Du-uu-ude"*) are examples of phatic communication.

phonetic refers to the production and/or comprehension of the sounds of a language. The science of phonetics studies the physics and physiology of how sounds are produced by speakers and perceived by listeners in the various languages of the world.

phonology the science of describing and analyzing the patterns of sound combinations of a language. Every language has its own unique patterns. For example, Spanish and English both have the sounds /s/ as in *sand*, /p/ as in *pan*, and /l/ as in *land*. English can put all three sounds together in a single syllable, for example, in the words *splice* or *splash*, but Spanish cannot combine the three sounds. On the other hand, Polish and English both have the sounds *d* as in *dine* and *v* as in *vine*; English cannot combine them in that order in a single syllable, but Polish can, as in the word *dva* (two).

pidgin a type of language that arises in situations of intense contact for specific purposes between groups of speakers of two languages, for example, as a consequence of trade or slavery. A pidgin usually has the vocabulary of one language and the grammatical structure of the other. A pidgin cannot be a native language for anyone because it has very limited expressive power. Pidgins are usually short-lived; they either outlast their usefulness and disappear or expand their communicative potential and become CREOLE languages.

Platonic refers to the ideas of Greek philosopher and writer Plato (c. 428-c. 348 B.C.E.). Plato sought knowledge and truth by means of reason and discussion among open-minded people, that is, by the use of dialectics. His methods are often contrasted with those of ARISTOTLE, who, as an empiricist, relied more on direct observation and information gained from the five senses.

prefix something added to the beginning of a word that changes or alters the word's meaning; for example, with the word *heated*: **un**heated, **re**heated, **pre**heated, and **over**heated. *See also* AFFIX and SUFFIX.

prescriptive grammar the set of rules devised and maintained by one or more authoritative bodies for the correct usage of a language. Prescriptive grammar attempts to instruct people in how they *should* talk and/or write. Some languages such as French or Spanish have official academies that make and change rules of correct usage; the rules of English are maintained *ad hoc* by usage manuals, dictionaries, and, to a lesser extent, newspapers and magazines—and, ultimately, by the language's users.

pro-drop language a language in which the subject of a sentence does not need to be explicitly expressed because other elements, such as verb endings, provide the necessary information. English is not a pro-drop language, since it requires every sentence to have a subject; for example, *I eat, you eat, we eat, they eat.* Spanish, on the other hand, is a pro-drop language; the same sentences—*como, comes, comemos, comen*—do not require pronouns because the verb *comer* (to eat) has a distinct form for each possible subject.

productive describes a grammatical structure, such as a word PREFIX or SUFFIX, that can easily combine to form new words or phrases. For example, the negative prefix **un-** is highly productive; not only can many new words be formed with it, but other speakers of English will be able to understand the word without further explanation. You could tell a friend that your blind date last night was *"very **un**wonderful,"* and although the word is not in the dictionary and may never have been heard before, your friend would understand it immediately.

Received Pronunciation (RP) pronunciation standards of British English that are associated with prestige and the highest levels of social status. It is also known as "Queen's English" or "BBC English." Until the 1970s, RP was the required pronunciation for all BBC announcers and newscasters. It remains the accent of Standard English in Britain.

register a variety of a language that is appropriate to specific situations or addressees. For example, the simple question *"where did you go last night?"* would elicit very different responses depending on whether you were answering your roommate, your mother, or a police officer. Registers can usually be placed on a continuum of formality; all natural languages have multiple registers, and all adult speakers of a language consciously or unconsciously select the register most appropriate to the situation. *Contrast* DIALECT.

rhetorical question a question that is not intended to be answered directly. Writers and speakers may use a rhetorical question to frame an argument they are about to make or to call attention to something. Rhetorical questions are often used sarcastically or ironically; for example, when a parent asks, *"Just what do you think you're doing?"* a literal answer is usually not what is being requested.

Sapir-Whorf hypothesis the theory, named for early-twentieth-century linguists Edward Sapir and Benjamin Lee Whorf, that the specific language(s) we speak shape our perceptions of our own lives and of the world. Sapir wrote, "The language habits of our community predispose certain choices of interpretation." For example, the colors of the visible spectrum are a seamless blend; the division of red, orange, yellow, green, blue, indigo, and violet is completely arbitrary and not universal. *See also* LINGUISTIC DETERMINISM.

second language a language learned in late childhood or adulthood for the purpose of regular use in daily life; for example, in the case of many immigrants to the United States or other countries, or people who, for personal or professional reasons, communicate frequently with speakers of another language. *Contrast* FOREIGN LANGUAGE.

semantic domain categories of meaning into which words may be grouped; for example, names of flowers; verbs that describe ways of eating (*devour, slurp, chomp, lick, bite, chew*); shapes of human bodies (*stocky, slender, roly-poly, rotund, curvaceous, angular, willowy*). Some semantic domains may have specific usage limitations. For example, in American and British English, verbs that express opinion or states of mind are seldom used in the **-ing** form; it would sound peculiar to say *"I am liking that car," "she is wanting more ice cream,"* or *"your parents are believing in you."*

semantics a linguistics subfield that deals with meaning. A semantics exercise, for example, may ask you to list words such as *mouse, window, boot, freeze, surf,* or *crash* and explain how their meanings as computer-related terms are similar to and different from their more general meanings.

sex a term that refers to physiology and genetics by dividing people categorically into either male or female based on physical characteristics. *Sex* and *gender* are often used interchangeably in informal usage, but each has a precise and distinct meaning. Neither sex nor gender is a reliable predictor of a person's sexuality or sexual orientation. *Contrast* GENDER.

sexist language language usage that takes maleness as the default human characteristic and specifies femaleness only in references that are specifically or exclusively female. The statement "Someone left his keys on the table" is an example of sexist language (unless the speaker knows for certain that the keys could not have been left by a woman). Words such as *mailmen* or *mankind* are sexist when used to refer to all mail carriers or all humans (slightly more than half of whom are female).

Signed English a system of manual communication that uses English words and English word order but is expressed manually rather than spoken. Signed English is different from ASL (American Sign Language), which uses different word order and different ways to refer to persons and time. Signed English, a system of manual communication rather than a natural language, lacks the subtleties that are possible in both spoken English and ASL. Therefore, it is more cumbersome and less precise than ASL but may be more easily learned by English-speakers and people who become deaf after childhood. CONTRAST FINGERSPELLING.

slang generally short-lived and faddish words or expressions that enter a language as creative innovations, often made by young people. Slang expressions frequently deal with taboo subjects such as sex and bodily functions and are often metaphorical euphemisms (*toss your cookies* [vomit]; *woody* [erection]), humorous insults (*bee-atch*); affectionate terms of address or reference (*dog; my peeps*); code words for illegal, prohibited, or restricted activities (*living the down low*); expressions of praise (*crunk; off the hook; phat*). Slang expressions are frequently in-group markers and therefore may have narrow distribution among regional and/or social groups; a large number of U.S. slang terms have their origin in African American communities.

sociolinguistics the branch of linguistics that considers social aspects of language use patterns and the ways that language is used to construct and maintain social structures. Some of the topics studied by sociolinguists include language and identity, language and gender, dialectical variation (Where do people say *soda? pop? Coke? soft drink?*), language change and language contact, bilingualism, and many others.

Spanglish a term used to describe a style of speech in which speakers CODESWITCH between Spanish and English. Although some people consider Spanglish a corrupt form of language, its speakers often value it as a stylistic choice that displays proficiency in both languages and/or demonstrates speakers' pride in their bicultural identities. Most linguists would argue that Spanglish is not a new language because there are no novel grammatical rules or forms not already found in English or Spanish. Instead, it is a complex way of combining the linguistic resources speakers have. Speakers in many bilingual communities have names for the practice of combining their two languages: in addition to Spanglish, we find such labels as Konglish (Korean and English), Singlish (Chinese in Singapore and English), Hinglish (Hindi and English).

speechreading the practice of comprehending speech by careful observation of the speaker's mouth, lips, and tongue. Many Deaf people are adept at speechreading, which is immensely difficult to learn and can never be completely accurate because many speech sounds look alike, for example, the consonants in the words *pack, back,* and *bag. Lip-reading* is a less-preferred term for speechreading.

Standard English the variety of English that is taught in schools, used in formal writing, and often heard on radio and television. It is considered by many to be the correct and proper English. Standard English is not the same in all of the countries where English is spoken. In the United States, for example, the words *labor, color,* and *center* are correctly spelled as written here, while in Canada, New Zealand, Great Britain, and other parts of the English-speaking world—in fact, nearly all of it— the same words are correctly spelled *labour, colour,* and *centre. See also* NON-STANDARD and RECEIVED PRONUNCIATION.

standardized language a language with widely accepted rules of correct usage. English, Spanish, French, and Japanese are examples of languages with highly elaborated rules, and each of these languages has dialects that do not conform to the "standard." *See also* STANDARD ENGLISH, NON-STANDARD, and RECEIVED PRONUNCIATION.

suffix something added to the end of a word that changes the word's meaning or adds extra information; for example, with the word *play,* the suffix -*er* indicates a person who plays, while *played* puts the action in the past, and *plays* confirms that the subject of the verb is third person singular. *See also* AFFIX and PREFIX.

syntax the order of words and phrases in an utterance; also, the study and analysis of the ways in which words and phrases can and cannot appropriately combine in a given language. For example, someone interested in English syntax might want to analyze why it is appropriate to say, "*I didn't see you put the keys* **on the table**," but not "*I didn't see you put the keys* **where**." Computer programmers also use the term *syntax* to describe the order of elements in a program or operation.

systematic and rule-governed a condition of every human language and dialect, regardless of whether it has a written form or explicit usage manuals. All languages and dialects are systematic because their speakers, in order to construct well-formed utterances, follow specific, recognized patterns and orders of sounds and words; linguists refer to these patterns as "rules." Utterances that disregard the rules may be perceived as inadequate or misunderstood entirely; for example, if a Texan said, "*I might could help you on Saturday,*" another Texan would understand perfectly. However, the similar statement "*I could might help you on Saturday*" would violate the syntactic rules of the dialect—*might* must precede *could*—and would sound strange to the Texan in reverse order.

terministic screen label used by philosopher and rhetorician Kenneth Burke to remind us that all terms, that is, words, encourage us to see certain parts of reality while ignoring other parts of it. (As he put it, words simultaneously reflect and deflect reality.) Burke also notes that once one has chosen a set of terms, arguments in many ways work themselves out. A corporation's use of "downsizing" makes the process appear to be the "logical" thing to do given our society's emphasis on cost cutting and efficiency and our prejudice against unnecessarily large bureaucracies. At the same time, it completely diverts attention from the plight of workers who have lost their jobs.

transgendered a person born of one sex who identifies socially as a member of the other sex. Transgendered people may be heterosexual, lesbian, or gay. The majority of transgendered individuals are male-to-female.

transliteration a form of translation from one language to another that gives a literal, word-by-word translation rather than a translation in units of equivalent meaning. For example, the Spanish sentence *Esta tarea es pan comido* would be transliterated as "This homework is eaten bread," which makes no sense because "*pan comido*" is an idiom. A translation that retains the meaning would be "*This homework is a piece of cake,*" which uses the equivalent English idiom for a task that is very easy. Transliteration can also refer to the interpretation of a written word from one writing system to another, for example, rendering Arabic words into English or other European languages that use the roman alphabet.

typography the art and technology of mechanically producing writing. Almost all commercial typography is now done with computers. Typographic designers may manipulate such elements as font, size, line and character spacing, as well as effects such as **bold**, *italics*, or CAPITALIZATION in order to create a desired effect and enhance the message of the text.

usage refers to two very different phenomena. First, it can refer to the way speakers use a language in their lives. There are different kinds of usage, for example, everyday, informal usage; academic usage; formal usage, etc. In everyday usage, for example, we may say or hear statements such as, "*someone left their key on the table,*" or "*awesome, dude,*" while the same meanings in more formal usage may be given as, "someone *left his or her key on the table*," or "*that is quite excellent, my friend*." More narrowly, "usage" refers to what many people consider "good grammar": using *lay* and *lie* correctly, not saying *ain't*, avoiding double negatives. In this latter sense, usage represents the linguistic equivalent of good manners.

vernacular a language of everyday use of a people or a nation, as opposed to an official or formal language. The vernacular language of a particular place may be a variety or dialect of an official language or it may be another language altogether.

voiced/voiceless one of the features that linguists use for describing the sounds of a language. In English, for example, all vowels are voiced, and consonants can be either voiced or voiceless. Voiced sounds are produced with vibration in the vocal cords. Place your fingers lightly on the front of your throat and say *Sue* and *zoo*. Can you feel that your throat vibrates more on *zoo*? Say *chum* and *joke*. Which word begins with a voiced sound? Which one ends with a voiced sound?

Rhetorical Index

CAUSE AND EFFECT

COMPARISON AND CONTRAST

CLASSIFICATION AND DIVISION

DEFINITION

ARGUMENTATION AND PERSUASION

TEXT ACKNOWLEDGMENTS

IMAGE ACKNOWLEDGMENTS

Chapter 1

Rothman: Subaru "Get Out and Stay Out" ad courtesy of Subaru of America, Inc; Coors "Straight Talk from Coors" ad courtesy of Coors; Delta "Variety Makes us Strong" ad courtesy of Delta Air Lines / The Jackson Heath Group. **<wordscanheal.org>:** screenshot from <www.wordscanheal.org>. **Quindlen:** Photo of gay rights protest, Nancy Siesel / the *New York Times*; Photo of civil rights marchers with "I am a man" signs © Bettman / Corbis; "Growth of Overt Homosexuality" headline, the *New York Times*; "3,000 Troops Put Down Mississippi Rioting" headline, the *New York Times*. **Duer Miller:** Drawing of "The Awakening" by Hy Mayer. From the Library of Congress Prints and Photographs Division Washington, D.C. 20540 USA. **Kakutani:** Cartoon by Barbara Smaller. © the *New Yorker* Collection 2004 Barbara Smaller from cartoonbank.com. All Rights Reserved.

Chapter 2

<freespeling.com>: screenshot from <www.freespeling.com.> **Biehl:** Map of German speaking nations. © the *San Francisco Chronicle*. Reprinted by permission. **Winchester:** Drawings of Roget and of a woman reading over man's shoulder courtesy of David Johnson; Photo of Roget towards the end of his life from the Royal College of Physicians of London. **Mercedes-Benz** ads courtesy of Mercedes-Benz USA.

Chapter 3

Jump Start cartoon by Robb Armstrong reprinted by permission of United Feature Syndicate, Inc. *Rose Is Rose* cartoons by Pat Brady reprinted by permission of United Feature Syndicate, Inc. **Bruder:** Grammar Lady icon from <www.grammarlady.com>. *Zits* cartoon by Jim Borgman and Jerry Scott © Zits partnership. Reprinted with special permission of King Features Syndicate. *FoxTrot* cartoon by Bill Amend © 2002 Bill Amend. Reprinted with permission of Universal Press Syndicate. All rights reserved. "The IM's of Romeo and Juliet" cartoon by Roz Chast © the *New Yorker* Collection 2002 Roz Chast from cartoonbank.com. All Rights Reserved. **Borkowsky:** Photo of Amy's mom from Amy Borkowsky. **Nussbaum Cohen:** Photo of Palm Pilot with Arabic script by Marty Katz.

Chapter 4

Luann cartoon by Greg Evans reprinted by permission of United Feature Syndicate, Inc. *Baldo* cartoons by Hector Cantú and Carlos Castellanos © 2001, 2002 Baldo Partnership. Distributed by Universal Press Syndicate. Reprinted with permission. All rights reserved. **Smith:** Photo of a woman studying. From the *Fort Worth Star-Telegram*/Kampha Bouaphanh. **Haberman:** Drawing from *Di Kats der Payats* (The Cat in the Hat) reprinted by permission of International Creative Management and Celeste Sollod and Zackary Berger of Twenty-Fourth Street Books, LLC.

Chapter 5

Troutt: Photo of Condoleezza Rice © Brooks Kraft/Corbis; Photo of Jesse Jackson © Ramin Talaie/Corbis; Photo of Jay-Z © Contographer/Corbis. *Jump Start* cartoon by Robb Armstrong reprinted by permission of United Feature Syndicate, Inc. *"I Has a Dream"* ad courtesy of Austin Kelley Advertising.

Chapter 6

Bizarro cartoon © Dan Piraro. Reprinted with special permission of King Features Syndicate. "If I were a car" cartoon by Peter Steiner © The New Yorker Collection 1995 Peter Steiner from cartoonbank.com. All Rights Reserved. Photo of Fiat billboard by Jill Posener. **Hairston and Ruszkiewicz:** Photo of Mia Hamm © Duomo/Corbis.

Chapter 7

Luann cartoon by Greg Evans reprinted by permission of United Feature Syndicate, Inc. **Solomon:** Photos of Miss Deaf America semifinalists and of Deaf students demonstrating from Marc Asnin. Redux. **Brueggemann:** Photo of Alexander Graham Bell and his wife from Parks Canada/Alexander Graham Bell National Historic Site of Canada.

Chapter 8

Woo: Washington Redskins photo © Reuters/Corbis. **Wise:** Cartoon © Lalo Alcaraz 2002. Reprinted by permission of Universal Press Syndicate. All rights reserved. **Pope:** Photo of a Baku ice cream shop © Staton R. Winter/the *New York Times*; Photo of the Arabic Diet Coke can courtesy of Jane and Nick Netherton. Photo of the Arabic Coke can and the Hebrew Pepsi can courtesy of the authors. **Tomorrow:** *This Modern World* cartoon © Tom Tomorrow.

Chapter 9

Crystal: Photo of a man on a bicycle, Amit Barghava for the *New York Times*; **Duff-Brown:** Photo of a customer service call center in India © Brian Lee/Corbis. **Walraff:** Drawings courtesy of Christopher Niemann.

Index